Sam A



# The Life of Abraham Lincoln: As President

Written by
Ward Hill Lamon

Edited by Bob O'Connor

Bob O'Connor

Cover Illustration by Lloyd Ostendorf
Dedication of the National Cemetery
Gettysburg, Pennsylvania, November 19, 1863
Ward Hill Lamon with white sash next to Lincoln
Used with permission

This item is reproduced with permission from
*The Huntington Library, San Marino, California.*

ISBN13 978-1-936680-01-6

Printed in the United States of America

Published November 2012

MONT CLAIR PRESS

Toll-free (877) BUY BOOK
Local Phone (610) 941-9999
Fax (610) 941-9959
www.MontClairPress.com

# Editor's Note:

This publication is produced from the original, never-before published manuscript of Ward Hill Lamon and written circa 1880 - 1890.

Who was Ward Hill Lamon? Mr. Lamon was a Virginian who grew up in Mill Creek in southern Berkeley County, now called Bunker Hill, West Virginia.

In 1846, at age eighteen, he moved to Danville, Illinois where his three cousins lived. There he read to become a lawyer. After passing his bar exam, he was assigned to the 8th Judicial Circuit of Illinois where he rode with Abraham Lincoln and others.

Although he was almost twenty years his junior, Mr. Lamon became a favorite of Mr. Lincoln. In 1852, they joined in the law partnership of Lincoln and Lamon, with Mr. Lamon seeking and securing the cases and Mr. Lincoln defending them. During the four years of the partnership, records indicate they defended 114 cases in Vermilion County. The partnership was dissolved in 1856 when Mr. Lamon was elected prosecuting attorney.

Their friendship continued. Mr. Lamon was among a group of Illinois supporters who helped secure the presidential nomination for Mr. Lincoln at the 1859 Republican National Convention in Chicago. When Mr. Lincoln was elected president, he insisted that Mr. Lamon go to Washington with him.

On the train to Washington in February 1861, Mr. Lincoln and Mr. Lamon learned of plots discovered by two separate sources that attempts would be made on Mr. Lincoln's life when the train passed through Baltimore. Mr. Lincoln chose Mr. Lamon to accompany him and sneak him through Baltimore in the middle of the night. From that moment on, Mr. Lamon assumed the mantle of being the personal bodyguard of Abraham Lincoln.

At six feet four, 260 pounds and heavily armed at all times with two Colt 44 pistols, two Bowie knives, a set of brass knuckles, and a blackjack, Mr. Lamon was physically up to the role. Mr. Lincoln, at the same time, trusted Mr. Lamon with his life.

In Washington, Mr. Lincoln appointed his friend as the U.S. Federal Marshall of the District of Columbia where Mr. Lamon would report directly to the president.

Mr. Lincoln's entire time in Washington was made safer under Mr. Lamon's watchful eyes. It was said of Mr. Lamon, "The faithful watch and vigil long with which he guarded Lincoln's person during those four years was seldom, if ever, equaled in fidelity of men to men."[1] On April 11, 1865 when Mr. Lincoln ordered him to go to Richmond, Mr. Lamon begged Mr. Lincoln to be careful, and particularly insisted that he not go to the theater.

Mr. Lincoln went to Ford's Theater on April 14, 1865. Metropolitan Police Officer John Parker was assigned to guard the president in Mr. Lamon's absence. You know the rest of the story.

Ward Hill Lamon is credited with writing two other books. They are: "The Life of Abraham Lincoln: From His Birth to His Inauguration as President," originally published in 1872 and "The Recollections of Abraham Lincoln 1847-1865," originally published in 1895 and reprinted in 1911.

Both have been recently reprinted by The University of Nebraska Press. "The Life of Abraham Lincoln: From His Birth to his Inauguration as President" was republished in 1999. (ISBN 0-8032-7985-X) "Recollections of Abraham Lincoln" was reprinted in 1994. (ISBN 0-8032-7950-7)

What is remarkable about this manuscript is that this is the first book actually written by Ward Hill Lamon. "The Life of Abraham Lincoln: From His Birth to His Inauguration" was ghost written by Chauncey Black,[2] who was paid to write the book from the papers belonging to Mr. Lamon and others sold to Mr. Lamon by William Herndon.[3] According to historians, Mr. Black had never met Mr. Lincoln, had never visited any of the states where Mr. Lincoln lived, and was himself a Jeffersonian Democrat.

---

[1] Recollections of Abraham Lincoln, pgs. xxxviii.

[2] Chauncey Black and his father Jeremiah Black were law partners of author Ward Hill Lamon in Washington, D.C. Lincoln in American Memory, pg. 77.

[3] Together Mr. Lamon and William Herndon had personally known Mr. Lincoln for the sum total of 38 years, Mr. Herndon from 1844 to 1865 and Lamon 1848 to 1865. Herndon joined Lincoln as a law partner in 1844 in Springfield, Illinois. It was Mr. Herndon who sold Ward Hill Lamon his papers for the book "The Life of Abraham Lincoln: From His Birth to His Inauguration as President." Lincoln and the Civil War pg 300, Seaport Autographs, pg. 39 and Lincoln's Herndon, pg. 253. See also pg. 3.

"Recollections of Abraham Lincoln" was actually put together by Dorothy "Dolly" Lamon Teillard, Lamon's daughter, from her father's papers after his death in 1893.

Mr. Lamon was troubled with all the criticism of the 1872 book. Robert Todd Lincoln,[4] the gatekeeper of his father's legacy, edited most books written about his father. Mr. Lamon would not let Robert Todd Lincoln see the manuscript. After its publication (a run of 2000 books) Robert Todd Lincoln purchased and destroyed most of the copies due to certain information in the book which he did not like. At the same time, Robert Todd Lincoln also claimed he never read the book. Those objectionable parts of the 1872 book according to Robert Todd Lincoln concerned the marital status of Mr. Lincoln's parents, Mr. Lincoln's religious beliefs and Mr. Lincoln's relationship to Ann Rutledge.

In a personal letter to Thales Lindsley dated August 12, 1882, Robert Todd Lincoln wrote, "Dear sir; In response to your letter of the 5th of August, inquiring as to where you can get a second volume of the Life of President Lincoln, by Ward H. Lamon, I have to inform you that no second volume was ever published. I regret that you possess the first as I consider it a book largely made up of inventions, some of them inspired by malice." Very respectfully yours, Robert T. Lincoln[5]

As the years went by, Mr. Lamon's friends urged him to write this second book. One letter in particular sums up the encouragement Mr. Lamon received from dozens of his friends. The letter, dated May 20, 1885, is from J. P. Usher of Lawrence, Kansas. Mr. Usher was President Lincoln's Secretary of Interior. Mr. Usher wrote "There are now but a few left who were intimately acquainted with Mr. Lincoln. I do not call to mind anyone who was so much with him as yourself. You were his partner for years in the practice of law, his confidential friend during the time he was president. I venture to say there is now none living other than yourself in whom he so much confided and to whom he gave free expression of his feelings toward others, his trials

---

[4] Robert Todd Lincoln was the president's oldest son. After his father's death, Robert became the gate keeper of his father's legacy. Born in August 1, 1843, he lived until 1926. He served as Secretary of War in the Cabinet of James Garfield and was present when President Garfield was shot. He also served as President of the Pullman Railroad Company. The Two American Presidents, pgs. 43 & 441 and Lincoln: The Prairie Years, pg. 181

[5] www.historycooperative.org/journals/jala/14.1/schwartz-1/html page 11

and troubles in conducting his great office. You were with him, I know, more than any other one. I think in view of all the circumstances and of the growing interest which the rising generation takes in all he did and said, you ought to take the time if you can, to commit to writing your recollections of him, his sayings, and doings, which were not necessarily committed to writing and made public. Won't you do it? Can you not, through a series of articles to be published in some of the magazines, lay before the public a history of his inner life, so that the multitude may read and know much more of that wonderful man? Although I knew him quite well for many years, I am deeply interested in all that he said and did, and I am persuaded that the multitudes of the people feel a like interest. Truly and sincerely yours, signed J. P. Usher"[6]

Historians have believed for well over one hundred years that Mr. Lamon never wrote this book. I had believed that myself for a long time. A letter and list of papers of Ward Hill Lamon belonging to The Huntington Library in California was shipped to me by my friend Reverend John Schildt in August 2007. Rev. Schildt wrote the book "Four Days in October" about President Lincoln's visit to Sharpsburg, Maryland following the battle of Antietam. Rev. Schildt studied Mr. Lamon because Mr. Lamon traveled on that trip with Mr. Lincoln to visit General McClellan. That correspondence first alerted me that this book might exist.

A trip to The Huntington Library in late 2007 confirmed the existence of this previously unpublished manuscript.

This book is the first time we actually hear from Mr. Lamon himself—the man Abraham Lincoln called his "particular friend"—about what was going on during the troubled times of the American civil war and the Lincoln White House.

Obviously, this manuscript was never seen or edited by Robert Todd Lincoln either.

I have added footnotes for clarification. I have also reorganized some of the passages which were not in sequential order. I have not changed the original manuscript—though in those paragraphs where his sentences went on and on for thirteen or so lines, I was very tempted to make shorter sentences using modern acceptable punctuation.

---

[6] Recollections of Abraham Lincoln, pg. xxvi.

It is obvious in the Civil War diary section of the manuscript by Mr. Lamon that battles have been left out. I did not attempt to add those battles.

I added the photographs and drawings to facilitate the manuscript.

It is my personal, albeit biased opinion, that Ward Hill Lamon was one of Abraham Lincoln's closest and certainly his most trusted friend.

I had quit on the project numerous times. Fortunately, several staunch supporters kept encouraging me to let the world see what Mr. Lamon wrote.

With this manuscript, Ward Hill Lamon is finally heard on the subject of Abraham Lincoln. I think you will find some of his incites pretty fascinating.

And I know Ward Hill Lamon's spirit is smiling down on me for my efforts.

Enjoy!!

Bob O'Connor

Author, Ward Hill Lamon

# Contents

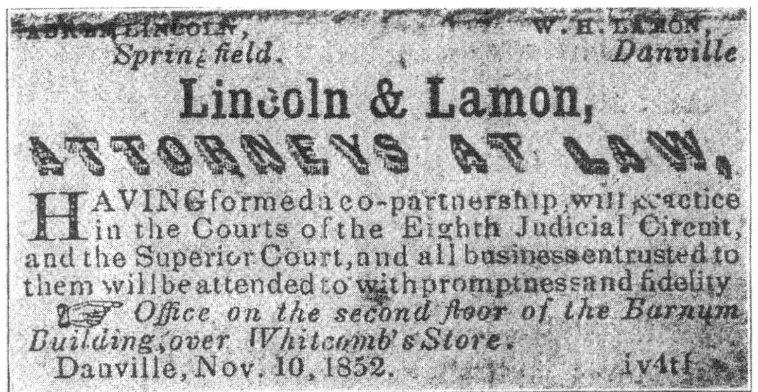

LINCOLN, W. H. LAMON,
Springfield. Danville

Lincoln & Lamon,

ATTORNEYS AT LAW,

HAVING formed a co-partnership, will practice in the Courts of the Eighth Judicial Circuit, and the Superior Court, and all business entrusted to them will be attended to with promptness and fidelity.

☞ Office on the second floor of the Barnum Building, over Whitcomb's Store.

Danville, Nov. 10, 1852. 1y4tf

Announcement in the *Danville Citizen* of the new law partnership of Lincoln and Lamon

*"May God make us worthy of the memory of Abraham Lincoln."*

Phillip Brooks
April 22, 1865[7]

# ORIGINAL PREFACE

## By Ward Hill Lamon

The Elder Walpole,[8] once in his old age, when he asked his son if he should read a book to him, he answered "Any thing but history, for history must be false." In all ages of the world, persons who have attempted to write histories have been more or less influenced, narrowed and biased by surrounding circumstances causing that want of fairness and impartiality indispensable to do "nothing to extenuate nor set down aught[9] in malice." Much of what is regarded as popular

[7] Lincoln Funeral Procession, Independence Hall, Philadelphia, Pennsylvania, Lincoln in American Memory, pg. 35.
[8] Elder Walpole was Robert L. Walpole, First Earl of Oxford, and generally regarded as the first Prime Minister of Great Britain. www.answers.com/topic/robert-walpole
[9] Aught means anything.

history was written under the influences of partiality, with judgment swayed less with truth in the light of the known facts than by draft upon the imagination to secure popularity to the author. History in the general sense is a narrative of the virtues, wisdom and worth or the follies, crimes, and miseries of man.

There has been much written about the events of President Lincoln's administration and the war of the rebellion. Most of the writers narrate from different standpoints, and the consequences is that there have been great discrepancies and many more speculative theories in regard to some of the events of the war and his connection therewith than there have been writers upon the subject.

The historical literature of the present century affords illustrations of incongruity[10] by authors influenced by different sentiments with the same state of facts for data. Napoleon[11] furnished a remarkable example of this kind of history. If a stranger to the great military chieftain—one who had never heard of the man—were to read Sir Walter Scott's life[12] of that eminent warrior and statesman and then read the historian Abbott's work[13] on the same subject, he would be perplexed and startled by amazement of the subject by the disparagement of the one and the deification[14] of the other. Prejudice and prepossession may have had much influence on these authors in the production of their respective works. From a monied stand point of view, they were both eminently successful. Sir Walter's book yielded him the sum of ninety thousand dollars for the disparagement it proclaimed and Abbott's work an immense sum for the deification it portrayed.

During the last twenty years there have been many biographies written of Abraham Lincoln. His peculiar character and position at the time of his death were singular and unique. Generally the works that have been written about him have been after the Abbot-Napoleon style with an evident tinge of purpose to omit reference to many important facts which if truthfully portrayed would but tend to

---

10 Incongruity is unsuitability.

11 Napoleon Bonaparte (Napoleon I) crowned himself as Emperor of France in 1804. www.lucidcafe.com/library/95avg/napolean.html

12 Sir Walter Scott's was a Scottish poet and novelist who wrote The Life of Napoleon Bonaparte in 1827. www.online-literature.com/walter-scott

13 John Stevens Cabot Abbott wrote The History of Napoleon Bonaparte in 1855. harpers.org/subjects/johnscabbott

14 Deification means making something godlike.

ennoble[15] his character instead of detracting from it; if perchance their publicity did prove him to be a man of flesh and blood like his fellow beings with whom he dwelt. No man at any time since his death could possible write his life truthfully that would give universally to the American people. Even to this day a large proportion of the people any of whom were not his friends while he lived, those who bitterly opposed his policy and traduced[16] his name now demanded the life—not of a man, but of a God.

His great service—his tragic death—so touched the imagination that Mr. Lincoln was transfigured. From that moment he became an ideal and to write a truthful life of him satisfactorily to many of his admirers has become impossible. During this generation no satisfactory biography of Mr. Lincoln can be written. In 100 years, when everything of the personal nature has been forgotten, when only the most public acts are remembered, and when the character has been separated from the man, then the life of Mr. Lincoln can be satisfactory—not truthfully—written.

Yet, dear reader, your humble servant, apprehends that by that time he will be incapacitated to write what he now submits for your consideration. Should this chronicle be deferred until the time that it would be acceptable to all people the natural frailty of memory doubtless would cause it to be abound with errors as great as the traditionary legends, recognized as history, written by Xenophon,[17] by Herodotus,[18] by Caesar,[19] by Hume,[20] by Lingard[21] and by Alison.[22]

---

[15] Ennoble means elevate.

[16] Traduced means defamed.

[17] Xenophon was a Greek writer and a student of Socrates who lived 430-354 BC. He wrote about the life in ancient Greece. www.ufm.edu/research/iep/x/xenophon.htm

[18] Herodotus is recognized as the Father of History in Western Culture. He lived 484-425 BC. www.livius.org/he-hg/herodotus/herodotus01.htm

[19] Julius Caesar is considered as one of the best writers of prose during his lifetime (100-44 BC). www.vroma.org/~bmcmanus/caesar.html

[20] David Hume is best known for writing a six volume History of England published between 1754 and 1762. plato.stanford.edu/entries/hume

[21] Dr. John Lingard was a Roman Catholic priest who wrote an eight volume set "The History of England, From the First Invasion by the Romans to the Ascension of Henry VIII." www.newadvent.org/cathen/09270.htm

[22] Archibald Alison was a Scottish author who wrote "The Life of Lord Woodhouseke" which was a volume of his sermons. He lived from 1757 to 1839. www.knowledgerush.com/kr/encyclopedia/archibald_alison_(Scottish_author)

The facts and events recorded in these pages are yet fresh in the minds of some of the living and are comparatively of recent occurrence. If doubted they can be either proved or disproved by living witnesses. If there be anything stated which taxes the credulity[23] of the people such as that General Grant,[24] like Hannibal,[25] had cut the way for his Army across the American Alps at Lookout Mountain "with fire, iron and vinegar," its truth or falsity can easily be established by those who handled the vinegar cruet on the occasion.

There is nothing that is not liable to misrepresentation. The very name of the country we occupy, the home of our Fathers, "the land of the free and the home of the brave" is a deception and a fraud. The historic name of America, perpetuated as it has been rank, is an injustice to the real discoverer of our continent.

The testimony of an eyewitness to the facts should be considered more authentic, everything else being equal, than traditional speculation, written or sanctioned, by the highest authority that ever wielded pen or gave ear to a story. Many public characters, strangers to the well-being of war and Mr. Lincoln while he was alive, whose private and public energies were so assiduously[26] devoted against him even to the indulgences of the manifest, unjust and unwarrantable opposition to his dearest purposes by abuse of his administration, extending even in some instances to the traduction[27] of his private character and the invasion of the sacred precincts of his domestic relations and the home circle of his dearest affections, now sing brutal and impious hymns of praise to his memory for having been so wise, good, and efficient in his great office. His death was a joyous event to them at the time of its occurrence, and his memory has been made a fruitful theme for the exercise of their hypocritical versatility and infamous buncombe[28] which by the real friend can be regarded only as akin to sacrilege. The keeping of Mr. Lincoln's sacred memory is now claimed by this class of patriots. They

---

23 Credulity means belief.

24 General Ulysses S. Grant, Union Lt. General was the commander of the Union forces and who accepted the surrender of Confederate General Robert E. Lee at Appomattox Courthouse, Virginia on April 9, 1865. General Grant later became President of the United States. Lincoln's War, pg. 404.

25 Hannibal was a Carthaginian military commander who is most famous for marching his army across the Pyrenees and Alps Mountains on board of war elephants during the Second Punic War. www.livius.org/ha-hd/hannibal/hannibal.htm

26 Assiduously means attentively.

27 Traduction means disgrace.

28 Buncombe means something done for mere show; hence, nonsense.

censoriously[29] judge of every man's loyalty to the great man by the amount of fulsome[30] flattery at the expense of truth he is capable of adding to the literature of romance upon their elevated and hypercritical standard of biographical adulation.[31]

The class of persons here referred to on the death of Mr. Lincoln were quick to realize that demagoguery would no longer be tolerated by an outraged people. A change of base was indispensable to their own safety. They were brought to see that zeal and enthusiasm for the man's worth were in the line of success and were in order to secure their own fame in the future, they just adopted such a course as to mislead the public sentiment from their former efforts to accomplish his political death.

They were not slow in finding undisclosed noble virtues and characteristics of the man they had so recently traduced. Ashamed of the cheap tricks they played for self-aggrandizement and political preferment, their tactics were to deify[32] instead of denounce the man. Public opinion instead of principle always actuates[33] such men. It was convenient now for them to smother their real sentiments and fall into rank in order to be in rapport with the healthy Christian sentiment that had been awakened by his death.

The author, after the publication of "The Life of Abraham Lincoln: From his Birth to his Inauguration as President" in 1872, had a lively and amusing appreciation of the employment of the versatile talent of some of those fresh from the purlieus[34] of political prostitution in attributing virtues to Mr. Lincoln never before that time discovered, even by his most intimate friends, family, associates, admirers or enemies—and the most sincere friends of Mr. Lincoln are now about the only skeptics regarding the newly discovered and established traits of character so graciously bestowed.

This book is not written for the entertainment of this class of latter day saints and hero worshippers. It is addressed alone to the lovers of truthful history, those who were the friends of Lincoln while alive—those who sincerely loved his memory and to honest people generally.

---

[29] Censoriously means severely.
[30] Fulsome means offensive or disgusting because it is insincere.
[31] Adulation means praise.
[32] Deify means to make a god of.
[33] Actuates means arouses.
[34] Purlieus means bounds.

*"I do not expect the Union to be dissolved–I do not expect the house to fall –but I do expect it will cease to be divided."*

Abraham Lincoln
June 16, 1858[35]

# — 1 —

# THE IMPENDING CRISIS

After the first shout of triumph, the first glow of exultation, the Republicans themselves in 1861 were half dismayed at the work they had done on the 6th of November, 1860. They had brought the nation face-to-face with the great peril, foretold by Washington,[36] Jefferson,[37] and Jackson[38] and by statesmen of every rank and form since the dawn of independence. The "geographical line" was distinctly drawn at last, a "sectional candidate" elected president, north of the "line" and not a solitary electoral vote south of it. A great people, comprising many millions, and inhibiting a vast region of our common country exasperated by calumny,[39] stung by defeat, and alarmed by the threats of furious fanatics who demigods held up to them as the only leaders of the triumphant party; it was the very contingency, the crisis, in which all venerable authority had declared from the beginning that the Union would surely perish, and the fragments, after exhausting each other by commercial restrictions and disastrous wars would find

---

[35] Lincoln: His Words and Deeds, pg. 19.

[36] George Washington is often referred to as "The Father of our country." He was the first commander of the Continental army (1732-1799) and the first President of the United States, 1789-1797. www.whitehouse.gov/about/presidents/georgewashington

[37] Thomas Jefferson was the 3rd President of the United States (1801-1809) and the co-author of the Declaration of Independence. www.whitehouse.gov/about/presidents/thomasjefferson

[38] Andrew Jackson was the 7th President of the United States, serving from 1829-1837. www.whitehouse.gov/about/presidents/andrewjackson

[39] Calumny means making false accusations or slander.

ignominious[40] safety in as many paltry[41] despotisms as there were fragments.

Out of the 1,800,000 voters who cast their ballots for Mr. Lincoln, it was the supreme desire of at least 1,700,000 that the Union might be preserved in peace and the limitations of the Constitution strictly preserved in regard to slaves in the states. The great northern democracy (both wings of it)—were unanimous for peace and Union. The Bell[42] party, which had polled nearly 700,000 votes, had gone into the campaign under no other platform. And in no other southern state except South Carolina was there a majority in favor of the great alternative, dissolution and the long chapter of bloody chances.

With this majority of the people for law and order, the statesmen of 1820, of 1832, of 1850—Jackson, Clay,[43] and Webster[44]—might have rescued the Union from the fate which overhung it, and deemed it stronger and more durable by the test; but there were slight difficulties in the way, now, with a multitude of demigods and few statesmen on either side of the dispute. The original nucleus of the Republican Party was that sturdy, long suffering band of implacable[45] abolitionists led by Garrison,[46] Phillips,[47] Lovejoy,[48] and their compeers.[49] They hated slavery because to them it was barbarous and inhuman. They hated the federal Constitution because it protected

---

[40] Ignominious means degrading.

[41] Paltry means worthless.

[42] John Bell of Tennessee was a seven-term Congressman who opposed both the Kansas-Nebraska Act and the Lecompton Constitution. He was one of the founders of the Whig Party and was the Constitutional Union party nominee for president in the 1860 election. Lincoln's Herndon, pg.136 and Appleton's Cyclopaedia of American Biography, Vol. I., pgs. 226-227.

[43] Henry Clay was a statesman and a Virginia Senator known for his oratory prowess. Appleton's Cyclopaedia of American Biography, Vol. I., pg. 640.

[44] Daniel Webster was a leading American statesman, lawyer, and member of Congress during the Antebellum Period. He lived from 1782 to 1852. www.marshfield.net/history/webster.htm

[45] Implacable means unable to be appeased.

[46] William Lloyd Garrison was an abolitionist who insisted that slavery be ended immediately. Two Roads to Sumter, pg. 61.

[47] Wendell Phillips was a radical abolitionist who was known as the nation's most gifted orator and its most extreme radical. Reelecting Lincoln, pgs. 70 and 136.

[48] Owen Lovejoy was a radical anti-slavery man and Congressman from Illinois. He was a friend of both Mr. Lincoln and author, Ward Hill Lamon. He advocated the immediate end of slavery. Lincoln's Herndon, pg. 74, Lincoln's War, pg. 254, and Ward Hill Lamon, Lincoln's "Particular Friend," pgs. 122 & 123.

[49] Compeers are equals.

slavery, and they hated the Union because it was a Union of slave holding communities. They wanted "no compact with hell, no covenant with death."

"We are disunionists," said they, "not from any love of separate confederacies, or as ignorant of the thousand evils that spring from neighboring and quarrelsome states, but we would get rid of this Union to get rid of slavery. All hail disunion; sacrifice anything for disunion. God forbid, sacrifice anything to keep South Carolina in. Rather build a bridge of gold and pay her toll across it. Let her march off with banners and trumpets and we will speed the parting guests. Let her not stand upon her order of going, but go at once. Give her the forces and arsenals and sub-treasuries and lend her jewels of silver and gold, and Egypt will rejoice that she has departed."

The South was a harlot whose presence in a pure sisterhood of states polluted all. Those who lived in fellowship of slaveholders shared their wickedness and must one day share the judgment. These men were crusaders, not politicians. Until very recently, the sober-minded people had detested and feared them. For years their fierce and reckless agitations had embarrassed and defeated the moderate Republicans. The latter tried Whigism, know-nothing-ism, anti-Nebraska, anything rather than assemble under the banner of these mad declaimers, but at Philadelphia they coalesced as thoroughly as honest fanatics and honest politicians ever coalesced, denounced slavery as one of the twin relics of barbarianism and built up a gigantic party upon our instinctive pity for the slave and our natural envy of lords of any kind, but especially of "lords of the lash." A little leaven leavens the whole loaf.

The abolitionists infused their spirit through the mass of the new party and those who joined them as allies soon followed them as disciples. They were the elder and the better branch. Their fidelity had been tried in the slow fire and the quick; many of them had individually periled life and fortune to succor[50] the slave when these their new allies formed the marshal's posse or compromised the mob which hunted alike the Negro and his friends through the streets and alleys of northern cities. They had seen their orators murdered, their presses burned, their houses sacked, men of exalted character guilty of no crime but compassion, and an unfortunate fellow creature tracked

[50] Succor means assist.

like felons from one hiding place to another. But they had done their printing in Garrett's,[51] made wood cuts and engravings in cellars, spoke in country school houses or obscure churches, circulated "incendiary matter" through the United States mails, and strained the "sacred rights of petition for redress of grievances" until they had brought a great party of northern public into substantial agreement with them.

They who had been foremost to stone them as false prophets, accepted them now as the very anointed and loved them as well for their heroism as their benevolence. Boston would decline now to beat down the foot-sore fugitive in her streets and deliver him sound and bleeding into the hands of his pursuers. When Mr. Garrison walked abroad he received the respectful salutations of his fellow citizens, instead of the rotten eggs and more hurtful missiles which occasionally greeted his appearance at an earlier period. Mrs. Stowe[52] had stung the ear of the world, slowly and reluctantly opened mellifluous[53] and fascinating Phillips; and the transcendent[54] genius of Parker[55] had touched the heart as well as the understanding of the generation. The American abolitionist had created a literature of their own; they had among them orators, philosophers, poets and pretty story tellers, whose works are familiar to every reader of the English tongue. The multiple books became the chief, almost the only, contributors to the periodical publications of the time, took very nearly exclusive possession of the religious press, got control of the great trade in school books, and sent an army of school masters, not only into the middle and western states, but even into the South.

The original abolitionists were, for the most part, pious and simple people who wished to remove slavery, not because they hated the masters or wanted the power themselves, but the practice was sinful in

---

[51] Thomas Garrett was a Pennsylvania abolitionist who aided fugitives slaves for more than forty years. According to his death wishes, colored men carried his body at his funeral. Appleton's Cyclopaedia of American Biography, Vol. II., pg. 609.

[52] Harriet Beecher Stowe wrote *Uncle Tom's Cabin* in 1852. This best selling book was a damning indictment against slavery. Two Roads to Sumter, pg. 94.

[53] Mellifluous means flowing smoothly.

[54] Transcendent means surpassing.

[55] Theodore Parker was a preacher from Massachusetts who also published the *Massachusetts Quarterly Revue.* He was an abolitionist who some say did as much as anyone to awaken and enlighten the conscience of the North on the subject of slavery. Appleton's Cyclopaedia of American Biography, Vol. IV., pgs. 654-656.

the sight of God. They were actuated[56] not by greed or ambition, but by an honest desire to save one race from the misery of slavery and the other from the guilt of maintaining it. They would have taken the slave from under the lash because he was their brother and they would have reminded the owner of him that any circumstances that reduced his power over flesh and blood was good for his soul. They would violate the rights of property to emancipate the soul and bodies of men. They would violate the Constitution and the laws of their country to practice a precept which they considered divine, but they had no thought of committing violence or shedding blood.

Most of them belonged to religious bodies which made non-resistance a part of their creed. The Quakers, for instance, would preach and pray and petition and rouse the passions of others to war-like pitch without the least thought of doing any fighting themselves. In the process of time, able and artful men began to perceive that this religious sentiment was capable of being indefinitely extended and intensified. Politicians began to look after it. Preachers and ecclesiastical bodies thought it worth recognition; men literally without religion themselves found their count in fanning this religious flame and men of most unorthodox opinions were loudest in delivering the sentiments against slavery in their true church. Altogether it was a party singularly compounded, priest and infidel, deist and covenanter, Calvinist and universalist—he who would not raise his hand against the invader of his own household and he who proposed to poison wells and invoke servile insurrection, met on a common platform and agreed in the name of religion to attack slavery in one way or another until it should be extirpated,[57] or a dissolution of the Union should release the northern states from all responsibility for its existence. As commonly happens when one class of men are severely exercised about the sins of another, the temper of the abolitionists grew gradually more intolerant until that which began in charity ended in hatred—until kindly sympathy for the slave became envenomed[58] hostility to the master, and religious sentiment was transformed into vindictive fanaticism. Through their literal, ecclesiastical and other channels they had easy access to the public mind and they never rested in the use of them. They agitated remorselessly. The pulpit and the

---

[56] Actuated means aroused.

[57] Extirpated means eradicated.

[58] Envenomed means embittered.

"moral lecture room" were among their chosen fields and swarmed with vehement orators, who had nothing on earth but anti-slavery to preach; they classed all their opponents under the comprehensive head of "the slave power" and this power they described as naughty, aggressive, cruel and treacherous.

They put the wolf's head on the shoulders of an entire population and then locally enough demanded that the monster should be hunted down and deprived of the power of doing mischief. Their appeals were addressed to the noblest and meanest passions of the human heart. They asked our sympathy for the slave with the scores of the lash on his back, bending to his unrequited toil or being torn from the bosom of his family gagged and chained to be sold in some distant mart. They excited our envy by depicting the luxurious life, the voluptuous habits, the naughty manners and the evil temper of the three hundred and forty thousand nobles who lived by the sweat and tears of an unfortunate and innocent race.

These, however, were not the most effective parts of their appeal. They managed to produce in the minds of the northern farmer and worker, the vague notion that this southern oligarchy[59] meant to enslave them also. It was alleged that those silly declaimers who talked about northern "mudsills" interpreted the real sentiments of their class that free labor and the mechanic arts were in danger of instant subversion by a barbarous despotism. "The slave power" had struggled for existence. Was this not ample proof that it sought dominion? It had entered the territories. How long would it be until it would invade the states? There was much said of the superior quality of our civilization as compared with theirs—our churches, colleges, common schools, arts, and sciences— the "dignity of labor" and inestimable value of "liberty" in general. All the stirring eloquence and the captivating phrases that had been used from time immemorial in the assertion of human rights fell naturally to the use of abolitionists in the prosecution of their self-imposed crusades. The word "free" with its pleasant and alluring compounds did amazing services—"freemen," freedom, free labor, free soil, and a multitude like them were irresistible catch words, and such a body of them were now brought into requisition as no party had had a monopoly on before. They were heard from every stump, pressed in every lecture, thundered from

---

[59] Oligarchy means a government where the power is vested in just a few.

every pulpit, garnished the most brilliant oration, and relieved the dullest of the most insufferable harangue.[60]

When all of the elements of opposition to the Democratic Party drifted together in 1858 on the anti-slavery platform, the Republican Party adopted the literature, as it did the spirit, of its parent and predecessors. It was a partnership in which the former furnished numbers and the organization and the latter vital sentiment and principle; without the transfusion of abolition blood, hot and invigorating, the new party would have sunk like the know-nothing party into premature decay for mere want of moral animation.

The Republican politicians stoutly denied that they entertained the principles, or shared the passions of the old time abolitionists, but they preached from its texts, borrowed its sermons and counterfeited its enthusiasm. There was no other way to argue the cause. Hostility to the slave power was their only apology for existence as a political organization. They sought votes in one section alone and to win them they must of necessity defame the other. In order to convince the North that slavery ought to be excluded from the territories, it was proper to show that slavery itself was a wicked and debasing institution—that if it was bad in one place, it was bad everywhere; that in the states where it was sheltered by the Constitution then its effects on both bond and free were baleful;[61] that it corrupted politics, blighted all moral life, stifled intellectual freedom, and repressed independent industry. It was founded on brutal conquest; it sought expansion by aggression and would never relent until "the wheat fields of New England" should be tilled by slave labor.

In 1858 Mr. Seward[62] reduced the faith of his party to a brief and pregnant formula: "It is," said he, "an irrepressible conflict between opposing and enduring forces and it means that the United States must, and will sooner or later become, either entirely a slave holding

---

[60] Harangue is a ranting speech.

[61] Baleful means deadly.

[62] William H. Seward of New York was the favored candidate for president going into the Republican National Convention in 1860. He served on Lincoln's Cabinet as Secretary of State. On April 14, the night Lincoln was shot, Seward was repeatedly stabbed by one of John Wilkes Booth's conspirators, Lewis Payne. Seward lived in spite of the attack. After the war, Seward negotiated the purchase of Alaska. Lincoln and The Civil War, pg. 33 & 36, Lincoln's War pg. 6, The Two American Presidents, pg. 423 and The Odd Couple Who Hanged Mary Surratt, pg. 71.

nation or a free labor nation."[63] Emulating him,[64] Mr. Lincoln put the same doctrine into a form equally startling: "A house divided against itself cannot stand. I believe this government cannot endure permanently half slave and half free. I do not expect the Union to be dissolved. I do not expect the house to fall. But I do expect that it will cease to be divided. It will become all one thing or all the other. Either the opponents of slavery will arrest the further spread of it, and place it where the public mind will rest in the belief that it is in the course of utter extinction, or its advocates will push it forward until it becomes alike lawful in all the states—old as well as new, North as well as South."[65]

Although it was not considered quite prudent to incorporate such opinions in the party platform, the floors of conventions rang with them and the whole body of our writers and editors engaged in the struggle of 1860 were more or less thoroughly committed to them. Many conservative Union men believed and charged that they served the evil turn they were intended to serve, scored the "geographical line" deeper through the hearts of the people, excited new apprehensions, embittered old hatreds and added fresh ones, consolidating the sectional party of the North and carrying the national election upon a storm of passionate declarations. A multitude of intelligent men voted the Republican ticket in the firm belief that the tenure of their lands and liberties depended upon its success.

Mr. Lincoln was chosen president. Mr. Seward was appointed Secretary of State. And the whole executive power of the nation they charged, had passed into the hands of rulers who regarded the Union as already divided, and proclaimed as ever enduring an "irrepressible conflict" between the several parts. But the election being over, the victory achieved, both Mr. Lincoln and Mr. Seward began to see the matter of dispute through a different medium; called at last to office and power, they wished to rule a united and opulent[66] country, instead of a single section whose political and commercial importance

---

[63] Spoken at Rochester, New York on October 25, 1858. The Story-Life of Lincoln, pg. 259.

[64] Author Lamon errs here. Mr. Lincoln could not have been emulating Mr. Seward when he gave his "house divided" speech. The "house divided" speech was June 17, 1858 before Mr. Seward's speech which was on October 25, 1858. The Story Life of Lincoln, pg. 259.

[65] Spoken at Springfield, Illinois on June 17, 1858. The Story Life of Lincoln, pg. 259.

[66] Opulent means wealthy.

depended greatly upon an intimate union with the rich planting commonwealths of the South. Mr. Seward was inclined to explain away the irrepressible conflict and Mr. Lincoln deliberately pronounced the crisis all "artificial." "Behind a cloud the sun is still shining."[67]

"I repeat, there is no crisis excepting such a one as may be gotten up at any time by turbulent men, aided by designing politicians. My advice to them under such circumstances is to keep cool. If the great American people only keep cool on both sides of the line, the troubles will come to an end, and the questions which now distracts the country, will be settled; just as surely as all other difficulties of a like character which have been originated in this government have been adjusted. Let the people on both sides keep their self-possession and just as other clouds have cleared away in due time, so will this great nation continue to prosper as heretofore."[68]

It is perfectly clear. It has been charged that Mr. Lincoln fully expected another compromise, but he had no intention of being chief among compromisers. He had said that the house was divided, and he now considered it imprudent to admit that the statement was untrue in point of fact—that there was in truth no line of division between the inmates.[69] They charge that his assertion to the contrary was merely a little trick to get possession of the house itself, while the real owners were quarrelling over imaginary difficulties. Doubtless Mr. Seward also regarded the conflict of which he had been the herald as a partisan chimera[70] had served its day; but after so long insisting that it was entirely "irrepressible," it seemed to him at least unwise to come forward in person and actually repress it. They had a party as well as a country to save. And any tender of the compromise which gave the South equal or indeed any rights in the territories and in the places under the exclusive control of Congress, which supposed rights were insisted upon by a large minority of the people, would instantly dissolve the party.

---

[67] Words spoken by Mr. Lincoln on February 11, 1861 in Toledo, Ohio on the train to Washington. The Life of Abraham Lincoln, pg. 508.
[68] Spoken by Mr. Lincoln on February 15, 1861 in Philadelphia on the train ride to Washington. The Life of Abraham Lincoln, pg. 509.
[69] Inmates in this case means inhabitants.
[70] Chimera is a shark.

Their associated leaders were equally embarrassed. They had not entered upon the anti-slavery crusade with the feeling that animated the abolitionists; their "oral" sentiments were only borrowed for the occasion. The elections being over, they had no further use for them. And they knew very well as Mr. Jefferson[71] had observed long ago that the extension of slavery into the territories did not reduce a single freeman from bondage or alter, except for the better, the condition of a single slave. They argued, in the mind of a sane man there could be no "moral idea" whatever connected with this branch of the controversy. And these leaders were all sane. They were therefore perfectly willing to surrender the substance of that by which the country had been convulsed[72] and the Union imperiled—the exclusion of slavery from the territories.

"At this session," says Mr. Greeley,[73] "after the withdrawal of the southern members in such numbers as to give the Republicans a large majority in the House and the practical control of the Senate, three separate acts were passed organizing the territories of Colorado, Nevada and Dakota respectively—the three together covering a large portion of all the remaining territory of the United States." All these acts were silent in regard to slavery leaving whatever rights had accrued to the South under the Constitution as interpreted by the Supreme Court in the Dred Scott decision[74] not merely unimpaired but unquestioned by any legislative action. "This was done," continued Mr. Greeley, "not in accordance with the feelings and views of the Republicans who reported and passed the bills, but as a peace offering and concession to those southern Unionists who were constantly protesting that they cared nothing for the extension of slavery; in fact were rather opposed to it but would not tamely submit to a stigma placed on their section and institution by northern votes."

---

[71] Thomas Jefferson—See pg. 16.

[72] Convulsed means agitated.

[73] Horace Greeley was editor of the *New York Tribune* and an abolitionist. He was opposed to slavery but did not like Northern interference. Greeley approved of colonization of the blacks and believed the total prohibition of slavery to be impractical. He was first a Whig, then an anti-slaver Whig and then a Republican. He was candidate for president in the 1864 election. Lincoln and The Civil War, pg. 69 and Appleton's Cyclopaedia of American Biography, Vol. II., pgs. 735 & 737.

[74] The Supreme Court decision of March 6, 1857 decreed that no slave or descendent of a slave could ever be a citizen of a state or of the United States. It also stated that Congress lacked the power to prohibit slavery in the federal territories, thereby making the Missouri Compromise unconstitutional. Two Roads to Sumter, pgs.134 -136.

It was in truth what the pure abolitionists regarded "dough-face" work to save a worthless Union, vain as a concession because it was never acknowledged to be a concession, and base because it was a faceless betrayal of the voters who had given the party the power on just the opposite principle. But this was not all. The House adopted by a very large majority Mr. Corwin's report[75] from the committee of 33[76] affirming the "justice and propriety" of a faithful execution of the Fugitive Slave Law[77] and adding a new and stronger guarantee to the existence of slavery in the states and yet more: the fervid[78] and frothy orators who had incited fourteen states to stain the statute books with "personal liberty" bills[79] intended "to hinder" the recovery of slave property, now united in a resolution imploring them to revise and expunge[80] them; and finally the House passed and the Senate concurred in the childish proposition to amend the federal Constitution so as to prohibit any further amendment that might give to Congress power to meddle with slavery in the states. All this was done by a majority of Mr. Lincoln's friends in Congress, while individuals and a great part of the Republican press were inclined to go still farther in the same direction. What became of the "free soil principles" when the territories were organized without reference to them and what became of the "irrepressible conflict" when slavery in

---

[75] Thomas Corwin was the Governor of Ohio and an old Whig who supported the Republicans. He was considered a great orator who had contempt for Negropiles. He served as Secretary to the Treasury in the Cabinet of President Fillmore and Minister to Mexico for President Lincoln. Appleton's Cyclopaedia of American Biography, Vol. I., pg. 751 and Lincoln and His Party in the Secession Crisis, pg. 37.

[76] The Committee of 33 of the House of Representatives studied the Crittenden Compromise but could not decide whether they should endorse it or not. Two Roads to Sumter, pg. 259.

[77] The Fugitive Slave Law of 1850 said that any federal marshal who did not arrest an alleged fugitive slave was subject to a $1000 fine. Officers who captured runaway slaves received a bonus. The fugitive slaves had no rights in court and could not defend themselves against any accusations. www.nationalcenter.org/fugitiveslaveact.html

[78] Fervid means zealous.

[79] Liberty bills were laws that required jury trials before alleged slaves could be moved. Political leaders feared slaves would be kidnapped into slavery. These laws were enacted in response to the Fugitive Slaves Act of 1793 and 1850. www.cliffnotes.com/wileycoa/cliffsreviewtopic/compromise-of-1850.topicarticleID-25073,articleID-25050.html

[80] Expunged means eradicated.

the states was buttressed anew by the proposed amendment to the Constitution?[81]

Undoubtedly Mr. Lincoln hoped that these practical concessions would avert the war. They were intended to have the effect of a compromise without the name. They were not indeed entitled to the name whether taken separately or as a whole; for a compromise implies a bargain between two or more—adjusting difficulties on the basis of mutual sacrifice and mutual benefit. Here there was no sacrifice but of Republican principles, and no benefit to the South.

But the South was not pacified by these concessions. On the contrary she was more than ever vexed and exasperated. It was well known that her principal men were anxious for the passage of the Crittenden compromise[82] which established the old line of 36 degrees 30 minutes, consecrating all north of it to freedom and leaving all south of it a battle ground whose ultimate political character would depend upon the character of its immigrants, as in the case of Kansas.

Even Mr. Davis[83] and Mr. Toombs[84] were willing to accept it when proffered and sustained by the ruling faction; that proffer the Republicans refused to make, with singular and ominous unanimity. It was charged the Republicans wanted to compromise, but they did not want to be called compromisers; the Republicans wanted to conciliate,

---

[81] Called the Corwin Amendment, the legislation was passed by Congress on March 2, 1861. It forbid any attempt to empower Congress to abolish or interfere with the domestic institution of the states including "persons held to labor or service" (a reference to slavery). The amendment was never ratified. *Harpers Weekly*, March 9, 1861

[82] John Jordan Crittenden, a member of the Senate's Committee of Thirteen, was the son of a Revolutionary War veteran. He proposed the Crittenden Compromise which guaranteed the permanent existence of slavery in the slave states and included permanent reestablishment of the Missouri Compromise prohibited north of the 36 degree, 20 minute parallel. A provision in the compromise was it could not be repealed or amended. Lincoln and the Civil War, pgs. 43 & 307, and Two Roads to Sumter, pg. 13.

[83] Jefferson Davis was a U.S. Military Academy graduate who served in the U.S. Senate from Mississippi from 1847-1851 and from 1857-1861. He was President of the Confederacy and was inaugurated on Feb. 18, 1861. After the war he was imprisoned, but freed after several years without a trial. U. S. Senators Home—State Information—Mississippi, and The Two American Presidents, pg. 452.

[84] Robert Toombs, of Georgia was Secretary of State for the Confederacy. He was at the battle of Antietam Creek in Maryland. His four hundred Georgia sharpshooters held off a Union force of 12,500 at the Burnside Bridge on Sept. 17, 1862. The Rise and Fall of the Confederate Government, pg. 242 and swartz.eng.auburn.edu/ACW/ant.docs/burnbrg.html

but they didn't want to be called "dough-faced;" they were willing to give up their principles if they could only be permitted to deny the fact; to purchase peace at any price if they could only escape the name of "peace-makers." Yet, when Mr. Lincoln was asked to say in plain English words that the operation of the Constitution as expounded by the Supreme Court should not be obstructed by a partisan legislature, he replied with an oath—"that would be treason." It was evident to those who were at all familiar with Mr. Lincoln that he hoped for some spontaneous action of his party friends which would confound the fire-eaters, satisfy the South and preserve the peace; yet when interrogated upon that very point he replied in a letter intended for the public eye that he would not consent to lowering the Republican standard "a hair's breadth." It was not the moral strength but the moral weakness of the Republicans which prevented him from offering a compromise, like the Crittenden proposition or the peace conference. It was not the thing itself that they dreaded but the name of it.

On the other hand, the South spurned all temporary expedients such as declaratory resolutions, proposed amendments to the Constitution and statutes, significant not for what they contain, but for what they do not contain. These, they said, might stand a day or a year, but that sooner or later they would be repudiated[85] by the party which had granted them reluctantly, and with a secret determination to disregard them in the end. When the South should be lulled to repose, when Mr. Lincoln should be firmly seated in power, the army and navy accustomed to obeying, his office holders swarming in the South as well as in the North, and the corrupting effects of his patronage beginning to be felt, then, they said, whenever it suited the inclinations or the purposes of his party, Mr. Lincoln would quietly put forth his hand, blot out this record of shame, repeal these measures by the very votes that had enacted them, and resume the attitude of open hostility to all the rights and interests of the South.

The South demanded a genuine compromise—a compromise in fact and in name—a covenant between equal parties whose very nature implied sacredness and perpetuity. It was the crisis of fate to them. They were engaged in a struggle for life. Up to the repeal of the

---

[85] Repudiated means rejected.

Missouri restriction[86] they had ostensibly equal chances with the North of settlement of territory south of 36 degrees 30 minutes. After the mad struggle in Kansas, after it became clear that the North could be easily induced to pour out its countless supplies of men and arms to make one free state after another as far as our limits extended, the effort for equality in the Senate was practically at an end. The balance of power was gone. The only question left was in regard to slavery in the states, as they supposed; but the Republican Party had not only declared for free territories; it had solemnly resolved in two national platforms, that slavery per se and wherever it existed, was a relic of barbarism. It proposed by the mouths of a thousand orators to enclose it as with a wall of fire and force the serpent to "sting itself to death."

The Republican Party won its voters, acquired power, and kept it by the simple process of magnifying the evils of slavery and portraying the masters not merely as ordinary criminals but as outlaws, pirates, man-stealers and man killers—enemies of the human race. It was indeed many years since the South had first heard a cry for the blood of its people ascend from the North, but that cry was then feeble and partially stifled by the very communities from which it arose. The abolitionists had long been in the habit of burning the Constitution in public and at the same time, declaring all slave holders worthy of death.

George Thompson[87] had freely advised his followers to begin the good work by cutting throats; and such men as Giddings[88] had gloated in advance over their calamities and mocked prospectively at their miseries.

But during all this time the abolitionists were a mere handful of raving fanatics as it was supposed, despised in the North as much as they were detested in the South. Massachusetts would have as soon gone to a mad house to select her rulers as to an abolitionist convention at Framingham; it was even proposed to treat abolitionists as criminals, and suppress them by the strong hand as enemies of society; but things were changed now.

---

[86] Missouri Compromise of 1820 called for permitting slavery south of the 36 degree 30 minute North latitude and prohibited slavery north of that line. Two Roads to Sumter, pgs. 57 & 58.

[87] George Thompson was an anti-slavery leader in the British Parliament. Lincoln The President, pgs. 354 -355.

[88] Joshua Giddings was considered to be the Grand Old Man of the anti-slavery cause. Lincoln and His Party in the Secession Crisis, pg. 31.

The abolitionists had taken possession of the very government which had threatened them with the pillory.[89] In 1840 they could muster not more than 7,000 voters. In 1844 they had gained over 62,000 and in 1852 the number was over 187,000. But in 1856 they took their place in front of the mighty party which cast over 1,342,000 ballots, and in 1860 with a spirit and purpose more undisguised became more powerful than ever, they led the van in the election of a president who owed his nomination to the declaration that "ultimate extinction" was the inevitable fate of slavery in the South.

It was charged in the meantime that their rifles and Bibles had done the business in Kansas. John Brown[90] had followed out their logic by murder and pillage in Virginia and as they said, ruffian and thief as he was, he had been canonized for his crime. The South no longer heard what they regarded as brutal libels of the abolitions in the small voice of a thousand fanatics assembled in some distance corner of New England but in the hoarse shout of victorious millions, intoxicated by the sudden acquisition of power; as they believed, burning to use it against those they were taught to regard as enemies of religion and society.

Mr. Lincoln stood at the head and said the "house must cease to be divided." Mr. Seward stood next. He pronounced the conflict "irrepressible" until we should become entirely a free labor nation. Mr. Greeley was publishing the organ of one wing of the party; Mr. Weed[91] the chief organ of the other. They united in a circular recommending a book, Helper's[92] *The Impending Crisis of the South*, offering to print 100,000 copies of a compendium as a electioneering document. This circular was "cordially" endorsed and the "enterprise" approved by sixty-eight Republican representatives in Congress, with Mr. Colfax[93]

---

[89] Pillory means public scorn.

[90] John Brown was an abolitionist who captured the federal arsenal at Harpers Ferry in October 1859 in an attempt to free the slaves. The Thundering Voice of Jehovah, pg. 29.

[91] Thurlow Weed was political manager for Mr. Seward from New York. He was a journalist and established the *Albany Evening Journal.* He was instrumental in helping found the Whig party. Lincoln and the Civil War, pg. 49 and Appleton's Cyclopaedia of American Biography, Vol. VI., pg. 419.

[92] Hinton Rowan Helper wrote to urge poor whites to band together for the immediate abolition of slavery and the overthrow of plantation rule. Two Roads to Sumter, pgs. 182 & 212.

[93] Schuyler Colfax born in New York. He moved to Indiana where owned the *St. Joseph Valley Register*, a Whig newspaper. He was Speaker of the House from 1863 -

to head the list. But Mr. Seward went farther. He prepared a separate paper by commending the work to public favor. "I have read *The Impending Crisis of the South* with great attention," said he. "It seems to me a work of great merit—rich, vet, accurate in statistical information and logical in analysis."

This book created intense excitement in the winter and fall of 1859 in the midst of which the Honorable John Sherman[94] one of the signers of the circular was placed in nomination for Speaker of the House of Representatives by the regular Republican caucus and voted for. The Republican members charged through eight long weeks of debate mainly because he was a signer.

In the book slave holders are spoken of as thieves, murders, licensed robbers, and likened to small pox, "mad dogs," and other nuisances to be abated. "Compensation to slave holders for Negroes!" cried Mr. Helper. "Preposterous idea. The suggestion is criminal, the demand unjust, wicked, monstrous, damnable! Shall we pat the bloodhounds for the sake of doing them a favor? Shall we feed the curs[95] of slavery to make them rich at our expense? Pay these whelps[96] for the purpose of converting them into decent, honest, upright men? A profound sense of duty incites us to make every possible effort until the very last freedom shall have been utterly vanquished. To the summons of the righteous monitor within, we shall endeavor to prove faithful: no opportunity for inflicting a mortal wound in the side of slavery shall be permitted to pass unimproved. Frown, sirs, fret, foam, prepare your weapons, threat, strike, shoot, stab, bring on civil war, dissolve the Union. Nay, annihilate the solar system, if you will. Do all this, more, less, worse, better, anything; do what you will, sirs. You can neither foil nor intimidate us. Our purpose is as firmly fixed as the eternal pillars of heaven. We have determined to abolish slavery and so help us God, abolish it we will. Take this to bed with you tonight, sirs, and think about it. Dream over it and let us know how you feel tomorrow. The thunder that cries in the South, rumbles all around us. The sky lowers above. The earth shakes beneath the great hive of the

---

1869. He was President Grant's Vice-President from 1869 -1873. Lincoln and the Civil War, pg. 162 and Seaford Autographs, pg. 9.

94 Honorable John Sherman was a Senator from Ohio. He was the brother of Union General William Tecumseh Sherman. Lincoln, The President, pg. 64 and Lincoln's War, pg. 16.

95 Curs are inferior dogs.

96 Whelps are young puppies.

North with the enemy pouring forth in numbers countless and ever growing, swayed by a single passion, impelled by a single purpose, expressed in a single motto: Alarm to the sleep, fire to the dwellings, poison to the food and water of the slave holders."

The writer here inserts the following letter at this point from the Honorable Joseph Holt:[97]

*Washington, November 30, 1860*

*My Dear Sir. I am in receipt of yours of the 27th instant, and thank you for your kindly allusion to myself, in connection with the fearful agitation which now threatens the dismemberment of the government. I think the President's message[98] will meet your approbation, but I have little hope that it will accomplish anything in moderating the madness that rules the hour. The indications are that the movement has passed beyond the reach of human control. God alone can disarm the cloud of its lightening. South Carolina will be out of the Union, and in the armed assertion of a distinct nationality probably before Christmas. This is certain, unless the course of events is arrested by prompt and decided action on the part of the people and the legislatures of the Northern States; the other slave States will follow South Carolina in a few weeks or months. The border States now so devoted to the Union, will linger a little while; but they may soon unite their fortunes with those of their South Carolina sisters. Conservative men have now no ground to stand upon, no weapon to battle with. All has been swept from them by the guilty agitations and infamous legislation of the North. I do not anticipate, with any confidence, that the North will act up to the solemn responsibilities of the crisis, by retracting those fatal steps which have conducted us to the very brink of perdition,[99] politically, morally, and financially.*

*There is a feeling growing in the free States which says, "Let the South go!" and this feeling threatens rapidly to increase. It is, in part, the fruit of complete estrangement, and in part a weariness of this perpetual conflict between North and South, which has now lasted thirty years. The country wants repose, and is willing to purchase it at any sacrifice. Alas for the delusion of the belief that repose will follow the overthrow of the government.*

*I doubt not, from the temper of the public mind, that the Southern States will be allowed to withdraw peacefully; but when the work of dismemberment begins, we shall*

---

[97] Honorable Joseph Holt was a Democrat from Kentucky who served in James Buchanan's Cabinet as Postmaster General and then as Secretary of War, replacing John B. Floyd when he resigned. He was Judge Advocate for the Union Army and founded and headed the Bureau of Military Justice. Lincoln and the Civil War, pg. 235 and Appleton's Cyclopaedia of American Biography, Vol. III., pg. 244.

[98] Judge Holt was referring to President James Buchanan.

[99] Perdition means ruin.

*break up the fragments from month to month, with the nonchalance with which we break the bread upon the breakfast table. If all the grave and vital questions which will at once arise among these fragments of the ruptured Republic can be adjusted without resort to arms, then we have made vast progress since the history of our race was written. But the tragic events of the hour will show that we have made no progress at all. We shall soon grow up a race of chieftains, who will rival the political bandits of South America and Mexico, and who will carve out to us our miserable heritage with their bloody swords. The masses of the people dream not of these things. They suppose the Republic can be destroyed today, and that peace will smile over its ruin tomorrow. They know nothing of civil war: the Marah*[100] *in the pilgrimage of nations has happily been for them a sealed fountain; they know not, as others do, of its bitterness, and that civil war is a scourge that darkens every fireside, and wrings every heart with anguish. They are to be commiserated,*[101] *for they know not what to do. Whence is all this? It has become the pulpit and the press and the cowering, unscrupulous politicians of the North have taught the people that they are responsible for the domestic institutions of the South, and that they have been faithful to God only by being unfaithful to the compact which they have made to their fellow men. Hence those Liberty Bills which degrade the statute books of some ten of the free States, and are confessedly a shameless violation of the federal Constitution in a point vital to her honor. We have presented, from year to year, the humiliating spectacle of free and sovereign States, by a solemn act of legislation, legalizing the theft of their neighbor's property. I say theft, since it is not the less because the subject of the despicable crime chances to be a slave, instead of a horse or bale of goods.*

*From the same teaching has come the perpetual agitation of the slavery question, which has reached the minds of the slave population of the South, and has rendered every home in that distracted land insecure. This is the feature of the irrepressible conflict with which the Northern people are not familiar. In almost every part of the South miscreant*[102] *fanatics have been found, and poisonings and conflagrations*[103] *have marked their footsteps. Mothers there lie down at night trembling beside children, and wives cling to their husbands as they leave their homes in the morning. I have a brother residing in Mississippi, who is a lawyer by profession, and a cotton planter, but has never had any connection with politics. Knowing the calm and conservative tone of his character, I wrote him a few weeks since, and implored him to exert his influence*

---

[100] Marah is a reference from the Torah identified as being traveled to by the Israelites where they found a fountain of water that were so bitter that they could not drink it. www.learningtorch.org/dvartorah/viewdurantorah.aspx?d+ID=706

[101] Commiserated means felt sorry for.

[102] Miscreant means unscrupulous.

[103] Conflagrations are raging fires.

*in allaying the frenzy and the popular mind around him. He had replied to me at much length, and after depicting the machinations*[104] *of the wretches to which I have alluded, and the consternation*[105] *which reigns in the homes in the South, he says it is the unalterable determination of the Southern people to overthrow the government as the only refuge which is left to them from these insupportable wrongs; and he adds: "On the success of the movement depends my every interest—the safety of my roof from the firebrand, and of my wife and children from the poison and the dagger."*

*I give you his language because it truthfully expresses the Southern mind which at this moment glows as a furnace in its hatred to the North because of these infernal agitations. Think you that any people can endure this condition of things? When the Northern preacher infuses into his audience the spirit of assassins and incendiaries in his crusade against slavery, does he think, as he lies down quietly at night, of the southern homes he has robbed of sleep, and the helpless woman and children he has exposed to all the nameless horrors of servile insurrections?*

*I am still for the Union, because I have yet a faint, hesitating hope that the North will do justice to the South, and save the Republic, before the wreck is complete. But action, to be available, must be prompt. If the free States will sweep the Liberty Bills from their codes, propose a convention of the States, and offer guarantees which will afford the same repose and safety for the Southern homes and property enjoyed by those in the North, the impending tragedy may be averted, but not otherwise. I feel a positive personal humiliation as a member of the human family in the events now preparing. If the Republic is to be offered as a sacrifice upon the altar of American servitude, then the question of man's capacity for self-government is forever settled. The derision of the world will henceforth justly treat the pretension as a farce; and the blessed hope which for five thousand years our race, amid storms and battles, has been hugging to its bosom, will be demonstrated to be a phantom and a dream.*

*Pardon these hurried and disjointed words. They have been pressed out of my heart by the sorrows that are weighing upon it.*

*Sincerely your friend,*

*J. Holt*[106]

In the practice which thus provoked the cry of his northern countrymen, the slave-holder could see nothing but what was right in the sight of God, and just as between man and man. Slavery he said was as old almost as time. From the hour of deliverance to the day of dispersion it had been practiced by the peculiar people of God with

[104] Machinations are plots.

[105] Consternation means fear.

[106] Recollections of Abraham Lincoln, pgs. 58—62.

the awful sanction of a theocratic[107] state. When the savior came with the palm in his hand he not only spared it from all rebuke, but recognized and regulated it as an institution in which he found no evil. The church had bowed to the authority and emulated the example of the master. With her aid and countenance, slavery had flourished in every age and country since the Christian era. In new lands she flaunted it. In the old she upheld and encouraged; even the modesty of the sectaries[108] had bought and sold the bondsmen who fell to their lot without a shade of doubt or became unprofitable. To this rule the Puritans and Quakers were no exception. Indeed it was but a few years since slavery in Massachusetts had been suffered to die of its own accord and the profit of the slave trade was still to be seen in the stately mansions and pleasant gardens of her maritime towns.

The southern man could see no reason of state, of law, or of religion which required him to yield his most ancient rights and his most valuable property to the new born zeal of adversaries, he more than expected of being actuated[109] by mere malignity[110] in the guise of philanthropy. All that he knew or had ever known of the policy of the state of religion or of law was on the side of slavery. It was his inheritance in the land descended from his remotest ancestors, recorded in their deeds and written in the wills of his nearest kindred, interwoven, more or less, intimately with every tradition and every precious memory, the basis of public economy and private prosperity, fostered by the maternal care of Great Britain and unlike any other domestic institution, solemnly protected by distinct provisions in the fundamental law of the federal Union. It was as much therefore a part of his religion to cherish and defend it, as it was part of the religion of the abolitionist to denounce and assail it. To him at least it was still pure and of good report. He held it as sacred as marriage; as sacred as the relation of parent to child. Forcible abolition was in his eyes lawless and cruel as arbitrary divorce or the violent abduction of his offspring. It bereft[111] his fire side, broke up his family, set his whole household in arms against him, and deluded to their ruin those whom the Lord had given into his hands for wise and beneficent purpose. He

---

107 Theocratic is government sanctioned by God.
108 Sectaries are people who are independent.
109 Actuated means sharpened.
110 Malignity means malcontent.
111 Bereft means to make uncomfortable.

saw in the extinction of slavery the extinction of society and the subservion[112] of the state. His imagination could compass no crime more daring in the conception or more terrible in the execution; itself the violation of every law including the divine from the Ten Commandments to the last act of the assembly. It was the inauguration of every disaster and of every enormity which man in their sober senses equally fear and detest. It was knife to his throat, the torch to his roof, a peril unutterable to his wife and daughter and certain penury[113] or worse, to such of his posterity as might survive to other times.

We smile at his delusion and laugh at his fears, but we forget they were shared by eight million people and have been entertained by the whole generation of patriots and statesmen who made the Union—by Mr. Jefferson who opposed slavery and "trembled for the judgment" as by the New England ship owner and Georgia planter, who struck hands to continue the African slave trade to 1808. Mr. Lincoln himself with that charity for honest but mistaken opinions which more than once caused him to pause long and reflect seriously before committing his administration to the extremities of party rage, declared in an elaborate speech that had his lot been cast in the South, he would no doubt have been a zealous defender of the "peculiar institution" and confessed that were he then possessed of unlimited power, he would not know how to liberate the slaves without disturbing the peace and prosperity of the country.

The late distinguished Judge Jeremiah H. Black[114] in a paper written by him in response to the memorial address on the late William H. Seward, by Charles Francis Adams,[115] enlarged upon this subject in the following language:

---

112 Subservion means subordination.

113 Penury means destitution.

114 Judge Jeremiah H. Black was the Attorney General and Secretary of State in the Cabinet of James Buchanan and was part of the Peace Conference for 1864. He and his son, Chauncey, were Ward Hill Lamon's law partners in Washington, D. C. following Mr. Lincoln's death. It was Chauncey Black who was the ghost writer for Lamon's book "The Life of Abraham Lincoln: From His Birth to His Inauguration as President," Lincoln and the Civil War, pg. 211, The Life of Abraham Lincoln, pg. v. and Lincoln's Herndon, pg. 253.

115 Charles Francis Adams was a radical in Congress from Massachusetts who became Minister to London. Lincoln and the Civil War, pgs. 126 & 257.

*"The southern people sprang from a race accustomed for two thousand years to dominate over all other races with which it came into contact. They supposed themselves greatly superior to Negroes. Most of them believed that if they and the Africans must "The southern people sprang from a race accustomed for two thousand years to dominate over all other races with which it came in contact. They supposed themselves greatly superior to Negroes. Most of them believed that if they and the Africans must live together the best and safest relation that could be established between them was that of master and servant. They thought it could not be abolished without a revolution disastrous to their material property and fatal to their organization. They did not think it sinful. The Bible furnished evidence satisfactory to them that God himself had framed the Constitution and the laws for his chosen people, which made Israel a pro-slavery commonwealth as much as Virginia or South Carolina. Their religious teachers had told them for many centuries that the canons of the Christian church did not oppose it, but would hold them morally responsible for the abuse of the power it gave them. They knew that the fathers of the republic and other men—the best and the greatest of all the ages—had lived according to this faith and had taken it with them to the valley of the shadow of death. Some of them believed it a dangerous evil but did not see how to get rid of it. This last class were especially resentful of outside interference."*

They felt as Jefferson did that they had the wolf by the ears. They could neither hold on with comfort nor let go with safety and it made them extremely indignant to be goaded[116] in the rear. In all the country from the Potomac River to the Gulf there was probably not one man who felt convinced that this difficult subject could be determined for them by strangers and enemies. Seeing that we in the North had held fast to every pound of human flesh we owned and either worked it to death or sold it for a price, our provision for freedom of unborn Negroes did not tend much to their edification.[117] They had no confidence in that ripening influence of humanity which turned up the whites of its eyes at a Negro compelled to hoe corn and pick cotton yet gloated over the prospect of insurrection and massacre. They were nearly unanimous in the opinion that this Yankee intrusion into their affairs was prompted by rancorous[118] hatred of the white people, or that it proceeded at best from that monkey-like spirit of mischief which is never content without thrusting its unwelcome nose into somebody's kitchen or somebody's church.

---

[116] Goaded means prodded.

[117] Edification means liking.

[118] Rancorous means spiteful.

They had a tradition among them that it was not their fathers who brought the Africans into this country. They charged the cruelties of the slave trade and the horrors of the middle passage upon the English and the Yankees. The planters merely received the savage Negroes, tamed them, taught them to work and converted them to Christianity, organized them into churches, and generally did more to improve their condition materially and spiritually than all the missionary societies that ever existed. Moreover, they had a suspicion that if they gave up their right of self-government on the subject, all their other rights would be taken away. Once placed without the pale of Constitutional protection, their northern enemies would then up root and branch.

Here we come to consider that emancipation of figures as well as feelings. The loss of four million of slaves at an average of $600.00 each constitute in the aggregate a sacrifice too vast to be contemplated for a moment, yet this was but a single item. The cotton crop of 1859 was worth $247,000,000 and the demand still in excess of supply. That crop of 1860 was worth the round sum of $189,000,000. It formed the bulk of our exchanges in Europe, paid our foreign indebtedness, maintained a great marine, built towns, cities, and railways, enriched factories, brokers and bankers, and made the foremost nations of the world commercially our tributaries and politically our dependents. A short crop embarrassed and distressed all western Europe. A total failure, a war, or total non-intercourse would reduce whole communities to famine and probably precipitate them into revolution. It was an opinion generally received and scarcely questioned anywhere, that cotton planting could only be carried on by African labor and that African labor was possible only under compulsion. Here then was but another item of loss which if put in perspective could neither be measured by statistics nor computed in figures. Add to this the sudden conversion of millions of producers into mere consumers, the depreciation of real estate, the depreciation of stock and securities as of banks and railways, dependent for their value upon inland commerce in the products of slave labor, with the waste, disorder and blood—shed inevitably attending a revolution like this, and you have a sum total literally appalling. Could any people on earth tamely submit to spoliation[119] so thorough and so fatal? The very Bengalese would muster the last man and stake the last jewel to avert it."

---

[119] Spoliation means ruin.

To many Christian people, this doctrine was regarded as fallacious[120] and heretical. Yet the dogma was formulated in even stronger language in a speech made by the Honorable A. H. Stephens[121] at Savannah, Georgia, on the 21st of March, 1861. He said, in speaking of Jefferson and the other founders of the government of the United States:

"The prevailing ideas entertained by him (Jefferson) and most of the leading statesmen of the time of the formation of the old Constitution, were that the enslavement of Africans was in violation of the law of nature; that it was wrong in principle, socially, morally, and politically. It was an evil they knew not well how to deal with, but the general opinion of that day was that somehow or other in the order of providence the institution would be evanescent[122] and pass away. This idea though not incorporated into the Constitution was the prevailing idea at that time. The Constitution, it is true, secured every essential guarantee to the institution while it should last and thus no argument can be urged against the Constitutional guarantees thus secured because of the common sentiment of the day.

Those ideas however were fundamentally wrong. They rested upon the assumption of the equality of races. This was an error. It was a sandy foundation and the government built upon it fell when the storm came and the wind blew. Our new government is founded on the exactly opposite idea—its foundations are laid, its cornerstone rests on the great truth that the Negro is not equal to the white man; that slavery, subordination to the superior race, is a natural and normal condition. This, our new government, the Confederate States of America, is the first in the history of the world, based upon this great physical, philanthropical, and moral truth."

It is true that some of these anticipations of the South have not been fully realized. Cotton was still grown although in more limited quantities for a number of years after the war. Lands may yet be sold for a third or fourth of their value. Immediately after the war there

---

120 Fallacious means misleading.

121 Honorable Alexander H. Stephens served with Mr. Lincoln in the House of Representatives and later became the Vice-President of the Confederacy. He never really believed in the Confederacy and spent time being critical of and obstructing the Confederate war efforts without resigning his position with the new government. Lincoln and the Civil War, pgs. 329 & 330, Lincoln's Herndon, pg. 27 and Two Roads to Sumter, pg. 265.

122 Evanescent means fleeting.

were places where the old masters, stripped of their power, influence and property, might venture to live among their freed men with no immediate prospects of assassination. And there were places where white men entertaining a certain class of political opinions might sow with a faint hope of reaping—but these immunities and privileges were by no means general. They depended on the favor of a distant government and may be withdrawn, upon information furnished by hostile spies or affidavits, filed by Negroes who sign by making a mark.

Complaints are sometimes heeded but heeded only to be answered with the scourge. Involuntary sighs were heard of a people in agony groaning under mountains of debt contracted for their oppression, and struggling merely for liberty, to live and be suppressed by blows which crush and mangle as they fall. Emancipation by the general government has produced only a part of the ruin accompanied by part of the horrors predicted by those who were its victims. That it did not produce more, that it did not leave the cotton states a howling wilderness, soaked by the blood of their former proprietors as it did in San Domingo and Haiti was doubtless owing to the fact that it took place under a ruler so mild in his nature, and so reluctant to the particular work in hand as Abraham Lincoln.

But the South dreaded the worst, and therefore presented in Congress the idea of definite and lasting peace or immediate separation. She would take nothing of mere grace and favor. She wanted not a statute but a treaty; not mercy but justice. The law she held had always been on her side but the part with which she was now dealing had no respect for the law and would never permit it to stand between them and their party. The "irrepressible conflict" had no other meaning and the higher law doctrine was invented to enable them to carry on the conflict without reference to the law of the land; about the fact itself, there was little or no dispute. The abolitionists did not disguise their intentions. The Republicans admitted the tendencies of their own teaching—the impending dangers of the South—by half-way and half-hearted measures of redress or security; measures which both parties to the contest regarded as hollow and delusive—the trick of today, the snare of tomorrow.

*"By the Constitution, the executive may recommend measures where he may think proper, and he may veto those he thinks improper, and it is supposed that he may add to these certain indirect influences to affect the action of Congress. As a rule, I think it better that Congress should originate as well as perfect its measures without external bias."*

Abraham Lincoln
Pittsburgh, February 17, 1861[123]

— 2 —

# THE DILEMMA OF THE 36TH CONGRESS

Nothing is now more certain than that a majority of the southern politicians who came to the front in this crisis were almost as much adverse to separation as to emancipation. Between these hard alternatives they were loath to choose; and although the belief was universal throughout the South that the dominant party was bent upon using the power of the common government for the ultimate ruin of that section, it was not until the peace conference[124] had met and adjourned, not until the Crittenden proposition had been voted down,[125] not until the last hope of reasonable accommodation had faded from the hearts of men, that anything like a general concert of action was to be seen outside of South Carolina. Up to that fatal

[123] Lincoln: His words and Deeds, pg. 23.

[124] The Peace Conference of 1861 was held in Washington at the Old Willard Hotel on February 8-27, 1861, at the request of the Virginia legislature, as a last ditch effort to avert war. Representatives from twenty-one of the thirty-four states attended. www.dcmemorials.com/index_indiv0000692.htm

[125] The Crittenden vote was taken in the last hours of the Congressional session in March 1861. Lincoln and His Party in the Secession Crisis, pg. 302.

moment a large majority of her people had been loyal to the Union of their fathers.

On the other hand the Republicans who were willing enough to concede any principle in a surreptitious[126] and doubtful fashion were as loud as ever against making compacts with a party defeated at the polls; they could not lower the Republican standard. They would make such laws as they saw proper for all the subjects of the federal government but declined to enter into any agreement with a beaten and factious[127] minority. Some of them looked forward to the day of final disruption with abounding pleasure and like Senator Wade,[128] painted the future glories of a northern confederacy, absorbing the entire continent north of the Potomac River harmonious within and all powerful without. Some of them would be pleased to see the Union exist as it was, though it was by no means worth the concessions which seemed necessary to preserve it. Many of them were sincerely attached to it, both by interest and conviction, but like Mr. Seward and Mr. Lincoln, believed it was the best policy to keep cool, do nothing, and let the storm "blow itself out." A few very corrupt politicians wanted a war of some kind for the plunder it would make; but this class was ever weak and timid at the beginning, although strong and shameless in the midst of civil strife. A few cruel and besotted[129] creatures ashamed of their own brutality and exposing their infamy only in private letters and telegrams between themselves decided at this supreme moment that our free institutions were worth nothing without "blood letting" and longed to see the carnage begin for the sweet savor of the gore.

With the greatest number, however, who had to do with the question of settlement, it was a matter merely of profit and loss to the party. As yet, they did not favor war, because war was a measure of doubtful issue at best, and of manifest unpopularity at the time. Concessions to retain the South in the Union were certain to divide if

---

126 Surreptitious means clandestine.

127 Factious means fractional.

128 Senator Benjamin Franklin Wade was a radical Republican in Congress from Ohio who had the nickname "Bluff Ben". He sat on the Joint Committee on the Conduct of the War. Senator Wade and Senator Zachariah Chandler of Michigan were critics of both President Lincoln and General McClellan and urged that the Union army go south to meet the enemy. The Word of Lincoln, pg. 58, and Lincoln and the Civil War, pgs. 146, 175 & 178.

129 Besotted means stupid.

not disperse the party, whereas separation would carry off the great body of their political opponents and probably leave them undisputed masters of the North nation for an indefinite period of time.

Between the two great parties—the secessionists and the Republicans—there stood another, formidable in its number of adherents in both sections but almost powerless in the federal councils, divided at Charleston, defeated at the polls, broken but not disheartened—the two wings of the Democratic Party. United in defense of interest and principles which neither had ever abandoned and which both had ever maintained, the Democratic Party was inspired by common love of liberty, order, and Union. The followers of President Buchanan[130] rallied under the leadership of Senator Douglas[131] and the followers of Senator Douglas under the leadership of President Buchanan with a force and alacrity[132] which party disciples could never produce. With them the duties of patriotism and the interests of partisanship were precisely the same. The love of county and the hope of power combined to make the Union, in their estimation, the most sacred of human institutions. Accordingly they devoted themselves to the work of saving it with a spirit and energy which have few parallels in the history of political parties. They knew, however, but one mode which might be considered perfectly adapted to the end—the mode which created the Union and the mode which being thrice tried by the purest patriots of all earth, had thrice preserved it from dissolution. They had been by no means unanimous upon all the phases of the slavery question. They had differed seriously about the annexation of Texas,[133] about the Wilmot Proviso,[134] about the Kansas-Nebraska bill,[135] and about the LeCompton constitution.[136]

---

[130] James Buchanan was the bachelor President from Pennsylvania who served from 1856 -1860. Harriett Lane, his niece served as the First Lady. Lincoln's Herndon, pg. 91 and www.whitehouse.gov/about/presidents/jamesbuchanan

[131] Stephen A. Douglas was born in Vermont and introduced the Kansas - Nebraska Bill into Congress. He debated Mr. Lincoln across Illinois in 1858 in what became known as the Lincoln-Douglas debates. The debates helped get Douglas elected to the U. S. Senate. Douglass died on June 3, 1861. www.illinoiscivilwar.org/douglas-sa.html

[132] Alacrity means briskness.

[133] Annexation of Texas occurred in 1845. www.u-s-history.com/1pages/h302.html

[134] The Wilmot Proviso was introduced by Pennsylvania congressman David Wilmot on numerous occasions in Congress from 1846 to 1849 without ever passing. The bill said "that neither slavery or involuntary servitude shall ever exist in any part of said territory"—the territory being land acquired from the result of the Mexican War.

Very lately Senator Douglas had succeeded in making a new doctrine popular among the many because it was anti-slavery in practice and tendency. But the Democrats were united generally in estimating the Union above all price and as worthy of any concession which might be necessary to save it. They thought the South had serious complaints which ought to be seriously heard and honestly met. Slavery they could not doubt was in imminent danger from the passions of the triumphant faction. And they knew well that when slavery was abolished, the interposition of the federal government, the rights of the states and the people would be abolished with it. They desired therefore that the Republican Party should subscribe some good and sufficient guarantee that the extremists among them had not spoken by authority. The South being satisfied on this vital point, it was a matter of indifference what particular form the compromise might take. A majority of the people could never be induced to secede. The Union would be safe, Mr. Lincoln inaugurated and this evil day departed forever; but in the 36th Congress the Democrats, although respectable in numbers and ability, were still a minority. They could only watch and wait; abide the tardy action of adverse committees and moderate as far as possible the tempest of acrimonious[137] debate.

From the beginning to the end of the session at every turn of fortune and at every crisis of the controversy through the weary days of contention and the long nights of shameful intrigue, while the secessionists matured their fatal plans in one committee room in the Capitol, and committees of the Republican caucus were smothering alike all measures of conciliation and preparation in another; the "little band of Union savers" were true to their sacred trust. Those

---

Lincoln's Herndon, pg. 21, Two Roads to Sumter, pgs. 59 & 60, and Appleton's Cyclopaedia of American Biography, Vol. VI., pg. 544.

[135] Kansas - Nebraska Bill was introduced by Senator Douglas in 1854 and passed on May 30, 1854. It called for opening more territories to slavery. It repealed the act of the Missouri Compromise that had barred slavery from above the 36 degree 30 minutes North Latitude. Lincoln and the Civil War, pg. 294 and Appleton's Cyclopaedia of American Biography, Part VI., pg. 30.

[136] The Le Compton Constitution was the pro-slavery constitution developed by the village of Le Compton in Kansas. It was illegally framed, but was endorsed and supported by President James Buchanan. Later Kansas voters in the state were allowed to vote for the constitution "with slavery" or "without slavery" and overwhelmingly voted 11,000 to 2,000 "without slavery." Two Roads to Sumter, pgs. 146, 147 & 151 and Lincoln, His Path to the Presidency, pg. 192.

[137] Acrimonious means angry.

Democrats voted solidly for every proposition that was calculated to allay the apprehensions of the South or to enshrine the Union deeper in the hearts of the people. They voted for the Crittenden proposition not precisely as the best and most equitable settlement that could be devised but as the best that could be obtained. When the work of the peace congress—a body august[138] in its origin and more august in its purpose—fell stillborn amid the clamor of revolutionists and the cold-blooded felicitations[139] of partisans, they alone looked on with increasing shame and dismay; but they did not despair. They closed their thin ranks for yet another struggle and to the last hour of that recreant[140] Congress pressed with abounding hope and fervid appeal, a proposal to take the sense of the whole people of the United States upon the matters at issue before plunging into a long and terrible war—at what cost to life, liberty and property no man could then foresee.

Had they succeeded, had the Bigelow proposition[141] passed, had partisan leaders turned patriots for a single hour, it is probable that the Union would have been saved without a drop of blood or the expenditure of a cent of money with no stain upon free institutions; no commonwealths in the dust; no peril to the liberty of the citizen. As the discussion went on, the following of these men vastly increased among the people, although they gained no recruits among their colleagues in Congress. To them the Union men of the South comprising the majority of the people of that section looked up at the forlorn hope of peace; with them the great body of the Bell[142] and Everett[143] voters now in perfect accord; and with them the larger part

---

138 August means imposing.

139 Felicitations are congratulations.

140 Recreant means cowardly.

141 John Bigelow was U. S. Counsel to Paris. A journalist by trade, he was editor of the *Plebian* and the *Democratic Revue* and was managing editor of the *Evening Post*. He also authored the book "The Complete Works of Benjamin Franklin." Lincoln and the Civil War, pg. 271 and Appleton's Cyclopaedia of American Biography, Vol. I., pg. 261.

142 John Bell—See pg. 8.

143 Edward Everett was a Governor and a Congressman from Massachusetts. He served on the Cabinet of President Fillmore as Secretary of State. He was President of Harvard College from 1846 to 1849. He was the vice-presidential candidate in 1860 for the Constitutional Union party with John Bell, receiving 646,124 votes. He was considered a great orator and gave the main address at the dedication of the National Cemetery on Gettysburg, Pennsylvania on November 19, 1862. His speech that day

of the rank and file of the Republican Party were in full although silent sympathy. But in Congress their power bore no proportion to the numbers they represented; their voice, though never still, was small and easily drowned in the roar of conflicting passions. An election for representatives or an election on the question of compromise would have changed all this; but an election was not to be had.

Regardless of the fact that Mr. Lincoln had been chosen by a minority[144] of the people; regardless of the manifest change of sentiment in the body of their own party, the Republicans alleged that the presidential election had settled every dispute and rendered another recurrence to the people unnecessary and improper. The verdict, having been legally obtained, although against the wishes of the majority of the jurors, must stand for all time. And they could not surrender one jot or title of the power acquired without "lowering the standard," "yielding to dictation" and sinking down to the level of mere "dough faces," and "Union savers." In the hollow of their hands lay the means of life and the means of death. They gave us one and withheld the other. They declined to take the responsibility of allaying the tumult; but they took the far greater responsibility of allowing the nation to drift unconsciously and unprepared into the most gigantic civil war that ever shook the earth.

The executive administration was still nominally in the hands of the Democrats, but the power of President Buchanan as limited by law and his moral influence had ceased with the rout of his party, in the most pressing exigency[145] of the nation's history. He could not get the collector of the fort of Charleston confirmed by the Senate although it seemed perfectly clear then that the initial struggle for the Union would take place under that power. All eyes were turned toward the rising sun. Mr. Lincoln's policy was as yet a profound mystery. It was not until he began his journey towards Washington that he let fall any intimation that might help the country to a conclusion concerning his opinions. When he did speak he left no room for doubt. It was clear that he thought a peaceful solution of the difficulty not only possible

---

lasted over two hours. Seaport Autographs, pg. 24, and Appleton's Cyclopaedia of American Biography, Part II., pg. 387.

[144] Election results show that Mr. Lincoln received 1,858,200 while his three opponents Bell, Douglas and Breckenridge received together 2,824,874. Southern History of the War, pg. 40.

[145] Exigency means urgency.

but supremely desirable and the employment of force or even the suggestion of it by his predecessor in office would disconcert his plan and disappoint his hopes. To the same spoke the principal newspaper organ of his party[146] at New York and the principal organ of his Secretary of State[147] at Albany. There was nothing to indicate that Mr. Lincoln would pursue a more warlike policy than Mr. Buchanan or that he desired his partisans in Congress to arm the president with powers which Mr. Buchanan implored them to give him.

Within forty-eight hours after the election of Mr. Lincoln, the legislature of South Carolina called a state convention. It met on the 17th of December and within three days one of which was occupied in organization and another in running away from small pox, the inevitable ordinance of secession was formally adopted and the little commonwealth began to act under the erroneous impression that she was a sovereign and independent nation. She indignantly accepted the postal service of the "late United States of America" and even permitted the gold and silver coins of the United States to circulate within her limits. But intelligence for the rest of the country was published in her newspapers under the head of "foreign news." Her governor appointed "a Cabinet," commissioned "ambassadors" and practiced so many fantastic imitations of greatness and power that but for the serious purpose and bloody event its proceedings would have been very amusing. It was a curious little comedy between the acts of a serious tragedy.

The example of South Carolina was followed by the remaining cotton states in rapid succession. In early February, a convention of delegates met in Montgomery, Alabama to frame a provisional constitution and form a provisional government for the Confederate States of America. Upon these proceedings and the prodigious[148] energies with which they were conducted, they moved ahead in the formation of a great and powerful government. The rest of the country looked on appalled, breathless and bewildered. Now at last the South seemed in terrible earnest. The protests of the opposition were seldom heard and now never respected. Resistance was crushed by strong measures and swift; complaints were suffered to proceed no

---

146 The principal organ of the party was Greeley's *New York Tribune*. See page 14.

147 President Lincoln's Secretary of State was William Seward. The principal organ of the Secretary of State was Thurlow Weed's *Albany Evening Journal*. See page 18.

148 Prodigious means vast.

farther than the chimney corner. The clamor of demigods, the shout of the rabble, military processions and rolling drums made remonstrance[149] as inaudible as it was perilous, and presented the illusion of popular unanimity which did not exist in fact.

It was certain that the people of South Carolina were nearly if not quite unanimous in their desire to be led out of the Union; but it was still a question of whether the movement would have received a majority in any other cotton state with a fair poll of electors. Conventions in most every instance declared states out of the Union without further reference to the people; a formal minority disclosed at the polls would have proved almost as fatal to secession as an adverse majority. As in all revolutions of magnitude, the daring and active spirits dragged the hesitating along with them and dragooned[150] their opponents into silence; but in the middle states—in Delaware, Maryland, Virginia, North Carolina, Tennessee, Kentucky, Arkansas, and Missouri—the sentiment in favor of the Union was almost as strong as it ever had been in the republic.

It was this sentiment—that majority in the border and that great majority in the Gulf States—which the Democrats desired to cherish and develop. And it was this sentiment which Mr. Lincoln and his party regarded as the best, perhaps the only hope of the country. It would have been greater, stronger, and everywhere victorious. It would by the confession of the disunionists themselves have overthrown them at every turn and routed them utterly but for the refusal of the Republican majority to pass the measures upon which its very life depended; that majority would have been glad to see it wax and conquer and no doubt Mr. Lincoln expected to see it; but they denied its help for reasons most of them would have blushed to have owned outside their partisan caucus.

Congress met on the 3rd of December. President Buchanan's message was in tone, temper and gravity of its recommendations, the most important paper ever presented to a legislative body; stern and solemn language befitting the dreaded theme, it traced the progress of disintegration and the several causes of it. Here are some excerpts from President Buchanan's speech to Congress that day—his State of the Union address.

---

149 Remonstrance is a protest.

150 Dragooned means compelled.

*"The long-continued and intemperate interference of the Northern people with the question of slavery in the Southern States has at length produced its natural effects. The different sections of the Union are now arraying against each other, and the time has arrived, so much dreaded by the Father of his Country, when hostile geographical parties have been formed.*

*I have long foreseen and forewarned my countrymen of the now impending dangers. This does not proceed solely from the claim on the part of Congress or the Territorial legislature to exclude slavery from the Territories, nor from the efforts of different States to defeat the execution of the fugitive slave law. All or any of the evils might have been endured by the South without danger to the Union (as others have been) in hope that time and reflection might apply the remedy.*

*The immediate peril arises not so much from these causes as from the fact that the incessant and violent agitation of the slavery question throughout the North for the last quarter of a century has at length produced its malign influence on the slaves and inspired them the vague notion of freedom. Hence a sense of security no longer exists around the family altar. This feeling of peace at home has given place to apprehensions of servile insurrections.*

*Many a matron throughout the South retires at night in the dread of what may befall herself and her children before morning. Should this apprehension of domestic danger, whether real or imaginary, extend and intensify itself until it shall pervade the masses of the Southern people, then disunion will become inevitable. Self-preservation is the first law of nature, and has been implanted in the heart of man by his Creator for the wisest purpose; and no political union, however fraught with blessings and benefits on all other respects, can long continue if the necessary consequences be to render the homes and firesides of nearly half the parties to it habitually and hopelessly insecure. Sooner or later the bonds of such a union must be severed. It is my conviction that this fatal period has not yet arrived, and my prayer to God that He would preserve the Constitution and the Union throughout all generations.*

*How easy it would be for the American people to settle the slavery question forever and to restore peace and harmony to this distracted country! They and they alone can do it. All that is necessary to accomplish this object, and all for which the slave states have ever contended, is to be let alone and permitted to manage their domestic institutions in their own way. As sovereign states, they, and they alone are responsible before God and the world for the slavery existing among them. For this the people of the North are no more responsible and have no more right to interfere than with similar institutions in Russia or in Brazil.*

*And this brings me to observe that the election of any one of our fellow citizens to the office of the president does not of itself afford just cause for dissolving the*

*Union. Reason, justice, a regard for the Constitution, all require that we shall wait for an overt and dangerous act on the part of the president elect before resorting to such a remedy.*

*I earnestly recommend the following explanatory amendment to the Constitution on three special points:*

*1. An expressed recognition of the right of property in slaves in the states where it now exists or may hereafter exist.*

*2. The duty of protecting this right in all the common Territories throughout their Territorial existence and until they shall be admitted as States to the Union, with or without slavery, as their constitutions may prescribe.*

*3. A like recognition of the right of the master to have his slave who has escaped from one State to another restored and delivered up to him, and of the validity of the fugitive slave law enacted for this purpose."*[151]

President Buchanan's address reminded Congress that they and they alone possessed the power to stay the revolution whether by force or by conciliation. It recited the painful apprehensions entertained in the South and fervently sought the representatives of the whole people to disappoint and remove them. It contained a singularly clear and very timely exposition of the nature of the federal compact. No state could lawfully withdraw from it. And no state could lawfully be expelled from it. The federal Constitution was as much a part of "the constitution of every state" as if it had been textually inserted therein. The federal government was sovereign within its own sphere and to the extent of its authority "acted directly upon the individual citizens of every state." Within these limits, its coercive power was ample to defend itself, its laws and its property. It could suppress insurrection, fight battles, conquer armies, dispense hostile combinations and punish away any or all of its enemies; but it could not declare war against a state. It could not make indiscriminate war against all the inhabitants of a state. Such was the opinion of the Attorney General[152] and we shall presently see how that officer interpreted his own opinion as the conflict deepened and new exigencies[153] arose. But if the coming insurrection was to be met by force, the law as it stood was miserably defective.

---

[151] Teachingamericanhistory.org—1860 State of the Union Address by James Buchanan.

[152] The Attorney General at that time was Jeremiah Black.

[153] Exigencies means urgencies.

The acts of 1795 and 1807 were wholly inadequate to the present occasion. They required the president to act in concert with the marshal and a civil *posse comitatus*[154] but in this case, South Carolina, the marshal, the judge, all the public officers, and all the people were on one side, and that was the wrong one. "Congress alone," said President Buchanan, "has the power to decide whether the present law can or cannot be amended so as to carry out more effectually the object of the Constitution." With Congress rested the whole responsibility of peace or war and with them the message was left.

The message had received the cordial approbation of every member of the Cabinet except for Mr. Cobb[155] and Mr. Thompson.[156] They, of course, objected to that part of it which denied the right of secession. Mr. Floyd[157] was still vehement on the side of the Union. The peculiar reasons for his change of ground were yet undeveloped. Mr. Cobb found a fault in the original draft which seems to have been detected by none of his colleagues. He thought the power of Congress to make war against a state ought to be denied in language stronger and more specific and it was so modified solely to meet his views.

But Congress behaved like a body of men who thought that the calamities of the nation were no special business of theirs. The members from the extreme South were watching for the proper moment to resign. Those from the middle states were the minority which could only stand and wait upon the movements of others while

---

154 *Posse comitatus* means the people to be summoned.

155 Howell Cobb was a member of the U.S. House of Representatives from Georgia when Mr. Lincoln was in Congress. He was one of the early supporters of secession and one of the richest slaveholders in the South. He presided at the Montgomery secession convention. He was Secretary of Treasury for the Cabinet of James Buchanan and Secretary of the Treasury in the Confederate Cabinet. The Story-Life of Lincoln, pg. 186, Two Roads to Sumter, pgs. 130 & 265 and Appleton's Cyclopaedia of American Biography, Vol. I., pgs. 666 & 667.

156 Jacob Thompson from Mississippi was a Congressman from 1838-1857 and was Secretary of the Interior during the James Buchanan administration. He was a proponent of surrendering the forts in the Charleston harbor and withdrawing Major Anderson and his men. He was Governor of Mississippi from 1862-1864 and an aid-de-camp to General Beauregard during the war. He was indicted in the conspiracy in Canada by Confederate officials to kidnap or kill President Lincoln. The Story-Life of Lincoln, pg. 363, The Lincoln Conspiracies, pg. 17, www.fulkerson.org/thompson.html and Appleton's Cyclopaedia of American Biography, Vol. VI., pg. 91

157 John B. Floyd was Secretary of War for the James Buchanan administration. He was a Brigadier General in the Confederate Army. Appleton's Cyclopaedia of American Biography, Vol. II., pgs. 487- 488.

the great and all powerful northern party was what the French minister called "a mere aggregation of individual ambitions." Of this last class each perused[158] his object steadily and keenly. They had suffered a long exile from office and they were returning now with a pleasure too great to be too much diminished by the troubles of the country. They busied themselves in dividing of the jobs and offices of the county while the government was perishing before their eyes. It is certain that they either did not think the Union in danger or else did not care to preserve it. The latter is not probable. It was "the evil heart of unbelief" with which they were cursed. They had always denied the possibility of dissolution in any conjunction of circumstances. And their habit of disregarding the evidence was too strong to be suddenly changed. In the philosophy of their politics it had not been dreamed of as a possible thing. Even when they saw it assume the shape of a fixed and terrible fact they could not comprehend its meaning. They looked on at the frightful phenomenon as a crowd of barbarians might look at an ellipse of the sun. They saw the light of heaven extinguished, and the earth covered with strange and unaccountable darkness, but they could neither understand its cause nor what it portended.[159]

President Buchanan recommended the calling of a convention to amend the Constitution, not to give any new privileges to the people of the southern states, but merely to confirm by express provision, the rights which they had already. If this had met a prompt and cheerful response from Congress it is at least possible that the dispute might have been settled—but it met with no favor and shared the fate of all similar propositions. It will naturally be supposed that the men who resolutely rejected all overtures of peace must at least have made ample preparations for war. If conciliation was out of the question then coercion or dissolution was the only alternative left. If the attitude of the southern men had become such that it was beneath the dignity of the North to treat them or to grant them redress, it was certainly necessary to see that a force was provided great enough to compel submission. But the country and the whole world saw with profound astonishment that the majority of Congress opposed or neglected all measures of force as steadily as they opposed or objected those which looked to a peaceful compromise. They would neither accept the sword nor take the olive branch. In the meantime

158 Perused means inspected.

159 Portended means signified.

opposition to the Union was growing in the cotton states with frightful rapidity. State after state announced her determination to retire from it, peaceably if she could, forcibly if she must. The disunionists were consolidating their powers skillfully as well as boldly and sympathy with them was increasing even in the border slave states. The nation was going to pieces and Congress left to its fate. The vessel freighted with all the hopes and all the wealth of 30,000,000 people was drifting to her doom and they alone who had power to control her course refused to lay a finger on her helm.

*"It is said that serious apprehensions are, to some extent, entertained, which I do not share, that the peace of this District might be disturbed before the 4th of March next. In any event, it will be my duty to preserve it, and this duty shall be performed."*

President James Buchanan
January, 1861[160]

# — 3 —

# THE LAST MONTHS OF THE JAMES BUCHANAN ADMINISTRATION

Since the meeting of Congress, President Buchanan's Cabinet had been materially changed. Lewis Cass[161] resigned as Secretary of State December 12, 1860 because the president refused to reinforce the forts in Charleston harbor and on the 17th of the same month Jeremiah S. Black[162] was appointed his successor. Howell Cobb resigned as Secretary of the Treasury on the 19th and assigned for the reason of doing so "his duty to Georgia required it." The vacancies had been filled by the appointment of Edwin M. Stanton[163] as

160 Abraham Lincoln: The Year of His Election, pg. 196.

161 Lewis Cass was from New Hampshire. He served as Secretary of War for President Andrew Jackson and Secretary of State during James Buchanan's presidency. www.answers.com/topic/lewis-cass

162 Jeremiah Black—See pg. 27.

163 Edwin M. Stanton was a Ohio attorney who was in the Cabinets of both James Buchanan and Abraham Lincoln. He was Mr. Buchanan's Attorney General and Mr. Lincoln's Secretary of War. Stanton was instrumental in helping forge the surrenders at the end of the war. He was appointed a justice on the Supreme Court by President Grant but died four days after his confirmation. Lincoln's War, pg. 107 & 119 The Two American Presidents, pgs. 142 & 244 and Appleton's Cyclopaedia of American Biography, Vol. V., pgs. 648-649.

Attorney General, and Philip F. Thomas,[164] of Maryland, as Secretary of the Treasury. Mr. Thompson's retirement from the Interior was simply a question of time.

On the 28th of December, three gentlemen,[165] styling themselves "commissioners" of South Carolina, sent a communication to President Buchanan offering to exhibit their credentials and proposing to "treat" with "the government of the United States" about sundry[166] questions of debt and property. But after their departure from home the whole aspect of the affairs had been changed by an important event. Major Anderson[167] the federal commander in Charleston had in pursuance of a plain order removed his little force from Fort Moultrie to Fort Sumter[168] and the commissioners threatened to suspend all discussions while in the very act of opening it until Major Anderson's proceedings were satisfactorily explained.

The commissioners had arrived on the 26th and the news of Major Anderson's removal had arrived on the 27th.[169]

---

164 Phillip Francis Thomas was Governor of Maryland from 1848 - 1851. He was a U. S. Congressman who replaced Howell Cobb as Secretary of the Treasury in the Cabinet of James Buchanan serving less than a month from Dec. 1860 to January 11, 1861. Appleton's Cyclopaedia of American Biography, Vol. VI., pgs. 85 & 86.

165 Messers. Jas. L. Orr, J. H. Adams and R. W. Barnwell. The Great Conspiracy, Volume II, Chapter 7.

166 Sundry means various.

167 Major Robert Anderson was commanding officer of the federal garrison at the forts in the Charleston, South Carolina harbor including Fort Sumter. He was a West Point graduate who returned to the school to teach artillery. He was a veteran of the Mexican War where he was wounded. He had known Mr. Lincoln from the Blackhawk War. He was instrumental in developing the Soldier's Home in Washington. Lincoln The President, pg. 447, The Story-Life of Lincoln, pg. 105, Fort Sumter National Monument, South Carolina, pg. 8 and Appleton's Cyclopaedia of American Biography, pg. 70.

168 Fort Moultrie and Fort Sumter were two forts in the Charleston harbor. Fort Sumter National Monument South Carolina, pg. 6.

169 Their message conveyed said in part: "We have the honor to transmit to you a copy of the full powers from the Convention of the people of South Carolina, under which we are authorized and empowered to treat with the real estate, with their appurtenances, in the limits of South Carolina; and also for the apportionment of the public debt, and for a division of all other property held by the government of the United States, as agent of the Confederate States, of which South Carolina was recently a member and generally to negotiate as to all other measures and arrangements proper to be made and adopted in the existing relation of the parties, and for the continuance of peace and amity between the commonwealth and the government at Washington." Harpers Pictorial History of the Great Rebellion, pg. 30.

From the evening of the 27th to the morning of the 31st of December 1860 (three days and four nights) the actions of Major Anderson and the answer to the commissioners were under discussion. The morning when the Cabinet assembled and the startling news from Charleston was announced, the Secretary of State expressed his strong approbation[170] of Major Anderson's movement and asserted that it was in perfect accordance with his orders. It happened that nobody else remembered the precise terms of those orders. The Secretary of War[171] denied that they contained anything that could justify the removal and the president was inclined to agree with him on the question of fact.[172] The orders were sent for and read and it was found that the instructions were explicit and clear to remove into any fort in the harbor which would increase Major Anderson's means of resistance as soon as he "had tangible evidence of a design" to attack him. Some discussion on the tangibility of the evidence ensued but this was soon settled. For the words could mean nothing unless they meant that he should move whenever he had a well-grounded apprehension that an assault would be made and he was left to judge of that for himself. The president could not choose but to support the officer who had apparently in good faith obeyed the instructions under which he was bound to act.

Mr. Floyd then insisted with much earnestness that the troops should be entirely withdrawn from all the forts in Charleston harbor and he put his proposition in writing. It received no support from any of his colleagues and no countenance from the president. President Buchanan thought as he afterwards said that the tone in which Mr. Floyd read his paper was loud and discourteous but at the time he rebuked it only with that quiet dignity under which the courage of many a stronger man had wilted before. Mr. Floyd's views or wishes

---

170 Approbation means approval.

171 Secretary of War was John B. Floyd. Appleton's Cyclopaedia of American Biography, Vol. VII, pgs. 487 & 488.

172 Major Anderson's orders were as follows: Instructions received December 11, 1860. "You are to hold possession of the forts in this harbor, and if attacked you are to defend yourself to the last extremity. The smallness of your force will not permit you, perhaps, to occupy more than one of the three forts, but an attack on or an attempt to take possession of any one of them will be regarded as an act of hostility, and you may then put your command into either of them which you deem most proper to increase its power of resistance. You are also authorized to take similar steps whenever you have tangible evidence of a design to proceed to a hostile act." Fort Sumter National Monument, South Carolina, pg. 6.

on any subject had for some time before ceased to have any force on the wind of the president or other members of the administration. Mr. Floyd was bold, brilliant and true-hearted to his friends but his political principles hung loosely upon him and he was entirely incapable of managing pecuniary[173] affairs. His private business was always in confusion and that of the War Department brought to a similar condition. His colleagues bore his shortcomings impatiently and the president was vexed and distressed of complaints of his mal-administration.

Mr. Buchanan's wrath was thoroughly aroused when he heard of the secretary's assent to the payment of a large claim in the face of the Attorney General's opinion that it was unjust and illegal. By the president's stern command, the money was stopped before it reached the hand of the claimant. When he discovered that Mr. Floyd had accepted bills of contractors long in advance of their earnings he sent Vice-President Mr. Breckinridge[174] to him with the request that Mr. Floyd would resign, couched in terms which gave him clearly to understand that he would be removed if he did not. This happened on the 23rd of December. From that time Mr. Floyd was regarded virtually out of office. Until then he was an outspoken opponent of secession. And when he came uninvited to the Cabinet meeting on the evening of the 27th and took the side of the secessionist on the questions under discussion, it was plainly seen that he wished to make an issue on which he could resign without reference to the real cause. John B. Floyd resigned as Secretary of War on December 29th, assigning as his reason therefore that the president refused "to withdraw Major Anderson's command from Fort Sumter and yield up that fort to the state of South Carolina." It was a cunning and well-managed maneuver and some of his colleagues who liked him personally were willing to see it succeed. The president was induced with some difficulty to accept his resignation without commentary.

---

173 Pecuniary means monetary.

174 John Cabell Breckinridge was born in Kentucky and was a Major in the Mexican War. He graduated from Transylvania University and became a lawyer. He served both as a Congressman and a U.S. Senator. He was Vice-President of the United States under James Buchanan's and a presidential candidate in the 1860 election. He was a Major General in the Confederate Army. After the war he fled to England, finally returning to Kentucky after the universal amnesty. Appleton's Cyclopaedia of American Biography, Vol. I., pg. 366 and Pride of the South, pgs. 74-76.

Three days later a criminal prosecution was ordered against Mr. Floyd for malfeasance in office and a conspiracy to defraud the United States based on the transactions already referred to. An indictment was found but it was never tried because he had testified on the whole subject before a committee of the House of Representatives.[175] There was an act that any person could not be "held to answer any act or fact" concerning which he had so testified.[176] It is impossible to state what would have been the result of the trial. There is no evidence against Mr. Floyd of anything worse than reckless impudence.[177] Not a cent of any money proceeding from these premature acceptances could be traced to his hands. And it is very clear that he had no connection in thought, word, or deed with the abstraction[178] of the Indian trust bonds from the Interior Department. Mr. Floyd left Washington empty-handed, so poor he had to borrow the money to take his family to Virginia. No man retired in this country from so high an office with such a weight of popular odium resting upon his head. But this arose mainly out of the false charge that he had treacherously and unlawfully sent arms and munitions to the South so as to leave the North defenseless in the anticipated civil war. The accusation persisted for years; asserted and reasserted constantly in the face of the known and proven truth.

Late in the evening of Saturday the 29th of December the president laid before the Cabinet the result of his own reflections in the form of an answer to the South Carolina commissioners. It was such a paper that none of them expected it to be. One member only approved the document and five opposed it for different reasons. Messrs. Black, Holt and Stanton objected that it conceded too much to the contumacious[179] state and Messrs. Thomas and Thompson thought that its whole tone was so hostile to the claim of South Carolina, that it would make the immediately outbreak of civil war inevitable. Mr.

---

[175] Mr. Floyd was indicted by a District of Columbia grand jury for conspiracy on January 27, 1861. He appeared in court on March 7, 1861 but the indictment was thrown out. See footnote that follows.

[176] The indictments against Floyd had been quashed by the court in Washington on two grounds—that there was no evidence of fraud on his part and because the charge of malfeasance in the matter of the Indian bonds was precluded from trial by the act of 1857 which forbid a prosecution when the party implicated has testified before a Committee of Congress previously. *Harpers Weekly*, March 30, 1861.

[177] Impudence means brazenness.

[178] Abstraction means dishonest taking.

[179] Contumacious means stubborn.

Toucey[180] was fully with the president. Not much criticism was bestowed upon the document at the time. The members all thought that further discussion would be useless. In their past experience they had seen how inflexible were Mr. Buchanan's resolutions when once formed. Each was left to decide for himself what his duty required him to do. It seemed certain that the Cabinet was about to explode and fly off in the opposite direction.

On the next morning, Sunday, December 30, Judge Black communicated to Messrs. Stanton, Holt and Toucey his conviction that the president's mind was fixed beyond all hope of change and his own determination to resign in consequence. Mr. Toucey told the president and Judge Black was sent for. He went reluctantly dreading the effect of his own feeling of the appeal which he knew Mr. Buchanan would make to the sacred friendship which had lasted through many years of prosperity and certainly ought not to be broken in that hour of trouble and adversity. What was said between them during this interview need not be told but it ended in the offer of the president to let Judge Black take the document in question, strike out what he thought objectionable and insert what was necessary to make it meet his own views; but this must be done immediately. Judge Black went to the Attorney General's office and there wrote the following paper which Mr. Stanton copied as rapidly as the sheets were thrown to him:

Memorandum for the president on the subject of the paper drawn up by him in reply to the commissioners of South Carolina.

*First—The first and the concluding paragraph both seem to acknowledge the right of South Carolina to be represented in this government by diplomatic officers; that implies that she is an independent nation with no other relations to the government of the Union than any other foreign power. If such be the fact then she has acquired all the rights, powers and responsibilities of a separated government by the mere ordinance of secession which passed her convention only a few days ago. But the president has always and particularly in his late message to Congress denied the right of secession and asserted that no state could throw off her federal obligations in that way. Moreover the president has very distinctly declared that even if a state could secede and go out of the Union at pleasure whether by*

[180] Isaac Toucey from Connecticut was U.S. Attorney General from June 1848 - March 1849 and Secretary of the Navy in the Cabinet of James Buchanan. He was also a U.S. Senator. The Story-Life of Lincoln, pg. 358 and Appleton's Cyclopaedia of American Biography, Part VI., pg. 142.

*revolution or the exercise of constitutional right he could not recognize her independence without being guilty of usurpation.*[181] *I think therefore that every word and sentence which implies that South Carolina is in an attitude which enables the presidency to treat or negotiate with her or to receive her commissioners in the character of diplomatic ministers or agents, ought to be stricken out and an exclusive declaration substituted which would reassert the principles of the message. It is surely not enough that the words of the message be transcribed if the doctrine there announced be practically abandoned by carrying on negotiation.*

*Second—I would strike out all expression of regret that the commissioners are unwilling to proceed with the negotiations since it is very clear that there can be no negotiations with them, whether they are willing or not.*

*Third—Above all, it is objectionable to intimate the willingness to negotiate with the state of South Carolina of the possession of the military posts which belong to the United States, or to propose any adjustments to the subject or any arrangement about it. The forts in Charleston harbor belong to this government, are its own, and cannot be given up. It is true; they might be surrendered to a superior force whether that force be a seceding state or the force of a foreign nation, but Fort Sumter is impregnable and cannot be taken, if defended as it should be. It is a thing of the last importance that it should be maintained if all the power of this nation can do it for the command of the harbor, and the president's ability to execute the revenue laws may depend upon it.*

*Fourth—The words "coercing a state by force of arms to remain in the confederacy," a power I do not believe the Constitution has conferred on Congress, ought certainly not be retained. They are too vague and might have the effect (which I am sure the president does not intend) to mislead the commissioners concerning his sentiments. The power to defend the public property, to resist an assailing force which unlawfully attempts to drive out the troops of the United States from one of their fortifications and to use military and naval forces for the purpose of aiding the proper officers of the United States in the execution of the law—this is as far as it goes. It is called coercion, and may be well called "coercing a state by force of arms to remain in the Union." The president has always asserted his right of coercion to that extent. He merely denies the right of Congress to make offensive war upon a state of the Union, as such might be made upon a foreign government.*

*Fifth—The implied ascent of the president to the accusation which the commissioners make of a compact with South Carolina by which he was bound not to take such measures as he saw fit for the defense of the forts ought to be stricken out and a flat denial of any such bargain, pledge or agreement inserted. The papers*

---

[181] Usurpation means seizing by force.

*signed by the late members of Congress from South Carolina do not bear any such construction. And this as I understand it is the only transaction between South Carolina and him which bears upon the subject either directly or indirectly. I think it deeply concerns the president's reputation that he should contradict this statement since if it be undenied,*[182] *it puts him in the attitude of an executive officer who voluntarily disarms himself of the power to perform his duty and ties up his hands so that he cannot, without breaking his word, "preserve, protect and defend the Constitution and see the laws faithfully executed." The fact that he pledged himself in any such way cannot be true. The commissioners have no doubt been so informed but there must be some mistake about it. It arose no doubt from the president's anxious, doubtless and laudable desire to avoid civil war and his often expressed determination to not even furnish an excuse for an outbreak at Charleston by reinforcing Major Anderson unless it was absolutely necessary.*

*Sixth—The remotest doubt about Major Anderson's perfect propriety of behavior should be carefully avoided. He is not merely a gallant and meritorious officer who is entitled to a fair hearing before he is condemned; he has saved the country, I solemnly believe, when its day was darkest and its perils most extreme. He has done everything mortal man could do to repair the fatal error which the administration has committed in not sending down troops enough to hold all the forts. He has kept the strongest one. He still commands the harbor. We still may exceed the laws if we try. Besides there was nothing in the orders sent to him by the War Department which is in the slightest degree contravened*[183] *by his act of throwing his command into Fort Sumter. Even if those orders, sent without your knowledge, did forbid him to leave a place where his men might have perished and shelter them under a stronger position, we ought all of us to rejoice that he broke such orders.*

*Seventh—The idea that a wrong was committed against South Carolina by moving from Fort Moultrie to Fort Sumter ought to be repelled as firmly as may be consistent with a proper respect for the high character of the gentlemen who compose the South Carolina commission. It is a strange assumption of right on the part of the state to say that our United States troops must remain in the weakest position that they can find in the harbor. It is not a menace to South Carolina or to Charleston or of any menace at all. It is simply self-defense. If South Carolina does not attack Major Anderson, no human being will be injured. For there certainly can be no reason to believe that he will commence hostilities. The apparent objection to his being in Fort Sumter is that he will be less likely to fall an easy prey to his assailants.*

182 Undenied means indisputable.

183 Contravened means opposed.

*These are the points in which I advise the paper to be amended. I admit that they are too radical to permit much hope of their adoption. If they are adopted the whole paper will need to be recast. But there is one thing not to be overlooked in this terrible crisis. I entreat the president to order the Brooklyn*[184] *and the Macedonian*[185] *to Charleston without the least delay and in the meantime send a hasty messenger to Major Anderson, to let him know that his government will not desert him, with reinforcement of troops from New York or Old Point to follow immediately. If this be done at once, all yet may be not well, but comparatively safe. If not, I can see nothing before us but ruin, and disaster to the country.*

The original of this paper went to the president but Mr. Stanton's copy was retained by him and by him endorsed "observations on s.c.com. by J.S.B."[186] Although Judge Black took the entire responsibility of it, edited every word himself and spoke throughout in the first person singular, it undoubtedly embodied the sentiments of Mr. Stanton also. He commented on it with strong expressions of delight and Mr. Holt who saw it the same day equally approved it. Mr. Stanton would have resigned with Mr. Black if the views of the latter (which were also his own) had not been adopted. Mr. Holt would perhaps have done the same but he did not say so. There was never any talk, or suggestion, or threat, absolute or conditional, by any northern member of the administration other than what is here stated.

The observations were the latest effort in the single-handed struggle of one man to alter a decision which had stood immovable against the united assault of himself and two of his colleagues. Unexpectedly it succeeded. The president yielded to this earnest appeal, much which he had previously denied with inflexible firmness. How much can the reader ascertain by comparison with this paper to the final answer to the commissioners? Mr. Buchanan had always felt in full the deep responsibility resting upon him. He was anxious to avoid a collision which would prevent accommodation, hurry the border states out of the Union, and precipitate a civil war for which the government was totally unprepared. But he had never for a

---

184 *Brooklyn* was a Union screw sloop with a crew of 335. She stood waiting for word to reinforce and re-supply Major Anderson at Charlestown harbor. Later she participated in bombardments of Grand Gulf, Mississippi, and Galveston, Texas and in the attack at Vicksburg. Warships of the Civil War Navies, pg. 35.

185 *Macedonian* was a federal sloop, 164 feet long, with 380 crew and 20 guns. After the war she became the Naval Academy practice ship. Warships of the Civil War Navies, pg. 133.

186 Stands for South Carolina Commissioners, by Jeremiah S. Black.

moment willingly contemplated the surrender of the forts at Charleston. On the contrary he had uniformly declared—before the election and after—that if those forts should be given up he would rather "die than live." His regular message having produced no apparent effect, the president determined to make another appeal to the patriotism of Congress. At his request Judge Black drew up a message in the spirit of his late "memorandum" of which two or three paragraphs were adopted by the president and the balance were rejected. Among the latter were the following, occurring just after a startling recital of South Carolina "manifold acts of aggressions and wrongs."

"Major Anderson was in command of all the forts in the harbor with orders to defend them. He had a right—nay, it was his imperative duty—to occupy that one of the three in which his own life and that of his men could be safest. I am bound to presume, being without evidence to the contrary, that he had a reason to fear an attack. But whether he had or not his movement being for purpose, purely defensive, cannot with any show of reason be construed as an injury to South Carolina.

If the state authorities had no intention to attack him, the transfer of his force from a weak point to a strong one must have been a matter of perfect indifference to them. If on the contrary their purpose was hostile, then his movement was clearly proper and necessary to his own safety and the performance of his duty.

If no adjustment be made by Congress, if no proposition settlement be made before the people, if no hope be afforded of the peaceful termination of the contest, I must frankly say that no power which the law has put into the hands of the executive is in my opinion sufficient to stay the progress of the revolution. I can retain the possession of Fort Sumter and command of the harbor of Charleston. This will enable me to collect the revenue of the fort and I intend to do so. But will that preserve the Union, when ten or twelve or fourteen states shall take up the attitude similar to that South Carolina now occupies?

I would be unfaithful to my duty if I did not warn you that the dangers which we are encompassed are far more extensive than those which arise from the non-execution of the laws at Charleston. I therefore recommend that Congress pass a law authorizing the executive to call into service of the United States such numbers of the military of this district or of the states as may be deemed necessary to suppress insurrection and preserve the public peace."

President Buchanan was solemnly assured by the highest authority that South Carolina would not attack any of the forts in the Charleston harbor in the circumstances that then existed. But "to guard against surprise" an exposition as powerful as his limited means would afford was prepared early in December and held in readiness to reinforce Major Anderson. An officer was dispatched to acquaint Major Anderson with the fact and order him to "defend himself to the last extremity." For nearly a month, the man-of-war *Brooklyn* lay at Fortress Monroe[187] awaiting the proper moment to take on board five hundred disciplined troops, with provision and munitions of war to be thrown into Fort Moultrie and now Fort Sumter.

At one time it appeared the Secretary of War[188] was urgent for sending her off immediately, but was met by a professional opinion from General Scott[189] that she ought not go at all. But on the 30th of December, the president made up his mind to succor[190] Major Anderson at all hazards. The latter had now removed to Fort Sumter. The South Carolinians had seized all unoccupied forts, and there was no longer any reason for the delay. But again General Scott interposed. He did not wish the great steamer with five hundred veterans to be sent from Fortress Monroe, but recommended instead a sloop-of-war and cutter with two hundred and fifty raw recruits from New York. The president promptly overruled him and dispatched the *Brooklyn*.

The necessary orders were issued through General Scott, who instead of transmitting them to the proper officers, put them into his pocket and called to "congratulate" the president that he had them there. But on that day, the 31st, the president had communicated his

---

187 Fortress Monroe guarded the Hampton Roads area where several rivers including the James River flow into the Chesapeake Bay. The Peace Conference in early 1865 was held on the *River Queen* anchored at this fort. It was at Fortress Monroe where the government held Confederate Jefferson Davis prisoner after the war. Smithsonian's Great Battles and Battlefields of the Civil War, pgs. 751 & 756.

188 John B. Floyd was Secretary of War.

189 General Winfield Scott was a veteran of the Blackhawk War, the Mexican War, the War of 1812 and the Seminole War. He was a presidential candidate in the 1852 election. He was the commanding officer of the U.S. Army prior to the Civil War. He retired in October 1861 because at age 75 he was too old to be active in the war. The Story-Life of Lincoln, pgs. 105, 191, and 222 and Appleton's Cyclopaedia of American Biography, Vol. V., pg. 440.

190 Succor means help.

answer to the South Carolina commissioners. Before they separated, both he and the General came to the conclusion that the order to the *Brooklyn* ought to await the reply of the commissioners. By the courtly soldier this was considered only "gentlemanly and proper." The delay for this purpose only lasted until the 2nd of January, when it was discovered that the general who had acquiesced in the plan of sending the *Brooklyn* had changed his mind again, and would now hear to nothing else than a merchant vessel and the troops from New York.

On the 2nd of January, the last day of the delay, occasioned by awaiting the answer of the commissioners of South Carolina, which General Scott considered so gentlemanly and proper, it was made the subject of a prolonged and heated discussion in the Cabinet. It ended in a resolution to send an officer to Major Anderson to ascertain whether he wanted or needed reinforcements. Here, Judge Jeremiah Black, apprehensive of another delay, interposed a question: "Does the sending of a messenger imply that no additional troops will be sent until his return?"

"Judge Black," said President Buchanan impatiently, raising both hands, "it implies nothing." Just at this juncture, while Mr. Holt[191] was writing down the interrogatories to be propounded[192] to Major Anderson, the answer of the commissioners arrived. It excited so much disgust and indignation, that there could be no question as to the proper disposition of it.[193] The president wrote across it his curt refusal to receive it, and caused it to be instantly returned. Then turning to the Secretary of War[194] he said "reinforcements must now be sent." The order was made in the Cabinet, but Mr. Thompson, the Secretary of the Interior, did not hear it fully. Perhaps it was not intended that he should.

With great reluctance the president yielded, and the unarmed *Star of the West*[195] was substituted for the armed and powerful *Brooklyn*. She

---

[191] Judge Joseph Holt—See page 23.

[192] Propounded means proposed.

[193] The Commissioners presented a copy of the Ordinance of Secession and asked President Buchanan to withdraw the federal troops from the Charleston harbor. www.teachingushistory/history.org/jtrove/buchananletters.htm

[194] Joseph Holt had just replaced John B. Floyd who had resigned.

[195] *Star of the West* thereby carried the raw recruits towards Charleston harbor from New York to reinforce Major Anderson. The ship was a 228 foot Union side-wheel steamer with 6 guns. Later in the war she was captured by the Confederate ship *General*

sailed on the 5th and while entering the harbor of Charleston on the 9th was fired at and struck by a shot fired from the battery of Morris Island when she bore around and put to sea again. Intelligence of this battery "among the sand hills" had been received in Washington on the evening of the 5th, but the *Star of the West* could neither be warned nor detained. It was hoped that the mission of the *Star of the West* would remain in profound secrecy with the few persons whom courtesy or necessity required to know it.

For many days Mr. Thompson had been exerting himself to prevent the South Carolinians from attacking Major Anderson, an event which he believed would be equally disastrous to both sections. To affect this purpose, which to say the least was not unpatriotic, many telegrams were passing between him and Judge Longstreet[196] an eminent and comparatively reasonable citizen of South Carolina. So late as the 5th, the very day the vessel sailed, Mr. Thompson answered a direct inquiry of his correspondence as follows: "I cannot speak by authority, but I do not believe any additional troops will be sent to Charleston while the present status lasts. If Fort Sumter is attacked, they will be sent, I believe." When under these circumstances he heard that the expedition was actually at sea, it was not surprising that he was both amazed and shocked. He felt he had been not only slighted but deceived, and used as an unconscious instrument to produce a gross and shameful deception upon those who had trusted in his word all along.

Was it a violation of his official duty to remove a delusion which owed its existence to him and him alone? He had reason to believe that his assurances had done much thus far to keep the peace and to keep Fort Sumter from assault. Was he bound to withdraw them now that he knew them to be false, and thus imperil the *Star of the West* with her freight of human life? He thought he was. Having given an unofficial opinion that reinforcements would not be sent at the very moment when they were actually embarking, he determined to send an unofficial dispatch saying that they had been in fact sent, but without his knowledge or consent. He wrote it at his house and exhibited it to Judge Black, who had gone there to persuade him from the act. The

---

*Rush* off Texas in April 19, 1861 and converted into a Confederate ship and renamed *St. Philip*. Warships of the Civil War Navies, pgs. 232 & 233.

[196] A. B. Longstreet was President of the College of South Carolina. *Richmond Daily Dispatch*, January 11, 1861.

messenger of the department, William W. Cowling, was waiting to carry the message to the telegraph office. Mr. Cowling caught a few words of the earnest dispute which followed—Judge Black in imploring him not to send it and Mr. Thompson insisting it was a matter which concerned his honor and he must be permitted to perform his sacred duty.

Mr. Cowling was convinced by the argument that Judge Black was right and Mr. Thompson wrong. Being a patriot as well as an official, he disobeyed the secretary's order—put the perilous dispatch in his pocket and let the Charlestonians find out the state of affairs as best they could. His conduct was cordially approved by Mr. Kelley,[197] of the Interior, Judge Black and the Honorable John Sherman[198] to each of whom he revealed it within a few hours. This dispatch, it is very clear, was never sent. But it is equally clear that another was. Mr. Thompson may have suspected Mr. Cowling, or may have received another telegram from Judge Longstreet. At all events he telegraphed "that the *Star of the West* had sailed for Charleston with two hundred fifty troops on board, and she ought to reach the city on that same day." The message did not reach Charleston until twenty minutes after five in the evening. It was none too early, for by daylight the next morning the ship was steaming up the channel. And of the rest the reader is already informed.

On the 8th of January, President Buchanan sent in the special message he had deliberated upon. He painted in a bold free hand the evils already upon the country and the still greater perils that were impending, recurring to the narrow limits of his own discretionary powers and reminding Congress again they alone had power to save the country. He besought them to act in one direction or the other. He communicated the wanton and unprovoked seizure of many forts, arsenals and magazines which the small force at its command would be powerless to recover as it had been to protect. There was still time to conciliate[199] public opinion in the seceded states, to prevent the other slave states from going out, and to restore greater harmony by no greater sacrifice than a little pride of opinion. But this appeal fell as

---

[197] William D. Kelley was a Pennsylvania Congressman who was the senior member of the House in terms of longevity when he died in 1890. Lincoln's War, pg. 221 and Appleton's Cyclopaedia of American Biography, Vol. III., pg. 505.

[198] Honorable John Sherman—See pg. 22.

[199] Conciliate means to win over.

a former appeal had fallen, upon ears that heard not and hearts that heeded not.

It is very true that if the president thought the northern majority capable of yielding the smallest point to that minority they had just beaten so triumphantly at the ballot boxes, he must have given them credit for great magnanimity[200] of character; the men who had expressed so much contempt for the southern character, must conserve their consistency by despising it still. Those who had denounced every expression of fear of the Union as the cowardice of "dough-faced" politicians were not likely to confess themselves under the influence of this same fear. They could not retreat all at once the assertions which they had vociferated[201] into the ears of the electors from every northern stump that the Union was in the slightest danger. Perhaps if their own rank had contained some great man, some real statesman who deserved their confidence and had it, they might have led them through the fearful passage as Wellington[202] and Peel[203] had led their party through the crisis of catholic emancipation, when the British nation was saved from revolution as dangerous as that which now threatened the Union. These men might have taught Congress that exemption from a great calamity such as even the temporary dismemberment of an empire accompanied the blood shed spoliation and anarchy of civil war would be cheaply purchased even at the expense of conceding in the way of compromise, much more than what was due from the strong to the weak. Such men being rare perhaps, it is not wondered that none were found among the Republican members of either House.

But it was amazing that no man could give his consent to a bill which would enable the executive to meet the revolution and put it down by force since that required no exertion of moral courage, no sacrifice of political consistency, and no humiliation of personal pride. This refusal of Congress to inaugurate a system of active coercion was not caused by a belief that the executive was already armed with

---

200 Magnanimity means loftiness.

201 Vociferated means cried out.

202 The Duke of Wellington was a hero of the battle of Waterloo and an advisor to Queen Victoria of England. Lincoln, His Path to the Presidency, pg. 123.

203 Sir Robert Peel was the Conservative Prime Minister of the United Kingdom, December 1834 to June 1846. He was instrumental in establishing the modern police force lading for police officers to become known as "bobbies." www.victorianweb.org/history/pms/peel/peel10.html

sufficient power to do it. Not a doubt was expressed of the president's own view on that subject. It was universally admitted that he had no authority under the Act of 1795 to call out the militia to suppress an insurrection against the federal government. No one suggested that he could of his own will increase the regular army or navy. It was not asserted in any quarter that he might execute the laws by military force without the intervention of judges and marshals. If he had hinted at his intention to usurp these powers or any others which legally did not belong to him, there was no reason to doubt that he would have been, as he certainly ought to have been, impeached within twenty-four hours. Nor can the omission be charged to the request of government. It was a deliberate refusal to give him the authority requested.

It is safe to say that no one in high positions during these times has received more praise or deserved it less as many good and loyal men believe than General Winfield Scott. Before the election of Mr. Lincoln, before a state had seceded, before it was even certain that any state would secede, he laid before the Secretary of War a paper which he called "his views." It was not inappropriately named, as he presented little else but dissolving views of the "great republic," rent into "fragments" of which he volunteered to trace the proper boundaries and locate the capital. He quoted Paley's "*Moral and Political Philosophy*"[204] to show that a nation might use force to preserve the continuity of its territory; but for a secession which made no gap in a union and left the continuity unbroken, merely carrying away a dozen or so of neighboring states, he could think of no remedy whatever. Thus if South Carolina seceded while North Carolina and Georgia remained, South Carolina might lawfully be coerced. But if all three went out together, there was nothing to be done but to bless them, unless perhaps it was to give them a little considerate advice about the selection of a capital.

"It will be seen," said General Scott, "that the views only apply to a case of secession which makes a gap in the present Union." The falling of say Texas or of all the Atlantic states from the Potomac River south was not within the scope of General Scott's provisional remedies. The foregoing views eschew[205] the idea of invading a seceding state. He dreaded, "the laceration and despotism of the sword" and considered

---

[204] *Moral and Political Philosophy* was published by William Paley in 1785 from a series of his lectures. www.answers.com/topic/william-paley

[205] Eschew means to abstain from.

the reduction of the Union to "fragments," "a smaller evil." Mr. Buchanan thought this part of the document "out of time and out of place"—a very mild judgment. It might have been penned at the headquarters of the South Carolina militia, and read with applause at the secession convention, after mentioning what his pat feelings were like, and what "ticket" had his "sympathies."

The general came to the military point in this dreary dissertation. It took only a short paragraph to state it and consisted of the naked advice to garrison nine forts in the South, so as to make an attempt to take them "ridiculous." There he broke off, omitting entirely to designate any force available for such a purpose. The next day, however, he supplied the information. "There were," he said, "in all five companies only within reach—not enough to make any single one of the forts impregnable" and to this statement he gave the imposing title of "supplemental views." The general repeated his advice on the 15th of December.

On the 8th of January, General Scott published his views to the world, South Carolina and the cotton states included. What aid and comfort they afforded to the latter can only be conjectured from the character of the document itself; but determined not to be misunderstood, he saluted the new administration on the evening of the 3rd of March in a letter in which he again aired his political opinion and after deprecating[206] the "enormous waste" and numberless horrors of civil war which could only end in the conquest of devastated and worthless "provinces," he put the sum of his views about which he had made such a bother into a single sentence. "Wayward sisters—depart in peace."

Jacob Thompson resigned as Secretary of the Interior on the 8th day of January 1861 because he had learned that additional troops had been ordered to Charleston in the *Star of the West.* When the *Star of the West* was fired upon on January 9, Major Anderson made no reply from the guns of Fort Sumter as he should have done, when he saw his own supply ship which he knew and recognized, suffering in the midst of an overwhelming cannonade. He sent to the governor to obtain a disavowal of the act, and in case of a failure to get it, said he would consider the act the beginning of hostilities and would fire upon any vessel in reach of his guns. But his zeal departed with his

[206] Deprecating means expressing disapproval of.

messenger. And when the governor transmitted, instead of an apology, the demand for the surrender of Fort Sumter itself, he calmly referred the matter to Washington—and made himself happy with a truce. The major might certainly have done better. For at that moment he considered his position impregnable, boasting of his power to command the harbor and defeat "any force that might be brought against him."

On the 10th of January, the House referred the special message to a secret committee of five—Messrs. Howard,[207] Branch,[208] Dawes,[209] Cochrane[210] and Hickman.[211]

On the 11th of January, Mr. Thomas[212] resigned from the Treasury Department because he disagreed with the president and Cabinet about affairs in Charleston, and especially about "the authority under existing law to enforce collections of customs at the port of Charleston." General Dix[213] took his place and henceforth the Cabinet was a unit. Joseph Holt who was then Postmaster General was

---

207 Benjamin Chew Howard was a Maryland lawyer who was also chairman of the House foreign relations committee. Appleton's Cyclopaedia of American Biography, Vol. III., pgs. 276 & 277.

208 Lawrence O'Brien Branch was a North Carolina lawyer who was a three-term Congressman. He was a Brigadier General for the Confederacy who was killed at Antietam on September 17, 1862. Appleton's Cyclopaedia of American Biography, Vol. I., pg. 358.

209 Henry Caurens Dawes was a Congressman from Massachusetts who served twenty years, from 1853 -1873. He was responsible for completing the construction on the Washington Monument. He also set up the education system for the American Indians in western territories after the war. Appleton's Cyclopaedia of American Biography, Vol. II., pg. 107.

210 John Cochrane was a Democratic Congressman from New York who became a Union Brigadier General. He was later nominated as General Frémont's vice-presidential candidate in the election of 1864. Lincoln's War pg. 235, Reelecting Lincoln, pg. 178-180 and www.mrlincolnandnewyork.org .

211 John Hickman from Pennsylvania was a four-term Congressman. He was the first Congressman to propose freeing the slaves and enlisting Negroes into the Union army. He was a Republican candidate for vice-president at the party convention in 1860. Appleton's Cyclopaedia of American Biography, Vol. III., pg. 195.

212 Phillip Francis Thomas—See pg. 46.

213 John Adams Dix of New York was an attorney and U.S. Senator. He became the Secretary of the Treasury in the Cabinet of James Buchanan, taking the place of Howell Cobb when Mr. Cobb resigned. Mr. Lincoln named Dix a Major General of the New York troops at the beginning of the Civil War. General Dix helped negotiate the terms of prisoner exchange with D. H. Hill of the Confederacy. The Story-Life of Lincoln, pg. 363, Lincoln's War, pg. 261, and Appleton's Cyclopaedia of American Biography, Vol. II., pgs. 183 & 184.

appointed with temporary charge to the War Department and on January 11 he was appointed Secretary of War. Joseph Holt resigned on the 18th of January and Horatio King[214] was appointed his successor. John A. Dix was then appointed as King's successor

President Buchanan's Cabinet was at no time harmonious for a year previous to the time of Mr. Lincoln's inauguration.
Perhaps the spirit by which they were animated as a body was never more candidly expressed than in the following letter:

*State Department, January 17, 1861*
*Dear sir:*

*I am much obliged by your letter. It undoubtedly would be a great party move as between Democrats and Black Republicans to let the latter have a civil war of their own making.*

*It would also be poetic as well as political justice to let them reap the whirlwind which must grow out of the storm they sowed. But can we avoid doing something? Is not the business altogether beyond party considerations? For South Carolina compels us to choose between the destruction of the Government and some kind of defense. They have smitten us on one cheek—shall we turn the other? They have taken our coat—shall we give them our cloak also? The gospel commands this in private affairs, but the rule is not understood, I think, as applying to public property held by a government in trust for its people. I am not in favor of war, but I can not resist the conviction that when war is made against us a moderate self-defense is righteous and proper. Coercion well, I would not care about coercing South Carolina if she could agree not to coerce us. But she kicks, cuffs, abuses, spits upon us, commits all kinds of outrages against our rights, and then cries out that she is coerced if we propose to hide our diminished heads under a shelter which may protect us a little better for the future.*

*I agree with you that we ought not to make a civil war. Do you disagree with me in the opinion that we are bound to defend our selves from an unjust and illegal attack? Whatever your answer may be, it can not prevent me from being your friend,*

*J.S. Black*

---

214 Horatio King was from Maine. He was editor of the Jeffersonian newspaper of Paris, Maine and was a practicing attorney. He worked hard to help assure that the District of Columbia enacted the Emancipation law of D.C. www.u-s-history.com/pages/h1233.html

Judge Black[215] also responded as Attorney General to a request of a legal opinion concerning secession from President Buchanan. The judge indicated that the federal government had a duty and a right to collect duties and to defend public property and to execute the laws. Judge Black said this right could only be enforced peaceably, and if force were necessary, only Congress could legislate such procedures. Black continued saying that Congress could not "arm one part of the people against another for the purpose beyond that of merely protecting the general government in the exercise of proper constitutional functions." Critics said Judge Black formed the position of the government on the issue by basically saying "You cannot do it, but we cannot stop you if you do." His opinion was that the secession was not constitutional but the federal government was powerless to try to coerce a state back into the Union.[216]

It was twenty days before the secret committee of the House was heard from at all. On the 30th of January the chairman reported a bill "to enable the president to call forth the military or to accept the services of volunteers to protect and defend the forts, magazines, arsenals and other property of the United States and to recover the possession of such as had been unlawfully seized." The bill was re-committed on the same day it was reported back; that is to say, reported back to the same committee. And there it slept the sleep that knows no waking. The committee made no further report and none was ever called.

The Peace Conference that met in Washington on February 4, 1861 at the request of the Virginia legislature composed of representatives from thirteen free and seven border states adopted and reported to Congress a number of resolutions making various concessions to southern demands.[217] Congress rejected all of these—passed as a substitute an amendment to the Constitution, proposed by Senator Douglas, which forbade Congress to ever interfere with slavery in the states. (But this amendment was never adopted by the necessary number of states.) While these measures were being uselessly

---

215 Judge Jeremiah Black—See page 27.

216 http://housedivided,dickinson.edu/main/index.php?q=node/12125

217 The Plan of Adjustment adopted by the Peace Commission proposed, in part, to maintain slavery in the present South, to have the Senators vote on the entry of new states or territories to decide the slavery issue, and that the Constitution should not be construed to give Congress the ability to regulate, abolish or control slavery within any state or territory. Harpers Pictorial History of the Great Rebellion, pg. 46.

debated and the time which should have been spent in preparation to make the federal government ready to assert its supremacy was wasted in dalliance[218] over theoretical remedies for incurable evils, the work of the South to effect secession was pressed with the utmost vigor, energy and ability.

Colonel I. W. Hayne[219] the governor's envoy and Lieutenant Hall[220] from Fort Sumter arrived in Washington on the 14th of February. The latter represented Major Anderson as perfectly secure, while the former bore demands of the surrender of his position. But nine of the Senators from the cotton states prevailed on Colonel Hayne not to deliver his note until they had time to ascertain whether Mr. Buchanan would agree not to reinforce the fort provided Governor Pickens[221] would also agree to let it alone. On the 19th the correspondence between them was laid before the president who employed the potent pen of Mr. Holt to say in reply "at the present moment it is not deemed necessary to reinforce Major Anderson because he makes no such request, and feels quite secure in his position. Should his safety, however, require reinforcements, every effort will be made to supply them."

On the 18th of February, nineteen days after Mr. Howard's bill had been finally disposed of by the re-committal, and nineteen days before the close of the session, Mr. Benjamin Stanton[222] of Ohio, chairman of the committee on military affairs, reported a bill which, without touching the subject of recovering of the forts or other public property, simply extended the power of the president to call out the militia in cases of insurrection against the United States. This raised a question of constitutional law not free from difficulty. It was earnestly

---

218 Dalliance means trifling.

219Colonel I. W. Hayne was attorney general for the state of South Carolina and envoy for Governor Pickens. *Richmond Daily Dispatch*, February 12, 1861.

220 Lt. Norman J. Hall risked his life during the siege at Fort Sumter trying to put back the fallen Union flag. Search.intelius.com/Norman-J-Hall

221 Governor Francis Wilkinson Pickens was a lawyer and Congressman. In 1836 he proposed that the District of Columbia shouldn't be allowed to abolish slavery without the consent of the states of Maryland and Virginia. Pickens served as Minister to Russia from 1858 - 1860. He was appointed Governor of South Carolina on December 16, 1860, four days before South Carolina voted to secede from the Union. The Confederate Governors, pgs. 162 & 162 and Appleton's Cyclopaedia of American Biography, Vol. IV., pg. 768.

222 Benjamin Stanton was a Congressman from Ohio who served from 1851 to 1853. He also served as Lt. Governor to David Tod. Plumbot.com/david_tod.html

discussed for several days. On Tuesday the 26th of February, Mr. Corwin[223] moved to postpone its consideration until the 28th. Mr. Stanton warned the House that if the motion prevailed it would be fatal to the bill. "It will be impossible," said he, "after that to have it passed by the Senate." But it was postponed by a vote of 100 yeas and 70 nos. This was as the House intended it should be, a finishing blow to the bill, and it was accordingly heard no more. Another bill was proposed looking to the forcible execution of the revenue laws in the disaffected states. This was a bill reported on the 3rd of January from the committee on judiciary and "entitled a further bill to provide for the collection of duties on imports." But it was not called up for consideration until the 2nd of March, the day before the last one of the session, and it was called up then only to be defeated.

On the 30th of January, Colonel Hayne had presented the governor's demand, and again Mr. Holt replied in a letter of overwhelming force which the style and sentiments will stand forever in his immortal honor.

*War Department, February 6, 1861*
*Honorable I. W. Hayne, Attorney General of the State of South Carolina*

*The President of the United States has received your letter of the 31st ultimo, and has charged me with the duty of replaying thereto.*

*In the communication addressed to the President by Governor Pickens, under the date of the 12th of January, and which accompanies yours now before me, his Excellency says: "I have determined to send to you Hon. I. W. Hayne, the Attorney General of the State of South Carolina, and have instructed him to demand the surrender of Fort Sumter, in the harbor of Charleston, to the constituted authorities of the State of South Carolina. The demand I have made of Major Anderson, and which I now make to you, is suggested because of my earnest desire to avoid bloodshed which a persistence in your attempt to retain possession of that fort will cause and which will be unavailing to secure you that possession, but induce a calamity most deeply to be deplored."*

*The character of the demand thus authorized to be made, appears, under the influence I presume of the correspondence with the Senators to which you refer, to have been modified by subsequent instructions of his Excellency, dated the 26th and received by yourself of the 30th of January, in which he says: "If it be so that Fort Sumter is held as property, then as property the rights, whatever they may be, of the*

223 Thomas Corwin—See pg. 17.

*United States, can be ascertained; and for the satisfaction of these rights the pledge of the State of the South Carolina you are authorized to give."*

*The full scope and precise purport of your instructions, as thus modified, you have expressed in the following words: "I do not claim as a military man to demand the surrender of a fortress, but as the legal officers of the State—its Attorney General—to claim for the State the exercise of its undoubted right of eminent domain, and to pledge the State to make good all injury to the rights of property which arise from the exercise of the claim."*

*And lest this explicit language should not sufficiently define your position, you add: "The proposition now is that her (South Carolina's) law officer should, under the authority of the Governor and his Council, distinctly pledge the faith of South Carolina to make such compensation, in regard to Fort Sumter and its appurtenances*[224] *and contents, to the full extent of the money value of the property of the United States delivered over to the authorities of South Carolina by your command."*

*You then adopt his Excellency's train of thought upon the subject so far as to suggest that the possession of Fort Sumter by the U. States, "If continued long enough, must lead to collision," and that "an attack upon it would scarcely improve it as property, whatever the result, and, if captured, it would no longer be the subject of account."*

*The proposal, then, now presented to the President, is simply an offer on the part of S. Carolina to buy Fort Sumter and contents as property of the United States, sustained by a declaration in effect, that if she is not permitted to make the purchase, she will seize the fort by force of arms. As the initiation of a negotiation for the transfer of property between friendly Governments, this proposal impresses the President as having assumed a most unusual form. He has, however, investigated the claim on which it professes to be based, apart from the declaration that accompanies it. And it may be here remarked that the stress has been laid upon the employment of the words "property" and "public property" by the President in his several messages. These are the most comprehensive terms which can be used in such a connection, and, surely, when referred to a fort of any other public establishment, they embraced the entire and undivided interest of the Government therein.*

*The title of the United States to Fort Sumter is complete and uncontested. Were its interest in this property purely proprietary, in the ordinary acceptation of the term, it might probably be subjected to the exercise of the right of eminent domain; but it has also political relations to it of much higher and more imposing*

---

[224] Appurtenances are adjuncts or appendages.

*character than those of mere proprietorship. It has absolute jurisdiction over the fort and soil on which it stands. This jurisdiction consists in the authority to "exercise exclusive legislation" over the property referred to, and is therefore clearly incompatible with the claim of eminent domain now insisted upon by South Carolina. This authority was not derived from any questionable, revolutionary source, but from the peaceful cession of South Carolina herself, acting through her Legislature, under a provision of the Constitution of the United States. South Carolina can no more assert the right of eminent domain over Fort Sumter than Maryland can assert it over the District of Columbia. The political and proprietary rights of the U. States in either case rest upon the precisely same ground.*

*The President, however, is relieved from the necessity of further pursuing this inquiry by the fact that, whatever may be the claim of South Carolina to this fort, he has no constitutional power to cede or surrender it. The property of the United States has been acquired by force of public law and can only be disposed of under the same solemn sanctions. The President, as the head of the Executive branch of the Government only, can no more sell or transfer Fort Sumter to South Carolina than he can sell and convey the Capitol of the United States to Maryland, or to any other State or individual seeking to possess it. His Excellency the Governor is too familiar with the Constitution of the United States, and with the limitations upon the powers of the Chief Magistrate of the Government it has established, not to appreciate at once the soundness of this legal proposition.*

*The question of reinforcing Fort Sumter is so fully disposed of in my letter to Senator Slidell*[225] *and others, under date of 22nd of January—a copy which accompanies this—that its discussion will not now be renewed. I then said: "At the present moment it is not deemed necessary to reinforce Major Anderson, because he makes no such request. Should his safety, however, require reinforcements, every effort will be made to supply them."*

*I can add nothing to the explicitness of this language, which still applies to the existing status. The right to send forward reinforcements, when in the judgment of the President the safety of the garrison requires them, rests on the same unquestionable foundation as the right to occupy the fortress itself.*

*Fort Sumter is in itself a military post, and nothing else; and it would seem that not so much as the purpose of its use should give to it a hostile or friendly character. This fortress is now held by the Government of the United States, for the same objects for which it has been held from completion of its construction. These are national and defensive; and were a public enemy now to attempt to the capture of Charleston or the destruction of the commerce of its harbor, the whole force of the*

225 John Slidell was a U.S. Congressman and U.S. Senator and then a Confederate Senator. www.answers.com/john-slidell

*batteries would be at once exerted for their protection. How the presence of a small garrison, actuated by such a spirit as this, can compromise the dignity or honor of South Carolina, or become a source of irritation to her people, the President is at a loss to understand. The attitude of that garrison, as has been often declared, is neither menacing nor defiant, nor unfriendly. It is acting under orders to stand strictly on the defensive, and the Government and people of South Carolina must well know that they can never receive aught but shelter from its guns, unless, in the absence of all provocation they should assault it, and seek its destruction. The intent with which this fortress is held by the President is truthfully stated by Senator Davis*[226] *and others, in their letters to yourself of the 15th January, in which they said: "It is not held with any hostile or unfriendly purpose towards your State, but merely as property of the United States, which the President deems his duty to protect and preserve."*

*In the letter, Senator Davis*[227] *and others to yourself, under date of the 15th ultimo, they say: "We, therefore, think it especially due from South Carolina to our States—to say nothing of other slaveholding States—that she should, as far as she can consistently with her honor, avoid initiating hostilities between her and the United States or any other Power," and you now yourself give to the President the gratifying assurances that South Carolina has every disposition to preserve the public peace; and, since he is himself sincerely animated by the same desire, it would seem that this common and patriotic object must be of certain attainment. It is difficult, however, to reconcile with this assurance, the declaration on your part that "it is a consideration of her (South Carolina) own dignity as a sovereign, and the safety of her people, which prompts her to demand that this property should no longer be used as a military post by a Government she no longer acknowledges," and the thought you so constantly present that this occupation must lead to a collision of arms and prevalence of civil war.*

*If the announcement, so repeatedly made, of the President's specific purposes in continuing the occupation of Fort Sumter, until the question shall have been settled by competent au view of the circumstances which have so severely tried it, be not*

---

226 Senator Henry Winter Davis was a Congressman from Maryland. He was a cousin of Mr. Lincoln's friend Judge David Davis. He had a law degree from the University of Virginia and was known as a great orator. He held anti-slavery views, though he himself was a slave owner thorough inheritance. He supported Mr. Lincoln in his attempt to try to keep Maryland from seceding. He was a bitter opponent of Lincoln's reconstruction views. His bill (Wade-Davis Act) defining reconstruction was passed by Congress but vetoed by Mr. Lincoln. Seaport Autographs, pgs. 18 & 19.

227 Henry Winter Davis was the co-author with Benjamin Wade establishing the fact that secesh states could rejoin the Union. www.ohiocivilwar150.org/tag/henry-winter-davis

*accepted as a satisfactory pledge of the peaceful policy of this Administration towards South Carolina, then it may be safely affirmed that neither language nor conduct can possibly furnish one. If, with all the multiplied proofs which exist in the President's anxiety for peace, and of the earnestness with he has pursued it, the authorities of that State shall assault Fort Sumter, and peril the lives of the handful of brave and loyal men shut up within its walls, and thus plunge our common country into the horrors of civil war, then upon them and those they represent must rest the responsibility.*

*Very respectfully yours, your obedient servant,*

*J. Holt, Secretary of War*[228]

The Honorable I.W. Hayne rejoined as follows:

*It was no part of my mission to discuss the political relations of the United States Government to anything with the territorial limits of South Carolina. South Carolina claims to have dissolved all political connection with your Government, and to have destroyed all political relations of your Government with everything within her borders. She is unquestionable at this moment de facte a separate and independent Government, exercising complete sovereignty over every foot of her soil except Fort Sumter. Now that the intention is avowed to hold this place as a military post, with acclaim of exclusive jurisdiction on the part of a Government foreign to South Carolina, it will be for the authorities to determine what is the course proper to be pursued. It is then to ignore the fact that South Carolina is yours a foreign Government. And how, with this patent fact before you, you can consider the continued occupation of the fort in her harbor a pacific measure and a parcel of a peaceful policy, passes, certainly, my comprehension.*

*You say that the fort is garrisoned for our protection, and is held for the same purpose for which it has been ever held since its construction. Are you not aware that to hold in the territory of a foreign power a fortress against her will, avowedly for the purpose of protecting her citizens, is perhaps the highest insult which one Government can offer to another? But Fort Sumter was never garrisoned at all until South Carolina had dissolved her connection with your Government. This garrison entered in the night, with every circumstance of secrecy, after spiking the guns and burning the gun-carriages, and cutting down the flag staff of an adjacent fort, which was then abandoned. South Carolina has not taken Fort Sumter into her own possession only because of her misplaced confidence in a Government which deceived her. A fortress occupied under circumstances above stated, is considered not only as no cause of irritation, but you represent it as held for our protection. Your*

---

[228] Judge Joseph Holt, *Richmond Daily Dispatch*, February 12, 1861

*Excellency's Secretary has indulged in irony on a very grave subject. As to the responsibility for consequences, if indeed it does rest on us, I can assure your Excellency we are happily unconscious of the fact.*

*I return to Charleston tomorrow. With considerations of high regard, I am, very respectfully.*

*I. W. Hayne, Special Envoy*[229]

On the 3rd of March, 1861, the 36th Congress reached the prescribed period of its existence, and died a constitutional death. Its last session of three months was spent in view of an awful public calamity which it made no effort to arrest nor to mitigate. It saw the nation compassed[230] round with a frightful danger, but it proposed no plan either of conciliation or defense. It adjourned forever and left the law precisely where it had found it.

Thus the executive was left alone to struggle against the revolution which the constitutional powers of both the legislative and executive would have been insufficient to check. He was almost powerless but none the less resolved to put forth the little strength he had.

After the transfer of Mr. Holt to the War Department, and the resignation of Messrs. Thomas and Thompson, the Cabinet consisted of Messrs. Black, Stanton, Dix, Holt, Toucey and King.[231] They continued in perfect harmony until the end. If any exception to this statement be required it must be made with reference to the arrangement which took place about Fort Pickens.[232] General Scott[233] urgently recommended this "truce" as he afterwards called it. Mr. Holt and Mr. Toucey gave it their approbation and Messrs. Black and Stanton opposed it. The other members gave no opinion. The president thought the general in chief[234] was right but there was very little discussion about it. On the general principles which controlled them and on the details of business they were in perfect accord. The account therefore by T. W.[235] in the *London Observer* "of certain most

---

229 *Richmond Daily Dispatch*, February 12, 1861

230 Compassed means enclosed.

231 Horatio King—See pg. 63.

232 Fort Pickens was a federal fort near Pensacola, Florida that General Winfield Scott thought should be abandoned. The Two American Presidents, pg. 155 & 158.

233 General Winfield Scott—See page 55.

234 The General in Chief was Attorney General Jeremiah Black—See pg. 27.

235 T. W. is Thurlow Weed. He asserted in the letter that President Buchanan was prevented from ordering Major Anderson back to Fort Moultrie by threat of

discreditable disputes as occurred in February 1861" is without foundation in fact.

At the close of Mr. Buchanan's administration his Cabinet stood: Jeremiah S. Black, Secretary of State; Edwin M. Stanton, Attorney General; Horatio King, Postmaster General; John B. Dix, Secretary of the Treasury; Joseph Holt, Secretary of War; Isaac Touchy, Secretary of the Navy; and Moses Kelly,[236] Acting Secretary of the Interior; there being but two of the original Cabinet left in Mr. Black and Mr. Touchy.

The whole subject was beyond controversy. The president had no notion of a surrender, and would not entertain the thought for a moment. In pursuance of this policy, now thoroughly established and well understood, another expedition for the relief of Fort Sumter was prepared at New York. It never sailed, for two reasons, either one was more than sufficient. First—because Major Anderson did not need or want it. Second—because South Carolina as well as the president was disposed to respect the appeal of Virginia, to avoid hostilities till the peace congress should meet and act.

---

resignation by four Cabinet members. Encyclopedia Britannica, 11th Edition, James Buchanan. See page 21.

236 Moses Kelly was the chief clerk who took over the Dept. of the Interior when Thompson resigned. www.gpoaccess.gov/serialset/cdocement/hd108-222/officers.pdf

*"I am in the Garden of Gethsemane now,*
*and my cup of bitterness is overflowing."*
Abraham Lincoln
Christmas, 1860[237]

# — 4 —

# THE TIMELINE OF SECESSION

## SOUTH CAROLINA

Governor William H. Gist[238] of that state, on the 6th of November, 1860, had recommended in his message to the legislature and the people, that in the event of the election of Abraham Lincoln to the presidency (the election came off on the same day the message was issued) a convention of the people of the state be immediately called to consider and determine for themselves the mode and measure of redress, and urged that the only remedy or alternative left was the secession of South Carolina from the Union.

On the 10th of November, Senators James H. Hammond[239] and James Chestnut, Jr.[240] resigned their seats in the Senate of the United

[237] Lincoln in American Memory, pg. 88.

[238] Governor William Henry Gist was the former Governor of South Carolina. He wrote letters to all the southern governors suggesting simultaneous secession if Mr. Lincoln were elected. When Mr. Lincoln was elected, he called his state to convention. The Confederate Nation, 1861 - 1865, pgs. 42 & 45 and Lincoln and His Party in the Secession Crisis, pg. 7.

[239] Senator James Henry Hammond was Governor of South Carolina from 1842 - 1844. He was publisher of the *Southern Times*. He served in Congress and the U.S. Senate. Hammond was known as "Mudsill Hammond" due to a speech he made on settlement of Kansas which provoked the North. He suggested impeaching President Jefferson Davis in 1862 for in competency. Appleton's Cyclopaedia of American Biography, Vol. III., pgs. 67 & 68 and The Confederate Nation, 1861 - 1865, pg. 140

[240] James Chestnut, Jr. was a Princeton graduate who served in the U.S. Senate. He later was a Colonel in the Confederate Army and an aid-de-camp to Confederate

States. A convention was called to meet on the 17th of December, and on that day, an ordinance of secession was immediately passed. On the 19th the total suspension of debts of the citizens of non-slave holding states was proclaimed.

The Honorable Francis W. Pickens, the newly elected governor of state, assumed the functions of a *soi-disant*[241] president of the new republic of the state of South Carolina with all the paraphernalia,[242] pomp and circumstance of a separate and independent nation. He appointed a Cabinet, consisting of A. G. McGrath,[243] Secretary of State; David S. Jamison,[244] Secretary of War; C. G. Memminger,[245] Secretary of Treasury; W. W. Harllee,[246] Postmaster General; and Albert C. Garlington,[247] Secretary of the Interior.

The new republic was now organized for government. This proclamation, issued by Governor Pickens on the 20th of December, 1860, announced the repeal of the ordinance of May 23, 1788[248] and the dissolution of the union between the states of South Carolina and other states under the name of the Confederate States of America, and proclaiming to the world, is, as she has a right to be, a separate, sovereign, free and independent state and as such has the right to levy war, conclude peace, negotiate treaties, leagues or covenants, and to do all acts whatsoever that rightfully pertain to a free and independent

---

President Jefferson Davis. Appleton's Cyclopaedia of American Biography, Vol. I., pg. 600.

241 *Soi-disant* means pretend.

242 Paraphernalia means furnishings.

243 A. G. McGrath was judge of the U.S. District Court and a secession leader. His most famous remark about secession was "the time for deliberating has passed—the time for action has come." *Daily Dispatch*, November 20, 1860.

244 David S. Jamison was a member of the South Carolina Cabinet in 1860 and president of the South Carolina Constitutional Convention, December 17-20, 1860.

245 Christopher G. Memminger was a lawyer who suggested a convention of disunion in the South. At the time of his suggestion, his home state of Virginia declined to attend any convention because they chose to wait and see. He was the first Secretary of the Treasury for the Confederacy. He helped develop Charleston as one of the most comprehensive school systems in the country. The Confederate Nation, 1861 - 1865, pg. 42.

246 W. W. Harllee was one of the signers of the South Carolina secession ordinances. Secession of South Carolina.

247 Albert C. Garlington later became a Confederate General. Files.usgarchives.net/ga/fulton/newspaper/alumni.txt

248 This was the date that South Carolina ratified the U. S. Constitution. Ordinance of Secession of the 13 Confederate States of America.

state. On the 24th of December, the state's representatives in Congress withdrew.

Messrs. Barnwell,[249] Adams,[250] and Orr[251] were appointed commissioners to proceed to Washington to treat for the possession of the United States property within the limits of the new nationality. All of the commissioners were gentlemen of the highest character, and men of great experience, at this time conservative in their views and imperative in their demands for recognition. They would have been content if South Carolina were to be let alone, as no factor of the Union as Rhode Island sought to be at the time of the adoption of the federal Constitution.[252]

They did not want Georgia and the gulf states to follow the example set. It was not at this time thought to be for the best interest of the state to be united with the great cotton growing gulf states, any more than it was to continue in the United States. The cotton growing states were already sapping their life blood, and she looked to the central west and upper Mississippi and Ohio regions as a source for protection to her best interests. They wanted no confederacy. They only wanted independence, to act in conformity with Governor Pickens' proclamation. Nothing except the eminent danger and threatening attitude of the United States by such acts as the occupancy of Fort Sumter could then have caused the state to assume a confederate instead of an independent movement.

---

[249] Robert Woodward Barnwell was a Harvard College graduate who served in the U.S. Senate. He was from South Carolina and a friend of Jefferson Davis. He was President of South Carolina College. Jefferson Davis asked him to be Secretary of State in the Confederate Cabinet but he chose not to. He was a supporter of separate countries for the Confederacy, but not war. He served in the Confederate Senate. The Two American Presidents, pgs. 55, 122 & 125, The Confederate Nation, 1861-1865, pg. 47 and Appleton's Cyclopaedia of American Biography, Vol. I., pg. 174.

[250] James H. Adams was one of three from South Carolina appointed to lay the ordinance of secession before the President and U.S. Congress. www.questia.com/read/599537?title2chapterXIII%3athefort_sumptercrisisdecember2%2c1860-January8%2c1861

[251] James Lawrence Orr was editor of the *Gazette* newspaper. He served in the U.S. House of Representatives where he was chairman of Indian affairs and Speaker of the House. After the war he was Governor of North Carolina and also Minister to Russia. Appleton's Cyclopaedia of American Biography, Vol. IV., pg. 593. See pg. 35.

[252] Between September 1787 and January 1790, the general assembly of Rhode Island rejected eleven attempts to convene a state convention to ratify the U.S. Constitution. Rhode Island History, Chapter III.

These commissioners seem not to have had a doubt but that the United States government would at once adjust the Fort Sumter trouble and recognize the government of South Carolina as an accomplished fact within the purview[253] of the organic act. This done, South Carolina would at once come forward, to check the impending danger of a new confederacy.

President Buchanan declined to treat with the commissioners, greatly to their surprise and chagrin. They left Washington for home on the 4th day of January, 1861. On the next day the convention appointed T. J. Withers,[254] L. M. Keitt,[255] W. W. Boyce,[256] James Chestnut, Jr., Robert B. Rhett, Jr.,[257] Robert W. Barnwell and C. G. Memminger delegates to the southern congress. The same day the legislature declared that any attempt to reinforce Fort Sumter would considered an open act of hostility and a declaration of war.

On the 9th of January the *Star of the West*, a United States vessel, which had been sent to reinforce the force, was fired on and driven back by order of the government, which act the legislature approved of by resolution.

---

253 Purview means scope.

254 T. J. Withers of South Carolina was a signer of the Confederate Constitution adopted on March 11, 1861.
www.sciway3.net/proctor/marion/military/wbts/confederateconstitution.html

255 Lawrence Massillon Keitt was a Congressman who left to join the army and became a Colonel in the 20th South Carolina volunteers. Colonel Keitt was wounded at the battle of Cold Harbor (June 3, 1864) and died the next day. He was an acquaintance of the author, Ward Hill Lamon and saved Lamon from an angry mod in the streets of Charleston, South Carolina just a few weeks before the shelling of Fort Sumter. Ward Hill Lamon: Lincoln's "Particular Friend", pg. 197, The Two American Presidents, pg. 286 and Appleton's Cyclopaedia of American Biography, Vol. III., pg. 504.

256 William Waters Boyce was from South Carolina and served in the U.S. Congress. He refused to serve on the Committee of 33. Lincoln and His Party in the Secession Crisis, pg. 92.

257 Robert Barnwell Rhett, Jr. of South Carolina was a lawyer, planter and politician and also the owner and editor of *The Charleston Mercury*. He was a troublesome opponent of Jefferson Davis. He was the one who proposed the Montgomery Convention which was held on February 13, 1861. In his newspaper editorials he said of the Davis war policy that it was "unwise and most disastrous and his conduct of the war weak and incompetent." Of the loss at Atlanta, Rhett wrote "What was wanted by our army was not a *change in generals* but *reinforcements*." Two Roads to Sumter, pg. 264, The Confederate Nation, 1861 - 1865, pg. 42 and The Two American Presidents, pgs. 122, 281, 282 & 410.

## GEORGIA

On November 18, 1860, the legislature of Georgia met and on the 3rd of December it appropriated one million dollars to arm the state. On January 2nd Georgia voted 50,243 for and 37,123 against immediate secession. A convention as held on the 16th of January, 1861 and commissioners from South Carolina and Alabama were received by the convention.

On the 19th of January, an ordinance of secession passed and on the 21st the Senators and Representatives in Congress withdrew from that body.

Three days later delegates were elected to the southern congress at Montgomery, Alabama, and shortly after this, commissioners were elected to go to other slave holding states and an address was adopted "to the South and world." It was not until the 11th of March that the Confederate constitution was ratified. An ordinance was then passed authorizing the confederate government to occupy, use and possess the forts, navy yard, arsenals, and custom houses in the state. Governor Brown[258] on the 26th of April subsequently issued a proclamation ordering the repudiation by the citizens of Georgia of all debts due northern creditors.

## MISSISSIPPI

Mississippi's convention assembled on the 7th of January, 1861 and defeated by a vote of 70 to 29 a motion to submit secession to the people for a popular ratification. The ordinance of secession passed by a vote of 83 to 15. Commissioners of other states were received and resolutions were adopted recognizing South Carolina as sovereign and independent. On the 12th day of January, the Mississippi representatives in Congress of the United States withdrew and on the 21st of that month, her Senators also withdrew. Afterwards on the 30th of March, Mississippi ratified the Confederate constitution by a vote 78 to 7.

---

[258] Joseph E. Brown was the four term Governor of Georgia and a U.S. Senator. A superior court judge and the Chief Justice of the Georgia Supreme Court, Judge Brown was an active secessionist. He was a strong Confederate Governor but no friend of Jefferson Davis. He was very critical of the Davis draft and *habeas corpus* acts of 1864. After the war he was President of the Western and Atlantic Railroad. The Two American Presidents, pgs. 399 - 401 and Appleton's Cyclopaedia of American Biography, Vol. I., pg. 408.

## FLORIDA

Florida Governor M. S. Perry[259] strongly recommended immediate secession. On January 3, 1861, their convention met. Commissioners from South Carolina and Alabama were received, the ordinance of secession passed by the vote of 62 to 7 and delegates were appointed to the Montgomery congress. Three days after this, Florida's Senators and Representatives in the federal Congress withdrew. Control of the government property was given to the Confederate government.

## LOUISIANA

The state convention met January 23, 1861. The South Carolina and Alabama commissioners were in attendance. The governor[260] was instructed to communicate with the governors of other southern states. The ordinance of secession passed by a vote of 113 to 17. The convention refused to submit the ordinance to the people for ratification. The Senators and all the Representatives in the Congress of the United States, except John. E. Bouligny,[261] withdrew. In secret session a resolution was passed to appropriate the money in the United States mint and custom houses, amounting to $536,000 and to turn it over to the Confederate states' government. This money was accepted with the most profound and grateful resolution expressive of the high sense of patriotic liberality of the state of Louisiana. The Confederate constitution was ratified in convention by a vote of 101 to 7. All United States property was turned over to the Confederacy.

## ALABAMA

The convention met January 7, 1861. South Carolina again being on hand with her commissioners, an ordinance was passed in secret

---

[259] Madison S. Perry was the fourth Governor of Florida, serving from 1857—1861. During his administration a boundary dispute was settled with Georgia, he established the state militia and encouraged the building or railroads. www.floridamemory.com/collections/governors/perry.cfm

[260] Thomas Overton Moore was Democrat Governor of Louisiana from 1860 - 1864. www.enlou.com/people/mooreto-bio.htm

[261] John Edward Bouligny was a Congressman from New Orleans who opposed secession. He was the only Congressman from the secession states who did not leave his seat during the war, preferring instead to move to Washington and support the Union. Appleton's Cyclopaedia of American Biography, Vol. I., pg. 32.

session by a vote of 61 to 39. The ordinance was not submitted to the people. Delegates were now elected to the congress at Montgomery. The Senators and Representatives withdrew from the federal Congress and commissioners were appointed to treat with the United States government concerning the forts, arsenals and other government property within the state. The convention adopted a resolution requesting the people of all southern states to meet the people of Alabama in convention on the 4th day of February for consultation. Commissioners were also appointed to other states. The constitution was ratified by a vote of 90 to 9. And the usual transfer of the federal property to the Confederacy was made.

## ARKANSAS

On March 4, 1861, her convention met and the vote being taken on the ordinance of secession was defeated, 25 for it and 30 against it. On the 18th a compromise was affected, agreeing to submit the question of secession to the people on the first Monday of the following August. Then on the 6th day of May, and not until then, was the ordinance passed by a vote of 69 to 1.[262] The customary transfer of the United States government property was made in the usual form.

## TEXAS

On February 1, 1861, Texas passed the ordinance of secession by a vote of 166 to 8. Delegates to the Confederate Congress were elected. The ordinance of secession was voted on by the people, with 46,153 for and 14,747 against its adoption. Thereupon the convention declared the state out of the Union on the 4th of March. The convention deposed[263] Governor Houston[264] by the vote of 127 to 4. The forts and other property were transferred with the usual ceremony. The constitution was ratified, with yeas 62 and nays 7.

---

[262] The only dissenting vote was cast by a 62 year old lawyer and teacher, Isaac Murphy. www.oldstatehouse.com/educational programs/

[263] Deposed means removed.

[264] Governor Sam Houston, became the President of the Republic of Texas following the Mexican War. When Texas became a state in 1845 he served in the U.S. Senate. He was deposed by the convention because he refused to take the oath of allegiance to the Confederacy. Appleton's Cyclopaedia of American Biography, Vol. III., pg. 274 and www.aoc.gov/cc/art/hsh/houston.cfm

## NORTH CAROLINA

The state Senate on the 18th of December, 1860 passed a bill appropriating $300,000 to arm the state. On the 6th of January the state House also passed this bill. The legislature also passed a bill to the affect that no ordinance shall be valid unless ratified by a majority of the voting population. On the 31st Thomas L. Clingman[265] was elected United States Senator. The vote by the people for a convention on the 28th of February was for 47,323, against 46,672. Afterwards, on May 1st, an extra session of the legislature met, being called by Governor Ellis[266] and a convention bill was passed. On the 20th a convention met at Raleigh, the ordinance of secession was passed, the constitution ratified, and the usual transfer and cession of property of the United States to the Confederacy was gone through.

## TENNESSEE

The people by popular vote defeated the bill for convention on February 9, 1861 by a vote of 67,360 to 54,156. In May following, the legislature passed a resolution authorizing Governor Isham Harris [267]to appoint commissioners to enter into a military league with the Confederacy. A secret session of the legislature was ratified. The league subsequently made, then appointed Messers. A. O. W. Totten,[268] Gustavus A. Henry,[269] Washington Barrow,[270] Tennessee's

---

[265] Thomas Lanier Clingman was a Whig from North Carolina who served in Congress and as a U.S. Senator. He was a topographical engineer. Clingman's Peak in the Smokey Mountains is named after him. He served as Brigadier General in the N.C. Infantry. Appleton's Cyclopaedia of American Biography, Vol. I., pgs. 658-659.

[266] Governor John Willis Ellis was a supporter of secession who served as Governor of North Carolina until his death in 1861. Appleton's Cyclopaedia of American Biography, Vol. II., pgs. 333 & 334.

[267] Isham Green Harris was a lawyer, Congressman and U.S. Senator. He served as Governor of Tennessee in 1857, 1859 and 1861. He owned the Carolina Life and Casualty Company. He gave Jefferson Davis a job following his release from prison in the late 1860s. The Two American Presidents, pg. 433 and Appleton's Cyclopaedia of American Biography, Vol. III., pg. 92.

[268] Archibald O.W. Totten was from Madison County, Tennessee. He too become a commissioner. *NY Times*, May 13, 1861.

[269] Gustavus Adolph Henry Sr. was a Whig lawyer who served in the Congress of the Confederacy. Appleton's Cyclopaedia of American Biography, Vol. III., pg. 176.

[270] Washington Barrow was a Tennessee lawyer who served in Congress. He was a Whig and editor of the *Nashville Banner* newspaper. Appleton's Cyclopaedia of American Biography, Vol. I., pg. 179.

Commissioners with Henry W. Hilliard[271] the Commissioner for the Confederacy. These Commissioners stipulated that Tennessee, until she became a member of the Confederacy, would place all her military forces under the control of the Confederacy, and made the usual transfer of public property. The legislature took high grounds in the face of popular will expressed by the vote of the people at the recent elections; made a declaration of independence; an ordinance of secession; an ordinance ratifying the Confederate constitution; propositions, however, which were to be voted on by the people. On the 24th of June the vote stood for separation 106,053 and 47,174 against, whereupon the governor declared the state out of the Union.

## VIRGINIA

This state was in great trepidation, being a border, slave-holding state, and knowing that in the case of war her soil would be the theatre of military action. It was necessary for her to use all her power and influence to avert war, if possible. During the latter part of the month of January, Judge Robertson[272] was sent as a commissioner to South Carolina to treat with that people and seek a conference and a co-operative course with the Virginians on these matters of difference. The policy of the Virginia legislature, as Commissioner Robertson explained it, was the procurement of amendments and new guarantees in the new Constitution of the United States. The legislature of South Carolina rejected Mr. Robertson's propositions and declared in their resolutions, and in candor, due to the long continuing respect subsisting between Virginia and South Carolina, induced them in their representative capacity to proclaim that they do not deem it advisable to the negotiations when they have no desire or intention to promote the ultimate object in mind. This was answered by resolutions to the South Carolina body declaring the separation of that state from the federal Union to be final; that they had no further interest in the Constitution of the United States; and that she could have no

---

271 Henry W. Hilliard was an attorney appointed by Jefferson Davis as the Confederate Commissioner from Tennessee. He became a Brigadier General in the Confederate Army. Later he served as minister to Brazil (1877—1881). www.bioguide.congress.gov

272 Judge John Robertson was a Virginia Congressman and judge of the circuit court. He was the brother of Virginia Governor Wyndham Robertson. Appleton's Cyclopaedia of American Biography, Vol. V., pg. 280.

appropriate negotiations with the federal government except such as may arise between them in their natural relations as a foreign state. It was further declared that the South Carolina people had no confidence in the federal government, that the most solemn pledges of that government had been disregarded, that under pretense of preserving property, hostile troops had been attempted to be introduced into one of the fortresses of this state, concealed in the hold of one of the vessels of commerce with a view to subjugate the people of South Carolina. Since the authorities at Washington were informed of the mediation of Virginia, a war vessel had been shipped to the South and troops and munitions of war were concentrated on the soil of Virginia and for this reason South Carolina declined to enter into any negotiations with Virginia.

On this subject the leading newspapers of the South, *The Charleston Mercury,* said of border embassies:

*"Hear them if you please, treat them with civility, feed them and drench them with champagne. Let them go. Let us act as if they had never come; as if they had not spoken; as if they did not exist; and let them seem to preserve their treasury as it passed through some more supple agency than ours. The time has come when the voice of a Virginia politician, though he coos like a dove, should not be heard in the land of the patriotic people."*

The feeling now in South Carolina was intense, not only against the United States as a nation, but also against Virginia as a faction of that nation. It was, however, only a question of time for the Virginians to fall in line with the southern confederation. Virginia had proposed the Crittenden resolutions as a basis of adjustment and requested the general government avoid collision with the southern states.

Now the New York legislature, about this time, sent the Virginia legislature resolutions expressing the utmost disdain for the actions of that body; and saying that the threat conveyed, can inspire no terror in freemen. This did not conduce to allay the unfriendly feeling already engendered between the sections. The resolutions were returned to the Governor of New York. Ohio sent resolutions. Pennsylvania and Michigan did the same. The Ohio resolutions were met with disfavor. Those of Pennsylvania were tabled and Michigan had hers sent back without comment. Resolutions from Tennessee were referred to the committee on federal relations.

On the 25th of January, ex-president Tyler[273] and James A. Seddon,[274] Commissioners to the peace conference presented their report and denounced in no mild terms the action and recommendation of that body as an insult to the South, a sham and a delusion. The next day one million dollars was appropriated by the legislature of Virginia for the defense of the state.

On February 4th, the Commonwealth of Virginia defeated a secession resolution 122 to 30.[275]

It was then resolved that in case all efforts to reconcile the differences failed, the Virginia's honor as well as interests imperatively demand that she united her destinies with the southern movement. They proclaimed the doctrine that no reconstruction of the Union would be satisfactory or could be permanent that did not secure irrevocably to each section self-protecting power against invasion and incursions by the federal Union against the reserved rights of the states—the logical conclusion of which was the general government attempting to control or direct its troops and government property within the state was a violation of the state's rights and gave a just cause for the rebellion against the authority and a right of revolution in government.

The Virginia Convention met February 13. Commissioners from South Carolina, Mississippi and Georgia were admitted and all made speeches picturing the dangers of Virginia remaining with the people of the North, that the Union was unnatural and monstrous, there was no human force, no sanctity of human touch, that could possibly reunite the two sections North and South. The economy of God would have to be changed before it was possible.

At this time the whole state of Virginia it might be said, the whole South and the whole country were in perturbation[276] and everything seemed clouded with sadness and apprehension for the result of the

---

273 John Tyler was a Whig from Virginia and the tenth President of the United States serving from 1841-1845. www.homeofheroes.com/presidents/10-tyler.html

274 James Alexander Seddon was a Congressman from Virginia who was appointed the Secretary of War for the Confederacy in November, 1862. He resigned that position under pressure in January, 1865 when he was accused of profiting from the sale of grain to the government. The charges were later proven false. He also was a member of the Confederate Congress. The Confederate Nation, 1861 - 1865, pgs. 206 & 286 and Appleton's Cyclopaedia of American Biography, Vol. V., pg. 449.

275 Lincoln and His Party in the Secession Crisis, pg. 309.

276 Perturbation means disturbance.

action and determination of the people of the southern states. The congress at Montgomery had passed a bill absolutely prohibiting the importation of slaves from the United States unless accompanied by their owners with an eye to settlement within the Confederacy. The sole object of this legislation was to secure Virginia and Kentucky, especially Virginia to secede and join the Confederacy. These were both border states and were in great danger in any event in case of war. Afterwards Mr. Wise[277] offered a resolution in recognition for independence of the seceding states which was accepted and on the 4th of April the ordinance of secession passed in secret session by a vote of 80 to 45. On the same day the constitution of the provisional government of the Confederate States was ratified. The ordinance would cease to have legal effect provided the people of Virginia voting on it, should they reject it. It was not until May 23, submitted to the people for election, the secession of Virginia temporarily became a fact. Now A. H. Stephens,[278] as Commissioner of the Confederacy and a committee of Virginia convention stipulated that until Virginia became a member of the Confederacy, that he, Mr. Stephens should administer the United States estate within Virginia for the benefit of the southern confederacy and be the agent to turn over to it all of her public property, naval stores, and munitions of war within the state. The vote on the ordinance of secession was announced on June 25th and stood 132,201 for and 37,451 against.

Sometime within the month of July the convention passed a prescription act[279] declaring that any citizen of Virginia holding office under the government of the United States after the 31st day of July, 1861 should be forever banished from the state and declared an alien enemy and also that any citizen of Virginia hereafter undertaking to represent the state of Virginia in the Congress of the United States should, in addition to the above penalty, be considered guilty of

---

[277] Henry Alexander Wise was Governor of Virginia during the John Brown raid in 1859. He oversaw the capture and execution of the abolitionist. He served in the U.S. Congress and also as Minister of Brazil. He was a Brigadier General in the Confederate Army. His son, O. Jennings Wise, was editor of the *Richmond Enquirer* prior to the war. O. Jennings Wise was killed at the battle of Roanoke Island in February 1862. The Confederate Nation, 1861—1865, pg. 86, Harpers Pictorial History of the Great Rebellion, pr. 246 and Appleton's Cyclopaedia of American Biography, Vol. VI., pgs. 579 - 580.

[278] A. H. Stephens—See page 30.

[279] Virginia Prescription Act of 1861

treason and his property be liable to confiscation. When Virginia seceded and placed her destinies with the southern states in revolt against the federal authorities, war, a terrible war, was inevitable, beyond reconciliation, except by the force of arms.

## KENTUCKY

Early in February, 1861 in the Senate, Kentucky passed resolutions appealing to the southern people to stop their revolutionary government, but they proved futile, and that body declared it expedient to call a state convention of the people. In this action of the Senate, the House concurred on March 22. The states rights convention assembled and denounced the attempt of the general government to collect revenue as coercion in which case they affirmed that it was the duty of the border states to make common cause with the new Confederacy and recommended a border states convention. On October 29 a southern conference met at Russelville[280] and adopted resolutions proclaiming a revolution, providing for a sovereignty convention at that place, pledged resistance to all federal and state taxes for the prosecution of the war on the part of the United States and appointed a committee to carry out the resolutions adopted. This committee consisted of John. C. Breckinridge,[281] late Vice-President of the United States; Humphrey Marshall,[282] late member of the federal Congress, commissioner and minister to China; William B. Preston,[283] ex-member of Congress and ex-minister of Spain; along with others—the most distinguished and influential men of Kentucky. On November 18, the convention met and passed a declaration of independence and an ordinance of secession. A

---

[280] Russellville is in Hamblen County, Tennessee between Morristown and Whitesburg.

[281] John Breckinridge—See pg. 48.

[282] Humphrey Marshall was a U.S. Congressman from Kentucky. He was an 1832 graduate of the U.S. Military Academy. He served in both the Mexican and Black Hawk Wars. During the civil war he was commander of the Confederate forces of Eastern Kentucky. He also served in the Confederate Congress. At the battle of Middle Creek, he opposed James Garfield, future U.S. President. Appleton's Cyclopaedia of American Biography, Vol. IV., pg. 227.

[283] William B. Preston had served as the Secretary of the Navy under President Zachary Taylor. He was a Whig lawyer from Virginia who served in the U.S. Congress and the Confederate Senate. Appleton's Cyclopaedia of American Biography, Vol. V., pg. 115.

provisional government was agreed upon consisting of a governor,[284] legislative council of ten, a treasurer and an auditor.

## MARYLAND

A commissioner was sent to this state from Mississippi in mid-December of 1860 but Governor Hicks[285] declined to accept or favor the overtures made to him in favor of secession. *The Baltimore Clipper* newspaper of the 31st denied the existence of an organization to prevent the inauguration of President Lincoln. At this time the sentiments of the people were very much mixed. The respectable element, leading men of the state, were pretty evenly divided on the subject of the old government or the new one. The leading Union men who favored the existing government were the Honorable Reverdy Johnson,[286] Governor Hicks, Henry Winter Davis,[287] and others. The opposition was led by Ross Winans,[288] Marshal Kane,[289] James Carroll,[290] Speaker of the House of Representatives, E. L. Kilbourn,[291] Ex-Senator, Anthony Kennedy[292] and others.

---

[284] George W. Johnson was named the Kentucky Governor. Southern History of the War, pg. 211.

[285] Governor Thomas Holliday Hicks was a U.S. Senator who served as Maryland Governor between 1858 - 1862. Southern History of the War, pg. 66 and Appleton's Cyclopaedia of American Biography, Vol. III., pgs. 196 & 197.

[286] Reverdy Johnson was the legal representative for the plaintiff in the Dred Scot case before the Supreme Court in 1857. The Story-Life of Lincoln, pg. 278.

[287] Henry Winter Davis—See pg. 69.

[288] Ross Winans was an inventor and builder of railroad locomotives for the B & O Railroad and one of the country's first multimillionaires. He was an outspoken anti-federalist. Americanhistory.si.edu/archives/d8155.htm

[289] George P. Kane was the marshal of the police during the Baltimore riots of 1861. He had also been implicated by Allan Pinkerton in part of the plot to kill Mr. Lincoln when the train taking him to his Inauguration passed through Baltimore. *Harpers New Weekly Magazine*, June 1868.

[290] James Carroll was a director of both the Chesapeake and Ohio Canal company and the Baltimore and Ohio Railroad. He gave the B & O Railroad the land where they built the Mount Clare station. www.montclaire.org/history/railroad.html

[291] Elbridge L. Kilbourn was from Anne Arundel County, Maryland. He served in the state House of Representatives from 1851-1861 and in 1870. www.msa.md.gov/msa/speccol/sc3550/sc3520/012500/0012512/html/msa12512.html

[292] Anthony Kennedy was a cotton grower and manufacturer. He served as U.S. Senator and also was instrumental in framing the state constitution for the state of Maryland in 1867. Appleton's Cyclopaedia of American Biography, Vol. III., pg. 517.

On the 20th the legislature reassembled at Frederick City, Annapolis being then occupied by the Union troops. Governor Hicks was now peculiarly situated. He had already issued his address against secession, although at this time he wrote to General Benjamin F. Butler,[293] protesting his landing his troops at Annapolis. General Butler replied that he intended to land them there and march to Washington. This was done and forcible possession was immediately taken by the troops of the Annapolis and Elm Ridge Railroad. The House of Delegates voted on April 29 against secession by a vote of 53 to 13 and the Senate voted unanimously against it. Resolutions were passed declaring that Maryland protests against the war, and earnestly beseeched and implored the President of the United States to make peace with the Confederate States.

A committee was appointed to visit with President Davis[294] and instructed to convey the assurances that Maryland sympathizes with the Confederate States and that the people of Maryland enlisted with their whole hearts on the side of reconciliation and peace. Messers. McKaig,[295] Yellot,[296] and Harding, commissioners to visit President Davis returned and made the report accompanied by a letter from Mr. Davis expressing his gratification to learn that the state of Maryland was in sympathy with "themselves," enlisted on the side of peace and reconciliation and giving assurance of his perfect willingness for secession of hostilities. He went so far as to say that he would receive any proposition for peace the United States government would make him, which was at the time considered to be a great condescension on the part of the president of the new government of the Confederacy.

---

[293] General Benjamin B. Butler was a self-made millionaire lawyer from Massachusetts. He brought the 8th Massachusetts regiment to Annapolis, Maryland enroute to Washington City. His troops arrived by train from Annapolis. On May 13th he seized Federal Hill in Baltimore without any orders to do so. In November, 1862 he raised 5,000 additional troops for the Union Navy in the Gulf area. Civil War a Narrative, Part II, pg. 83 and Lincoln's War, pgs. 39 - 40, & 47- 48.

[294] Jefferson Davis—See pg. 18.

[295] Thomas J. McKaig was a State Senator from Allegheny County, Maryland. *Richmond Daily Dispatch*, October 25, 1861.

[296] Coleman Yellot was a Maryland State Senator who supported revolution and fled to Virginia when Maryland opposed secession. *Richmond Daily Dispatch*, March 9, 1863

## MISSOURI

Missouri held a convention of her people which on its assembling opposed secession and opposed the passage of any laws of the federal Congress granting supplies to men and money to coerce the seceding states into submission or subjugation, and in case such acts were passed, they declared it the duty of their delegation in the United States Congress to withdraw. They defeated secession by a popular vote of 110,000 to 30,000. At the convention delegates opposed secession by a vote of 89 to 1. The Crittenden resolutions were recommended as a basis of settlement but the state followed the lead of the other southern states in casting her destinies with the hazardous new government.

It will be observed that all of the slave-holding states which had not joined the southern Confederacy at the time of Mr. Lincoln's inauguration as president, joined soon after, making a solid cooperative government whose dearest interests were opposed to the old federal rule. Revolutionary in principal, the people had committed the palpable[297] act of treason and placed themselves in the position that it was to their successful revolution or death. The federal government had been greatly weakened during the last months of Mr. Buchanan's administration by the distribution of the inadequate number of arms it possessed, the majority of them being sent to southern forts and arsenals, which forts and arsenals were speedily seized and appropriated to the cause of the South and turned upon the legitimate government.

---

[297] Palable means obvious.

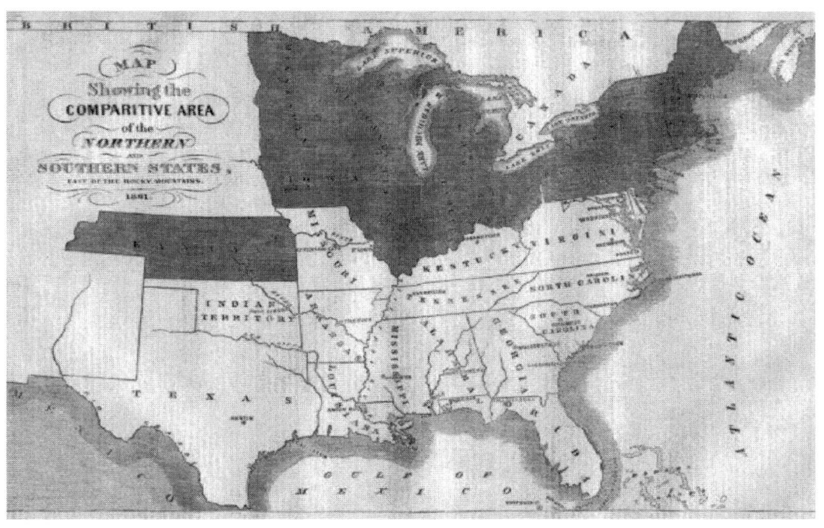


*Harpers Weekly* Map of the Confederate States
February, 1861

*"Here I have lived a quarter of a century, and have passed from a young man to an old man... I now leave,*
*not knowing when, or whether ever,*
*I shall return, with a task before me greater that*
*that which rested upon Washington."*

Abraham Lincoln
Springfield, Illinois
February 11, 1861[298]

# — 5 —

# ABRAHAM LINCOLN BECOMES PRESIDENT

When Mr. Lincoln went from Springfield, Illinois to Washington to assume the duties of the President of the United States, his long continued and eventful trip from the scenes of his quiet western home to the great capital of the nation, the country was filled with hopes and fears such as never before influenced a peaceful or warlike people about a private citizen or prospective actor. Nothing or little, at least, was known that had been published as to what would be the policy of his administration.[299]

Before his arrival there was well-founded apprehension for his safety in his transit.[300] It was believed by many of his partisan friends

[298] Showcase.netins.net/web/creative/Lincoln/speeches/farewell.htm

[299] Mr. Lincoln deliberately adopted a policy of silence between his Cooper Institute speech of February, 1860 and his inaugural address of March, 1861. He did not make one campaign speech or write one public letter to reaffirm his position on any subject. Lincoln and His Party in the Secession Crisis, pgs. 135 & 136.

[300] Both Allan Pinkerton, detective, and Mr. William Seward, Secretary of State Designee, had separately discovered plots to assassinate Mr. Lincoln when his train passed through Baltimore. *Trains Magazine*, February 2009, pg. 29.

as well as by those who were opposed to him and his party that a conspiracy had been formed to prevent his reaching Washington, by taking his life. These apprehensions being timely made known to him induced him to change his program of movement after arriving in Harrisburg, Pennsylvania and addressing the people there on 22nd of February en-route. Under cover of the night of the same day, he secretly took a special train on the Pennsylvania Central Railroad, taking one man only with him.[301] He went to Philadelphia and about midnight took in a sleeper on the regular train of cars, and arrived safely in Washington the next morning about six o'clock without suspicion of anyone (except his escort) on the cars in Philadelphia, Baltimore, Harrisburg and Washington knowing of his whereabouts.

It is proper, however, to state that besides his escort and suite[302] left in Harrisburg, Governor Curtin[303] of Pennsylvania, Mr. Felton[304] of the Philadelphia, Wilmington and Baltimore Railroad, Mr. Seward, General Scott, Senator Trumball,[305] and Representative Washburne,[306] a Congressional representative from the Galena district of Illinois, all knew of his purpose to go through this clandestinely, all favoring and

---

301 That man was the author, Ward Hill Lamon. Trains Magazine, February 2009, pg. 29.

302 Suite means personal staff.

303 Governor Andrew G. Curtin of Pennsylvania studied law at Dickenson College in Carlisle, Pennsylvania. He was instrumental in throwing Pennsylvania's support behind Mr. Lincoln at the Republican National Convention in 1859. He helped purchase land for the National Cemetery in Gettysburg. He served in Congress from 1861 - 1887 and then was appointed the Minister to Russia by President Grant. Lincoln's War, pgs. 305 & 376.

304 Samuel Morse Felton was the president of the railroad. He was a civil engineer from Massachusetts and a Harvard College graduate. Appleton's Cyclopaedia of American Biography, Vol. II., pg. 429.

305 Senator Lyman Trumball was a lawyer born in Connecticut. He moved to Illinois in 1837 and served as a justice of the Illinois Supreme Court from 1848—1853. He had defeated Mr. Lincoln in the election of 1855 in that state. He was elected to the U.S. Senate and served from 1855—1873. His proposal in Congress to have the Union army capture Richmond by July 20, 1864 failed to get enough support to pass. He was co-author of the Thirteenth Amendment. He voted to acquit President Andrew Johnson. He supported the formation of Yellowstone National Park in debates in 1871. The town of Trumbull, Arizona is named after him. Lincoln's War, pgs. 20, 63, 74 & 75.

306 E. B. Washburne was a Republican Congressman from Galena, Illinois. He was chairman of Mr. Lincoln's committee to investigate government contracts. It was his proposal to name General Grant a Lieutenant General. Lincoln and the Civil War, pgs. 49 & 105, Lincoln's War, pgs. 100 & 356 and www.mrlincolnandfriends.org/iniside.asp?pageID=82&subjectID=6

advising the policy of the expedient. Allan C. Pinkerton,[307] a Chicago detective in the employment of Mr. Felton accompanied him with Mr. Lincoln's friend[308] in the train from Philadelphia to Washington and to the friend mainly Mr. Lincoln was indebted for securing the sleeping berth and concealing his identity on the train.

On Mr. Lincoln's arrival at the Washington depot he was met by the Honorable E. B. Washburne, and was conveyed to Willard's Hotel. He was there met by Mr. Seward of New York. He took possession of the rooms and accommodations negotiated by telegraph by his friend who accompanied him from Harrisburg to Washington. In the course of the morning after his arrival, accompanied by Mr. Seward and the friend before referred to, Mr. Lincoln paid a visit of courtesy to President Buchanan. Mr. Lincoln had a protracted interview with the president after which he again went to his quarters at the hotel. For several days after this, his time was employed in receiving calls, entertaining, and receiving all kinds of propositions about what should be his policy of administration and who should be his Cabinet counselors. He was thus employed during the remaining nine days until he was inaugurated president.

In this time, the great questions of policy and the minutia of the administrative economy were gravely and earnestly discussed. Those with the most patriotic motives gave their counsel favoring conciliation. Those honestly advocating a vigorous war policy, those earnestly recommending delay of demonstrative action for or against a war, together with those irresponsible persons who desired war for the sake of war, which would afford them the opportunity to prey upon the public treasury to enrich their personal fortunes, were all heard. Due consideration was given to the respective counsel and advice of all.

---

[307] Allan Pinkerton was the detective who alerted Mr. Lamon and Mr. Lincoln of the plot in Baltimore. He was at various times also known as E. I. Allen, J. H. Hutcheson, and "Plums." He founded the Pinkerton Detective Agency. Pinkerton had documented seventy-eight threats to Mr. Lincoln while Mr. Lamon, the author, had investigated over eighty threats. Abraham Lincoln, The War Years, Vol. III, pg. 823 and Allan Pinkerton, The First Private Eye, pg. 177, *Harpers New Monthly Magazine*, June 1868 and "Incognito in Baltimore" pg. 36.

[308] The friend was Ward Hill Lamon, the author of this manuscript. *Trains Magazine*, February 2009, pg. 29.

On the 27th of February, the outgoing city council of Washington accompanied by the mayor[309] went to the presidential mansion to take their farewell leave of President Buchanan after which they went to Mr. Lincoln's quarters to pay their respects to him. Mr. Lincoln spoke to the mayor and city council as follows:

*Mr. Mayor*

*I thank you, and through you the municipal authority, by who you are accompanied for this welcome; and as it is the first time in my life since the present phase of politics has presented itself in the country that I have said anything publicly within a region of the country where the very institution of slavery exists. I will take the occasion to say, I think very much of the ill feeling that has existed and still exists, between the people of the section from which I came, and the people here, is owing to the misunderstanding between each other which unhappily prevails. I therefore avail myself of this opportunity to assure you, Mr. Mayor, and all of the gentlemen present, that I have not now, and never had, any other than kindly feelings toward you as to the people of my own section.*

*I have not now, and never have had any disposition to treat you with any respect otherwise that as my own neighbors. I have not now any purpose to withhold from you any of the Constitutional rights, under any circumstances, that I would not feel myself constrained to withhold from my own neighbors; and I hope, in a word. When we shall become better acquainted—and I say it with great confidence—we shall like each other more. Again, I thank you for the kindness of this reception.*[310]

About this time there were in Washington City active military preparations in the militia and volunteer companies on foot for service. The various companies were actively drilling and generally tinctured with secession, and publicly passed resolutions favoring secession and holding themselves in readiness for an opportunity to strike the first blow against the government in favor of their favorite movement. Soon after this they were made aware of the stringent measures taken for the protection of the city, the public property and the preservation of the public peace, and disbanded their organizations and went South,

---

[309] James G. Berret was Mayor of Washington from 1858-1861. The mayor delivered a brief address expressing hope that Mr. Lincoln will "restore peace and harmony to our distracted country." He was force to resign during the Lincoln administration for refusing to take the oath of allegiance to the Union. He claimed his oath of office should suffice. TheLincolnLog.org

[310] *New York Herald*, February 28, 1861 from TheLincolnLog.org

separating in Washington for service in the Confederacy. Few of this organized band of patriots remained in Washington or within the Union lines that were shortly afterwards drawn.

Up to the second day of March, none of the politicians knew what the inaugural address was to be. Mr. Seward had no intimation to its purport.[311] It was an instrument prepared by Mr. Lincoln alone without consulting anybody. Mr. Seward acknowledged conservatism had inspired great hopes in the disturbed minds of men in and out of his party. If he was at the head of Mr. Lincoln's administration, war would be averted between the sections. The episode of Cabinet appointment destroyed these hopes of settlement through his insistence. The conclusion was inevitable. If he was to be at the head of the administration he would not have been left so long in the dark as to the purport of the first act of Lincoln's official life. When the last faint hope was destroyed that Mr. Seward was virtually to be president the outlook to him seemed discouraging.

Mr. Lincoln's inauguration on March 4, 1861 was a wonderful pageant. There were fearful apprehensions by the authorities favorable to his administration of danger to his person, and extensive preparations were made for his protection under direction of General Scott around in front of the platform from the point where the president-elect would leave his carriage until he passed into the Capitol, a distance of over one hundred feet. There was a temporary fence built of stout boards, to guard against a surprise or the apprehended danger. On the way up Pennsylvania Avenue to the Capitol, Mr. Lincoln was accompanied in the same carriage by President Buchanan, the retiring president, and Senators Baker[312] of Oregon and Pearce[313] of Maryland.

---

[311] Purport means substance.

[312] Senator Edward Baker was born in London but moved to the United States in 1816. He was a veteran from the Mexican War where he commanded the Illinois volunteers. He had served in the U.S. Senate from Oregon and in the U.S. Congress from Missouri. He was a personal friend of Mr. Lincoln's who was killed at Balls Bluff early in the Civil War. Abraham and Mary Todd Lincoln named their second son Edward Baker Lincoln in honor of their friend. Lincoln's War, pgs. 48 & 49. Southern History of the Civil War, pg. 187 and Don't Know Much About the Civil War?, pg. 200.

[313] Senator James A. Pearce was a Democratic U.S. Senator from Chestertown, Maryland. When Congressional Radicals attacked author Ward Hill Lamon, Pearce defended Lamon's actions. *Charleston Mercury*, June 18, 1858 and Ward Hill Lamon: Lincoln's "Particular Friend," pg. 263.

President Buchanan's manner was as usual grave, thoughtful and dignified, silent and uncommunicative. Mr. Lincoln appeared in his usual composed thoughtful habit, apparently unmoved and indifferent to the excitement around him. To an interested spectator or disinterested observer the preparations and arrangements alike showed apprehension of a murderous design against the life of Mr. Lincoln, or danger of a fearful outbreak among the people to prevent the inauguration of the newly elected president. The carriage to which he rode to the Capitol was closely surrounded by marshals[314] on horse back and cavalry selected with due care from the most loyal and efficient companies of veteran troops and marines. There were thirty thousand people present to witness this inauguration, which was by many of them regarded as the new era in our country's history; the inauguration was of a reform government, new and dangerous, as shown by the result of the administration that followed.

When Mr. Lincoln was escorted to the Senate chamber it was crowded to excess with the most prominent officers of the government with Senators and representatives and foreign ministers. Mr. Breckinridge, the retiring Vice-President, administered the oath of office to Mr. Hamlin,[315] the Vice-President elect, who at once after making his address assumed the duties of the chair as presiding officer of the United States Senate. Mr. Lincoln was then escorted to the platform on the east side of the Capitol and was introduced by Senator Baker to the vast audience awaiting his appearance. His appearance and introduction were greeted with prolonged cheers, after which in a calm, deliberate but impressive voice, he delivered his address. Part of this remarkable state paper is included below as a summary.[316]

---

[314] The author, Ward Hill Lamon was assistant marshal-in-chief of this event. One newspaper described Mr. Lamon as "a giant garbed in the coat of military cut, with two pistols and a Bowie knife in his sash of red, mounted on splendid horse who was in the center of the guards in the rear of the vehicle"—that vehicle being the carriage carrying Mr. Lincoln and Mr. Buchanan. Ward Hill Lamon: Lincoln's Particular Friend, pg. 183.

[315] Hannibal Hamlin from Maine was Lincoln's vice-president during his first term as president. The Two American Presidents, pg. 139.

[316] A brief summary of his long speech—Mr. Lincoln disavowed any intention of interfering with the institution of slavery in the states where it exists…said that the Fugitive Slave Law should be enforced…the intention was to pursue a peaceful course of his administration. He said that no state, upon its own mere motion, could lawfully go out of the Union; that Ordinances of Secession were void; that resistance to the authority of the United States was insurrection; and that his official power should be

We cannot however from here refrain from repeating the concluding words of this wonderful production which so forcibly exemplifies his character and great good heart, which were as follow: *"I am loathe to close. We are not enemies but friends. We must not be enemies. Though passions may have strained, it must not break our bonds of affection. The mystic cords of memory stretching from every battle field and patriotic grave, to every living heart and hearthstone all over the broad land, will yet swell the chorus of the Union when again touched, as surely they will be, by the better angels of our nature. The immense audience present was deeply impressed and with awe viewed the momentous character of the occasion. They were given to contemplate. It produced comparative silence of applause and no manifestation of disapprobation. All were impressed with a deep conviction of great interest concerning their own individual states as citizens and the future of their country. The sentiments that they had just heard uttered from the chief executive foreshadowed the storm awaiting their future."*

After the oath of office was administered to him by the venerable Chief Justice of the United States, Roger B. Taney,[317] Mr. Lincoln was escorted to the presidential mansion in the same order that he had attended to the Capitol, amid the firing of cannon and the sounds of music. Mr. Buchanan accompanied him and in taking his leave, expressed his wish and hope in earnest and befitting language that Mr. Lincoln's administration of the government would be a happy and prosperous one. The inauguration over, everyone seemed to feel a sense of relief. No accidents. No demonstration which could be construed to portend[318] disturbance. There was however no relaxation in the vigilance and arrangements made and making for the defense of the city and protection of the executive. Troops were stationed in different portions of the city and every precaution was taken by General Scott and the public authorities to guard against disturbances of any kind or nature. There were many suspected persons in official

---

used to "hold, occupy, and possess the property and places belonging to the government." Harpers Pictorial History of the Great Rebellion, pgs. 47 & 48.

[317] Chief Justice Roger Brooke Taney was from Frederick, Maryland. He had served as U.S. Attorney General for President Andrew Jackson starting in 1831. Justice Taney had become Chief Justice of the Supreme Court on March 15, 1836 and served until is death on October 12, 1864. He rendered the famous Dred Scott decision on March 6, 1857. He swore Mr. Lincoln in as President for Lincoln's first inauguration in March 1861. Mr. Lincoln and Judge Taney clashed over the *habeas corpus* issue. Ironically, Justice Taney died the same day the state of Maryland abolished slavery. The Life of Abraham Lincoln, pg. 536 and The Cyclopaedia of American Biography, Part VI., pgs. 28 - 31.

[318] Portend means threatened.

positions in the city who were narrowly watched. Among them was the Chief of the Capital Police, a potion of dangerous authority at the time. He was a recognized sympathizer of the South and soon joined his fortune with his friends in the rebellion.

The New York delegation on the night of the inauguration paid their respects to the president. Mr. Lincoln said to them he was rejoiced to see good feeling manifested by them, and said he hoped that "our friends South would be when they read his inaugural, satisfied." He said he had made it as near right as it was possible for him to make it in accordance with the Constitution, which he thought was as good for the people who lived south of the Mason and Dixon line as it was for those who lived north.

On the 4th of March, 1861, the affairs of the nation looked desperate indeed. Seven states had already revolted and others in sympathy with them were not only ready and willing to join them but were anxious and impatient for an excuse to do so. The first attempt to exert the national authority was then a justifiable excuse. Soon the manifestations of this authority developed and soon the other slave-holding states followed in the revolt.

There had been a fierce struggle among the Republican politicians as to whom Mr. Lincoln should appoint to his Cabinet. The people at large expected Mr. Seward would, without doubt, be one of the number. The Honorable Benjamin Wade of Ohio, Mr. Greeley of New York, and others were bitterly opposed to it, and endeavoring to make it impossible for Mr. Lincoln to bring Mr. Seward to his counsel. Mr. Cameron,[319] Mr. Blair[320] and Mr. Smith[321] all had their opponents

---

[319] Simon Cameron of Pennsylvania was a business man and a politician. He was a candidate for the nomination for president at the Republican National Convention in 1860. He pulled out on the second ballot and threw Pennsylvania's votes to Mr. Lincoln. He served on the Lincoln Cabinet as Secretary of War. Lincoln's War. pg. 8 and Two Roads to Sumter, pgs. 221 & 225.

[320] Montgomery Blair was a West Point graduate. He was counsel for the plaintiff in the Dred Scott case before the Supreme Court in 1857. He had been Mayor of St. Louis but moved to Maryland where he was a judge. He was a Republican and was Mr. Lincoln's Postmaster General. He attended the dedication of the National Cemetery in Gettysburg with Mr. Lincoln. The Story-Life of Lincoln, pgs. 278 & 547, Lincoln's War, pg. 73 and Appleton's Cyclopaedia of American Biography, Vol. I., pg. 282.

[321] Caleb Blood Smith was originally from Massachusetts but moved to Indiana. He was editor of the *Sentinel* newspaper of Connersville, Indiana. He was a Whig Congressman from 1843 - 1849. He helped secure Mr. Lincoln's nomination in the Republican National Convention in 1859. He resigned as Secretary of the Interior until

and enemies who strongly advised against their appointments. These opposing elements carried matters to such extremes that Mr. Lincoln despaired of harmonizing the Seward men with the Chase[322] men. There was a plan afoot urging with great earnestness to put Mr. Corwin[323] into the State Department and sending Mr. Seward to England as minister and giving the appointment of the Secretary of Treasury to New York. Had this program been successful, it would have successfully closed Mr. Chase out. True, the personal relations between Mr. Corwin and Mr. Lincoln were very close and intimate, much more so than Mr. Lincoln's relationship with Mr. Chase, but there was no public man whose character for ability and integrity Mr. Lincoln had a greater respect and veneration for than that of Mr. Chase.

There was a widespread and prevailing opinion among the politicians who did not know Mr. Lincoln, that Mr. Seward had an overpowering will and control over him. The belief was general that Mr. Seward, in whose ability and moderation the conservative people of the North seemed to have the most confidence, would be the real head of the administration. This supposition was a great mistake. It underrated the man who had been elected to wield the helm of the government in the troubles waters in the brewing storm. Mr. Lincoln was as self-reliant a man as ever breathed the atmosphere of patriotism. He was not then in the hands of Mr. Seward, nor had he ever been. Nor was he afterwards ever in his or in any other man's hands; in the sense of subserviency[324] of will, or as a supple tool of assumed superiority.

---

December, 1862 and became a circuit judge in Indiana. Appleton's Cyclopaedia of American Biography, Vol. V., pg. 558.

322 Salmon Portland Chase was a New Hampshire native. He graduated from Dartmouth College and became a lawyer. He was fervent opponent of slavery. In 1837 as an attorney he defended a colored woman in court who was a fugitive slave. He was twice Governor of Ohio and a U.S. Senator. Mr. Chase was a serious contender for the Republican nomination for president during the Republican National Convention of 1860. He became Secretary of the Treasury during the Lincoln administration. Upon resigning in June 1864, Mr. Lincoln appointed him as Chief Justice of the Supreme Court. The Story-Life of Lincoln, pgs. 313, 345, & 588, Lincoln and the Civil War, pgs. 33, 130 & 134, Appleton's Cyclopaedia of American Biography, Vol. I., pgs. 585-588, and Seaport Autographs, pg.6.

323 Thomas Corwin—See pg. 17.

324 Subserviency means being ruled by someone else.

As late as March 20, 1861, a large and respectable delegation of persons visited Mr. Lincoln to bring matters to a conclusion. The object of these parties was to prevent the appointment of Mr. Chase to the Cabinet, at the risk of everything. They were received civilly and treated courteously. Mr. Lincoln listened to them with great patience. They were unanimous in their opposition to the appointment. Mr. Seward's appointment they urged was absolutely and indispensably required to secure either the support of the North or respectful hearing at the South from the administration. The danger to the Union cause was portrayed of a man like Mr. Chase being put in the Cabinet, who was so notoriously identified with and supported by men who did not desire the perpetuation[325] of the Union.

The delegation was strongly urged that Mr. Chase would an unsafe counselor and that he and his supporters favored a northern republic extending from the Ohio River to Canada, rather than supporting the Union of our fathers, maintained on the principles of its founders. Another argument was urged which to them seemed of vital importance and conclusion. The men thought that was it would not be possible for Mr. Seward to sit in the Cabinet with Mr. Chase a member. To think of it was revolting to them, and that they or their state could nor would not tolerate it.

These attempts so earnestly put forth, distressed Mr. Lincoln greatly. At length, after a long pause, he replied that it was very difficult to reconcile conflicting claims and interests; that his greatest desire was to form an administration that would command the confidence and respect of the country and with the party which placed him in power. He spoke of his high respect for Mr. Seward, his eminent service, his great genius and the respect he was held in by the country. He said Mr. Chase also had great claims that no one could gainsay.[326] His claims were perhaps not so great as Mr. Seward's, but this he would not then discuss. The party and the country wanted the hearty and harmonious cooperation with all good men without regard to sections. There was an ominous[327] pause. Mr. Lincoln then went to a drawer and took out a paper, saying "I had written out my choice and selection of members for the Cabinet after most careful and deliberate consideration. And now you are telling me I must break the slate and begin the thing all over again." He

---

[325] Perpetuation means permanency.

[326] Gainsay means to contradict.

[327] Ominous means fateful.

admitted that he had some times apprehended that it might be as they had suggested, that he might be forced to reconsider what he considered his judicious conclusions. In view of the possibility he had constructed an alternative list so well as the original. He had hoped to make Mr. Seward as Secretary of State and Mr. Chase as Secretary of the Treasury. He expressed his regrets that he could not be gratified in this desire and added that he could not reasonably expect to have things just as he wanted them.

Silence prevailed for quite a space of time and then he added, "This being the case gentlemen, now it would do for us to agree upon a change like this. To appoint Mr. Chase Secretary of the Treasury and to offer the State Department to William L. Dayton[328] of New Jersey." The delegation was shocked, disappointed and outraged. Mr. Lincoln continued in the same strain again and referred to his high appreciation to the abilities of Mr. Seward. He said Mr. Dayton was an old Whig, like Mr. Seward and himself and that he was from New Jersey and was "next door to New York." "Mr. Seward," he added, "could go minister to England where his genius would find wonderful scope in keeping Europe straight about home troubles." The delegation was non-plussed.[329] They, however, saw and appreciated the inevitable. They, for the first time realized the indomitable[330] will of the president, that afterwards became so notable throughout the trying times of his administration. They saw that the "mountain would not come to the Mohammed with conditions imposed, so Mohammed had to go to the mountain."

The difficulty was accommodated by Mr. Seward coming into the Cabinet with Mr. Chase and the administrative organization was affected to Mr. Lincoln's satisfaction. Mr. Seward was a Republican with centralizing tendencies and had been a prominent and powerful member of the old Whig Party which had gone to decay. Mr. Chase was a states' rights federal Republican, not having been strictly attached to either the Whig or Democratic organizations. Mr. Chase had for years been a conspicuous leader of the anti-slavery movement which had risen on the ruins of the Whig Party. Mr. Seward had

---

[328] William L. Dayton of New Jersey was a former U. S. Senator and Mr. Lincoln's Minister of France from 1861-1864. He successfully lobbied Napoleon III to not recognize the Confederacy. Lincoln, the Prairie Year, pg. 222.

[329] Non-plussed means baffled.

[330] Indomitable means unconquerable.

cautiously abstained from any connecting with the anti-slavery party per se, while Mr. Chase had been its active and efficient advocate, regardless of party organization.

Mr. Lincoln adopted, whether consciously or unconsciously, the policy of President George Washington in bringing men of opposite principles into his Cabinet as far as he could do so, hoping that they would harmonize in administrative measures. In doing so, in the cases of Mr. Seward and Mr. Chase, Mr. Lincoln entirely reversed the original arrangement by giving Mr. Seward, a Republican centralist the post of Mr. Jefferson, a states' rights federal Republican, and to Mr. Chase, a federal Republican, the post assigned to Mr. Hamilton,[331] a centralist.

An extra session of the Senate was at once called for executive business. Mr. Lincoln sent in the names of the members of the Cabinet. The Senate promptly confirmed their appointment.

The Cabinet was composed of as follows:

Hon. William H. Seward[332] Secretary of State

Hon. Salmon P. Chase Secretary of the Treasury

Hon. Gideon Welles[333] Secretary of the Navy

Hon. Caleb B. Smith Secretary of the Interior

Hon. Montgomery Blair Postmaster General

Hon. Edward Bates[334] Attorney General

Hon. Simon Cameron Secretary of War

After the 4th of March, 1861, Mr. Lincoln having been inaugurated, his Cabinet having been selected and appointed, immediately the consideration of the state of the country was paramount. South Carolina had led off and had become disenjoined from the body politic of the sisterhood of states of the Union.

---

331 Alexander Hamilton was the first Secretary of the Treasury. He was a founding father and co-author of the Federalist papers which emphasized a strong central government. He helped create the national bank. Ameri-canrevwar.com/files/hamilt.htm

332 William H. Seward—See page 13.

333 Gideon Welles of Connecticut was editor of the *Hartford Times* newspaper, the official organ of the Democratic Party. He opposed the extension of slavery. He served as Secretary of the Navy until 1869. Appleton's Cyclopaedia of American Biography, Vol. VI., pg. 427.

334 Edward Bates was a Quaker from Virginia. He was against slavery. He was the presiding officer of the Whig convention in 1856. He moved to Missouri where he was a lawyer and Congressman who was the oldest man in Mr. Lincoln's Cabinet. He served as Attorney General. The Two American Presidents, pg. 88, 139 & 141 and Appleton's Cyclopaedia of American Biography, Vol. I., pg. 193.

At this time Mr. Seward was in favor of immediately calling a national convention. Senator Douglas was urging this course on Mr. Lincoln as the only means of saving the country from a territorial war. Everything now seemed in disturbed condition. Men who ought to have united and cooperated together to enforce the conservative will of the whole country on the desperate and despicable intriguer[335] of both sections seemed paralyzed, disorganized and dormant, while the enemies of the Union were alert, determined and hopeful.

No call for national convention was made. Mr. Lincoln assumed the duties of administering the government in its distracted condition. At the time he called the extraordinary extra session of the Senate on the 4th of March, there were only left of the southern Senators in that body Messrs. Bragg[336] and Clingman[337] of North Carolina, Andrew Johnson[338] of Tennessee, Messrs. Hemphill[339] and Wigfall[340] of Texas, and Messrs. Hunter[341] and Mason[342] of Virginia.

---

335 Intriguer means plotter.

336 Thomas Bragg was Governor of North Carolina from 1854 - 1858. He was a U .S. Senator and became Attorney General in the cabinet of Jefferson Davis. Appleton's Cyclopaedia of American Biography, Vol. I., pg. 356.

337 Senator Thomas Lanier Clingman—See pg. 80.

338 Andrew Johnson was a war Democrat from TN who supported President Lincoln's military policies. He was elected Vice-President during Lincoln's second term and became President upon Lincoln's assassination. He was the first U.S. President to be tried for impeachment. www.answers.com/topic/andrew-jackson.

339 John Hemphill had replaced Sam Houston in the U.S. Senate from Texas. Hemphill was expelled from the Senate when Texas voted to secede. He became a confederate Congressman. www.cemetery.state.tx.us/pub/user_firm.asp?step=1&pers_id=59

340 Louis Trezaunt Wigfall was a U.S Senator from Texas. He served in the Confederate Senate and was one of its most able defenders of the slave power. Wigfall was an aid to General Beauregard at the bombardment of Fort Sumter in April 1861. He was leader of a secret organization that made an unsuccessful attempt to kidnap President Buchanan in late 1860 and early 1861. Appleton's Cyclopaedia of American Biography, Vol. VI., pg. 499.

341 Robert Mercer Taliaferro Hunter of Virginia was a cautious secessionist who became President Pro-Tem of the Confederate Senate after resigning as Confederate Secretary of State. The Confederate Nation, 1861 - 1865, pgs. 86 & 148.

342 James Murray Mason was a former U.S. Senator (chairman of the committee on foreign relations) and Congressman from Virginia. He was a graduate of the University of Pennsylvania and authored the Fugitive Slave Law of 1850. He was a lawyer and a states rights Democrat. He was sent to England as a minister in January 1862 by Jefferson Davis to convince the British to support the Confederate cause. Lincoln's War. pgs. 102 - 105 and Appleton's Cyclopaedia of American Biography, Vol. IV., pg. 243, Southern History of the War, pg. 214 and Don't Know Much About the Civil War? pg. 198.

An animated debate took place in Congress over President Lincoln's inaugural address. Mr. Dixon[343] offered a resolution that the usual number of copies of the address be printed for the use of the Senate. Mr. Clingman made a speech not to approve its being printed, as a matter of course, but he desired to be understood in asserting against the printing of it as he did not endorse its positions. He said its purpose and objects seemed to clearly and directly lead to war, and argued that if the principles enumerated in it were adopted, this result could not be avoided.

Mr. Douglas replied that from the address, he came to the conclusion that it was the wish and purpose of the president to pursue a peaceful policy and to avoid war. He was rejoiced in being able to come to that conclusion.

Mr. Wigfall asked Senator Douglas the pointed question whether he would advise that the troops at Fort Sumter be withdrawn, the flag of the United States be removed from the borders of the Confederate states, and that there should be no attempt to levy tribute upon a foreign people.

Mr. Douglas replied that as the gentleman he was not the guardian of the honor of the country but was looking to the interests of another, which is hostile to this country, he felt under no obligation to give him his views, because Mr. Wigfall might soon be found in the enemy's country and be commanding its armies.

Mr. Foster[344] of Connecticut offered a resolution to expel Mr. Wigfall because he had declared in debate that he was a foreigner and that he owed no allegiance to the government—that he belongs to and owes his allegiance to another and foreign government.

Mr. Clingman offered as a substitute, "Whereas it is understood that the state of Texas has seceded from the Union and is no longer one of the United States, therefore resolved that she is not entitled to be represented in this body." Mr. Foster would not admit that a state of this Union had any right or any power under the Constitution or to take itself out of the union of states which go to make up the United States of America. Mr. Mason of Virginia then said; "I aver it here, as a Senator of Virginia, in the face of the country, that I owe and

---

343 James Dixon of Connecticut was a Whig leader in the U.S. Senate. Appleton's Cyclopaedia of American Biography, Vol. II., pg. 186.

344 Henry Allen Foster was a Democratic Congressman and then U.S. Senator from Connecticut. Appleton's Cyclopaedia of American Biography, Vol. II., pg. 511.

recognize no allegiance to the government of the United States." The matter in quotation marks was referred to the judiciary committee.

A resolution was then offered by Mr. Fessenden[345] of Maine to strike from the rolls of the Senate Messrs. Davis[346] and Brown[347] of Mississippi, Mr. Mallory[348] of Florida, Mr. Clay Jr.[349] of Alabama, Mr. Toombs[350] of Georgia, Mr. Benjamin[351] of Louisiana; they having previously withdrawn from the Senate and announced that they were no longer members of that body. The resolution was amended and carried, and their seats were declared vacant and their names were to be omitted at the call of the rolls.

Mr. Douglas offered a resolution calling on the Secretary of War to inform the Senate what forts, navy yards, and other property within the limits of South Carolina, Georgia, Alabama, Florida, Mississippi, Louisiana and Texas were now within the active possession and occupation of the United States. He asked for the number of men by which each was garrisoned and held, whether reinforcements were necessary to retain the same and if so, whether the government had the power and means under existing laws to supply such reinforcement within such time as the exigencies and necessities of the case demand.

---

[345] William P. H. Fessenden from New Hampshire was a Bowdoin College graduate and an attorney. He was a Whig and an anti-slavery man. www.virtualology.com .
[346] Jefferson Davis—See page 18.
[347] Albert G. Brown was a U.S. Senator from Mississippi from 1854-1861. U. S. Senators Home—State Information—Mississippi
[348] Stephen Rossey Mallory was a Democrat from Florida who served in the U. S. Senate from 1851-1861. He was the chairman of the Committee on Naval Affairs for Congress and later became Secretary of the Confederate Navy. U.S. Senators Home—State Information—Florida and The Confederate Navy, pg. 6.
[349] Clement Claiborne Clay was an attorney who graduated from the University of Alabama. He was a U.S. Senator and later a Confederate Senator. He was a long time friend of Jefferson Davis but did not take the appointment of Secretary of State offered by Davis. He was arrested and imprisoned as part of the conspiracy to assassinate President Lincoln until a pardon was issued and he was freed on April 17, 1866. The Two American Presidents, pg. 126 & 331 and Civil War a Narrative, Part IX, pg. 301 and Appleton's Cyclopaedia of American Biography, Vol. I., pgs. 638 & 639.
[350] Robert Toombs—See pg. 18.
[351] Judah Phillip Benjamin was born in St. Croix and then moved to Key West, Florida. He was Chairman of the Navel Affairs Committee during his time as a U.S. Senator. He was Secretary of the Navy and later Attorney General for the Jefferson Davis Confederate Cabinet. Following the war he was arrested and incarcerated at Fort Lafayette for ten months before being released in March 1866. The Confederate Nation, 1861 - 1865, pgs. 78, 79 & 148 and Appleton's Cyclopaedia of American Biography, Vol. I., pg. 235.

He also wanted to know whether the defense and protection of the United States and their interests made it necessary and wise to retain military possession of such forts, places and other property except at Key West and Tortugas and to recapture and re-occupy such others as the United States had been deprived of by seizure or surrender for any other purpose and with a view to any other end, than the subjugation[352] and occupation of those states which have assumed the right to secede from the Union. And within whose limits such forts and other public property were situated and if such be the motives for recapturing and holding the forts and other property, what military force including regulars and volunteers would be necessary to enable the United States to reduce the states aforesaid as such others as were supposed to sympathize with them, subjugation and obedience of the laws of the Union and to protect the federal capital.

Mr. Douglas made a speech in support of the resolution in which he depicted the dangerous tendencies of the country; and thought the information which the resolution proposed to elicit was very important to the quiet and peace of the country. He argued that the inaugural address of the president was understood by many of both sections of the Union as indicating a war policy. If these apprehensions were allowed to ripen into a conviction that the administration did mediate a war policy to subjugation the seceding states by military force, he feared that they would find a terrific issue precipitated upon them sooner than they imagined. As for himself, he did not believe such to be the policy of the president; he did not understand the inaugural in that way. Mr. Douglas in his speech went further and formulated the state of the country as involving one of three issues.

First—The restoration and preservation of the Union by such amendments to the Constitution as will ensure the domestic tranquility, safety and equality of all states and the restored peace and fraternity to the whole country.

Second—A peaceful dissolution of the Union by recognizing the independence of such states as refusing to remain in the Union without such Constitutional amendments and the establishment of a liberal system of commercial and social intercourse with them by treaties of commerce and amity.

---

[352] Subjugation means annexation.

Third—War with a view to the subjugation and military occupation of those states which have seceded or may secede from the Union.

These promulgations[353] startled many members of the Senate. They were like bomb shells thrown into the camp. Here was the public status reduced to three distinct issues as alternatives, one of which must necessarily be adopted. There was no middle course, no other path leading to safety and security, but to accept one of these three horns of the dilemma. These utterances had been made by as tried and true patriot as lived on the continent. He was a sincere lover of his country and its flag; his only aim and ambition being to save the country with honor to all sections, if possible. True he formerly had an ambition to be chief executive of the nation, and submitted his chances to the suffrages of the people. Mr. Lincoln, Mr. Breckinridge and Mr. Bell, inspired by the same laudable ambition, did the same. In the struggle, the will of the people was expressed in the election of Mr. Lincoln, and Mr. Douglas bowed in submission to that will. He was too pure and noble to entertain any of the rancor[354] of jealousy; his country's life was at stake and he nobly and eagerly used his efforts to save it.

Senator Wilson[355] of Massachusetts and Senator Hale[356] of New Hampshire, attacked the resolution introduced by Mr. Douglas just referred to, and indulged in very undignified and discourteous personalities towards him. Whether this was prompted by jealousy or the more unworthy motive which had been attributed to them of favoring a northern as well as a southern confederacy—dissolution of the Union—it is not our purpose now to inquire into. The sequel may

---

[353] Promulgations are declarations.

[354] Rancor is ill will.

[355] Henry Wilson was a Senator from Massachusetts who was an ardent abolitionist. He was editor of the *Boston Republican* newspaper. A shoemaker by trade, he was called the "Natick cobbler." He first proposed to the Massachusetts legislature in 1853 that colored men be enlisted in the state militia. He later proposed a resolution in Congress to legalize all of Mr. Lincoln's activities since 1861. He also served as Vice-President for President Ulysses S. Grant. Lincoln's War, pg. 63 and Appleton's Cyclopaedia of American Biography, Vol. VI., pgs. 548 - 550.

[356] Representative James Parker Hale was a graduate of Bowdoin College and an anti-slavery man. He served in both the U.S. Senate and U.S. Congress. He ran as the Free Soil candidate for President in 1852. He tried to introduce an amendment to the Constitution making it legal for slavery in the states where it already existed but it failed to be adopted. The Two American Presidents, pg. 114 and Appleton's Cyclopaedia of American Biography, Vol. III., pgs. 33 & 34.

be found in the facts. Mr. Wilson commenced his tirade by saying that Senator Douglas was a man of anxieties, that the inaugural address had hardly been flashed over the country before he sets forth unasked to give an interpretation of it; that nobody on the Republican side of the chamber had undertaken either to sanction or disavow that interpretation. He went on to say "The Senator struts up before the Senate and the country and talks about what he will not permit; what he will not do. I beg leave to say to the Senator and to the country he is clothed with no power to dictate to us or to any considerable body of men. He has not a Senate at his heels. He stands here alone and is hardly more powerful before the nation. I say to the Senator that I want him and his friends in the country to understand that the administration which has just come to power will take its own time to deliberate, to act, to declare its own policy, and will do it through men in whom it has confidence, who have a right to speak for it. The Senator made here today what I regard as a mischievous, a wicked and unpatriotic speech. He talks about the alarm that pervades the country. Sir, that Senator, by the course he has chosen to take during the last few days, assumes to be the alarmist of the country, and he is the only man I see alarmed. The great portion of this country at this day and this hour are coming to look at these questions that have distracted and divided the country as they are. There is today less excitement, ill will and anxiety in the country. Matters are clearing up. The skies brighten. The sober judgment and patriotism of the nation are rising to meet the wants of the time and occasion."

At this distance of time in taking a perspective view of Mr. Wilson's speech, and the time and circumstances under which it was made, it seems not only ridiculous and silly, but funny as well. The idea of Mr. Douglas at the time being the only man alarmed about the state of the country is remarkable. "The matters were clearing up"—if the Senator meant by this that the Confederates were "clearing up" our customs house, forts and arsenals in the South, he was right. What else was being "cleared up"? No one but himself could see the "clearing." As to "the sober judgment and patriotism of this nation, who were rising to meet the wants of the time and occasion," it might be well said that at the battle of Bull Run in July following the session, when Mr. Wilson went there himself with plug hat, white breeches, and kid gloves, to meet the "wants of the occasion" that if he had looked behind him when he was making the best time on record for

Washington, or had looked into a mirror upon his arrival, he would doubtless have seen others besides the Senator from Illinois who were alarmed and scared nearly to death.

Mr. Douglas in reply to Mr. Wilson's speech merely said "I can pardon the petulant[357] remarks and personal attacks of the Senator from Massachusetts. He winced under what I said. He unconsciously admits that I was right in my construction of the inaugural; that those general clauses about enforcing the laws and collecting the revenues and possessing the forts did not indicate what Mr. Lincoln was going to do. A confession that my construction was right when I said that Mr. Lincoln's policy was going to depend on the necessities of the case, and be changed from time to time with a view to preserve the peace of the county." Mr. Douglas conclude by saying, in effect, that his object was to demonstrate that the wing of the party to which Senator Wilson belongs—the war party—the disunion wing—were not authorized to speak for the president in regard to his policy. "Senator Wilson's line of policy and mine differ. Mine is to preserve the peace. I do not understand that to be his. There are Union men on that side of the house and I know there are disunionists there too. Hence I do not expect to be in harmony on the Union question with the whole of that side of the chamber. I will act and harmonize with every Union man in America, no matter what his politics or where he comes from, who will forget party and act with reference to country."

Mr. Fessenden of Maine, who was proverbial for his courtesy and moderation, misunderstood Mr. Douglas in the course of the debate and arose to a personal explanation, out of which grew an acrimonious[358] discussion between the two Senators. Mr. Hale remarked with that levity for which he was so notorious, apt and effective. He intended to say something in reply to the Senator from Illinois. It occurred to him that there was in an old book that he used to read an answer to his speech. It was very short and he would read it. It is written in the 15th chapter of Second Samuel, fourth verse. "Assalom said, 'Moreover, oh, were I made judge of the land that any man that hath any suit or cause might come to me and I would do him justice.'" This stroke of wit, like the most of his sallies[359] in doing the funny business for the Senate brought down the house and caused

[357] Petulant means saucy.
[358] Acrimonious means angry.
[359] Sallies are flights of fantasy.

great laughter. He was one of those men who in dealing with law or public policy preferred to be popular rather than right. He afterwards learned by said experience that there were political virtues which sound morality held in admiration.

Like some others in both sections it was said of Mr. Hale that if his theological opinions conformed to his ideas and profession of political duty he would esteem the luck of Barabbas,[360] as more meritorious than the fidelity of John or the devotion of all Marys. There were some men at this time who were taught and who taught that enmity[361] to the Constitution was the sum total of public and private virtue and the time had arrived for them to "show their faith by their works" and in doing so, it cannot be denied that their moral perceptions were much distorted. It was obvious that both Mr. Wilson and Mr. Hale as well as most of the fair-minded men of the Senate knew that Mr. Douglas was really uttering the sentiments and sketching the policy of Mr. Lincoln in this debate, and the wonder is that they did not admit this fact, and turn their Senatorial batteries upon the White House. They had at least the discretion and self-command sufficient to forebear from doing this until later in the period.

Mr. Lincoln had shown great wisdom in appreciating the importance of holding such Democrats as Mr. Douglas close to the administration on the issue of a unified country or a dissolution of the Union. He had said, "They are just where we Whigs were in 1848 about the Mexican War. We had to take the locofoco[362] preamble when Taylor[363] wanted help or else vote against Taylor. The Democrats must vote to hold the Union now without bothering whether we or the southern men got things where they are. We must make it easy for them to do this because we cannot live through the case without them." He further said, "Some of our friends are opposed to an accommodation because the South began the trouble and was entirely responsible for the consequences, be they what they may. This reminds me of a story told out of Illinois where I lived. 'There was a vicious bull in the pasture and a neighbor passing

---

[360] Barabbas is a Biblical figure. He was the man the crowd asked Pontius Pilate to release at the trial of Jesus of Nazareth. www.answers.com/topic/barabbas

[361] Enmity means hostility.

[362] Locofoco refers to Democrats.

[363] President Zachary Taylor was the 12th President of the United States. He had a forty year career in the U.S. Army. He died after just 16 months in office from gastroenteritis. www.whitehouse.gov/about/zacharytaylor

through the field. The animal took after him. He ran to a tree and got there in time to save himself. And being able to run around the tree faster than the bull he managed to seize him by the tail. His "bullship" seeing himself at a disadvantage pawed the earth and scattered gravel for a while then broke into a full run, bellowing at every jump. The man was holding onto his tail cussing him, and asking the question. 'D__m you, who commenced this fuss?' Now our plain duty is to settle the fuss we have before us, without reference to who commenced it.'"

Mr. Lincoln told another anecdote in connection with the probable adjustment of the difficulties. Said he, "Once upon a time a number of very pious gentlemen all strict members of the true church were appointed to take in charge and superintend the erection of a bridge over a very dangerous and turbulent river. They found great difficulty in securing the services of an engineer competent for the work. Finally Brother Jones said that Mr. Meyers had built several bridges and he had no doubt that he could build this one. Mr. Meyers was sent for. The committee asked, 'Can you build this bridge?' 'Yes' was the answer. 'I can build a bridge to the infernal regions if required.' The committee was shocked and Brother Jones felt called upon to say something in defense of his friend. He commenced by saying, 'Gentlemen. I know my friend Mr. Meyers so well. He is so honest a man and so good an architect, if he states positively that he can build a bridge to hell, why I believe he can do it; but I feel bound to say that I have my doubts about the abutment on the infernal side.'

"So," said Mr. Lincoln, "when the politicians told me that the northern and southern wings of the democracy could be harmonized, why I believe them, of course, but I always had my doubts about 'the abutment on the other side.'"

Mr. Douglas resolution was laid on the table by a vote of yeas 23, nays 11. The Senate closed its extraordinary session on March 28, 1861. Shortly after this, on June 3, 1861, Senator Douglas died while putting forth his best energies to prepare the people of the state of Illinois for the coming conflict of arms between the northern and southern sections.

During these debates the farewells and departures of the southern Senators and representatives would announce another seceding state without waiting to see if a reconciliation could be effected.

Mr. Lincoln would have been glad of an accommodation if he could have seen any way of affecting it with honor to the flag. He and his entire Cabinet agreed that it was the duty of the federal government to enforce the laws, protect the public property and preserve the Union of the states. On the 12th of April, 1861 President Lincoln, in answer to the Virginia commissioners, recommended to them a grateful reading of his inaugural address and added "In that I expressed my policy and with deep regret and mortification[364] I now learn there is great and injurious uncertainty in the peoples' minds as to what that policy is and what course I intend to pursue. Not having seen occasion to change, it is now my purpose to pursue the course marked out in the inaugural address. I now repeat that the power confided in me will be used to hold, occupy and possess the property and public buildings of the government and to collect the duties on imports. Beyond what is necessary for these objects, there will be no invasion of force against and among the population anywhere."

He also at that time stated that he would carry out all the laws concerning the forts in the seceding states belonging to the government. All this was in the line of policy enunciated by Thomas Jefferson in a letter from Paris written on the 13th day of November, 1787 in which he said "The tree of Liberty must be refreshed from time to time with the blood of patriots and tyrants. It is its natural manure. The most expensive fertilizer—acting like guano on the impoverished soil."

[364] Mortification means humiliation.

*"We must settle this question now, whether in a free government the minority have the right to break up government whenever they choose. If we fail, it will go far to prove the incapability of the people to govern themselves."*

Abraham Lincoln
as told to his secretary John Hay[365]

# — 6 —

# THE EARLY STAGES OF THE WAR

After President Lincoln re-announced his purpose to re-supply Fort Sumter, an attack[366] was precipitated on it by the rebel forces around it. It was bombarded for 30 hours. When the American flag for the first time in its history was lowered under the fire of insurgent citizens, the fort surrendered on the 14th of April, 1861. The force at Fort Sumter had held General Beauregard[367] in check with his command at Charleston. When it fell, General Beauregard marched to Virginia and precipitated its secession. If we could have held Fort Sumter there would have been no bloodshed and no war. It was the coercing process of Virginia into the Confederacy by General Beauregard's army that caused the war.

In 1833, President Jackson[368] held nullification in check and compelled the repeal of the South Carolina ordinances in the first

---

365 Lincoln in American Memory, pg. 385.

366 April 12, 1861 at 4:30 am. NPS Fort Sumter, pg. 1.

367 General Pierre G. T. Beauregard graduated second in his class of 1845 from the U.S. Military Academy. He was Superintendent of West Point in January 1861. He was in command of the South Carolinians in Charleston. Ironically, at West Point, Beauregard's artillery instructor was Major Robert Anderson. Later he was transferred to Petersburg by General Lee to defend the south side of Richmond. After the war, he served as president of several railroads and was state adjutant general of Louisiana. The Confederate Nation, 1861 - 1865, pg. 75, Civil War a Narrative, Part VII., pg. 121, Lincoln's War, pg. 24 and Pride of the South, pgs. 69 & 70.

368 President Andrew Jackson—See pg. 7.

attempt of obtaining a virtual secession by sending General Scott with one thousand men and orders to hold Fort Moultrie.

Major Anderson's position in Fort Sumter was infinitely stronger now than General Scott's was then, and the North was then infinitely as much greater or stronger than the South in 1860 and 1861 as Fort Sumter was stronger than Fort Moultrie in 1833. But President Jackson's administration was not chided as the administrations of Presidents Buchanan and Lincoln were with disunion representatives—mugwumps from the North as well as from the South who were willing and ready to invite and encourage secession by agreeing to yield with impunity[369] to the exactions[370] of South Carolina and to allow the forces sent for purpose of the protecting the national honor to be driven back, the old flag unprotected and groveling in the dust.

As a speculative question it is to be submitted; when President Buchanan's hands were tied by the embarrassments of having no judges and no marshals to enforce the laws in the southern states and no *posse comitatus*[371] to command which rendered him helpless and Congress persistently refusing to comply with his earnest appeals to pass laws empowering and authorizing him to meet the emergency by military enforcement of the laws in subjugating conformity to obedience to the law and order of the states in rebellion and President Buchanan under the short tenure of his office and the circumstances surrounding him had patriotically done what President Lincoln in his wisdom did, unauthorized which was sanctioned by the inherent and indestructible power of the incoming rules of the nations—declared war without the sanction of Congress—the only war making power under the Constitution; how long would it have been with a Democratic majority in Congress—with secession tendencies, until he would have been impeached, dethroned, and disgraced? This may be considered a delicate subject to consider. Therefore we will not discuss it.

We are, however, authorized in saying that President Buchanan was at least tardy in the reinforcement at Fort Sumter, which ought to have been speedily reinforced. As much might be said of President Lincoln. He neglected doing this, which, if done, may have averted war. The destinies of the government were thrown into extremes, and the policy

---

[369] Impunity means freedom from punishment.

[370] Exactions are extortions.

[371] *Posse comitatus* means temporary police force.

of the new government seemed to be, that in as much as the South had forced the existing state of things, that the Confederacy should commit the overt act of war, which resulting in the firing on Fort Sumter, placing it in the aggressive attitude of submitting to a trial by battle—and the inevitable issue of declaring of war followed. (On the anniversary of this day four years afterwards, the flag was again to be lowered, but only at half mast, announcing the assassination of Mr. Lincoln.)

The news of the firing on and the surrender of Fort Sumter to the Confederates aroused the North from a long continued sleep or trance. The majority of both the Democrats and Republicans of the North were furious. The North almost as a unit clamored for arms. The war was now fully inaugurated and begun. The war Democrats soon became absorbed into the Republican organization and a fusion of sentiments, object and purposed followed, all combining to reestablish the supremacy of the law and maintain the old flag all over the territory of the united government.

The firing of Fort Sumter by the Confederate forces sounded the tocsin[372] of alarm throughout the whole North. There was a considerable minority of the people in that section who looked upon this misguided act of southern fanaticism with a glow of heartfelt pleasure. They had earnestly prayed for the justification for war and the speedy settlement of the troubles and the total extinction of the institution of slavery as a disturbing element in the country. Part of the federal army had already surrendered to the Confederacy and most of the rest were scattered in isolated forts which were besieged by the enemy.

General Scott had reported to Mr. Lincoln that he had but 16,000[373] regulars available for immediate service. Most all of the federal ships had been sent to distant seas, and many of the most experienced officers of the army and navy had already taken service under the rebel flag. The United States Treasury was almost in a bankrupt condition and many of the government employees were only too anxious to secure all the plunder possible and decamp to the South. This course was perhaps natural enough. They only emulated the conduct of servants of dying dynasties all over the world. The indisposition of northern politicians to arm the president with power

---

[372] Tocsin means signal.
[373] Fort Sumter National Monument, South Carolina, pg. 11.

for war purposes prevailed up to this time and now the combined northern people clamored for legal authorization to bring back the South to law, order and obedience at the point of the bayonet.

In the history of the government for the first time it was now under control of what might be termed loose constructionists. The war Democrats became absorbed with the Republicans and in joint cooperation sacrificed all other consideration to the common cause of suppressing the rebellion. This was a hazardous experiment and deviation from that policy which had characterized the Democrats from the foundation of the government to that time. At no time had they ever advocated or tamely submitted to a strain on the Constitution, even to conform to the necessities of the hour. In this case the life of the nation was in jeopardy and if the Constitution interfered in the struggle and got worsted, it was considered of subordinate important to the lives of the people and the life of the nation. Self-protection, the first law of nature, inspired the people of the North and unified them as one man, subordinating the principles of the Constitution to the impending people, alike to it and to the people, and in the four years of dreadful struggle the Constitution was fortunately not damaged beyond repairing nor did it suffer as much as might have been anticipated from its surroundings. It withstood all innovations and remains today the same pliant old instrument of our original guidance, direction and protection.

Soon after the treasonable provisional government (the Confederates States of America) was formed in Montgomery, Alabama and the insurgents had committed the flagrant bombardment and capture of Fort Sumter of immediate conciliation,[374] all roads and avenues to Washington City were obstructed, and the capital was put in the condition of a siege. The mails in every direction were stopped, the lines of telegraph cut off and the military and naval forces were called out by the president for the defense of the capital. The Lincoln administration was cut off from all communications by the organized and combined treasonable resistance in the state of Maryland and this at a time when there had yet been no adequate and effective organization for its public defense. Congress had adjourned and the whole responsibility rested upon the executive. Congress had made no provision for the state of things that existed. Here was an emergency.

[374] Conciliation means avoiding hostilities.

Should the president allow the government at once to fall into ruin or to avail himself to the broader powers as conferred by the Constitution in cases of insurrection? Assume, if you please, authority that is not expressly granted by any authority, by any direction or warrant. This was the issue Mr. Lincoln then had to grapple with.

He promptly decided to make the effort to save the country, with all its blessings for the present age and for all of posterity. In this emergency the California Treasury ships on the way to the Atlantic coast became an object of consideration and protection to the commercial marine generally was most important. Mr. Lincoln directed the purchase or charter and the arming as quickly as possible of five steam ships for the purpose of public defense. This order was given to the commandant of the Navy Yard at Boston. Orders were also given to the commandant of the Philadelphia Navy Yard for the purchase, charter and arming of the equal number of vessels for the same purpose. An equal number of vessels were ordered to be placed into the armed service by purchase or charter of the commandant of New York. Commander Gillis[375] was also ordered to purchase two other vessels and similar orders were given to Commodore DuPont[376] with a view of opening a water passage to and from the capital. These several officers were ordered to advise with and obtain the counsel and directions of the Honorable E. D. Morgan[377] of New York or in his absence George D. Morgan,[378] William M. Evarts,[379] E. W.

---

[375] Commander John P. Gillis commanded several U.S. Naval ships including the U.S. Steamer *Monticello* and the U.S. S. *Pocahontas*. www.usnlp.org/navychronology/1861a.html

[376] Commodore Samuel A. DuPont was flag officer of the South Atlantic Blockade Squadron which consisted of 26 ships. Southern History of the War, pg. 217 and Smithsonian's Great Battles and Battlefields of the Civil War, pg. 116.

[377] Edwin D. Morgan was chairman of the National Republican Party from 1856 - 1864. He helped raise funds for Mr. Lincoln's presidential election. He was Governor of New York from 1858 - 1862. Appleton's Cyclopaedia of American Biography, Vol. IV., pg. 398 and www.nysl.nysed.gov/msscfa.sc11818.htm

[378] George D. Morgan helped secure funding for the stone fleet of the U. S. Navy. He owned an import business in partnership with Edwin Morgan who was his cousin. He was born in Pennsylvania and was Counsel to Marseilles and Minister to Portugal prior to the war. He joined with General Mitchel to drive the rebel troops out of eastern Tennessee. He commanded the 13th Corps of the Union Army. He had to resign his command in June 1863 due to ill health. He was a Congressman from 1868 - 1872. Civil War a Narrative, Part II., pg. 103, The Armies and The Leaders, pgs. 189, 216 & 233 and *New York Times* January 17, 1862.

Blatchford,[380] and Moses H. Grinnell,[381] who were by his special direction empowered by the Secretary of the Navy to act for his department in that crisis in the matters pertaining to the forwarding of troops and supplies for the public defense.

In this emergency the president was impressed with the necessity for an agency that should be authorized by the War Department—Secretary Simon Cameron—to make all necessary arrangements for the transportation of troops and munitions of war in aid and assistance of the officers of the army of the United States until communication by mail and telegraph should completely be re-established between the city of New York and the capital.

After the firing on Fort Sumter, General Beauregard marched his hostile army into the state of Virginia, then a loyal state of the Union, and threatened the seizure of the capital of the nation. The whole North went into active preparation to meet the invading hosts and in an incredibly short space—four days after the flag was lowered on Fort Sumter, Col. Cake[382] with 400 men of the 25th Pennsylvania volunteers arrived at Washington.[383] Special mention is made of this because they were the first troops to enter the city for its defense. The 6th Massachusetts Regiment was then on its way to the capital and on the day after, April 19, while passing through Baltimore was attacked by a mob. Three soldiers were killed and eleven were wounded. The troops fired on the mob killing eleven of them and wounding many more. On the day these troops were fired upon, Mr. Lincoln declared a blockade of southern ports, and appointed General Patterson[384] of Pennsylvania to command the Department of Washington.

---

[379] William M. Evarts of New York served in the U.S. Senate and as both Secretary of War under Rutherford B. Hayes and U.S. Attorney General under Andrew Johnson. www.answers.com/topic/william-m-evarts

[380] E. W. Blatchford was the treasurer of the Sanitary Commission during the Civil War. www.refs.ilgenweb.net/bios.ilbios1915-1/bl.html

[381] Moses H. Grinnell was a U.S. Naval officer. Mr. Lincoln stopped at his daughter's house on his train trip to his Inauguration and many important New York political and business leaders. www.mrlincolnandnewyork.org/inside.asp?ID=46&subjectID=3

[382] Colonel Henry Lutz Cake was a newspaper publisher of the *Pottsville Mining Record* in Northumberland, Pennsylvania. antietam.actw.org/officers.php?officer_id=440

[383] This occurred on April 18th.

[384] General Robert Patterson was born in Ireland but moved to Pennsylvania in 1797. He served in both the War of 1812 and the Mexican War. He was president of the Electoral College in 1836 at the election of Andrew Jackson. When the war started he was the oldest major general in the U.S. Army and one of the largest mill owners in the United States. He commanded the federal forces at Harpers Ferry, Virginia.

Governor Hicks[385] of Maryland and Mayor Brown[386] of Baltimore promptly notified the president that troops passing through Baltimore would have to fight their way, there being a strong disloyal element in the city. On the same day the 7th New York Regiment left the City of New York for Washington. Lt. Jones[387] with his federal command reached Carlisle, Pennsylvania having marched thirty miles the previous night from Harpers Ferry where he had destroyed the arsenal and public property at that place.

The Baltimore mob succeeded in checking railroad traffic and the passage of troops through the city from the north and west by destroying the railroad tracks and various bridges. Immediately after the riot commenced in Baltimore, a monster Union meeting was held in New York. A Union defense committee was formed by the wealthiest and foremost citizens. This committee provided for money, ships, supplies and marching regiments.

About this time there was happening a series of most startling disasters to the cause of the Union. Fort Sumter had fallen on the 14th of the month. Three days after this Virginia seceded from the Union. The day following, Harpers Ferry was lost; on the next day the riot in Baltimore, and all communications was cut off from the north and west. The following day (April 20th) the Gosport Navy Yard[388] with its contents was destroyed by Commander McCauley[389] to prevent it from falling into the hands of the secessionists. The sloop of war *Cumberland*

---

Lincoln's War, pg. 59 and Appleton's Cyclopaedia of American Biography, Vol. IV., pgs. 673 & 674.

[385] Governor Thomas Hicks—See pg. 86.

[386] Mayor George W. Brown was the Mayor of Baltimore. He told Mr. Lincoln that "It is not possible for more soldiers to pass through Baltimore unless they fight their way every step." Lincoln's War, pg. 36.

[387] Lt. Edward F. Jones was the commander of the 6th Massachusetts. Lincoln's War, pg. 37.

[388] The Gosport Naval Yards near Portsmouth, Virginia were destroyed by the federal government to keep the ships from falling into enemy hands. The destruction included the loss of the ships as follows: *The Pennsylvania*, *The Columbus*, *The Delaware*, *The Germantown*, *The Dolphin*, *The Columbia* and *The Merrimac*. *The Merrimac* parts including the engine and boiler were later salvaged and made into an ironclad by the Confederates. Southern History of the War, pgs. 71 & 72.

[389] Commodore Charles Stewart McCauley was a naval veteran who had served on the USS *Constellation* in 1813. He was the commander of the U.S. Naval Yard at Gosport. Appleton's Cyclopaedia of American Biography, Vol. IV., pg. 78.

[390]and the frigate *United States*[391] were the only vessels of value or things saved from the wreck. The government lost by this destruction about fifty million dollars. The arsenal at Liberty, Missouri was the same day seized by the rebels, and the 4th Massachusetts Regiment arrived at Fortress Monroe.[392]

On the next day (April 21st), Robert E. Lee[393] who had just resigned his commission in the United States Army and who had been acting as chief of staff for General Scott was appointed by Governor Letcher[394] as the commander of the Confederate military forces and naval forces of Virginia. The arsenal at Fayetteville, North Carolina surrendered to the state and Arkansas took possession of the arsenal at Napoleon.

The riot in Baltimore had now assumed proportions of an insurrection throughout the whole of Maryland and was of threatening and dangerous proportions. The authorities of Baltimore made it known to Mr. Lincoln their utter inability to restrain the turbulence of that city and beseeched him to avoid further blood shed by ordering the cessation of future transit of troops through the city. This fire from the front as well as one from the rear embarrassed Mr. Lincoln. What he then most wanted was troops for the defense of the Washington. He consulted with General Scott and it was agreed if no resistance was offered coming to Washington either in their march around Baltimore or by way of Annapolis[395] he would not force their march through that city. This concession for the time being was

---

[390] The *Cumberland* was built in 1825 to carry a crew of 400 with 24 guns. She was 175 feet long with three masts and sails. Warships of the Civil War Navies, pg. 127.
[391] The *United States* was built in 1796. It was 198 feet long with 44 guns and a crew of 467 sailors. Warships of the Civil War Navies, pg. 125.
[392] Fortress Monroe was a military instillation located at Hampton Roads, Virginia on the tip of the Virginia Peninsula. Along with Fort Wool, the two forts guarded the shipping lanes between the harbor and the Chesapeake Bay.
[393] Robert E. Lee was a U.S. Military Academy graduate (Class of 1829) and was named commandant of that school. He was a veteran of the Mexican War. He was in charge of the capture of John Brown at Harpers Ferry in October 1859. He was the commanding officer of the Army of Virginia and then the commanding officer of all the Confederate army. After the war he was President of Washington College in Lexington, Virginia (today that college has been renamed Washington and Lee). Virginia Southern History of the War, Part II., pg. 512.
[394] John Letcher was Governor of Virginia was from 1860-1864. After the war he served in the Virginia State Assembly and on the Board of Visitors for the Virginia Military Institute (WMI). www.civilwarcauses.org/letcher.htm
[395] Annapolis was a port city and the capital of Maryland.

satisfactory to the Baltimore authorities. This was the first instance in which the United States government ever treated with rebels in armed rebellion. Just now some detachments of Pennsylvania regiments were enroute to Washington from Harrisburg and Mr. Lincoln to show his good faith, ordered the troops back to Harrisburg and to come around by way of Annapolis. This order occasioned a political bumblebee's nest about Mr. Lincoln's care. The non-affiliated radicals who could not appreciate the situation and misapprehended the necessity and spirit of the order, made a great outcry and condemned the act as imbecile and cowardly.

On the arrival of the 6th Massachusetts and the 7th New York regiments under their respective commanders, General Butler[396] and Col. Lefferts,[397] at Philadelphia, the former on the same afternoon and the latter on the next morning, the commanders were informed by the railroad officials of the riot, burning of bridges and destruction of railroads stating the impossibility of reaching either Washington or Baltimore by rail. The alternative was then taken of going to Annapolis, Maryland by water and from there march to Washington. These regiments went to Washington by different routes, General Butler moving about daylight on April 21, and Colonel Lefferts arrived the next day. On their respective arrivals, they were met by Governor Hick's protest, warning them not to land. The governor was now panic stricken, was fuddled, was in doubt whether he was a Union man or a secessionist, was not intimately acquainted with himself and did not understand the situation or himself either. He was soon given to understand by these two commanders who did understand themselves and the situation, that the sacred soil of Maryland, however deluded, and that her citizens were in their claim of state supremacy, was not too sacred for the national flag to float over.

In his bewilderment, Governor Hicks immediately wrote to Mr. Lincoln, urging him to order the troops away. He made in his communication the modest proposition that Mr. Lincoln request the

---

[396] General Benjamin Butler—See. pg. 87.

[397] Col. Marshall Lefferts was a successful businessman in New York who was president of several New York telegraph companies from 1849 - 1860. He also patented a couple of devices for use on the telegraph. He commanded the first Union unit to leave New York for the war. His forces were sent back to New York City in July 1863 to keep order during the draft riots. Appleton's Cyclopaedia of American Biography, Vol. III., pg. 677.

British Minister, Lord Lyons,[398] to mediate and settle the trouble between the government and the rebels. To this proposition he received a merited rebuke. In repeated conversations with Mr. Lincoln, Governor Hicks had impressed him as an orthodox Union man, so much so that great reliance was placed on his loyalty and discretion. But after this the governor wrote: "We are ranging and organizing forces to protect the city and preserve order and we want arms."

Mr. Lincoln granted that "if the arms were furnished, they would be used to kill Union soldiers and the capture of the capital," and deemed it prudent "to place the arms in the hands of more reliable patriots."

The rebels now took possession of the telegraph wires and offices, leaving the capital a beleaguered and blockaded city. The greatest alarm was manifested in the city of Washington. Business operations had almost ceased. The city gave greater evidence in its deathlike stillness, of being a grand old cemetery than the habitable, bustling capital of a great nation. Visitors and residents were alike alarmed and made their way from it as they would from a pestilence,[399] by private conveyance and otherwise. The hotels were deserted. Scarcely a professional politician was left in the city and for the time being Mr. Lincoln felt a relief in all the gloom in the absence of marplots,[400] civil and military.

After years it may be doubted which he had the greatest reason to fear, the open hostilities of the rebels or the calamity of secret intrigues in his own party. The latter class now commenced to increase in numbers and grow in great magnitude to their opposition to his most patriotic efforts and most holy ambitions. About this time too, Mr. Henry Winter Davis and another gentleman from Baltimore had a conversation about the situation with him. Mr. Lincoln said, "Gentlemen. The people of your city are of a more dangerous type of traitor than the rebels of South Carolina. Let me ask you. Supposing a goddess of secession was to appear in your city, instead of a living harlot, and the whole people who were without the sin of rebellion were commanded to cast a stone at her. How many of such projectiles would be required for the occasion?" Mr. Davis promptly replied, "Mr.

---

398 Lord Richard Bickerton Pernell Lyons was British Minister to the United States—from 1861 to 1865. www.factbites.com/topics/Lord-Lyon

399 Pestilence means plague.

400 Marplots are people who frustrate a plan.

President. The way things are now there would not be one stone cast in the day time, but the old jade would catch the devil after nightfall."

On the 23rd of April, martial law was declared at Baltimore. On the arrival of these two regiments in Washington on the 24th they marched up Pennsylvania Avenue to the White House amidst the wildest shouts of enthusiasm of the people left in the city who had attended to welcome them. After receiving the grateful salute, and thanks of Mr. Lincoln, they marched to the quarters prepared for them. Their arrival gave a great sense of security and soon changed the aspect of things to its former condition.

On the 25th Major Sibley[401] surrendered four hundred fifty troops in Texas to Colonel Van Dorn[402] and Captain S. D. Sturgis[403] made his escape with two companies of cavalry with horses, equipment and provisions from Forth Worth. The same day Captain Stokes[404] of the regular army with a detachment of Illinois troops removed from the arsenal at St. Louis, 22,000 stands of arms and a great amount of fixed ammunition &c. to Springfield, Illinois.

The North had to depend almost entirely on volunteer troops and the president thought that the 75,000 men which he proclaimed called for would be sufficient for the purpose of war. He also called for an extra session of Congress to meet on the 4th of July. In the meantime, war was fully inaugurated. In the absence of the only war making power under the Constitution, (Congress has the exclusive right to

---

401 Henry Sibley was a graduate of the U.S. Military Academy in 1838. He was from Louisiana. Sibley served in both the Seminole War and the Mexican War. He was a Confederate who led raids in the Rio Grande area and was a brigadier General of the Department of Mexico. He also invented and patented a tent used in the civil war which was designed from wigwams of Sioux Indians. Civil War a Narrative, Part II., pg. 20 and Appleton's Cyclopaedia of the American Biography, Vol. V., pgs. 520-521.

402 Colonel Earl Van Dorn was born in Mississippi. He received an appointment to the U.S. Military Academy from his great uncle Andrew Jackson. He later was involved in the Mexican War. The general was head of the 2nd Corps of Sidney Johnson's cavalry and also led Confederate troops attached to General Sterling Price. Van Dorn's men were defeated at both Pea Ridge and Corinth and won a victory at Holly Spring. Lincoln's War, pgs. 140 & 191-193 and Civil War a Narrative, Part II., pg. 3.

403 Captain Samuel Davis Sturgis was from Pennsylvania. He graduated from the U.S. Military Academy in 1846 and was a veteran of the Mexican War. He was chief of the Union Cavalry, Department of the Ohio who saw action at South Mountain, Antietam and Fredericksburg. His son, Garland, was killed at the battle of Little Big Horn on June 25, 1876. Appleton's Cyclopaedia of American Biography, Vol. V., pg. 734.

404 Captain James Stokes was a Marylander but move to Illinois where he was a manufacturer and railroad man. He served as captain of the Illinois volunteers. Appleton's Cyclopaedia of American Biography, Vol. V., pg. 699.

declare war) lines were distinctly drawn before the time set for the meeting of the extra session of Congress. The rebellion was general in the states of Virginia and the ten other slave-holding states. About forty counties in the western part of Virginia refused to be bound by the action of the rest of the state and took the necessary steps afterwards to form a legislature which claimed to be the real, true and veritable[405] authorized legislature of the state of Virginia. And it was that body that gave assent and cooperation required by the Constitution to the formation of a new state and the state of West Virginia was now formed—it first being called the state of Kanawha. Its right as a state was recognized by Congress and it was admitted in the year 1863.[406]

## MAY 1861

On the 2nd of May, the 69th New York Regiment reached Washington. Colonel Ellsworth[407] with his New York Fire Zouaves arrived the same day. The next day the 1st New Jersey Brigade left its state for the seat of war, and on that day fourteen companies of Kentuckians offered their services to the federal government, not withstanding the governor of that state had refused to respond to the call by Mr. Lincoln for 75,000 men. On this day Mr. Lincoln made another call for men—42,000 three year volunteers, including troops for the regular army and seamen.

On May the 4th General McClellan[408] was appointed commander of the Department of the Ohio. Virginia became a member of the Confederate States on the 6th of that month. On the 10th the president

---

[405] Veritable means real.

[406] West Virginia statehood was approved on April 20, 1863 to be effective on June 20, 1863. History of West Virginia, pg. 334.

[407] Colonel Ephraim Elmer Ellsworth was a friend of Mr. Lincoln and author Ward Hill Lamon in Springfield, Illinois. William Herndon, Ellsworth and Lamon were with Abraham Lincoln on November 6, 1860 when Lincoln voted at the Sangamon County courthouse. Ellsworth organized Zouave units in both Illinois and New York. He wrote "Manuel of Arms for Light Infantry Adopted to the Rifled Musket, With or Without Priming Attachment." Lincoln's War, pgs. 6 - 8 and Appleton's Cyclopaedia of American Biography, Vol. II., pg. 335.

[408] General George McClellan was a vice-president of the Illinois Central Railroad before the war. He twice commanded the Union Army of the Potomac. He ran against President Lincoln in the 1864 election and was defeated. He was known as a procrastinator. www.civilwarhome.com/macbio.htm

ordered all the officers of the army to subscribe a new oath of allegiance. On this day Captain Lyon[409] captured Camp Jackson, near St. Louis, commanded by Brigadier General Frost[410] of the Missouri militia. This was done by suddenly completely surrounding the camp that surprised the troops and a large quantity of arms and munitions of war were captured. Captain Lyon was made Brigadier General for his gallantry on this occasion. At this time a convention composed of delegates from thirty-eight counties met in Wheeling, Virginia to take measures to form a new state.[411]

The Confederates were now fortifying Harpers Ferry. On the 14th Major General Butler unauthorized by his superiors and under cover of a terrible thunderstorm, marched in the nighttime with one thousand men and took possession of Federal Hill in Baltimore. General Scott regarded this as a most hazardous movement and gave General Butler a severe reprimand for the venture. This daring act proved to be the proper thing. The little garrison was soon reinforced and the result was that open rebellion disappeared not only in Baltimore, but throughout the state.

The military Department of Virginia was formed on the 17th of May, comprised of eastern Virginia, North Carolina, and South Carolina, with headquarters at Fortress Monroe under command of General Benjamin Butler. The federal government now ordered the seizure of all telegraphic dispatches throughout the North. Governor Magoffin[412] declared the neutrality of Kentucky in the impending contest. On the May 24, 13,000 troops crossed the Potomac River from Washington into Virginia and occupied Alexandria, where the

---

409 Captain Nathaniel Lyon was from Connecticut and graduated in 1841 from the U.S. Military Academy. He fought in both the Seminole War and Mexican War. He gave $30,000 of his own money to the government to support the Union cause. He was a Union commander during the Missouri campaign. In one battle he was shot in the breast and had his horse killed out from under him at the same time. He was killed at Wilson's Creek on August 10th, 1861. Civil War a Narrative, Part II, pg. 8 and Appleton's Cyclopaedia of American Biography, Vol., IV., pgs. 67 - 69.

410 Brig. General D. M. Frost was a Confederate general who commanded a Missouri brigade against General Price. The Armies and The Leaders, pg. 279.

411 These were the counties in western Virginia who were meeting to secede from Virginia and form their own state in support of the Union. The History of West Virginia, pg. 334.

412 Beriah Magoffin was Governor of Kentucky from 1859-1862. He was an Irish immigrant and lawyer who supported the Fugitive Slave Laws. He refused to send soldiers to support the Union and then also refused to send soldiers to support the Confederacy. www.absolutestronomycom/topics/Beriah_Magoffin

Confederate flag had been flying in full view of the White House ever since Mr. Lincoln had first occupied it. The flag had become a great source of annoyance to him. The gallant Colonel Ellsworth of the New York Fire Zouave Regiment rushed to the top of the old hotel, Marshall House,[413] and tore down the offensive flag. As he was descending the stairs with the flag he was met by the proprietor of the house by the name of Jackson[414] who shot and killed him instantly. He had scarcely fallen when one of Colonel Ellsworth's men[415] instantly killed Jackson. Immediately after Mr. Lincoln learned of the death of Colonel Ellsworth, he directed his body to be brought to the presidential mansion from which he was afterwards buried.

Few events of the war gave Mr. Lincoln greater pain than the death of this young, gallant and most promising officer. The young man had studied law with Mr. Lincoln for a time before the war and Mr. Lincoln had become personally very much attached to Colonel Ellsworth, so much so that he was one of the invited guests to accompany Mr. Lincoln to Washington when he went there to be inaugurated. Colonel Ellsworth's untimely death, before he had an opportunity of displaying his wonderful military genius which was known and acknowledged by all, cast a gloom not only over Mr. Lincoln who loved him but brought sadness to an admiring multitude of people throughout the North. Great achievements had been expected of Colonel Ellsworth during the progress of the war.

With this formidable army which had just entered Virginia, now a Confederate State, and General Beauregard in command of the Confederate forces at Manassas Junction,[416] but a few miles distant, all hope of peace, accommodation or peaceful settlement was dissipated. There was no alternative now but war. There had prevailed a boastful superiority of southern people over the northern people in courage and fighting qualities. This was braggadocio.[417] They were all one people. One section could not properly claim superiority over the other and cowardice could never be charged against the American

---

413 The Marshal House was located at the corner of Pitt and King Streets in Alexandria, Virginia. www.zazzle.com

414 Jackson was a captain in a local Confederate artillery company. With his death he became a martyr to the rebel cause. Southern History of the War, pg. 81.

415 The man who killed Jackson was Frank E. Brownell of the New York Fire Zuoaves. Appleton's Cyclopaedia of American Biography, Vol. II., pg. 335.

416 Also called Bull Run

417 Braggadocio means boastful.

soldier whether he hailed from the North or from the South. An unbiased history will record that as an incontrovertible fact. Things had now progressed to a most formidable attitude in Virginia and a great battle was imminent. Lieutenant Thompkins,[418] with a small body of men under his command had attacked the enemy at Fairfax Courthouse in Virginia. Colonel Kelley[419] had fought him at Philippi[420] in which engagement Colonel Kelley defeated him but was badly wounded in the engagement.

On the 26th of the month, the western Virginia counties gave a large majority in favor of the Union.[421] The steamers *Freeborn*[422]and A*nacosta*[423] attacked the batteries at Acquia Creek.[424] There had been a skirmish between the Confederates and a company of Home Guards on the border at Williamsport, Maryland.[425] The steamer *Harriet Lane*[426] made an attack on the batteries at Pig Point near Fortress Monroe.

The Cabinet of Mr. Lincoln was not a unit on some of the measures and the course of policy which the government should pursue towards the secessionists in 1861. The administration had questions to deal with which in many respects were novel and without

---

418 Lieutenant Colonel Charles F. Thompkins led a small contingent of New York troops against a much larger Confederate force. www.mycivilwar.com/battles/610601.htm

419 Colonel Benjamin Franklin Kelley led the Union 1st Virginia Infantry and Company A of the 2nd Virginia Infantry. He was from Wheeling, in western Virginia (now West Virginia). His nickname was "old Ben Kelley." He was captured at Cumberland, Maryland on February 1, 1865 and was sent to Libby Prison. He was quickly exchanged. www.blueandgraytrial.com

420 Philippi was located in Barbour County, Virginia (today West Virginia). The battle took place on June 3, 1861 and is considered the first organized land battle of the civil war.

421 This was the effort of the counties to form their own separate state from Virginia. www.wvculture.org/history/statehood.htm

422 *The Freeborn* was a steam driven tug boat. Southern History of the War, pg. 58

423 *Anacosta* was a fourth rate Union small screw combatant with a crew of 67. Warships of the Civil War Navies, pg.103.

424 Acquia Creek is a tributary of the Potomac River in northern Virginia.

425 Williamsport, Maryland is located along the Potomac River and was the crossing point of the Confederate Army in their advance to Gettysburg in June,1863 and their retreat from Gettysburg in July, 1863.

426 *The Harriet Lane* was a steam cutter named after President Buchanan's niece who was hostess at the White House for her bachelor uncle. She was originally a U.S. revenue cutter. She fired the first naval shot of the war. Southern History of the War, pg. 58, U. S. Navy Ships—*Harriet Lane* and Warships of the Civil War Navies, pg. 234.

precedent. The insurrection itself was of a character unprecedented. The administration had scarcely become inaugurated when hostilities were precipitated and forced an administrative policy before time was given to develop any course other than that adopted, which was indispensable to the dignity and protection of the Union.

The call for 75,000 men would have little availed with the declaration of the blockade of the southern ports. The blockade clause of the proclamation caused a difference and want of entire unanimity in the Cabinet. This policy was debated and questioned as a doubtful and irregular proceeding. Whatever the opposition to the laws in the southern states—"insurrection" or "rebellion"—it was purely domestic. It was a civil war and not a foreign war. The arguments used were that the internal dissentions in our territory should be confined within our borders. The majority of the Cabinet contended for a mere embargo, or suspension of intercourse with the southern people rather than a complete blockade—and to interdict commerce with the insurgents until the rebellion was suppressed.

There was a division of opinion whether a blockade was a domestic or international question—it was not doubted that it was the proper thing to do between two belligerent nations—the doubts were as to whether we could properly blockade our own ports and prohibit traffic from abroad by law and make its violation a criminal offense. It was contended that by the blockade of the whole territory in rebellion that it would be calculated to raise the insurgents to the character and dignity of the belligerents, which would virtually admit that the Confederacy was a quasi-government. The blockade was opposed, therefore, by the greater number of the Cabinet through the apprehension that it would lead to embarrassments by giving the organization a position among foreign nations that we could not accord to at home.

The right to close the ports was by no one controverted.[427] The right to blockade was the issue. After much discussion Mr. Seward dispatched Mr. Adams[428] our minister to England, on the 8th of June, 1861 with the following message: "We claim to have the right to close the ports which have been seized by the insurrectionists for the purpose of suppressing the attempted revolution and no one could

---

427 Controverted means denied.

428 Charles Francis Adams—See pg. 27.

justly complain if we had done so decisively and peremptorily."[429] The difference in opinion expressed in the Cabinet on the subject soon reached the English government. That government, with characteristic diplomacy at once sought to take advantage of the want of harmony in the American Cabinet by creating debate in Parliament ostensibly on the affairs of New Granada, which was unequivocally and unmistakably intended as an admonition and menace for the United States. Sir John Russell[430] took occasion in this debate to the monstrous interpolation[431] of a new doctrine in international law by menacingly declaring to the feeble government of New Grenada: "It is not competent for a government to close its ports that are *de facto* [432]in the possession of insurgents." About this time our minister in London wrote to our secretary Mr. Seward that he had just had an interview with Lord John Russell and said: "something about difficulties in New Grenada and the intelligence that the insurgents had undertaken to close several of their ports. But the law offices here told him that this could not be done, as against foreign nations except by the regular form of blockade. He did not know what we thought about it, but he had observed that some such plan was likely to be adopted at the coming session of Congress in regards to the course of those of whom we consider as insurgents."

Mr. Adams continued, "His lordship also announced in Parliament that the opinion of her majesty's government after taking legal advice is that it is perfectly competent for the government of a country in a state of tranquility to say which ports shall be open to trade, and which shall be closed; but in the event of insurrection or civil war in that country it is not competent for the government to close those ports that are *de facto* in the hands of the insurgents as that would be an invasion of international law with regard to the blockade." But the menace and subterfuge[433] of the English were disregarded by the

---

[429] Peremptorily means imminently.
[430] Sir John Russell was a British Prime Minister from 1846-1852 and then from 1865-1866. He met with minister Adams regarding British ships and their relationship with the Confederacy. He and Lord Palmerston had decided in September 1862 with one more Confederate victory, England would enter the war. Instead the Confederates lost at Sharpsburg. He was also a correspondent for the *London Times* newspaper. Lincoln and the Civil War, pgs. 257, 267-270 and The Two American Presidents, pg. 294.
[431] Interpolation means altering.
[432] *De facto* means in reality.
[433] Subterfuge means evading the issue.

Americans. The *lifty dictum*[434] "the opinion of her majesty's government after taking legal advice" did not prove convincing, and her American cousins took legal advice from their American counsels (astute statesmen too) whether recognized by the economies of the nations or not.

## JUNE 1861

The battle of Big Bethel[435] was fought on the 10th of June when General Pierce,[436] with three regiments of Union troops, was defeated with considerable loss.[437] Major Winthrop[438] among others was killed. The Confederates now evacuated Harpers Ferry,[439] burned the bridges and destroyed all the valuable property except the armory machinery which had not before been destroyed by Lt. Jones,[440] which they took to Richmond. On the 17th of June, a train of cars with two hundred seventy-five Ohio Volunteers under the command of Colonel Robert Schenk[441] was fired into by a masked battery near Vienna, Virginia. A

---

434 *Lifty dictum* is a legal opinion based on a point other than the precise issue involved.
435 Great Bethany Church is about 9 miles leading south from Hampton, Virginia on the James River at the tip of the Peninsula. Southern History of the War, pg. 83 and Civil War a Narrative, Part II., pg. 122.
436 General Byron K. Pierce from Massachusetts originally was a Colonel who commanded the 3rd Mass. Infantry. He originally led the 5th Michigan Infantry. www.pathsofhistory.com and The Armies and The Leaders, pg. 215.
437 Confederate commander at this battle was Colonel John Bankhead Magruder who had 12,000 men entrenched in front of Fortress Monroe. Southern History of the War, pg. 83 and Civil War a Narrative, Part II., pg. 122.
438 Major Theodore Winthrop was a Yale College graduate from Connecticut. He was one of the men who surveyed the Isthmus of Panama in 1853 for the building of the Panama Canal. He was the author of several novels. He died standing high on a log to rally his troops when he was shot through the heart. Appleton's Cyclopaedia of American Biography, Vol. VI., pg. 577.
439 General Joseph Eggleston Johnston was a graduate in the class of 1829 of the U.S. Military Academy (a classmate of Robert E. Lee). He was wounded four times in the Mexican War. He commanded the Shenandoah Valley for the Confederate army in 1861. He said Harpers Ferry was untenable and set fire to the town and blew up the bridge across the Potomac River. Later he commanded the forces protecting Atlanta during General Sherman's March to the Sea. He was known as one of the South's most able generals. Civil War a Narrative, Part VII., pgs. 117 & 318, Southern History of the War, pg. 87 & 88 and Pride of the South, pgs. 95, 96 and 105-107.
440 Lt. Edward Jones—See pg. 118.
441 Colonel Robert Cumming Schenk was a Whig Congressman from Ohio who graduated from Miami University. He was an attorney and a railroad man. His right

number of the troops were killed or wounded, the Colonel being among the wounded.

On the 20th the Union convention of the western Virginia counties elected Francis D. Pierpont[442] Governor of Virginia[443] which was an entire repudiation of Virginia under Governor Letcher. General McClellan assumed command in person of the Army of Western Virginia. On the 26th President Lincoln acknowledged the Wheeling government as the real government of Virginia. A sharp fight was had at Buchanan, Virginia where the Confederates were defeated.

During the first year of his administration, Mr. Lincoln appointed the following ministers, residents and envoys extraordinaire and plenipotentiary[444] to foreign courts:

Austria—Anson Berlingame[445] from Massachusetts, who was not received and then sent to China. John Lothrop Motly[446] was then appointed. He also afterwards was appointed Minister to England by President Grant.[447]

Belgium—Henry S. Sanford[448] from Connecticut

Bolivar—David K. Cartter[449] of Ohio

Brazil—James Watson Webb[450] of New York

---

arm was shattered at the second battle of Bull Run. After the war he was re-elected to Congress. Appleton's Cyclopaedia of American Biography, Vol. V., pgs. 417 & 418.

442 Francis H. Pierpont is called the "father of West Virginia." After the war he was named Provisional Governor of Virginia by President Johnson. www.britannica.com/cbchecked/topic/459873Francis-H-Pierpont

443 The convention also sent W. T. Willie and John S. Carlisle as Virginia's representatives to the U.S. Senate. Southern History of the War, pg. 96.

444 Plenipotentiary means someone given the power to transact business.

445 Anson Berlingame was born in New York. Following his graduation from Harvard Law School he became a lawyer and a legislator. The towns of Berlingame, California and Berlingame, Kansas are both named after him. www.answers.com/topic/berlingame-anson—See pg. 97.

446 John Lothrop Motly was a graduate of Harvard College and a published author. He served as Minister of Austria from 1861 - 1867. Appleton's Cyclopaedia of American Biography, Vol. IV., pgs. 438 & 439.

447 General Ulysses S. Grant—See pg. 4.

448 Henry S. Sanford graduated from the University of Heidelberg. He served as Minister to Belgium from 1861 to 1869. He was founder of the International African Association which later became the Congo. He founded the city of Sanford, Florida and brought lemons to the citrus industry in that state. Appleton's Cyclopaedia of American Biography, Vol. V., pg. 370.

449 David K. Cartter served as Minister to Bolivia from June 28, 1861 to March 10, 1862. bioguide/congress.gov/scripts/biodisplay.pl?index=C000206

450 James Watson Webb was editor of several New York newspapers including the *Morning Courier* and *The New York Enquirer* which eventually merged into *The World*

Chili—Thomas H. Nelson[451] of Indiana
China—Anson Berlingame of Massachusetts
Columbia—Allen A. Burton[452] of Kentucky
Costa Rica—Charles N. Riotte[453] of Texas
Denmark—Bradford R. Wood[454] of New York
Ecuador—Frederick Hassaurack[455] of Ohio
Guatemala—Elisha O. Crosley[456] of New York
Hawaii—Thomas J. Dryer,[457] Commissioner of Oregon
Honduras—Hezekiah G. Wells[458] of Michigan, who declined it. Jacob Howard[459] of Michigan was then appointed but resigned and James Partridge[460] of Maryland was appointed.
Italy—George P. Marsh[461] of Vermont

---

newspaper. While Minister of Brazil he procured the withdrawal of France from Mexico. Appleton's Cyclopaedia of American Biography, Vol. VI., pg. 493.

451 Thomas Henry Nelson was a Whig. While Minister of Chili, he was credited with saving numerous persons from the burning of the Santiago Cathedral on December 6, 1864. He also served as Minster to Mexico from 1869 - 1873. Appleton's Cyclopaedia of American Biography, Vol. IV., pgs. 492 & 493.

452 Allen A. Burton was a Kentucky judge. Burton family website.

453 Charles N. Riotte was Minister of Costa Rico from 1861—1867. U.S. State Department—Costa Rica

454 Bradford R. Wood was a graduate of Union College in New York who became a teacher and a lawyer. He served as Minister to Denmark from 1861—1865. Later he was elected to Congress. Biographical Directory of the U.S. Congress.

455 Frank Hassaurack served from 1861-1866 and was the editor of the *Cincinnati Volkblatt*. www.findagrave.com/cgi-bin/fg.cgi?pagegr&grid=18546386

456 Elisha O. Crosley was born in New York but moved to California where he was a delegate to California's 1st Constitutional Convention. www.joincalifornia.com/candidate/10779

457 Thomas J. Dryer was a free mason, mountain climber and politician. He was publisher of the *Portland Oregon* and editor of the *California Courier* of San Francisco. He served as Minister to Hawaii from 1861-1863. politicalgraveyard.com/geo/HI/ofc/diplo.html

458 Hezekiah G. Wells was appointed August 7, 1861 as Minister to Honduras during a recess of the Senate but he refused to serve. www.history.state.gov/department/history/people.wells_hezekiah_g

459 Jacob Merritt Howard was a U.S. Senator and Congressman who is credited with giving the Republican Party the name "Republican." Appleton's Cyclopaedia of American Biography, Vol. III., pg. 277.

460 James Partridge was appointed Minister to Honduras on February 10, 1862 but left the post shortly after that. He was later appointed Minister to El Salvador, Venezuela, Brazil and Peru. www.history.state.gov/department/history/people.partridge_james_rudolph

461 George P. Marsh was a Whig Congressman who graduated from Dartmouth College. He had served as Minister to Turkey from 1849—1853. He served as Minister

Japan—Robert H. Pruyn[462] of New York
Mexico—Thomas Corwin[463] of Ohio
Netherlands—James S. Pike[464] of Maine
Nicaragua—Andrew B. Dickinson[465] of New York
Paraguay—Charles A. Washburn[466] Commissioner of California
Peru—Christopher Robinson[467] of Rhode Island
Portugal—James E. Harvey[468] of Pennsylvania
Prussian—Norman B. Judd[469] of Illinois
Russia—Cassius M. Clay[470] of Kentucky. He took leave. Simon Cameron of Pennsylvania was appointed January 17, 1862.
Spain—Carl Schurtz[471] of Missouri, who resigned April, 1862 and Cassius M. Clay was appointed but did not serve. In June of 1862 Gustavus Koerner[472] of Illinois was appointed.

---

to Italy from 1861- 1882. Appleton's Cyclopaedia of American Biography, Vol. IV., pgs. 261 & 217.

462 Robert H. Pruyn was a lawyer who was named Minister to Japan, serving from 1861 to 1865. Later he became the President of the National Commercial bank and Trust in Albany and was one of the founders of the Albany Law School. *New York Times*, February 27, 1882

463 Thomas Corwin—See pg. 17.

464 James S. Pike was an anti-slavery man who was a published author, journalist and associate editor of the *New York Tribune*. He served as Minister to the Netherlands from 1861 - 1866. Appleton's Cyclopaedia of American Biography, Vol. V., pg. 18.

465 Andrew B. Dickinson served as Minister to Nicaragua from 1861 to 1863. U.S. Department of State, Office of the Historian.

466 Charles A. Washburn was a graduate of Bowdoin College. He was editor of the *Alta California* and the San Francisco *Daily Times* newspapers. During his ministry in 1868 a war broke out between Paraguay and Brazil. Washburn escaped but several of his aids were killed. Appleton's Cyclopaedia of American Biography, Vol. VI., pg. 372.

467 Christopher Robinson was a graduate of Brown University who became a lawyer and Congressman. He served as Minister of Peru from 1861—1866. topics.breitbart.com/Chris+Robinson

468 James E. Harvey was Minister to Portugal from 1861 -1869. www.politicalgraveyard.com/geo/zz/pt.html

469 Norman Buell Judd was a friend of Mr. Lincoln's from Illinois and chairman of the Illinois Republican state central committee. He helped run Mr. Lincoln's 1860 presidential campaign. He served as minister between 1861 and 1865. He was elected to Congress from 1867-1871 and then became President of the Rock Island Railroad. The Two American Presidents, pg. 81 and Appleton's Cyclopaedia of American Biography, Vol. III., pg. 482.

470 Cassius M. Clay was an abolitionist who printed the newspaper *True American*. He attended Yale College and had a distinguished military career in the Mexican War. As Minister of Russia he wanted to come home to be a general. When he got his wish, he refused to serve in the army unless slavery was abolished immediately. He later returned to Russia. Seaport Autographs, pg. 8 and Lincoln's War, pgs. 17, 20 & 199.

States of the Church[473]—Alex W. Randall[474] of Wisconsin in 1861, William M. Blakford of New York in 1862
Turkey—Edward Joy Morris[475] of Pennsylvania
Venezuela—Henry T. Blow[476] of Missouri

These appointments in the main were made by recommendations of Secretary Seward in whose department they properly belong, which gave rise again after the administration got into running order, to the impression that Mr. Seward was to be the *de facto* president and like the prime minister of the British government would direct the affairs of "the nation in the name of another" which made the relations embarrassing particularly in Mr. Lincoln's Cabinet. The Senators from New York and Mr. Seward did not agree about the local appointments for that state. A conference was held on the subject at the State Department to which the president was especially invited. He

---

471 Carl Schurtz was an immigrant from Prussia who came to the U.S. in 1852 and who is called "America's most celebrated citizen of foreign birth." After his service as Minister of Spain, he became a Major General in the Civil War. He also served in the U.S. Senate and was Secretary of the Interior for President Rutherford B. Hayes. He was commander of the 12th Corps of the Union Army. He was editor of the *New York Evening Post* and served as the Secretary of the Interior (1877 - 1881). The Armies and The Leaders, pgs, 23, 24, & 214 and www.johnib.wordpress.com/category/carl_schurtz

472 Gustav Koerner was born in Germany and graduated from the University of Heidelberg. He moved to Illinois where he was a judge on the Illinois Supreme Court from 1845 - 1851 and the state's Lieutenant Governor from 1854 - 1857. He served as Minister to Spain, 1861 - 1865. Appleton's Cyclopaedia of American Biography, Vol. III., pg. 570.

473 States of the Church were the territories under the rule of the Pope established by the Catholic Church in 754 and operating until 1870. Encyclopedia2.thefreedictionary.com/states+of+the+church

474 Alex Williams Randall was a two-term Governor of Wisconsin. He also served as Postmaster General from 1866-1869. Appleton's Cyclopaedia of American Biography, Vol. V., pg. 170.

475 Edward Joy Morris was a Harvard College graduate and a published author. He was a Whig Congressman and charge d'affaires to Naples 1850 - 1854. He served as Minister to Turkey 1861 - 1870. Appleton's Cyclopaedia of American Biography, Vol. IV., pg. 412.

476 Henry T. Blow was a successful businessman in Missouri. He was an anti-slavery leader in Congress. He also served as Minister to Brazil, 1869 - 1871. Appleton's Cyclopaedia of American Biography, Vol. I., pg. 297.

attended. There was also present besides Mr. Seward, Mr. King[477] and Mr. Harris,[478] the two Senators, and Secretary Welles.

The president opened the conference by saying, "Gentlemen. I will at once relieve you of the responsibility of considering the question in relation to the appointment of collector to the port of New York as I intend on my own authority to appoint Hiram Barney[479] to that position. Mr. Barney," he said, "from my personal knowledge of him, is a man of integrity and I have full faith and confidence in him." The New York gentlemen were not pleased with this appointment but acquiesced to it after which the other appointments embracing nearly all of the important ones to be made in the state of New York were discussed.

The navy agent at New York City was soon disposed of. There was no disagreement about it. There was a serious disagreement about some of the other appointments. Mr. Seward insisted upon the list which he made out being accepted and the nominations sent forthwith[480] to the Senate, to which the Senators objected. The question then arose as to whether the Secretary of the Treasury and the Attorney General had been consulted and concurred in the list of selections. Mr. Seward argued that was unnecessary, that these were strictly New York appointments and that he and the Senators knew better than any others what was best of the party and the administration. He was answered with the argument that the Cabinet officers were responsible to the people for the proper administration of the affairs in their respective departments, that they should have confidence in their subordinates and their subordinates should have reciprocal confidence in them. Such appointments should be made with their concurrence or otherwise difficulties might arise. Mr. Lincoln was of the opinion that this was the wiser course, and declined to make the appointments indicated until the other heads of

---

477 Preston King was born in New York and was a U.S. Senator from 1857-1863. He was a good friend of Andrew Johnson. Famousamerican.net/prestonking/

478 Ira Harris filled the vacancy in the Senate when Mr. Seward was named to the Lincoln Cabinet. His daughter, Clara, and her fiancé Henry Rathbone were both present in the box with President Lincoln and Mrs. Lincoln at Ford's Theater when the president was shot. www.absoluteastronomy.com/topics/Ira_Harris

479 Hiram Barney was a lawyer and abolitionist who raise money for Mr. Lincoln's election. He was the collector of the port of New York from 1861 to 1864. www.mrlincolnandnewyork.org/inside.asp?ID=52&subjectid=3

480 Forthwith means promptly.

departments interested in them were advised. The meeting then adjourned and the appointments were afterwards satisfactorily made.

## JULY 1861

On the 4th Congress convened (in special session) for the first time in the history of the government with whom as parties are organized the Republicans had a majority in both branches of the body. The free states and borders states only were represented. The House resolved to consider at this session only bills concerning the military, naval and financial operations of the government. The disastrous battle of Bull Run followed on the 21st of July. This had the effect to stimulate the energies of members of Congress. Bills were passed by the House to close the southern ports against commerce, to authorize a loan, to appropriate money for the army and navy, to call out five hundred thousand volunteers, to define and punish conspiracy against the United States and to confiscate all private property, including slaves, employed against the United States. The House pledged itself to vote any amount of money and any amount of men necessary to suppress the rebellion. There were some extreme Democrats who constantly offered propositions looking to the negotiations of peace. Those propositions were as constantly voted down by the overwhelming majorities on the grounds that negotiations with states in armed rebellion was not only undignified, but unconstitutional.

In the face and eyes of all this bluster, Congress declined to commit itself to the blockade and in the most explicit and emphatic language authorized by an Act of July 13 in the closing of the ports.

The southern ports were never closed under the act of Congress of July 13, 1861 until after the fall of Richmond. On the 11th of April, 1865, only three days before his assassination, Mr. Lincoln issued his proclamation pursuant to the act of Congress to close the ports of the southern states. There was an anomalous state of things growing out of all this: the United States while treating the Confederates as belligerents, and their organization as a quasi-government, perpetuated the strange inconsistency as denouncing their cruisers as pirates.

The Union troops were forced to retreat and reached Springfield (Missouri) on the 5th of July. The battle of Rich Mountain[481] was

---

[481] Rich Mountain was in Randolph County, Virginia (now West Virginia).

fought on July 12. Colonel Pegram[482] commanded the Confederate forces and the Union troops were commanded by General Rosecrans.[483]

On the 13th and 14th of July, General Patterson[484] crossed the Potomac River with his army at Williamsport, Maryland and advanced against the Confederates under General Jackson,[485] who gave battle at Falling Waters. The Confederates opened fire with four pieces of artillery but soon retreated with small loss to either side. The news of the battle of Carthage, in Missouri between the Confederate General Jackson[486] of that state and Colonel Sigel's command[487] numbering 15,000 reached Washington.

On the 16th of July, Congress authorized the president to call for militia and raise 500,000 men for the service. On this day there arose a difficulty among the rebel prize crew on the steamer *S. J. Waring.*[488] A Negro man named William Tilghman[489] killed three of the crew,

---

482 Brigadier General John Pegram of Virginia was the first former U.S. Army officer to be captured fighting for the Confederacy. He was wounded in the leg at Wilderness. Civil War a Narrative, Part VII., pg. 156.

483 General William S. Rosencrans was a native of Ohio and a U.S. Military Academy (class of 1842) graduate who lived in Charleston, Virginia. He was an architect and civil engineer who taught at the military academy. He was president of several coal companies prior to the war. He was ordered to capture Chattanooga Tennessee but lost the opportunity when he sat and waited instead. He thought he should outrank General Grant. People of the South admired him as one of the North's best generals. Two American Presidents, pgs 294, 298 & 304, Appleton's Cyclopaedia of American Biography, Vol. V., pgs 323 - 325 and Southern History of the War, pg. 175.

484 General Robert Patterson—See pg. 117. Battle was actually on July 2.

485Thomas J. Jackson was a graduate of the U.S. military academy and was a Mexican War veteran. General Jackson, better known as "Stonewall," was an artillery, tactics and philosophy instructor at Virginia Military Institute before the war. He had served in the Mexican War and was at the hanging of John Brown in Charlestown, Virginia in December 1859. His nickname came from the stand he and his man made at first Bull Run when it was said "There was Jackson, standing like a stonewall rallying the Virginians." He was General Robert E. Lee's most trusted general. He was shot by mistake by his own men on May 2, 1863 and died a few days later. Appleton's Cyclopaedia of American Biography, Vol. III., pgs. 391 & 392.

486 General Claiborne Fox Jackson was Governor of Missouri and a Confederate General. www.mogenweb.org/mocivwar/clairbornefoxjackson.htm

487 Colonel Franz Sigel was born in Baden, Germany and moved to New York in 1852. He was later editor of the *Baltimore Wecker* newspaper. Appleton's Cyclopaedia of American Biography, Vol. V., pg. 524.

488 *S. J. Waring* was a schooner captured on July 6, 1861 by the Confederate privateer *Jefferson Davis.* www.history.navy.mil/photos/pers_us/uspers_+/w_tilgmn.htm

489 The civilian ship was captured 150 miles east of Sandy Hook, New Jersey by the privateer *Jefferson Davis.* The captures put a prize crew on board to take her to a

recaptured and brought the vessel safely into New York Harbor and delivered it to authorities. General McDowell's army,[490] consisting of 50,000 commenced moving towards Manassas Junction. On the same day General Patterson had an engagement with rebel General Stuart[491] at Bunker Hill[492] a small place about halfway between Martinsburg and Winchester. The federal forces followed the enemy about two miles.

On the 17th General Johnston reported his command to consist of 6,500 men and General Patterson's to be about 18,000. General Patterson admitted he had seventeen regiments. General Patterson was deluded by a supposition that General Johnston had 45,000 men at his command. After this the Confederate authorities sent General Johnston reinforcements making his effective strength 9,000 men besides 2,000 local militia in the process of organization. This was at a time when a political campaign was going on in western Virginia.[493] The east had claimed to have seceded from the United States. Western Virginia was striving to secede from the eastern part of the state, and continue its union with the federal government, which in a political point of view made the occupation of Harpers Ferry and the Shenandoah Valley very desirable. There followed an engagement at

---

southern port. On July 16, William Tilghman a member of the original crew killed the prize crew with an ax and took the ship into the New York Harbor. www.history.navy.mil/photos/sj-civsh-s/sj-waring.htm

490 General Irvin McDowell was a U.S. Military Academy graduate (1838) from Ohio and a soldier in the Mexican War. He returned to the school to teach infantry tactics. He replaced General Winfield Scott as the commanding general of the Union Army in 1861. He was sent with the Army of the Potomac towards Richmond. He commanded the First Corps of Union troops at the battle of Bull Run (First Manassas) on July 21, 1861. He was defeated and dismissed following the battle. The Story-Life of Lincoln, pgs. 415 -417, The Armies and The Leaders, pg. 186 and Two American Presidents, pg. 178 & 180.

491 General John Ewell Brown (JEB) Stuart was a graduate of the U.S. Military Academy class of 1854. In 1859 he acted as aide to Colonel Robert E. Lee in the capture of John Brown at Harpers Ferry, Virginia. He was commander of the Confederate Cavalry Corps. He was what General Lee called the "eyes of the army." He was known for his daring raids. He was killed at Yellow Tavern on May 12, 1864. Civil War a Narrative, Part II, pg. 223 and The Armies and The Leaders, pgs. 114 & 252.

492 The author Ward Hill Lamon lived in Bunker Hill from 1830 - 1846. Ward Hill Lamon: Lincoln's "Particular Friend," pgs. 21 & 26.

493 The Blue Ridge Mountains was the line between Eastern Virginia and Western Virginia. In 1850, Eastern Virginia had 401,540 whites, 409,793 slaves, and 45,783 free blacks. Western Virginia in the same year had 492,609 whites, 62,233 slaves and 8,123 free blacks. Harpers Pictorial History of the Great Rebellion, pg. 140.

Corrick's Ford[494] in which the rebel General Garnett[495] was killed. And the same day the battle of Scarytown[496] occurred.

The disaster of General Pegram and General Garnett at Cheat Mountain[497] was anticipated by the rebels and they apprehended that General McClellan with his entire command would reinforce General Patterson. General Patterson, with full knowledge of all this, knowing the importance of giving battle to General Johnston and preventing his joining of General Beauregard at Bull Run, where he knew a battle was imminent, failed to act. This allowed General Johnston to join General Beauregard in time to turn the tide of battle in favor of the rebels, without following him up to counteract the effect of his strength on that occasion.

This battle of Bull Run or Manassas, as it is sometimes called, was the first great battle and one of the most important and deadly of the war. There were six divisions of the federal troops commanded respectively by Generals Hunter,[498] Heinzelman,[499] Tyler,[500]

---

[494] Corrick's Ford is on the Cheat River in what was western Virginia (now West Virginia).

[495] General Robert Selden Garnett was originally the commanding officer of the Confederate Army of the Northeast. He has the distinction of being the first general killed in the civil war. He was killed opposing General McClellan's forces at Rich Mountain in western Virginia on July 13, 1861. Smithsonian's Great Battles and Battlefields of the Civil War, pgs. 777 & 778. and The Armies and The Leaders, pgs. 146 & 242.

[496] Scareytown, Virginia on July 17, 1861.

[497] Cheat Mountain was an outpost in western Virginia overlooking the Staunton-Parkersburg Turnpike and guarding the Tygart Valley. The Smithsonian's Great Battles and Battlefields of the Civil War, pg. 778.

[498] David Hunter was an 1822 graduate of the U.S. Military Academy who saw action in the Mexican War. He was controversial in that without authorization he emancipated slaves in his district in 1862. He was president of the military court which tried the Lincoln Conspirators. He was the commander who replaced General Sigal in the Shenandoah Valley campaign of May 1864 and later was replaced by General Sheridan. After Mr. Lincoln's death, Judge Hunter was the president of military commission that tried the Lincoln Conspirators. Grant Takes Command, pg. 248 & 346, The Armies and The Leaders, pg. 178, Appleton's Cyclopaedia of American Biography, Vol. III., pg. 321.

[499] General Samuel Peter Heinzelman commanded a corps for the Union troops under General McClellan. He led the 3rd Corps at Fair Oaks and at the second battle of Bull Run. Civil War a Narrative, Part II., pg. 137 and The Armies and The Leaders, pg. 194.

[500] General Daniel Tyler was from Connecticut. He led the federal advance at the first battle of Bull Run. The Armies and The Leaders, pg. 197.

Richardson,[501] Runyan[502] and Miles.[503] There was a general engagement of troops on both sides. The battle raged with terrible destruction to each. After fighting over six hours, the battle was in effect won by the federals, who began to be jubilant and the Confederates disheartened. General Jackson opportunely for the Confederates came up and threw his whole force on the right wing of the federal forces. The Union troops greatly exhausted and the suddenness and strength of this attack produced great disorder and demoralization. The result was a panic followed by a general rout and the loss of the battle. There were in the aggregate over five thousand killed and wounded in this battle according to the respective reports of the commanders of the armies at that time. There were 60,000 men in actuality engaged in the fight—20,000 Union and 40,000 Confederates.

Mr. Lincoln always believed and repeatedly said that if General Patterson had pursued into Winchester and had given battle to General Jackson, the battle would have been different at Bull Run. It was pretty generally believed that by proper military exercise on the part of General Patterson, and if he had obeyed the order of General Scott, General Jackson's command would have been prevented from joining General Beauregard at Bull Run and without doubt the battle would have gone in favor of the Union side, which would have had the effect of shortening the duration of the war. But General Jackson with his command was allowed to go on unmolested, and arrived just in time to save the Confederates from defeat.

War now had assumed fearful proportions. The defeat of our army at Bull Run although discouraging to many, had not that effect on Mr. Lincoln. He did not for a moment doubt the final success of the Union troops in suppressing the rebellion. His faith never wavered; he philosophized over the outlook; he keenly felt that a bad start had been made and fully realized that a long and desperate struggle was in

---

501 General Israel B. Richardson was commander of a federal division of General Sumner's Union forces. He was wounded at Antietam on September 17, 1862 and died November 3, 1962. Civil War a Narrative, Part II., pg. 143 and The Armies and The Leaders, pg. 131.

502 General Theodore Runyan was a native of New Jersey. He commanded the 1st brigade sent by New Jersey to defend the capital. All-biographies.com

503 General Dixon Miles commanded the federal garrison at Bolivar Heights. He was killed on September 15, 1862 when "Stonewall" Jackson's men overwhelmed his position and took 12,500 prisoners. Smithsonian's Great Battles and Battlefields of the Civil War, pg. 782.

prospect. His only fear for the future was his apprehension of the late disaster producing discouragement among his compatriots in the North and encouraging the compromise and peace policy in the minds of those who in the commencement were loudest in their cries for war. But he was soon relieved from this apprehension.

Mr. Lincoln had good cause to believe the masses of the people of the North were honestly in favor of a vigorous prosecution of the war and were instigated by nothing but patriotic motives. He could safely rely on their support to the bitter end. Yet there was also a large class of persons belonging to his own party, among them some prominent politicians who were in favor of war for revenue only. This latter class now had their harvest, the opportunity for speculation and fraud, in preying upon the volunteers and their grasp upon the public money, plunder and spoil which satisfied them. The conduct of many of them excited in the mind of Mr. Lincoln as well as in that of all honest men a feeling of loathing and disgust.

After the disaster at Bull Run the federal troops retreated to Washington. General McDowell was again placed in charge of the defenses on the Virginia side of the Potomac River, Arlington Heights &c. General Banks[504] took command at Harpers Ferry, General Dix was placed in command at Baltimore, General Rosecrans was in command in western Virginia. General Patterson's time having expired was mustered out of the service.

The Union army after the battle of Bull Run was for a time greatly demoralized; not that the men were discouraged or wavered in loyalty to the cause of their choice but war was new to them and did not open satisfactorily. Many of them never had personal experience of its reality until then. They went into the fight being impressed with the justice of their cause and believing implicitly in the old adage "twice armed is he who hath his quarrel just," soon realized that faith and justice unassisted by the use of deadly weapons amount to but little in a fight, and that eternal vigilance, courage, determination and keeping the powder dry were necessary for conquest. Immediately after the battle General McClellan was placed in command. His popularity soon

---

504 Nathaniel Prentiss Banks was Governor of Massachusetts, the first Republican to ever serve as Speaker of the House, and a Major General of the Union volunteers. He commanded the Army of the Gulf. His troops were routed in the Shenandoah Valley by Jackson's Stonewall Brigade at Winchester, Virginia in August, 1862. Lincoln's War, pgs 47 & 176 and Civil War a Narrative, Part VII., pg. 15.

infused great confidence into the soldiers. For the time they idolized him, and he won the sobriquet[505] of "Little Mac," and endearing epithet that they applied to him until he quit the army. To add to the embarrassment of the army's condition, the three month volunteers began to return to their homes, and fresh and inexperienced troops had to be enlisted to take their places to make the army effective.

The time of the 6th Massachusetts Regiment, the regiment which had been fired on by the mob in Baltimore on the 19th of April, had expired but they agreed to remain ten days longer. On the 24th 80,000 volunteers were offered and accepted by the government. On the 25th General Frémont[506] assumed command at St. Louis. On this day Robert Toombs,[507] the Confederate Secretary of State resigned and was succeeded by Robert M. T. Hunter[508] of Virginia. The steamer *Resolute*[509] belonging to the Potomac River fleet arrived in Washington, convoying three prizes[510] and bringing valuable information about the movement of the rebels along the Potomac River. The privateer *Sumter*[511] up to this time had captured nine vessels belonging to the Union. On the 26th 21,000 men known as the Pennsylvania Reserve Corps entered the field under the command of General McCall.[512]

---

505 Sobriquet means nickname.

506 General John C. Frémont from Georgia, was a teacher of mathematics in the U.S. Navy and a topographer. He explored and mapped numerous regions of the west including Nevada, Utah and California. Frémont Peak is named for him. He ran for President in 1856. He had emancipated slaves during his military days in Missouri in 1861 and had gotten in trouble with the president because he acted without Mr. Lincoln's approval. After the war he was Governor of Arizona and the civilian Governor of California. Reelecting Lincoln, pg. 145-146, The Armies and The Leaders, pgs. 177 & 186 and Appleton's Cyclopaedia of American Biography, Vol. II., pgs. 545 - 548.

507 Robert Toombs—See pg. 18.

508 Robert M. T. Hunter—See pg. 102.

509 *Resolute* was a small schooner used by the federal Revenue Service. Warships of the Civil War Navies, pg. 193.

510 Prizes were enemy vessels captured or destroyed. Many Confederate blockade runners captured by the Union Navy were put back in service as part of the Union naval fleet.

511 *Sumter* was an 184 foot ship converted into a cruiser. She was the first Confederate raider. She took 18 Union ships as prizes. Warships of the Civil War Navies, pg. 214.

512 General George B. McCall was from Pennsylvania and commanded a 9,500 man division of General McClellan's Union Army at the Seven Days Battle. He was captured by General Longstreet. Civil War a Narrative, Part II., pgs. 192 & 233 and The Armies and The Leaders, pg. 293

Phillip Kearny[513] was appointed a Brigadier General in the regular army. Resolutions on the next day were presented and passed in the Senate approving the acts of the president. On the day following a battalion of Union troops under Colonel Mulligan[514] ambushed Confederate troops at Mt. Pleasant, Missouri and captured a number of troops and several officers. On the 30th nearly all of the government clerks from Virginia in Washington resigned their positions on account of the ordinance passed by that state prohibiting any citizen of that state from holding any office under the federal government. The government made no serious objections to accepting their resignations and dispersing with their services. Mr. Lincoln quietly remarked when told of it, "Well, I think I can do without so much state loyalty mixed with so little loyalty with the general government. Let them go where they belong."

---

513 Phillip Kearny was born in New York but lived in New Jersey. He had lost an arm in the Mexican War. He commanded a division of the Union Army in General Heitzelman's corps. General Winfield Scott called Kearny "the bravest man I ever saw." As a Union General who developed a system of colored ribbons to identify troops in the field. Civil War a Narrative, pg. 233.

513 Brigadier General Isaac I. Stevens was born in Massachusetts. He graduated first Civil War a Narrative, Part II., pgs. 143 & 240 and The Sword of Lincoln, pg. 75.

514 James A. Mulligan was a Union general ordered to hold Lexington, Mississippi at all costs in September 1864. He was mortally wounded leading a division in the second battle at Kernstown, Virginia in June, 1863. Smithsonian's Great Battles and Battlefields of the Civil War, pgs. 410 & 638-39.

*"This is essentially a people's contest. On the side of the Union it is a struggle for maintaining in the world, that form and substance of government, whose leading object is to elevate the condition of men–to lift artificial weights from all shoulders–to clear the paths of laudable pursuit for all–to afford all an unfiltered start and fair chance, in the race of life."*

Abraham Lincoln
Address to Congress, July 4, 1861[515]

# — 7 —

# AFTER BULL RUN

## AUGUST 1861

On the 3rd of August the Baltimore Police seized the steamer *George Reems* laden with military stores destined for the rebels. On this day Congress passed the Confiscation Act.[516] On the day following General Magruder[517] with a body of Confederate troops endeavored to draw the Union troops into an engagement, but failing to do so, he entered the town of Hampton, Virginia and totally destroyed it by fire. That same day the *Democratic Standard* office in Concord, New

[515] Lincoln in American Memory, pg. 385.

[516] The Confiscation Act of 1861 said that government could confiscate property used to aid the Confederacy (primarily slaves) to weaken the insurrection. www.answers.com/topic/confiscation-acts

[517] General John Bankhead Magruder was from Winchester, Virginia. He was a graduate in the U. S. Military Academy Class of 1830. He served in both the Seminole and Mexican Wars. He was in charge of the artillery in and around Richmond. He is best known for having tricked General McClellan during the Peninsula Campaign. He kept marching his troops around in circles in view of the Union sentries making General McClellan think he was constantly being reinforced. After the war he commanded troops in Mexico. Don't Know Much About the Civil War?, pg. 243, The Pride of the South, pg. 108 and The Armies and The Leaders, pg. 251.

Hampshire was destroyed by soldiers because of the disloyal utterances of that paper.

Congress adjourned August 6, 1861. Up to the time of the convention of this Congress, the president had taken the responsibility upon himself of doing many things as a war necessity which were unauthorized by law, such as inaugurating war to repel invasion and suppress rebellion, and in expending large sums for which no appropriation had been made by Congress. His course was approved heartily by the extra session and necessary appropriations were cheerfully made to legalize his expenditures of the public funds. Great harmony between the branches of Congress and the President existed. Not so, however, later on in the course of the war.

The battle of Wilson's Creek[518] was fought on the 10th of August. General Ben McCulloch[519] commanding 22,000 Confederate troops was attacked by General Lyon[520] with 5,200 men mostly volunteers. General Lyon, a braver soldier than whom never drew sword, fell early in the action with a ball through his body. Major Sturgis[521] at once took command. Colonel Sigel[522] commanded one column of General Lyon's army in this engagement and with his command had marched fifteen miles for the purpose of cutting the enemy's flank. The fight was progressing with fair prospect of being won by the federals but being mistaken in the identity of an approaching regiment of rebel reinforcements Colonel Sigel allowed it to approach too near. On its first fire his advance was thrown into disorder and he was driven back with a loss of five guns. Major Sturgis finally fell back to Springfield, Missouri but was not pursued by the enemy. The Union loss in this battle was 1,235 killed, wounded or missing. The Confederate loss was

---

518 Battle of Wilson Creek (also called Oak Hill) occurred ten and a half miles south of Springfield, Missouri. This was the most significant battle fought west of the Mississippi River. Southern History of the War, pgs. 145 & 192 and Smithsonian's Great Battles and Battlefields of the Civil War, pg. 415.

519 General Benjamin McCulloch served in the Mexican War and also the battle of San Jacinto in the Spanish War. He commanded the Confederate forces in Indian Territory which includes Creeks, Seminoles, Cherokees, Chickasaws and Choctaws. He also founded the "Texas Rangers." His orders were to rid Missouri of Yankees. He was killed at Pea Ridge on March 7, 1862. Don't Know Much About the Civil War?, pgs. 30 & 410, The Armies and The Leaders, pg. 147, Southern History of the War, pgs. 285 & 286 and Civil War a Narrative, Part II., pg. 4.

520 Nathaniel Lyon—See pg. 124.

521 Major Samuel D. Sturgis—See pg. 122.

522 Colonel Franz Sigel—See pg. 136.

officially stated as 421 killed and 1,300 wounded. The next day Major Sturgis and Colonel Sigel fell back with their commands to Rollo, Missouri. About this time Justice Catron[523] of the Supreme Court of the United States was expelled and driven out of Nashville, Tennessee, because of his loyalty to the government. Charles J. Faulkner[524] of Virginia on his return from France, where he had been sent by Mr. Buchanan as Minister Plenipotentiary[525] was arrested in Washington City charged with treason and furnishing arms to the rebels. On the 13th instant, $50,000,000 of the government loan was taken by the cities of New York, Philadelphia and Boston.

On the 22nd of August transportation of the mails was refused for the *Daily News*, *Day-Book* and other treasonable newspapers at New York. The office of the *Christian Observer* in Philadelphia was seized by the United States Marshal. On the day following James D. Berret[526] of Washington was arrested and sent north. The use of the U. S. mails was denied to *The New York Journal of Commerce*, *Freeman's Journal* and the *Brooklyn Eagle*.

On the 29th the expedition under Colonel Butler[527] and Commodore Stringham[528] after bombarding for two days captured Forts Clark and Hatteras.[529] The garrisons surrendered as prisoners of war. Great quantities of ordinance and commissary stores were captured. On the 31st the Captain General of Cuba[530] by proclamation admitted the

---

523 Supreme Court Justice John Catron served from 1837—1865. He supported slavery but opposed secession. www.answers.com/topic/john-catron

524 Charles J. Faulkner was from Martinsburg, Virginia (now West Virginia). He was a law graduate of Georgetown University. He served in Congress and then as Minister to France during the James Buchanan administration. He was charged with negotiating with the French for the sale of arms to the Confederacy. www.wvculture.org/history/faulknercharlesobit.html

525 Minister Plenipotentiary is one who has power to transact official business.

526 James D. Berret—See pg. 93 footnote.

527 Colonel Benjamin Butler—See pg. 87.

528 Commodore Silas Stringham was the commander of the Union warships which included the *USS Wabash*, *USS Cumberland*, and *USS Minnesota* and included 149 guns. Smithsonian's Battles and Battlefields of the Civil War, pgs. 419 & 420.

529 Fort Clark and Fort Hatteras were both located on the outer banks of North Carolina on Hatteras Island. They guarded the entrance to Pamlico Sound. Confederate ships often hid in this area to attack Union vessels from there. Southern History of the War, pg. 217 and Smithsonian's Great Battles and Battlefields of the Civil War, pgs. 419 & 420.

530 Francisco Serrano y Dominguez, Duke de la Torre, was Captain General of Cuba from 1859-1862.

Confederate vessels into Cuban ports and promised them protection while in port, giving other guarantees to the belligerents. This looked like recognition of the belligerent rights of the South by Spain's viceroy in Cuba, which would result in a rupture between the United States and Spain. This was anything but desirable by the American government as it had fully as much domestic war on hand as it could attend to at this time, without the addition of a foreign war. It was generally apprehended that a war with Spain would involve other nations and bring on a general war among them with us.

The Fugitive Slave Law[531] was at the beginning of the war the most embarrassing and vexatious question with which the administration had to deal. On August 31, General Frémont, who was at the time in command of the Department of the Missouri, declared the slaves owned by the rebels in the state free. The order of General Frémont declared martial law be established throughout the state of Missouri and that all persons taken with arms in their hands within the lines of his department should be tried by court martial and if found guilty, should be shot, including all persons in arms against the authority of the United States or who were taking an active part with the public enemy. Their property, real and personal, were declared confiscated to the public use, and slaves belonging to them were declared free men. Mr. Lincoln, believing that the time had not yet come to properly do this, annulled the order.

## SEPTEMBER 1861

On the 2nd of September, the second day after the proclamation was issued, Mr. Lincoln wrote to General Frémont in the spirit of kindness setting forth his fears that the proclamation in relation to the liberating of the slaves would alarm our southern Union friends and turn them against us, particularly in Kentucky, and asked him of his

---

www.1911encyclopedia.org/Francisco_Serrano_y_Dominguez%2C_Duke_de_la_Torre_and_Count_of_San_Antonio

[531] The Fugitive Slave Law was approved on September 18, 1850 as part of a group of laws called "The Compromise of 1850." Anti-slavery supporters gained admission of California as a free state and prohibition of slave trading in the District of Columbia. Pro-slavery factions gained concessions regarding slavery in Texas. The passage of the law encouraged the continuation of the Underground Railroad and infuriated abolitionists. It had a provision allowing fugitive slaves to be pursued into free states and returned to their owners. www.nationalcenter.org/fugitiveslaveact.html

own motion to modify the order so as to conform to a recent act of Congress passed on August 6, 1861,[532] a copy of which act he sent him. Mr. Lincoln professed in the letter which he wrote, a spirit of caution and not of censure. General Frémont declined to make the modification unless the president agree it be done.

The first invasion of the Confederate forces into Kentucky was by General Polk,[533] in command of a large body of troops. He took possession of Columbus[534] on the 4th and while he was thus engaged a naval battle took place opposite Hickman in Kentucky between the federal gun boats *Tyler* and *Lexington* and the Confederate gunboat *Yankee.* On the 5th the United States marshal disbanded an organization of secessionists at Stralenburg, New Jersey.[535] On the next day Paducah[536] was taken by General Grant, with two regiments opposed by a rebel force of four thousand men. On the 7th instant General Polk was reinforced at Columbus by General Pillow,[537] with seven thousand men. The battle of Carnifax Ferry on the Gauley River,[538] was fought on September 10. This battle was fought by the opposing Generals Floyd[539] and Rosecrans. General Floyd had 5,000 men with sixteen guns in position as well as entrenched. At the first fire, Col. Lowe[540] of the 12th Ohio was killed. The battle was fought

---

532 The Act was the First Conscription Act which said that the government could confiscate property used to aid the Confederacy (primarily slaves) to weaken the insurrection. www.answers.com/topic/confiscation-acts

533 General Leonidus Polk was graduate of the U.S. Military Academy Class of 1827 (a classmate of Jefferson Davis). He was an Episcopal Bishop of Alabama. He organized the Army of the Mississippi and led a corps at Shiloh, Perryville and Chickamauga. He commanded one of the five Confederate infantry corps under General Bragg in Georgia. He was killed by cannon fire at Pine Mountain on June 14, 1864. Smithsonian's Great Battles and Battlefields of the Civil War, pgs. 13 & 137, The Armies and The Leaders, pg. 143 and Pride of the South, pgs.111 - 113 and 116.

534 Columbus is locate in the far western part of Kentucky along the Mississippi River just downstream from Cairo, Illinois.

535 Stralenburg, New Jersey was a small village near Hackensack.

536 Paducah, Kentucky is on the Ohio River just upstream from where the Ohio River flows into the Mississippi River.

537 Gideon J. Pillow was a lawyer and politician from Tennessee. He is most noted as the Confederate General who failed at Fort Donelson. www.encyclopedia.com/topic/Gideon_John_Pillow

538 Carnifax Ferry on the Gauley River is in western Virginia near Summersville.

539 John B. Floyd—See pg. 42.

540 Colonel John W. Lowe was from Xenia, Ohio. He was killed when struck in the forehead by a musket ball leading eight companies of the 12th Ohio in battle. www.dragonbbs.com/members/ww8566.histartcivilwar3.html

with great fury until night came on, when the men were withdrawn, and they slept on their arms. During the silent watches of the night Confederate General Floyd evacuated his entrenchments and precipitately retreated across the river, destroying the bridge after him and sinking the boats. The loss on either side of the battle was great.

On the same day, Lexington, Missouri[541] was surrendered to the Confederates under General Price.[542] Colonel Mulligan's garrison at Lexington did not exceed 2,000 men. The attacking party of General Price consisted of 20,000 men. It is said to have been utterly impossible for Colonel Mulligan to hold out longer as the engagement had lasted four days. His water supply had been cut off fifty-nine hours before the surrender. The federal loss was thirty-nine killed and 120 wounded, the troops being in entrenchments. The Confederate loss was estimated at 100 killed and wounded.

With his usual disposition to be charged with responsibility whenever an emergency arose, Mr. Lincoln promptly on the 11th of September, made the order[543] in the following language: "It is therefore ordered that the said clause of the said proposition be so modified, held and construed to conform to and not to transcend the provisions on the same subject contained in the act of Congress entitled &c, and that said act be published with this order."

On the 11th instant the legislature of Kentucky ordered the Confederate troops to leave the state, which order was not just then respected. The next day the Confederate forces attacked the Union forces on Cheat Mountain,[544] but were repulsed and Colonel John A.

---

[541] Lexington, Missouri is just east of Kansas City and on the Missouri River.

[542] General Sterling Price was originally from Virginia where he graduated from Hampton-Sydney College. He moved to Missouri in 1831 to practice law. He was a veteran of the Mexican War. A former Congressman, he was the Governor of Missouri from 1853 to 1857. He opposed secession. He was commander of the Confederate forces on both sides of the Mississippi River in the area called Trans-Mississippi. He was the Confederate commander of the cavalry at the attack of the Union Forces at Lexington, Missouri. Lincoln's War, pg. 90, Pride of the South, pgs. 113- 115,Civil War a Narrative, Part VII., pg. 36, Southern History of the War, pgs. 160, 161, & 162, Pride of the South, pgs. 113—115, and The Armies and The Leaders, pg. 276.

[543] This order was made to John Frémont to rescind his order to free all slaves in Missouri. www.blueandgraytrail.com/event/abraham_lincoln

[544] Cheat Mountain is located in Randolph and Pocahontas Counties, in western Virginia (today West Virginia.). It was here that Confederate General Robert E. Lee commanded his first troops in battle.

Washington[545] former proprietor of Mt. Vernon while on a reconnoiter trip near Elk Water, was killed. General McClellan received as aides on his staff Count De Paris[546] and Duc de Chartres[547] on September 14. On the next day James B. Clay[548] was arrested on his way to join the Confederate army. The day following was observed as a day of fasting in accordance with the president's proclamation of August 13.

On the 15th Colonel Francis P. Blair, Jr.[549] was ordered under arrest for using disrespectful language in speaking of his superior officers contrary to the army regulations. On the 19th *The Louisville Courier* was suppressed. On the 22nd of September, General Albert Sidney Johnston,[550] one of the most experienced generals in the American war on either side, assumed command of the Confederate Western Department. On the 23rd Ross Winans,[551] a man of great wealth and a resident of Baltimore, was released as a prisoner from Fortress

---

545 John Augustine Washington was Lt. Colonel on General Lee's staff. He was a direct descendent of the George Washington family. www.findagrave.com/cgi-bin/fg.cgi?page=g&grid=6045745

546 Louis-Phillippe Albert of New Orleans was the Court de Paris. He was an aid to General McClellan. www.encyclopedia.com/doc/1E1-X-Paris-Lo.html

547 Robert Phillippe, Louis Eugene Ferdinand of Orleans was Duc de Chartres from 1840-1910. He was the brother of the Count de Paris and also an aid to General McClellan. www.oac.cdlib.org/findaid/ark:/13030/kt5f59s0n5

548 James B. Clay was a Congressman from Kentucky. He was the son of Henry Clay and a member of the 1861 Peace Commission. He died of tuberculosis in 1864. www.wvculture.org/history/civilwar/carnifax01.html

549 Colonel Francis P. Blair, Jr. was from Kentucky and was the brother of Montgomery Blair, Mr. Lincoln's Postmaster General. He was also a friend of General William Tecumseh Sherman. He was an attorney and editor of a newspaper in St. Louis. He served as a Congressman from Missouri. He commanded a Union brigade under General Steele. He was responsible for saving Missouri for the North. After the war he was a U.S. Senator for one term. Civil War a Narrative, pg. 76, The Armies and The Leaders, pg. 224 and Civil War a Narrative, Part VII., pg. 353.

550 General Albert Sidney Johnston, who was born in Kentucky and was the brother-in-law of Brigadier General William Preston. He was an 1826 graduate of the U.S. Military Academy where he finished second in his class. His roommate was Confederate General Leonidus Polk. He fought in the Blackhawk War. He was offered high command in both the Confederate and Union armies. He led 40,000 Confederate men who faced General Grant at Pittsburg Landing in Mississippi. To Grant he was the Confederate's toughest general. He was killed at the battle of Shiloh on August 6, 1862. Don't Know Much About the Civil War?, pgs. 222 & 225 and Pride of the South, pgs. 94 & 95, The Civil War a Narrative, pgs. 50 & 99, and The Armies and The Leaders, pgs. 143 & 260.

551 Ross Winans—See pg. 86.

Monroe where he had been imprisoned for treasonable utterances &c. He took the oath of allegiance.

General Price evacuated Lexington on the 29th and sought safer quarters. Two Union regiments, one under the command of Colonel Ed Baker,[552] the California regiment, the other the Irish regiment of Pennsylvania mistaking each other for Confederates fired into each other near Munson's Hill and before they had discovered their mistake a number of men were killed and wounded, with several officers among the wounded.

## OCTOBER 1861

On the 1st of October the chief of the tribe of the Cherokee Indians joined the Confederates and on the next day $33,000 deposited in the St. Louis Savings Association belonging to the Cherokee nation was seized by the government and confiscated. On the 3rd there was a battle at Greenbrier, Virginia between General Reynolds[553] of the Union forces and the Confederate General Henry Jackson.[554] The fight lasted over an hour. The latter was driven from the ground with a loss of forty men killed and wounded and a few prisoners taken. The federal loss was not so great—8 killed and 32 wounded. Four thousand Confederates drove the 20th Indiana from their camp near Hatteras Inlet and the 20th Indiana retreated to the lighthouse on the island. The *Monticello*,[555] a Union gunboat, at once came to the relief of the Union troops and shelled the Confederates for four hours while they were endeavoring to embark in their boats. There was terrific slaughter in this engagement. Night caused the secession of hostilities. The gunboat hauled off and under the cover of

---

[552] Colonel Edward D. Baker—See pg. 94.

[553] General John Fulton Reynolds was from Lancaster, Pennsylvania. He had served in the Mexican War. When the war started he was commandant at West Point. He was a brigadier commander of McCall's brigade. He commanded the Union's 1st Corps at Gettysburg where he was killed on July 2, 1863. Civil War a Narrative, Part II., pg. 219 and The Armies and The Leaders, pgs. 129 & 188.

[554] General Henry R. Jackson was from Georgia. He graduated from Yale University. He was captured at the battle of New Orleans but was later paroled. He became Minister to Mexico (1885 - 1886). www.dbpedia.openlinksw.com.8890/resource/Henry_R_Jackson

[555] *Monticello* was a 180 foot long wooden hulled ship that was active in the blockade. It accidentally sank the *Peterhoff* in a collision on March 9, 1864. Warships of the Civil War Navies, pg. 93.

night and the Confederates retreated. The *Susquehanna*[556] frigate remained in range all night.

On the 8th General Anderson[557] was relieved of command in Kentucky on account of ill health. At this time there was a bitter feud between General Frémont, the commander of the Department of the Missouri, and Colonel Francis P. Blair Jr. commanding the 1st Missouri Artillery. Colonel Blair had been placed under arrest for using disrespectful language to General Frémont. On the 9th Colonel Blair preferred charges against General Frémont. On the 11th Confederate General Twiggs[558] was relieved at his own request from command at New Orleans on account of ill health. On the 12th the Confederate steamer *Theodora*[559] ran the blockade at Charleston carrying on board rebel commissioners and ministers representing the Confederate States of America in the foreign governments—Messrs. Mason[560] and Slidell.[561] On the same day Confederate Commander Hollins[562] undertook to destroy the federal fleet in the southwest pass with a ram, fire ships &c. He was not successful at this, as the vessels kept well out of the way of the fire, and parried[563] the butt of the ram. Finally the rebel gunboats were beaten off and their ram much injured. About this time there was continuous skirmishing in the neighborhood of Washington. Being apprehensive from the disposition manifested by the action and tone of some of the powerful nations represented at Washington, Mr. Lincoln caused the Secretary of State to issue a

---

556 *Susquehanna* was a 257 foot side wheel frigate with nine guns and a crew of 300. She participated in the Union bombardment of Port Royal and the capture of Hatteras Inlet. Warships of the Civil War Navies, pg. 23.

557 Robert Anderson—See pg. 46.

558 David E. Twiggs was a federal commander in the Texas division. He surrendered to a small posse of volunteers and was dismissed from the army. He switched sides and became a Major General in the Confederate Army and commanded the Army of Eastern Louisiana. Civil War a Narrative, Part II., pgs. 20 & 21 and The Armies and The Leaders, pg. 263.

559 *Theodora* was a 175 foot long blockade runner that successfully ran the blockade many times. She was captured off the coast of Wilmington, North Carolina by the *Victoria* and *State of Georgia* on May 28, 1862. Warships of the Civil War Navies, pg. 225.

560 James Mason—See pg. 102.

561 John Slidell—See pg. 68.

562 Commander George N. Hollins was a navy man from Baltimore, Maryland whose career started in 1814. He left the U.S. Navy to join the Confederacy. www.famousamericans.net/georgenicholshollins

563 Parried means to ward off.

circular to the governors of states bordering on the ocean and lake coasts urging the necessity of putting the defenses in proper condition to repel any attack that may be made in case of a foreign war growing out of the rebellion which to him then seemed to be inevitable. The circular gave assurances that the expenses would be refunded to the states by the government.

On the 15th the Connecticut Senate passed a resolution requiring the portraits of two distinguished politicians, the Honorable Isaac Toucy[564] and Honorable T. H. Seymour[565] be removed from the Connecticut Senate chamber until the loyalty of these gentlemen could be established. These gentlemen were very prominent in their state and had held many high offices of state and government. Mr. Toucy had been a Representative in Congress, Governor of the state, United States Senator, Attorney General under President Polk,[566] and was Secretary of the Navy in Mr. Buchanan's Cabinet. Mr. Seymour had been a member of Congress, served as a Major in the Mexican War, was four time Governor, and minister to Russia under President Pierce.[567]

After the general evacuation of Lexington, Missouri by General Price, the town was still held by three hundred Confederate soldiers until the 16th when Major White[568] with one hundred fifty men surprised the garrison and captured the town. The Confederates threw away their arms and fled. On the 19th Major Lynde[569] in the Union service disgracefully surrendered Fort Fillmore[570] in Texas with its

---

[564] Isaac Touchy—See pg. 50.

[565] Thomas H. Seymour was born in Hartford, Connecticut and was editor of the *Jefferson* newspaper. He was the Democratic Governor of Connecticut and a Copperhead. Reelecting Lincoln, pgs. 103 and 287 and www.famousamericans.com/thomashartseymour

[566] President James K. Polk was the 11th President of the United States, serving from 1845-1849. www.jameskpolk.com/new

[567] President Franklin Pierce was the 14th President of the United States serving 1853 - 1857. www.answers.com/topic/franklin-pierce

[568] Frank J. White led the "prairie rangers" and was captured in battle. His men returned to rescue him from his captors. www.thelibrary.springfield.missouri.org/lochistory/historicalsites/17.cfm

[569] Major Isaac Lynde was a thirty-four year U.S. infantry veteran and commander of the Union forces at Fort Pillow, forty miles up river from El Paso, Texas. Civil War a Narrative, Part II., pgs. 12 & 22.

[570] Fort Fillmore, New Mexico was located 38 miles upstream on the Rio Grande protecting Mesilla. Smithsonian's Great Battles and Battlefields of the Civil War, pg. 84.

garrison to inferior numbers of Confederates, having in the garrison three times the number of the attacking party. For this he was later dismissed from the service.

General Wool[571] commanding at Fortress Monroe ordered that all contrabands employed in his department should receive; the males eight dollars and the females four dollars per month. *The Journal and Democratic* office of Terre Haute, Indiana was destroyed by the soldiers for publishing treasonable sentiments. The battle of Ball's Bluff[572] occurred on the 21st of October. General Stone[573] ordered Colonel Edward D. Baker[574] with two thousand men to cross the Potomac River at Harrison's Island and Ball's Bluff in order to support the reconnaissance above and below that point on the Potomac River. Colonel Baker's forces were attacked about four o'clock in the evening by five thousand Confederates under command of General Evans.[575] Colonel Baker was killed at the first fire and great regret was felt and expressed throughout the country. The Union forces were soon driven back to the river. There was no means of crossing the river, it being too deep to ford and many of the federals were slaughtered or drowned in attempting to escape by swimming to the Maryland side of the river. Of the two thousand men he crossed the river with, one thousand of them were either killed, wounded or taken prisoner.

---

[571] General John E. Wool was 78 years old and a friend of General Winfield Scott. He served twenty-five years as Inspector General. His forces arrived to capture Norfolk shortly after the government had burned the Groton Naval Yards. Civil War a Narrative, Part II., pg.140

[572] Ball's Bluff is within just a few miles of Leesburg, Virginia and on the Potomac River.

[573] General Charles P. Stone from Massachusetts was dismissed from the war by the Joint Commission on the Conduct of the War. He was arrested and held 189 days in prison, but was never charged and never cleared. His military career was ruined, but he became an engineer. He built the platform in New York harbor in 1887 for the Statue of Liberty. Don't Know Much About the Civil War? pg. 203 and www.factaisy.com/civilwar/content/brigadier-general-charles-p-stone

[574] Edward D. Baker—See page 94.

[575] General Nathan George Evans was from South Carolina, He graduated from the U.S. Military Academy Class of 1848. He engineered and built five miles of entrenchments around Secessionville, South Carolina. Nicknamed "Shanks," because of the thinness of his legs, he commanded the Confederate brigade at Kingston, North Carolina in December 1862. He later commanded a district on the Atlantic coast. After the surrender he was principal of a high school in Alabama. Smithsonian's Great Battles and Battlefields of the Civil War, pgs. 425 & 518, Pride of the South, pgs. 12 & 14 and The Armies and The Leaders, pg. 285.

In military circles there was great dissatisfaction expressed about General Stone's order to Colonel Baker and a strong suspicion was aroused of foul play and a deliberate purpose on the part of General Stone to have Colonel Baker and his command slaughtered by pre-concerted arrangements with the rebels. General Stone was arrested and confined in Fort Lafayette,[576] but was afterwards released from imprisonment and relieved from further service in the army. It was due to General Stone to add that Colonel Baker exceeded his orders by making an attack on the enemy.

The battle of Fredericktown in Missouri was fought on the same day. The federal troops under Col. Plummer[577] of Indiana attacked a large force of Confederates under General Jeff Thompson[578] and Colonel Lowe.[579] The engagement lasted two hours when the Confederates fled in great disorder. Colonel Lowe was killed together with two hundred others of the Confederates besides a large number wounded. Union loss was slight. The same day General Schoepf[580] commanding Union forces attacked the Confederate General Zollicoffer[581] commanding about 7,500 men at Camp Wildcat,

---

[576] Fort Lafayette is an inland coastal fort in the New York Harbor at what is now Bay Ridge (Brooklyn). It was a prisoner of war camp located on an island at the point in New York City where the lower ends of Staten Island and Long Islands came together. It opened to Confederate prisoners on July 15, 1861.

[577] Colonel John B. Plummer was of Cape Girardeau and led 1500 Union troops into battle. www.arlingtoncemetery.net/jbplummer.htm

[578] General Meriwether Jeff Thompson was born in Harpers Ferry, Virginia. He was a veteran of the Mexican War. He moved and became pro-slavery in Indiana. He had been at Fort Sumter with Major Robert Anderson and commanded the "Swap Fox Brigade" in Missouri. He commanded the 14th Union Army Corps under General Sherman. After the war he was commander of the U.S. troops in Alaska. He moved to Missouri where he helped build the Hannibal and St. Joseph Railroad. He was Mayor of St. Joseph (1857 -1860) and presided over the first Pony Express delivery on April 3, 1860. He was a civil engineer after the war. Don't Know Much About the Civil War? pgs. 387-388 and Southern History of the War, pg. 157.

[579] Alden Lowe was shot in the head while commanding the 3rd Missouri Infantry. www.chrisanddavid.com/wilsoncreek/roles/soldiersmsgl-r.html

[580] General Albin A. Schoepf was commander of the Union prison at Fort Delaware where he was given the nickname "General Terror." Fort Delaware State Park

[581] Brigadier General Felix Zollicoffer was a newspaper editor and Congressman from Tennessee who always voted with those having southern sympathies. He was killed at Mill Springs, Kentucky on January 19, 1862. Southern History of the War, pg. 232 and Smithsonian's Great Battles and Battlefields of the Civil War, pg. 265.

[581] *Itasca* was a Unadilla class Union gunboat that captured four enemy ships. Warships of the Civil War Navies, pgs. 49 & 52.

Kentucky and put them to rout. On the 23rd, General Lander[582] who was a great favorite in the Union army was severely wounded while making a recognizance. On the next day the battle of West Liberty[583] in Kentucky was fought and the Confederates were routed with great loss of troops and much valuable material. On the 24th of October the rebel ministers, plenipotentiary[584] and commissioners abroad, Messrs. Mason and Slidell, were formally received at Havana in Cuba. The American counsel at the port signaled the American sloop of war, *The Jacinto*[585] lying off the port. Captain Wilkes[586] of *The Jacinto* afterwards arrested Messrs. Mason and Slidell and took them prisoner of war, and delivered them to the United States authorities in New York. They were confined in Fort Lafayette.

*The Richmond* Virginia *Examine* at this date triumphed over the fact that Mr. Mason and Mr. Slidell[587] had safely run the gauntlet and got through the American fleet and were on their way to Europe. Soon the newspaper was destined to learn that such was not the fact, both of them being at that time at Fort Lafayette.

On the 26th the battle of Romney[588] in Virginia was fought. The Confederate outposts at Mill Creek about five miles from Romney were attacked by General Kelley[589] with 2,500 men. The Confederates were driven back to their main force near the town. General Kelley ordered a charge on the rebel batteries which was made in gallant style when the Confederates precipitately[590] broke and fled through the

---

[582] General Frederick W. Lander was from Massachusetts. The Armies and The Leaders, pg. 213.

[583] West Liberty is located about 80 miles east of Lexington, Kentucky.

[584] Plenipotentiary means someone who has authority to conduct official business.

[585] *The Jacinto* stopped the British mail steamer *The Trent*, causing the South to welcome the news thinking that the incident would bring England into the war on the side of the Confederates. Southern History of the War, pg. 214.

[586] Captain Charles Wilkes of the U.S. Navy was raised by his aunt Elizabeth Ann Seton who became the first American born woman named a saint by the Catholic Church. Wilkes led the U. S. Exploration of the world logging 81,000 miles in what is now called the Wilkes Expedition. His arrest of Messers. Mason and Slidell has become known as the Trent Affair. www.arlingtoncemetery.net/cwilkes.htm

[587] James Mason and John Slidell were diplomats appointed by the Confederacy to try to get France and England to sign treaties in support of the Confederate states. www.civilwarhome.com/trent.html

[588] Romney, Virginia is on the South Branch of the Potomac River about 25 miles south of Cumberland, Maryland.

[589] General Benjamin Franklin Kelley—See pg. 126.

[590] Precipitately means abruptly.

town in the direction of Winchester. General Kelley took four or five hundred prisoners at this battle and considerable war material. About two hundred men on both sides were killed. About this time there were about four hundred rebels in arms near Concord, Missouri who laid down their arms upon condition of promised protection against arrest by the federal government.

On the 28th President Lincoln appointed a military commission to examine the financial affairs of the western department. The commission consisted of Messrs. Joseph Holt[591] of Kentucky, David Davis[592] of Illinois and Thomas Benton[593] of Missouri. On the 30th John C. Breckinridge formally resigned his seat in the United States Senate, having before this joined the Confederacy and now enlisted in its actual service. On the next day all the rebel prisoners confined at Fort Lafayette were transferred to Fort Warren.[594]

## NOVEMBER 1861

On the 1st day of November, 1861, General Winfield Scott was retired from command of the United States Army. Major General George B. McClellan was appointed his successor as commander in chief of the Union forces. On the same day Generals Frémont and Price signed an agreement for the exchange of prisoners[595] and Colonel Mulligan[596] was exchanged for Brigadier General D. M. Frost.[597] An artillery fight took place at New River (Virginia) a short distance from Gauley Bridge.

On the 2nd General Frémont was relieved of command of the Department of the West and General Hunter[598] placed in command in

---

[591] Joseph Holt—See pg. 23.
[592] David Davis was a judge on the 8th Judicial Circuit of Illinois when Mr. Lincoln and author Ward Hill Lamon rode the circuit. Davis later was named Chief Justice of the U.S. Supreme Court by President Lincoln. Ward Hill Lamon: Lincoln's "Particular Friend," pg. 284.
[593] Thomas Hart Benton from Missouri met Abraham Lincoln in 1847 when he was a U.S. Senator. The Prairie Years. pg. 152 and 181.
[594] Fort Warren was on George's Island at the entrance of Boston Harbor.
[595] This agreement was signed without President Lincoln's approval. Cyrus F. Jenkins Civil War Diary, November 1, 1861.
[596] Brigadier General James A. Mulligan—See pg. 142.
[597] Brigadier General D. M. Frost—See pg. 124.
[598] General David Hunter—See pg. 138.

his stead. On the 6th John C. Breckinridge, Humphrey Marshall[599] and others were indicted for treason by the grand jury of Frankfort, Kentucky. The battle of Belmont[600] was fought on November 7. Generals Grant and McClernand[601] with a force of 2,850 men advanced on the Confederates, who made stubborn resistance, but at length were driven from their position and pursued some distance. Their camp was burned. The Confederates were soon reinforced when General Grant withdrew his forces to his gunboats, *Lexington*[602]and *Tyler.*[603] The gunboats had covered both his advance and his retreat. The federal loss in this battle was 84 killed, 288 wounded and 235 prisoners. The Confederate loss was 261 killed, 427 wounded and 278 prisoners.

On this day the bombardment of Port Royal[604] commenced. The Confederate forces were commanded by General Thomas F. Drayton[605] and the affiliated Union naval forces commanded by Captain Percival F. Drayton[606] USA. These opposing leaders were once a product of West Point, Annapolis. General Drayton was the direct descendent of Wm. Henry Drayton, Governor of South

---

599 General Humphrey Marshall—See pg. 85.

600 Battle of Belmont was fought in Mississippi County, Missouri.

601 Major General John A. McClernand was from Kentucky and fought in the Blackhawk War. He settled in Illinois and became a lawyer in Springfield, and was a friend of Abraham Lincoln. He was a Union commander of a division at Pittsburg Landing and commanded the Union's XIII Corps at Vicksburg. He suggested to General Sherman that an army/navy assault on Arkansas Post in January 1863 might be successful. He was along when Mr. Lincoln and Mr. Lamon made the trip to Sharpsburg, Maryland to visit General McClellan in October 1862. Civil War a Narrative, Part II., pg. 67, Five Days in October, pgs. 6—8, and Smithsonian's Great Battles and Battlefields of the Civil War, pgs. 39, 314, and 365 and The Armies and The Leaders, pgs. 177 & 218.

602 *Lexington* was a timber clad side wheeler, 177 foot in length. Warships of the Civil War Navies, pg. 159.

603 *Tyler* was a timber clad side wheeler, 177 foot in length. Warships of the Civil War Navies, pg. 159.

604 Port Royal is about 50 miles south of Charleston, South Carolina and about halfway between the harbors of Charleston, South Carolina and Savannah, Georgia.

605 Brigadier General Thomas F. Drayton was a southern aristocrat who owned an expansive plantation at Hilton Head, South Carolina. He was a graduate of West Point. His military aide was William Seabrook Drayton, his cousin. He faced his brother in fighting—Union Commander Percival Drayton of the USS *Pocahontas*, a gunboat which was part of Admiral Farragut's fleet. He commanded the Confederate forces at Port Royal. Southern History of the War, pg. 218 and Smithsonian's Great Battle and Battlefields of the Civil War, pg. 526.

606 Percival F. Drayton was the brother of Thomas F. Drayton—see above footnote.

Carolina. The Union fleet was several days in reconnoitering and preparing for an attack on Fort Walker with General Beauregard commanding the entrance of this harbor. After the attack, the fighting lasted for over five hours when both forts[607] surrendered, and for the first time since the war began, the national flag waved over the soil of South Carolina. This is regarded as the most brilliant action of cannonading that occurred during the war. The rebel loss was great. The federal loss was inconsiderable, and the carnage created by the shot and shells from the fleet was described as terrible. The loss of the batteries at Port Royal and the commanding position of the harbor were most serious to the Confederate cause and excited great consternation among the people in Charleston and Savannah.

On the same day Beaufort and Hilton Head in South Carolina were occupied by Union troops. The first intelligence was received at Charleston of the capture and burning of the *Royal Yacht*[608] a rebel privateer by a party from *The Santee.*[609] This occurred on the 8th instant. The Confederates at Piketon, Kentucky were on the 9th attacked by General Nelson.[610] They surrendered unconditionally with two thousand prisoners. On this day General Joseph E. Johnston[611] was placed in charge of the Confederate forces in Virginia. The day following General Halleck[612] was placed in charge of the Union forces of the West and General Buell[613] in command of Kentucky. About one

---

607 Fort Walker and Fort Beauregard

608 *Royal Yacht* was a Confederate schooner in the Texas gulf area. Warships of the Civil War Navies, pg. 235.

609 *The Santee* was a 202 foot frigate with 44 guns. After the war she became a school ship for the U.S. Naval Academy. Warships of the Civil War Navies, pg 128.

610 Major General William Nelson was from Kentucky. He commanded the Union forces of General Buell at Shiloh. Smithsonian's Great Battle and Battlefields of the Civil War, pgs. 263 & 267 and The Armies and The Leaders, pg. 207

611 General Joe Johnston—See pg. 129.

612 General Henry Halleck graduated from the U.S. Military Academy in 1839 and was a veteran of the Mexican War. He was a New Yorker. He was a Union General named by Mr. Lincoln as General-in-Chief in October 1862. Halleck later became Mr. Lincoln's chief of staff in Washington. Southern History of the War, pg. 222, The Armies and The Leaders, pgs. 64 & 165 and Lincoln and the Civil War, pgs. 73, 90 & 121.

613 General Don Carlos Buell was a native of Ohio and a participant in the Mexican War. He was one of General Halleck's Union commanders in the West. After the war, he became President of Green River Iron Company. The Armies and The Leaders, pgs. 172 & 173, Civil War a Narrative, pgs. 40 & 41 and Southern History of the War, pg. 221.

hundred fifty federal soldiers in Guyandotte, Virginia[614] were enticed into a house and most of them were treacherously murdered by the inhabitants. Afterwards the town was burned and entirely destroyed in retaliation for the outrage. On the 11th the United States gunboat *Connecticut*[615] captured the British schooner *Adelaide* laden with arms and provisions for the Confederates. This capture was made near Cape Canaveral.[616] On the 13th Lieutenant Worden[617] who was taken prisoner at Pensacola while carrying dispatches to Fort Pickens[618] was exchanged for Lieutenant Sharpe[619] of the Confederate Army. On the 19th the American steamer *Harvey Biron* captured and burned the rebel steamer *Nashville*[620] in the British Channel. Also on the 19th the Stone Fleet[621] had sailed for Charleston harbor and the victory of Port Royal was celebrated all over the country. The citizens of Charleston were called on by the mayor[622] to aid in the defense of the city. In reply to the request of General Wool, General Huger[623] in command of the

---

614 Guyandotte, Virginia was located along the Ohio River in western Virginia. Today it is called Huntington, West Virginia.

615 *Connecticut* was a 251 foot large combatant with two masts and side wheels. She was used as a transport and supply ship, but also captured eleven enemy ships as war time prizes. Warships of the Civil War Navies, pg. 71.

616 Cape Canaveral is along the Atlantic coast of Florida just east of Orlando.

617 Lt. John L. Worden was the commander of the *Monitor* with its crew of 57 sailors. He was captured at Montgomery, Alabama and held prisoner for months. He is considered the first Prisoner of War in the Civil War. Don't Know Much About the Civil War?, pg. 217, www.arthurmokin.com, The Civil War a Narrative, pg. 226 and www.mariner.org/library/connections/pdf/m5016johnwordenpapers.pdf

618 Fort Pickens was part of the three fort defense of the harbor at Pensacola, Florida built to guard the Naval Yard. It was a pentagon shaped fort which was designed for 200 guns. Smithsonian's Great Battle and Battlefields of the Civil War, pg. 102.

619 Lt. Sharpe was in the Confederate Navy. www.suvcw.org/ny/camps/worden/history.htm

620 *Nashville* was a 215 foot long Confederate cruiser with two guns and side wheels. She was the first Confederate ship to enter European waters. She was destroyed by the *Montauk* on February 28, 1863. Warships of the Civil War Navies, pg. 212 & 213.

621 The Stone Fleet was old whaling ships purchase by the government to blockade Southern ports. Among those ships used were the *Robin Hood, Potomac, Fortune, L.C. Richmond, South America, Courier* and others. *Harpers Weekly*, December 14, 1863, pg 798.

622 Charles Macbeth served as mayor of Charleston, South Carolina from 1857 until he surrendered the city to Union Gen. Alexander Schimmelfennig. www.halseymap.com/flash/mayors.esp and timelines.com/1865/2/18/the-mayor-of-charleston-surrenders-the-city-to-alexander-schimmelfennig

623 Benjamin Huger was the Confederate commander of one of the seven corps. He took part in the Seven Days Battles in Virginia. Smithsonian's Great Battle and Battlefields of the Civil War, pgs. 323 & 699.

rebel army agreed that blankets and clothing necessary for the comfort of the federal prisoners might be sent to him. This was notably the first concession of such a privilege given up to this time during the war.

On the next day Confederate General Floyd[624] became panic stricken at Gauley River, broke camp and retreated leaving behind him a great deal of arms, ammunition and camp equipage.[625] It would seem General Floyd was a greater military success in making a retreat than at an advance, or in holding a position.

On the 22nd the rebel steamer *Time*[626] undertook to enter the harbor at Pensacola (Florida) and was fired upon from Fort Pickens. This provoked Forts McRee and Barrancas[627] to fire on Fort Pickens and the dual was kept up all day. In the morning the fight was renewed and Fort McRee was silenced with Fort Barrancas and the naval yard being greatly damaged. On the 23rd General Butler with the advance of his expedition left Portland for New Orleans. On the following day the Union troops took possession of Tybee Island[628] in Georgia. On the day after Union troops landed at Buckingham on the main land of South Carolina, General Lee declared Charleston under martial law.

On the 26th there was a submarine cable laid from Fort Moultrie to Fort Sumter by the Confederates. The black flag was displayed by the rebel cavalry at Concordia in Louisiana. General Sherman[629] took possession of the crops at Beaufort, South Carolina on military account and upon military orders from the War Department. This day was observed throughout the North as a day of national thanksgiving. On the 27th there was a very exciting condemnation meeting held in

---

624 John B. Floyd.—See pg. 42.

625 Equipage means furniture of the army.

626 *Time* was a Confederate steamer. Warships of the Civil War Navies, pg. 237.

627 Forts McRee and Barrancas were the other two forts guarding the harbor and naval yard at Pensacola, Florida, in triangulation with Fort Pickens. Fort McRee was a circular fort built in the 1840s as part of the coastal fortifications. It was designed for 125 guns. Fort Barrancas was built in 1844 upon the ruins of an old Spanish fort built in 1797. This fort was designed for 44 guns. www.nps.gov/archive/guis/extended/FLA/history/forts.htm

628 Tybee Island was located near Fort Pulaski. It was 18 miles downstream from Savannah, Georgia and protected the channel. The Union troops place eleven batteries on Tybee Island to bombard Fort Pulaski. Smithsonian's Great Battles and Battlefields of the Civil War, pg. 235.

629 General William Tecumseh Sherman was the second best known Union general. He is most noted for his famous March to the Sea where he lead 62,000 Union troops. The Blue and The Gray, pg.949 and 950 and www.civilwarhome.com/sherbio.htm

Liverpool, England over the arrest of Mr. Mason and Mr. Slidell on a British steamer. The meeting characterized the arrest with great indignation as an "outrage upon the British flag." That city it will be remembered was at that time interested extensively in commerce with the Confederate government and strange as it may appear, on that same day the United States authority assumed exclusive control of the commerce of the Mississippi and Ohio Rivers. Hitherto these rivers had been regarded as public navigable highways open to the free intercourse of all nations. On the 30th twelve hundred Creek Indians arose in rebellion against the Confederate states authorities.[630]

## DECEMBER 1861

On December 1, 1861 the schooner *Albion* of Nassau was captured by the gunboat *Penguin*[631] in the attempt to run the blockade at Charleston. She had on board military stores for the rebels valued at one hundred thousand dollars. About this time all east Tennesseans who refused to acknowledge the southern Confederacy, the journals of the state advocated and advised, should be hung.

On the 4th *The Memphis Avalanche* urged that the black flag should be raised. The English government prohibited the exportation of firearms, lead, brimstone,[632] nitrate of soda[633] and gunpowder. The reports to Congress on the 5th by the War and Navy Departments showed the Union forces regular and volunteers, seamen and marines to aggregate 682,971 men.

On the 10th the Congress of the United States met in regular session.[634] Their first act was to request the president to place the prisoners Mr. Mason and Mr. Slidell in solitary confinement in

---

630 Creek Chief Opoth-ley-aho-la led a Union band of Creek and Cherokee Indians in Oklahoma. He revolted when the Confederate soldiers captured their villages on the Arkansas River, taking women and children as prisoners. These men later formed the 1st regiment of Indian Home Guards. Southern History of the War, pg. 266 and Smithsonian's Great Battles and Battlefields of the Civil War, pgs. 468 - 470.

631 *Penguin* was a three-masted Union schooner with a crew of 69 that captured four enemy ships. Warships of the Civil War Navies, pg. 94.

632 Brimstone is sulfur used in manufacturing explosives.

633 Nitrate of soda is a derivative of nitrous acid used in manufacturing explosives.

634 This was the first time Congress met in regular session since the beginning of the war. www.libraryunt.edu/govinfo/browse-topics/government-and-politics/politics/years-and-sessions-of-congress

retaliation for the same treatment to Colonels Corcoran[635] and Wood[636] by the rebels.

A diplomatic correspondence arose out of the arrest of Mr. Mason and Mr. Slidell between England and the United States government, the result of which was the prisoners were to be discharged from prison and allowed to go to England, their destination when the arrest was made. Diplomacy determined that the arrest was not warranted by international law.

On the 13th a battle was fought at Camp Allegheny[637] near Staunton, Virginia by Colonel Johnston's rebel troops[638] numbering two thousand and General Milroy[639] with seven hundred fifty Union men. The fight lasted from daylight until three o'clock in the afternoon when the Union troops retired. Confederate loss was over two hundred men. The Union loss was comparatively small. The British ship *Admiral*[640] while attempting to run the blockade at Savannah, Georgia was captured. The Earl of Darby[641] in the British House of Lords suggested to the English government that outward bound ships should signal all English vessels that were inbound. He said war with America was probable. There was at this time great excitement throughout the United States owing to the imperative and threatening tone of the English press in relation to the arrest of Mr. Mason and Mr. Slidell. On the 18th 1,300 prisoners were captured at Milford,

---

635 Colonel Michael Corcoran led a Union division against General George Pickett's right flank at Suffolk, Virginian in April, 1862. Smithsonian's Great Battles and Battlefields of the Civil War, pg. 762.

636 Colonel Alfred M. Wood was in the 14th Reg. of the New York State Militia and was wounded and captured at Bull Run.
www.simmonsgames.com/research/authors.USWarDept/ORA/OR-S2-V2-C3.html

637 Camp Allegheny was at the summit of the Allegheny Mountains overlooking the Staunton-Parkersburg turnpike near Staunton, Virginia. Smithsonian's Great Battles and Battlefields of the Civil War, pgs. 779-780.

638 Colonel Edward "Allegheny" Johnson graduated from the U.S. Military Academy in 1830 and served in the Seminole War and Mexican War. He received the nickname leading six infantry regiments at this battle.
www.associatepublisher.com/e/e/ed/edward_johnson_(general).htm

639 Brigadier General Robert Milroy led Union forces in the Shenandoah Valley during the campaign of May 1862. Civil War a Narrative, Part II., pgs. 149 & 150.

640 *Admiral* was a 220 foot long fourth-rate British ship with four guns. She captured four enemy craft. Warships of the Civil War Navies, pg. 109.

641 The Earl of Darby was Edward Smith-Stanley who served three different times as Prime Minister of the United Kingdom.
www.victorianweb.org/history/pms/derby1/html

Missouri by federal Colonel Jeff. C. Davis[642] with slight loss. The next day a prize crew from the fleet off Charleston delivered over to the authorities in New York the British ship *Eshire,* as a prize taken in the attempt to run the blockade, having on board a cargo of valuable merchandise. Charles James Faulkner[643] the ex-minister to France who had been arrested in Washington for treason to the government while minister and confined in Fort Warren[644] was released on parole. He went through the line to Richmond and his arrival there created great excitement. He was enthusiastically received by his Confederate friends. The Stone Fleet was sunk on the 22nd on Charleston Bar.

On the next day George W. Jones[645] late minister of the United States government to Bogotá was arrested for treason and sent to Fort Lafayette. Congress thanked Colonel Mulligan and his command for their gallant defense of Lexington. On the same day a severe engagement took place in Dranesville, Virginia by the Union soldiers under General Ord[646] and the rebel cavalry under General Stuart.[647] The fighting lasted two hours when the Confederates retreated leaving a large number of their dead and wounded on the field. There was now great rejoicing in the South at the prospect of a war between the United States and England. On the 28th the rebel commissioners Mr. Mason and Mr. Slidell were released from imprisonment. On the 30th there was a demand by Congress upon the Secretary of War to furnish the correspondence between General Scott and General Patterson in relation to the conduct of the war which demand the secretary declined to comply with. On the day following specie payments were virtually suspended throughout the North. About this time the newspapers throughout the whole country and Canada were full of

---

642 Colonel Jeff. Columbus Davis was with the 22nd Indiana Infantry and commanded the 3rd Division of the Union Army. Stellar-one.com/civil_war/battle_of_pea_ridge_17/htm

643 Charles James Faulkner—See pg. 145.

644 Fort Warren was in the Boston Harbor.

645 George W. Jones was a U.S. Senator from Iowa and the minister to Granada in 1859. He was charged with being disloyal to the Union and held in jail for 64 days. www.knowledgerush.com/kr/encyclopedia/George_W_Jones

646 Edward O. C. Ord was born in Maryland. He was roommate to William T. Sherman at the U.S. Military Academy class of 1839. He was the man who designed Fort Sam Houston. He commanded the Army of the James and was instrumental in the Union breakthrough at Petersburg at the end of the war. www.blueandgray.com/event/edward_o_c_ord

647 JEB Stuart—See pg. 137.

adverse comments about the release of the rebel commissioners. *The Toronto Leader*, a Canadian Journal spoke of their surrender as "the greatest collapse since the beginning of time" and *The Montreal Gazette* said "it was a bitter pill for the fire-eaters to cram down their throat."

*"Every one seems relieved at the change in the War Department."*

Letter sent home by George Meade[648]

# — 8 —

# MR. STANTON REPLACES MR. CAMERON AS SECRETARY OF WAR

The Honorable Simon Cameron,[649] Secretary of War, resigned his position as such and the Honorable Edwin M. Stanton was appointed his successor. Mr. Cameron was at once appointed the minister to Russia to fill the vacancy made by the recall of Honorable Cassius M. Clay who had been tendered a Major General's commission to take part in the war. The appointment of Mr. Stanton[650] in Lincoln's Cabinet in place of the Hon. Simon Cameron the Secretary of War was a great surprise to the country. Those who were acquainted with the relations between Mr. Lincoln and Mr. Stanton when they were both practicing lawyers were not only astonished with the appointment, but were apprehensive that there could not possibly be harmony of action and cooperation between them.

There were perhaps seldom if ever two really great men who were as unalike in all respects as Mr. Lincoln and Mr. Stanton. Their habits of life, disposition and taste—in fact—they were dissimilar in every respect in the general make up of man. Mr. Stanton had been a member of Mr. Buchanan's Cabinet, and Mr. Lincoln appreciated his great ability displayed not only as a Cabinet counselor but as a lawyer who stood among the head of his profession in the United States. The president needed the ablest counsel he could obtain and allowed no personal consideration to influence him in seeking the right man for the service.

---

648 The Sword of Lincoln, pgs. 56 and 57.

649 Simon Cameron—See pg. 97.

650 Edwin Stanton—See pg. 45.

In order to make the history of this appointment complete in all its meaning and bearings it will be necessary to go back to the year 1858 when Abraham Lincoln was practicing law in Springfield, Illinois and Edwin M. Stanton was at the head of his position in Cincinnati, Ohio. The celebrated McCormick Reaper and Mower case[651] was before the United States Court in Cincinnati. Mr. Stanton was retained as counsel in chief in the case and Abraham Lincoln of Illinois—Mr. Lincoln being McCormick's attorney in Chicago.[652]

When Mr. Lincoln arrived in Cincinnati to attend the trial he called upon Mr. Stanton. Mr. Stanton treated him in so rude and impolite a manner Mr. Lincoln went to Mr. McCormick and informed him that he would have to withdraw as his counsel in the case and stating his reasons therefore. Mr. McCormick begged him to remain and went to Mr. Stanton and talked to him about the matter. Mr. Lincoln was in a room adjoining where the conversation occurred and overheard Mr. Stanton saying he would not associate with "such a damn gawky long-armed ape as that; if he could not have a man who was a gentleman in appearance associated with him in the case he would himself abandoned it." When Mr. McCormick returned to Mr. Lincoln the latter refunded him his $500 retainer fee and peremptorily declined to keep it. He then returned to Urbana, Illinois where court was in session. Mr. Lincoln related the facts and his mortification to his friend, Judge David Davis, then on the bench and other members of the bar as an excuse for his unexpected return. After this event Mr. Lincoln never met Mr. Stanton until the events now briefly related brought them together, yet it is certain that Mr. Lincoln never forgot the gratuitous insult then cast upon him.

When Mr. Mason and Mr. Slidell as commissioners of the Confederacy to England and France were captured (November 8, 1861) on the English mail vessel *Trent*, there was, it will be remembered, great exultation among loyal people all over the country which Mr. Lincoln, Seward, Chase, Blair, Sumner[653] and the rest shared, except Mr.

---

[651] Cyrus McCormick filed suit against John H. Manny for patent infringement. McCormick was the inventor of the reaper. His company today is called International Harvester. Mr. Manny eventually won the court case. *Illinois - Springfield Times*, June 2, 2005 and www.lib.niu.edu/1995/ihy950230.htm

[652] The Prairie Years, pg. 212—says Lincoln and Stanton were on the side of Mr. Manny.

[653] Edwin Vase Sumner was born in Massachusetts and entered the U.S. Army in 1819 as a second lieutenant. He fought in the Seminole War and the Mexican War and was

Stanton. Mr. Lincoln shook his head and expressed great fear of grave complications with England. All remembered the single danger that the government escaped through Mr. Seward's diplomacy.

By December, 1861, Mr. Lincoln and his Cabinet were in a state of alarm in fear of war with England. Mr. Chase one day came to the president and told him that Mr. Stanton who had been Attorney General under President Buchanan had talked to him on the subject of the troubles with Great Britain and had expressed the opinion that the action the American Government in arresting Mr. Mason and Mr. Slidell was legal and could be sustained by international law. Mr. Lincoln told Mr. Chase that Mr. Stanton did not like him and had treated him rudely on one occasion, but if Mr. Chase thought Mr. Stanton would meet him, he would be glad to have him do so and give his views on the subject. In an hour Mr. Chase had Mr. Stanton in Mr. Lincoln's presence. Mr. Lincoln expressed his gratification at hearing Mr. Stanton's views and asked him to repeat them to Mr. Lincoln. Mr. Stanton proceeded to the discussion of the case and the laws bearing thereon, with Mr. Lincoln listening intently. Mr. Lincoln expressed his thanks and asked Mr. Stanton to put his opinion in writing which he promised to do by ten o'clock the next morning.

The opinion was brought at the appointed time. Mr. Lincoln read it and filed it and then said, "Mr. Stanton. This is a time of war. You are as much interested in sustaining the government as myself or any other man. This is no time to consider party issues. The life of the nation is in danger. I need the best counselors around me. I have every confidence in your judgment and have concluded to ask you to become one of my counselors. The office of the Secretary of War will be vacant and I want you to accept the position. Will you do it?"

Mr. Stanton was amazed and said, "Why Mr. President you take me by surprise. This is an embarrassing question but will you give me a day or two to consider? I will give you an answer." The next day he called on the president and signified his intention to accept. On the 13th day of January 1862 the folio of Secretary of War was placed in his hands. His connection with the administration through the remainder of the term of troublesome times is part of the history of the country.

---

the oldest field commander in the Civil War for either side. He commanded the Second Corps for the Union Army. www.answers.com/topic/sumner-edwin-vase

*"If the government and the marshall intend to putting this rebellion down soon, I think it is time they were whipping somebody."*

Letter from Stephen Logan, of Springfield, Illinois
to his son-in law, Ward Hill Lamon[654]

# — 9 —

# THE WAR OF 1862

## JANUARY 1862

January 1, 1862 another battle was fought at Port Royal in which the Unionists succeeded. At Pensacola, Fort Barrancas was again fired upon by Fort Pickens and received great damage. On the next day the steam ship *Ella Warley* ran the blockade at Charleston with a valuable cargo on board, and was bearer of most important dispatches for the Confederate government.

On the 17th an appropriation was made by Congress for $5,960,000 for fortifications and coast defenses. On the 18th John Tyler,[655] ex-President of the United States died in Richmond, Virginia. He was seventy-two years of age. Mr. Tyler was an ardent Union man at the commencement of the war and counseled peace and compromise; but when he became satisfied this course was futile he cast his fortune with the Confederates. Confederate Generals Zollicoffer[656] and Crittenden[657] attacked the corps of General George H. Thomas,[658]

[654] Ward Hill Lamon: Lincoln's "Particular Friend," pg. 313.

[655] John Tyler—See pg. 83.

[656] Felix K. Zollicoffer—See pg. 154.

[657] George B. Crittenden was born in Kentucky and graduated in the class of 1832 from the U.S. Military Academy. He served in the Black Hawk War. He commanded the Military District of Eastern Tennessee for the Confederacy. His brother Thomas H. was a Union general. www.answers.com/topic/george-b-crittenden

commanding the Union forces at Mill Springs, Kentucky. They fought severely until late in the afternoon when the Confederate forces gave way and retreated in great confusion across the Cumberland River. The Confederate losses in killed and wounded was two hundred thirty-one besides one hundred fifty prisoners with a large amount of stores.[659] The Union loss in killed and wounded was two hundred forty-seven; thirty-nine of that number being killed. The Union gunboat *Itasca*[660] captured the schooner *Lizzy Weston* belonging to Apalachicola, Florida[661] laden with cotton bound for Jamaica.

Also on the 27th the protest of Earl Russell[662] was entered against British vessels after capture while running the blockade being taken into port with the British flag floating beneath that of the United States. The American Secretary of State apologized saying that the flying of the British flag under the American flag was ignorantly done and gave orders to prevent the repetition of such acts which satisfied Great Britain for the time being. Also on the 27th Mr. Mason and Mr. Slidell arrived in South Hampton, England. They were greatly disappointed at their cold reception by the people and the authorities. On the 31st Mr. Seward directed the release of all prisoners taken on vessels running the blockade. The president was authorized by Congress to take military possession of all telegraph and railroad lines in the United States. Queen Victoria[663] the same day declared her purpose to remain strictly neutral in the matter of the American conflict.

## FEBRUARY 1862

On February 3, 1862 in accordance with Earl Russell's manifestation of England's neutrality, the privateer *Nashville* a rebel vessel was

658 George H. Thomas was known as "the rock of Chickamauga" because he fought General Bragg's army to a draw although outnumbered more than three to one. www.homeearthlink.net

659 Confederate General Zollicoffer was killed in this action. Southern History of the War, pg. 232.

660 *Itasca* was a Unadilla class Union gunboat that captured four enemy ships. Warships of the Civil War Navies, pgs. 49 & 52.

661 Apalachicola, Florida is on the Gulf of Mexico west of Tallahassee near Panama City.

662 Earl Russell—See pg. 128.

663 Queen Victoria was queen of England from 1837-1901. www.answers.com/topic/queen-victoria

ordered out of South Hampton harbor. The American warship *Tuscarora*[664] on the watch for the *Nashville* was in the act of pursuing her as she left the harbor but the British frigate *Shannon* caused the *Tuscarora* to desist and compelled her to wait twenty-four hours after clearing port to comply with the rule and requirements of international law. The capture of the privateer was thus prevented at that time. On this day the government of the United States decided and declared that the crews of captured privateers should be treated as prisoners of war. On the 4th the leading newspaper of the South *The Richmond Examiner* gave voice to the following remarkable sentiments: "It is better to fight at the risk of losing battles than to remain inactive to fill inglorious graves; better that the government and the people should be aroused to duty by defeat than that the army should go to sleep." The British schooner *Mars* was captured by the American vessel *Keystone State*[665] while attempting to run the blockade off of Fernandina, Florida.[666] On the same day the English government removed the prohibition against shipping of arms, gunpowder, lead, &c. from England.

On the 6th the bombardment of Fort Henry[667] on the Tennessee River commenced. Commodore Foote[668] the United States flag officer with his fleet of seven gunboats opened fire on the fort about a mile distant. After severe cannonading for several hours Fort Henry surrendered. General Grant with the land forces arrived about an hour after the surrender. There were not more than sixty or seventy prisoners taken. The main body of the garrison with General Lloyd Tilghman[669] the commanding officer had made their escape before the

---

664 *Tuscarora* was a 198 foot Wyoming class screw sloop carrying a crew of 198 with three guns. Her job was to seek and capture Confederate raiders in European waters. Warships of the Civil War Navies, pg. 40.

665 *Keystone State* was a 219 foot Union vessel with four guns and a crew of 162. She captured fifteen prize ships. Warships of the Civil War Navies, pg. 73

666 Fernandina, Florida is the northernmost Atlantic coast town in Florida. It is north of Jacksonville.

667 Fort Henry, built in 1861,was the most important fortification to guard the Tennessee River. It was situated at the southernmost point in the Confederate lines. Southern History of the War, pg. 243 and Smithsonian's Great Battles and Battlefields of the Civil War, pg. 539.

668 Commodore Andrew Hull Foote of the Union Navy was assigned to clear all waterways to the Gulf, a 500 mile stretch from the mouth of the Ohio River to the mouth of the Mississippi River. Civil War a Narrative, Part II., pgs. 34-36.

669 General Lloyd Tilghman commanded Fort Henry for the Confederacy. He was killed at Champion's Hill on May 16, 1863. Smithsonian's Great Battles and Battlefields of the Civil War, pg. 539 and The Armies and The Leaders, pg. 151.

capture. There were however taken twenty guns, seventeen mortars and great amounts of stores. On the same day an issue of one hundred and fifty million dollars of legal tender notes was authorized by Congress. On the 8th the battle of Roanoke Island[670] was fought. The fighting had been commenced the day previous and resulted in some of the rebel gunboats being disabled and some of their guns dismounted. That morning General Burnside[671] landed about five thousand federal troops on the island and a stubborn resistance was made to their attack.[672] The works of the enemy had to be carried at the point of the bayonet. That evening the fort surrendered. In the six forts three thousand prisoners were taken together with forty-two guns, three thousand stands of small arms, and an immense quantity of military stores. There were killed and wounded on the federal side about 335 men. On the Confederate side the loss was not one-fourth that number.

On the 10th Jefferson Davis[673] was by the Confederate Congress reelected President of the Confederate States of America and A. H. Stephens[674] Vice-President of that same time. They had respectively received all the electoral votes cast in the states claimed by the new government. The battle at Fort Donelson[675] was fought on the 14th,

---

[670] Roanoke Island is located between the Croatan and Roanoke Sounds near Nags Head, North Carolina and was a strategic key to the defense of Norfolk. The forts here guarded two sounds, eight rivers, four canals, and two railroads. The forts included Fort Huger, Fort Blanchard, Fort Forrest, Fort Bartow, Fort Forest and Fort Roanoke Island. Harpers Pictorial History of the Great Rebellion, pg. 242 and Southern History of the War, pg. 238.

[671] General Ambrose Burnside was a merchant tailor from Indiana. An 1847 West Point graduate, he is credited with inventing a breech loading rifle. He worked for the Illinois Central Railroad when George McClellan was the railroad's vice-president. Burnside led his men across a bridge at the battle of Antietam Creek which today is called "Burnside Bridge." He was the commanding Union General at the battle of Fredericksburg on December 13, 1863, replacing General McClellan. It is his "chops" that made famous the term "side burns." He was Governor of Rhode Island from 1866 - 1869 and a U.S. Senator. The Story-Life of Lincoln, pg. 494 and Appleton's Cyclopaedia of American Biography, Vol. I., pgs. 462 - 465, The Armies and The Leaders, pgs. 166, 169 & 296, and Antietam Battlefield brochure, National Park Service.

[672] The rebel forces were led by General Henry Wise. His son, Captain O. Jennings Wise, was killed at this battle. Southern History of the War, pg. 237. See pg. 63.

[673] Jefferson Davis—See. pg. 18.

[674] A. H. Stephens—See pg. 30.

[675] Fort Donelson was located on the Cumberland River in Tennessee. It was commanded by Brigadier General Gideon J. Pillow and then reinforced by General

15th and 16th of February, 1862. The federal gunboat *St. Louis*[676] opened fire on the fort about three o'clock in the afternoon on February 14. A vigorous fire was kept up about an hour and a half and the water batteries were silenced. The *St. Louis* became disabled from a plunging shot through her pilot house disabling her wheel. All the vessels engaged had suffered more or less and Commodore Foote ordered the fleet to drop down the river which ended the fighting for that day. Early next morning a heavy force of Confederates attacked the Union lines in front of the fort—it being the extreme right of the Union line. Their expectation was to cut their way through. In this at first they were not successful. The Confederates, however, were soon reinforced and successful in pushing back the Union lines. The federals were then reinforced and drove the Confederates back. The battle was waged with great determination on both sides during the day with varying advantages to either side. In the evening the federals after a hand-to-hand fight made for the Confederate's right line and the Union forces were in possession of the outer line of the fortification. On the 16th Fort Donelson surrendered to General Grant. General Buckner[677] in command of the fort and 11,500 men were taken prisoner, together with twenty thousand stand of arms and a great quantity of ammunition. During the night Generals Floyd and Pillow with about five thousand men made their escape. General Floyd

---

John B. Floyd and General Simon B. Buckner. Civil War a Narrative, Part II., pg. 31, Southern History of the War, pg. 244 and Smithsonian's Great Battles and Battlefields of the Civil War, pgs. 541 & 542.

[676] *St. Louis* was a Union river ironclad. She was 175 feet long with two guns and a center wheel. She was hit fifty nine times at Fort Donelson. Warships of the Civil War Navies, pgs. 151 & 152.

[677] General Simon Bolivar Buckner was born in Kentucky and graduated from the U.S. Military Academy in 1844. He served in the Mexican War and was an instructor of tactics at West Point. He was the Confederate general sent to reinforce the troops at Fort Donelson. When things got hot, General Floyd and Brigadier General Pillow fled. General Buckner surrendered the fort to his West Point classmate General Ulysses S. Grant. Buckner was a defender of his native state of Kentucky. He led his troops to victory at Chickamauga. After the war he was Governor of Kentucky. When Grant died, General Buckner was a pall bearer. When General Buckner died he was the last surviving Confederate who was a Major General and above. After the war he served as Governor of Kentucky and was editor of the *Louisville Courier*. When he died in 1914 he was the last surviving Confederate General of rank Major General and above. Civil War a Narrative, Part II., pg. 31, Southern History of the War, pg. 244, The Armies and The Leaders, pg. 258, Pride of the South, pg. 76, Smithsonian's Great Battles and Battlefields of the Civil War, pgs. 541 & 542 and The Pride of the South, pg. 76

had many times before thus distinguished himself as a masterly officer of a retreat. Perhaps no officer in either army during the war so distinguished himself in this peculiar quality of military strategy as was credited to him.

Fort Henry, Fort Roanoke Island and Fort Donelson after a stubborn resistance were all now in the hands and under the control of the Union forces. This caused a general rejoicing all over the North. On the next day after the surrender of Fort Donelson two rebel Tennessee regiments not knowing of the surrender innocently marched into the fort for the purpose of reinforcing them. They numbered fourteen hundred and seventy men and they were at once taken prisoner. A battle was fought at Fort Craig[678] in New Mexico on the 21st between General Canby[679] commanding the federal forces and Colonel Steele[680] commanding the Confederates continuing all day and into the evening. The federal forces were compelled to retreat into the fort with a loss of sixty-two killed and one hundred sixty-two wounded. On February 22, the anniversary of the birth of the father of the republic and the country—George Washington—was celebrated throughout the North with the appropriate ceremonies while the South celebrated it by inaugurating the president and the vice-president for a fragment of the country bequeathed as a sacred legacy by him to the people. On the 25th General William Nelson commanding the advance of General Buell's Union army took possession of and occupied Nashville, Tennessee. On this day the president ordered all the telegraph lines in the northern states taken into military possession. On the 27th Lieutenant Worden[681] in command of the ironclad *Monitor*[682] went to sea and the

---

678 Fort Craig is located on the Rio Grande River south of Albuquerque, New Mexico. The Civil War a Narrative, Part II., pg. 23.

679 General Edward Richard Sprigg Canby was from Kentucky and a graduated in the class of 1839 from the U.S. Military Academy. He was a soldier in the Seminole and Mexican Wars. He prevented the Confederate invasion of California territory. He was named the commander of the division of western Missouri and then commander of the federal army of Louisiana on May 7, 1864. He accepted the surrender of General Kirby at Baton Rogue, Louisiana on May 26, 1865. In 1873 he was murdered by an Indian chief. Southern History of the War, pg. 524, Grant Takes Command, pg. 174, The Armies and The Leaders, pg. 182 and Lincoln and His Generals, pg. 309.

680 Colonel William Steele headed the 7th Regiment of Sibley's brigade, CSA. www.angelfire.com/tx/Randystexas/pages64.html

681 Lt. John Worden—See pg. 159.

evacuation of Columbus[683] commenced. On the next day another British ship *The Lebanore* with a valuable cargo was brought into New York captured while attempting to run the blockade. The same day the rebel steamship *Nashville* was more successful as it ran the blockade at Beaufort, South Carolina.

## MARCH 1862

On March 2, 1862, General Lander[684] died from the affects of a wound he received at Edwards Ferry in October last. On the next day Columbus, Kentucky was occupied by Union soldiers. It had been entirely deserted by the Confederate troops and most of the prominent citizens. On the same day Fernandina, Florida was taken by the land and naval forces under General Wright[685] and Commodore DuPont.[686] On the 4th General James Shields[687] was appointed to take command of the late General Lander's brigade and Andrew Johnson[688] was appointed the military Governor of Tennessee and also commissioned a Brigadier General in the Union service. The next day the federal steamer *Waterwitch*[689] captured the rebel schooner *William*

---

682 *Monitor* was a 179 foot long federal ironclad with a rotating turret containing two guns and a crew of 49 men. She was the first ironclad built without rigging or sails. She was called "a cheese box on a raft." The *Monitor* was accidentally sunk while being towed by the *Rhode Island* near Hatteras on December 31, 1862 with the loss of 16 sailors. The Civil War a Narrative, pg. 125 and Warships of the Civil War Navies, pg. 4.

683 Columbus, Kentucky is on the Mississippi River in the westernmost part of the state and downstream from Cairo, Illinois.

684 General Frederick Lander—See pg. 155.

685 General Horatio G. Wright was from Connecticut and graduated 2nd in the class of 1841 at the U.S. Military Academy. He helped to destroy the Groton Naval Yard to keep the ships from falling into rebel hands. He was the commander of the Union's 6th Corps in the Shenandoah and Peninsula campaigns. He re-enforced Union lines entrenched at Petersburg in February 1865. After the war, as an engineer he completed the Washington Monument and the Brooklyn Bridge. Lincoln's War, pg. 366, The Armies and The Leaders, pgs. 183 & 202, and Civil War a Narrative, Part IX., pg. 53.

686 Commodore Samuel DuPont—See pg. 116.

687 General James Shields challenged Abraham Lincoln to a duel in 1842 following articles in the newspapers written by Lincoln and critical of Shield's handling of the state auditor's office. Lincoln: The Presidential Archives, pg. 41.

688 Andrew Johnson—See pg. 102.

689 *Waterwitch* was a Union side-wheel sloop captured by the Confederates at Nossabaw Sound in Georgia on June 3, 1864 and used in the Confederate Navy. Warships of the Civil War Navies, pgs. 24 & 241.

*Malery* in St. Andrew's Bay, Florida. On the day following the president sent a message to Congress asking pecuniary[690] aid for the states for emancipating their slaves.

The battle of Pea Ridge[691] was commenced on the 6th of March. On that day the Confederates attacked the Union army on its right wing the main line being on Sugar Creek. The action ceased about four o'clock in the afternoon for that day owing to the reinforcements of the Union troops coming up which caused the Confederates to withdraw. The armies of both sides slept on their arms at that time. At eleven o'clock the next morning the Confederates again attacked the right flank of the Union army. They fought all day with great loss to both sides. General McCulloch[692] was mortally wounded. He was in command of the rebel forces. At sunrise the following day the fight was again renewed by Union General Curtis[693] and his right and center lines. The whole rebel line responded with determined energy. General Curtis ordered the center and left wings of his command to the front and was successful in turning the Confederate right wing. Then a charge was ordered of the Union line which resulted in the complete rout of the whole rebel force. The Union loss was two hundred and twelve killed, nine hundred twenty-six wounded and one hundred seventy-five missing. The Confederate loss was very heavy but never ascertained though it was supposed to be about five thousand, killed, wounded or missing. On this day the president issued his order No. 2[694] dividing the Union army into five *corps d'armie* to be commanded respectively by Generals Banks,[695] McDowell, Heintzleman, Sumner

---

690 Pecuniary means financial.

691 Pea Ridge also called Elk Horn was near Leetown, Arkansas is in the northwestern corner of the state. Southern History of the War, pg. 282.

692 Benjamin McCulloch—See pg. 144.

693 Major General Samuel Ryan Curtis was originally from New York. He was a graduate of the U. S. Military Academy Class of 1831 and was active in the Mexican War. He was a former Congressman from Iowa and an abolitionist. He was a Union general in the Trans-Mississippi theater. One of his scouts was the infamous Wild Bill Hickok. After the war, he helped promoted the transcontinental railroad. The Civil War a Narrative, pg. 140, The Civil War a Narrative, Part II., pg. 7, The Armies and The Leaders, pg. 176, and www.nps.gov.peri

694 The President made these military appointments without consultation from General McClellan. The general was upset that he was not in on the discussions of the appointments. The Sword of Lincoln, pgs. 61 & 62.

695 Nathaniel Banks—See pg. 140.

and Keyes.[696] On March 8th there was a naval fight between the rebel ironclad *Merrimac*[697] and the United States frigates *Cumberland*[698] and the *Congress*.[699] The *Cumberland's* fire upon the *Merrimac* did not disturb her. The ironclad then struck the *Cumberland* amid ships and sunk her immediately. The *Merrimac* then went for the *Congress* and that vessel surrendered and was burned. The Union vessel *Minnesota*[700] endeavored to make her escape but in doing so ran aground. The Union *Monitor*[701] having arrived that evening from New York went immediately to the aid of the *Minnesota.* Next morning the fight was renewed; this time between the two ironclads, the *Merrimac* and the *Monitor* and after a severe fight of about four hours the *Merrimac* retired greatly damaged and the *Monitor* received no injury.

In general nothing is attempted to being given in these pages in relation to the history of the battles fought during the American civil war either by the land or naval forces except to outline briefly the engagements and the results. A more extended history would require greater space than can be here given. The naval engagement between the rebel *Merrimac* and the federal *Monitor*, the two vessels which had justly become the wonder of the world in the sea warfare, however, requires a more extended notice than is accorded to many of the

---

696 General Erasmus Darwin Keyes was a West Pointer from Massachusetts who became chief engineer for the City of St. Louis. He commanded the Union's 4th Corps on the peninsula campaign. The Armies and The Leaders, pgs. 181 & 196.

697 *Merrimac* (also known as *The Virginian)* was a U.S. frigate salvaged from the destruction of the Groton Naval Yards and made into a Confederate ironclad by Commander John M. Brooke. Her commander was 62 year old Franklin Buchanan who served as the first Superintendent of the U.S. Naval Academy. She was 263 feet long with a crew of 320. She had ten guns, two inches of iron plate on the sides and a ram at the bow. On May 11, 1862 she was burned by her crew to prevent her capture by the Union Navy. Southern History of the War, pg. 274, Warships of the Civil War Navies, pg. 202 and Don't Know Much About the Civil War?, pg. 215.

698 *Cumberland* was a Union frigate that was manned by a crew of 400 with 44 guns. She was 175 feet long. Warships of the Civil War Navies, pg. 127.

699 *Congress* was a Union frigate, 179 feet long with 44 guns and a crew of 480. She was destroyed by fire at Hampton Roads on March 8, 1862. Warships of the Civil War Navies, pg. 128.

700 *Minnesota* was a 264 foot long screw frigate with 47 guns, 3 masts, and a crew of 646. She was destroyed by the *Merrimac (Virginian)* on March 8 - 9, 1862 at Hampton Roads. Warships of the Civil War Navies, pg. 28.

701 *Monitor* was the U. S. Navy's most famous ironclad. Built of 3/8 inch double thick iron, the vessel was 140 feet long and 30 feet wide. When afloat, the vessel was a raft with a revolving circular turret, twenty feet in diameter, with two 11-inch guns. Harpers Pictorial History of the Great Rebellion, pgs. 251 and 253.

important contests between the contending armies. These two vessels were respectably terrors to the federal and Confederate navies. It is no exaggeration to state that there was a most formidable Union squadron in Hampton Roads, including the *Minnesota,* then regarded as the most formidable war vessel known in American waters. The *Merrimac* with her superior advantages being ironclad, cooperating with the tremendous Confederate naval forces, the federals met an enemy equally powerful for destruction. Through the wonderful power and terrible execution of the *Merrimac* it is evident that the whole federal fleet and every vessel in Hampton Roads would have been captured or destroyed but for the timely arrival of the *Monitor.* The death and destruction which it dealt saved alike the squadron and the honor of the American flag and secured immortality for the name of the commander[702] and the builder[703] of that wonderful man-of-war. The following account of those vessels and the naval fight in Hampton Roads is taken from the Secretary of Navy Report (Union) of Operations in southeastern Virginia.

*January 11-March 17, 1862*
*Extract from Annual Report of the Secretary of the Navy*[704] *concerning the Battle of the Monitor and the Merrimac*
*DECEMBER 1, 1862.*

*It was the intention and constant effort of the Department and contractors that the Monitor should be completed in the month of January, but there was delay in consequence of difficulties incident to an undertaking of such novelty and magnitude, and there were also some slight defects, which were, however, promptly remedied, and she left New York early in March, reaching Hampton Roads on the night of the 8th.*

*Her arrival, though not as soon as anticipated, was most opportune and important. For some time the Department had heard with great solicitude of the progress which the insurgents had made in armoring and equipping the large war-steamer Merrimac, which had fallen into their hands when Norfolk was abandoned. On the afternoon of the 8th of March this formidable vessel, heavily armored and armed and fully prepared to operate both as a ram and a war steamer, came down the Elizabeth River, accompanied by several smaller steamers,*

---

702 John L. Worden—See pg. 159.

703 Builder of the *Monitor* was John Ericsson a Swedish immigrant. The Civil War a Narrative, pg. 225.

704 The Secretary of the Navy was Giddeon Welles.

*two of them partially armored, to attack the vessels of the blockading squadron that were in and about Hampton Roads. When the Merrimac and her attendants made their appearance the Congress and the Cumberland, two sailing vessels, were anchored off Newport News, and the remaining vessels were in the vicinity of Fortress Monroe, some 6 miles distant. The Minnesota, the Roanoke, and the St. Lawrence got immediately under way and proceeded toward the scene of action.*

*The Congress, being nearest to the Merrimac, was the first to receive her fire, which was promptly returned by a full broadside, the shots falling apparently harmlessly off from the armored side of the assailant. Passing by the Congress, the Merrimac dashed upon the Cumberland, and was received by her with a heavy, well-directed, and vigorous fire, which, like that of the Congress, produced unfortunately but little effect. A contest so unequal could not be of long continuance, and it was closed when the Merrimac, availing herself of her power as a steam ram, ran furiously against the Cumberland, laying open her wooden hull, and causing her almost immediately to sink. As her guns approached the water's edge her young commander, Lieutenant Morris,*[705] *and the gallant crew stood firm at their posts, delivered a parting fire, and the good ship went down heroically, with her colors flying. Having thus destroyed the Cumberland, the Merrimac turned again upon the Congress, which had, in the mean time, been engaged with the smaller rebel steamers, and after a heavy loss, in order to guard against such a fate as that which had befallen the Cumberland, had been run aground. The Merrimac now selected a raking position astern of the Congress, while one of the smaller steamers poured in a constant fire on her starboard quarter. Two other steamers of the enemy also approached from the James River, firing upon the unfortunate frigate with precision and severe effect. The guns of the Congress were almost entirely disabled, and her gallant commanding officer, Lieut. Joseph B. Smith,*[706] *had fallen at his post. Her decks were strewn with the dead and dying, the ship was on fire in several places, and not a gun could be brought to bear upon the assailants. In this state of things, and with no effectual relief at hand, the senior surviving officer, Lieutenant Pendergrast,*[707] *felt it his duty to save further useless destruction of life by hauling down his colors. This was done about 4 o'clock p.m. The Congress continued to burn till about 8 in the evening and then blew up.*

---

[705] Lt. George U. Morris was commanding officer at this battle due to the absence of Captain Wallace Radford. www.history.navy.mil/branches/org/12-6f.htm

[706] Joseph B. Smith was born in Maine and was appointed a midshipman at the Naval Academy in 1847. He died in the loss of the *Congress* in this battle. Search.intelus.com/q/joseph-smith

[707] Lt. Austin Pendergrast wrote the report to Secretary of War Giddeon Welles regarding this battle. www.cssvirginia.org/vacsn3/crew/congress/index.htm

*From the Congress the Merrimac turned her attention to the remaining vessels of the squadron. The Roanoke had grounded on her way to the scene of the conflict; and although she succeeded in getting off, her condition was such, her propeller being useless, that she took no part in the action. The St. Lawrence also grounded near the Minnesota and had a short engagement with the Merrimac, but suffered no serious injury, and on getting afloat was ordered back to Fortress Monroe.*

*The Minnesota, which had also got aground in the shallow waters of the channel, became the special object of attack, and the Merrimac, with the Yorktown and Jamestown, bore down upon her. The Merrimac drew too much water to approach very near; her fire was not therefore particularly effective. The other steamers selected their position, fired with much accuracy, and caused considerable damage to the Minnesota. She soon, however, succeeded in getting a gun to bear on the two smaller steamers and drove them away—one apparently in a crippled condition. About 7 p.m. the Merrimac also hauled off, and the three stood toward Norfolk.*

*All efforts to get the Minnesota afloat during the night and into a safe position were totally unavailing. The morning was looked for with deep anxiety, as it would in all probability bring a renewed attack from the formidable assailant. At this critical and anxious moment the Monitor, one of the newly-finished armored vessels, came into Hampton Roads, from New York, under command of Lieut. John L. Worden, and a little after midnight anchored alongside the Minnesota. At 6 o'clock the next morning the Merrimac, as anticipated, again made her appearance, and opened her fire upon the Minnesota. Promptly obeying the signal to attack, the Monitor ran down past the Minnesota and laid herself close alongside the Merrimac, between that formidable vessel and the Minnesota. The fierce conflict between these two ironclads lasted for several hours. It was in appearance an unequal conflict, for the Merrimac was a large and noble structure, and the Monitor was in comparison almost diminutive. But the Monitor was strong in her armor, in the ingenious novelty of her construction, in the large caliber of her two guns, and the valor and skill with which she was handled. After several hours' fighting the Merrimac found herself overmatched, and, leaving the Monitor, sought to renew the attack on the Minnesota; but the Monitor again placed herself between the two vessels and reopened her fire upon her adversary. At noon the Merrimac, seriously damaged, abandoned the contest and, with her companions, retreated toward Norfolk.*

*Thus terminated the most remarkable naval combat of modern times, perhaps of any age. The fiercest and most formidable naval assault upon the power of the Union which has ever been made by the insurgents was heroically repelled, and a new era was opened in the history of maritime warfare.*

On the 10th Centreville, Virginia was occupied by the United States troops. On this day the rebel Generals Floyd and Pillow were suspended from their commands for misconduct at Fort Donelson by Jefferson Davis. The Union flag was raised by the inhabitants at St. Augustine, Florida,[708] that city and its adjacent fort having surrendered to Commodore DuPont. On the day following Winchester, Virginia[709] was taken and occupied by the Union troops and a lively skirmish ensued on the next day. General Halleck was appointed to command the new Department of the Mississippi which had just been created. On the same day the city of Jacksonville, Florida[710] was occupied by Union forces and General McClellan took possession of Manassas, Virginia.

On the 13th there was a battle at Salem, Arkansas with the Confederates having one thousand men; the federals having two hundred and fifty. The former were defeated with the loss of one hundred men and the federal loss was twenty-five killed and wounded. At New Madrid, Missouri[711] on the 13th General Pope[712] after having placed sunken batteries during the night before mounted with heavy field pieces commenced the attack with his heavy siege guns upon the garrison. The attack was replied to by the Confederates with their heavy guns, both from the land and the fleet. General Pope with his forces continued to close around the garrison until they were in dangerous proximity for both of them. The Confederates, fearing the anticipated assault that was inevitably coming the next morning, fled during the night leaving everything they had. The stores captured were valued at a million dollars. The Union forces captured several thousand stand of small arms, whole batteries of field artillery and twenty-five heavy siege

[708] St. Augustine, Florida is on the Atlantic coast about 50 miles south of Jacksonville.
[709] Winchester, Virginia is at the northern end of the Shenandoah Valley.
[710] Jacksonville, Florida is in the northeast corner of Florida on the Atlantic coast.
[711] New Madrid, Missouri is along the Mississippi River in the southeastern portion of Missouri and about 40 miles downstream from Cairo, Illinois.
[712] General John Pope was an 1842 graduate of West Point a veteran of the Mexican War. From Kentucky, he was a topical engineer in the U.S. Army. His claim to fame is that he was the only Union General to receive the personal ire of General Robert E. Lee due to Pope's handling of secessionist population. General Pope led the Union attacks on Memphis, winning the battle of Shiloh. After asking to be relieved of his command, he fought the Sioux Indians in the West. Lincoln's War, pgs. 141 & 143, The Armies and The Leaders, pgs. 173 & 176 and Appleton's Cyclopaedia of American Biography, Vol. V., pgs. 68 & 69 and www.civilwarhome.com/popebio.html

guns. Besides the artillery and men of the nine boats, the rebel force was estimated at nine thousand men. There were but fifty-one men killed and wounded on the Union side. The next day the battle of New Bern[713] was fought. The Confederates[714] were entrenched behind strong fortifications two miles in extent with a force of ten thousand men, having for their defense a large quantity of field artillery and twenty-one guns in position. One after another their batteries were taken by Union forces and when the last one yielded the Confederates fled precipitately in the direction of Goldsboro,[715] most of them taking the cars[716] in preference to the more common mode of transportation by soldiers from an engagement such as they had just participated in. The federal loss at this battle was about one hundred killed and four hundred wounded.

On the 18th the bombardment of Island No. 10[717] which had been commenced on the 15th was continued and a ship called the *Emily Pierre* while attempting to run the blockade at Charleston harbor was captured. On the same day General Pope at New Madrid permitted a rebel gunboat to approach within fifty yards of one of his masked batteries and then sunk her. He now had five rebel steamers hemmed in by his batteries so that it was impossible for them to make their escape. On the 21st General Burnside entered and occupied Beaufort, South Carolina.[718] On the 22nd there was a battle near Winchester, Virginia in which the federal General Shields was wounded in the arm by a fragment of a shell. The Confederates were driven back but on the next day the very important battle of Kernstown[719] was fought near Winchester. General Shields command numbering ten thousand

---

713 New Bern, North Carolina is located on the Neuse River inland from Cape Hatteras. It was where the Confederates lost three forts (Fort Lane, Fort Thompson, and Fort Ellis) and 50 cannon. Southern History of the War, pg. 294.

714 The Confederates were commanded by General Lawrence O'Bryan Branch. See pg. 62.

715 Goldsboro, North Carolina was sixty miles from New Bern and had the main north-south railroad connection and supply route to Richmond—the Wilmington and Weldon Railroad.

716 Cars refer to train cars

717 Island No. 10 is in the northwestern tip of Tennessee on the Mississippi River. It was named because it is the tenth island below the mouth of the Ohio River. It was fortified with 39 guns. Civil War a Narrative, Part II., pgs. 33 & 34.

718 Beaufort, South Carolina is on the St. Helena Sound near Port Royal and midway between Charlestown and Savannah. It had an important rail connection to Raleigh and Richmond.

719 Kernstown, Virginia is just south of Winchester.

men was attacked by twelve thousand Confederates commanded by General Jackson.[720] After fighting until noon when the Confederates were driven back a half a mile, they rallied and in turn drove the federals back. Both sides fought desperately until three o'clock p.m. General Shields had given orders to turn the left flank of the enemy and it was done successfully. Then the Confederates became panic stricken and fled toward Strasburg. The Union loss was one hundred fifty killed and four hundred fifty wounded. The Confederates loss in killed, wounded and missing was 1,500. On the 26th—28th there was a battle at Apache Canyon[721] known as the battle of Glorietta Pass, New Mexico between twelve hundred Union troops commanded by Col. J. P. Slough[722] and Major Chivington[723] and two thousand troops of the Confederates from the state of Texas who were lying in the bush. Colonel Slough attacked them in front while Major Chivington with his command from Colorado attacked them in the rear. The battle continued until four o'clock in the afternoon when flags of truce were interchanged and the dead were buried and the wounded were cared for. The federal losses were twenty killed, fifty-four wounded and thirty-five prisoners. The Confederate loss was about one hundred fifty killed, two hundred wounded and ninety-three prisoners. The Confederates also lost their entire train consisting of wagons, mules, &c.

## APRIL 1862

On April 2, General McClellan arrived at Fortress Monroe.[724] On the next day the mortar boat fleet disabled the rebel floating battery at

---

720 Thomas J. "Stonewall" Jackson—See pg. 136.

721 Apache Canyon at Glorietta Pass is in New Mexico.

722 Colonel John P. Slough was a thirty-three year old lawyer from Colorado who commanded the 1st New Mexico Volunteers and the 2nd Colorado Volunteers, including several Union cavalry and infantry units. Smithsonian's Great Battles and Battlefields of the Civil War, pgs. 90 & 91 and The Armies and The Leaders, pg. 195.

723 Major John M. Chivington commanded a unit made up of volunteer from California, New Mexico and Colorado who saw action at Apache Pass in Indian Territory. Smithsonian's Great Battles and Battlefields of the Civil War, pgs. 79 & 90.

724 General McClellan arrived with 100,000 men, 15,000 horses and mules, 1224 wagons, 44 artillery batteries and supplies. The Sword of Lincoln, pg. 66.

Island No. 10. On the 5th the federal gunboat *Carondelet*[725] ran the batteries at Island No. 10 and arrived at New Madrid in safety. General McClellan in his march of the peninsula with his command reached Yorktown, Virginia on this day.

Perhaps no battle of the American civil war caused as great as amount of comment, criticism and speculation as the battle of Shiloh.[726] What the comment, criticism and speculation were is not our purpose to record or deal with. It is the intention to only give a succinct statement of the history and facts in regard to this and other battles of the war as the writer understands them. This battle was commenced on the 5th of April. The Confederate forces under Generals Beauregard and Johnston[727] numbered 45,000 men, with the federals having 35,000 men under the command of General Grant.[728] The battle raced furiously all day. The Union army was at length driven back to the river with the loss of 3,500 men, thirty pieces of artillery and a great amount of camp equipage.[729] Union General Prentiss[730] was taken prisoner. The gunboats operating on the rebel right wing saved the federal army from total defeat and annihilation. Confederate General Sidney Johnston, one of the most distinguished military men of the age, was killed. On the night following General Buell with his Union army from Nashville arrived and crossed over the river to the aid of General Grant. The engagement began again early the next morning. The Confederates were soon checked and the entire battle was turned in favor of the federals. On the advance of the Union lines en masse the Confederates were forced back and put in rapid motion, pursued by General Sherman[731] and his command. On this day

---

[725] *Carondelet* was a Cairo Class Union river ironclad commanded by Henry Walke. The ship was 175 feet long, had 14 guns and a crew of 251. Warships of the Civil War Navies, pg. 151.

[726] Shiloh gets its name from a little church, Shiloh Chapel. It is located on the Tennessee River in southern Tennessee about 75 miles east of Memphis.

[727] General Albert Sidney Johnston—See pg. 149.

[728] This was the largest battle in the war up to this point. Civil War a Narrative, Part II., pg. 76.

[729] Equipage is furniture for the army.

[730] General Benjamin M. Prentiss was a Virginia native and an Illinois lawyer. He was commander of one of the Union divisions under General Grant in Tennessee. He is the general who is known for saving General Grant at Shiloh. The Civil War a Narrative, pg. 603 and Civil War a Narrative, Part II., pgs. 52 & 71.

[731] General William Tecumseh Sherman—See pg. 160.

Brigadier General W. H. L. Wallace[732] of Ottawa, Illinois was killed. He was a distinguished lawyer and intimate personal friend of Mr. Lincoln. When the news came of the death of General Wallace, Mr. Lincoln was affected to tears. He remarked that the victory gained in this battle however gratifying was but silent compensation for the loss of poor General Wallace and other noble men who fell in this struggle. The Union loss in this battle was 1,614 killed, 7,721 wounded and 3,963 prisoners and missing. The Confederates left 3,000 dead and wounded on the field but their entire loss was 1,723 killed, 8,012 wounded and 959 missing.

On the same day under cover of gunboats a Union detachment crossed the river at New Madrid shortly after the Union divisions of Generals Hamilton,[733] Paine,[734] Stanley[735] and Granger[736] crossed and prepared to attack Island No. 10 fortifications in the rear. The garrison at the island was bombarded for twenty-three days and when the Confederate command realized the fact that it was completely surrounded, surrendered to Commodore Foote. Many of the men of the garrison escaped to the main land. There were taken five hundred and sixty prisoners besides seventeen officers and a quarter a million dollars worth of property. After this General Pope stopped the retreat of the escaping Confederate forces and compelled them to surrender

---

[732] Brigadier General W. H. L. Wallace commanded a division of Grant's Union army in Tennessee. Civil War a Narrative, Part II., pgs. 50 & 52 and The Armies and The Leaders, pg. 133.

[733] General Charles S. Hamilton was from Wisconsin. He commanded a Union division at Corinth. The Armies and The Leaders, pg. 309.

[734] General Halbert E. Paine was from Wisconsin and was the only officer in General Bank's army who had not attended West Point. He commanded a division at Port Hudson where he was badly wounded on June 1863. The Civil War a Narrative, pgs. 394 & 402 and The Armies and The Leaders, pg. 309.

[735] General David Sloan Stanley was an Ohio native and a graduate of the Class of 1852 of West Point. He served in the Indian Territory and dealt with most every Indian tribe from the Mississippi River to the Rio Grande valley. He was the commander of the 4th Corps of Sherman's Army. He was chief of the Cavalry Corps of the Cumberland. He was severely wounded at Franklin, Tennessee on November 20, 1864. Appleton's Cyclopaedia of American Biography, Vol. V., pgs. 644 & 645 and The Armies and The Leaders, pgs. 93, 196 & 237.

[736] General Gordon Granger was from New York. He was an 1845 graduate of the U.S. Military Academy. He served in both the Seminole and Mexican Wars. He was cited for bravery during the Mexican War. He served on General McClellan's staff of the Army of the Potomac. He was the Union commander of the Army of Kentucky and later commanded the 4th Corps. Appleton's Cyclopaedia of American Biography, Vol. II., pg. 706, and The Armies and The Leaders, pgs. 175 & 182.

to him including four generals besides two hundred thirty-three other officers, six thousand privates, ten thousand stands of arms, two thousand horses and mules, one thousand wagons and $40,000 worth of provisions. On the day following great rejoicing on account of the reduction of this stronghold for Confederate protection and a single victory of the federal army over the enemy was manifested in the North. On the 10th Mr. Lincoln recommended the people on the next day of worship to offer thanks to almighty God for the recent victory.

On the next day April 11th Fort Pulaski[737] was bombarded by Union forces during the entire day. During the night four new batteries were planted which in the morning did great execution. The bombardment was vigorously kept up until two o'clock in the afternoon when the fort was surrendered. Three hundred eighty-five prisoners were taken with the fort. The loss in men killed and wounded was not great on either side. Forty-seven guns and a large quantity of ammunition were captured. On the same day Union General Mitchell[738] with his command took Huntsville, Alabama[739] and greatly surprised the people in it. He captured seventeen railroad locomotives, one hundred fifty cars and one hundred seventy prisoners. From Huntsville then there was sent an expedition to Stevenson[740] on the Memphis and Charleston Railroad where he captured two thousand prisoners and a large amount of rolling stock including five locomotive engines. On the 13th the rebel schooner *Selma*[741] with a great amount of rebel mail on its way to Baltimore was

---

737 Fort Pulaski was a brick pentagon shaped fort on Cockspur Island that guarded the mouth of the Savannah River. It is located along the Atlantic cost in the northeast corner of Georgia. Civil War a Narrative, Part II., pg. 78.

738 General Ormsby McKnight Mitchell was from Kentucky and graduated in the West Point class (1829) as Robert E. Lee and Joseph Johnson. He was an assistant professor of math at West Point. He led one of Buell's Union divisions. He helped drive the Confederates out of eastern Tennessee. Later Mitchell commanded the Union's 10th Corps. He was captured at Huntersville. He died of yellow fever in October 1862. Civil War a Narrative, Part II., pg. 103, Harpers Pictorial History of the Great Rebellion, pg. 238, and The Armies and The Leaders, pgs. 187 & 210.

739 Huntsville, Alabama is located in the northern part of the state along the Tennessee River.

740 Stevenson, Alabama is in the northeastern corner of the state just south of Chattanooga, Tennessee.

741 *Selma* was a 252 foot long Union side wheeler schooner carrying 55 men with four guns. She was originally a Confederate vessel, captured and converted to use by the federal navy near Fort Morgan in Mobile Bay on August 5, 1864. Warships of the Civil War Navies, pg. 86.

captured. The blockade was considered ineffective up to this date, April 13, 1862. Fifty-eight vessels had run the blockade into southern ports. How many had run out to sea is not known. On the 14th the Secretary of War Simon Cameron was arrested at the suit of Pierce Butler[742] for false imprisonment. On the 15th the president signed a bill passed by Congress abolishing slavery in the District of Columbia.[743]

On the 18th the town of Fredericksburg, Virginia surrendered to Union General Augur.[744] On the same day the Forts Jackson and St. Philip[745] below New Orleans on the Mississippi River were bombarded by the national fleet[746] under Commodore Farragut.[747] The bombardment was continued for six days when Commodore Farragut decided to run his fleet past the forts. It was done successfully but afterwards he met the rebel fleet and a desperate fight ensued in which he had one of his vessels sunk, but destroyed thirteen rebel gunboats and three of their transports. The Union fleet then came to anchor within thirty miles of the city of New Orleans. The Confederate's loss was one hundred eighty-five killed, one hundred ninety-seven wounded and four hundred prisoners. The Union loss was thirty killed and one hundred ten wounded. On the following day Commodore Farragut commanded the city of New Orleans to surrender. Forts on Lake Poncharitrain in the rear of the city were evacuated. The

---

742 Pierce Butler was a South Carolina man by birth but lived in Philadelphia. He was pro secession. He sued for false imprisonment, trespass, and assault and battery. The charges were later dropped. www.hti.umich.edu/cgi/t/text/text-idx?c=lincoln;tgn=div1;view=text;idno=lincoln5;hode=lincoln5%3a342

743 Mr. Lincoln had introduced a referendum in 1849 when he was a Congressman. The proposal called for the elimination of slavery in the District of Columbia. The proposal did not get the support it needed to be adopted. Lincoln's Emancipation, pg. 82.

744 General Christopher Colon Augur was from New York, He was a 1839 graduate of the U.S. Military Academy and was a veteran from the Mexican War. He commanded twenty-two Union regiments at Port Hudson and also later commanded the garrisons surrounding Washington, D.C. The Armies and The Leaders, pgs. 193 & 230 and Grant Takes Command, pg. 313.

745 Forts Jackson and St. Philip were forts located seventy-five miles south of New Orleans on the Mississippi River. For Jackson had 74 guns. Fort St. Philip had 52 guns. Civil War a Narrative, Part II., pgs. 80 & 90.

746 The national fleet was a Union naval force of 18 warships, seven screw sloops, and nine gunboats with armaments totaling 243 guns that took part in the bombardment of New Orleans. Civil War a Narrative, Part II., pg. 84.

747 Admiral David Glasgow Farragut was a native of Knoxville, Tennessee. He had over fifty years of naval service as he started on the *Essex* in the War of 1812 at age 9. Civil War a Narrative, Part II., pg. 84

Confederate General Lovell[748] who had been in command of that city with twenty thousand troops had evacuated it. Union batteries were planted near Fort Macon and a bombardment of that fort was commenced in conjunction with the federal troops which lasted pretty much through the day. On the following day the fort surrendered to General Burnside and Commodore Lockwood.[749]

The same day Mr. Lincoln visited the French frigate *Cassender* in the Washington harbor. This was a respect shown to such a vessel unknown to the established legacy of American presidents. It was the first time a President of the United States had gone on board to visit a foreign man-of-war. He was received and entertained with the same honors paid to the Emperor of France.[750] Forts Philip and Jackson on the 28th being cut off from supplies and surrounded by the enemy surrendered to Commodore Porter[751] commanding the mortar fleet. On the 29th there was a fight between the rebel General Kirby Smith[752] and the Union General Mitchell at Bridgeport, Alabama[753] which resulted in favor of the federals with a loss to the Confederates of seventy-two killed and three hundred fifty prisoners.

---

748 General Mansfield Lovell was a Maryland native who went to West Point and then became the Street Commissioner for the City of New York. He was sent by the Confederate command to New Orleans to replace General Twiggs and assigned command of the Lower Mississippi. Civil War a Narrative, Part II., pg. 86 and The Armies and The Leaders, pg. 273.

749 Commodore Samuel Lockwood attempted to shell the fort from his fleet but the storm and high waves prohibited shells from the ships reaching the fort. thomaslegion.net/battle_of_fort_macon_history.html

750 Napoleon III, also known as Louis Napoleon, was emperor of France from 1852-1870. www.answers.com/topic/louis-bonaparte

751 Commodore William D. Porter was the son of Admiral David Porter and the foster brother of Admiral Farragut. He had retired from the U.S. Navy but returned during the Civil War to command the mortar fleet. www.history.navy.mil/photos/pers-us/uspers-p/wd-portr.htm.

752 General Edmund Kirby Smith was born in Florida and was a graduate of the U.S Military Academy Class of 1845. He fought in the Mexican and Indian Wars. He was the Confederate commanding officer of an area known as the Trans-Mississippi and included five western states and then the Army of East Tennessee and the Army of Kentucky at Chickahominy. Grant Takes Command, pg. 10, Civil War a Narrative, Part VII., pg. 28. Civil War a Narrative, Part II., pg. 138, Pride of the South, pgs. 115 & 116 and The Armies and The Leaders, pgs. 243 & 258.

753 Bridgeport, Alabama is about ten miles north of Stevenson in the northeast corner of Alabama.

## MAY 1862

On May 1, the United States steamer *Mercedita*[754] captured the Confederate schooner *Bermuda.* The next day the port of New Orleans was opened to commerce. The day following Yorktown, Virginia was evacuated by the Confederates. They left all their heavy guns, camp equipage &c. and the town was occupied by General McClellan. On the same day a British steamer *The Circassian*[755] was captured by the federal gunboat *Summerset* having on board a cargo valued at five hundred thousand dollars. The battle of Williamsburg[756] was fought on the 5th of May. The rear of the Confederate army was overtaken by General McClellan's forces and fighting commenced which lasted all day, waged on both sides with terrible affect. In the evening General Hancock[757] turned the Confederates left which caused them to stampede. During the night they retreated. The federal loss was 2,249. The Confederate loss was 1,703. On the next day General McClellan occupied the town. On the 7th General McClellan drove the Confederates across the Chickahominy River[758] and reached a point within thirty-three miles of Richmond. The next day Generals Schenk[759] and Milroy with a large force of troops attacked 14,000 Confederates under the command of General Jackson at McDowell,

---

754 *Mercedita* was a wooden hulled Union three mast schooner. She was 195 in length, with nine guns and a crew of 121. Warships of the Civil War Navies, pgs. 92 & 93.

755 *The Circassian* was a 255 foot three mast iron hull Union ship carrying a crew of 142 and having six guns. Originally a Confederate blockade runner captured by the federals, she was determined to be too slow and was used as a supply ship by the Union Navy. Warships of the Civil War Navies, pg. 110.

756 Williamsburg, Virginia is on the James River about 50 miles upstream from Norfolk.

757 General Winfield Scott Hancock was from Pennsylvania and an 1844 graduate of the U.S. Military Academy. He served in the Mexican War. He was wounded at Gettysburg but returned to serve again. He was active in both the Mexican War and the border troubles in Kansas. He was the commander of the 2nd Corps, taking over command in place of General Meade. He was severely wounded at Gettysburg. He commanded a corps longer than any Union general. He also ran for President against James Garfield. Grant Takes Command, pg. 331, The Armies and The Leaders, pgs. 190 & 192 and
www.civilwarhome.com/hanbio.htm

758 Chickahominy River is a tributary to the James River near Richmond, Virginia. Civil War a Narrative, Part II., inside back cover.

759 General Robert Schenk—See pgs. 129 & 130.

Virginia.[760] The federals were forced to fall back and retired to Franklin[761] which they did in good order. It was not definitely known what the Confederate loss was, yet it was heavy. The federal loss was about two hundred fifty killed and wounded. On the 9th of the month Pensacola, Florida was evacuated by the Confederates and the forts, navy yards, barracks, and marine hospital were by them set fire. On the 9th General McClellan was thanked by Congress. The battle of Farmington, Mississippi[762] was fought with General Bragg[763] in command. During the fight he was heavily reinforced. Colonel Payne[764] commanded the Union troops and deemed it prudent to retired across the Tennessee River. The Union loss in killed and wounded was one hundred eighty men and the Confederate loss was about one hundred twenty. On the next day General McClellan's advance occupied the white house on the Pamunky River.[765] This became a very important point afterwards in a military point of view. On this day General Butler's Union forces seized $800,000 in specie at the consulate of the Netherlands at New Orleans.

General David Hunter on the 9th day of May, tried this experiment of liberating and declaring the slaves free in the department under his command consisting of the states of South Carolina, Georgia and Florida and without consulting the chief executive. This action of General Hunter greatly astonished Mr. Lincoln. On May 11th the

---

[760] McDowell, Virginia is in the Shenandoah Valley about 25 miles northwest of Staunton.

[761] Franklin is just north of McDowell and about 25 miles into what is now West Virginia.

[762] Farmington, Mississippi is in the northeast corner of Mississippi just a few miles from Corinth.

[763] General Braxton Bragg was a North Carolina planter who was a graduate from the U.S. Military Academy Class of 1837. He served in both the Mexican and Seminole Wars. He defeated General Rosencrans at Chickamauga. He was the commander in chief of the Confederate army at Richmond. He also served as chief of staff of General Beauregard. After the war he was chief engineer for the state of Alabama. Civil War a Narrative, pg. 957, Civil War a Narrative, Part II., pg. 51, The Pride of the South, pgs. 70—73, and The Armies and The Leaders, pgs. 243 & 262.

[764] Colonel Oliver Hazard Payne was a graduate of Yale class of 1832. He organized Company F of the 64th Illinois Infantry. www.64thill.org/patritismillinois.htm and www.academic2.martist.edu/fox/esopus/esopo42.htm.

[765] Pamunky River is north of Richmond and flows into the James River. Civil War a Narrative, Part II., inside back cover.

commander[766] of the ironclad *Merrimac* blew her up off Crany Island, Virginia.[767] On the 13th at Charleston the rebel armed steamer *Planter*[768] was run out of the harbor by the colored pilot[769] and crew and presented to the federal steamer *Augusta.*[770] On the same day General Butler prohibited the observance of a fast day ordered and appointed by Jefferson Davis. It was not that General Butler objected to fasting, humiliation and prayer but he thought the less Mr. Davis had to do with a sacred matter the better it would be for the souls of the people. On the 17th, Bottom Bridge,[771] fifteen miles from Richmond, Virginia was reached by the advance of the Army of the Potomac. On the 19th John T. Monroe,[772] Mayor of New Orleans was arrested by order of General Butler and sent to Fort Jackson.

On the 19th of the same month, Mr. Lincoln issued a public announcement rescinding the proclamation of General Hunter[773] without any conference with General Hunter on the subject whatsoever. In this instrument Mr. Lincoln took occasion to use very expressive and emphatic language in defining the powers of general officers in the field to meddle with questions so totally different from police regulations, from armies and camps. Mr. Lincoln distinctly stated that neither General Hunter nor any other commander or person had been authorized by the government of the United States to make proclamations declaring slaves in any of the states free and that the supposed proclamation now in question whether genuine or false, was void so far as respects to such declarations. He went on further to

---

766 John M. Brooke was her commander. She was destroyed to avoid capture thereby not allowing the Union to convert her into a Union naval vessel. Warships of the Civil War Navies, pg. 202.

767 Crany Island, Virginia is an island in the James River.

768 *Planter* was a 147 foot long Confederate side wheeler. Warships of the Civil War Navies, pgs. 86 & 241.

769 The colored man who stole the ship from the harbor was Robert Small. Warships of the Civil War Navies, pg. 241.

770 *Augusta* was a 220 foot long large Union combatant with a wooden hull and three masts. She had a side wheel, a crew of 157 and nine guns. She was part of the fleet that occupied Port Royal and Beaufort and took two rebel ships captive. Warships of the Civil War Navies, pg. 69.

771 Bottom Bridge crosses the Chickahominy River east of Richmond. Civil War a Narrative, Part II., pg. 225.

772 John T. Monroe was Mayor of New Orleans from June 1860 - May 1862 and May 1866 - March 1867. nutrius.org/~nopl/info/louinfo/admins/Monroe.htm

773 Proclamation by General David Hunter on previous page—to free all the slaves in his district.

say: "I further make known that whether it be competent for me as Commander in Chief of the army and navy to declare the slaves of any state or states free, and whether in any time in any case it shall have become a necessity indispensable to the maintenance of the government to exercise such supposed power, are questions which under my responsibility I reserve to myself and which I cannot feel justified in leaving to the discretion of a commander in the field." The general officers were more careful after this in coming to the front as liberators of the slaves.

General B. F. Butler, commanding in Virginia, did not go as far at this time as General Frémont had in declaring slaves free, but he declared them contraband of war, and liable to confiscation, by military law, which proved to be one of the most effective orders ever issued in the field by a military officer. To the policy promulgated,[774] adopted and resulting from this course for the ultimate extinguishment of slavery in the South was made plain and was the auxiliary and forerunner of President Lincoln's proclamation of emancipation issued in January, 1863.

On the 22nd a portion of General McClellan's Army of the Potomac crossed the Chickahominy at New Bridge and Bottom Bridge.[775] On the next day the Union General Kenly[776] commanding at Front Royal, Virginia[777] was driven out by a large force of rebels under General Ewell.[778] General Kenly's loss was very heavy. On the day following the advance of General McClellan's army under General Stoneman[779] went to Mechanicsville, five miles from Richmond.

---

774 Promulgated means declared.

775 New Bridge is near Savage Mill, Virginia and crosses over the Chickahominy River east of Richmond. Civil War a Narrative, Part II., pg. 225.

776 General John R. Kenly was from Maryland and led the 1st Maryland Regiment. The Armies and The Leaders, pg. 211.

777 Front Royal, Virginia is in the Shenandoah Valley just southeast of Winchester.

778 General Richard Stoddert Ewell was a 45 year old District of Columbia native who was a U.S. Military Academy graduate and a veteran of the Mexican War. He served under General "Stonewall" Jackson during the Shenandoah Campaign. He commanded part of Jackson's Confederate army. He fought for three years on a wooden leg lost at Groveton. The Armies and The Leaders, pgs. 245 & 248, Civil War a Narrative, pg. 434, Pride of the South, pgs. 14 & 15, and Civil War a Narrative, Part II., pgs. 157 & 178.

779 General George Stoneman was from New York and an 1846 graduate of the U.S. Military Academy. He was commander of Fort Brown in Texas when the civil war started . He succeeded Major General Heintzelman as commander of the Union's 3rd Corps and later led the Cavalry Corps and 23rd Army Corps. He was the commander

Another British steamer *The Settin* was captured while attempting to run the blockade at Charleston. On the same day the steamer *Swan*[780] was captured by the United States brig *Brainbridge*[781] off the coast of Cuba. It was today ascertained that the expense of the United States army was one million dollars a day from the first of April. Today there were 800 men sent to the relief of General Kenly. All of the men but 150 were captured by the Confederates.

On the 25th Generals Jackson and Ewell with 15,000 men again attacked General Banks with a force of 4,000 men at Winchester and forced him back through Martinsburg[782] and across the Potomac River into Maryland. At this time great concern was felt for the safety of the capital of Washington and on the 20th the 7th New York Militia left New York for that city in answer to a call to defend it. On this day General Banks with his command reached Williamsport, Maryland.[783] He had marched thirty-five miles that day. A desperate march was necessary for the safety of himself and his command. He lost fifty of his wagons. On the same day another British blockade runner the *Paris* laden with ordinance and medical stores for the Confederacy was captured off Charleston. At Hanover[784] General Fitz John Porter[785] defeated the Confederates, killing one hundred men and capturing five hundred prisoners. On the 28th the rebel schooner *Angus H. Ward* was captured by the steamer *Northern Light.* General Butler arrested Pierre

---

of one of the two the cavalry corps in General Sherman's March to the Sea. After the war he served as Governor of California from 1883-1887. Lincoln's War, pg. 239, Civil War a Narrative, Part VII., pg. 352, Grant Takes Command, pg. 407 and The Armies and The Leaders, pg. 194.

780 *Swan* was a Confederate steamer and blockade runner. Warships of the Civil War Navies, pg. 237.

781 *Brainbridge* was a 100 foot long Union brig with ten guns. She took three prize ships before her capture off of Cape Hatteras on August 21, 1863. Warships of the Civil War Navies, pg. 134.

782 Martinsburg, Virginia (today West Virginia).

783 Williamsport, Maryland is in western Maryland near Hagerstown and was the place where the Confederates crossed the Potomac River going to and coming from Gettysburg, Pennsylvania.

784 Hanover, Pennsylvania is in southern Pennsylvania just 12 miles east of Gettysburg.

785 General Fitz John Porter was a West Point grad and a veteran soldier from the Mexican War. He was also an instructor at West Point. He was General McClellan's most trusted subordinate during the Peninsula Campaign. He commanded the 5th Corps of the Union army at Chickahominy. He served on the staffs of both Generals Banks and Patterson. He was court-marshaled during the war but his commission was later restored. Civil War a Narrative, pg. 726, The Armies and The Leaders, pgs. 183 & 198, The Sword of Lincoln, pg. 72 and Civil War a Narrative, Part II., pg. 143

Soule[786] in New Orleans. General Banks was reinforced. On the next day another British blockade runner the *Elizabeth* was captured at Charleston by the federal gunboat *Keystone State*. On the 30th General Halleck occupied Corinth.[787] On that day another English ironclad steamer *The Cambria* was taken as a prize by the federal gunboat *Huron*.[788] She was also loaded with war materials for the Confederacy. The rebel schooner *Cora* was also captured off Charleston by the *Keystone State*.

The commencement of the fight for Richmond began on the 31st of May as the Union advance had crossed the river at Fair Oaks[789] and Seven Pines[790] and were attacked by the Confederate forces of General Joe Johnston. The division commanded by the federal General Casey[791] was soon overpowered and were forced to fall back. General Couch's division[792] came to his rescue and checked the Confederate advance. The fight then became desperate and continued until it was stopped by the darkness of the night.

## JUNE 1862

On June 1, at Fair Oaks, the battle was renewed in the morning and was continued with cessation until night when the Confederates lost the ground they had gained and were driven back towards Richmond. In this battle the federals lost 4,384 in killed and wounded

---

[786] Pierre Soule was a U.S. politician and diplomat most noted for the Ostend Manifesto in 1854 which was an attempt to annex Cuba. He was imprisoned as a southern supporter but later escaped. www.answers.com/topic/ostend-manifesto

[787] Corinth is in northeastern part of Mississippi and was a railroad hub.

[788] *The Huron* was a 158 foot long Union Unadilla Class screw gunboat with a crew of 114 and 6 guns. During the war she was able to capture seven enemy vessels. Warships of the Civil War Navies, pgs. 49 -52.

[789] Fair Oaks, Virginia is just east of Richmond along the York River Railroad. Civil War a Narrative, Part II., pg. 171.

[790] Seven Pines is just south of Fair Oaks along the Nine Mile Road. Civil War a Narrative, Part II, pg. 171.

[791] General Silas Casey was a U.S. Military Academy graduate and a veteran of both the Seminole and Mexican wars. He commanded a division of the Second Corps in the Army of the Potomac. www.historyantral.com/bio/UGENS/USACasey.html

[792] General Darvius Nash Couch was a senior corps commander for the federal army. He was from New York and served in the Mexican War and Seminole War. He commanded the II Corps at both Fredericksburg and Chancellorsville. He also led a division of the 23rd Corps at Nashville in 1863. Civil War a Narrative, pg. 250 and The Armies and The Leaders, pgs. 179 & 190.

besides 647 missing. The Confederates lost eighteen general officers and 6,100 men, killed, wounded and missing. They left 1,200 of their dead on the field to be buried by the enemy.

On the 2nd General Hunter's force whose objective point was Charleston, South Carolina landed with safety without opposition on James Island.[793] The forces under Generals Jackson and Frémont respectively met at Strasburg, Virginia[794] and had an engagement in which General Jackson was defeated. On the 3rd General Robert E. Lee[795] was placed in command of the Confederate forces at Richmond. General Pope with 40,000 Union soldiers was thirty miles south of Florence, Alabama in pursuit of the retreating forces of the Confederacy. He had captured 10,000 prisoners, 15,000 stand of arms and nine locomotives. On this day the Confederates paroled 16,000 federal prisoners taken at Shiloh on account of being unable to feed them. They reported at Nashville, Tennessee. Memphis, Tennessee was surrendered to federal forces on the 6th after a brilliant naval fight near that city between the Confederate and federal troops. On the 7th William Mumford[796] was hung at New Orleans for hauling down the American flag that had been flying over the United States Mint after the surrender of that city.

On the 8th Stonewall Jackson attacked General Frémont at Cross Keys, Virginia[797] ten miles from Harrisonburg. A severe fight ensued at the end of which General Jackson and his command was forced to retreat. The Union loss was about six hundred killed and wounded. The Confederate loss is unknown. General Ashby,[798] a dashing Confederate cavalry general, was killed in this engagement. On the 16th another fight occurred on James Island at Secessionville, South Carolina[799] when the Union troops were repulsed with a loss of over

---

[793] James Island is immediately south of Charleston, South Carolina and on the south side of the Charleston harbor.

[794] Strasburg, Virginia is in the Shenandoah Valley just south of Winchester.

[795] Robert E. Lee—See pg. 119.

[796] William Bruce Mumford was born in North Carolina and lived in New Orleans. www.absoluteastronomy.com/topics/New_Orleans_Mint

[797] Cross Keys, Virginia is in the Shenandoah Valley just east of Harrisonburg. Civil War a Narrative, Part II, inside back cover.

[798] General Turner Ashby was a legendary Confederate horsemen from Virginia. His men were known as "the Mountain Rangers." Southern History of the War, pgs. 396 - 398.

[799] Secessionville, South Carolina is south of Charleston on the Atlantic coast. Civil War a Narrative, Part II., inside back cover.

500 men. The battle of Oak Grove was fought on the 25th of June. This battle was fought by General Hooker's division[800] of the Army of the Potomac and lasted seven hours, when the Confederates were driven back. The Union loss in killed and wounded and missing was about 500. The Confederate loss was supposed to be about the same number. On this day all the property of the rebel General David E. Twiggs,[801] formerly of the Unites States Army and now a Confederate General, was confiscated by order of General Butler at New Orleans. The next day the rebel batteries at Vicksburg[802] were shelled by Admiral Porter's mortar fleet.[803] On the same day the commands of Generals Banks, McDowell[804] and Frémont were consolidated in one army corps under the command of General Pope. On this day the battle of Mechanicsville[805] near Richmond was fought. It lasted throughout the day. It was thought to be one of the most terrific engagements that were fought during the war. General Lee commanded the Confederate forces in person and first attacked General McCall's division.[806] The battle lasted until night but was not renewed again. Federal loss in killed and wounded was 256 with the rebel loss reported at 1,484.

On the 27th the Union fleet renewed its bombardment of Vicksburg. General Frémont requested that he be relieved of his command which was granted. On this day the battle of Gaines Mill[807] was fought. The Confederates attacked the Union forces with greatly superior numbers. Both sides fought gallantly until night closed the battle. The federals were forced across the river to the south side. There was great loss on both sides. The Union losses included 284 dead with the

---

800 Joseph Hooker was from Massachusetts. He was an 1857 graduate of West Point and a veteran of the Mexican War. His nickname was "fighting Joe." He was a Union Commander wounded at Gettysburg. Legend has it that his name became associated with prostitutes (called "hookers") when he rounded them up in Washington. *Harpers Weekly*, July 5, 1862 and www.militarymuseum.org/hooker.html

801 David E. Twiggs—See pg. 151.

802 Vicksburg, Mississippi is in the western part of the state, along the Mississippi River and was a strategic point on the river.

803 Admiral David Dixon Porter was commander of the mortar_flotilla under Admiral Farragut. www.arlingtoncemetery.net/ddporter.htm

804 General Irvin McDowell—See pg. 137.

805 Mechanicsville is just a few miles northeast of Richmond along the Chickahominy River.

806 General George A. McCall –See pg. 141.

807 Gaines Mill, Virginia is just northeast of Richmond along the Chickahominy River. Civil War a Narrative, Part II., pg. 225.

wounded and missing numbering almost 6,000. The federals lost several thousand prisoners in this battle. Total Confederate dead, wounded and missing totaled 8,751. On the 28th was fought the battle of Chickahominy, Virginia.[808] The brunt of this battle was borne by the corps commanded by General Fitz John Porter. The battle of Peach Orchard[809] and Savage Station[810] followed the next day without victory to either side. The battle of White Oak Swamp[811] followed with like results. On the 30th John W. Andrews[812] an indiscreet citizen of New Orleans was arrested by General Butler for publicly showing a cross he possessed and boasting that it was made out of the bones of a Yankee soldier. He was ordered to be confined at hard labor on the fortifications for two years, kept in close confinement at Ship Island and allowed no communication with anyone. General Butler on the same day also arrested Mrs. Phillips[813] and Fidel Keller[814] for like offensives, wicked sentiments expressed by them openly.

The aggregate losses June 15th through July 1st in what was known as the Seven Days battle was 15,849 Union and 20,614 Confederate.

---

[808] Chickahominy, Virginia is the river east of Richmond where much of the Seven Days battle took place.

[809] Peach Orchard is east of Richmond and south of the Chickahominy River. Civil War a Narrative, Part 11., pg. 225.

[810] Savage Station is east of Richmond and south of the Chickahominy River. Civil War a Narrative, Part II., pg. 225.

[811] White Oak Swamp is just southeast of Richmond and south of the Chickahominy River. Civil War a Narrative, Part II., pg. 225.

[812] John W. Andrews exhibited a religious cross made of bones of a Yankee soldier. He was sentenced to two years of hard labor at Ship Island. www.simmonsgames.com/research/authors/USward??/ORA/OR-S2-V4U.html and www.civilwar.bluegrass.net/officersandenlistedmen/benjaminfranklinbutler.html

[813] Mrs. Phillips, the wife of Phillip Phillips, was arrested and held on Ship Island for more than two months for laughing at the funeral of a Union officer as it passed her house. www.simmonsgames.com/research/authors/USward??/ORA/OR-S2-V4U.html and www.civilwar.bluegrass.net/officersandenlistedmen/benjaminfranklinbutler.html

[814] Fidel Keller reportedly exhibited bones in his store window labeled "Chickahominy" intending that the public to be the bones of a Yankee soldier. He was sentenced to two years of hard labor at Ship Island. www.simmonsgames.com/research/authors/USward??/ORA/OR-S2-V4U.html and www.civilwar.bluegrass.net/officersandenlistedmen/benjaminfranklinbutler.html

## JULY 1862

The battle of Malvern Hill[815] took place on the 1st of July, 1862. Under cover of the gunboats the federal army took a position on Malvern Hill and at once the whole Confederate army in range attacked them. The conflict lasted until dark when the Confederates were repulsed. The aggregate Union loss in the battles near this point is estimated at 724 killed, 4,245 wounded and 3,067 missing—the sum total of 8,036 men. The Confederate loss is supposed to be in all 9,477 men. The battle of Booneville, Mississippi[816] was fought on the same day. It continued throughout the day under General Sheridan[817] of the 2nd Michigan Cavalry. A body of infantry fought and defeated 4,700 Confederates after a terrible struggle. On this day President Lincoln made another call for 200,000 more troops. On the same day the swords of General Twiggs which had been presented to him by Congress for gallant services during the Mexican War were seized by General Butler in New Orleans and sent to Washington where they are now deposited in the archives of the government. At this juncture the inactive movements on the York Peninsula of the army under the command of General McClellan and the reverses and repulses of the army before Richmond began to dishearten the whole country and greatly annoy Mr. Lincoln who was held responsible for all the failures by the people not in accord with him in his efforts, and particularly the ambitious politicians of his own party who had a single eye to his succession to themselves or their chosen friends.

When Mr. Cameron resigned his portfolio of the War Department the change brought the hostility of Secretary Stanton to General McClellan who was then general-in-chief of the United States Army. Mr. Lincoln's admiration of General McClellan whose wondrous talent was displayed to such advantage in the summer of 1861 when he took command at Washington in enforcing order and proper military discipline and administration, was not in the main weakened. In many respects Mr. Lincoln regarded General McClellan greatly superior to

---

815 Malvern Hill is southeast of Richmond along the James River. Civil War a Narrative, Part II., pg. 225.

816 Booneville, Mississippi is in the northeast corner of the state between Corinth and Tupelo.

817 General Phillip H. Sheridan was born in New York and was an 1853 graduate of the U.S. Military Academy. He led the Shenandoah Campaign for General Grant with the goal to "lay waste the Valley." www.civilwarhome.com/sheridanbio.htm

any other military man with whom he had come in contact. The general's hesitation and want of dash lessened Mr. Lincoln's confidence in the general's efficiency in this emergency. Mr. Lincoln had lost no confidence however in the superior military capacity and great intelligence. What he found fault mostly for was that General McClellan was never quite ready to strike a blow at the right time, when he was so able to accomplish great results.

To add to the complications, the general during the month of July met with Mr. Lincoln in relation to his civil administration and his political conduct of affairs in a tone unauthorized by the relations and bordering on the utmost limits of allowance and toleration. A combination of causes among them notably the hostility of the Secretary of War to General McClellan brought General Halleck, who was by no means equal to General McClellan as a military genius nor equal to the occasion, to the forefront. General Halleck was appointed General-in-Chief of the United States Army and an executive order was issued creating the Army of Virginia. General Pope was placed in command of the forces in front of Washington. The appointment of General Pope gave great dissatisfaction to some of the older generals of the service. General Pope, unfortunately for himself and the country, issued an impolitic[818] and injudicious proclamation on taking the command which was construed to reflect upon the course of proceedings of his predecessor. However much General McClellan was opposed by the administration in military affairs or abused by the politicians, the soldiers were attached to him with sincere and affectionate regard such as perhaps as never before in the history of war entertained for a commander. General McClellan was eventually suspended and General Halleck was placed in charge of the military affairs at Washington. The first thing General Halleck did after the suspension of General McClellan was to issue an order withdrawing the Army of the Potomac from the vicinity of Richmond. The cry had been "on to Richmond" until it had become the most unwelcome sound that could possibly offend Mr. Lincoln's ears. Now the order was "back from Richmond." The news of this order and the retreat of General McClellan's army "back from Richmond" caused excitement at the North, great exaltation at the South and had a very discouraging affect upon the Union people generally.

---

[818] Impolitic means unwise.

On the 7th of July a body of four hundred men under the command of Colonel Charles E. Hovey[819] engaged in a fight with a body of Confederates 2,000 strong and defeated them. About the close of the fight Colonel Hovey was reinforced by about two hundred cavalry. For the number engaged this was one of the liveliest and most deadly engagements of the war. The Confederates had over two hundred men killed besides a great number of wounded and prisoners. On the 9th a public meeting was held in England which called for the British government to mediate in our American civil war and if necessary to acknowledge the independence of the South. On the 15th General Twiggs[820] died at Augusta, Georgia. On the 17th Congress passed the Second Confiscation Act.[821]

On the 18th there occurred an exciting debate in the British House of Commons on the motion of Mr. Lindsey[822] to offer mediation between the United States and the Confederate States of America. On the 19th another English brig *The Napier* while endeavoring to run the blockade at Wilmington[823] was captured by the federal steamer *Mystic*. On the 19th the report of the rebel General Morgan's performance[824] formed one of the most remarkable episodes in all military history

819 Colonel Charles E. Hovey was born in Vermont and a graduate of Dartmouth College. He was an educator who founded several schools including the University of Normal at Normal, Illinois. He organized the 33rd Illinois infantry. He saw action in Missouri and was commended for his actions at Arkansas Port where he was wounded in the arm but continued to command. The Armies and The Leaders, pg. 199 and www.arlingtoncemetary.net/cehovey.html .

820 General David E. Twiggs—See pg. 151.

821 The Second Confiscation Act, section 11 and the Militia Act, sections 12, 13 and 15, which passed the same day, "authorized the President to receive into the service of the United States, for the purpose of constructing entrenchments or performing camp duty, or any labor, or any military or naval service for which they were found to be competent, persons of African descent, and provided that such persons be enrolled and organized, under such regulations, nor inconsistent with the Constitution and the laws the President might prescribe." Men of Color, pg. 1.

822 William S. Lindsay was the leader of the British Parliament and a wealthy ship owner who traded with both the North and the South during the war. www.blogs.dickenson.edu.archive/?cat=1216

823 Wilmington, N.C. is a large port city in the southeastern part of the state.

824 Colonel John Hunt Morgan from Alabama was a daring Confederate raider. He was captured along with his men which included his brothers, at Salinesville on July 26, 1863 and was sent to prison at the Ohio Penitentiary in Columbus. He and his men escaped from the prison on November 27, 1863. He was killed September 4, 1864 at Greenville. Civil War a Narrative, pg. 8, The Armies and The Leaders, pg. 155 and 286 and The Civil War a Narrative, Part VII., pgs. 245.

surpassing in reality Sir Walter Scott's fiction[825] commingling with reality in Scott's novel letters. This report shows in twenty-four days during which time General Morgan and his men had captured seventeen towns, destroyed large amounts of stores, dispersed and put to flight fifteen hundred home guards, paroled one thousand regular troops and had lost but ninety of his troops he took from Kentucky; the greatest accomplishment of the war in reckless dash and imperturbable[826] persistency.

On the 22nd an exchange of prisoners convention[827] was held. General Dix[828] acted for the federals and General D. H. Hill[829] acted for the Confederates. They agreed on the basis of exchange. On the next day General Kilpatrick[830] defeated a body of Confederates on the North Anna River[831] and also destroyed a railroad train carrying large quantities of stores. He also cut the telegraph wires and returned without loss to his quarters in Fredericksburg. On the 24th the steamer *Tubal Cane* was captured by the federal gunboat *Octoria*. The schooner *Emma*[832] was also taken by the *Adirondack*.[833] *The Richmond Enquirer* stated that the rebel steamer *Nashville* had again run the blockade with twenty-two pieces of artillery captured at the battle of Inkerman[834] and

---

825 Sir Walter Scott—See pg. 2.
826 Imperturbable means calm.
827 The convention established guidelines for prisoner exchanges. www.spartacus.schoolnet.co.uk/USACWexchange.htm
828 General John A. Dix—See pg. 63.
829 General Daniel Harvey Hill was born in South Carolina. He was a graduate of the U.S. Military Academy Class of 1842. He was engaged in the Mexican War and taught mathematics prior to the civil war. He was known as D.H. Hill. He commanded the 2nd Corps Army of Tennessee and was involved in the Seven Days battle. He led a Confederate division at Fort Magruder. After the war he was an editor of a newspaper and President of Arkansas Industrial University. Civil War a Narrative, Part II., pgs. 171 & 236, Pride of the South, pgs. 88—90, and The Armies and The Leaders, pgs. 345 & 266.
830 General H. Judson Kilpatrick led a division of Union cavalry which included George Custer. Civil War a Narrative, pgs. 437 & 571.
831 North Anna River is north of Richmond. It flows into the Pamunkey River near Hanover, Virginia where there was an important rail junction.
832 *Emma* was a 156 foot Union schooner. She had been a former blockade runner captured and put into service in the federal navy. She had 8 guns and a crew of 68. Warships of the Civil War Navies, pg. 90.
833 *Adirondack* was a 205 foot Union Ossipee Class sloop with nine guns and a crew of 160. Warships of the Civil War Navies, pg. 42.
834 Inkerman was a Crimean War battle fought November 5, 1854 where the British and French defeated the Russians. www.britishbattles.com/crimean-war/inkerman.htm

presented to the Confederate States of America by the merchants of Great Britain. On the next day the rebel steamer *Cuba* ran the blockade and entered Mobile. On the 27th and 28th there was fighting at Bayou Bernard[835] in the Cherokee nation in which the Confederates lost one hundred twenty-five men killed. On the 31st the Secretary of War issued an order revoking the furloughs and leaves of absence heretofore granted by commanders to special friends and meritorious officers and ordered them to join their federal commands forthwith. At the same time he ordered a muster of each regiment and detachment to note and detect absentees. On the same day the rebel steamer *Memphis*[836] which had been a source of annoyance to the blockade squadron was captured by the *Magnolia*[837] after having run the blockade at Charleston.

## AUGUST 1862

On August 1st the Confederate government issued an order that Generals Pope and Von Steinwehr[838] and the officers under them should not be treated as soldiers and not be entitled to the privileges of parole, and threatened to execute any officers in their hands in retaliation if the Union officers should carry out their orders in regard to spies, guerrillas, &c. The next day the famous woman spy, Belle Boyd,[839] (whom the humble author of these pages well knew and who was at her respected father's house - Ben Boyd - at Bunker Hill[840] in Berkeley County, Virginia on the night of her birth) was arrested and sent to Washington and was afterwards released at the instance of the

---

835 Bayou Bernard is near Gulfport, Mississippi

836 *Memphis* was a 227 foot long large combatant with 100 men and seven guns. She was captured and converted to Union service. She captured four prizes. Warships of the Civil War Navies, pg. 80.

837 *Magnolia* was a 242 foot long former blockade runner, captured and converted into a Union naval vessel. She was a side wheeler with a crew of 95 with three guns. She captured five enemy vessels. Warships of the Civil War Navies, pg. 74.

838 General Adolph Von Steinwehr was a Russian immigrant who moved to New York. He commanded a federal division under General Howard at Gettysburg. Civil War a Narrative, pgs. 475 & 487 and The Armies and The Leaders, pg. 227.

839 Belle Boyd was a Confederate spy who passed Union secrets to Stonewall Jackson. The Civil War, Strange and Fascinating Facts, pg. 147 and www.civilwarhome.com/boydbio.htm

840 Bunker Hill, Virginia (now West Virginia) is located between Martinsburg, Virginia and Winchester, Virginia. The author, Ward Hill Lamon grew up in Bunker Hill. *Berkeley County Journal*, 1979, pg. 16 and Miss Dolly, pg. 1.

writer through the instigation of friendship for her father and family, induced by early association. On this same day the first French vessel *The Harriet Rali* was captured for attempting to run the blockade. On the next day there was another British vessel the propeller *Columbia* was captured after a chase of several hours by the United States steamer *Santiago*[841] off the Bahamas for attempting to run the blockade. She had on board twelve Armstrong guns and a vast amount of munitions of war.

On the 4th General McClellan protested against General Halleck's order withdrawing the troops from the peninsula, and urged that if such a course was persisted it would result fatally. There was on the 5th a battle fought at Baton Rouge, Louisiana[842] in which the Confederates were routed and left their dead on the field. General Williams[843] who was in command of the federal forces was killed. There was a Union loss in this battle of two hundred fifty men killed, wounded and missing. The Confederate loss was six hundred killed and a large number of wounded and prisoners. On the 6th the rebel ironclad *Arkansas*[844] was attacked near Baton Rogue by the federal gunboat *Essex* and destroyed. On the next day there was a fight between the federal forces under Colonel Canby[845] and the Confederate forces under General Sibley[846] near Fort Fillmore, New Mexico after which the Confederates charged General Sibley with drunkenness and general inefficiencies.

Cedar Mountain battle was fought on August 9. General Jackson commanded the Confederate forces, crossing the Rapidan River and advancing against the federal forces commanded by General Banks at

---

841 *Santiago de Cuba* was a 237 foot Union side wheeler with a wooden hull and two masts. She had ten guns and a crew of around 160 men. She captured fourteen enemy vessels. Warships of the Civil War Navies, pg. 76.

842 Baton Rogue, Louisiana is located on the Mississippi River about eight miles upstream from New Orleans.

843 General Thomas Williams was from Albany, New York. He was an 1837 graduate of the U.S. Military Academy. He fought in the Blackhawk, Seminole and Mexican Wars. He commanded six infantry regiments, two artillery batteries, and a troop of cavalry at Baton Rogue. Americanhistory.about.com/od/civilwarbattles/p/cwbattle_baton.htm

844 *Arkansas* was a Confederate casemate ironclad with 18 inch iron and wood sloping sides and a ram in the bow. She had 8 guns and a crew of 200. She was burned by her crew on August 6, 1862 to prevent her capture. Warships of the Civil War Navies, pg. 202.

845 Colonel Edward R. S. Canby—See pg. 173.

846 Brigadier General Henry Hopkins Sibley—See pg. 122.

Cedar Mountain near Culpeper Courthouse.[847] The battle did not commence until after six o'clock in the afternoon and after two hours of very hard fighting the Confederates fell back under cover of darkness. The federal loss was 1,500 men killed, wounded, or missing. The Confederate loss was not known but is supposed to be about 2,500. On the 11th John Slidell's property[848] was confiscated. On the 13th the French blockade runner *Harriet Rali* captured on the 2nd instant was released by the United States government. General Hovey defeated the Confederate General Hyndman[849] at Clarendon, Missouri and captured seven hundred prisoners with great loss of life on both sides. On the 14th General Breckenridge at Baton Rogue complained to General Pine of certain acts committed by him which he protested were not in accordance with the usages of civilized warfare and threatened on the reputation the alternative of raising the black flag. On the next day the counsel of Spanish government at New Orleans protested against the stringency of the quarantine laws and regulations established by General Butler at that port. On the following day Colonel Corcoran,[850] Colonel Wilcox,[851] Lieutenant Colonel Brown and Major Rogers having been exchanged as prisoners of war, arrived at Fortress Monroe. On the same day Governor Magoffin[852] resigned as the President of the Senate and J. F. Robinson[853] succeeded him.

---

847 Culpeper Courthouse, Virginia is east of Fredericksburg and was an important north/south rail junction.

848 Slidell was the Minister to France who was captured and then let go. See pg. 68.

849 General Thomas Hyndman was a politician and attorney. He was a major player in the secession of Arkansas. He commanded a CSA brigade at Corinth and was wounded at Shiloh. www.encyclopediaofarkansas.net/encyclopedia/entry-detail.aspx?entryid=1672

850 Michael Corcoran was wounded in the leg and captured at Manassas and held prisoner in Richmond. www.irishidentity.com/geese/stories/corcoran.htm—See pg. 215.

851 Colonel Cadmus Marcellus Wilcox was from North Carolina and was a graduate of the U.S. Military Academy in 1846, the same class as Thomas J. Jackson and George Pickett. He was a veteran of the Mexican War. He served as an assistant instructor of infantry tactics at the academy. He commanded Confederate troops at both Gettysburg and Fredericksburg. After the war he was chief of the railroad division of the land office and published "The History of the Mexican War." Civil War a Narrative, pgs. 310 & 510, Pride of the South, pgs. 58 & 59, and The Armies and The Leaders, pg. 282.

852 Governor Magoffin—See pg. 124.

853 James F. Robinson was from Kentucky and served as the state's 22nd Governor. li-brary.georgetowncollege.edu/special_collections/James_Fisher_Robinson_papers.htm

General Grant ordered all persons in his department enrolled "who if they were at home would be liable to draft."

On the next day at St. Patrick's Cathedral in the city of New York Archbishop Hughes[854] preached a sermon and gave utterance to patriotic sentiment. He urged the United States government to speedily place enough men in the field to bring what he termed "this unnatural and suicidal strife" to a close. On the following day Colonels Corcoran and Wilcox were appointed Brigadier Generals dating back to the time of the battle of Bull Run. On the 21st of August, Jefferson Davis ordered that Generals Hunter and Phelps[855] should be treated as outlaws and no longer be recognized as soldiers and in case of their capture should be hung. The federal and Confederate armies on the Rappahannock River[856] in full force faced each other. The Confederates attempted to cross the river for a more intimate interchange of military courtesy but were driven back by the command of General Reno.[857] The same day 40,000 Union troops under the command of General Rosencrans marched to Iuka, Missouri. On the next day all of General Pope's papers were destroyed at Catlett's Station by Confederate General Stuart's Cavalry.[858] General Schurtz[859] crossed the Rappahannock River and drove the Confederates back temporarily. When they rallied a very serious battle occurred which lasted until night when the federal command was again forced to cross the river and retire from conflict. On this day the Army of the Peninsula commenced arriving in Alexandria, Virginia. Colonel Rodney Mason[860] of the 71st Ohio Regiment was dismissed from service for having surrendered Clarksville, Tennessee to the Confederates on the 18th instant without firing a gun. Clarksville, at

---

854 Archbishop John Joseph Hughes was the head of the Catholic Church in New York. He began building the new St. Peter's Church in 1858 in New York City. www.newadvent.org/cathen/07516a.htm

855 General John Woolcott Phelps was a graduate of the U.S. Military Academy Class of 1836. thomaslegion.net.unitedstatesmilitaryacedemy.html

856 Rappahannock River lies between the Potomac River and the York River through Fredericksburg and then to the Chesapeake Bay.

857 General Jesse L. Reno was from Wheeling, Virginia (now West Virginia). He was an 1846 graduate of the U.S. Military Academy and fought in the Mexican War. He commanded the Union's Ninth Corps. The Ninth Corps, pg. 10

858 General JEB Stuart—See pg. 137.

859 General Carl Schurtz—See pg. 133.

860 Col. Rodney Mason was the organizer of the 71st Ohio Regiment. www.ohiocivilwar.com/cw71.html

that juncture was regarded as a strong strategic point and an important one for the interests of the federal forces. On the 23rd the respective forces along the Rappahannock River renewed their fight. The Confederates made a successful crossing of the river at or near the Sulphur Springs at Warrenton where they were given battle by the federal forces, which resulted in the Confederates being driven across the Great Run. After this General Pope with his command fell back to Warrenton.

On the next day the fighting was renewed at Sulphur Springs and Waterloo Bridge with varying success to either army. On the same day Charles J. Ingersol[861] a distinguished gentleman of rebel proclivities was arrested in Philadelphia, Pennsylvania. On the 26th Generals Heintzelman[862] and Porter reinforced General Pope at Warrenton Junction. General Ewell's division attacked General Pope's right flank and turned it. There they overpowered that force of Union soldiers who were at Bull Run. General Pope marched with his command toward Alexandria and Washington City. At Kettle Run the Confederates were overtaken and attacked by General Hooker's division. The fight lasted until dark when the Confederates were driven from the field losing three thousand men in the conflict. On the next day a severe fight was had between General Jackson of the Confederate Army and the federal Generals McDowell[863] and Sigel[864] at Centreville. General Jackson's forces were driven back with fearful loss. The battle of Grovetown was fought on the 28th; commanded on the Confederate side by Generals Jackson and Longstreet[865] and on the federal side by General Pope. This was a fearful fight and resulted in the Confederate's defeat and being driven from the field of action.

---

[861] Charles J. Ingersol was arrested for language used at a meeting in Philadelphia on August 23rd. *New York Times*, August 26, 1862.
[862] General Peter Heintzelman—See pg. 138.
[863] General Irvin McDowell—See pg. 137.
[864] General Franz Sigel—See pg. 136.
[865] General James Longstreet was from South Carolina. He graduated from the U.S. Military Academy in 1842. He was severely wounded in the Mexican War. He was wounded again at Wilderness but returned to his command. He was a Confederate commander of a division at Gettysburg. He was openly critical of General Lee's strategy on the third day of that battle. After the war he became a Republican which did not sit well with his Confederate colleagues. He was Minister to Turkey and also served as Commissioner of the Pacific Railroads. Civil War a Narrative, Part II., pg. 128 & 172, Pride of the South, pgs. 34, 43—45, and The Armies and The Leaders, pgs. 245 & 246.

On the same day was commenced the battle of Richmond, Kentucky.[866] The whole Confederate line engaged the Army of the Cumberland in front of Richmond. After a severe fight of an hour the Confederate forces were driven back. At an early hour the next morning the Confederates again advanced and in turn forced the federals back. The fighting continued all day without material advantage to either side and at dark the federal forces were compelled to retreat with a loss of 206 killed, 844 wounded and over a thousand prisoners. The Confederates lost forty-eight killed and 372 wounded. At Bolivar, Tennessee[867] a battle was fought on the same day which lasted for seven hours after which the Confederates withdrew.

In this battle Lieutenant Colonel Harvey Hogg[868] of the 2nd Illinois Regiment was killed. Colonel Hogg was a native of Tennessee but had made his residence in Bloomington, Illinois[869] for several years before the war. Colonel Hogg was a highly educated and accomplished man, very popular in his state, and a lawyer by profession. He possessed in a very wonderful degree those qualities of head and heart which make men loved while living and sincerely mourned when dead. His death caused universal regret throughout the state of Illinois and was a source of sincere sorrow for Mr. Lincoln, whose intimate acquaintance and warm friendship Colonel Hogg, had the pleasure of enjoying from the time he entered the state until he was called thence to the service of his country and to death.

The second battle of Bull Run was fought on August 30, on the same ground positively being reverent that the first disastrous battle of Bull Run was fought on the 21st day of July 1861 and with like results. General Pope now commanded the Union Army; General Beauregard then in command, General Lee now commanding the rebel forces.

---

866 Richmond, Kentucky is about 25 miles south and slightly east of Lexington.

867 Bolivar, Tennessee is about 50 miles east of Memphis, Tennessee.

868 Lieutenant Colonel Harvey Hogg moved to Bloomington, Illinois from Tennessee in 1855. He was a member of the Illinois State Legislature. Mr. Lincoln said "Hogg was well known to me personally as a most reliable gentleman." Author Ward Hill Lamon and Hogg were law partners in Bloomington, Illinois where Lamon was prosecuting attorney. They had an office above the Crother's and Chew's Drug Store. The partnership lasted until Lamon went with Mr. Lincoln to Washington with Mr. Lincoln. Ward Hill Lamon: Lincoln's "Particular Friend," pgs. 57 & 58 and www.lib.niu.edu/2007/iho10705.html

869 Bloomington, Illinois is about 65 miles northeast of Springfield and was part of the 8th judicial circuit of Illinois.

The very soil upon which these battles were fought seemed to be token disaster for the Union cause and fatal calamity to the federal army. The tide of the battle in favor of the Confederates did not materially change until the sanguinary[870] battle of South Mountain[871] and Antietam afterwards fought in the month of September the 14th and 17th consecutively when hope was revived and success for the Union was in a measure insured.

This second battle of Bull Run fought on the 30th of August raged fearfully all day and the slaughter on both sides was very great. The right wing of the federals was maintained, though their left wing had been driven back half a mile or more. At close of the day the whole Union army fell back to Centreville. On the next day the most intense disappointment prevailed all over the North of General Pope's defeat. In the last three days of fighting, the North had sustained almost 11,000 casualties with the South losses estimated at 8,400.

## SEPTEMBER 1862

On the 1st day of September the last of the battles of the Army of Virginia on their retreat was fought at Chantilly.[872] Major General Kearny[873] and Brigadier General Stevens[874] were killed. In this fight the Confederates were driven back at all points with immense slaughter on both sides. The federal army lost in this battle one thousand killed, six thousand wounded and two thousand prisoners. The loss of the Confederates was great but not definitely known. The engagement did not exceed one hour, but was terrible in its results. On the 2nd Mr. Lincoln, without the concurrence or knowledge of his Cabinet and without consulting the Secretary of War or anyone else, again appointed General McClellan to command the defenses of Washington. What followed demonstrated Mr. Lincoln's superior

---

870 Sanguinary means bloody.

871 South Mountain, Maryland is a mountain ridge between Frederick and Boonsboro.

872 Chantilly, Virginia is about ten miles north of Manassas, where the battle of Bull Run took place.

873 Major General Phillip Kearny—See pg. 142.

874 Brigadier General Isaac I. Stevens was born in Massachusetts. He graduated first in his class in 1839 from the U.S. Military Academy. He served in the Ninth Corps under General Pope. His son Hazard was also wounded in this battle. After the war he was named Governor of the Washington Territory. www.absoluteastronomy.com/topics/Issac_Stevens

wisdom in emergencies of danger. The Army of Virginia which had been created for the command of General Pope for the purpose of dispensing with the disfavored tardiness of action manifested by General McClellan, the hope of securing speedy victories was now most sadly and fearfully demoralized. The whole War Department including Secretary Stanton and General Halleck, the General-in-Chief of the Army of the United States, were now greatly alarmed. General McClellan was fortunate enough to bring order out of chaos and soon refitted the discouraged but brave and noble army for speedy active service, and very soon there was an opportunity afforded them of showing that valor and heroism imperishable in the hearts of every true American whether well-directed or ill-advised in every section of the states of this broad Union of confederation. General Pope then continued his retreat towards Washington without further loss on the 3rd day of the month when his whole army safely entered the entrenchments around the city of Washington.

Whether at this momentous period the fact of professional pride and jealousy were allowed to encroach on patriotic duty it is not here the purpose to discuss. No opinion is ventured as to whether or not General Pope was the most judicious and able officer then in the United State Army to meet the experience General Robert E. Lee and the dashing General Jackson. At the time much discussion was indulged as to the whether welfare of the republic was or was not jeopardized to gratify personal, official or professional resentments and there discussions and speculations were not confined alone in respect to the general officers. Why the Army of the Potomac was recalled from in front of Richmond and brought back to Washington and was required to retrace its march to regain its abandoned position was never understood by the initiated. And at no period in the history of the country was the whole community so entirely stirred and confused. Things looked gloomy beyond anything that ever had occurred before or is ever likely to occur again in the history of this country.

On the 3rd of September 1862 General Pope asked to be relieved of his command; which request was granted. Honorable Joseph Holt[875] on that day was appointed Judge Advocate General of the United States Army. On the next day Union troops evacuated Frederick City,

---

875 Judge Joseph Holt—See page 23.

Maryland.[876] On the same day the Peace Society of Great Britain[877] recommended that the people of the United States accept mediation and put a stop to the civil war. The same date the bark *Annie Laurie* was captured while attempting to run the blockade. The rebel schooner *Rising Sun* was captured the next day. General Lee with his Confederate command now occupied Frederick City, Maryland. The following day the people of Harrisburg, Pennsylvania were thrown into intense excitement by news of the report of the approach of Confederate troops towards Hagerstown, Maryland and Gettysburg, Pennsylvania. On the next day General McClellan took the field and went with all possible speed up the Potomac River towards Frederick. General Banks[878] was put in command at Washington. On the 8th a fight occurred at Poolesville, Maryland[879] which resulted in a defeat for the Confederates. On this day a proclamation to the people was issued and signed by the Confederate commanding Generals Lee and Bradley Johnson[880] (the latter being a native of Frederick City, Maryland) stating that they had come to assist the citizens of Maryland in regaining their rights. (What these rights were the proclamation failed to state.) The militia turned out in force everywhere in Pennsylvania and Maryland to resist the invasion. On the next day the Confederates made an attack on Williamsport, Maryland and were repulsed. At the same time General Stuart's Cavalry were driven back by General Keyes[881] with the loss of ninety men in attempting to cross the Potomac River at Edward's Ferry. The 8th Illinois Cavalry and the 3rd Indiana Cavalry on their march up the Potomac River to join the main force of the federal army had several engagements with the Confederates in their march; on the 9th of September at Monocacy

---

[876] Frederick City, Maryland (today Frederick, Maryland)

[877] The Peace Society of Great Britain was founded in 1816. The organization was principally against war upon any pretense.
www.swathmore.edu/library/peace/cdgb/intpeacesociety.htm

[878] General Nathaniel Banks—See pg. 140.

[879] Poolesville, Maryland is located about 20 miles south of Frederick.

[880] General Bradley Tyler Johnson was born in Frederick, Maryland. He was a graduate of Princeton University and a writer. He was a lawyer who practiced law in Baltimore before the war and in Richmond after the war. He helped form the First Maryland Infantry and later was a Brigadier General in the Confederate Cavalry.
Stonewall.hut.ru/leaders/Johnson_bt.htm

[881] General Erasmus D. Keyes—See pg. 176.

Church[882] and Barnesville[883] near Frederick City. On the same day Middletown, Maryland was occupied by the Confederate forces and they commenced a conscription of the citizens for rebel service.

On the 10th there was spirited fight at Fayette, Virginia in which the federals were defeated with a loss of over one hundred killed and wounded. Natchez,[884] Mississippi was being bombarded and forced to surrender. On the 10th General Lee evacuated Frederick City and a fight occurred at Sugar Loaf Mountain in which the federals got the worst of it and were compelled to retreat. The Confederates entered and occupied Hagerstown, Maryland. The next day and the following there was a fight in Charlestown, Virginia[885] near the Potomac River and that town was burned.[886] On that same date General Burnside's federal forces occupied Frederick City, which caused great rejoicing among the people as this had now become a very important point in view of the situation of the two armies. During this time Maryland Heights[887] opposite Harpers Ferry was attacked and the fighting continued until sun down.

On the 12th General Lew Wallace[888] was in full pursuit of General Kirby Smith[889] in his retreat from Cincinnati. Early the next morning the fighting was renewed at Maryland Heights and lasted until two o'clock in the afternoon. Then the guns were spiked and under orders from headquarters the federal troops were removed to Harpers Ferry. On the 14th the Union troops under the command of General

---

882 Monocacy Church is just south of Fredrick and was the junction of the B & O Railroad.

883 Barnesville is about five miles northeast of Poolesville, Maryland.

884 Natchez, Mississippi is on the Mississippi River about 60 miles downstream from Vicksburg.

885 Charlestown, Virginia county seat of what is now Jefferson County, West Virginia. It is about five miles west of Harpers Ferry.

886 The author uses the term "burned" whereas the town was badly damaged by a bombardment but was not actually burned. Jefferson County Historical Society

887 Maryland Heights is the 1,100 foot high overlook across the Potomac River from Harpers Ferry.

888 General Lewis Wallace was born in Indiana. He had been a lawyer and a soldier in the Mexican War. He supervised the defenses of the town of Cincinnati and commanded the 8th Corps of the Union Army. After the war he was the President of the Military Court that tried and hanged Henry Wirz the commandant of Andersonville Prison. He also wrote the famous book *Ben Hur* which was published in 1880. Lew Wallace: Autobiography, pg. 938, Civil War a Narrative, Part XI., pg. 309 and The Armies and The Leaders, pgs. 23 & 206.

889 General Edmund Kirby Smith—See pg. 187.

Burnside moved towards the ferry. General McClellan and his troops overtook the Confederates near Middletown, Maryland and the terrific battle of South Mountain occurred. The Heights were carried by the commands of Generals Hooker and Reno while General Franklin[890] took and held Burkettsville Gap.[891] The fight lasted until night and was one great slaughter, resulting in the defeat of the Confederates who were forced from the field leaving their dead and wounded upon it. The federals lost 325 killed,[892] 1,403 wounded and 85 prisoners. The Confederates lost 2,685 killed, wounded and missing. The Confederates now occupied Maryland Heights and continued their attack on Harpers Ferry. Lieutenant Colonel Davis[893] with the 12th Illinois Cavalry did some desperate fighting in cutting his way out from the ferry. Later that same day he captured General Longstreet's wagon train and halted his command at Greencastle, Pennsylvania.

On the 14th General Butler ordered enrollment of all neutral foreigners in New Orleans. On the same day there was a severe engagement at Munfordville,[894] Kentucky which lasted eight hours and resulted in a victory to the federals and great loss to the Confederates. On the same day Union troops at Bolivar Heights[895] were forced to surrender to the Confederate General Jackson. At this surrender the Confederates took 12,500[896] prisoners, forty-seven pieces of artillery, and a vast amount of stores of various kinds. There were a number of the Union soldiers killed also one hundred twenty wounded before the

---

890 General William Buell Franklin was from Pennsylvania. He graduated in the class of 1842 from the U. S. Military Academy. He commanded the 6th Corps under General McClellan at Peninsula and at Antietam. Franklin was captured by the Confederates while riding on the Pennsylvania and Baltimore Railroad in July 1864 but escaped the next day. After the war he was Vice-President of Colt Firearms Company and was the American Commissioner General to the Paris Exposition in 1889. Later he was responsible of the completion of the U.S. Capitol building. Lincoln's War, pg. 174, Appleton's Cyclopaedia of American Biography, Vol. II., pgs. 575 & 576, and The Armies and The Leaders, pgs. 183 & 202.

891 Burkettsville Gap is a low point in the South Mountain range adjacent to Burkettsville, Maryland.

892 Among those killed at South Mountain was Union General Jessie Reno. See pg. 204.

893 Lieutenant Colonel Jeff Davis—See pg. 163.

894 Munfordville, Kentucky is about 72 miles south and slightly west of Louisville.

895 Bolivar Heights is the high ground behind Harpers Ferry, Virginia to the west.

896 This was the largest surrender during the civil war. johnsmilitaryhistory.com/harpersferrybattle.html

surrender. The federal General Miles[897] was killed in this battle. The Confederate loss was unknown.

On the 15th Cincinnati was again threatened by the advance of the Confederate forces that had been driven back by General Wallace previously. After four days fighting in Mumfordville, Colonels Dunham[898] and Wilder[899] in command of the federal forces were compelled to surrender to a superior force of the Confederates under the command of General Bragg[900] with over four thousand prisoners and as many stands of arms and a large amount of stores captured from the federals.

On the next day was commenced the battle of Antietam on the 17th of September. On this day General Hooker's Corps attacked the Confederate left. First one army and then the other would advance and then fall back. There was deadly execution done by both armies. A piece of woods in front of the Union line was considered by both armies as the key position and this was held by the federals. At one o'clock the stone bridge on the left was carried by General Burnside at the point of the bayonet. At four o'clock General Franklin moved his batteries forward and held his ground. The Confederates were driven from the hills in front by General Burnside, but were at once reinforced and drove him back to his former position. General Jackson of the Confederate troops after having captured Harpers Ferry reinforced the Confederate Army at Antietam. The battle on all sides raged fiercely and desperately. At dark the firing on all sides ceased and the fighting was suspended for the day. It was a ferociously contested battle and its equal in carnage is unknown in American history. General McClellan stated the Confederate loss at 25,542 men. The Confederates at the time acknowledged a loss of 14,000. The Union lost 20,010 killed, 9,416 missing and 1,043 missing.[901] There were engaged in this battle 200,000 troops. Among the federal loss, General

---

897 General Dixon Miles—See pg. 139.

898 Colonel Cyrus L. Dunham and Colonel Wilder were principal commanders of the Union forces at Mumfordville. www.americancivilwar.com/statepic/ky/ky008.htm

899 Colonel John Wilder was an industrialist from Indiana who led the horse-back infantry known as the "Lightning Brigade." Civil War a Narrative, pgs. 668 & 671 & 672.

900 General Braxton Bragg—See pg. 189.

901 The official count for the combined casualties of both armies at Antietam are now listed as 23,115, making it the single bloodiest day in American history. Antietam Battlefield, NPS brochure.

Mansfield[902] an old and experienced officer was killed, Generals Rodman[903] and Richardson[904] were mortally wounded and nine other general officers were also wounded. The federals retained all of their own guns and lost none of their colors during the battle.

On the 18th the Confederates again evacuated Harpers Ferry. On the same day General Bragg at Mumfordville informed the citizens of Kentucky that his army had come to restore them to their liberties, without defining or alluding to what those liberties were which he imagined they had lost. On the same day authorities at the Confederate seat of government, laboring under a like delusion, issued a proclamation for thanksgiving and prayer in the Confederate States for the victory of Manassas/Bull Run, not taking into account their defeats at South Mountain and Antietam of the three days previous nor in any way making provision for proper acknowledgement to almighty God for the turn in the tide of the war that a few days had wrought. On the 19th of September the battle of Iuka, Mississippi[905] was fought between General Price on the one side and General Rosencrans on the other. This battle continued for two hours and resulted in the loss to the Confederates in killed, wounded and missing of 1,262 men. The federal loss in killed, wounded and missing was 752 men. The federal forces under General McClellan had now on the 19th recovered from the fatigue of battle and commenced a pursuit of the Confederates engaged in it on their way into the state of Virginia. Too much time had been lost in recuperation to overtake the Confederate Army at any point where it would have been prudent to renew hostilities. The abundant caution of General McClellan after the tremendous fight at Antietam in not promptly pursuing the defeated Confederates resulted in disfavor of the war administration of General McClellan's conduct and speedily resulted in his deposition[906] from command. Whether justly or unjustly, he was relieved.

No man either in the military or civil life during the war who played a leading part in the drama of life then being enacted, had

---

902 General Joseph K. Mansfield was wounded at Antietam on September 17, 1862 and died the next day. The Armies and The Leaders, pgs. 129 & 216.

903 General Isaac P. Rodman was wounded at Antietam on September 17, 1862 and died on September 30, 1862. The Armies and The Leaders, pg. 133.

904 General Israel B. Richardson—See pg. 138.

905 Iuka, Mississippi is in the northeast corner of Mississippi on the border with Alabama.

906 Deposition means removal.

warmer friends in the army or bitter enemies among the politicians in the country than General McClellan. The constant wonder of those persons in the heat of passion evoked by his failure at one time to capture Richmond and to crush the rebellion at the outset was a justification of their charge upon him of want of fidelity to his trust which involved indirectly the charge of treason. Yet he retained in such a marked degree the personal devotion of his officers and affection of his soldiers.

When he took command of the Army of the Potomac it was composed of a mass of untrained, undisciplined and but poorly armed men. Yet after fighting some of the hardest battles of the war covering eighteen months, he left it a splendid military organization well-prepared for the accomplishment of the splendid achievements attained afterwards by General Grant. At the time General McClellan first took command of the army the South was powerful in all the elements of successful warfare. In his aggressive movements he had much to contend with. He was impressed with the belief that he was not supported by the authorities at Washington as he should have been while the Washington authorities continually protested that they were giving him all the support in their power.

At this time the political managers of the party had greater power and more influence in making and unmaking generals and planning military campaigns than were conceded to them at a later period. It could well be doubted whether any commander could have crushed the rebellion in the time during which General McClellan was at the head of the army. The South had greatly changed from the time he retired from the service and the time General Grant took command of the eastern army. When the latter came to the command long strain had weakened and exhausted the forces and resources of the South. There had come a change from the former buoyant bravery of hope to the desperate bravery of doubtful success. "On to Richmond" was the popular policy and the incessant cry of irresponsible non-combatants and political enthusiasts all over the North, so much so that it had become very embarrassing to the administration. The commander of the army, General McClellan, was not sufficiently aggressive to suit these enthusiasts and allay their clamor.

At the beginning, possible by a bold dash under a more aggressive leader, the Confederate capital might have been captured, but added to his natural caution General McClellan had the fiasco of the Bull Run battle constantly before his eyes. It was ever fresh in his memory that the defeat of our army at this battle resulted from its being prematurely fought in subservient obedience to popular clamor. It was what might be called a political battle. But in its results it was strictly military and taught a bad lesson to the army as well as to the directors of popular opinion and the officious[907] meddlers in military affairs who forced the battle prematurely. Neither Mr. Lincoln or General McDowell believed at the time that the Union Army was prepared for this fight, but solely in deference to the legislature and political clamor they yielded to prevalent opinion and striped[908] for the fray, the obedient little army plunged in and then plunged in again, and then retired and acknowledged they were whipped. The federal army took refuge in flight while many of the instigators of the disaster sulked from the danger and calamity they caused and fled to a safe harbor little abashed[909] because of their audacity and slightly concerned for the ruin they had caused.

As a rule the average American politician is no better fitted than the aggressive newspaper editor or no more competent to direct and command a hostile army than an educated military general but this fact did not seem to be appreciated until after the first battle of Bull Run was fought. The outcome of the peninsular campaign might have been very different had the army been in the start what General McClellan afterwards made it before his removal.

It was thought by a great many people, many of them conservative in politics as well as in regard to war that General McClellan's course in this particular, whatever personal wrongs or imaginary wrongs he may have suffered, was not warranted by the spirit of the times nor consistent with his high character as a military commander, his former connection with the war, or as a civilian gentleman. But he lived long enough to see the prejudices his conduct engendered to a great extent disappear. He was a man of wonderful magnetism and enjoyed the respect of the American people at the time of his death which occurred on the 29th day of October, 1885.

On the 21st the federals again drove out the Confederates and reoccupied Mumfordville, Kentucky, General Bragg and his forces

---

[907] Officious means dutiful.
[908] Striped means having uniforms decorated with their rank.
[909] Abashed means confused.

deeming it prudent to evacuate. A fight at Ashby Gap, Virginia[910] on this day resulted in the defeat of the Confederates with great loss of men.

On the 22nd of September[911] Mr. Lincoln issued his preliminary proclamation of freedom to the slaves declaring that he would proclaim on the 1st day of January, 1863 freedom to the slaves in any state or part of a state, in rebellion against the government of the United States.

Political discord and military jealousies naturally arose in the progress of the affairs which seriously affected the relation on concord[912] existing at this time between the two branches—executive and legislative. The subject of emancipation of slaves gave the first trouble between them. Individual members of Congress were far in advance of the president on this subject. A large portion of the members were in favor of immediate emancipation. Mr. Lincoln saw that freedom of the slave was inevitable, yet he knew the people at large were not yet ready for it. He was determined that the government should not be in the attitude to justify the charge that the war was inaugurated for the emancipation of slaves of the South without compensation to their owners. This state of things existed until the summer of 1862. The president then determined to use slavery itself as a means of coercion and punishment. Mr. Lincoln issued a proclamation in which he foreshadowed his purpose. He gave the South another and last opportunity to retain their property in slaves by proposing to the revolutionary states to return to their allegiance or otherwise, he would be compelled as a military necessity to declare the slaves in such states, free men. No notice was taken of this.

General Nelson[913] who had been in command had on the 22nd instant ordered all of the women and children out of Louisville, Kentucky preparatory for an anticipated battle on the arrival of these

---

910 Ashby Gap, Virginia is a low point in the Blue Ridge Mountains allowing people and troops to move easily across to and from the Shenandoah Valley.

911 Mr. Lincoln wanted to wait until after a Union victory to make the announcement. Mr. Lincoln told his Cabinet, "If God gave us a victory in the approaching battle, I would consider it an indication of Divine will, and that it was my duty to move forward in the cause of emancipation." That victory had come on September 17 at Sharpsburg, Maryland. He said with the victory, "God has decided this question in favor of the slaves." The Eloquent President, pg. 169.

912 On concord means in harmony.

913 Major General William Nelson—See pg. 158.

two hostile armies. On the 24th a convention of the governors of the loyal states was held pursuant to a call for a council on the state of the country at Altoona, Pennsylvania.[914] The president ordered the arrest of all persons who have discouraged enlistments or in any way aided the rebellion and suspended the writ of *habeas corpus* in all such cases. On the next day the respective armies under the commands of Generals Buell[915] and Bragg proceeded under forced marches to occupy Louisville, Kentucky. General Buell's army arrived first and took possession of the city.

On the 26th resolutions were passed by the Confederate House of Representatives offering the free navigation of the Mississippi River and contributory rivers and the market of the South to the North and western states under certain conditions. When Mr. Lincoln was informed of this generous proposition he remarked "if he had before then read something about the Pope issuing a bull against the comet, whether the comet was affected by that bull, history gave no account. However that may be, it shall not prevent me from appointing a Provost General for the whole United States. So Mr. Secretary Stanton, please issue an order for the creation of such an office; such an officer may become useful." General Nelson was on the 29th instant shot and killed by federal General Jeff C. Davis at the Galt House,[916] Louisville. The shooting was the result of a private quarrel between these two gentlemen. On the 30th of the month Simeon Draper was appointed to the office of Provost General. Three days after the Confederate Congress had "opened up" the Mississippi River to conditional navigation and trade the Confederate House of Representatives was seriously considering the propriety of raising the black flag during the period for which the war should last. This was, however, a military resort for the greater security of life, liberty and the pursuit of happiness that was not put into practical affect.

---

914 The Convention of Governors in Altoona, Pennsylvania was hosted by Governor Curtin in the Logan House on September 24—26. Fourteen loyal state governors attended. They pledged to continue their support for the Union and President Lincoln. www.altoonalibrary.org/books/keystonecity/keystonecity0002.htm

915 General Don Carlos Buell—See pg. 158.

916 Galt House is a famous Louisville riverside hotel still in operation today.

## OCTOBER 1862

Mr. Lincoln on the 2nd, 3rd and 4th visited the army at Harpers Ferry and the battle field of Antietam at Sharpsburg, Maryland. He was accompanied by Mr. John W. Garrett[917] president of the Baltimore and Ohio Railroad Company of whom Mr. Lincoln was very fond, General McClernand,[918] the Honorable O. M. Hatch,[919] both from Illinois, the Marshal of the District of Columbia[920] and others. From Harpers Ferry to Antietam the party had to travel by ambulance the route necessary to be taken on account of the military state of affairs through a desolate, dreary part of Maryland. The party became very tired before reaching their destination and it was on this occasion a long distance from the sight of any battlefield that Mr. Lincoln weary and feeling unusually sad turned to the marshal and asked him to sing a song which was a great favorite of his called "Twenty Years Ago." The song was sung. "The Sword of Bunker Hill" was called for and sung. After the singing was over, and the conversation had ceased the ambulance went suddenly over a rough broken place in the road which well might throw the party out of it and onto the ground. The marshal whose spirits were exuberant upon all occasions instantly struck up the Negro minstrel "Picayune Butler" commending with "In New Orleans where I was born, my ol massa did blow his horn, but all us nigger run aroun crying old Ben Butler's come to town."[921]

Although this amused the party at the time, the singer was gently rebuked for his thoughtless levity, he having forgotten the sad occasion of their mission. To make amends as he said, he would now give them a hymn written by the Rev. Dr. Watts in the original. In the most sonorous[922] and ludicrous[923] tone of voice sang "Come hungry,

---

917 John W. Garrett was a banker, and philanthropist. He served as President of the Baltimore and Ohio Railroad from 1858 until his death in 1884. www.nps.gov/mono/history/culture/john_w_garrett.htm

918 General John Alexander McClernand—See pg. 157.

919 O. M. Hatch was the Secretary of State for Illinois. He worked for Lincoln's nomination at the Republican National Commission in Chicago. Lincoln: The Prairie Years, pg. 283.

920 Ward Hill Lamon, the author, was the Marshal of the District of Columbia. Ward Hill Lamon: Lincoln's "Particular Friend", pg. 216.

921 Ward Hill Lamon played the banjo and sang. He frequently entertained Mr. Lincoln to help lift his spirits. Many of his songs were Negro dialect ballads or minstrel tunes, some more "off color" than others. Ward Hill Lamon: Lincoln's "Particular Friend," pg. 6.

922 Sonorous means loud.

come thirsty, come naked, come bare, come filthy, come lousey, come just as you are." Whereupon the marshal was in great danger of being thrown out of the wagon. Peace at length was again restored to this branch of the human family and the culprit was again restored to favor by Mr. Lincoln saying to him, "Now sir. We want nothing more from you but silence and a great deal of that." This jocular bull of Mr. Lincoln created a general laugh and no thought was entertained at that time of any of the party that these incidences would ever become subjects of comment and adverse criticism of the conduct of Mr. Lincoln on that occasion. It was soon published in the newspapers of the country that were unfavorable to Mr. Lincoln; that he had called for a Negro song on the battle field and the journals and adverse political orators of the country during the political campaign of 1864 belched this unkind and ungenerous misinterpretation from every crossroad, grocery and convenient stump. (See page 295) It served its base purpose as an engine of defamation of that well-known, pure and sympathetic character as a man. The vile misinterpretation annoyed him very much. Yet when it was proposed to him that it would be the proper thing to contradict this slander, through the public press, he replied, "No, there has already been enough said about this falsehood; let the thing alone. If I have not established character enough to give the lie to this charge, I can only say I have been mistaken in my own estimate of myself. But in politics everyone has to skin his own skunk. The hide of this one, these fellows are welcomed to as this body has already given forth its unsavory odor."

On the 2nd of October the rebel House of Representatives passed a resolution proposing to the Pacific states and territories to join in a league with the Confederacy, offensive and defensive. These states and territories however did not favor the proposition and the proposed league proved a failure. On the 3rd of this month the battle of Corinth[924] commenced early in the morning and lasted until night. Confederate Generals Van Dorn,[925] Price[926] and Lovell[927] with their commands attacked the Union lines. The federal forces were driven

---

923 Ludicrous means ridiculous.

924 Corinth is in the northeast corner of Mississippi and only a few miles from the Tennessee border.

925 General Earl Van Dorn—See pg. 122.

926 Sterling Price—See pg. 148.

927 Mansfield Lovell—See pg. 187.

back into the town. Early the next morning hostilities were renewed by the Confederates again attacking and fighting continuously until noon when the Confederates were repulsed. General Rosencrans commanded in person the federal forces in this battle with 20,000 men, the Confederates numbering 38,000 men. Union General Hackleman[928] was killed. The Confederate loss was 473 killed and their wounded estimate was 1,997. There were 137 Confederate officers and over one thousand men taken prisoner, 3,300 stands of arms, fourteen stands of colors and a great amount of stores of all kinds taken. The federals loss was 355 killed, 1,841 wounded and 324 prisoners. After the battle the Confederates were pursued by the federals to Fort Miles, with the main body of the pursuing Union army called to a halt, but with the Union cavalry continuing the pursuit thirty miles further. The retreating forces on the 5th made a stand at Hatchie River where Generals Ord[929] and Hurlbut[930] overtook them and gave them battle. After seven hours of desperate fighting and the loss of four hundred prisoners and a great number of killed and wounded who were left on the field unburied and uncared for, they fled in great disorder. The Union loss here was five hundred men killed and wounded.

The battle of Perryville or as it is sometimes called Chaplin Hills, Kentucky[931]—was fought at this place being situated on the Chaplin River. General McCook's Corps[932] was attacked by the Confederates. The fighting lasted several hours and was desperate. The Confederates

---

[928] General Pleasant A. Hackleman was born in Indiana. He was a lawyer and politician. He nominated Abraham Lincoln in a speech at the Republican National Convention in Chicago. He was Union commander of the First Brigade, 2nd Division of the Army of Tennessee. He was shot in the neck at Corinth and died. The Armies and The Leaders, pg. 137

[929] Edward O. C. Ord—See pg. 163.

[930] Steven A. Hurlbut was a lawyer from Charleston, South Carolina who moved to Illinois in 1845. He was sent as an envoy with the author, Ward Hill Lamon, just prior to the shelling of Fort Sumter. In spite of being from South Carolina he stood by the North during the war. Hurlbut also ordered the arrest of any five secessionists in retaliation of a Union officer arrested in Hannibal, Missouri during the war. After the war he served as Minister to Peru. The Two American Presidents, pg. 322, Civil War a Narrative, Part II., pg. 50, Ward Hill Lamon, Lincoln's "Particular Friend," pg. 192, and The Armies and The Leaders, pgs. 191, 222 & 294.

[931] Perryville/Chaplin Hills is about 30 miles southwest of Lexington, Kentucky.

[932] General Alexander McD. McCook was Ohio born, a graduate of West Point (class of 1863) and an instructor there. He was one of eight of his parent's sons to serve in the civil war. He commanded the 12th Corps at Chickamauga. He served as aide-de-camp to General Sherman after the war. The Armies and The Leaders, pgs. 193 & 228.

were driven across the river with great loss. They lost in killed and wounded and missing 3,396 men. The federal loss was 845 killed and about 2,851 wounded and 515 missing in action. Federal Generals Jackson[933] and Terrill[934] were killed. General Bragg's command would have been captured here by General Buell had he not fallen back to Bryantsville. On the 10th the Confederate General JEB Stuart with his cavalry command made a raid across the Potomac River into Maryland crossing the river at McCoy's Ferry, capturing the Union pickets, and then proceeding towards Mercersburg, Pennsylvania. They captured the town and then marched to Chambersburg.[935] They occupied Chambersburg and after levying contributions on the citizens of that town, they destroyed the depots and workshops of the railroad companies, several trains of cars, and five thousand stands of arms and other property. General Stuart and his men then passed into Maryland through Emmitsburg[936] and during the night obstructed the Baltimore and Ohio Railroad at Poolesville. They then attacked General Stoneman's cavalry[937] and drove them across the Monocacy River.[938] Then they re-crossed the Potomac River at Whites Ford[939] into Virginia. This was a most successful raid. History gives few parallels to it. In this whole expedition General Stuart had not one man killed and only seven men taken prisoner.

On October 18th a citizen in Palmyra, Missouri[940] had been murdered for doing some service to the Union cause by a gang of notorious guerillas. Generals Porter[941] and John McNeil[942] executed

---

933 General James E. Jackson was a Union commander who was killed at Chaplin Hills on October 8, 1862. The Armies and The Leaders, pg. 133.
934 General William R. Terrill was a Union artillery commander at the battle of Shiloh. The Armies and The Leaders, pg. 137. and www.encyclopediavirginia.org/Terrill_William_R_1834_1862
935 Chambersburg is about 15 miles northeast of Mercersburg.
936 Emmitsburg, Maryland is in Frederick County, north of Frederick City.
937 General George Stoneman—See pg. 191.
938 Monocacy River is a river in Frederick, Maryland that flows into the Potomac River near Point of Rocks.
939 Whites Ford is near Leesburg, Virginia and was used to cross the Potomac River.
940 Palmyra, Missouri is in the northeastern part of the state and on the Mississippi River upstream about 100 miles from St. Louis.
941 General Joseph C. Porter was from Kentucky. He led many guerilla raids for the CSA at Vassar Hill, Moore's Mill and Kirlesville. www.camppope.com/sale/nporter.htm
942 General John McNeil was from Michigan and originally commanded the 3rd Michigan Infantry. The Armies and The Leaders, pg. 217.

ten rebel prisoners at that place in retaliation for that murder. On the 20th a provisional court was established in Louisiana and Mr. Lincoln appointed Charles A. Peabody[943] of New York judge of said court. On October 21 General Pleasanton's force[944] attacked General Hampton's[945] command at Martinsburg, Virginia and drove them from the town. General Pleasanton then returned to Shepherdstown.[946] When near that place his command was attacked by the Confederates and the latter were repulsed with considerable slaughter, leaving sixty men dead. The federal loss was not so great.

On the 22nd General Buell was ordered back to the Ohio, General Bragg's army having eluded him and General Buell made a safe entrance into Tennessee. On this day General Blount's command at Marysville, Arkansas attacked 5,000 rebels and routed them with a loss to the Confederates of all one hundred fifty men killed and wounded and the loss of their artillery. On the 24th another British schooner was captured by *The Restless*[947] at Bull's Bay.[948] She was laden with arms and ammunition for the Confederates. Another British steamer the *Anglia* was captured by *The Restless* inside of Bull's Bay. General Buell was relieved of command on the 30th by order of the president and General Rosencrans was appointed in his place.

---

943 Charles Augustus Peabody was born in New Hampshire. He attended Harvard Law School. He was appointed the Chief Justice of the Supreme Court of Louisiana. Famousamericans.net/charlesaugustuspeabody

944 General Alfred Pleasanton was an 1844 graduate of the U.S. Military Academy. He served in the Mexican War. His cavalry men drove the enemy across the river and out of Maryland following the battle of Antietam. He was commander in chief of the Union cavalry corps of the Army of the Potomac. After the war he served as President of the Terre Haute and Cincinnati Railroad. The Two American Presidents, pg.274, Appleton's Cyclopaedia of American Biography, Vol. V., pg. 40 and The Armies and The Leaders, pg. 238.

945 General Wade Hampton was South Carolina born and one of South Carolina's largest slave holders. He was a U.S. Senator and Governor of South Carolina. During the war he led Confederate forces in defense of Trevilian Station. In September 1864 he conducted the "great beefsteak raid" by commandeering over 2,500 cattle and driving them to the Confederates side to feed their soldiers. Following the war he was a commissioner of the railroads. The Armies and The Leaders, pgs, 247 & 252 and The Confederate Nation, pg. 289.

946 Shepherdstown, Virginia is on the Potomac River just a few miles from Sharpsburg, Maryland.

947 *The Restless* was a 108 foot long Union bark carrying a crew of 66 and four guns. She captured sixteen enemy prizes. Warships of the Civil War Navies, pg. 142.

948 Bull's Bay is just north of Charleston, South Carolina.

Visit to McClellan's headquarters
Author Ward Hill Lamon is second from the left

## NOVEMBER 1862

On November 1 General Brannan[949] assumed command of the 10th Corps at Port Royal. Up to this time the rebel vessel *Alabama* had captured twenty-two federal vessels, nineteen of which she had destroyed. On the 5th the 14th Army Corps was divided into three corps under command of Major General Thomas,[950] General Crittenden[951] and General McCook. On this day General Burnside was appointed commander of the Army of the Potomac in place of General McClellan relieved. On the 8th Colonel Ford[952] of Ohio was dismissed from the army for having abandoned his position on Maryland Heights in September last in the face of the enemy. On the same day charges of disobedience of orders were preferred against General Fitz John Porter[953] by General Pope and he was ordered to Washington for trial. On the 11th 1,596 Confederates and 1,016 Union officers and 2,100 privates were exchanged. On the 12th General Hooker was appointed to General Porter's former command of the 5th

---

949 General John Milton Brannan was born in the District of Columbia and was active in the Mexican War. He commanded the Union's Tenth Corps. Civil War a Narrative, pg. 716 and The Armies and The Leaders, pgs. 187 & 210.

950 George H. Thomas—See pg. 169.

951 Thomas Crittenden—See pg. 168 footnote.

952 Colonel Thomas Ford commanded five companies of the 8th Ohio. www.ohiogenealogyexpress.com/mmilitary/8th_ohi-xiv-departbattlefield.htm

953 General Fitz John Porter—See pg. 192.

Corps. On the 14th the Army of the Potomac was again divided into three grand divisions, under command of Generals Sumner,[954] Franklin and Hooker with the 11th Army Corps as a reserve. On the 16th a strict observance of the Sabbath Day in the army and navy was ordered by President Lincoln. On the 17th Jefferson Davis demanded the surrender of General McNeil and threatened in case of refusal to hang the first ten officers who should fall into his hands.

## DECEMBER 1862

On December 1st Mr. Lincoln in a message to Congress[955] recommended compensated emancipation of the slaves of the loyal states before the year 1900. On the 2nd General Hovey[956] with 20,000 men occupied Grenada, Mississippi.[957] On that same day General Geary[958] had a fight with the Confederates near Charlestown, Virginia and defeated them. On the next day the Confederates surrendered Winchester, Virginia to General Geary.

After three days skirmishing, the battle of Prairie Grove[959] opened and after fighting until night, the Confederates retreated over Boston Mountain abandoning their dead and wounded. The Confederates lost 1,317 dead, wounded of missing with a thousand of them being buried on the field. The federal loss was seventy-five killed, 813 wounded and 263 missing. On the same day the California steamer *Ariel*[960]was captured by the privateer *Alabama* off the coast of Cuba. The next day the *Ariel* was released on bond of $230,000 payable at the close of the war. On the 10th Congress passed a bill admitting West Virginia as a state.[961] The battle of Fredericksburg, Virginia was fought on

---

954 General Edwin V. Sumner—See pg. 166.

955 Lincoln's State of the Union message

956 General Charles R. Hovey—See pg. 199.

957 Grenada, Mississippi is about 75 miles north of Jackson, Mississippi.

958 General John White Geary organized the 28th Pennsylvania Infantry. He was a civil engineer and studied law at Jefferson College. He commanded the Second Division of the Union's Tenth Corps during Sherman's Atlanta campaign. www.paroots.com/pacw/officers/geary.html

959 Prairie Grove, Arkansas is in the far northwestern part of the state, north of Fort Smith near the Oklahoma border.

960 *Ariel* was a small Union schooner. She captured three rebel ships as prizes. Warships of the Civil War Navies, pg. 144.

961 The bill stated that West Virginia would become a state on June 20, 1863. History of West Virginia, pg. 334.

December 13. After two days of bombardment of the city, General Burnside advanced across the river and took possession of the city and then advanced on the Confederate works just south of it. General Franklin advanced against the rebel right while General Hooker attacked the center. There were a number of gallant charges made by the federal troops to take the rebel line, but without avail. At night the two armies were found in the same positions they had occupied in the morning. The Union loss was killed 1,284, wounded 9,600 and about 1,769 missing or taken prisoner. The Confederate loss was 585 dead, 4,061 wounded and 653 missing or taken prisoner. This was a disastrous battle for the federals. On the next day there was no general engagement but continual skirmishes along the lines. On the 15th General Burnside still held the city and General Lee's army was inside of their entrenchments. During the night and next morning General Burnside's army re-crossed to the north side of the river. On this day General B. F. Butler was relieved of his command at New Orleans and General Banks appointed in his stead.

On the 18th the Secretary of State and the Secretary of the Treasury Messrs. Seward and Chase tendered their resignations to President Lincoln, but subsequently withdrew them. On the 23rd the Confederate President issued his proclamation denouncing General Butler as an outlaw and threatening to hang him and any of his officers that he captured in retaliation for the hanging of W. D. Mumford[962] in New Orleans. On the 27th General Sherman attacked the outworks at Vicksburg while the gunboats engaged the Haines Bluff batteries. A detachment was sent across the Mississippi River to destroy the Vicksburg and Shreveport Railroad in order to prevent reinforcements reaching the garrison. The federals continued to advance driving the Confederates out of their entrenchments. On the next day the first and second lines were taken and the federals advanced to within two miles of the city. The day following, the federals were repulsed after taking the main battery and rifle pits in the rear of the city. The Confederates were strongly reinforced and threw their whole force on General Sherman's command. After a hand-to-hand fight, General Sherman was forced to retreat to the outer line of works. General Grant at this time prevented cooperation with General Sherman on account of the disaster at Holly Springs. The Union loss was supposed to be between

---

[962] W.D. Mumford—See pg. 194.

four and five thousand men. The day after this battle the gallant little ironclad *Monitor* so effective in the Hampton Roads naval fight sank off Cape Hatteras.[963]

On the 29th Generals McCook, Crittenden and Thomas attacked the Confederates near Stuart's Creek and drove them back to their entrenchments on Stone River, three miles from Murfreesboro. The battle of Murfreesboro[964] was fought on December 31. About daylight General McCook's command was attacked by General Hardee[965] and the right wing of the federal army was driven back with the loss of twenty-eight pieces of artillery. The left wing which had commenced to advance was halted after which a new line of battle was formed. General Rosencrans massed the artillery in the center and by a destructive fire completely crushed the enemy and then ordered a charge when the Confederates broke. General Rosencrans exposed himself very daringly during the whole of this fight which lasted ten hours. General Rains[966] one of the Confederate generals was killed. It was anticipated that the battle would be renewed on the 1st of January, 1863 and he adjusted his lines preparatory to it.

---

963 The *Monitor* sank during a gale while being towed by the *Rhode Island*. Sixteen Union sailors were lost in the accident. Warships of the Civil War Navies, pg. 4.

964 Murfreesboro is just about 25 miles south east of Nashville, Tennessee.

965 General William Hardee was a West Point graduate from Georgia. He commanded one of General Johnston's infantry corps. Civil War a Narrative, Part VII., pgs. 321 & 327.

966 General James Edward Rains of Tennessee commanded the 11th Tennessee Regiment and the 2nd Brigade of the Confederate army. The Armies and The Leaders, pg. 151.

*"The act of signing the Emancipation Proclamation on January 1, 1863 will be "the crowning event" of the Lincoln administration and would "fulfill the mission for which he had been raised up by an over-ruling Providence"*

Nettie Colburn, psychic, as told to Abraham Lincoln at the White House in December, 1862[967]

# — 10 —

# THE WAR IN 1863

## JANUARY 1863

The first of January arrived, and President Lincoln issued his emancipation proclamation in words and figures as follows, to wit:

*By the President of the United States of America:*
*A Proclamation.*

*Whereas, on the twenty-second day of September, in the year of our Lord one thousand eight hundred and sixty-two, a proclamation was issued by the President of the United States, containing, among other things, the following, to wit:*

*That on the first day of January, in the year of our Lord one thousand eight hundred and sixty-three, all persons held as slaves within any State or designated part of a State, the people whereof shall then be in rebellion against the United States, shall be then, thenceforward, and forever free; and the Executive Government of the United States, including the military and naval authority thereof, will recognize and maintain the freedom of such persons, and will do no act or acts to repress such persons, or any of them, in any efforts they may make for their actual freedom.*

*That the Executive will, on the first day of January aforesaid, by proclamation, designate the States and parts of States, if any, in which the people thereof, respectively, shall then be in rebellion against the United States; and the fact that*

[967] Lincoln in American Memory, pg. 229.

*any State, or the people thereof, shall on that day be, in good faith, represented in the Congress of the United States by members chosen thereto at elections wherein a majority of the qualified voters of such State shall have participated, shall, in the absence of strong countervailing testimony, be deemed conclusive evidence that such State, and the people thereof, are not then in rebellion against the United States.*

*Now, therefore I, Abraham Lincoln, President of the United States, by virtue of the power in me vested as Commander-in-Chief, of the Army and Navy of the United States in time of actual armed rebellion against the authority and government of the United States, and as a fit and necessary war measure for suppressing said rebellion, do, on this first day of January, in the year of our Lord one thousand eight hundred and sixty-three, and in accordance with my purpose so to do publicly proclaimed for the full period of one hundred days, from the day first above mentioned, order and designate as the States and parts of States wherein the people thereof respectively, are this day in rebellion against the United States, the following, to wit: Arkansas, Texas, Louisiana, (except the Parishes of St. Bernard, Plaquemines, Jefferson, St. John, St. Charles, St. James Ascension, Assumption, Terrebonne, Lafourche, St. Mary, St. Martin, and Orleans, including the City of New Orleans) Mississippi, Alabama, Florida, Georgia, South Carolina, North Carolina, and Virginia, (except the forty-eight counties designated as West Virginia, and also the counties of Berkley, Accomac, Northampton, Elizabeth City, York, Princess Ann, and Norfolk, including the cities of Norfolk and Portsmouth), and which excepted parts, are for the present, left precisely as if this proclamation were not issued.*

*And by virtue of the power, and for the purpose aforesaid, I do order and declare that all persons held as slaves within said designated States, and parts of States, are, and henceforward shall be free; and that the Executive government of the United States, including the military and naval authorities thereof, will recognize and maintain the freedom of said persons.*

*And I hereby enjoin upon the people so declared to be free to abstain from all violence, unless in necessary self-defence (sic); and I recommend to them that, in all cases when allowed, they labor faithfully for reasonable wages.*

*And I further declare and make known, that such persons of suitable condition, will be received into the armed service of the United States to garrison forts, positions, stations, and other places, and to man vessels of all sorts in said service.*

*And upon this act, sincerely believed to be an act of justice, warranted by the Constitution, upon military necessity, I invoke the considerate judgment of mankind, and the gracious favor of Almighty God.*

*In witness whereof, I have hereunto set my hand and caused the seal of the United States to be affixed.*

*Done at the City of Washington, this first day of January, in the year of our Lord one thousand eight hundred and sixty three, and of the Independence of the United States of America the eighty-seventh.*

*By the President: ABRAHAM LINCOLN*
*WILLIAM H. SEWARD, Secretary of State.* [968]

There was, however, no general engagement but considerable skirmishing throughout the day at Murfreesboro. On the next day the Confederates had amassed their columns on the left wing of the federals and advanced to within one hundred yards when they were met with heavy fire and broke, losing two thousand men. General Sherman was suspended from command by General McClernand. On the day following General Rosencrans was greatly annoyed by heavy skirmishing in front of Murfreesboro and he ordered his four commanders to clear their fronts. He ordered General Rosseau's division[969] to dislodge the Confederates, which they did. On the 4th it was found that the Confederates had retreated from the town the night before. There was no battle during the war that was more hotly contested resulting in greater destruction to life and more important in its results. General Rosecrans who was in command of the Union forces received the grateful plaudits and the heartfelt thanks of the Union people of the country. There was a general acknowledgement that this battle was fought under great disadvantage to the federal command and with greatly inferior numbers, and the battle would have inevitably been lost but for the great generalship of General Rosencrans and the indomitable pluck and bravery of the gallant troops of his command. On the day following General Thomas took possession and occupied the town of Murfreesboro. There were engaged in this battle on the federal side 43,400 men and an estimated number on the Confederate side of 62,520. There were about 25,000 casualties in this battle. The Union losses were 1,677 killed, 7,542

[968] www.archives.gov/exhibits/featured_documents/emancipation_proclamation/transcript.html

[969] General Lovell H. Rosseau led 4,000 cavalry and mounted infantry against Nathan Forrest and his men near Nashville. Harpers Pictorial History of the Great Rebellion, pg. 671.

wounded and 3,686 missing while the rebel losses were 1,294 killed, 7,945 wounded, and 2,476 missing.

Middle Tennessee was by this victory effectually cleared of the Confederate forces and Kentucky saved from any further formidable invasion of a hostile army. War had now been in active operation for more than a year and a half. During a great portion of that time there was a gloomy outlook for the Union people. Many of the staunchest Union men had become discouraged and despaired of the ability of the Union army to crush the rebellion. Not so with Mr. Lincoln. At no time during the war was he discouraged or did he waiver or doubt the final success of the United States Army. The results of this battle were a source of great gratification to him. He realized now that many of his friends who had become discouraged and were ready for peace upon any condition would see as he had seen from the beginning their way clear to success in re-uniting the country. He said this battle had done more to secure good results and a quick termination of the war than any other that had been fought since the commencement of hostilities. "The victories of Mill's Springs, Fort Donelson and Shiloh, the capitulation of Columbus, Island No. 10 and Memphis, gave us control of the upper Mississippi; the capture of New Orleans effectually controlled the river against the egress of the rebel navy and placed under our control the sugar growing districts of Louisiana. The federal armies had brought under subjugation Missouri and the Army of the frontier had pushed across the borders into Arkansas. We now occupy the whole coast of North Carolina and nearly all of South Carolina. The capture of Fort Pulaski has done amazing things; our overpowering the principal seaport town of Savannah, Georgia and our guns command the town and island of Galveston, Texas. The advanced of our armies recently has given us victories on all sides. Our friends have sown discouragement without cause, and our enemies have now great cause for discouragement. These occupations by the federal forces of the territory claimed as belonging to this new-fledged government has led to commotions and dissentions among these secession people which must at no distant day result in an overthrow of their hopes of a separate government." Mr. Lincoln expressed the hope that it was only a question of time when this country would be re-united.

On the 8th *The Pocahontas*[970] captured the English steamer *San-blas.* On the 10th the forces under General McClernand landed on the Arkansas River about a mile below Arkansas Post.[971] The same day the southern papers reported the steamer *Giraffe* as having successfully run the blockade laden with government stores and bringing a special important messenger to the Confederate government. The English ships *Avenger* and *Julia* from Nassau were brought in as prizes by the gunboat *Sangamon*[972] from Key West. On the same day the privateer *Retribution* captured the Brigantine *J. P. Elliot* and put a prize crew on board. They left on board the wife of the mate. She succeeded in getting the officers drunk and while so ironed them; then with the assistance of the crew most of whom were Negroes, she took the vessel to St. Thomas and delivered it to the United States Consul. On the same day *The Rising Dawn*, an English steamer while endeavoring to run the blockade at Charleston was captured by the United States steamer *Aurora.*

The battle of Arkansas Post was fought on the 11th of January, as the land forces under General McClernand assisted by the gunboats under Admiral Porter[973] stormed this place. General Churchill[974] was in command of the Confederate forces. The garrison soon surrendered. The Union loss was one hundred thirty-four killed, eighty-nine wounded and twenty-nine missing. The Confederate loss was one hundred nine killed and wounded and there were 5,000 prisoners taken including the commanding general. The next day, after the fortifications were surrendered, two regiments from Texas marched into the fort with the intention of reinforcing the Confederates and instead were captured by the federal garrison in

---

970 *The Pocahontas* was originally named the *Despatch.* She was a 169 foot long second-class Union sloop with a crew of between 95 and 173. She collected four war prizes. Warships of the Civil War Navies, pg. 89.

971 Arkansas Post, Arkansas is about 20 miles upstream from where the Arkansas River meets the Mississippi River.

972 *Sangamon* was a Union Passaic Class ironclad with two guns in a turret. She was 200 feet long with a crew between 67-88 and was part of the flotilla protecting the James River. Warships of the Civil War Navies, pgs. 8 & 10.

973 Rear Admiral David Porter—See pg. 187.

974 General Thomas James Churchill was from Arkansas. He was a graduate of Transylvania University and a lawyer. He commanded the Confederate garrison at Fort Hindman. He led the Division of the Army of the West defending Arkansas and the Red River region. He was Governor of Arkansas from 1881—1883. The Armies and The Leaders, pg. 257

possession of the fort. On the 11th United States Naval Commander Buchanan[975] was killed on the gunboat *Calhoun* which had run aground at Bayou Teche, Louisiana and was fired upon by the Confederates. On the 20th General Fitz John Porter was dismissed from the United States Army by sentence of court martial for disobedience of orders. On the 25th of this month, General Burnside was relieved of command from the Army of the Potomac and General Joseph Hooker was appointed his successor.

About this time *The Richmond Examiner* published the following remarkable but truthful statement, namely: "The pledge once deemed foolish by the South that he would 'hold, occupy and possess all the forts belonging to the United States government' has been redeemed almost to the letter by Lincoln." It is also in this statement admitted that another year of such progress as this will find Mr. Lincoln master of the southern Confederacy. The article further truthfully stated that with the exception of Forts Sumter and Morgan, all the strongholds on the seaboard between Fortress Monroe to the Rio Grande were in the possession of the North and the onward march of General Rosencrans towards Alabama, the presence of General Grant in north Mississippi and General Curtis[976] in Arkansas to say nothing of General Banks at New Orleans and Baton Rouge, set at rest the silly dream that "a slim strip of seacoast is in possession of the foes." The newspaper then went on to say that "if within the next two months the Confederates do not add 75,000 or 100,000 to our forces in the southwest, we shall come to grief."

Elsewhere we have said something about Mr. Lincoln's status as a politician of the country. The same dissatisfaction entertained by then his administration of affairs was partaken of to a considerable extent by the military department of the government so far as the political-generalship of the army at this time was concerned. The jealousies engendered had caused a state of things in the field that involved the military operations a little less political than the legislative branch of the government. It was well for the fame of Mr. Lincoln that the people at large and the rank and file of the

---

975 Commander Thomas McKean Buchanan was a graduate of the U.S. Military Academy in 1855. He was involved in many battles in the lower Mississippi. Famousamerican.net/mckeanbuchanan

976 General Samuel Ryan Curtis—See pg. 175.

army did not participate in the sentiments then engendered by the base influence of jealousy.

The military operations at the beginning of the war were directed, to a great extent, by amateurs influenced by political preference. A general in command was often thwarted in his well-considered and purposed operations by diseased public opinion brought to bear through the amateur directors—so much so indeed that it may well be wondered that any military victories were achieved during this state of political and military direction—and that victories gained were owed entirely to the great confidence, love and admiration of the rank and file of the army for their commander-in-chief Abraham Lincoln. Of the soldiers, be it said to their honor, they were not fighting for place, for self-aggrandizement, but to repress the rebellion and to restore their country to its pristine splendor and majesty. Of them the remark would well apply, made by Napoleon at Turrenne[977] when he said he was "the only example of a general grew bolder as he grew older." Mr. Lincoln was by no means ignorant of what was going on around him.

Generals Franklin and Sumner were relieved of their commands about the same time that General Burnside was relieved. On the 28th *The Philadelphia Evening Journal* was suppressed for alleged disloyal sentiments. On the same day Henry S. Foote[978] introduced resolutions into the federal Congress offering offensive and defensive alliances with the northwestern states as would lay down their arms and desist from a further prosecution of the war against the South, generously making the same offer to the northwestern states that Mr. Lincoln had made to the South.

On the 29th another British steamer, *The Princess Royal* was captured off Charleston while running the blockade. She had on board eight Wentworth guns,[979] four steam engines, a great many rifles and a considerable amount of powder. On the same day the federal gunboat *Isaac P. Smith*[980] was forced to surrender to the Confederates after a hot engagement in Stone River. The *Isaac P. Smith* had eleven guns and one

---

977 Refers to Napoleon Bonaparte's war strategies.

978 Henry Stuart Foote was a U.S. Senator from Mississippi from 1847-1852 and also served as Governor of Mississippi. www.answers.com/topic/Foote-henry-stuart

979 Wentworth guns were manufactured by the R. W. Wentworth Company.

980 *Isaac P. Smith* was a 171 foot Union vessel. She carried a crew of about 100 men and had nine guns. She had been engaged in the bombardment of Port Royal. She wrecked on June 5, 1863 at Fort Moultrie, South Carolina. Warships of the Civil War Navies, pg. 92.

hundred eighty men. General Beauregard and Commodore Ingraham[981] issued a joint proclamation announcing that the blockade of the southern ports was legally raised.

## FEBRUARY 1863

On the 2nd of February the Commander of the 2nd district of Missouri, General Sloan, issued an order for the prompt execution of all Confederate recruiting offers, guerillas, bush-wackers and other emissaries caught in his district. He also issued an order that the property of all such persons be seized, confiscated and applied to the indemnification[982] of Union citizens. On this day two thousand Confederates with three pieces of artillery attacked the gunboat *New Era*[983] at Island No. 10 but were forced to retire. On the following day General Wheeler[984] with about four thousand Confederates renewed the assault upon Fort Donelson but were repulsed after a severe fight which lasted into the night with a loss to the Confederates of two hundred killed, five hundred wounded and fifty prisoners. The federals being in their entrenchments lost but twelve killed and fourteen missing. This attack would have undoubtedly been successful if it had not been for the timely arrival of the federal gunboats dispersing the rebels just as the garrison had fired their last shot. Another British bark,[985] *The Springbock*, was captured by *The Sonoma*.[986] She was sailing under a false manifest.

On the 8th Lebanon, Tennessee was occupied by the Union forces and there Colonel Morgan, the ubiquitous[987] guerilla chief met with his greatest loss of men, having six hundred of his command captured.

---

981 Commodore Duncan N. Ingraham was put in charge of the Confederate Navy. tomaslegion.net/the_creation_of_the_Confederate_Navy.htm

982 Indemnification means reimbursement.

983 *New Era* was a 137 foot Union tinclad stern wheeler with six guns. She was part of the Mississippi River fleet. She took four prizes. Warships of the Civil War Navies, pg. 175.

984 General Joseph Wheeler was an 1859 graduate of the U.S. Military Academy. He ws the commanding officer of the Army of Tennessee cavalry. tennesseeencyclopedia.net/imagegallery/php?entryID=W048

985 A bark is a three masted ship.

986 *The Sonoma* was a 233 foot long Sonoma Class federal side wheel gunboat with a crew of 120 and four guns. She took five prizes during the war. Warships of the Civil War Navies, pg. 61.

987 Ubiquitous means omnipresent.

On the 12th General Grant cut the levees of the river at Yazoo Pass.[988] On this day President Lincoln submitted to the Senate a correspondence with the French government in relation to its mediation in our present struggle. On the 14th at Gordon's landing on the Red River through the treachery of the pilot, captured *The Queen of the West*[989] the pilot having run aground under the guns of the rebels. Captain Ellet[990] escaped from the boat to *The DeSoto*[991] which was pursued by the rebel gunboat *Webb*.[992] *The DeSoto* burned and the crew was transferred to *Era No. 5*[993] which had before that time been captured by the Confederates. *The Indianola*[994] made her appearance and *The Webb* ceased to pursue.

On the 17th the first representatives of the Congress of the United States from Louisiana were admitted—Messers. Flanders[995] and Hahn,[996] from the first and second districts. On the next day a proclamation was issued by General Beauregard to the people of Charleston and Savannah stating the apprehension of an early attack upon those two cities and calling upon all able bodied men to rally with arms, pikes, scythes, spades and shovels for the defense of their homes and families. On this date *The Richmond Examiner* expressed the greatest indignation at the peace propositions of the French minister

---

988 Yahoo Pass was upstream from Vicksburg on the Mississippi River.

989 *The Queen of the West* was a 181 foot Union Ellet Ram. She carried a crew of 120 and had five guns. Her war prizes totaled four. When captured, all of the crew except thirteen escaped. Warships of the Civil War Navies, pg. 161.

990 Captain Charles H. Ellet, Jr. was a bridge builder. He commanded the Ellet's Ram Fleet of nine steamboats which operated in the Mississippi River. Ellet was shot in the knee at the Battle of Memphis and died from the wound. www.civilwarstudies.org/articles/vol_5/charles_ellet.shtm

991 *The DeSoto* was a 253 foot federal wooden hull side wheeler. She had nine guns and a crew of 185. She captured 21 rebel vessels. Warships of the Civil War Navies, pgs. 70 & 71.

992 *Webb* was a 206 foot Confederate side wheeler with a cotton clad ram. She was used mostly as a transport ship. Warships of the Civil War Navies, pg. 231.

993 *Era No. 5* was a Confederate stern wheeler used as a transport. Warships of the Civil War Navies, pg. 246.

994 *The Indianola* was a 175 foot long federal river ironclad with three inch casemate armor plating. She had four guns and a crew or 144. Warships of the Civil War Navies, pg. 155.

995 Benjamin H. Flanders was a former Congressman who served as the Mayor of New Orleans and the Governor of Louisiana. Bi-oguide.congress.gov/scripts/biodisplay.pl?index=f000189

996 Michael Hahn was and immigrant from Germany and was the 19th Governor of Louisiana. politics.kosmix.com/topic/Michael_Hahn

of foreign affairs, and said the only peace commissioners were Generals Lee, Johnston, Beauregard, Jackson and Longstreet. This voiced the sentiment of the masses of the southern people and was not encouraging to a peaceful settlement of the question. Amid all this the 22nd of February, the anniversary of President Washington's birthday, was celebrated with appropriate ceremonies throughout the North, giving evidence of the great respect cherished for the memory of the father of this distracted family of states.

## MARCH 1863

On the 3rd of March Congress passed the bill to indemnify the President of the United States and his Cabinet against the consequences of illegal arrests. On this day Mr. Lincoln approved the Conscription Act. On the 4th Brigadier General Corcoran[997] shot and instantly killed Lieutenant Colonel Kimball[998] of the Hawkin's Zouaves near Suffolk, Virginia. Brigadier General Corcoran was tried by court martial but was acquitted. On the 5th Colonel Coburn's force[999] consisting of three regiments of infantry, five hundred cavalry and one battery at Thompson's Station in Tennessee was attacked by General Van Dorn[1000] with 18,000 Confederates. The fighting was kept up throughout the day. Most of the federal infantry was either killed or captured, their ammunition having been expended. The Union loss was sixty-five killed, two hundred fifty wounded and over 1,000 prisoners. The Confederates had eighteen killed and four hundred wounded. The federal cavalry and artillery escaped. On the next day in New York the stock quotations showed confidence in the final success of the Union army as gold fell from one hundred seventy-two to one hundred forty-five. On the 8th Colonel Hurlbut at Memphis had ordered all resigned officers to leave the department under pain of arrest. Colonel Grierson[1001] in command of the 6th and 7th Illinois

---

997 Michael Corcoran—See pg. 162.

998 Lt. Colonel Nathan Kimball was born in Indiana. He led the First Brigade of Genera and French's Third Division at Antietam and Fredericksburg. www.nps.gov/frsp

999 Colonel John Coburn led the U.S. military operations in middle Tennessee. www.nps.gov/history/hps/abpp/battles/tn013.htm

1000 Earl Van Dorn –See pg. 122.

1001 Colonel Benjamin H. Grierson was from Illinois. He led the Union cavalry in Mississippi. Civil War a Narrative, pg. 334.

Cavalry captured General Richardson's guerillas[1002] near Covington, Tennessee[1003] by surrounding them. About the same time Colonel Lee[1004]captured General Lowery[1005] and his guerillas at Wythe Depot, Germantown, Tennessee.[1006] On the same day a brigade of Negroe troops captured Jacksonville, Florida. On the 9th another British steamer, *The Druro*, was captured off Cape Fear by the United States steamer, *Quaker City*.[1007] On that day the Confederates cut the levee at Lake Providence and flooded over one hundred miles of Louisiana. General Banks' expedition of 18,000 troops left New Orleans for Port Hudson. On the next day Mr. Lincoln warned all the deserters to return to their commands by the 1st day of April and called upon all patriotic citizens to give their aid and assistance in returning deserters to their command and enforcing the conscript act.

On the 11th a proclamation to the citizens of Delaware was issued by Governor Connon[1008] enjoining them to hold their allegiance to the general government paramount to that of the state and promising protection to all who should aid by act or information the national magistracy in suppressing the rebellion against the operation of "the act to prevent illègal arrests" passed by the legislature of Delaware. On the same day a party of Confederates attempted to cut the levees opposite Vicksburg. On the 14th the gunboats *Carondelet*,[1009] *Mound City*,[1010] *Louisville*,[1011] *Pittsburg*[1012] and *Cincinnati*[1013] under the command

---

1002 General Israel Richardson—See pg. 139.

1003 Covington, Tennessee is 30 miles northeast of Memphis. .

1004 Colonel Albert L. Lee commanded the 7th Regiment of Kansas Volunteer Cavalry. www4.pair.com/justfolk/reghis1.htm

1005 General Mark B. Lowery led a brigade of Confederate infantry in the Army of Tennessee. The Armies and The Leaders, pg. 277.

1006 Germantown, Tennessee is a couple of miles southeast of Memphis

1007 *Quaker City* was a 244 foot Union large combatant side wheeler. She had a crew of 142 and four guns. She took 22 enemy prizes. Warships of the Civil War Navies, pg. 76.

1008 Governor William Connon was Governor of Delaware from 1863—1865, dying in office. He supported the thirteenth amendment which was blocked by the Democrats from his state. www.freebase.com/view/in/william_cannon

1009 *Caronelet* was a 175 foot long Cairo Class river ironclad with a center wheel. She was protected by a 2.5 inch casement armor. She was part of the Mississippi River fleet of the Union Navy. She had 14 guns and a crew of 257. Warships of the Civil War Navies, pg. 151.

1010 *Mound City* was a 175 foot long Cairo Class Mississippi River ironclad. She had 14 guns and a federal crew of 251. Warships of the Civil War Navies, pgs. 151 & 153.

1011 *Louisville* was a federal Mississippi River Cairo Class ironclad with a crew of 251 and 14 guns. Warships of the Civil War Navies, pgs. 151 & 213.

of Admiral Porter left the mouth of the Yazoo River for the upper Yazoo by way of Black Bayou and Rolling Forks. On the following day the United States officials at San Francisco seized the rebel steamer *Chaplain* as a privateer. She had on board six Dahlgren guns[1014] with a party of rebels whose purpose it was to capture the mail steamer *Oregon*.[1015] On the 15th President Davis issued an address to the people of the South urging them to devote their agricultural labor to the production of food. He said that to oppose an invading force of 1,300,000 men they had only the unconquerable valor of a people destined to be free; that the federal army had been baffled in their attempts on Vicksburg, Port Hudson and elsewhere and that in a few weeks the falling of the waters and heat of the summer would complete their discomfiture.[1016] He closed with an appeal to that patriotism which they had exhibited from the beginning of the war.

On the 16th seven of the gunboats and three transports of the fleet of Admiral Porter ran the batteries at Vicksburg. One of the transports was burned but with this exception, that of one man being killed and three being wounded, there were no other casualties. On the same day the gunboat *Vanderbilt*[1017] captured another British steamer the *Gertrude* while attempting to run the federal blockade at Charleston. The captured vessel had on board a large cargo of gunpowder and military stores intended for the rebels. On the next day the federal batteries opposite Vicksburg opened fire on the town. On the 20th the citizens of Baltimore, Maryland held an immense Union meeting. This day it is

---

1012 *Pittsburg* was a federal Cairo Class river ironclad, used in the Mississippi River fleet. She had 14 guns and a crew of 251. Warships of the Civil War Navies, pgs. 151 & 153.

1013 *Cincinnati* was a Union Mississippi River Cairo Class ironclad. She had a crew of 251 and 14 guns. Warships of the Civil War Navies, pgs. 151-152.

1014 Dahlgren guns were muzzle loading naval artillery pieces designed by John A. Dahlgren of the U.S. Navy. Dahlgren was a U.S. Navy Admiral who commanded the South Atlantic Blockading Squadron. www.civilwarartillery.com/inventors/dahlgren.htm

1015 *Oregon* was part of the Confederate's Mississippi River defense fleet stationed in the Louisiana area. She was a 216 foot side wheeler with four guns and a mast. She also served successfully as a blockade runner. She was destroyed by her crew in 1862 to avoid capture. Warships of the Civil War Navies, pg. 230.

1016 Discomfiture means rout.

1017 *Vanderbilt* was a 340 foot side wheeler with two masts built originally for trans-Atlantic passenger travel by Cornelius Vanderbilt. Mr. Vanderbilt gave the ship to the federal navy when the war started. It was converted into a fast cruiser with 15 guns and a crew of 209. She took four prizes. Warships of the Civil War Navies, pgs. 77 & 78.

to be observed was the second anniversary of the massacre of Union soldiers in that city while in transit to Washington to defend it and resist rebellious invasion. The treasonable assaults by the mob of the city two years before did more than any one thing to accelerate the general uprising of patriotism throughout the North. The *Alabama* and *Florida* had destroyed three other vessels belonging to the United States.

On the 17th Colonel James E. Fry[1018] was appointed Provost Marshal General under the Conscription Act. On the same day General Avery's Union cavalry[1019] consisting of two hundred men crossed the Rappahannock River at Kelley's Ford. The ford being very narrow they were compelled to cross singly in the face of a calling fire. They charged the rebel rifle pits and entrenchments, capturing nearly the whole force. Immediately after this they encountered General Fitzhugh Lee's cavalry.[1020] General Granger[1021] was attacked at Franklin, Tennessee[1022] by General Van Dorn with his whole command and after a severe fight of two hours General Van Dorn was defeated and retreated leaving his dead on the field. The killed, wounded and missing for the combined forces did not exceed four hundred.

On the 26th his advance under Colonel Prince[1023] captured and destroyed the train of cars laden with all kinds of military stores. On the next day he reached Hazelhurst forty miles south of Jackson. On the next day he reached Brookhaven, captured two hundred prisoners, paroled them and destroyed a large camp of instruction with its equipment. Also on the 27th a detachment of his force captured Mayhew, twelve miles from Columbus, Mississippi and tore up twenty miles of the Central Mississippi Railroad. On the next day he reached the town of Philadelphia, Mississippi after a perilous march through

---

1018 James E. Fry was the Assistant Adjutant General who was in charge of calling and enrolling the Union troops. *New York Times*, March 19, 1863

1019 General Isaac E. Avery commanded the Georgia Dragoons. www.shilohbattlefield.org/commission.pages/mississippi/hardee/wood.htm

1020 General Fitzhugh Lee (also known as "Roonie") was a West Pointer, graduating in 1856 and a classmate of General Mosby. He commanded a cavalry brigade. He was the nephew of Confederate General Robert E. Lee. Civil War a Narration, pgs. 244 & 245.

1021 General Gordon Granger—See pg. 184.

1022 Franklin is about 15 miles south of Nashville, Tennessee.

1023 Colonel Prince was battalion commander part of Grierson's cavalry. www.historynet.com/americas-civil-war-colored-benjamin-grierson's-cavalry-raid-in-1863.htm/1

swamps and rivers from Starkville. On the following day he reached Newton Mills and destroyed thirty-nine train cars laden with quartermaster and commissary stores. His raid through the state up to this time created the greatest excitement in central Mississippi. The following day he reached a point seven miles north of Montross burning and destroying the railroad in his route. Also on the 28th Cape Girardeau, Missouri was attacked by eight thousand Confederates under General Marmaduke.[1024] The fighting lasted two hours when they were repulsed and retreated toward Bloomfield with a loss of sixty killed, three hundred wounded and a large number of prisoners. The Union loss was inconsiderable not exceeding twenty men killed and wounded. On their retreat Colonel Newton[1025] commanded the vanguard.[1026] They were surprised by the Union forces under General Vandervoort[1027] and were completely routed; the whole command was either killed or taken prisoner. On the 29th the Rappahannock River was crossed by the Army of the Potomac, surprising the rebel pickets and capturing four hundred prisoners. Thirty-five thousand men comprising the left wing crossed four miles below Fredericksburg where an engagement occurred and lasted twelve hours resulting in the rebels being driven from their rifle pits a distance of eight miles. On that day the Union ships *Oneida*[1028] of New York and the bark *Henrietta* of Baltimore were captured with cargoes between $500,000 and $1,000,000. The *Oneida* was burned by the privateer *Florida*. The fight of Fairmont, Virginia[1029] occurred on April 30. This place was defended by three hundred fifty men and was attacked by a heavy

---

1024 Brigadier General John S. Marmaduke was born in Missouri and attended West Point. He was commander of the Confederate Cavalry west of the Mississippi. Civil War a Narrative, pg. 139 and The Armies and The Leaders, pg. 279.

1025 Colonel Robert C. Newton commanded the First Battalion of the 10th Arkansas Cavalry. www.couchgen.com/civilwar/10thregt.htm

1026 The vanguard is the front of the army.

1027 General Paul Vandervoort was from Nebraska. He enlisted at age 15. During the war he spent time in Confederate prisons at Libby, Belle Island and Andersonville. After the war he served as commander in Chief of the Grand Army of the Republic in 1882. The Armies and The Leaders, pg. 296 and www.nebraskahistory.org/publish/publicat/timeline/vendervoort-paul.htm

1028 *Oneida* was an Iroquois Class Union sloop, 198 feet in length with a crew of 124 and ten guns. Warships of the Civil War Navies, pg. 39.

1029 Fairmont, Virginia is located about 15 miles southwest of what is today Morgantown, West Virginia.

force of cavalry under Generals Imboden[1030] and Jones.[1031] The fighting continued all day long. The garrison was forced eventually to surrender. The Union loss did not exceed more than five men killed and wounded. The rebel loss was over five hundred men. General Meade's Corps[1032] occupied Chancellorsville four miles south of Fredericksburg. On the same day the rebel batteries up the Yazoo River were attacked by General Sherman with a fleet of gunboats and transports. On that same day General Geary landed at Bruinsburg below Vicksburg. Colonel Grierson[1033] with his cavalry made a wonderful raid through Mississippi, starting from LaGrange, Tennessee on the 17th of April 1863. And he moved his command to Bayou Chittou Station destroying bridges, railroads, &c. enroute.

## MAY 1863

On May 1 Colonel Grierson with his command arrived in Baton Rogue and aroused great enthusiasm among the people. He had traveled over eight hundred miles through the rebellious country having encountered no obstacle which he did not overcome, He and his men fought and dispersed the rebels wherever they encountered them, captured over one thousand prisoners, took two hundred horses, and destroyed over $400,000 worth of property. His raid was not equaled by any during the war except General Morgan's wonderful ride through Ohio, Indiana, Kentucky and Tennessee.

The battle of Magnolia,[1034] fought on the 1st saw a portion of General Pendleton's rebel army[1035] under the command of General

---

1030 Brigadier General John B. Imboden was the commander of the 7th Brigade of the Confederate Cavalry. After the battle at Gettysburg, he commanded the seventeen mile long wagon train carrying the Confederate wounded back to Virginia. Civil War a Narrative, pg. 463 and The Armies and The Leaders, pg. 105.

1031 General William E. Jones was commander of a brigade of General Stuart's Confederate cavalry. He was killed at Piedmont, June 5, 1864. The Armies and The Leaders, pg. 155 and Civil War a Narrative, pg. 438.

1032 General George Meade was born in Spain. He graduated from the U.S. Military in 1835. He held various commands including relieving General Hooker as commander of the Union forces in June of 1863 just prior to the battle of Gettysburg. He lost his command shortly after that battle as he was criticized for allowing Lee's army to escape. www.civilwarhom.com/meadebio.htm

1033 Benjamin Henry Grierson—See pg. 236.

1034 The Battle of Magnolia, Louisiana is also called the Battle of Baton Rogue.

1035 General George H. Pendleton was a Democratic Congressman from Ohio. Reelecting Lincoln, pgs. 90 and 291.

Bowen[1036] fight with a portion of General Grant's army resulting in the rebels being driven back and the occupation of Fort Gibson. On the 1st General Sykes[1037] division was attacked at Chancellorsville by the rebels when a warm engagement ensued lasting an hour and a half. The battle of Chancellorsville on the next day at noon fairly opened. General Jackson with forty thousand men attacked General Hooker's right. The first shock was received by the Eleventh Corps of the United States Army causing them to break. Reinforcements being promptly supplied, the rebels were checked after capturing several pieces of artillery. General Sickles[1038] had penetrated the rebel column but the retreat of the Eleventh Corps compelled his recall. Night coming on at eleven o'clock, General Hooker ordered an attack. Finding the communications with General Sickles interrupted it was restored and the rebels were driven back. General Sickles brought with him four hundred prisoners. This was a desperately fought battle. On the day following the battle was renewed about 5½ a.m. and was continued with wonderful determination and terrible slaughter until 11½.

General Sedgwick[1039] stormed and captured Martee Hill in Fredericksburg about four miles below Chancellorsville and drove the rebels on to the rear of General Lee which brought the Confederates between his command and that of General Hooker. General Lee then recovered Chancellorsville and drove General Hooker towards the United States ford. Two thousand prisoners were captured by the federals. General "Stonewall" Jackson was severely wounded in this battle by mistake of his own troops, while he was making a

---

[1036] Brigadier General John S. Bowen from Missouri commanded the Confederate forces at Grand Gulf on the Mississippi River just south of Vicksburg. Civil War a Narrative, pg. 346

[1037] Major General George Sykes from Delaware was a graduate of the U.S. Military Academy class of 1842 and served in the Seminole and Mexican Wars. He saved General Pope's army from total destruction at the battle of second Bull Run. Civil War a Narrative, pg. 277 and The Armies and The Leaders, pgs. 183 & 200.

[1038] General Daniel Edgar Sickles was a New York born Congressman. He commanded the Union's 3rd Corps at Chancellorsville. He lost his leg at Gettysburg but continued in the Union Army. After the war he served as Minister to Spain from 1869 - 1873, served in Congress and was county sheriff in New York. The Armies and The Leaders, pgs. 181 & 194.

[1039] General John Sedgwick commanded the VI Corps. He was killed by a sharpshooter at Spotsylvania May 9, 1864. www.civilwarbattlefields.us/spotsylvania/segwick,html

recognizance in person after nightfall on May 2. From the result of this unfortunate wounding the great and successful Confederate chieftain died ten day after. General Lee was feelingly sad afterwards, saying he lost his right arm, and his most trusted lieutenant. General Jackson's name and presence was so powerful an incentive to valor with his troops that the fact of his being wounded was kept from them and his corps was led the next day by General JEB Stuart splendidly and effectively.

From what we can learn of "Stonewall" Jackson's character he was a pious belligerent; he had led a life of purity and did his fighting as he had ever performed other duties in life, prompted by conscientious convictions of right however diligent his enemies may have thought him to be in his course.

General Sedgwick was forced to retreat the next day across the river to join General Hooker and the rebels retook Fredericksburg. On the 3rd General Lee was heavily reinforced and drove General Hooker back, forcing him to re-cross the Rappahannock River. The Union loss in this battle was 1,575 killed, 9,594 wounded and about 5,676 missing. The rebel loss was 1,665 killed, 9,081 wounded and 2,018 missing. The rear of General Hooker's army got back to the main on the 6th.

On the 3rd Colonel Streight's command[1040] was captured near Rome, Georgia[1041] consisting of 1375 men with all their horses by Generals Forrest[1042] and Rody. During Colonel Streight's whole raid up to that time he had lost seventy-two men killed, wounded and missing, while the rebels had lost between five and six hundred. On the 4th a portion of General Stoneman's command[1043] under General

---

1040 Colonel Adel D. Streight was a New York native who commanded a Indiana regiment in the Union Army. He was captured on May 3 and incarcerated for ten months at Libby Prison in Richmond, Virginia. Civil War a Narrative, pgs. 189 & 683.

1041 Rome, Georgia is in the northwestern part of the state about 55 miles northwest of Atlanta and near the Alabama border.

1042 General Nathan Bedford Forrest was a slave trader in Memphis, Tennessee. Although barely literate, he was considered the greatest cavalry man in the country. He was the Confederate cavalry commander most feared by General Grant. His brother Jeffrey, one of his horseman, died in Mississippi in January 1864. After the war he had several large plantations. He became the first leader of the Ku Klux Klan. He was President of the Selma, Marion, and Memphis Railroad. Civil War Narrative, pg. 65, Pride of the South, pgs, 82 -84, and The Armies and The Leaders, pgs. 21, 48, 249 & 278.

1043 George Stoneman—See pg. 191.

Kirpatrick[1044] made an entrance into the fortifications of Richmond. On the 7th Dr. Peters[1045] at Morris County, Tennessee killed General Van Dorn of the rebel army as a result of a private quarrel. On the 9th another British schooner the *Linette* was captured off Mobile, Alabama[1046] by the steam transport *Union*. On the 10th General Grant invaded Jackson, Mississippi.[1047] On the 11th the court of inquiry into the military conduct of General Buell was adjourned. This court had been in session 165 days.

On the 11th the Provost Marshal of New Orleans ordered that all public resorts except places of worship should display the national flag and the theaters were required to play national airs every evening much to the disgust of many of the inhabitants of that city. The battle of Raymond, Mississippi[1048] occurred on the 12th. This was a stubborn fight that lasted two hours. General McPherson's Corps[1049] captured the place after killing seventy-five men and capturing one hundred eighty-six prisoners. On the 13th General Schoepf[1050] was relieved of the command of the Department of the Missouri and was succeeded by General Curtis.[1051] On the 14th the battle of Jackson[1052] was fought. General Grant captured the city. On that day resolutions were made by the rebel Congress threatening the hanging of all commissioned officers of Negro regiments who might be captured. At Mississippi Springs, General Grant defeated Generals Green[1053] and Walker[1054]

---

1044 H. Judson Kilpatrick—See pg. 200.

1045 Dr. George B. Peters was protesting General Van Dorn's attention to the doctor's young wife, though some said the shooting was politically motivated. Civil War a Narrative, pg. 178.

1046 Mobile, Alabama is located on the Gulf of Mexico between Pensacola, Florida and New Orleans.

1047 Jackson, Mississippi is 50 miles due west of Vicksburg.

1048 Raymond, Mississippi is about 10 miles southwest of Jackson.

1049 General James Birdseye McPherson commanded the center of General Grant's Union army at Vicksburg. Civil War a Narrative, pgs. 61 & 145.

1050 General Albin Schoepf—See pg. 154.

1051 General Samuel R. Curtis—See pg. 175.

1052 Jackson, Mississippi was the capital of Jefferson Davis' home state. Civil War a Narrative, pg. 363.

1053 General Martin E. Green was a Confederate commander killed at Vicksburg, July 27, 1863. The Armies and The Leaders, pgs. 151 & 153.

1054 General William Henry Talbot Walker was a Confederate commander at Jackson, Mississippi and Lookout Mountain, Tennessee. He was born in Georgia and was a Mexican War hero. He was wounded three times at the battle of Olustee, Florida on February 20, 1864. He was killed at Atlanta on July 22, 1864. Civil War a Narrative, pgs. 263 & 690 and The Armies and The Leaders, pgs. 145 & 278.

while General McPherson captured and occupied Clinton, Mississippi.[1055]

The battle of Champion Hill was fought on the 16th of May and the result of the battle was the rebels under Lieutenant General Pemberton[1056] were utterly defeated. There were twenty five thousand men on each side of this engagement. The rebels lost three hundred eighty-one killed, 1,769 wounded with 1,670 missing or prisoners and sixteen pieces of artillery. The Unionists had four hundred ten killed, 1,844 wounded and one hundred eighty-seven missing or prisoners.

On the 16th Clement L. Vallandigham[1057] was sentenced by General Burnside to be confined in Fort Warren during the war. Vallandigham applied to Judge Levitt[1058] of Cincinnati for a writ of *habeas corpus*. He declined to issue it. Mr. Lincoln afterwards modified the sentence of General Burnside to transportation of the prisoner beyond federal lines. On the next day was fought the battle of Big Black. General Grant on the advance towards Vicksburg met and opened hostilities. General Pemberton's forces were driven back into Vicksburg with the loss of 2,600 men and seventeen pieces of artillery. General Pemberton burned the bridges upon his retreat. On the date the Tredegar Iron Works[1059] at Richmond were burned. On the next day

---

1055 Clinton, Mississippi is just a few miles northwest of Jackson.

1056 Lt. General John Clifford Pemberton was born in Pennsylvania. He graduated in 1837 from the U.S. Military Academy and was a hero of the Mexican War. He commanded the Confederate Departments of South Carolina, Georgia and Florida. Pride of the South, pgs. 110 & 111.

1057 Clement C. Vallandigham was the editor of the *Dayton Empire* newspaper. He was a Democratic Congressman from Ohio. He was known as "the king of the Copperheads." He attacked the Lincoln administration with violence and boldness. He was arrested by General Burnside and banished behind Confederate lines. After the war he was a practicing attorney. He accidentally shot himself while demonstrating a gun in a trial in 1871 and died. Lincoln and the Civil War, pg. 192, Appleton's Cyclopaedia of American Biography, Vol. VI., pgs. 227 & 228. and Reelecting Lincoln, pgs. 14-15.

1058 Judge Humphrey Howe Levitt was a former Ohio Congressman and Judge of the District Court of the Southern Division of Ohio. The judge's opinion was later upheld by the U.S. Supreme Court. www.ca6.uscourts.gov/hb-hist/courts/district%20/OH/SDOH/judges/hhl-bio/html

1059 Tredegar Iron Works in Richmond was constructed as an iron works in the early 1800s. At the beginning of the Civil War over half of the 900 employees at the operation were slaves. They made iron here used in the construction of the ironclad USS Virginia and over 1,100 artillery pieces. After the war it was a profitable business up until 1873 with over 1200 employees. www.nps.gov/archive/rich/8pt006.html

Vicksburg was invested.[1060] General Grant had constructed pontoon bridges across the river on which he crossed and made a close investment of the city. Haines Bluff was occupied at this time by the command of General Sherman and all the approaches to the city were now occupied. In the various engagements of General Grant's approach on Vicksburg the rebels had lost 9,000 prisoners and sixty-five pieces of artillery.

The majority of the original commanding officers of the Union Army were appointed from the ranks of the Democratic Party. The commanders of the Army corps afterwards were:

First Army Corps—General John Norton[1061]
Second Army Corps—General Gouveneur K. Warren[1062]
Third Army Corps—William H. French[1063]
Fourth Army Corps—General Gordon Granger[1064]
Fifth Army Corps—General George Sykes[1065]
Sixth Army Corps—General John Sedgwick[1066]
Seventh Army Corps was consolidated with the 18th
Eighth Army Corps—General Robert C. Schenk[1067]
Ninth Army Corps—General John G. Parke[1068]
Tenth Army Corps—General Q. A. Gillmore[1069]

---

1060 Invested means surrounded.

1061 General John Norton was from Illinois and a friend of both Mr. Lincoln and author, Ward Hill Lamon. Ward Hill Lamon, Lincoln's "Particular Friend," pg. 122

1062 General Gouveneur Kemble Warren from New York, graduated second in his class at West Point in 1850. He became a topographer, mapping the Dakotas and Nebraska territories and helping to find possible routes for a transcontinental railroad. During the civil war, he built the fort on Federal Hill in Baltimore. Appleton's Cyclopaedia of American Biography, Vol. VI., pgs. 362 & 363.

1063 William Henry French was born in Baltimore, Maryland and was an 1837 graduate of the U.S. Military Academy. He was an aide-de-camp to General Franklin Pierce during the Mexican War. He also served in the Seminole War. Appleton's Cyclopaedia of American Biography, Vol. II., pg. 549 and The Armies and The Leaders, pgs. 181 & 196.

1064 General Gordon Granger—See pg. 184.

1065 General George Sykes—See pg. 242.

1066 General John Sedgwick—See pg. 242.

1067 General Robert C. Schenk—See pgs. 129 & 130.

1068 General John Grubb Parke was an 1849 graduate of the U.S. Military Academy and became a topographer. He was from Pennsylvania. He replaced General Burnside in 1864 as commander of the 9th Corps. After the war he was Commandant of West Point in 1887 and also became the Chief Engineer for Washington, D.C. Grant Takes Command, pg. 368, The Armies and The Leaders, pgs. 185 & 208 and Appleton's Cyclopaedia of American Biography, Vol. IV., pg. 649.

Eleventh Army Corps—General Oliver O. Howard[1070]
Twelfth Army Corps—General Henry W. Slocum[1071]
Thirteenth Army Corps—General Edward O. C. Ord[1072]
Fourteenth Army Corps—General John McCauley Palmer[1073]
Fifteenth Army Corps—General John A. Logan[1074]
Sixteenth Army Corps—General Stephen A. Hurlbut[1075]
Seventeenth Army Corps—General James B. McPherson[1076]
Eighteenth Army Corps—General Benjamin F. Butler[1077]
Nineteenth Army Corps—General William B Franklin[1078]
Twentieth and Twenty-First consolidated as the Fourth Corps
Twenty-Second Army Corps—George L. Hartsuff[1079]

---

1069 General Quincy Adams Gillmore was commander of the Union troops at Charleston, South Carolina. He also helped defend Washington against General Early's raid in July 1864. The Armies and The Leaders, pgs 175 & 210 and Grant Takes Command, pg. 149.

1070 General Oliver Otis Howard was from Maine and a graduate of Bowdoin College and West Point (class of 1854). He returned to West Point to teach mathematics from 1854 to 1861. He was wounded twice, had five horses shot out from under him and lost his right arm in the fighting at Fair Oaks. He commanded the Army of the Tennessee. He was at the surrender of Confederate General Joe Johnston. Later Mr. Howard was a Congressman and was in charge of the Freedman's Bureau from 1865 to 1874. He was Commandant of West Point from 1880 - 1882. Appleton's Cyclopaedia of American Biography, Vol. III., pg. 278, The Sword of Lincoln, pg. 88 and The Armies and The Leaders, pgs. 76, 170 & 171.

1071 General Henry Warner Slocum was from New York and was a graduate of West Point (1852). He was severely wounded at Bull Run but returned. His troops were the first to enter Atlanta on September 2, 1864 as part of General Sherman's March to the Sea and he notified the War Department of Sherman's victory there. Later he was a commissioner for the Brooklyn Bridge in New York City. Grant Takes Command, pg. 359 and Appleton's Cyclopaedia of American Biography, Vol. V., pg. 551.

1072 General Edward Otho Cresap Ord —See pg. 163.

1073 General John McCauley Palmer was born in Kentucky. He moved to Illinois and became a lawyer. He was a friend of Abraham Lincoln and a delegate to the Republican National Convention in Chicago where Lincoln was nominated. He served as Governor of Illinois from 1868—1872. Mr. Palmer was a Presidential candidate for the Democratic party in the 1896 election. www.daylife.com/topic/john_m_palmer

1074 General John A. Logan was born in Illinois. He was often referred to as "Black Jack Logan" due to his black eyes and black hair. He graduated from the University of Louisville with a law degree. He served in the Mexican War and in both the U. S. Congress and U. S. Senate. He was a union commander of General McPherson's army at Vicksburg. He was nominated for Vice-President in the 1884 National election. www.illinoiscivilwar.org/john_logan.html and Civil War a Narrative, pg. 409.

1075 General Stephen Augusta Hurlbut—See pg. 220.

1076 General James Birdseye McPherson—See pg. 244.

1077 General Benjamin F. Butler—See pg. 87.

1078 General William Buell Franklin—See pg. 211.

Cavalry Corps
Army of the Potomac—General Alfred Pleasanton[1080]
Army of Cumberland—General David S. Stanley[1081]

At the time of the fall of Fort Sumter, the population of the loyal states was about 23,000,000 and the whole army included the troops at the beleaguered forts, together with those which had already been surrendered to the Confederacy consisting of nineteen regiments, two corps of engineers, numbering in all not over 14,000 effective men. Up to the first day of July 1862 there had been enlisted in the service of the United States, 1,750,000 men, which constituted the greatest army according to numbers that the history of the world given any account of since that of Xerxes[1082] when he invade Greece.

The following table will show the number of men furnished by each state up to the time of June 1, 1863:

| | | |
|---|---|---|
| Maine | 29,960 | 6,500 to the Navy |
| New Hampshire | 20,000 | 17,000 to the Navy |
| Vermont | 18,508 | |
| Massachusetts | 75,000 | 1,400 to the Navy |
| Rhode Island | 18,755 | |
| Connecticut | 38,219 | |
| New York | 250,000 | |
| New Jersey | 21,002 | |
| Pennsylvania | 195,326 | |
| Delaware | 13,651 | |
| Maryland | 15,000 | |
| West Virginia | 20,000 | |
| Kentucky | 43,908 | |
| Tennessee | 18,500 | |
| Missouri | 40,000 | |
| Ohio | 90,228 | |
| Indiana | 130,000 | |

1079 General George L. Hartsuff was a graduate of the U.S. Military Academy class of 1852. He was severely wounded at Antietam on September 17, 1862. Fort Hartsuff in Florida is named in his honor. Freepages.genealogy.rootsweb.ancestry.com/~crackerbarrel/Hartsuff.html

1080 General Alfred Pleasanton—See pg. 222.

1081 General David S. Stanley—See pg. 184.

1082 Xerxes was King of Prussia from 485—465 B. C. www.encyclopedia.com/topic/xerxes_I.aspx

| | |
|---|---|
| Illinois | 150,000 |
| Wisconsin | 40.646 |
| Michigan | 44,572 |
| Iowa | 40,127 |
| Kansas | 10,000 |
| Minnesota | 13,317 |
| Oregon | 700 |
| California | 7,500 |
| Washington territory | 100 |
| Dakota Territory | 278 |
| Colorado Territory | 3,000 |
| Nebraska Territory | 3,000 |
| Nevada Territory | 150 |
| District of Columbia | 2,000 |

## JUNE 1863

June the 1st the *Chicago Times* was suspended and *the New York World's* circulation in the Department of the Ohio was prohibited by General Burnside. This order gave great dissatisfaction in Illinois of that suspension. Federal Judge Drummond[1083] at Chicago granted a temporary injunction to restrain the military from taking possession of the *Chicago Times* office. On the 3rd the Illinois House of Representatives passed resolution denouncing General Burnside's order and demanding its withdrawal. Mr. Lincoln was appealed to and he revoked the order by General Burnside both in relation to the *Times* and the *World.*

On the 5th the Union troops in their operations reached within speaking distance of the rebel works at Vicksburg. The siege guns were opened on them; there were thrown into the city in the short space of one hour, 3,600 shells. On the 8th of June gold was at a premium in Richmond, Virginia of six dollars and silver at five fifty.

On the 9th the siege of Vicksburg was progressing slowly. The rifle pits and parallels were being forwarded by General Grant as rapidly as prudence dictated. The rear of General Grant's army was now being constantly threatened with an attack from General Johnston who

---

1083 Judge Thomas Drummond was born in Maine and graduated from Bowdoin College. He moved to Galena, Illinois where he served in the Illinois General Assembly with Abraham Lincoln. He organized a protest against General Burnside's actions. www.powerset,com/explore/go/thomas-drummond

continued to mass troops behind him. On the same day Colonel Lawrence W. Orton[1084] chief of artillery on General Bragg's staff, alias Lawrence Williams of the United States Army, and Major W. D. Pettis,[1085] C.S.A. were executed as spies at Franklin, Tennessee. By forged certificates and assertions that they had been deputed[1086] to examine fortifications they gained admission into the federal lines. Colonel Baird[1087] commanding the post had his suspicions excited and arrested them. Their executions followed under the development of facts. On that same day there was a fight in Beverly Ford between 1,500 cavalry under General Stuart and 900 under General Pleasanton. The fight lasted from five o'clock a.m. until late in the afternoon when General Stuart was reinforced and General Pleasanton was forced to withdraw. Before this the rebel cavalry had been driven back four miles. It was the purpose at the time for the Confederates to make an invasion of Pennsylvania, but this delayed the movement. About this time apprehensions were felt about the tone and temper of the Illinois legislature which was then in session and Governor Richard Yates[1088] always ready to take responsibilities, assumed the high prerogative of proroguing[1089] that body until January, 1865. This step was at the time regarded as an unusual assumption of power by the governor of a state not in rebellion.

Up to this time, June 11th it was estimated that 50,000 colored soldiers had been enlisted into the service of the United States. On this day a large number of rebel officers and prisoners that had been sent

---

[1084] Lawrence W. Orton was born in New York. When his parents died, his appointed guardian was George Washington Parke Custis, father of Robert E. Lee's wife Mary. In June 1863, he was hanged as a spy in Franklin, Tennessee. www.civilwarcavalry.com

[1085] W. D. Pettis and his cousin Walter Gip Peter were also hanged. www.civilwarcavalry.com

[1086] Deputed means assigned.

[1087] Colonel Abasolom Baird later became a Brigadier General. He led a Virginia Union loyal division against General Robert E. Lee at Gordon's Mill, Tennessee. Civil War a Narrative.

[1088] Governor Richard Yates was a member of Congress (1851—1855) from Illinois. He was as Governor of Illinois from 1861—1865. He gave the honorary title of Colonel to Ward Hill Lamon prior to Lamon's leaving for Washington with Mr. Lincoln. Governor Yates also write a letter introducing Lamon to Secretary Seward. During the war, he sent more troops to the Union army than any other state. He served as a U.S. Senator from 1865—1871. He was appointed by President Grant to inspect a land subsidy railroad. His son, Richard Yates Jr., also served as Governor of Illinois. Ward Hill Lamon, Lincoln's "Particular Friend," pgs. 143 & 145.

[1089] Proroguing means postponing.

to Fort Delaware in the steamer *Maple Leaf*. About ninety in number enroute overpowered the crew and took them prisoners and locked them below. The rebels then steamed for the Virginia shore, sixty miles below Fortress Monroe and escaped. On the 12th the Department of the Susquehanna was assigned to General Couch.[1090] General Lee commenced his movement on the Rappahannock on his march to Pennsylvania. His force was estimated at 78,000 men. Meanwhile General Johnston with the intention of attacking the rear of General Grant's army continued to mass his forces near Vicksburg.

On the 13th General Grant was within thirty yards of the rebel works and the bombardment continued with such great vigor that it almost silenced the rebel batteries. On the same day the rear of General Lee's Army consisting of Hill's Corps[1091] left Fredericksburg. On the 14th General Ewell commenced the attack on Winchester and carried the outer works. General Milroy[1092] was nearly surrounded by 18,000 men. General Milroy retreated to Martinsburg, pursued by General Ewell and a demand was made by General Ewell for the surrender of Martinsburg but it was refused by General Tyler then in command. An artillery fight ensued resulting in the retreat of General Tyler[1093] and his command to Harpers Ferry.

It was found necessary now to remove the Army of the Potomac north to counteract the movement of General Lee's Army and to keep him out of the states of Maryland and Pennsylvania. General Milroy on his march to Martinsburg after spiking his guns was attacked four miles from Winchester and was compelled to cut his way through the Confederates. In doing so he lost two thousand men, three batteries, six hundred muskets and two hundred wagons. On the 15th General Jenkin's rebel cavalry[1094] entered Chambersburg, Pennsylvania. On the same day General Tyler was forced to retreat from Harpers Ferry and

---

1090 General Darvius Couch—See pg. 193.

1091 General A. P. Hill commanded a brigade of Longstreet's division. He was a graduate of the U.S. Military Academy. He was shot and killed at Petersburg on April 2, 1865. www.civilwarhome.com/aphillbio.htm

1092 General Robert Milroy—See pg. 162.

1093 General Robert O. Tyler was an 1853 graduate of the U.S. Military Academy. He was part of the force sent to Fort Sumter in Charleston harbor to relieve the troops there. He commanded heavy artillery units throughout the war. www.findagrave.com/cgi-bin/fg.cgi?page=gr&GRid=19739

1094 General Albert G. Jenkins commanded a brigade in General JEB Stuart's Confederate cavalry. He was wounded at Cloyd's Mountain in Pulaski County, Virginia. Civil War a Narrative.

Maryland Heights. On the 17th 2,000 rebel cavalry advanced eleven miles beyond Chambersburg in the direction of Harrisburg, Pennsylvania. On the 18th General Jenkin's cavalry abandoned Chambersburg. On the same day the rebels burned a train of thirty-eight cars at Point of Rocks, Maryland[1095] taking the passengers prisoner. General Lee now occupied Thoroughfare Gap, Virginia and General Rodes[1096] with 3,000 men occupied Hagerstown, Maryland.
On the 18th General Grant relieved General McClernand from command of the Thirteenth Army Corps and appointed General Ord to succeed him. On the 19th General Jenkin's cavalry plundered the town of McConnelsburg, Pennsylvania. On the 20th Mr. Vallandigham ran the blockade at Wilmington. On the 20th General Grant captured the outer works of Vicksburg and a considerable number of prisoners. On the 21st there was terrific cannonading from the batteries and gunboats around Vicksburg. General Grant captured two batteries on the hills north of the city and turned the guns on the city. On the 21st Hagerstown (Maryland) was fortified by the rebels and the rebel cavalry reached Gettysburg, Pennsylvania. On the 22nd General Grant assaulted the works but was repulsed at the loss of one thousand men. The offer was then made by General Pemberton to surrender the city, provided the garrison would be allowed to march out after laying down their arms. The proposition was rejected, and the siege was commenced and vigorously prosecuted. Also on the 22nd Mr. Vallandigham reached Nassau. The following day *The Richmond Whig* in a lengthy article on the state of the war in the southwest spoke very despondingly[1097] of the prospects saying that if General Pemberton was whipped and Vicksburg captured, they would have material for large armies under better and braver generals, and called upon the southern people to rally to their standard and swell the ranks of the army.

In an editorial in *The London Times* about this time there appeared what we here quote: "The end of this war is not to be looked for from any return to conscientiousness or humanity, any conviction that the

---

1095 Point of Rocks, Maryland was along the Baltimore and Ohio Railroad, the Chesapeake and Ohio Canal and the Potomac River between Baltimore and Harpers Ferry.

1096 General Robert Rodes was a VMI graduate of the class of 1848. He led a Confederate division at Gettysburg, Wilderness and Spotsylvania. americancivilwar.com/south/general_robert_s_rodes

1097 Despondingly means hopelessly.

cause is unjust and success hopeless; the end must come by the slow process of exhaustion either of men or of that real enthusiasm which fights instead of preaches."

On the same day, Mr. Vallandigham reached Nassau. On the 24th Generals Lee and Longstreet were in Winchester, Virginia. General Longstreet retreated towards Virginia pursued by General Burnside while another army under General Foster[1098] started from Cumberland Gap to cut off his retreat.

On the 25th Mr. Vallandigham was delivered to the Confederate outposts at Murfreesboro, Tennessee. On the same day there was skirmish at McConnellsburg and the federals were forced to retire. That same day Carlisle, Pennsylvania[1099] was evacuated. On the 25th General Early's division[1100] of Longstreet's Corps reached Gettysburg and Rodes division occupied Chambersburg. Colonel Spear's 11th Pennsylvania Cavalry[1101] captured one hundred eleven men including General William Henry Fitzhugh Lee[1102] together with a number of horses, mules, &c. On the 27th General Hooker was relieved from the command of the Army of the Potomac and was succeeded by General Meade.[1103] The advance of the rebel army now reached Kingstown, which is but thirteen miles from Harrisburg, the capital of Pennsylvania. The main body of the army then was at Carlisle, Pennsylvania. On that same day General Lee reached Chambersburg. On the following day the people throughout Pennsylvania were in great excitement. All business was suspended in Philadelphia. The ancient towns of York and Mechanicsburg were occupied by rebels. On the 29th there was a fight at Mechanicsburg resulting in no great

---

1098 General Foster was one of General Burnside's three commanders at Roanoke Island. Civil War a Narrative, pg. 257.

1099 Carlisle, Pennsylvania is about 16 miles east of Harrisburg, the capital of Pennsylvania.

1100 General Jubal Early was a Virginian and a veteran of both the Mexican and Seminole Wars. He graduated from the U.S. Military Academy in 1837 and was a classmate of both General Hooker and General Bragg. He led an assault on Washington, D.C. on July 11, 1864 but was turned away. He was sounded at Williamsburg but continued to command. After the war, he refused to take an oath of allegiance to the United States. Lincoln's War, pgs. 366 - 368 and The Armies and The Leaders, pgs. 160, 245 & 248.

1101 Colonel Samuel P. Spear commanded the 11th cavalry brigade which was also known as Harlan's Light Brigade. www.pa-roots.com/pacw/cavalry/11thcav/11thcavorg.html

1102 General William Henry Fitzhugh Lee—See pg. 239.

1103 General George Gordon Meade—See pg. 241.

loss on either side. General Lee and staff now arrived at Carlisle and requisition was made on the inhabitants for a large quantity of provisions $30,000 of which was collected and turned over to him. On the 30th the rebels were driven from Gettysburg by General Pleasanton's cavalry and the place was occupied by his command. York was now abandoned by General Jubal Early's force and a rebel army of 40,000 men and forty pieces of artillery left Carlisle for Gettysburg. On the same day rebel lines were cut by the Army of the Potomac and the Pennsylvania towns of York and Hanover were occupied by that army. On the 31st all the siege guns at Vicksburg opened fire at midnight and the bombardment was continued until daylight the next morning.

## JULY 1863

On the 1st of July, General Grant demanded the unconditional surrender of Vicksburg, giving three days to consider. The reply of General Pemberton was that he did not want fifteen minutes. On the 2nd General F. B. Blair[1104] with his command returned to Vicksburg and the atolls between the Black and Yazoo Rivers. On the 3rd of July, a flag of truce was sent from Vicksburg to General Grant asking for an armistice to arrange terms of capitulation. No armistice was granted. General Grant refusing any other terms than unconditional surrender. General Pemberton had an interview with General Grant at three o'clock in the afternoon. In this interview it was arranged for the federal occupation of the city at 10 o'clock a.m. the next day. By the terms agreed upon the Confederate officers were to have their horses and four days rations and the men were to be paroled at once.

On the 4th General Steele's division[1105] marched into and occupied Vicksburg and the federal flag was raised over that city. 27,277 prisoners, fifteen general officers, one hundred two field officers, thirty siege guns and 50,000 stands of small arms besides thirty-seven stands of colors were among the trophies taken. For the last four days

---

[1104] General Francis Preston Blair—See pg. 149.

[1105] General Frederick Steele of New York was a U.S. Military Academy graduate from the class of 1843 and a veteran of the Mexican War. He was the commanding officer of the Army of the Arkansas engaged at Little Rock. He commanded one of the four divisions of General Sherman's Union forces at Vicksburg. Civil War a Narrative, and The Armies and The Leaders, pgs. 175 & 176.

the garrison had subsisted on mule meat and had become physically prostrated. Near the city there were 1,200 women and children living in caves. The number of persons who had been killed during the siege was five hundred two Union along with 2,550 wounded and one hundred forty-seven missing. Confederate losses were not known.

The battle of Gettysburg was commenced on the 1st day of July. The rebels under Generals Longstreet and A. P. Hill attacked the Union's First and Eleventh Corps at 9 o'clock a. m. This fight was very severe and attended with great loss, Union General Reynolds[1106] having been mortally wounded in the early part of the fight. There was also a cavalry fight in Hanover, Pennsylvania lasting all the afternoon. The Union loss there was two hundred men; the rebel loss killed and wounded was four hundred men. On the 2nd the battle of Gettysburg was renewed about 4 o'clock p.m. by the rebels attacking the Union lines but they were repulsed at all points. It was reported that 6,000 prisoners were taken this day by the federals. On the 3rd the fiercest of the three day fight occurred. The rebels attempted to turn General Meade's left flank but were repulsed, losing 3,000 prisoners. The fighting was furious and the slaughter was terrible. A great loss of officers occurred on both sides. The rebel casualties were estimated at 28,063 (3,903 killed, 18,735 wounded and 5,425 missing). The federal loss 3,155 killed, 14,529 wounded and 5,365 missing. On the night of the 4th the rebels commenced their retreat towards Chambersburg and Greencastle leaving their dead and wounded[1107] but leaving their surgeons to tend to the wounded. The 4th of July was celebrated not only because of its being the anniversary of the independence of the republic, but it was celebrated throughout the North with appropriate ceremonies and rejoicing over the twin victories at Vicksburg and Gettysburg.

Mr. Vallandigham reached Halifax, Nova Scotia on the 5th of July. On the same day General Lee's dispatch from Jefferson Davis was intercepted. It stated he could not reinforce General Lee and ordered his return to Richmond. It was estimated that General Lee lost 4,000 men by desertion during the progress of this battle. General Lee's retreat was impeded by General Pleasanton's command which occupied the mountain passes. At Mercersburg there was a battle

---

[1106] General John Reynolds—See pg. 150.

[1107] General John Imboden led the wagon train of Confederate wounded from Gettysburg —See pg. 241.

fought between General Fitz Lee and General Pierce.[1108] At the time a portion of Pleasanton's cavalry under General Gregg[1109] had a fight with the rebels at Fayetteville, Pennsylvania[1110] taking four hundred prisoners. On the 6th 10,000 prisoners arrived in Baltimore, sent there by General Meade. General Lee was now retiring towards the Potomac River closely followed by General Meade.

That night the Potomac River rose to such a degree that it destroyed the rebel pontoon bridges at Williamsport, Maryland. On the 7th the rebel army reached Hagerstown, Maryland on its retreat. On the 9th the federal cavalry destroyed five hundred of General Lee's wagons. On the 10th the ammunition and supplies of General Lee's Army were crossed over the Potomac River at Williamsport and his main body that evening fell back to Falling Waters. A fight occurred on this day at Sharpsburg lasting from daylight until dark, resulting in General Longstreet's division being driven back. General Jenkins was captured and sent to Fort McHenry.[1111] On the 10th of July the private library of President Davis was captured near Jackson, Mississippi and destroyed. On the 11th a storming party under General Strong[1112] assaulted Fort Wagner at Charleston, South Carolina. The federal flag was raised over the fort, but was soon taken down again owing to the fact that the assaulting party was not properly supported. The federals were repulsed with a loss of three hundred fifty killed, wounded and prisoners. On the 12th a riot commenced in New York in opposition to the Conscription Act. On the next day it continued and increased in vigor and twenty persons were killed. *The Tribune* building was attacked and would have been destroyed but for the police force driving the rioters off. They burned the colored orphan asylum and many other outrages were committed. George W. L. Bickley,[1113] who was chief of

---

[1108] General Byron R. Pierce—See pg. 129.,

[1109] Brigadier General David McM. Gregg commanded a Union brigade in the Mississippi campaign of 1863. Civil War a Narrative, pg. 360.

[1110] Fayetteville, Pennsylvania is just west of Chambersburg.

[1111] Fort McHenry was a Union prison in the harbor in Baltimore. Fort McHenry is most famous for being the sight of the writing of the National Anthem by Francis Scot Key in 1814.

[1112] General George C. Strong commanded the First Brigade at the assault on Fort Wagner. Among his men were two colored regiments, the 54th Massachusetts and the 2nd South Carolina. www.absoluteastonomy.com/topics/George_Crockett_Strong

[1113] George Washington Lafayette Bickley was born in Virginia. He taught alternative medicine at Eclectic Medical Institute in Cincinnati, Ohio. He was the founder of the Knights of the Golden Circle.

the Knights of the Golden Circle,[1114] was arrested at Albany and sent to prison at Louisville, Kentucky.

On the 12th the rebel rear of General Lee's army was pressed hard by the Army of the Potomac. It was at this time that Confederate General Johnson Pettigrew,[1115] was fatally wounded. On the 14th the rear of Lee's Army crossed the Potomac River at Williamsport and Falling Waters. On the same day General Kilpatrick's cavalry[1116] captured 1,500 prisoners, three battle flags, and a section of artillery in General Lee's rear. Mr. Vallandigham arrived at the Clifton House on the Canada side of Niagara Falls on the 15th of the month. There he issued an address to the people of Ohio accepting the nomination of Governor which had been tendered him by his friends in that state. Mr. Vallandigham's friends made the race for him while he was in exile. He had many sympathizers in that state but not sufficient to make him chief magistrate of that state in time of war. On the 15th while the riot was progressing though almost checked in New York City, like disturbances occurred in Newark, New Jersey; Boston, Massachusetts; Brooklyn, Yorkville and Harlem, New Jersey. All were speedily quelled. On that day Mr. Lincoln appointed the 6th of August as another day of thanksgiving and prayer for the successes recently had by the federal army. On the 16th the British flag was saluted and returned the salute to the privateer *Florida* at Bermuda. On the 17th the riot of New York City was nearly quelled. The military that were dispersed over the city were withdrawn. The citizens were advised by Mayor Opdyke[1117] to remain quiet in their homes and places of business but to be prepared for any emergency.

---

1114 Knights of the Golden Circle (also known as the Order of the American Knights and the Order of the Sons of Liberty) was a secret organization promoting the "golden circle" of territories of Mexico, Central America and the Caribbean to be taken in as Southern slave states. Clement Vallandigham was its supreme commander. The organization promoted the destruction of the Union and the perpetuation of slavery. www.sonofthesouth.net/mexican-war/knights-golden-circle.htm

1115 General Johnston J. Pettigrew was wounded at Falling Waters on General Imboden's retreat from Gettysburg. He was enroute to a hospital in Winchester, Virginia but died in a house in Bunker Hill called Edgewood and owned by the Boyd family. Bunker Hill is just north of Winchester. The author, Ward Hill Lamon, lived in Bunker Hill from ages two to eighteen. The Armies and The Leaders, pg. 153 and Berkeley County Historical Society Journal, 1979, pg. 23

1116 General H. Judson Kilpatrick—See pg. 200.

1117 George Opydyke was a retailer, manufacturer and banker and one of New York's wealthiest merchants. www.mrlincolnandnewyork.org/inside.asp?ID=63&subjectID=3

On the 20th General Lee commenced to move his army up the valley to Winchester where he arrived on July 22. On the 24th General Meade engaged the rebels. The battle resulted in the loss to the rebels of 2,300 killed and wounded. On the 25th the Confederates evacuated Front Royal and marched towards Culpepper and Orange County Courthouse.

On the 25th of July Jefferson Davis called for a day of fasting, humiliation and prayer. On the 26th there died one of Kentucky's greatest statesmen, at his house in Frankfort, the Honorable John J. Crittenden.[1118] He was a great patriot, loyal citizen and commanded the respect of the people of all sections of the country. On that day the great guerilla, General Morgan[1119] finding that his hour had come, surrendered to Captain Beckwith on condition of his parole. Just then General Shackleford[1120] made his appearance and refused the condition, taking General Morgan into his custody. On the next day 1,500 rebels under Colonel Pegrau crossed the Cumberland River and moved northward it is supposed with the design to free General Morgan. On the same day the Union forces occupied the north bank of the Rappahannock River near a station of that name. Gold at this time had risen in the Confederacy to a premium of eleven hundred percent. The Confederates arrived below Culpepper, Virginia on July 27. On the same day General Grant's forces pursued General Johnston in his retreat beyond Pearl River.

## AUGUST 1863

On the 1st of August Mr. Lincoln issue a proclamation that he would retaliate in kind for any ill treatment of federal soldiers black or white by rebels and that the federal uniform must be respected. On the 3rd Governor Seymour[1121] of New York asked the president to order a

---

1118 John C. Crittenden—See pg. 18 footnote.

1119 John Morgan—See pg. 199.

1120 General James M. Shackleford was a Union general from Kentucky who pursued Morgan's raiders. The Armies and The Leaders, pg. 207.

1121 Governor Horatio Seymour was a lawyer who was elected twice as Governor of New York, serving from 1853-54 and then again 1863-1864. He criticized Lincoln's conduct of war, centralization of power, and restrictions of civil liberties as well as opposing the emancipation policies. He was later named a Democratic nominee for President opposing Ulysses S. Grant. Lincoln and the Civil War, pgs. 189, 192, and 207 and Appleton's Cyclopaedia of American Biography, Vol. V., pgs. 475-478.

new enrollment and suspend the draft. General Lee's Army on this day arrived between Rapidan Station and the Orange County Courthouse, Virginia. On the 5th Jefferson Davis issued an earnest appeal to the Confederate deserters to return immediately to their camps. On the 7th Mr. Lincoln replied to Governor Seymour that he could not consent to suspend the draft in that city, time being important, but that the enrollment for some districts should be revised.

We here give a letter from General Lee to President Davis tendering his resignation as commander of the Confederate States Army. This letter was written while he was on the retreat from Pennsylvania and is as follows:

*Camp Orange August 8, 1863*
*His Excellency, Jefferson Davis, President*
*Mr. President*

*Your letters of 28th July and 2nd August have been received and I have waited for a leisure hour to reply, but I fear that it will never come. I am extremely obliged to you for the attention given to the wants of this army and the efforts made to supply them. Our absentees are returning and I hope the earnest and beautiful appeal made to the country in your proclamation will stir up the whole people, and that they may see their duty and perform it. Nothing is wanted but that their fortitude should equal their bravery to insure the success of our cause. They are sent to teach us wisdom and prudence, to call forth our greater energies and to prevent our falling into great disasters. Our people have only to be true and united to bear manfully the misfortunes incident to war and all will come right in the end.*

*I know how prone we are to censure, and how ready to blame others for the non-fulfillment of our expectations. This is unbecoming in a generous people and I grieve to see its expression. The general remedy for the want of success in a military commander is his removal. This is natural and in many instances proper. For no matter what may be the ability of the officer if he loses the confidence of his troops, disaster must sooner or later ensue.*

*I have been prompted by these reflections more than once since my return from Pennsylvania to propose to your excellency the propriety of selecting another commander for this army. I have seen and heard expressions of discontent from the public journals at the result of this expedition. I do not know how far this feeling extends in the army. My brother officers have been too kind to report it, and so far the troops have been too generous to exhibit it. It is fair, however, to suppose that it does exist and success is so necessary to us that nothing should be risked to ignore it.*

*I therefore request in all sincerity your excellency to take measures to supply my place. I do this with the more earnestness because no one is more aware than myself of my inability for the duties of my position. I cannot even accomplish what I myself desire. How can I fulfill the expectations of others? In addition I sensibly feel the growing failure of my bodily strength. I have not yet recovered from the attack I experienced the past spring. I am becoming more and more incapable of exertion, and am thus prevented from making the personal examinations and giving the personal supervision to the operations in the field which I feel to be necessary. I am so dull that in making use of the eyes of others I am frequently misled. Everything therefore points to the advantage to be derived from a new commander and I the more anxiously urge the matter upon your excellency from my belief that a younger and abler man than myself can readily be obtained. I know that he will have as gallant and brave an army that ever existed to second his efforts and it would be the happiest day of my life to see at its head a worthy leader; one that would accomplish more than I could perform and all that I have wished. I hope your excellency will attribute my request to the true reasons, the desire to serve my country, and to do all in my power to insure the success of her righteous causes.*

*I have no complaints to make of anyone but myself. I have received nothing but kindness from those above me, and the most considerate attention from my comrades and companions in arms. To your excellency I am specially indebted for uniform kindness and consideration. You have done everything in your power to aid me in the work committed to my charge, without omitting anything to promote the general welfare. I pray that your efforts may at length be crowned with success and that you may long live to enjoy the thanks of a grateful people.*

*With sentiments of great esteem, I am very respectfully and truly yours,*

*R.E. Lee, General*

It is obvious to the writer that Confederate President Jefferson Davis did not accept General Lee's resignation.

The battle of Chickamauga[1122] started at 11 o'clock on August 19. General Bragg was detected in attempting to flank the left of General Rosencrans' army. General Thomas' Corp,[1123] in order to counteract this movement, moved from the center to the left bringing his and General Longstreet's Corps opposite each other. The whole corps advanced and the rebels were forced to retreat. General Thomas was compelled to halt after driving them one mile and a half, his center not advancing as he

1122 Chickamauga is on the west side of Chattanooga, Tennessee near Lookout Mountain and near the Tennessee River.

1123 George H. Thomas—See pg. 169.

expected. At 2 o'clock p. m. Generals McCook's and Crittender's commands were hurled against Generals Polk's[1124] and Hill's Corps and the former were driven back. The federals then being reinforced and the rebels being driven back, the Union army again occupied its original ground. On the 26th the fight was renewed by General Thomas making a fierce assault on the left of the rebel line the assault which was by no means successful. Repeated assaults were made by the enemy. Breastworks of rails and logs had been constructed by General Thomas's men that enabled them to hold their ground. At this time the right and center was broken by vigorous attack made by the Confederates which caused serious confusion. General Thomas retreated to the base of the spur of Missionary Ridge finding himself alone and unsupported but being here reinforced by two brigades of reserves he made another assault, repulsed the rebels and maintaining his position which saved the army from utter defeat. During that night he fell back to Rossville. The Union loss in these two battles was 1,657 killed, 9,756 wounded and 4,757 missing. By the rebel report their loss is placed at 2,312 killed, and 14,674 wounded besides 1,468 missing.

On the 20th of August *The Richmond Whig* stated that while the number of soldiers of the roll of General Lee's Army during the fights before Richmond were 120,000 men, the number actually present in the battles were only 46,000. At Sharpsburg the numbers showed 140,000 men while there were present only 35,000 men while at Gettysburg about the same, the balance being absentees and deserters.

On the 21st the infamous guerilla Quantrill[1125] with his command of outlaws crossed the Missouri River about sixty miles below Lawrence, Kansas[1126] and indiscriminately murdered the citizens, men, women and children, burning their bodies, robbing houses of all valuables even to robbing the jewelry from the women's fingers. He killed one hundred ninety unoffending people besides wounding six hundred. General

---

1124 Leonidus Polk—See pg. 147.

1125 William Charles Quantrill was the leader of a Confederate band of irregular guerillas. Among his men were two outlaw brothers, Frank and Jessie James. The Odd Couple Who Hanged Mary Surratt, pg. 36 and Civil War a Narrative, pgs. 140 & 915.

1126 Lawrence, Kansas is in the northeastern part of the state between Topeka and the Missouri state line. Here General David O. Laws and his men killed nine raiders, but lost their track and the rest got away. The Odd Couple Who Hanged Mary Surratt, pg. 36.

James M. Lane[1127] was among the persons attacked but escaped on horseback, returning with two hundred men and gave Quantrill battle about twelve miles below Lawrence. Quantrill fled pursued by General Lane's little band. On the 21st General Thomas was again attacked at noon by the rebels but they were repulsed. On the 22nd gold had risen to 1600 percent and greenbacks to 1200 per cent premium. On the 28th Generals Crittenden and McCook were relieved from their commands, and their corps, the 20th and 21st were consolidated and numbered as the 4th Corps. General Gordon Granger was put in command of it.

On the 28th General Gilmor[1128] opened his "Swamp Angel." This "angel" sent one of its iron messengers seven mile from the point of firing across the city of Charleston. On the 24th General Gilmor reported Fort Sumter practically demolished. It had been bombarded for seven days. On this day there was a riot in Danville, Virginia in which a number of men were killed. Dr. James H. Farris was among the number. On the 26th there was captured at Natchez over 100,000 bales of Confederate States cotton. On the day General Gilmor captured a rifle pit in the rear of Fort Wagner. On the 27th Confederate General John B. Floyd,[1129] late Secretary of War of the United States died in Abington, Virginia. On the 29th Belle Boyd,[1130] notorious rebel spy was captured near Martinsburg, Virginia her former home and sent to the Old Capitol Prison.[1131]

## SEPTEMBER 1863

On the 1st General Meade's official report was made from which it appears that the loss in the Gettysburg campaign was 2,834 killed,

---

1127 General James M. Lane was from Indiana. He was involved as an abolitionist and fought against slavery in the Kansas territory. He served in U.S. Congress (1853—1855) and the U.S. Senate (1861—1866) from Kansas. He was a Confederate General. He died in Kansas in 1866 from a self-inflicted gun shot wound. Civil War a Narrative, pg. 513 and The Odd Couple Who Hanged Mary Surratt, pgs. 29 & 38.

1128 General Harry Gilmor was born in Maryland. His daring Confederate raiders were called "Gilmor's raiders." They wrecked two trains near Magnolia Station. He was imprisoned at Fort McHenry during the war. Later he was Police Commissioner in Baltimore in the 1870s.

1129 General John B. Floyd—See pg. 42 footnote.

1130 Belle Boyd—See pg. 201.

1131 As Marshal of the District of Columbia the author, Ward Hill Lamon, was in charge of the Old Capitol Prison. Ward Hill Lamon, Lincoln's "Particular Friend," pgs. 213 & 258.

13,703 wounded and 500 prisoners, aggregating 23,186. The federals also captured three guns, forty-one standards, 13,620 prisoners and 24,975 small arms.

On the 3rd President Lincoln issued another proclamation appointing the last Thursday in November as a day of thanksgiving and prayer.

## OCTOBER 1863

On the 11th of October General Meade retreated from the Rapidan and was pursued by General Lee. On the 12th he had been attacked by Colonel Hatch[1132] - the fight having lasted two hours resulting in the enemy's defeat. Colonel Hatch was now reinforced and gave General Chalmers[1133] a fight at Wyatt, on the Tallahatchie River and again defeated him. On the 13th General Chalmers withdrew across the Coldwater River having on the 11th attacked the garrison at Collinsville, Tennessee and driven them into their fortifications. On the 14th there was a battle fought at Bristow Station, Virginia when General Lee attempted again to turn the right flank of General Meade which was prevented by the assistance of the Second and Fifth Corps. The rebels lost four hundred killed and wounded and as many prisoners. On this day President Davis issued an edict to General Bragg's army in which he claimed the battle of Chickamauga. On the 15th General Meade's army reached the neighborhood of Manassas. On this day General Grant assumed command of the Military Division of the Mississippi. This division comprised of the divisions of the Ohio, Cumberland and Tennessee. There were no headquarters designated.

On the next day at Manassas the Army of the Potomac remained in line of battle expecting an attack by General Lee. On the 17th 300,000 more men were called by Mr. Lincoln to be drafted on the 5th of January if not raised before that time by volunteers. The federal artillery on this day drove back the rebel army in its attempt to cross Bull Run, at Union Mills and Blackburn Ford. On the 18th General Lee retired to the Rapidan. On the next day a skirmish occurred between

---

1132 Colonel Edward Hatch was originally from New England but commanded a Iowa brigade in the Union army. He was known as a brilliant cavalry commander. Civil War a Narrative, pg. 409 and The Armies and The Leaders, pg. 205.

1133 General James R. Chalmers commander of a Confederate cavalry in Mississippi and Tennessee. Civil War a Narrative, pgs. 338 & 783.

General Lee's rear guard and General Buford's cavalry[1134] at Thoroughfare Gap. The enemy withdrew and General Lee's army crossed the Rappahannock River at Rappahannock Station. On this day General Rosencrans was relieved from the command of the Army of the Cumberland and General Thomas succeeded him. General Lee on the 20th continued his retreat with General Meade in pursuit. On the 20th General Butler was ordered to the command of the 20th Army Corps relieving General Foster.[1135] On the 27th General Sherman was appointed to command the Department of the Tennessee and General John A. Logan[1136] to the command of General Sherman's Corps. On the 29th General Hooker at Waumatchie, near Lookout Mountain at 2 o'clock p.m. was attacked by rebels and after two hours of savage fighting the rebels were repulsed and driven across Lookout Creek. The rebel loss was 350 officers and men killed and wounded. On the 31st a conspiracy was discovered to release the prisoners at the Ohio Penitentiary, at Camp Chase, and McClain's Barracks.

## NOVEMBER 1863

On the 4th General Banks force occupied the town of Fort Brown after landing at Brownsville, Texas. A battle was fought on the 6th at Leesburg, Virginia by a detachment of General Averill's cavalry[1137] and a rebel force under General Patton. The rebels were defeated. On the same day a battle was fought at Droop Mountain, in Western Virginia[1138] by General Averill's cavalry and a force under General Echols.[1139] On the 7th General Meade commenced his forward

---

1134 General John Buford was the Union cavalry commander who delayed the Confederate troops on the first day (July 1, 1863) at the battle of Gettysburg. Harpers Pictorial History of the Great Rebellion, pg. 506.

1135 General John G. Foster—See pg. 253.

1136 General John. A. Logan—See pg. 247.

1137 General William W. Averill was born in New York. He invented methods of manufacturing steel castings and insulated electrical cables and asphalt pavement. He was an 1855 graduate of West Point. He commanded a cavalry brigade at Fredericksburg and during the Shenandoah Campaign under General Sheridan. After the war he was appointed General Counsel to British North America and served from 1866—1869.

1138 Today it is West Virginia. The new state became official on June 20, 1863. www.wvculture.org/history/statehood.html

1139 Brigadier General John Echols studied law at Harvard. He was wounded at Kernstown in March of 1862. He commanded a brigade in the Army of Western Virginia. www.historycentral.com/bio/cwcgens/csaechols.html

movement from Cedar Run and a spirited engagement took place at Rappahannock Station and Kelly's Ford. The Third and Sixth Corps of the United States Army having crossed the river took the rebel rifle pits and four hundred prisoners, killing one hundred and wounding two hundred. The Union loss was three hundred seventy. On the next day there was considerable skirmishing on the advance of General Lee's army. The rebels now retired across the Rapidan and General Meade occupied Culpepper Courthouse. On the 12th a plot was discovered among the refuges in Canada to release the prisoners of Johnson Island in Buffalo and other lake cities. This discovery was very timely as there had been and afterwards discovered combinations and plots to destroy railroads and towns and cities by an organized band of rebel sympathizers. General Dix[1140] was now ordered to Buffalo. The French government on the 13th sent advices to the United States authorities that they had prohibited the building of rams for the Confederate States. On the 14th General Johnston was placed in command of General Bragg's army. On the 17th Knoxville was besieged by General Burnside forming a line of battle around the town. General Longstreet had advanced and occupied Knoxville at the time. On the 18th the fight was renewed. The loss in the battles on the 17th and 18th amounted to one hundred fifty killed and wounded. On this day owing to the occupation of the Texas coast by General Banks 250,000 bales of cotton were brought into market. The *New London*[1141] while going into the Rio Grande captured the British brig *Dashing Wave* with her cargo of medicine, clothing, &c. together with $700,000 in gold. On this day General Hitchcock[1142] made a proposition to the Confederate States government to receive on parole rebel prisoners and to feed and cloth those in the hands of the Confederates. This was declined by Robert Ould,[1143] the Confederate States' commissioner.

---

1140 General John A. Dix—See pg. 63.

1141 *New London* was a 135 foot long Union three mast schooner with a crew of 135 and five guns. She captured thirteen prizes. Warships of the Civil War Navies, pg. 105.

1142 General Ethan A. Hitchcock was born in Vermont. He was an 1817 graduate of the U.S. Military Academy and became the commandant of the school from 1829—1833. He was commissioner of the prisoner exchange throughout the war and Chairman of the War Board. He played the flute and amassed a huge collection of music. www.biographicon.com/view/v6yuy

1143 Robert Ould of Virginia was the chief of the Confederate Bureau of Exchange. www.civilwarhome.com/confederategovernment.htm

On the 19th Mr. Lincoln dedicated the National Cemetery at Gettysburg, Pennsylvania.[1144] On the 21st General Meade occupied Madison Country Courthouse. On the 22nd part of the city of Knoxville had been burned and the town closely invested by General Longstreet. On the next day from Chattanooga General Thomas threw out a reconnoitering force consisting of Generals Sherman's and Ward's Divisions[1145] of the Fourth Corps under General Granger. In the afternoon of that day the rebel rifle pits were carried. Ball's Knob about half way to Mission Ridge was also carried, and two hundred prisoners were captured. A little over a hundred of the Union forces were killed or wounded. On the 24th of November the storming of Lookout Mountain began. A demonstration was made against General Bragg's position by General Grant's army and at daylight General Sherman moved across the Tennessee River at the mouth of Chickamauga Creek and carried the north end of Mission Ridge. The rebel left was turned by General Hooker who had moved up Lookout Valley and formed a line of battle in the rear, and the rebels were driven into their works at the summit of the mountain. This battle lasted from 8 o'clock a.m. until 9 o'clock p.m. and was fought above the clouds. On the 25th General Bragg was forced to abandon Lookout Mountain and General Hooker occupied the same position. On the same day General Sherman made two unsuccessful assaults upon Mission Ridge occupied by the rebels. General Grant about the middle of the afternoon perceiving that by the rebels massing heavily against General Sherman they had weakened their center, at once directed two columns against it and took it and broke it. He drove the main body of the rebels toward General Sherman who opened on them a terrific fire. The rebels then broke and fled in confusion toward Ringgold. In this battle being blinded by success, the divisions of General

---

[1144] The author fails to mention here that he was the Marshal-in-Chief of the dedication of the National Cemetery, inviting all states to participate, borrowing buggies and horses for the celebrities, organizing the procession from the downtown area to the cemetery and then acting as Master of Ceremonies for the event. He introduced Mr. Lincoln for what has become known as his "Gettysburg Address." Ward Hill Lamon, Lincoln's "Particular Friend," pgs. 318 & 319 and Official Program of the Dedication of the National Cemetery in Gettysburg, November 19, 1863.

[1145] General William Thomas Ward commanded the second brigade under General Granger in the Department of the Cumberland. bi-oguide.congress.gov/scripts/biodisplay.pl?index=w000145

Wood's[1146] and Sheridan's[1147] being ordered to carry the rifle pits and slopes of the ridge at all hazards were so elated that they actually rushed in and carried the crest of the ridge without orders. This terminated the battle. The Union losses on Lookout Mountain and Mission Ridge were 500 killed and 2,500 wounded. The Confederate loss was 2,000 killed and wounded, 7,000 prisoners, 62 pieces of artillery and 70,000 small arms. This same day General Longstreet attacked one of General Burnside's divisions strongly fortified two miles from Knoxville, with three brigades. After a stubborn fight they were repulsed with the loss of one hundred fifty men.

The battle of Chattanooga, Tennessee[1148] was fought from the 23rd to the 25th of November and was one of the most hotly contested battles of the war. The fighting was desperate on both sides. This battle properly includes the engagement at Orchard Knob, Lookout Mountain, and Mission Ridge. The troops engaged in it consisted of the Fourth and Fourteenth Corps of the Army of the Cumberland, the 11th Corps and Geary's division of the Twelfth Corps, and the Fifteenth Corps of the Army of the Tennessee.[1149] Orchard Knob was fought on the first day, Lookout Mountain on the second day, and Mission Ridge on the third. In these engagements on the Union side there were, according to official reports, seven hundred fifty-three killed, 4,722 wounded and three hundred forty-nine missing, total 5,824. The total loss of the Confederates was 6,667 including three hundred sixty-one killed, 2.160 wounded and 4,146 missing. On the 26th of November John Morgan[1150] and six of his officers tunneled the wall of their prison and made their escape from the Ohio Penitentiary. On the 29th General Longstreet's command made a desperate attack on Fort Saunders[1151] one of the strongest defenses of Knoxville and was repulsed with the loss of one hundred men.

---

1146 General Thomas J. Wood was a Georgian who graduated from the U.S. Military academy and served in the Mexican War. He commanded division for the Army of Ohio and the Army of the Cumberland. gastate-parks.org/net/content/go.aspx?ran=1885820027&s=123225.0.1.5

1147 General Phillip Sheridan—See pg. 197.

1148 Also called the battle of Missionary Ridge.

1149 Union commander was U.S. Grant. Troop strength for the Union was 85,000 and for the Confederates commanded by General Bragg it was less than half. Southern History of the War, pg. 163.

1150 John Hunt Morgan—See pg. 199.

1151 Fort Saunders is in Louisville, Kentucky.

*"This war is harried."*

Diary of Union surgeon, May 6, 1864[1152]

# — 11 —

# THE WAR IN 1864

## JANUARY 1864

During the month of January 1864 little was accomplished in the army except recruiting and administering the oath under the amnesty proclamation. On the 9th of February 1864, Colonel Streight[1153] with a large number of federal prisoners made their escape from Libby Prison.[1154]

## FEBRUARY 1864

On the 15th of February General Sherman with his command started on a great raid into the heart of the enemy's country and arrived at Meridian, Mississippi.[1155] Having completed the object of his raid he returned to Vicksburg with immense booty.

---

1152 The Sword of Lincoln, pg. 342.

1153 Colonel Streight—See pg. 243.

1154 Libby Prison was a prison opened in 1861 for Union officers, located in Richmond, Virginia. it was a three story tobacco warehouse concerted into a prison. There were three buildings each four stories high. Because of the number of deaths in the prison it was second in notoriety only to Andersonville. richmondthenandnow.com/Libby_Prison_Official_Publication_12.html

1155 Meridian, Mississippi is in the eastern part of the state near the Alabama border, east of Jackson.

**MARCH 1864**

On March the 8th General Grant was formally presented with his commission as Lieutenant General and on the 12th was assigned to the command of the United States Army. On the 14th Union forces under General A. J. Smith[1156] captured Fort De Russy, Louisiana[1157] with three hundred twenty-five prisoners, twelve pieces of artillery, 2000 barrels of powder, and an immense amount of ammunition and stores. On the 28th there was a riot in Charleston, Illinois[1158] where what were called Copperheads made an attack on the Twelfth Illinois Regiment.

---

1156 General Andrew Jackson Smith was from Pennsylvania and an 1828 graduate of the U.S. Military Academy. He was soldier in the Mexican War. He commanded the Sixth Union Corps during the siege of Vicksburg. He was wounded in the hip on December, 1862. After the war he was postmaster of the city of St. Louis. Civil War a Narrative, pgs. 76, 347, 370, 371 and The Armies and The Leaders, pgs. 222 & 224.

1157 Fort De Russy, Louisiana was on the Red River about three miles from Marksville. It was an earthen fort with an iron plated battery to resist fire from ironclads. www.fortderussy.org

1158 Charleston, Illinois is about seventy-five miles southeast of Springfield and straight west of Terre Haute, Indiana.

*"It (Lincoln's election of 1864) has demonstrated that a people's government can sustain a national election in the midst of a great civil war. Until now, it had not been known to the world that this was a possibility."*

Abraham Lincoln[1159]

# — 12 —

# THE ELECTION OF 1864

Notwithstanding, there was generous response by the patriotic men of all parties in the non slave-holding states, to the calls of the executive for assistance throughout the existence of the civil war. Yet there was an element composed of the broken Democratic organization and the disaffected Republicans which everlastingly throughout the terrible struggle most persistently opposed every reasonable measure of the administration to sustain the government intact and keep unsullied the American flag. The base intrigues hatched in the hotbeds of disaffected Republicans were, if possible, more embarrassing to the successful administration in the early part of the year 1864 than the open hostilities of the southern enemies to the party in power. Now the people were about to take action to put in motion the machinery to place in nomination a successor to the chief magistrate for the ensuing four years. The elements referring to war were anything but homogenous. Many patriotic men were in accord with the base elements of the Republican Party in their opposition to Mr. Lincoln's policy but they were not actuated by the same motives. They were consciously united in the prosecution of the war, but they disagreed as to the method of conducting it and differed as to the results to be obtained. Congress itself was not composed entirely of statesmen. Many of its members did not rise to the dignity of intelligent politicians. Both factions in the main were violent partisans.

---

1159 Lincoln in American Memory, pg. 334.

Neither extreme in Congress was satisfied with Mr. Lincoln's policy, and failing to control him with their dictation, his course was accepted to and his policy as indicated in his amnesty proclamation was attacked under the assumption that the legislative branch of the government was supreme and absolute. Under this delusion there was a counteracting policy projected by the radical members of the House.

During the first session of the 38th Congress there had been contrived a plan for the reconstruction of the states in rebellion. This mode of reconstruction was a novel one, most adroitly prepared by the disaffected element towards Mr. Lincoln, under the leadership of the Honorable Henry Winter Davis[1160] a very talented member of counsel from Maryland whose zeal sometimes got the better of his judgment. The Congressional plan was in antagonism to and was intended at all hazards to counteract the mild, humane and tolerant policy indicated by Mr. Lincoln. It proposed to deny the states in rebellion the right to representation and to prevent a re-union of the states without the express concurrence and assent of Congress and to compel their new constitutions to be so constructed as to embrace certain conditions in their proposed law which very clearly the legislative body had no constitutional authority to exact. The proposition was regarded by Mr. Lincoln and the conservative adherents to the administration as well as by most all venerable authority as unconstitutional and mischievous. The mischievous purpose it was intended to serve gained much importance by being reported at the opportune time pending the presidential election and the sending of delegates to the Republican National Convention which convened at Baltimore on the 7th of June, 1864.

This act of Congress known as the Davis Act passed the House of Representatives by a majority of eight votes. There were but six Republicans who voted against this bill and twenty of them voted against the preamble of the act which was in terms viciously partisan, uncourteous and unbecoming of the high source from which it emanates. The offensive preamble was stricken out, but the revolutionary enactment, in the strife for power received the sanction of the House of Representatives. Senator Wade[1161] of Ohio, a bitter and uncompromising Republican opponent of Mr. Lincoln's being chairman of the committee on territories in the Senate was now acting

---

[1160] Congressman Henry Winter Davis—See pg. 69.
[1161] Senator Benjamin Franklin Wade—See pg. 33 footnote.

in concert and confederation with Mr. Davis of the House. Ten days before the nominating convention met, Senator Wade reported the bill with slight amendments and it passed the Senate. Six Republicans and every Democrat voted against it. The bill was then submitted to Mr. Lincoln on the eve of the adjournment of Congress and there was no time left for the preparation of a veto message. This unwarrantable assumption of power by the legislative branch of the government was looked upon with amazement by Mr. Lincoln who was most earnestly and sincerely desirous of a speedy restoration of peace and unity. Yet he could not, if he had had an opportunity to do so, give his approbation[1162] to this arbitrary scheme of reconstruction which was the result of an intrigue to lessen and, if possible, to destroy his individual chances of being his own successor as chief magistrate of the nation as well as being in its terms subversive of true republican government in the assumption by the legislative branch of almost omnipotent unlimited power beyond and above all other departments of the government and beyond the power delegated by the Constitution itself.

Congress had assumed under the war powers incident to that branch of the government both executive and judicial authority and as the war commenced advancing to the close arrogated[1163] to itself the right to reduce the states to the condition of territorial dependencies and of making for these territories their constitutions and of arbitrarily altering and dictating to them the framework and their form of government and to be the sole judges of its being republican in form that would be guaranteed by the Constitution of the United States.

Mr. Lincoln, always adverse to controversy, was at this particular juncture reluctant to make a conflict with his radical friends who claimed that they were better Republicans than himself, but that the executive must exercise no power or policy, do no act or take any step towards restoration, reorganization, reconstruction of the Union or recognition of the states without first receiving the permission or consent of Congress. To such dictatorial usurpation of Mr. Lincoln's rightful authority he could not submit, and issued his proclamation on June 6, 1864. Congress assumed that the Union was broken and was greatly dissatisfied with the tolerant and conservative course Mr. Lincoln was disposed to take. They took issue with him as well in the

---

1162 Approbation means approval.
1163 Arrogated means assumed.

manner of conducting the war as in re-establishing the government owing to this unnecessary controversy the progress of the war was impeded and the meager results owing greatly to the dissentions between the executive and legislative branches of government and the waste and expense of summer campaigns of 1864 tended to the exhaustion of the patience and enthusiasm of the people.

There is little doubt but that this controversy was gotten up on the part of the disaffected radicals for the purpose of turning the national discontent resulting from the favor of generals in the field, upon Mr. Lincoln himself. Members of the Senate now generally gave Mr. Lincoln the cold shoulder. Few of them visited him except under the pressing necessity of business. All social intercourse between him and that body for a time was at an end. The six Republican member of the Senate who voted against the radical reconstruction bill still kept up their social relations to Mr. Lincoln. They were Messrs. Doolittle[1164] of Wisconsin, Henderson[1165] of Missouri, Lane[1166] of Indiana, Ten Eyck[1167] of New Jersey, Trumbull[1168] of Illinois and Van Winkle[1169] of West Virginia. It was regarded as preposterous by the conservative people of the country that the constitutional provision, which required the Constitution of the United States shall guarantee to every state a republican form of government, that Congress could dictate to the states which had been in rebellion, frame their constitution and compel them to abandon their fundamental laws and governmental

---

[1164] James Rood Doolittle was born in New York. He graduated from Hobart College and became a lawyer. Following a move to Wisconsin in 1851, he became a judge. Later he was President of the University of Chicago and President of the Democratic National Convention in 1872. bi-
oguide.congress.gov/scripts/biodisplay.pl?index=D000428

[1165] John Brooks Henderson was from Virginia. He was a lawyer and the man who co-authored the thirteenth amendment to the Constitution. He was one of six Republicans who voted to acquit in President Johnson's impeachment trial and later wrote a book about the Johnson Impeachment proceedings.
www.civilwarstlouis.com/history2/henderson.htm

[1166] James M. Lane—See pg. 262.

[1167] John C. Ten Eyck was born in New Jersey. He was a politician and a lawyer. He served in the U.S. Senate from 1859—1865. He was elected a commissioner to revise the state constitution of New Jersey in 1875.
www.freebase.com/view/en/john_c_ten_eyck

[1168] Lyman Trumbull—See pg. 91.

[1169] Peter G. Van Winkle was a lawyer born in New York. He later moved to Western Virginia where he helped frame the constitution for the new state of West Virginia in Wheeling. He was elected to the U.S. Senate and served from 1863 -1869. He voted to acquit President Johnson. bioguide.congress.gov/senpts/biodisplay.pl?index-V000066

traditions and usages that their fathers had prescribed and force them to embrace principles and doctrine unacceptable to them and which had not been brought in issue by the war. The word "guarantee" was so contorted by the new definitions given to it by Mr. Davis and Mr. Wade as to clothe Congress with unlimited power and control the reconstruction of the states. It was insisted by them that to "guarantee" was not to secure their own form of government adopted by them and under which they had lived prior to the war but it was to create, direct, control and impose upon them new fundamental laws embracing the right of suffrage and local self-government which the states from the foundations of the government had reserved and never delegated.

In order to show the sentiments of the southern people in regard to reconstruction, about the time of Mr. Lincoln's second presidential campaign, we make available the following extracts from the speeches and editorials of prominent men and generals of the South.

On the 7th day of January 1863 *The Richmond Enquirer* quotes Jefferson Davis as saying: "Do they hope to reconstruct the Union by striking at everything that is dear to men, by showing themselves so utterly degraded that if the question was proposed to you whether you would combine with hyenas or Yankees, I trust every Virginian would say give me the hyenas."

*The Richmond Dispatch* of January 11, 1863 has these words italicized: "*We warned the Democrats and conservatives of the North to dismiss from their minds at once the miserable delusion that the South can ever consent to enter again upon any terms the old Union. If the North will allow us to write the Constitution ourselves and to give us every guarantee we should ask, we would sooner be under the government of England or France than under a Union with men who have shown that they cannot keep faith and are the most barbarous and inhumane and most treacherous of mankind.*"

About the same date the *Richmond Sentinel* referring to an address by a New Hampshire Democrat declaring that if the South would come back into the Union the democracy of the North would guarantee their rights, &c. flouts the idea that the democracy will be able to warrant any such security and scorns the thought of any re-union with any such people as the Republican majority. "Rather tell one to be wedded to a corpse—rather than join hands with a fiend from the pit."

On the 23rd of July, 1861, *The Richmond Dispatch* quoted Alexander Stephens[1170] (the Vice-President of the Confederacy) as saying: "As for reconstruction such a thing is impossible. Such an idea must not be tolerated for an instant. The only terms upon which we can obtain permanent peace is final and complete separation. Rather than submit to anything short of that, let us all resolve to die like men worthy of freedom."

The Honorable Robert Toombs[1171] in a letter dated August, 1863 wrote: "I can conceive of no extremity to which my country could be reduced in which I could for a single moment entertain any proposition for any union with the North on any terms whatever. When all else is lost I prefer to unite with thousands of our countrymen who have found honorable death if not graves on the battlefield."

About the same time Extra Billy Smith,[1172] Governor of Virginia denounced as an utter impossibility in bitter terms the thought of reconstruction as reported in *The Richmond Examiner.*

In 1864, Governor Zebulon Vance[1173] of North Carolina in a speech upon the possibility of reconstruction said: "I tell you frankly there is no more probability of reconstruction of the old Union and reinstating things as they were four years ago than exists for you to gather up the scattered bones of your sons who have fallen in this struggle, re-clothe them with flesh, fill their veins with the blood they have shed, and their lungs with the same breath with which they breathed out their last prayer for their country's triumph."

Governor H. W. Allen[1174] of Louisiana said: "Peace is not so sweat as to be purchased at the cost of reconstruction. Lose Negroes, lose

---

[1170] Alexander H. Stephens—See pg. 30.

[1171] Robert Toombs —See pg. 18.

[1172] Governor Billy Smith was a lawyer and U.S. Congressman, serving from 1841—1843. He was a veteran of the Mexican War. He served two times as Governor of Virginia—from 1845—1849 and then from 1864—1865. He commanded a brigade in Jubal Early's Confederate division at Antietam and was wounded three times, but would not give up his command. www.extrabillysmith.com

[1173] Governor Zebulon Baird Vance was a U.S. Senator before and after the war. He also served as the governor of North Carolina. www.answers.com/topic/zebulon-baird-vance

[1174] Governor H. W. Allen was a lawyer, teacher and Whig Democrat. He volunteered for Confederate service where he served as Colonel in the 26th North Carolina. He was twice Governor of North Carolina, serving from 1862—1865 and from 1877—1879. He was a proponent of individual rights and self-government and often at odds

land, lose everything, lose life itself, but never think of reconstruction: rather than go back into the Union, the people of Louisiana will in convention assembled without a dissenting voice cede the state to any foreign power."

*The Richmond Dispatch* in March, 1864, discussing Mr. Lincoln's amnesty proclamation said: "No one knows better than Abraham Lincoln that any terms he might offer the southern people which contemplate their restoration to his bloody and brutal government will be rejected with scorn and execration.[1175] Instead of devoting to death our president and civil and military officers, if he had proposed to make Jefferson Davis his successor and General Lee the commander-in-chief of the Yankee armies, and our domestic institutions not only recognized at home but re-adopted in the free states—provided the South would re-enter the Yankee Union. There is not a man, woman or child in the Confederacy who would not spit upon the proposition. We desire no companionship upon any terms with a nation of robbers and murderers. The miscreants[1176] whose atrocities in this war have caused the whole civilized world to shutter must keep henceforth their distance. They shall not be our masters—we would not have them for our slaves."

A joint resolution of the legislature of Louisiana about this time read: "Resolved that the barbarous manner in which our enemies have waged war against us deserves the execration of all men, and has confirmed and strengthened us in the determination to oppose to the last extremity a reunion with them."

These excerpts culled at random present clear and convincing indices[1177] of the bitter and implacable[1178] feeling of the South against the North at this period. They are fervid[1179] with hate and passionate resentment and doubtless to their utterers and writers seemed the truthful and righteous exposition of the southern people's sentiments.

On August 5, 1864 Messrs. Henry Winter Davis and B. F. Wade through *The New York Tribune* published a terrible arraignment of Mr.

---

with Jefferson Davis. He was wounded at Shiloh and Baton Rogue. Appleton's Cyclopaedia of American Biography, Vol. I., pg. 53.

1175 Execration means abhorrence.

1176 Miscreants are villains.

1177 Indices are indicators.

1178 Implacable means unopposed.

1179 Fervid means zealous.

Lincoln for his course on the reconstruction bill in the following words:

"The president by preventing this bill a law holds the electoral votes of the southern states at the dictation of his personal ambition. If those votes turn the balance in his favor, is it to be supposed that his competitor defeated by such means will acquiesce if the rebel majority assert their supremacy in those states and send votes which elect an enemy of the government, will we not repel his claims? And is not civil war for the presidency inaugurated by the votes of rebel states? A more studied outrage upon the legislative authority of the people has never been perpetuated. Congress passed a bill. The president refused to approve it; then by proclamation puts as much of it in force as he sees fit and proposes to execute those parts by officers unknown to the laws of the United States and not subject to the confirmation of the Senate. The president after defeating the law proposes to appoint without law and without the advice and consent of the Senate, military governors of the rebel states. He has already exercised this dictatorial usurpation in Louisiana and he defeated the bill to limit its limitation. The president has greatly presumed on the forbearance which the supporters of the administration have so long practiced in view of the arduous conflict in which we are engaged and the reckless ferocity of our political opponents, but he must understand that we are supporters of a cause and not a man; that the authority of Congress is paramount and must be respected; that the whole body of the Union men in Congress will not submit to be impeached by him of rash and unconstitutional legislation, and if he wishes their support he must confine himself to executive duties; to obey, execute and not make the laws; to suppress by arms the rebellion and leave political reorganization to Congress."

With all this Mr. Lincoln could not be made to subscribe to the new doctrine that states where slavery existed and where Negroes were excluded from suffrage could be republican in form, nor could he be made to admit that the guarantee prescribed in the abolition of slavery was the destruction of existing state governments at the commencement of the war. No one could deny that Virginia, Missouri, Louisiana and South Carolina were Republican, yet they were not less Republican after slavery was abolished in them. It was a matter of paramount duty with the administration and a matter of deep and general interest of the people that after the suppression of the insurrection and rebellion, the Union of all the states should be re-established on principles that preserved the rights of each and of the federal government. It was not to be wondered that there was great difference of opinions on this subject when we take into view the political aspirations of partisan leaders, and the passions, prejudices, hopes and fears of the distracted elements of the North. Mr. Lincoln's persistency in not yielding and identifying himself with these revolutionary schemes greatly disappointed the radical leaders. He was in favor from the commencement of reconstructing the old government and never changed his views or gave countenance to the construction of the new one. With him the old Union of the states was above any and all party consideration.

Wendell Phillips[1180] followed up all this at a speech at Cooper Institute in New York City on the presidential election on which occasion the Rev. Dr. Cheever[1181] opened the meeting and proceeded before introducing Mr. Phillips to read a long speech, which he had prepared for the occasion. As usual with that gentleman's efforts, he was very prosy and tedious. The audience, after listening patiently for three quarters of an hour, concluded that they had had enough, and called from all parts of the house, "Phillips, Phillips." Rev. Dr. Cheever was unable to proceed for some time, and when comparative silence was restored said he had but one more sentence to speak and they might rest assured he would not leave that stage until he said it. This he did and then introduced the orator of the evening who addressed the audience.

These were Wendell Phillips remarks:

*"For thirty years he has been working to break up the Union in the interest of justice, and now he labored to save it for the same interest. The same curse he invoked on the Old Union would he invoke on a new Union if it is not founded on justice to the negro. "Science must either demonstrate that the negro is not a man, or politics must afford him equality at the ballot box and in the offices of trust." He judged Mr. Lincoln by his words and deeds, and so judging he was "unwilling to trust Abraham Lincoln with the future of the country. Let it be granted that Mr. Lincoln is pledged to Liberty and Union; but his pledge is wrung out of him by the Cleveland movement, and was a mere electioneering pledge. Mr. Lincoln is a politician. Politicians are like the bones of a horse's fore-shoulder—not a straight*

---

[1180] Wendell Phillips—See pg. 8.

[1181] Rev. Dr. George Barrell Cheever was pastor of "the Church of the Puritans" and was anti-slavery. *New York Times*, May 9, 1860.

*one in it. A reformer is like a Doric column*[1182] *of iron—straight, strong, and immoveable. It is a momentous responsibility to trust Mr. Lincoln where we want a Doric column to stand stern and strong for the nation. I am an abolitionist, but I am also a citizen watchful of constitutional Liberty; and I say if President Lincoln is inaugurated on the votes of Tennessee, Louisiana and Arkansas, every citizen is bound to resist him. Are you willing to sacrifice the constitutional rights of seventy years for your fondness for an individual?"*

Mr. Phillips then quoted some opinions from prominent men in the Republican party. "A man in the field said, 'The re-election of Abraham Lincoln will be a disaster.' Another said, 'The re-election of Abraham Lincoln will be national destruction.' Said another, 'There is no government at Washington—nothing there.' Winter Davis of Maryland testified to his (Lincoln's) inability. Said another, 'That proclamation will not stand a week before the Supreme Court; but I had rather trust it there than Abraham Lincoln to make the judges.' Mr. Lincoln has secured his success just as the South used to secure its success. He says to the radicals in the Republican Party. 'I am going to nominate myself at Baltimore; risk a division of the party if you dare!' and the radicals submitted. Political Massachusetts submitted, and is silent; but Antislavery Massachusetts calls to the people to save their own cause." Mr. Phillips said he "wanted by free speech to let Abraham Lincoln know that we are stronger than Abraham Lincoln, and that he is a servant to obey us. I distrust a man who uses whole despotism in Massachusetts and half despotism in South Carolina, and that man is Abraham Lincoln."[1183]

Mr. Lincoln when asked if he had seen the Wade-Davis Manifesto, the Phillips speech, &c. he said no he had not seen them and did not care to see them. He has seen enough to satisfy him that he was a failure in the opinion of many distinguished politicians of his own party as well as among the people in rebellion. "Time will show whether I am right or whether they are right and I am content to abide the decision of time."

It was urged that this opposition must be embarrassing to his administration as well as damaging to the party. He replied, "Yes, that

[1182] A Doric column was a plain Greek column developed in the 7th Century B.C. and used in buildings. www.guidetocolumns.com/Doric_column.htm

[1183] *New York Times*, May 13, 1863.

is true, but our friends Wade, Davis, Phillips, Grantz Brown,[1184] Greeley,[1185] Cheever and others are hard to please. I am incapable of doing this. I cannot please without wantonly violating not only my oath but the Constitution and statute laws, as well as the theory and most vital principles upon which our government was founded. I have enough to look after without giving much of my time to the consideration of the subject of who shall be my successor in office. The position is not a bed of roses and the occupant, whoever he may be, for the next four years will have little leisure to pluck a thorn or plant a rose in his own pathway. As for Wade, Davis and the others who see fit to deprecate my policy and criticize my official action, I shall not complain. I accord to them the fullest liberty of press and freedom of speech, but so far as any action of them however exercised, amicably and openly, strategically, clandestinely, hostilely[1186] or revolutionary, it will not change the policy I adopted in the belief that I am right. I feel on this subject as an old Illinois farmer felt when eating cheese and was interrupted by his son who said, 'Hold on Dad, there's skippers in the cheese.' Said he, 'Never mind Tom. If they can stand it, I can.' That is about the way I feel about these politicians."

There seemed to be as much irrepressible conflict and irreconcilable differences of principle between the members of the Republican Party and Mr. Lincoln as there was between Mr. Lincoln and the misguided Unionists. He had no disguises. There was no guile in him. He was straightforward, true, and honorable. It was said of him that he was acquainted with tears and smiles, complex in the power of his brain, and single in the dictates of his heart. His words reflected as a mirror and never failed to convey the perfect image of his convictions. Although cunning, he never wore a mask of hypocrisy to conceal his honest purposes. He was what might be called the child of uncultivated and uncorrupted nature, natural in life, conception and action. He possessed the great distinctive characteristic which is the product of intelligence and sincerity, which makes the logician—was

---

1184 Benjamin Grantz Brown was a graduate of Yale College and a leader of the Free Soil party. In 1856 he was shot in the leg in a dual and limped the rest of his life. He served in the U.S. Senate from 1863—1867. He was elected Governor of Missouri in 1871 and was also editor of the *Missouri Democrat* newspaper. He was an unsuccessful candidate with Horace Greeley for the 1872 election. www.bioguide.congress.gov/scripts/biodisplay.pl?index=B0000905

1185 Horace Greeley—see pg. 16.

1186 Hostilely means unfriendly.

ever candid and by his intellect intinctured[1187] with arrogance and his genius, devoid of pride, he was able to avoid successfully the snares and pits set as cunning devices for entangling him in devious alliances and in inevitable destruction. In all this he stood as a mighty statue, his own spokesman, simple and true, as a beacon to posterity—needing the fewest words and the least drapery to consecrate it as freedom's eternal monument.

Now, when passion has subdued and calm reflection and reason have resumed their sway, no one is weak or base enough to say or believe that in case the conservative course had not been pursued by Mr. Lincoln keeping the northern people clearly right, so that when the shock came, impartial nations saw and said there was no excuse for rebellion and no justification for secession could the Union have been maintained. He early drew the line between radical and conservative Republicans and maintained an issue on that line throughout the whole period of the war. Can it be doubted that but for the conservative sentiments awakened in the Republican Party and so persistently maintained by Mr. Lincoln, the North would not have been fatally divided?

There can be no doubt that this conservative administration of executive power throughout the war that was persistent so far as the executive was concerned prosecuted alone for the maintenance of the government and preserving the Union that caused the Democratic masses with many of the leaders to remain loyal. While on the other hand if the administration and the united Republican Party had proclaimed it a war for the abolition of slavery that the united South would have proved too strong for a divided North.

Since Mr. Lincoln's election to the presidency in 1860, there has been a "tidal wave" in politics. Seymour[1188] had been elected Governor of New York, and Indiana and Pennsylvania had swung around the Democratic banner against the administration of Mr. Lincoln. At one time it looked like the war was to be paralyzed by the success of the Democratic Party in the great states of the North. The Republican Party had its immense advantage. It was in power. It was the party of the war; the party around which would cluster the brightest memories of the generation; it was party of sentiment formed by the enthusiasm of the young men who were fighting for the Union as well as the non-

---

[1187] Intinctured means dripping.

[1188] Horatio Seymour—See pg. 258.

combatant element at home. It was the party of the noble achievements; to it was largely due the emancipation of the slaves and the preservation of the Union, if it were saved in the future. It had given some of the noblest men in history; yet with all its prestige and discipline, it was in danger of an opposition secession. Any event occurring in the extraordinary or humiliating character either in the military or civic departments of the government was usually, whether justly or unjustly, attributed to the fault of the executive. This was eagerly seized upon by his opponents and made as available as possible to cover his administration with shame and himself with obloquy[1189] and detraction.

The party as an organization had gained much by its power of absorption; it had not hesitated to appropriate the sentimental platform of the Bell-Everett[1190] ticket of 1860 which embodied "the Union, the constitution and the enforcement of the laws." There was never a more romantic or potent declaration of principles uttered which could be addressed by a law abiding citizen with greater effort for cooperation, but the trouble in all this was that there was a want of harmony in the party itself. There was an abiding and absorbing, growing and dangerous difference of opinion about policy ways and means reaching the common object of all in restoring peace to the country as well as the ambitious differences and preferences in the question of who should be Mr. Lincoln's successor. With this division in the Republican Party, Democrats might have had an even chance of political success at the election of 1864 had they not in their platform antagonized the active and settled sentiment of the country.

The American people had never seen the time when there was more active political discussion than now. Besides the question of war with its natural responsibilities, the finances, credit, currencies and revenues of the country interested as well as disturbed the people of all parties. The issues of the war, political preferment, and the welfare of the nation caused wonderful diversity of sentiment and correspondingly a diversity of action among the partisan adherents and advocates of the principles severally adopted by them. Radical rule or conservative rule was one issue. Democratic or Republican rule was another; each momentous in itself, and dangerous to the peace and well-being of the distracted country already involved in a bloody war.

---

1189 Obloquy means blame.

1190 John Bell (See pg. 8) and Edward Everett (See pgs. 36 & 37 footnotes).

In speaking of the differences of himself and his party during the campaign while the acrimonious[1191] fight was being made against him, Mr. Lincoln said: "A great wrong originating in political differences has been committed by which we and they (the rebels) are sufferers. The question is—are we ever again to be united and fellow countrymen? And so there is by my theory much to forgive. Those who are in the new movement seem to think there is nothing to forget. I am for conciliation. They seem to be governed by resentment. They believe we can be made one people by force and vengeance. I think we are not likely to bring about unity by hatred and persecution. If there is really this difference, our paths are difference and there is no need for secrecy or concealment." There is a remarkable degree of independence in every aspect of its import in these utterances in the face of the Democratic Party declarations, and the Pomeroy escapade.[1192] The people's provisional committee promulgating[1193] the principle of one term with its concomitant[1194] calamities, the call published and signed by a great number of Republicans from different parts of the country headed by the recent governor of the state of New York, named Lucius Robinson,[1195] inviting the citizens of the United States "who meant to uphold the Union and suppress the rebellion without infringing the rights of individuals or states," thereby charging in the new suggestion of turpitude[1196] of the president and his administration in terms by the call, super added by still another call, in the interest of the opposition made by the "central Frémont club" and others for all persons to meet at Cleveland, Ohio on the 31st of May.

The presidential election was seized upon as an opportune occasion to dispose of and crush Mr. Lincoln. There was, however, no great harmony among the mal-contents and aspirants for his place. Mr.

---

1191 Acrimonious means angry.

1192 The Pomeroy escapade was Samuel Pomeroy's attempt to entice Mr. Chase to run for President against Mr. Lincoln. Samuel Clarke Pomeroy was a U.S. Senator. While in Kansas, he colonized the town of Lawrence, Kansas, the first settlement in the territory. He also had proposed to Mr. Lincoln the idea of having an all-black colony in Central America. The Two American Presidents, pg. 271 and Appleton's Cyclopaedia of American Biography, Vol. V., pg. 60.

1193 Promulgating means declaring.

1194 Concomitant means accompanying.

1195 Lucius Robinson was a New York lawyer who was elected Governor of New York in 1876. One of the entrances to Niagara Falls is named for him. Appleton's Cyclopaedia of American Biography, Vol. V., pg. 287.

1196 Turpitude means depravity.

Chase,[1197] the Secretary of the Treasury, at first seemed to be the most eligible candidate upon who the opposition could concentrate. He had a laudable ambition to be president, and under more favorable circumstances would have proudly not only accepted the nomination if tendered to him, but would have eagerly sought it by hearty cooperation with his friends who had been alienated from Mr. Lincoln, if it had been possible to have acted without bad faith, to the incumbent and candidate respectively, one of whose trusted advisers he had been during the whole of his official course. Mr. Chase eventually became convinced that however much the politicians were opposed to Mr. Lincoln, the people of the country were for him, and they were determined to re-nominate and elect him. It was plain to be seen that Mr. Lincoln was the choice of the people. No one was more surprised at this than Mr. Lincoln himself.[1198]

Mr. Lincoln had been so confined in his duties in dealing with the politicians that he could only form an estimate of the popular voice by the manifest opposition he being evinced[1199] by the jealous interestedness of the partisan rivalry of the disaffected administration Republicans. However disparaging to his pride, Mr. Lincoln had become forced to the conclusion in the light of the knowledge derived from his political associations, and the tenor and temper of the public press, that he was a failure and unlikely to be his own successor in office.

It was soon demonstrated in these trying times of doubt and suspense that the favorite opposition candidate for the succession of all the political influence sought to be brought to bear in him by the influential members in Congress, the treasury officials, and other influence had not the strength or hold on the public mind in New Hampshire, Mr. Chase's native state, or in Ohio, the state of which he was now a citizen, to secure a public expression of preference in Mr. Chase's favor. The party conventions soon assembled in each of those states, and greatly to the astonishment of Mr. Lincoln and many of his political friends who had not taken into consideration the great and irresistible power of the people, emanated from the so-called leaders and politicians of the country, the sentiment was not only overwhelm-

---

1197 Salmon P. Chase—See pg. 98.

1198 No President of the United States in the last thirty years had been re-elected. Abraham Lincoln, The War Years, pg. 466.

1199 Evinced means subdued.

ing in favor of Mr. Lincoln's continuance in office, there was also great unanimity in favor of Mr. Lincoln in other states. The conclusion became inevitable and Mr. Chase, on the 3rd of March, wrote his famous letter of qualified declination to become a candidate for the presidency, reiterating what he claimed he had previously said in this language: "Should our friends manifest a preference for another, I should accept their decision with ready acquiescence due" and he withdrew from the contest much to the regret of his admiring friends. He gave no indication, however, of favoring the choice of many of his favoring admirers, for Abraham Lincoln with whom he had so been intimately associated.

A secret organization, in the interest of the opposition of Mr. Lincoln had been formed during the winter of 1863 and 1864. One Samuel C. Pomeroy was at its head. The character of this gentleman can be correctly estimated by the secret intrigue by which he was engaged. He was formerly a Massachusetts adventurer, sent to Kansas in the days of her territorial existence by a philanthropical association formed in Boston with unlimited funds to resist the encroachments of slavery and to make, if possible, a free state of the territory. Whether the funds furnished in Massachusetts contributed in any degree to the object for which they were entrusted to him as their disbursing agent does not appear yet, the irresistible force of events in time made Kansas a non slave-holding state, and the reserved Massachusetts funds, there is reason for knowing that they were appropriated to the electing of Mr. Pomeroy one of the first United States Senators from that state. Fresh from his political "prostitution constitution" in Kansas, having always his personal and pecuniary interests at heart above all other considerations, he was on the alert for new schemes to further unraveling[1200] ambition. To this end he was not slow in embracing the coveted prospect of Mr. Lincoln's downfall by the promotion of Mr. Chase to the presidency. He promptly ingratiated[1201] himself with the treasury employees and other adherents to the opposition of Mr. Lincoln, speedily formed a committee and constituted himself chairman of it; deluded by the hope and expectation that the national Republican organization would be superseded or subordinated to cooperation with him or to his associates in making Mr. Chase president. Mr. Pomeroy knew Mr.

---

[1200] Unraveling means disentangling.

[1201] Ingratiated means to bring into favor.

Lincoln was facing charges now being made by the Democratic Party for prosecuting what they now characterized as "a relentless war which was ruinous to the country," while the disaffected Republicans, were charging him with imbecility, a want of energy, and too great forbearance towards the enemies of the government in the South. The treasury patronage was greatly relied on in this movement and in view of the fact that this anti-Lincoln element had recently showed its opposition to the administration in so decided and marked a manner in Congress on the reconstruction policy, confidence was inspired of certain success.

Backed by all the elements of the opposition this self-constituted radical Republican Party impersonated by Senator Samuel C. Pomeroy, Senator from Kansas, supported by whom it might concern including many Congressmen, a most careful and elaborate secret circular was prepared and issued to the people, dignified by imposing and most illustrious signature at its conclusion of Samuel C. Pomeroy, chairman of the national executive committee. It is as follows:

Those in behalf of whom this communication is made have thoroughly surveyed impossible against the union of influences which will oppose him.

First, that even were the reelection of Mr. Lincoln desirable, it is practically impossible against the union of influences which will oppose him.

Second, that should he be reelected, the manifest tendency towards compromises and temporary expedients of policy will be stronger during a second term than it has been in the first, and the cause of human liberty, and the dignity and honor of the nation, suffer proportionately, while the war may continue to languish during his whole Administration, till the public debt shall become a burden too great to be borne.

Third, that the patronage of the Government through the necessities of the war has been so rapidly increased, and to such an enormous extent, and so loosely placed, as to render the "one-term principle" absolutely essential to the certain safely of our republican institutions.

Fourth, that we find united in Hon. Salmon P. Chase more of the qualities needed in a President during the next four years than are combined in any other available candidate; his record, clear and unimpeachable, showing him to be a statesman of rare ability and an administrator of the very highest order, while his private character furnishes the surest obtainable guarantee of economy and purity in the management of public affairs.

Fifth, that the discussion of the Presidential question, already commenced by the friends of Mr. Lincoln, has developed a popularity and strength in Mr. Chase unexpected even to his warmest admirers and while we are aware that this strength is at present unorganized, and in no condition to manifest its real magnitude, we are satisfied that it only needs systemic and faithful effort to develop it to an extent sufficient to overcome all opposing obstacles. For these reasons the friends of Mr. Chase have determined on measures which present his claims fairly and at once to the country…[1202]

After the decided expression of public sentiment in New Hampshire and Ohio by the people in convention as before stated, Mr. Chase became discouraged, and was induced in explanation, to state publicly: "I consider it more a privilege than a duty and that no further consideration be given to my name." Mr. Pomeroy, afterwards when his Waterloo came, in open Senate in an elaborately prepared speech, supplemented by the most careful consideration and suggestions of the combined influences of defeated hopes and the faction of hostility after Mr. Chase proposed to withdraw, added outrage to his corrupt intrigue by denying that his circular was a secret one, or considered as confidential. He passed a high and telling eulogy upon Mr. Chase and openly declared: "We still believed him to be the man whom the people will delight to honor" and urged that if Mr. Chase were elected he would secure "the confiscation of rebel property to the end, that there would be secured a Republican form of government with such subordination of the states' rights as would secure a free nationality according to the prevalent view of the representatives of the people in Congress assembled."

Mr. Pomeroy and his friends and confederates were combatting the humane policy of the president who was incapable of engaging in a persecution against a misguided and erring people who sought to break up the Union. Mr. Lincoln had no desire to kill and murder them, no wish to subjugate them, no intemperate desire to confiscate their property, and reduce them to beggary, nor to irritably deprive them of all legal and constitutional rights because of their mistaken views of his administration as to the security of their rights of property

[1202] Lincoln and Greeley, pg. 336.

in the peculiar institution. One of the most important issues now made was that the executive was subordinate to the legislature, that Mr. Lincoln had issued an emancipation proclamation as well as one of amnesty and his opponents in his own party denied the independence of the three great departments and insisted that the executive was a subordinate branch, and that no war necessity could warrant an executive order in such cases without the assent of Congress first obtained. Besides this the opposition was looking with jealous interest to the proscription[1203] and subjugation[1204] of intelligent and belligerent whites and the enfranchisement of the Negroes to the end of securing a more consolidated government of supreme central power in the undoubted interest of the dominant Republican Party regardless of the republican form of government guaranteed by the Constitution.

After the special miscarriage of the Chase movement, the Republican national executive committee was earnestly importuned[1205] to postpone the nominating convention until the month of September. This recommendation was headed by the distinguished William C. Bryant,[1206] a veteran politician, editor, and poet, backed by many gentlemen of high character. The object of this delay was obvious. Evidentially the purpose was not allaying[1207] the acrimonious[1208] presidential fight, but to cause diversion and to gain time in promoting discord and dissentions which might result to their advantage and to the detriment and destruction of Mr. Lincoln's chances. The national executive committee had singular unanimity, there being but one solitary member who disfavored the movement for postponement. It was at this time understood that the executive committee favored a nominating convention to be held in June. To forestall this action the anti-Lincoln Republicans early in the month of May styling themselves "the people's provisional committee" made a call for a convention to

---

1203 Proscription means prohibition.
1204 Subjugation means to make subservient.
1205 Importuned means urged.
1206 William Cullen Bryant was a Massachusetts poet who was born in 1794. He was editor of *The New York Evening Post.* He worked for Mr. Lincoln's nomination in the 1860 Republican National Convention to block Mr. Seward's nomination. Reelecting Lincoln, pg. 144, Appleton's Cyclopaedia of American Biography, Vol. I., pgs. 422 - 427 and Two Roads to Sumter, pg. 192.
1207 Allaying means calming.
1208 Acrimonious means angry.

be held at Cleveland on the 31st of the same month.[1209] This call was signed by many distinguished politicians headed by B. Gratz Brown, United States Senator from Missouri, Rev. Dr. Cheever of New York and others. Wendell Phillips, Fred. Douglass[1210] and others wrote letters approving the call, the object and the action of the convention.

Those called to assemble favored the immediate extinction of slavery by the action of Congress without regard to the executive action "the equality of all men before the law without regard to race or color;" together with such a plan for reconstruction the effect of which Congress might prescribe regardless of executive protest or constitutional restraint. This last call having capped the climax of all intolerant presumptions is in the remarkable phraseology of its convocation in these terms: "The imbecile and vacillating policy of the present administration in the conduct of the war being just weak enough to waste its men and its means to provoke the enemy, but not strong enough to conquer the rebellion, and its treachery to justice, freedom and its genuine democratic principles in its plan of reconstruction whereby the honor and dignity of the nation has been sacrificed to conciliate[1211] the still existing and arrogant slave power, to further the ends of unscrupulous partisan ambition, call in thunder tones on the lovers of justice and their country to come to the rescue of imperiled nationality and the cause of impartial justice and universal freedom, threatened with betrayal and overthrow, winding up with this remarkable figure of rhetoric: the way to victory and salvation is plain. Justice must be thrown in the seat of national legislation to guide the national will."

---

1209 May 31, 1864.

1210 Frederick Douglass was a slave born in Maryland but ran away and got his freedom. He was an orator and a publisher of the *North Star*. He became the leading black leader of his time. He visited Mr. Lincoln at the White House on two different occasions. He also helped enlist colored soldiers in the 54th and 55th Massachusetts regiments. From 1876 - 1881 Douglass was U.S. Federal Marshal of the District of Columbia. Reelecting Lincoln, pg. 92, Appleton's Cyclopaedia of American Biography, Vol. II., pg. 217

1211 Conciliate means to unite.

## THE CLEVELAND CONVENTION

There were some 350 persons who styled themselves delegates and who met pursuant to the call. The Honorable John Cochrane[1212] was made president of the body. General John Frémont[1213] was nominated for president by acclimation, and the Honorable John Cochrane was nominated for vice-president with but few dissenting votes. Both gentlemen accepted the nominations. Their candidacy continued until within six weeks of the presidential election. At no time had the ticket given that promise of success hoped for it by its promoters. The disastrous result was at length foreseen and some prominent gentlemen from Boston, anti-Lincoln in sentiment, on the 20th of August addressed a letter to Mr. Frémont asking this question: "If in case Mr. Lincoln will withdraw, will you do so and unite with the thorough and earnest friends with a vigorous prosecution of the war in a new convention?" The candidate of the Cleveland convention was willing to accede to this proposition but Mr. Lincoln having been from principle throughout the war opposed to treating the enemy in rebellion, declined to the soft impeachment the proposition involved as a last resort of his opponents to crush him and decided to continue in the presidential ring, after which the Cleveland convention's presidential candidate withdrew from the canvas on the 21st of September.

## THE REPUBLICAN NATIONAL CONVENTION

The call for the regular Republican national convention had been made in the regular way addressed to all "who desire the constitutional maintenance of the Union, the supremacy of the Constitution, and the complete suppression of the existing rebellion, with the cause thereof, by vigorous war and all and efficient means." This convention met at Baltimore, June 7, 1864 and was presided over temporarily by the Rev. Robert I. Breckinridge,[1214] of Kentucky, and as permanent president

---

1212 John Cochrane—See pg. 62.

1213 General John Frémont—See pg. 141.

1214 Rev. Robert I. Breckinridge of Kentucky was a pro-Union man who had two sons who were secessionists and high ranking officers in the Confederate Army. Reelecting Lincoln, pg.189.

by ex-governor William Dennison,[1215] of Ohio. On a formal vote for president, Mr. Lincoln received all the votes of every state, except those of Missouri, which were cast according to instructions for General U.S. Grant. Mr. Lincoln's nomination was made unanimous. When a ballot was taken for vice-president it resulted as follows: 200 for Andrew Johnson, 150 for Hannibal Hamlin,[1216] 108 for Daniel S. Dickinson,[1217] and 61 scattering votes. Before the vote could be announced a great many changes were made, resulting in 491 votes for Johnson, 17 for Dickinson and 9 for Hamlin. The vote was announced and Mr. Johnson was declared the candidate for vice-president.

## THE DEMOCRATIC CONVENTION

This convention met August 9, 1864 in Chicago. Ex-governor William Bigler,[1218] was named temporary president and Horatio Seymour[1219] of New York, permanent president. General George B. McClellan[1220] was nominated president on the first ballot. When the vote was first taken, there were 174 for General McClellan, 38 for Thomas H. Seymour[1221] of Connecticut, 12 for Horatio Seymour of New York, one-half a vote for Charles O'Conor[1222] of New York, and one-half a vote blank. Changes at once took place before the vote was

---

1215 William Dennison was a political friend of Mr. Lincoln and an anti-slavery man from Ohio. He was a banker and railroad executive who was also Governor of Ohio. He served as Postmaster General in Lincoln's Cabinet. He founded Dennison College in Ohio. Reelecting Lincoln, pg. 306, Seaport Autographs, pg. 14 and Appleton's Cyclopaedia of American Biography, Vol. II., pg. 142.

1216 Hannibal Hamlin—See pg. 95.

1217 Daniel S. Dickinson was born in Connecticut and moved to New York where he was a Congressman and U.S. Senator. He was chairman of the Senate finance committee. He was a former Democrat who had defected and threw his support to Mr. Lincoln. Reelecting Lincoln, pgs. 88 & 271, Appleton's Cyclopaedia of American Biography, Vol. II., pgs. 172 & 173 and Seaport Autographs pgs. 14 & 15.

1218 William Bigler was the former Democratic Governor of Pennsylvania. A printer by trade, he was editor of the *Clearfield Democrat* newspaper. He was also a U.S. Senator. Reelecting Lincoln, pg. 283 and Appleton's Cyclopaedia of American Biography, Vol. I., pg. 262.

1219 Horatio Seymour—See pg. 258.

1220 General George B. McClellan—See pg. 123.

1221 Thomas H. Seymour—See pg. 152.

1222 Charles O'Conor was an attorney from New York. After the war, he was hired by Varina Davis in 1865 to defend Confederate President Jefferson Davis. The attorney also obtained a writ for Davis' release from prison in May 1867. The First Lady of the Confederacy, pg. 171

announced and afterwards it was announced to be General George McClellan 202 1/2, for Thomas Seymour 28 1/2, all of the latter votes being given by the delegates from Indiana, Ohio and the border states. On motion of Mr. Vallandigham[1223] of Ohio, the nomination of General McClellan was made unanimous.

For vice-president the vote stood 65 1/2 for James Guthrie[1224] of Kentucky, 55 1/2 for Geo. H. Pendleton[1225] of Ohio, 32 1/2 for Lazarus W. Powel[1226] of Kentucky, 26 for George W. Cass,[1227] 13 for Daniel W. Vorhees,[1228] 16 for J. D. Caton[1229] of Illinois, 9 for Augustus C. Dodge,[1230] 8 for John Phelps,[1231] and 1/2 vote scattered in the darkness. Before another vote was taken all the candidates except Mr. Pendleton withdrew and Mr. Pendleton was declared the unanimous nominee. (By the way, it was never satisfactorily settled whether the scattered one-half vote concurred in the announcement or not.)

The platform of principles adopted at this convention was denounced by the opposing party as a base and cowardly surrender to the enemy and as an encouragement of the enemy in arms against the government to persevere in their hostilities. Their course would result in a peace party in the North that would secure and force terms of settlement of the sections on the basis of peaceable secession. This platform at first was unpopular with the masses and grew more so as

---

[1223] Clement C. Vallandigham—See pg. 245.

[1224] James Guthrie of Kentucky was a wealthy banker and the builder of railroads. He helped frame the state constitution for Kentucky. He was Secretary of the Treasury on the Cabinet of both Franklin Pierce and James Buchanan. Two Roads to Sumter, pg. 16 and Appleton's Cyclopaedia of American Biography, Vol. III., pg. 15.

[1225] George H. Pendleton—See pg. 241.

[1226] Lazarus W. Powel was the Governor of Kentucky, 1851-55 and a U.S. Senator 1859-1865. politicalgraveyard.com/bio/powell.html

[1227] George W. Cass was an industrialist and President of the Northern Pacific railroad. www.absoluteastronomy.com/topics/United_States_presidential_election%2c_1864

[1228] Daniel Wolsey Vorhees was a "Copperhead" Congressman from Indiana. He was an attorney who defended John Cook in the John Brown raider's trials in November 1859. He was both a Congressman (1861 - 1866) and a U.S. Senator (1877 - 1887). Reelecting Lincoln, pgs. 90 & 335 and Appleton's Cyclopaedia of American Biography, Vol. VI., pg. 307.

[1229] John D. Caton was a justice of the Illinois Supreme Court from 1842-1864. politicalgraveyard.com/bio/cas/cberry-caton.html

[1230] Augustus Caesar Dodge was Missouri born. He was a veteran of both the Mexican War and the Blackhawk War. He was a Congressman from Iowa Territory and later a U.S. Senator. Appleton's Cyclopaedia of American Biography, Vol. II., pg. 93.

[1231] John W. Phelps—See pg. 204.

the canvass progressed. The issue made was a vital one. It involved the necessity of all Union men to support the armies in the field by voting for Mr. Lincoln or the alternative of voting for General McClellan, whose party to be consistent with the principles annunciated in the platform, would be forced to submit to making a disgraceful peace.

In justice, however, to General McClellan, it must be said that he repudiated its obvious meaning in his letter of acceptance. The convention demanded "A cessation of hostilities with a view toward ultimate convention of the states." To this General McClellan responded that "so soon as it is ever clear or probable that our present adversaries are ready for peace on the basis of the Union, we should exhaust all the resources of statesmanship....to secure such peace." On this issue he stood with Mr. Lincoln. The convention explicitly declared that there was "four years of failure to restore the Union by the experiment of war" and declared that it was the sentiment of the American people that "public liberty and private rights were trodden down and the material prosperity of the country essentially impaired—justice, humanity, liberty, and the public welfare demanded that immediate efforts be made for the cessation of hostilities with the view to an ultimate convention of the states or other peaceable means to the end that at the earliest practicable peace may be restored on the basis of a federal Union of the states." In reply to this General McClellan wrote: "I could not look into the faces of my gallant comrades of the army and navy and tell them that their labors and sacrifice of so many of our slain and wounded brethren had been in vain; that we had abandoned that Union which we had for so often periled our lives." The sentiment of the convention was peace first and the Union would follow. The sentiment of the policy of General McClellan was the Union first and peace must follow.

The great mass of the northern people favorable to the Union became very much incensed at General McClellan for having accepted the nomination for president in 1864 from a political party whose platform contained a plank which annunciated as a principle the war a failure and that we would never succeed in suppressing the rebellion. This had a serious affect and a damaging tendency, it was claimed among the troops of the North and encouraged and inspired hope among the leaders as well as the rank and file of the southern people.

There was at no time during the canvass a reasonable doubt about the final result of the election yet doubtless this open repudiation of the heresy of his party General McClellan brought many votes to his support that would have otherwise been given to Mr. Lincoln. In due time, the strife resulted in the election of Mr. Lincoln for a second term. He received the electoral votes of the states of Maine, New Hampshire, Vermont, Massachusetts, Rhode Island, Connecticut, New York, Pennsylvania, Maryland, West Virginia, Ohio, Indiana, Illinois, Michigan, Iowa, Wisconsin, Minnesota, Kansas, Missouri, California and Oregon; in all 212 electoral votes, one of the electors from Nevada having died before votes were taken in the electoral college. Of the popular civic vote in the states he received 2,213,065 votes. General McClellan received the electoral votes of the states of New Jersey, Delaware and Kentucky, amounting to 21 in the electoral college, and of the popular civic votes of all the states he received 1,802,237 votes. There was also an army vote which had been legally provided for which was counted in canvassing the returns for electors, aggregating 116,887 for Mr. Lincoln and 33,748 for General McClellan. The total vote cast as counted amounted to 4,939,967. Mr. Lincoln's plurality was almost 500,000 votes.

One of the curious facts connected with General McClellan's candidacy for the president in 1864 is he having received only the electoral votes of three states; yet it is true that a change of less than 100,000 votes in five leading northern states would have defeated Mr. Lincoln and elected General McClellan President of the United States.

*Harpers Weekly* political anti-Lincoln campaign cartoon
Lincoln, Lamon (his back showing) and General McClellan
Sharpsburg, Maryland from October 1862 trip
(See page 219)

*"In giving freedom to the slave, we assure freedom is free."*

Abraham Lincoln[1232]

# — 13 —

# THE WAR IN 1864—PART II

## APRIL 1864

The next important battle was that of Sabin Crossroads,[1233] Texas which was fought on the 8th of April, 1864. This battle is also known as the battle of Mansfield and Pleasant Hill.[1234] The troops engaged on the Union side were cavalry divisions, Third and Fourth of the Union Army Corps, the first division of the Nineteenth Army Corps, Department of the Gulf, under General N. P. Banks.[1235] The Union loss in this battle was one hundred fifty killed, eight hundred forty-four wounded, and three hundred seventy-five missing, Confederate total loss was 5,707 killed, wounded and missing or captured.

The battle of Fort Pillow[1236] followed on the 12th of April, in which the Union loss was three hundred fifty killed, sixty wounded and one hundred fifty missing. The Confederate loss was inconsiderable, amounting to only eighty men. The Union troops engaged were Eleventh U. S. Colored Troops, Sixth U.S. Colored Heavy Artillery (and First Alabama), Battery F, U.S. Colored Light Artillery and

---

1232 Lincoln in American Memory, pg. 124.

1233 Sabin Crossroads was three miles from Mansfield, Texas at the intersection of four roads. Civil War a Narrative, Part VII., pg. 42.

1234 Pleasant Hill is near Shreveport, Louisiana. Southern History of the War, Part II, pg. 257

1235 Major General Nathaniel P. Banks—See pg. 140.

1236 Fort Pillow is 65 miles upstream from Memphis on the Saline River at Columbia, Kentucky. It sits on a high bluff about forty feet above the Mississippi River. The fort is mostly known from the 262 Union colored troops stationed there many who were taken prisoner and "massacred" by the Confederates. Civil War a Narrative, Part VII., pg. 63.

Bradford's Battalion of the Thirteenth Tennessee Cavalry—about six hundred men.[1237] On the 17th through the 20th of April inclusive the battle of Plymouth in North Carolina was fought. The troops engaged in this battle were the Eighty-fifth New York, the One Hundred Third Pennsylvania and the Sixteenth Connecticut assisted by the navy under Lt. Commander Flusser.[1238] This battle includes the engagements of Forts Grey, Wessel and Williams. The Union lost twenty killed, eighty wounded, and 1,500 missing. Total rebel loss was five hundred.

On the 30th of April the battle of Jenkin's Ferry was fought on the Saline River, Arkansas, with a loss of two hundred killed and nine hundred fifty-five wounded. The Confederate loss was 1,100. The Union troops engaged were the 77th Ohio, the Fourth, Nineteenth, Twenty-ninth, Thirty-sixth and Fortieth Iowa, the First Arkansas, Twelfth Kansas, Ninth and Thirty-seventh Wisconsin, and Forty-third Illinois Volunteers, the Seventy-ninth (First) Kansas) and Eighty-third (Second) Kansas) U. S. Colored Troops, Battery A Third Illinois, Second Indiana Battery, First Iowa, Second, Sixth and Fourteenth Kansas, First and Second Missouri, and the Thirteenth Illinois Cavalry, Third Division of the Seventeenth Corps, also under General N. P. Banks.

## MAY 1864

Following this, the great battle of the Wilderness, Virginia[1239] was fought on the 5th, 6th and 7th of May which resulted in the terrible slaughter to the Union forces. According to official report 2,246 Union men were killed, 12,137 wounded and 3,383 missing while the total rebel loss was 11,400 in killed, wounded or missing. The Union troops engaged were the Second Corps, Fifth Corps, Eighth Corps,

---

1237 Confederate commanders were General Nathan Bedford Forrest and Brigadier General James Chalmers. The Union commander was Major General Lionel F. Booth. Southern History of the War, Part II., pg. 260.

1238 Lt. Commander Charles W. Flusser was from Annapolis and a graduate in 1853 of the U.S. Naval Academy. He was killed in action on April 18, 1864 in a battle between the *Miami* and the Confederate Ironclad *Albemarle*. www,history.navy.mil/photos/pers-us/uspers-f/c-flusser.htm

1239 The Wilderness is just west of Fredericksburg, Virginia. Civil War a Narrative, Part VII., inside front cover.

Ninth Corps, Calvary Corps, led by R. L. Stone,[1240] under the Command of General Grant of the U.S. Army; the Confederates were commanded by General Robert E. Lee. During the progress of the battle there was another battle raging which lasted from the 5th to the 9th of May, known as Rocky Face Ridge, Georgia including Tunnel Hill, Mill Creek Gap, Buzzard Roost, and Snake Creek Gap, near Dalton, Georgia in which the Union forces lost in killed two hundred, and wounded six hundred twenty-seven; the Confederates loss was six hundred.

From the 8th to the 18th of May inclusive the great battle of Spotsylvania, Virginia was fought. The battle includes engagements on the Fredericksburg Road, Laurel Hill, and Ni River. The Union loss in this battle was 1,143 killed, 11,747 wounded, and 2,190 missing. The Confederate loss was estimated at 9,000 total, killed, wounded and missing. The troops engaged in this battle on the Union side (General Grant commanding in person) were the Second, Fifth, Sixth and Ninth Corps and Cavalry Corps, Army of the Potomac. On May the 12th to the 16th inclusive the battle of Fort Darling, or Drewry's Bluff, Virginia[1241] was fought by the Tenth and Eighteenth Corps of the Army and the *Virginia*[1242] and *North Carolina.*[1243] This battle includes the engagement at Weir's Bottom, Proctor's and Palmer's Creeks. The federal loss was four hundred thirty-two killed, 2,380 wounded and two hundred missing. The Confederates total loss was 2,500. The battle of Resaca, Georgia[1244] was fought on the 15th of May to the 18th inclusive. The federal loss was six hundred killed, and 2,147 wounded. The Confederate loss was 2,800. The Union troops engaged were the Fourteenth, Fourth and Twentieth Corps—Cavalry—Army of the

---

[1240] Colonel Ray L. Stone led the Third Brigade, Fourth Division which included the 121st PA, 142nd PA, 143rd PA, 149th PA and 150th PA. www.civilwarhome.com/wildernessbattleorderunion.htm

[1241] Fort Darling or Drewry's Bluff, Virginia is on the James River below Richmond. Civil War a Narrative, Part VII., inside back cover.

[1242] *Virginia* was built in Scotland in 1861 and became a Confederate blockade runner. She was 175 feet long with seven guns, an iron hull and a crew of 61. She was captured on January 18, 1863 and refurbished so she could be used by the Union Navy. Warships of the Civil War Navies, pg. 95.

[1243] *North Carolina* was a 196 foot Ship of the Line built in 1816. She was manned by 820 sailors, had armaments of 74 guns, and was 196 feet long. Warships of the Civil War Navies, pg. 125.

[1244] Resaca, Georgia is located on the Oostanaula River in the northwest corner of Georgia. Civil War a Narrative, Part VII., inside back cover.

Cumberland, the Fifteenth and Sixteenth Corps, Army of the Tennessee, and the Twenty-third Corps, Army of the Ohio.

The battle of New Market, Virginia,[1245] was fought on May 15th by a portion of the Army of West Virginia. The Union loss was one hundred twenty killed, five hundred sixty wounded and two hundred forty missing. The Confederate loss was four hundred five. On May the 16th to 30th inclusive, the battle of Bermuda Hundreds was fought, with two hundred Union soldiers killed and 1,000 wounded. The Confederate total loss in this engagement was 2,000. The Union troops engaged were the 10th and 18th Corps, Army of the James. The battle of North Anna River, Virginia, was fought from the 23rd to the 27th of May. Total Union loss was 1,973. Total Confederate loss was 2,000. The Second, Fifth and Ninth Corps of the Army of the Potomac did the fighting in this battle.

## JUNE 1864

The second battle of Cold Harbor, Virginia,[1246] was commenced on the 1st and ended on the 12th of June. The federal loss was 1,925 killed, 10,570 wounded and 2,456 missing, while the total loss of the Confederates was not know but was believed to be considerably less. The Union forces engaged were the Second, Fifth, Sixth and Ninth Corps and Cavalry Corps, Army of the Potomac and the Eighteenth Corps, Army of the James.

On the 5th of June, the battle of Piedmont, Virginia was fought, with a loss of seven hundred eighty men on the Union side, and 2,970 on the Confederates. The fighting was done on the Union side by the Cavalry and Infantry of the Army of West Virginia. On the 9th of June to the 30th inclusive, the battle of Kenesaw Mountain including Pine Mountain, Pine Knob, Golgotha, and Culp's House, was fought with the general assault on June 27th, at McFee's Crossroads, Latimore Mills and Powder Springs. The Union loss was 6,670. The Confederate loss was 4,600. Troops in this engagement on the federal side were the Fourth, Fourteenth and Twenty-Fourth Corps, Army of the Cumberland, Fifteenth, Sixteenth and Seventeenth Corps Army of the

---

1245 New Market, Virginia is located in the Shenandoah Valley south of Winchester, Virginia.

1246 Cold Harbor, Virginia is north east of Richmond and north of the Chickahominy River. Civil War a Narrative, Part II., pg. 225.

Tennessee, and the Twenty-third Corps, Army of the Ohio. This battle is sometimes designated as Lost Mountain, Lost Creek, Mannita and Big Shanty. On the 10th of June Brice's Cross Roads battle, near Guntown, Mississippi, was fought with a Union loss of 2,220 and a Confederate loss of six hundred.

On the 13th to the 19th a battle at Petersburg, Virginia was fought. This battle includes Baylor's Farm, Walthall Junction and Weir's Bottom Church. The Union loss in killed was 2,013, wounded 9,935 and missing 4,621. Confederate losses was not given but was believed to be around 3,000. Troops engaged on the Union side of this battle were the Tenth and Eighteenth Corps, Army of the James, and the Second, Fifth, Sixth and Ninth Corps, Army of the Potomac. On the 17th and 18th the battle of Lynchburg, Virginia was fought with a loss of seven hundred on the Union side and two hundred on the Confederate side. The troops engaged were the 1st and 2nd Divisions Averill's[1247] and Duffies' Calvary, Army of West Virginia. On the 20th to 30th of June there was a battle at Petersburg, Virginia where the federal loss was five hundred six killed and wounded and eight hundred missing. Confederate loss was not known. The troops engaged on the Union side were the Fifth and Ninth Corps, Army of the Potomac, and Tenth and Eighteenth Corps, Army of the James.

On June 19, the death struggle between her pet of pirates of the ocean, *Alabama*, alias *Hull 290* and the loyal *Kearsarge*[1248] may have wounded the pride of England—to know that the hope of her people in a fair fight near the shores where they had fitted her for service, was sunk to rise no more. She had nothing to unbraid herself for she had done all for her beloved *Hull 290* that could have been expected of any friend, and her faithful greyhound true to the genuine diplomatic instincts not incompatible with the import of her name was conveniently there to the last to render service to her companion and to perform the last funeral rites over her watery grave. Then they surreptitiously and feloniously did steal, take, and carry away the

---

1247 William Averill—See pg. 264.

1248 *Kearsarge* was the Mohican class sloop, a Union ship with 7 guns including two 11" Dahlgren guns and a crew of 163 men under the command of Captain John A. Winslow. She sank the *Alabama* outside Cherbourg harbor on June 19, 1864 as thousands of people watched. Lincoln and the Civil War, pg. 275, Warships of the Civil War Navies, pg. 38, Civil War a Narrative, Part VII., pg. 381 and the Confederate Nation, 1861 - 1865, pgs. 278 & 279.

piratical prize leaving Commander Winslow[1249] of the *Kearsarge* to look on in amazement and see the speed the English hound made plowing through the waters to land the outlandish wrecker of American commerce, Captain Semmes[1250] on English soil, that he might find protection from just punishment under the British flag.

Timon[1251] of Athens, said: "The sea is a thief." It may be wondered what Timon would have called the greyhound had he seen him when: "He laid his hand upon the ocean's mane, and played familiar with his hoary looks."

Wilson's raid[1252] on the Wilson Railroad, Virginia, commenced on the 27th of June and ended on the 30th of June, in which he lost 1,418 men.

On the 27th of June a general assault was made the Union forces at Kennesaw Mountain. This was the second battle at this place, and resulted in the loss of Union forces of 2,051 casualties, and three hundred forty-two casualties for the Confederates. This battle was fought by the armies of the military division of the Army of the Mississippi.

---

1249 John A. Winslow was a South Carolina native and Mexican War participant. He had about 40 years service in the navy. The Confederate Nation. 1861-1865, pgs. 278 & 279 and Civil War a Narrative, Part VII., pg. 381.

1250 Captain Raphael Semmes was from Maryland. Semmes had served in the Mexican War, entered the U.S. Navy in 1826 and had a long naval career. He was known as "Old Beeswax" because of his handlebar mustache. He was commander of the *Alabama*. During the twenty-two months the *Alabama* was in service to the Confederacy, Semmes and his men were a menace to the Union ships. The Confederate Nation, 1861-1865, pgs. 182 & 183, The Confederate Navy, pg. 54 and Civil War a Narrative, Part VII, pg. 381.

1251 Timon of Athens is a play by William Shakespeare about a legendary Athenian. absoluteshakespeare.com/plays/timon_of_athens/Timon_of_athens.htm

1252 James H. Wilson commanded 13,000 Union cavalry troops. He was also involved in the last skirmish of the war east of the Mississippi River on May 6, 1865 in pursuit of Jefferson Davis in Georgia. He was a friend of General Grant who commanded a cavalry division of General Sheridan's army. Grant Takes Command, pg. 555 and Civil War a Narrative, Part VII., pg. 186 and Civil War a Narrative, Part IX., pgs. 6 & 277.

*"Mr. President, you must really get down from this exposed position. I cannot allow you to remain here longer and if you refuse, I shall deem it my duty to have you removed under guard."*

Major General Horatio G. Wright to Abraham Lincoln at Fort Stevens as the President stood on the parapet to watch the fighting.[1253]

# — 14 —

# ATTACK ON WASHINGTON CITY

There was perhaps no movement during the progress of the war which involved greater interests and consequences than General Early's attempt[1254] to capture the capital and his successfully being repulsed in the month of July of 1864; and there is perhaps no important event of the war about which there is so little known. The histories that have been written about the war give little or nothing of the stirring events which occurred on this occasion, when the fate of the capital of the nation was in its greatest peril. During the time of this raid telegraph wires were cut, and all communication between the scene of action and northern cities were cut off, which deprived the northern newspapers of the facts as they occurred. At the time it will also be remembered stirring events crowded on each other and history was being made very fast, so much so that failure to record it at once operated in many instances to permanent omissions and loss to posterity.

During the early summer of 1864, General Grant in his desperate fighting to take Richmond needed reinforcements and 18,000 of the most experienced artillerists from the forts around Washington were sent to him. General Lee was aware of this transfer of troops and the consequent weakening of the defense around the capital. During the

---

1253 Reelecting Lincoln, pg. 241.

1254 General Jubal Anderson Early—See pg. 253.

month of June while General Grant was threatening Petersburg, General Lee made a diversion. The Army of the Potomac was south of the James River. General Hunter[1255] had been defeated at Lynchburg and the Shenandoah Valley was clear. No resistance was to be apprehended, and the whole frontier of the loyal states lay unprotected. General Grant's army at this time was in great force and General Lee deemed it necessary to break it, by compelling him to withdraw a sufficient force to meet an invading army which he proposed to send to Maryland and the District of Columbia so as to weaken General Grant in his desires of capturing Petersburg and Richmond. Accordingly, General Early with a large force marched down the valley[1256] to Martinsburg, reaching that place on the 3rd of July, marching thence to Frederick, Maryland and there on the 7th, going thence to Rockville which is within fourteen miles of the capital. General Bradley Johnson[1257] with a Confederate cavalry brigade on the 9th moved north from Frederick City the only result which was a desperate scare to the people of Pennsylvania and the northern and eastern cities. The whole North was startled. The bridge across the Gunpowder River on the Philadelphia and Baltimore Railroad was burned by Major Harry Gilmor.[1258] He also captured federal General Franklin[1259] on the train stopped at that place.

General Grant was not long in finding out about the purpose of General Early's invasion and on the 5th or 6th, he ordered the Sixth Corps of the Army of the Potomac, commanded by Major General H. G. Wright[1260] to Washington. Fortunately at this time the Ninth Corps under General Emory[1261]was in transport to Fortress Monroe and Grant also ordered them to Washington without debarkation.

---

1255 General David Hunter—See pg. 138.

1256 The term "down the valley" used in describing their march north seems backwards. The Shenandoah River flows south to north, Therefore, when you are marching downstream (north), you are marching down the valley.

1257 General Bradley Tyler Johnson—See pg. 209.

1258 Major Harry Gilmor—See pg. 262.

1259 General William Franklin—See pg. 211.

1260 Horatio G. Wright—See pg. 174.

1261 General William Hemsley Emory was an engineer and astronomer from Maryland who graduated from the U.S. Military Academy in 1831. Emory led one of General Sheridan's infantry corps. He also engineered the boundary between Mexico and the United States. Grant Takes Command, pg. 360 and The Armies and The Leaders, pgs. 191 & 228.

The battle of Monocacy, Maryland, was fought on the 9th of July, resulted in ninety killed, five hundred seventy-nine wounded, 1,290 missing of the Union troops and four hundred Confederates total loss.[1262] This battle was fought by the 1st and 2nd brigade of the Sixth Corps and a detachment of the Eighth Corps of Union forces. General Wallace[1263] with an inferior force of about 5,000 men consisting of General Ricketts' Division[1264] of the Sixth Corps and an undisciplined force he had collected together, having a fight at Monocacy, was forced to retreat to Baltimore.

When General McCook[1265] was ordered a day or two before to take command of a reserve camp on the Piney Branch Creek near the line he went with the staff to the place of the encampment designated but could not find the reserve. A force had been collected for him to command composed of invalids, veteran reserves, dismounted cavalry, clerks, laborers, and men from every station and occupation of life. He also had some District of Columbia volunteers—a curious mass of soldiery but they had a singleness of purpose ever ready to discharge any duty required of them. Many of the veterans in this command were just from the hospitals—some of them lame and many of them unable to carry their guns. Before the fight was over another curious body of hard fighting was engaged. This was about 1,500 Union sailors who faced the enemy at Fort Lincoln.

On the 10th Mr. Lincoln sent a cipher dispatch to General Grant (not an order) but advising him to leave a sufficient force to maintain his position in front of Petersburg and to bring the residue of his troops to Washington with him personally, in which dispatch he said: "And make a vigorous effort to defeat the enemy's force in this vicinity. I think there is really a fair chance to do this if the movement is prompt." This is remarkable language for Mr. Lincoln and is difficult of explanation. There was at this time great consternation in Washington. General Early had about 20,000 men and on the day this

---

1262 The battle of Monocacy, though not a major engagement, delayed General Early's march to Washington just enough for Washington to be reinforced. The battle of Monocacy is considered to be the battle that saved the capital." Monocacy Battlefield, National Park brochure

1263 General Lewis Wallace—See pg. 210.

1264 General James B. Ricketts led a division of 5000 infantry and 4,000 of General Sheridan's unhorsed cavalry including 1,500 who had no weapons that were routed in the Wilderness. Grant Takes Command, pg. 200 & 310.

1265 General Alexander McD. McCook—See pg. 220.

dispatch was written, which was Sunday, he was on his way with his command to Rockville, expecting on the next day to throw his whole force into Washington. General Augur[1266] was now in command of the department at Washington. Fort Stevens, Fort De Rusey, and Fort Totten were all connected by rifle pits.[1267]

There were in the northern forts but 3,726 men, half of them volunteer artillery and the other half infantry. About one-fifth of the infantry were needed to man the parapets, and provide hardly a single relief to the great guns. General Early made his approaches by the 7th Street Road on the 11th, and when in sight of Fort Stevens, he discovered that the works were but feebly manned and at first anticipated its easy capture by a surprise. He was soon put at rest on this subject by seeing a cloud of dust at the rear of the works between the fort and Washington City and immediately followed a column of federal troops piling into the fort on the right and left. Then an artillery fire was opened on his forces from a number of batteries.

General Early then reconnoitered. General McCausland[1268] with his command at this time made an inspection of Fort Reno on the Georgetown Pike and reported to Early that that fort was too strongly manned for him to attack.

About noon the pickets of General McCook were driven into the rifle pits. Then he gave orders to open fire on the enemy from his heavy guns in Fort Stevens, which proved to be a very destructive one. Immediately after which General Briggs[1269] with a force of dismounted cavalry from the Army of the Potomac arrived from Washington and at once attacked the skirmishers of General Early's army and drove them back about three quarters of a mile. At 3 o'clock p.m. two divisions of the Sixth Corps arrived under the command of General Wright who immediately reported to General McCook for duty. There was also at this time close at hand a portion of the Eleventh Corps.

---

1266 General C. C. Augur—See pg. 186.

1267 There were sixty-eight forts in a semi-circle built to defend the capital. www.civilwar.org/battlefields/fortstevens/fort-stevens-history-articles/washington-civil-war.html

1268 General John McCausland was born in St. Louis, Missouri. He led a cavalry brigade in the Shenandoah Valley. He captured Chambersburg on July 30, 1864. He asked for $200,000 in ransom, and then burned the town when the ransom was not raised. Grant Takes Command, pg. 343 and Harpers Pictorial History of the Great Rebellion, pg. 708.

1269 General John G. Briggs commanded a detachment of 25th New York Cavalry dismounted. www.fortunecity.com/pottery/1080/fort_stevens_wash_dc_12jul64.html

Orders were given by the telegraph directing that Major Gilmor with this part of the 19th Corps should assume command from Fort Lincoln to Fort Totten; General Meigs[1270] who had just reported with about 1,800 men to take the command from Fort Totten to Fort De Russy, and General M. D. Hardin[1271] from there to the Potomac River. The Sixth Corps was to be held in reserve and General McCook should be in command of all forces.

By midnight greater confidence for the safety of the capital was felt, however, as the federal forces had been put in readiness with great confidence for the next day's fight, which was inevitable. The aspect of things had greatly changed by Monday noon, the 11th, but that was the most anxious time of the fight. The Confederate commander became convinced that his artillery could not be made available in the fight because too many of the federal guns bore on every position within range that they could have taken, rendering it impossible for them to put them in position, and made no attempt to do so. This accounts for not one piece of Confederate artillery being fired in front of Washington.

Before the second day of the attack however, Assistant Secretary Dana[1272] was very nervous, earnest and uneasy. He then telegraphed to General Grant as follows: "Nothing can possibly be done here towards pursuing and cutting off the enemy for want of a commander. General Auger commands the defenses of Washington with General McCook and a lot of Brigadiers under him, but he is not allowed to go outside. General Wright commands his own corps, Gilmor has been assigned to the temporary command of these

---

1270 General Montgomery C. Meigs was from Pennsylvania and served as Quartermaster for the Army of the Potomac. He developed a plan before the start of the war with Lt. Colonel Keyes which was presented to Mr. Lincoln regarding ways that he could fortify Fort Sumter. Later he took possession of the Custis - Lee mansion (Robert E. Lee's father-in-law estate in Arlington, Virginia) and developed the Arlington National Cemetery on the property. He was also in charge of the completion of the Capitol dome in Washington because Mr. Lincoln wanted the people to see that "we intend this Union shall go on." Lincoln's War, pgs. 24, 25, 52, 223 & 342.

1271 General Martin D. Hardin of the U.S. Volunteers was assigned to Hooker's division.
www.nps.gov/history/history/online_books/civilwar/hrsa1-g.html

1272 Honorable Charles A. Dana was the Assistant Secretary of War during Mr. Lincoln's administration. He had been the editor of the *New York Tribune*. He was also a personal friend of Mr. Stanton. The Story-Life of Lincoln, pg. 552 and Lincoln's War, pg. 251.

troops of the Nineteenth Corps in the City of Washington, General Ord is in command of the Eighth Corps and all other troops in the middle department, leaving General Wallace to command the City of Baltimore. But there is no head to the whole and it seems indispensable that you should appoint one. General Halleck[1273] (then chief of staff) will not give orders accept as he receives them. The president will give none, and until you direct positively and explicitly what is to be done everything will go on in the deplorable and fatal way it has gone for in the past week."

On the 12th there was considerable fighting. There was a house on one side near the Silver Spring Road and Mrs. Lay's[1274] house on the other side of this road, which had been seized and from which great annoyance had been given to the Union troops. Several ineffectual attempts had been made to dislodge rebels from these houses. A company of sharp shooters first failed in this. The houses were then shelled from Fort Stevens without success. General McCook then called upon General Wright for a brigade of veterans. General Frank Wheaten[1275] with his force attacked the houses and in a ravine just beyond the houses were found a large force of the enemy. Fighting now commenced in earnest and with desperation, resulting in the Confederates being driven from their position with a loss to General Wheaten's command of two hundred eighty killed and wounded. This battle brought a close to the attack on Washington and on the next day, the 13th, General McCook telegraphed General Wright with this dispatch: "The enemy left my front last night." Whereupon the Honorable Charles A. Dana, then assistant Secretary of War, telegraphed to General Grant "The enemy have disappeared along the entire line."

The only order given during this whole siege by General Halleck was issued on the 12th wherein he announced that: "Orders are given that every officer and man who leaves his post will be shot." That order proved to be a disastrous one. Every general officer was acting under prescribed orders and dare not under General Halleck's order operate outside the District of Columbia without subjecting himself

---

1273 Henry Halleck—See pg. 158.

1274 Mrs. Lay's house just outside of Fort Stevens was damaged when a shell exploded in the house. Centennial History of the City of Washington, D.C. pg. 274.

1275 General Frank Wheaton was from Rhode Island. He was a brigade and division commander for the Army of the Potomac. The Armies and The Leaders, pg. 305.

and his men to the penalty of being shot. On the following day General Grant telegraphed to Mr. Dana, the Assistant Secretary: "Boldness is all that is wanted to drive the enemy out of Maryland in confusion; I hope and believe Wright is the man—assume that."

General Early's command, although vanquished and defeated in the District of Columbia, "was not driven out of Maryland in confusion." Not withstanding there was much trammeled boldness ready and eager for the service of the pursuit of the enemy among the commanding officers at the head of the conquering troops in Washington as ever inspired or characterized an army. Yet, after the battle, the enemy was allowed "to strut in mimic majesty" about our border and by night most cunningly the Arab did fold his tent and silently steal away keeping the noiseless tenor of the war; the boldest holding his breath for a time as he passed over the white sand and between the silent rocks as their shadows, he penetrated the glade while no sound was uttered but a deep and solemn harmony pervaded the solemn values from steep to steep—crossing through Maryland uninterrupted in his march, entering the state of Pennsylvania and by way of hilarious recreation to compensate for long continuous restraint, burned and destroyed Chambersburg on the 30th day of the same month. He and his men held picnics down the Shenandoah Valley and returned in triumph to General Lee's command in the defense of Richmond where he might have reported to his superior officers in the language of the great Shakespeare: "Oh, Cassius, you are yoked with land, that carries anger as flint bears fire, who much enforced shows a hasty spark, and straight is cold again."

The house of the Postmaster General Montgomery Blair[1276] was burnt during this raid, but it is due to General Early to state that he denies being responsible for its destruction.

---

1276 Montgomery Blair—See pg. 97.

*"We accepted the war for an object, a worthy object. The war will end when the object is obtained. Under God, I hope it will never end till that time."*

Abraham Lincoln[1277]

# — 15 —

# THE WAR IN 1864—PART III

## JULY 1864

On the 1st of July until the 31st, the attack was again made and continued in front of Petersburg, Virginia by the Second, Fifth and Ninth Corps, Army of the Potomac, and the Tenth and Eighteenth Corps, Army of the James. The assault resulted in the loss to the Union forces not including the loss at the crater or Deep Bottom four hundred nineteen killed, 2,076 wounded and 1,200 missing.

On the 20th of July the battle of Peach Tree Creek, in Georgia, was fought. The loss of the Union forces was seven hundred ten, while the Confederate loss was 4796. This battle was fought by the Army of the Cumberland. On the 22nd of July, General Hood[1278] made his first sortie at Atlanta, Georgia. There were four hundred thirty men of the Union forces killed, 1,599 wounded and 1,733 missing. The Confederates total loss was 3,741. This battle was fought on the Union side by the Army of the Tennessee. On the 24th a battle was fought at Winchester, Virginia, with a loss of 1,200 Union soldiers and six hundred Confederates. A portion of the Army of West Virginia fought

---

1277 Lincoln in American Memory, pg. 199.

1278 General John Bell Hood was a graduate of the West Point class of 1853 from Kentucky. He fought the Comanche's in Texas before the war. He led the Texas brigade. He was also a Confederate General charged with defending Atlanta. He was sent there by President Jefferson Davis to replace General Joe Johnston. It was said of him, "none led with more glory than Hood, yet many led and there was much glory." Lincoln's War, pg. 388, The Armies and The Leaders, pgs. 243 & 262, and Grant Takes Command, pg. 357.

this battle. General Stoneman[1279] in making his raid to Macon, Georgia from the 25th to the 31st of July lost 1,000 men. At Ezra's Chapel, Atlanta, General Hood's second sortie on the 28th of July resulted in a total loss seven hundred to the Union forces and 4,643 for the Confederates. This battle was fought by the Army of the Tennessee. On the 30th of July the mine explosion[1280] at Petersburg occurred with a loss of four hundred nineteen killed, 1,679 wounded and 1,910 missing on the Union side and 1,200 on the Confederates. The troops engaged were the Ninth Corps, supported by the Eighteenth Corps, with the Second and Fifth Corps in reserve.

## AUGUST 1864

From August the 1st to the 31st there was loss to the Union forces of five hundred twenty-one killed in the trenches before Petersburg. August the 14th to the 18th, the battle of Strawberry Plain, Deep Bottom Run, was fought, with a Union loss of four hundred killed, 1,755 wounded and 1,400 missing; Confederate total loss was 1,100. This battle was fought by the Second Cavalry Division and the Second Corps, Army of the Potomac, and the Tenth Corps Army of the James. On the 18th, 19th and 21st of August, a battle was fought at Six-Mile House, Weldon Railroad, Virginia. The Union loss two hundred twelve killed, 1,155 wounded, and 3,176 missing. Confederate loss was 4000. Union troops engaged were Kautz Cavalry, Second Cavalry Division, the Fifth and Ninth Corps, Army of the Potomac. The battle of Summit Point,[1281] Virginia occurred on the 21st of August. The loss was six hundred Union troops and a Confederate loss of four hundred. On the 25th the battle of Ream's Station, Virginia took place. The Union loss was one hundred twenty-seven killed, five hundred forty-six wounded, and 1,700 missing. Total loss of the Confederates

---

1279 Brigadier General George Stoneman—See pg. 191.

1280 This was actually the explosion of a 500 foot long tunnel dug by the Union forces under the enemy lines and filled with explosives. The tunnel was engineered by Lt. Commander Henry Pleasants and dug by the 48th Pennsylvania Volunteers from the coal fields area of that state. The explosives were blown up on July 30. A Stillness at Appomattox pgs. 220-222, and 237.

1281 Summit Point is where the author, Ward Hill Lamon was born in 1828. This battle occurred at Cameron's Depot, Summit Point and Flowing Springs on General Early's return from his attempt to capture Washington City. www.lamonhouse.org—Lamon family tree and www.nps.gov/hps/abpp/battles/wv014.htm

was 1,500. The Second Corps and the 2nd Cavalry Division, Army of the Potomac fought this battle. The battle of Jonesboro, Georgia was fought on the 31st of August and 1st of September with a loss to the Union forces of 1,453 (two hundred thirty-three killed, 1,125 wounded and one hundred five missing) and a loss to the Confederates of over 2,000. The troops engaged were the cavalry and Davis' Division, the Fourteenth Corps, Army of the Cumberland, and the Fifteenth, Sixteenth and Seventeenth Corps, the Army of the Tennessee.

From the 5th of May to the 8th of September, the campaign in northern Georgia from the Chattanooga to Atlanta, Georgia the Union forces lost 5,284 men killed, 26,129 wounded, and 5,786 missing, making a total loss of 37,199 men. The Confederate loss was not known.

## SEPTEMBER 1864

On the 19th of September a desperate fight occurred at Opequon, Virginia, in which six hundred ninety-seven men were killed, 3,983 wounded, and three hundred thirty-eight missing in action on the Union side and two hundred seventy-six killed, 1,827 wounded and 1,818 missing in action on the Confederate side. The troops engaged were the Ninth Corps and the Cavalry Division, Army of West Virginia, the Sixth Corps and First and Third Cavalry Division, Army of the Potomac, First and Second Division of the Ninth Corps, of the Army of the Middle Military Division.

The battles of Fort Davidson, Pilot Knob or Ironton was fought on the 26th and 27th of September by the Forty-seventh and Fiftieth Missouri, the Fourteenth Iowa Volunteers, the Second and Third Missouri Cavalry, and Battery H, Second Missouri Light Artillery. These battles were the result of Price's invasion[1282] of Missouri. The federals lost five hundred six men, while the Confederates losses are unknown. On the 28th, 29th and 30th, the battle of New Market Heights, Virginia, was fought, which resulted in three hundred eighty-three killed, 2,299 wounded, six hundred forty-five missing to the federals, and a total Confederate loss of over 2,000 casualties. This battle includes Chapin's Farm, Laurel Hill, Fort Harrison, and Gilmore, and was fought by the Tenth and Eighteenth Corps and the

---

1282 Major General Sterling Price—See pg. 148.

Cavalry of the Army of the James. On the 30th of September and 1st of October occurred the battle at Pressle's Farm, at Popular Springs Church in Virginia. The Union loss one hundred forty killed, seven hundred eighty-eight wounded, and 2,685 missing. The Confederates total loss was nine hundred.

## OCTOBER 1864

On October 5 occurred the battle of Altoona, Georgia. Union loss was seven hundred six, and the Confederate loss was 1,142. On October 19th, the battle of Cedar Creek, Middletown, Virginia was fought on the Union side by the 1st and 3rd Divisions Cavalry and the Sixth Corps, Army of the Potomac, Eighth Corps and Cavalry of the Army of West Virginia, and 1st and 2nd Divisions of the Nineteenth Corps, and resulting in the federals losses as killed six hundred and forty-four, wounded 3,430, and missing 1,591. The total Confederate loss being three hundred twenty killed, 1,540 wounded and 1,050 missing. On October 27th Hatcher's Run fight occurred on the South Side Railroad in Virginia, in which the Union troops lost one hundred fifty-six men killed, 1,057 wounded and six hundred ninety-nine missing. Confederates lost 1,000 men total. Troops engaged were the 2nd Cavalry Division, the 2nd and 3rd Division, and the Second, Fifth and Ninth Corps, Army of the Potomac. This battle also includes Boydtown Road, Baugh Road, and Burgess Farm. On the 27th and 28th October occurred the battle of second Fair Oaks, near Richmond, Virginia. The union loss was one hundred twenty killed, seven hundred eighty-three wounded, and four hundred missing. Confederate loss total was four hundred twenty-one. In this engagement there were the Tenth and Eighteenth Corps and Cavalry, Army of the James.

The Rebel Ram *Albemarle*[1283] was on the 28th of October destroyed by Lt. W. B. Cushing[1284] of the United States Navy with thirteen men under his command. In the trenches before Petersburg from the 1st to

---

[1283] *Albemarle* was an 85 foot Confederate schooner with a ram and a crew of twenty-two. Warships of the Civil War Navies, pg. 143.

[1284] Lt. William B. Cushing was expelled from the U.S. Naval Academy for poor scholarship and pranks, but was reinstated and went on to an exemplary naval career. His plan to attack the CSS *Albemarle* by firing a torpedo into the enemy ship at close range sank the Confederate ship. www.coastalguide.com/civilwar/css-ram-albemarle.shtml

the 30th of October, the Union lost one hundred seventy men killed, eight hundred twenty-two wounded, and eight hundred twelve missing, while the total Confederate loss was about 1,000 men.

## NOVEMBER 1864

On the 28th of November the battle for Fort Kelly at New Creek, West Virginia occurred. Seven hundred Union troops were lost in this engagement, and an unknown number of Confederates. At Franklin, Tennessee a battle was fought on the 30th of November in which one hundred eighty-nine men were killed, 1,033 wounded, and 1,104 missing of the Union troops; and a total Confederate loss of 1,750 killed, 3,800 wounded and seven hundred two missing. The Union troops engaged in this battle were the Fourth Army Corps of the Cumberland, and Twenty-Third Army Corps of the Ohio.

## DECEMBER 1864

The battle of Nashville, Tennessee commenced on the 15th and closed on the 16th of December. This battle is sometime called Brentwood and Overton's Hill. There were engaged in it the Fourth Corps Army of the Cumberland, the Twenty-Third Corps Army of the Ohio; the 1st and 3rd Divisions of the Fifteenth Army Corps of the Army of Tennessee. The battle also included detachments of colored troops, convalescence, &c. and Cavalry Corps. The result of the battle was the loss to the Union forces of three hundred seven killed, and 2,562 wounded and one hundred twelve missing with the total Confederate loss being unknown.

*"Oh, this awful, awful war!"*

Abraham Lincoln, upon visiting the wounded soldiers at City Point in early 1865.[1285]

# — 16 —

# THE WAR IN 1865

## JANUARY 1865

There was fight at Beverly, West Virginia, on the 11th of January, 1865 between the Union forces of the 24th Ohio volunteers and the 8th Ohio Cavalry and the rebels which resulted in a loss of six hundred three men to the Union forces; the rebel loss was unknown. On the 13th, 14th and 15th of January, the battle of Fort Fisher, North Carolina occurred with the result of one hundred eighty-four killed, seven hundred forty-nine wounded and twenty-two missing on the Union side. The total Confederate loss was 2,483. The Union troops engaged in this battle were the 2nd Division, the 2nd Brigade, the 1st Division of the Twenty-Fourth Corps, the 3rd Division of the Twenty-Third Corps, Army of the James, and sailors and marines of the Atlantic Blockading Squadron.

## FEBRUARY 1865

On the 3rd of February during the so called peace conference held at Hampton Roads[1286] between Lincoln and Mr. Seward on the one

[1285] Lincoln in American Memory, pg. 105.

[1286] Peace Conference at Hampton Roads were held aboard the steamer *River Queen* at Fortress Monroe. Civil War a Narrative, Part IX., pg. 43.

side and Messrs. A. H. Stephens, J. A. Campbell[1287] and R. M. T. Hunter[1288] on the other. Mr. Hunter remarked that his recognition of President Davis's power was the first indispensable step towards peace. He at once entered into an ingenious argument to enforce the necessity of its recognition and cited as an incident and precedence[1289] of a constitutional ruler treating with rebels the case of King Charles I[1290] and his rebel parliament. Mr. Lincoln was secretly very much amused and turning to Mr. Hunter, he said: "Upon the question of history, I must refer you to Mr. Seward who is posted in such matters. As for myself I don't pretend to be but I have a distinct recollect in the case you refer to that history records King Charles lost his head, and I have no head to spare."

During this same conference Mr. Hunter also remarked on the subject of emancipation that the slaves had always been accustomed to work upon compulsion, under an overseer, and he apprehended that they would, if suddenly emancipated, precipitate themselves and the entire social fabric of the South into irredeemable ruin. In that case neither the whites nor the blacks would work: they would all starve together. Mr. Lincoln waited for a while, expecting Mr. Seward to reply to this speech. Seeing he was not going to do so, Mr. Lincoln replied: "Mr. Hunter, you ought to know a great deal better about this matter than I, for you have always lived under the slave system. The way you state the case, however, reminds me of an Illinois farmer, who was by no means noted for his fondness of work, and was given to shirk work whenever it was practicable. To this end he conceived a scheme of hog culture. He bought a large herd of swine, having a good farm, and planted an immense field of potatoes, with a view of turning the whole herd into the field late in the fall and supposed they would be able to provide for themselves in the winter without the necessity of labor on his part for their sustenance. Meeting a neighbor one day his scheme was discussed between them. The neighbor asked him how the thing would work during the winter in his opinion when the

---

1287 Judge John Campbell was a former U.S. Supreme Court judge from Alabama. He was Assistant Secretary of War for the Confederacy. www.mycivilwar.com/battles/650204.htm.

1288 General R. M. T. Hunter—See pg. 102.

1289 Precedence means importance.

1290 King Charles I was King of England, Sweden and Ireland, from 1625 to his execution on January 30, 1649. www.newworldencyclopedia.org/entry/charles_I_of_England

ground would be frozen one r two feet deep. He seemed not to have contemplated this contingency and was somewhat perplexed over it but at length answered: 'Well, neighbor, it will be a little hard on their snouts, but those snouts will have to root hog or die.'"

The battle of Dasney's Mill, Hatchers Run, Virginia was fought on the 5th, 6th and 7th of February, with the Union loss of two hundred thirty-two killed, 1,062 wounded and one hundred eighty-six missing. Confederate loss total was 1,200. This battle is also known as Rowanty Creek and Vaugh Roads. Fought by the Union troops—the Second Cavalry Division, the Third and Fifth Corps and the First Division of the Sixth Corps, Army of the Potomac.

*"In weaker hands, such a Cabinet would have been a hot bed of strife, under him it became a tower of strength."*

John Nicolay, Abraham Lincoln's Secretary[1291]

# — 17 —

# Cooperation with the Cabinet and the President

Throughout Mr. Lincoln's administration as much harmony as could be reasonably expected existed between him and his Cabinet ministers. Differences arose between them at times in regard to minor considerations of policy, but never to the extent that they were not harmonized, compromised or accommodated.

To this day there is a settled belief that there was a lack of hardy cooperation and unity of purpose and sentiment in administrative counsels. This is a mistake. Whenever there were differences they were in the main amicably adjusted, and the joint council worked in harmonious order. When Mr. Lincoln returned from Fortress Monroe and the conference had with the Confederate representatives Messers. Stephens, Campbell and Hunter,[1292] he prepared a message for Congress recommending an appropriation of three hundred million to pay for the slaves of the South on condition of the rebels laying down their arms and renewing their allegiance to the government of the United States and manumitting their slaves. When he submitted his proposed message to his Cabinet, they were unanimously opposed to it. Thereupon he yielded and abandoned the idea of sending the

---

1291 Lincoln in American Memory, pg. 121.

1292 Messers. A. H. Stevens (See pg. 30), Judge John Campbell and R. M. T. Hunter (See pg. 102). Judge John Campbell was a U.S. Supreme Court Justice who resigned to join the Confederacy. www.answers.com/topic/ john-archibald-campbell

message to Congress in deference to the opinion and counsel of his advisors.

There is also a prevailing opinion that the Secretary of War, Mr. Stanton, at times arbitrarily refused to obey or carry out Mr. Lincoln's orders. This is also not true. Largely this opinion is based on Mr. Stanton's refusal of permits of person desirous of going through the lines into insurgent districts. The persons who were disobliged in this respect were very severe in their comments of Mr. Stanton's course, which they considered harsh, disobliging and some times cruel. On refusal of Mr. Stanton to accommodate in many cases, Mr. Lincoln was appealed to and his invariable reply was "I cannot always know whether a permit ought to be granted and I want to oblige everybody when I can. Mr. Stanton and I have an understanding that is when I send an order to him which cannot be consistently granted, he is to refuse it. This he sometimes does." And on one occasion in response to one of the appeals to him from one of Mr. Stanton's refusals to give a permit after he had requested it to be given, he said "this state of things led to the jocular remark I made the other day to a man who complained of Mr. Stanton that I had not much influence in this administration—that I expected to have more with the next."

Mr. Lincoln was often disappointed and grieved at many things which occurred during the fearful war struggle about which he and his Cabinet differed in their estimates and conclusions. Of instances of his great disappointment he expected General McClellan would be successful on the Peninsula and afterwards he would follow up his victory at Antietam and that General Meade[1293] would follow up his victory at Gettysburg. In speaking of that battle and the omission of General Meade to pursue the enemy overcome him and capture him, Mr. Lincoln said, "He did so well at the Gettysburg fight that I cannot complain of him." Yet, immediately after the battle of Gettysburg was fought the congratulatory order which General Meade published to the troops was telegraphed to the War Department. During those trying times Mr. Lincoln watched the War Department day and night with sleepless anxiety and was the first person to receive the news as it came over the wires. He had hoped and expected great and substantial results from this battle—not only did he expect a mere victory over

[1293] George Meade—See pg. 241.

the enemy but total annihilation of General Lee's forces or surrender of his troops.

It will be remembered that the Union cavalry had destroyed the pontoon bridges over which the Confederates had cross the Potomac River into Maryland[1294] and upon which they depended on re-crossing back into Virginia. The river was now very much swollen; the pontoons and bridges destroyed. General Lee's army was penned up for nine days on the Maryland side of the Potomac River unable to get back to more safe quarters. Mr. Lincoln was intensely anxious to have General Meade attack them, destroy them, or capture them and thus end the war and its further cost of bloodshed. Being disappointed in this after reading the congratulatory order which said "Drive the invaders from our soil," in tones of anguish and despair, Mr. Lincoln said, "My God is that all?"

So far as the Peninsular campaign was concerned and the subsequent events, particularly General McClellan's relation to those events that had occurred and were occurring, there was a wide difference of opinion between the president and his constitutional advisors, but the difference was promptly settled by the masterly independence of Mr. Lincoln in cutting the Gordian knot[1295] and resuming the responsibility in defiance of all opposition, which resulted in the speedy achievement of the sanguinary battle of Antietam which to a great extent compensated for the Peninsular failure and the accompanying fiasco of the second battle of Bull Run.

As the war approached its conclusion and Mr. Lincoln foreseeing the inevitable submission of the insurgents in his mind did not become less seriously effected in contemplation of the new responsibilities which would devolve[1296] upon him as chief magistrate of the reorganized and reconstructed state of things. His second inaugural address mirrored his frame of mind to a great extent. He was oppressed with great care resulting from a conscientiousness that changes would occur in the near future which would impose upon him new and difficult duties in which he might possibly find himself in

---

[1294] At Williamsport, Maryland.

[1295] A Gordian knot is a legend associated with Alexander the Great. The knot was said to be so entangled that no one could untangle it. If a man could, he would be made ruler of Asia. It became a metaphor for an intractable problem. www.gordiansolutions.com/theknot.htm

[1296] Devolve means to transfer.

conflict not only with the men of his own party who already persistently opposed him, but with many other public men who had supported his administration throughout the existence of the war.

There seemed to be no settled policy for the contemplated new state of things and few men thought alike on the subject. There were almost as many theories as there were distinguished men to advance them. This state of things devolved the greater responsibility upon Mr. Lincoln and he keenly felt the force of it.

After capitulation of General Lee, what was to be done with the leaders of the rebellion became a most serious question. Persons who had been throughout the war the fiercest and most radical opponents of the rebels (such men as Horace Greeley[1297] and others) became suddenly most conservative, and the converse course was pursued by many of the most conservative persons, now urging relentless punishment of the offending leaders. General Grant asked for special instructions from Mr. Lincoln whether he should try to capture Mr. Jefferson Davis or let him escape from the country if he wanted to do so. Mr. Lincoln replied by relating a story of an Irishman who had taken a pledge of Father Mathews and having become terribly thirsty applied to a bartender for a lemonade, and while it was being prepared he whispered to the bartender, "and couldn't you put a little brandy in it unbeknownst to myself?" Mr. Lincoln told the general to let Jefferson Davis escape all unbeknown to himself—for he had no use for him.

The President of the Southern Confederacy was however, after Mr. Lincoln's death, captured and imprisoned at Fortress Monroe for two years and charged with treason &c. and at length admitted to bail in 1867. Mr. Horace Greeley, the great radical journalist, became one of his bondsmen. Mr. Davis was never brought to trial and eventually the charges against him were ignored. He went to Canada but subsequently he returned to Mississippi and lived in retirement, and wrote a book about the rebellion.

In referring to the different opinions entertained by Mr. Lincoln and the members of his Cabinet it will be observed that the matter of reconstruction of the state governments after the war was according to Mr. Lincoln's proclamation, the persons who were to re-establish such governments were to be qualified voters of their respective states

---

[1297] Horace Greeley—See pg. 16.

before the acts of secession. Mr. Cameron[1298] alone of all the Cabinet objected to this clause of the proclamation and insisted that it be changed so as to read "qualified voters - citizens of the state." The Attorney General in the year 1862 had given the opinion that men born in the United States were citizens of the United States and one-tenth of the "qualified voters required to organize if one-tenth of the 'citizens' the organization might be literally composed entirely of colored men." Mr. Lincoln was set in his purpose that the restored governments in the seceded states should be organized by the qualified voters of those states before secession was attempted and Mr. Cameron did submit to the inevitable.

---

1298 Simon Cameron—See pg. 97.

*"Fondly do we hope–fervently do we pray–that this mighty scourge of war may pass away. Yet, if God wills it to continue, until all the wealth piled by the bondsman two hundred and fifty years of unrequited toil shall be sunk, and every drop of blood drawn from the lash, shall be paid by another drawn sword, as was said three hundred years ago, so still it must be said 'the judgments of the Lord, are true and righteous altogether.'"*

Abraham Lincoln[1299]

# — 18 —

# THE WAR IN 1865—PART II

## MARCH 1865

During the night of the 3rd of March, Mr. Lincoln with several members of his Cabinet went together to the Capitol. They were waiting for the final passage of the bills by Congress so the president might sign them. At intervals between signing and reading these documents, they discussed the military situation. General Grant had telegraphed a glowing account of his mastery of the situation and his belief that in a few days more would see Richmond in his possession and the army of General Lee either dispersed utterly or captured bodily. A telegram from General Grant was just then received, that General Lee had asked an interview with reference to peace. Mr. Lincoln was much elated by this dispatch and he manifested the kindness of his heart by the expression of favorable terms to be granted to the conquered enemy. Secretary Stanton was also much excited over the contents of this news, but from other causes than that which inspired Mr. Lincoln. He listened in silence, restraining himself as much as possible for some time. At length he burst forth saying: "Mr. Lincoln, tomorrow is Inauguration Day. If you are not to be

1299 Lincoln in American Memory, pg. 39.

president of an obedient and united people, you had better not be inaugurated. Your work is already done. If any other authority than yours is for a moment to be recognized, or any terms made that do not signify that you are the supreme head of the nation—if generals in the field are to negotiate peace or any other magistrate is to be acknowledged on this continent, then you are not needed and you had better not take the oath of office."

Mr. Lincoln reflected for a moment, looked very serious and then said, "Mr. Stanton, you are right." His whole tone seemed to change. His mind seemed to be engrossed and he sat down at a table and wrote as follows: "The president directs me to say to you that he wishes you have no conference with General Lee unless it be for the capitulation of General Lee's army, or on some minor or purely military manner. He instructs me to say that you are not to decide, discuss or confer upon any political question—such questions the president holds in his own hands and will submit them to no military conferences or convention. In the meantime, you are to press to the utmost of your ability your military advantage."

He then read over what he had written and said, "Now Mr. Stanton date and sign this paper and send it to General Grant. We will see about this peace business." After this time and not long before the death of Mr. Lincoln, Mr. Stanton tendered his resignation as Secretary of War. His letter of resignation was couched in the kindest language paying a heartfelt tribute to Mr. Lincoln's uniform and constant friendship and his faithful devotion to the country. It also stated that he had accepted the position of Secretary of War for the purpose of holding it only till the war should end and that now he felt that his work was completed and that it was his duty to resign.

Mr. Lincoln was by the tone of the letter greatly moved. He said, "Mr. Stanton, you have been a good friend and a faithful public officer and it is not for you to say when you will no longer be needed here." And at Mr. Lincoln's earnest solicitation the letter of resignation was withdrawn and Mr. Stanton continued to occupy the war office until after Mr. Lincoln's death.

Wilcox Bridge battle, Wise's Fork, North Carolina, was fought on the 8th, 9th and 10th of March. Union loss was eighty killed, four hundred twenty wounded, and three hundred missing. Confederate loss was 1,500. The troops engaged were the First and Second Division of the district of Beaufort and the First Division, Twenty-third Corps, the Army of the Ohio. On the 15th of March the battle of Averysboro, North Carolina, was fought with a loss of 554 Union troops total and 856 Confederates. A battle at Bentonville, North Carolina was fought March 19th, 20th and 21st with a loss of 139 killed, 784 wounded, and 170 missing on the Union side; total Confederate loss was 195 killed, 1,313 wounded, and 610 missing. The Union troops engaged in the battle were the Fourteenth and Twentieth Corps left wing, the Fifteenth and Seventeenth Corps right wing, and Cavalry Division of Sherman's army. At Fort Steadman[1300] a battle was fought on March 25th resulting in a loss of 911 to the Union side and a loss of 2,681 to the Confederates. The Union troops engaged were the First and Third Division of the Ninth Army Corps of the Army of the Potomac. On March 25th the battle of Petersburg was fought, resulting in 103 killed, 164 wounded, and 209 missing of the Union troops. Confederate loss was 834. The federal troops in the battle were the Second and Sixth Corps, Army of the Potomac. From March 22nd to April 24th General Wilson[1301] made his raid from Chickasaw, Alabama to Macon, Georgia in which he had a number of engagements, resulting in a total loss to him of 725 men, with a loss to the Confederates of 8,020 men.

## APRIL 1865

April 1st the battle of Five Forks was fought. The Union loss in the battle was 134 killed, 706 wounded, 54 missing, with a total loss to the Confederates unknown, but with General Warren's[1302] men capturing between 5,000 and 6,000 rebel prisoners. The federal troops engaged in this battle were a Division of Cavalry, Army of the James, the 1st, 2nd and 3rd Division Cavalry Corps, and the 5th Corps of the Army of the Potomac. On April 2nd the city of Petersburg, Virginia was captured, with a federal loss of 625 men, 3189 wounded and 326 missing. Confederate loss was about 3,000. Troops engaged for the Union were the 2nd, 6th and 9th Corps, Army of the Potomac, and 24th Corps Army of the James. The last and final battle of the war of any note was fought at Saylor's Creek, Virginia on the 6th of April, resulting in a

---

1300 Fort Steadman was a Union army fortification in the siege lines around Petersburg, Virginia.
1301 Brigadier General James Harrison Wilson—See pg. 301.
1302 Gouveneur Kemble Warren—See pg. 246.

Union loss of 156 killed, 1,014 wounded and a total loss to the Confederates of 7,000 men. There was after this an engagement at High Bridge, Appomattox River, on that same day—resulting in a loss total of 1,041 on the Union side; Confederate loss unknown. On the 7th and 9th other engagements at Farmville, Virginia took place. And at Fort Blakely, Alabama, a battle occurred with an aggregate total loss of 1,284 men to the Union side and 2,900 to the Confederates.

On the 9th of April, General Lee surrendered with 26,000 men.

Correspondence between Ulysses S. Grant and Robert E. Lee is enclosed, discussing surrender terms at Appomattox. These reports were extracted from a Report of Lieut. Gen. Ulysses S. Grant, U. S. Army, commanding Armies of the United States, The Richmond (Virginia) Campaign.

*APRIL 7, 1865*
*General* R. E. LEE:
GENERAL: *The result of the last week must convince you of the hopelessness of further resistance on the part of the Army of Northern Virginia in this struggle. I feel that it is so, and regard it as my duty to shift from myself the responsibility of any further effusion of blood, by asking of you the surrender of that portion of the C. S. Army known as the Army of Northern Virginia.*
*U.S. GRANT,*
*Lieutenant-General*

*HEADQUARTERS ARMY OF NORTHERN VIRGINIA, APRIL 7, 1865*
*Lieut. Gen. U.S. GRANT:*
GENERAL: *I have received your note of this date. Though not entertaining the opinion you express on the hopelessness of further resistance on the part of the Army of Northern Virginia, I reciprocate your desire to avoid useless effusion of blood, and therefore, before considering your proposition, ask the terms you will offer on condition of its surrender.*
R. E. LEE,
*General*

*APRIL 8, 1865*
*General* R. E. LEE:
GENERAL: *Your note of last evening, in reply to mine of same date, asking the condition on which I will accept the surrender of the Army of Northern Virginia, is just received. In reply I would say that, peace being my great desire, there is but one*

*condition I would insist upon, namely, that the men and officers surrendered shall be disqualified for taking up arms again against the Government of the United States until properly exchanged. I will meet you, or will designate officers to meet any officers you may name for the same purpose, at any point agreeable to you, for the purpose of arranging definitely the terms upon which the surrender of the Army of Northern Virginia will be received.*
*U.S. GRANT,*
*Lieutenant-General*

*HEADQUARTERS ARMY OF NORTHERN VIRGINIA, APRIL 8, 1865*
*Lieut. Gen. U.S. GRANT:*
*GENERAL: I received at a late hour your note of to-day. In mine of yesterday I did not intend to propose the surrender of the Army of Northern Virginia, but to ask the terms of your proposition. To be frank, I do not think the emergency has arisen to call for the surrender of this army, but as the restoration of peace should be the sole object of all, I desired to know whether your proposals would lead to that end. I cannot, therefore, meet you with a view to surrender the Army of Northern Virginia, but as far as your proposal may affect the C. S. forces under my command, and tend to the restoration of peace, I should be pleased to meet you at 10 a.m., to-morrow; on the old stage road to Richmond, between the picket-lines of the two armies.*
R. E. LEE,
*General*

*APRIL 9, 1865*
*General* R. E. LEE:
GENERAL: *Your note of yesterday is received. I have no authority to treat on the subject of peace; the meeting proposed for 10 a.m. to-day could lead to no good. I will state, however, general, that I am equally anxious for peace with yourself, and the whole North entertains the same feeling. The terms upon which peace can be had are well understood. By the South laying down their arms they will hasten that most desirable event, save thousands of human lives, and hundreds of millions of property not yet destroyed. Seriously hoping that all our difficulties may be set-tied without the loss of another life, I subscribe myself, &c.*
*U.S. GRANT,*
*Lieutenant-General*

*HEADQUARTERS ARMY OF NORTHERN VIRGINIA,*
*APRIL 9, 1865*
*Lieut. Gen. U.S. GRANT:*
*GENERAL: I received your note of this morning on the picket-line, whither I had come to meet you and ascertain definitely what terms were embraced in your proposal of yesterday with reference to the surrender of this army. I now ask an interview in accordance with the offer contained in your letter of yesterday for that purpose.*
R. E. LEE,
*General*

*APPOMATTOX COURT-HOUSE, VA.*
*April 9, 1865*
*General* R. E. LEE:
*GENERAL: In accordance with the substance of my letter to you of the 8th instant, I propose to receive the surrender of the Army of Northern Virginia on the following terms, to wit:* Rolls *of all the officers and men to be made in duplicate, one copy to be given to an officer to be designated by me, the other to be retained by such officer or officers as you may designate. The officers to give their individual paroles not to take up arms against the Government of the United States until properly exchanged; and each company or regimental commander sign a like parole for the men of their commands. The arms, artillery, and public property to be parked and stacked, and turned over to the officers appointed by me to receive them. This will not embrace the side-arms of the officers, nor their private horses or baggage. This done, each officer and man will be allowed to return to his home, not to be disturbed by U. S. authority so long as they observe their paroles and the laws in force where they may reside.*
*U.S. GRANT,*
*Lieutenant-General*

*HEADQUARTERS ARMY OF NORTHERN VIRGINIA, April 9, 1865*
*Lieut. Gen. U. S. GRANT:*
*GENERAL: I have received your letter of this date containing the terms of surrender of the Army of Northern Virginia as proposed by you. As they are substantially the same as those expressed in your letter of the 8th instant, they are accepted. I will proceed to designate the proper officers to carry the stipulations into effect.*
R. E. LEE,
*General*[1303]

---

[1303] Official Records of the War of Rebellion

*The terms of the surrender are as follows: Agreement entered into this day (April 9, 1865) in regard to the surrender of the Army of Northern Virginia:*
*1. The troops shall march by brigades and detachments to a designated point, stock their arms, deposit their flags, sabers, pistols, &c. and from thence march to their homes under charge of their affairs, superintended by their respective division and corps commanders, officers retaining their side arms and the authorized number of private horses.*
*2. All public horses and public property of all kinds to be turned over to Staff Officers designated by United States authorities.*
*3. Such transportation as may be agreed upon as necessary for the transportation of private baggage of the officers will be allowed to accompany the officers to be turned over at the end of the trip to the nearest U.S. Quartermasters, receipts to be taken for same.*
*4. Couriers and wounded men of the artillery and cavalry whose horses are their own private property will be allowed to retain with them.*
*5. The surrender of the Army of Northern Virginia shall be construed to mean all the forces operation with that army on the 8th instant, the date of commencement of negotiations for surrender, except such bodies of cavalry as actually made their escape prior to the surrender, and except also such forces of the artillery as were more than twenty (20) miles from Appomattox Courthouse at the time of the surrender on the 9th instant.*
*Signed*
*General Ulysses S. Grant Robert E. Lee*[1304]

On the 18th of April, General Joe Johnston[1305] surrendered with 29,904 men. On May 4th, General Dick Taylor[1306] surrendered 10,000 men.[1307] On May 10th, General Sam Jones[1308] surrendered 8,000 men.

---

1304 www.eyewitnesstohistory.com/appomatx.htm.
1305 General Joseph E. Johnston —See pg. 129.
1306 General Richard Taylor was the son of Zachary Taylor former U.S. President and the brother of Jefferson Davis' first wife. He was a Yale graduate from Louisiana and a veteran of the Mexican War. He was a sugar planter in Louisiana. He originally commanded the Trans-Mississippi Region. He was the Confederate General who defeated General Banks and his army at Sabine Crossroads on April 18, 1864. Grant Takes Command, pg. 173, The Armies and The Leaders, pgs. 249 & 274, The Pride of the South, pg. 188 and Civil War a Narrative, Part VII., pg. 34.
1307 General Taylor surrendered to General Canby at Citronville, Alabama. Southern History of the War, Part II., pg. 522.
1308 General Sam Jones was a Virginian who graduated from the U.S. Military Academy in 1841. He commanded Confederate forces in Florida, Georgia and South Carolina. He commanded 6,000 men in southwestern Virginia to guard against the

On May 11th, General Jeff Thompson[1309] surrendered 7,454 men. On May 26th, General Kirby Smith[1310] surrendered the last of the Confederate army, consisting of 20,000 men, which closed the rebellion as far as armed resistance was concerned. General Lee's surrender was made to General Grant; General Johnston to General Sherman;[1311] General Taylor to General Canby;[1312] General Jones to a detachment of Wilson's Cavalry;[1313] General Thompson to General Dodge's forces;[1314] and General Kirby Smith to General Canby's command.

The scrupulous[1315] regard of Mr. Stanton for paramount executive authority in a most marked way was manifested after the death of Mr. Lincoln in the matter of the negotiation and convention between General Sherman and General Johnston for the surrender of the latter's army and indirectly for the adjustment of the whole matter of return of the insurgent states to the Union. This agreement, which was submitted to President Johnson for his approval, was well-matured and evidentially had been prepared with great care and ability. It was evident from its terms that General Sherman was not negotiating alone with General Johnston as two soldiers who had seen the end of the war that could no longer be maintained; the very terms of the signed instrument bears evidence of dealings with master minds. Advised by President Jefferson Davis and his Cabinet officers, making in character a political traiting[1316] with protection of a far reaching *ad vital* nature to the vanquished belligerents, required the most careful considerations instead of a purely military negotiation authorized by law and usages of the general officers commanding opposing armies in the field. In saying this no purpose is meant to disparage the great and acknowledged of these honored generals. Their astuteness is too well-known and acknowledged in all things pertaining to their profession to justify or tolerate any such insinuation; yet, we may be pardoned for saying that the attempt by settlement of the detail of the greatest and

---

thrust of General Burnside and to protect the salt works and lead mines. Grant Takes Command pgs. 58 & 59 and The Armies and The Leaders, pgs. 251 & 256.

1309 General Meriwether Jeff Thompson—See pg. 154.

1310 General Edmund Kirby Smith—See pg. 187.

1311 The surrender took place at Durham Station, North Carolina. Southern History of the War, Part II., pg. 520.

1312 General Edward Richard Sprigg Canby—See pg. 173.

1313 General James H. Wilson—See pg. 301.

1314 General Augustus Dodge—See pg. 292.

1315 Scrupulous means careful.

1316 Traiting means characteristic.

most important question ever to the arbitrament[1317] of a government by military instead of political authority was a mistake. This agreement implied a perfect restoration of all rights to the condition prevailing at the commencement of the hostilities with an added acknowledgement of a recognition of belligerent rights and the validity of the Confederate states government, with complete and unconditional amnesty and restoration of all former rights under the federal constitution and laws ante-dating the rebellion with full protection under the existing state of things. As it was learned afterwards the terms of the surrender[1318] then agreed upon by these generals met the entire view and approbation of the Davis administration, excepting one thing viz.[1319] in not providing for the auditing of the debt of the Confederacy and its payment in common with the war debt of the United States. This condition was not persisted in, and "the agreement was sent to Washington without it" and was disapproved by the president a few days later. General Johnston had surrendered on much different terms as had been accorded to General Lee at Appomattox.

The final condition of the surrender of the Confederate Army was due to the sagacity of Edwin M. Stanton, more than any other man. He saw that peace on any other terms than the settlement which was made would forfeit utterly all the true and vital fruit of the war and give a triumph to the revolutionary spirit of the South by a nominal purchase of peace and sacrifice of nearly everything that had been contended for during the four years of terrible struggle and bloodshed. The Sherman—Johnston cartel as it was apprehended might not secure permanent peace to the sections and it was deemed advisable to continue fighting rather than secure a peace that signified a trust or temporary dispersion of the southern army, still armed with the power and clothed with imaginary right giving them courage to renew hostilities at any time to enforce concessions which might be mockery of justice and an indignity to the royal citizens of an outraged government.

The following is the cartel of agreement between Generals Sherman and Johnston signed on April 18, 1865:

*I. The contending armies now in the fields to maintain the status quo until notice is given by the commanding general of any one of his opponent, and reasonable time, say forty-eight hours allowed.*

---

1317 Arbitrament means the right to decide for oneself.

1318 Terms of surrender Southern History of the War, Part II, page 50

1319 Viz. is the abbreviation for videlicet which means namely.

*II. The Confederate armies now in existence to be disbanded and conducted to their several state capitals, there to deposit their arms and public property in the state arsenal, and each officer and man to execute and file an agreement to cease from acts of war, and to abide by the action of both state and federal authorities. The number of arms and munitions of war to be reported to the chief ordinance officer at Washington City, subject to the future action of the Congress of the United States, and in the meantime to be used solely to maintain peace and order within the borders of the states respectively.*

*III. The recognition of the executive of the United States of the several governments, on their officers and Legislatures taking the oath prescribed by the Constitution of the United States and where conflicting state governments have resulted from the war, the legitimacy of all shall be submitted to the Supreme Court of the United States.*

*IV. The reestablishment of the federal courts in the several states, with powers as defined by the Constitution and the laws of Congress.*

*V. The people and the inhabitants of several states be guaranteed, so far as the executive can, their political rights and freedoms, as well as their rights of person and property, as defined by the Constitution of the United States, and of the states respectively.*

*VI. The executive authority or government of the United States not to disturb any of the people by reason of the late war, so long as they live in peace and quiet, and abstain from acts of armed hostility, and obey the laws in existence at the place of their residence.*

*VII. In general terms, it is announced that the war is to cease; a general amnesty, so far as the executive of the United States can command, or condition of the disbandment of the Confederate armies, the distribution of the arms, and the resumption of peaceful pursuit by the officers and men hitherto composing said armies.*

*Not being fully empowered by our respective principals to fulfill these terms, we individually and officially pledge ourselves to promptly obtain authority, and will endeavor to carry out the above programme.*

*Signed*

*General Joseph E. Johnston*
*Commanding the Confederate Army*
*General W. T. Sherman*
*Commanding the Army of the United States*[1320]

1320 Harpers Pictorial History of the United States during the Great Rebellion, pg. 774.

These pages furnish an interesting history of the closing scenes of the war.

No political question was considered at the surrender of General Lee's army. The surrender was purely a military event. The convention, however, between Generals Sherman and Johnston contemplated not only the termination of the war but the speedy settlement of all the questions involved by it. The assumed right of General Sherman to offer or accept the terms imposed was repudiated by the federal administration. The important records here given demonstrate beyond question that the Confederate leaders did not regard the question of slavery as the vital issue of the unequal contest which they had so long sustained and they omitted to exact or insist on terms for its protection. They seemed to assume that the "peculiar institution" would be continued in force as though the war had never occurred and it's evident that General Sherman held the same view. Soon, however, the indissolvable[1321] unity was affected on the basis of liberation of the slaves by the passage of the 13th Amendment to the Constitution of the United States which was passed in Congress on January 31, 1865 and was afterwards submitted to the popular vote and ratified by three-fourths of the states and proclaimed to be in force by December 6, 1865.[1322] This amendment was modeled on the language of the ordinance of 1787, which thus after a struggle of 80 years became the law of the land, and slavery ceased to be a "peculiar institution" of the country.

The question that will most interest the impartial student of history in studying the situation during the last hours of the Confederacy as shown by these documents we have no doubt will be the contract presented between the acknowledged weakness of the expiring Confederacy and the brave spirit evince[1323]—faithful to its representatives to the last to the cause which had been entrusted to the direction of its representatives.

Slavery, which was not only the pretext but the real cause of the war, had now been disposed of by the war itself. The institution of slavery was no longer secured to the states, and its perpetuity or extension dependent of the people of the respective states. The Constitution of the United States no longer gave special protection and guarantees vouchsafed before the war—necessity abolished the

---

1321 Indissolvable means non-rescinded.
1322 The U.S. Constitution, pg. 49.
1323 Evince means displayed.

institution; yet the policy and sole object of the administration was peace, maintenance of the federal system, reconstruction and restoration with as little disturbance to the reconstruction of the government and reinstatement of the Constitution as possible. All Mr. Lincoln required as an acquiescence of things this war of their making had brought about, and the speedy adjustment of the political, federal and state relations under the organic law of the nation.

Federal authority had been suspended in the southern states and the resumption of it in harmony with the state authority was a paramount interest. Mr. Lincoln had no idea of cooperating with that element strong in the country favoring the revolutionary opportunity—of promoting one or breaking down the other. All he desired was reconstruction, restoration and permanent peace by legal and constitutional means—not by negotiations with rebels in arms nor by the medium of commissioners appointed by the respective belligerent parties which would recognize the confederacy of the southern states as a foreign power legal and national.

Mr. Lincoln never acknowledged or yielded to the claim of the people in insurrection that they were other than citizens of the United States in revolution against the laws and defying the federal authorities. When these rebellious citizens should resume their allegiance and duties by laying down their arms and abandoning their usurped *de facto* government, their respective commonwealths should have the opportunity of resuming their original right of membership in the federal Union. His intent was to not ask for anything from the rebellious states and would deal as if they never left.

The matter of negotiations between the independent governments from the beginning of the outbreak of the rebellion had been made an ultimatum even from the day Fort Sumter was fired upon. At no time from the incipiency[1324] of the rebellion to the time of the capitulation of peace did Lincoln ever acknowledge by word, act, or deed the insurrection as legal. This amnesty proclamation of pardon and invitation of the states to resume their inter-state and national functions intended as the imitative measure in the interest of peace gave great offense to the anti-administration Republicans who at once arrayed themselves against the policy of the re-establishment of the government on the basis of the Constitution.

---

1324 Incipiency means beginning.

*"The dead of this war–there they lie, strewing in the fields and woods and valleys and battlefields...the dead, the dead, the dead–our dead–of South or North, ours all...our young men once so handsome and so joyous, taken from us–the sons from the mother, the husband from the wife, the dear friend from the dear friend..."*

Walt Whitman[1325]

# — 19 —

# SUMMARY OF THE WAR

In giving the losses of the various battles of the war, it is impossible to give them absolute certainty. They are here given from estimates, reports of commanders of the battles, and the official medical returns, which in many instances vary as to numbers. From the records of the war department we are able to ascertain the number of engagements and battles that were fought, in each of the states and territories of the Union North and during the existence of the war. They were as follows:

**Battles by state and territory**

New York, 1 riot
South Carolina, 60
Pennsylvania, 9
Georgia, 108
Maryland, 30
Florida, 32
District of Columbia, 1
Alabama, 78

1325 The Union in Crisis, 1850—1879, pgs. 200 & 201.

West Virginia, 80
Mississippi, 186
Virginia, 519
Louisiana, 18
North Carolina, 85
Texas, 14
Arkansas, 167
Tennessee, 298
Kentucky, 138
Oregon, 4
Ohio, 3
Nevada, 2
Indiana, 4
Washington Territory, 1
Illinois, 1
Utah, 1
Missouri, 244
New Mexico, 19
Minnesota, 6
Nebraska, 2
California, 6
Colorado, 4
Kansas, 7
Dakota, 11
Indian Territory, 17
Arizona, 4
Idaho, 1

In 1861, there were 156 engagements. In 1862, there were 564. In 1863, there were 627. In 1864, there were 779. In 1865, there were 175. During the war of the rebellion there was one Union Lieutenant General.[1326] Major Generals there were 11 with full rank, and 152 by brevet. Major Generals of volunteers there were 128 full rank, and 288 brevet. Brigadier Generals of the United States Army there were 36

1326 The one Lt. General was Ulysses S. Grant. The only other Lieutenant Generals in the country's history were Winfield Scott and George Washington. Lincoln's War.

full rank, and 187 brevet. Brigadier Generals of the volunteers there were 561 full rank, and 1170 by brevet.[1327]

In giving the rank of the general officers here stated, volunteers and also from the general orders issued, in time to time by the war department, some of those officers who had served in the Union army did not obtain their appointments until after the rebellion had closed. There were but a few of them and those appointments were confined to the regular army.

General Union officers killed in action numbered 38, and are as follows:[1328] Brigadier General Thomas Williams, Brigadier General Robert L. McCook, Brigadier General Henry Bohlen, Major General Phillip Kearney, Major General Isaac I. Stevens, Brigadier General Pleasant A. Hackleman, Brigadier General James S. Jackson, Brigadier General William R. Terrill, Brigadier General Conrad F. Jackson, Brigadier General Joshua W. Bell, Major General Hiram G. Barry, Major General John F. Reynolds, Brigadier General Stephen H. Weed, Brevet Major General S. K. Zook, Brevet Brigadier General A. Van Horn Ellis, Brevet Brigadier General Lewis Benedict, Brevet Major General Alex. Hayes, Brevet Major General James S. Wadsworth, Major General John Segwick, Brigadier General Thomas G. Stevenson, Brigadier General James C. Rice, Brevet Brigadier General Henry H. Giesy, Brevet Brigadier General John McConihe, Brevet Brigadier General Thomas W. Humphrey, Brevet Brigadier General William Blaisdell, Brevet Brigadier General George A. Cobham, Jr., Major General James B. McPherson, Brevet Brigadier General Griffin A. Stedman, Brevet Brigadier General George E. Elstner, Brevet Major General David A. Russell, Brevet Brigadier General Frank H. Peck, Brigadier General Hiram Burdham, Brevet Brigadier General George D. Wells, Brigadier General Daniel D. Bidwell, Brevet Brigadier General Sylvester G. Hill, Brevet Major General Frederick Winthrop, Brevet Brigadier General George W. Gowan, and Brevet Brigadier General Theodore Reed.

---

[1327] Out of 583 Union Generals, forty-seven were killed in action. By comparison, out of 425 Confederate Generals, seventy-seven were killed in action. Out of two million Union soldiers, there were 640,000 casualties, including 365,000 killed or died of disease and another 275,00 who were wounded. By comparison, out of 750,000 Confederate soldiers, 256,000 were killed or died from disease, with another 194,000 wounded for a total of 450,000 casualties. The Civil War, A Narrative—Five Forks to Appomattox, pgs. 308 & 309.

[1328] Phisterer's Records, pg. 318.

Union officers who died of wounds received in the action were 29 in number as follows:[1329] Brigadier General William H. L. Wallace, Brigadier General George W. Taylor, Brevet Brigadier General Thornton F. Broadhead, Major General Jesse L. Reno, Major General Joseph K. F. Mansfield, Brigadier General Isaac P. Rodman, Major General Isaac B. Richardson, Brigadier General George D. Bayard, Major General Averl W. Whipple, Brigadier General Edmund Kirby, Brevet Brigadier General George H. Ward, Brevet Brigadier General Paul Joseph Revere, Brevet Brigadier General Louis R. Francine, Major General George C. Strong, Brigadier General William H, Lytle, Brigadier General William P. Sanders, Brevet Brigadier General William M. Green, Brevet Brigadier General Arthur H. Dalton, Brevet Brigadier General William H. Babcock, Brevet Brigadier General George L. Prescott, Brigadier General Charles G. Barber, Brigadier General Samuel A. Rice, Brevet Brigadier General James A. Mulligan, Brevet Brigadier General Henry Lyman Patton, Brevet Brigadier General Willoughby Babcock, Brevet Brigadier General Alexander Gardiner, Brevet Brigadier General J. Howard Klitching, Brevet Major General Thomas A. Smyth, and Brevet Brigadier General Francis Washburn.

Federal officers who died of disease and other causes numbered 35:[1330] and are as follows: Brevet Brigadier General John Garland, Brevet Major General John Gilmore, Brigadier General Frederick W. Lander, Brevet Brigadier General Charles F. Smith, Brigadier General William H. Keim, Brigadier General Joseph B. Plummer, Major General William Nelson, Major General Ormsby M. Mitchell, Brigadier General Charles D. Johnson, Brigadier General Francis M. Patterson, Major General Edwin V. Sumner, Brigadier General James Cooper, Brigadier General E. N. Kirk, Brigadier General Thomas Webb, Major General John Buford, Brigadier General Michael Corcoran, Brigadier General Stephen G. Camplin, Brevet Major General Joseph G. Totten, Brigadier General Joseph P. Taylor, Brigadier General Daniel P. Woodbury, Brigadier General Joshua B. Howell, Brevet Brigadier General Thomas J. C. Amery, Major General David B. Birney, Brevet Major General T.E.G. Ransom, Brevet Brigadier General Charles Wheelock, Brevet Brigadier General David P. Shunk, Brevet Brigadier General Cleveland J. Campbell, Brigadier

[1329] Phisterer's Records, pg. 119.
[1330] Phisterer's Records, pg. 321.

General George Wright, Brigadier General M. M. Crocker, Brevet Brigadier General Alanzo G. Draper, Brigadier General Alexander Schimmelpfennig, Brevet Brigadier General William R. Revere, Jr., Brevet Brigadier General Reno R. DeRany, and Brevet Major General William W. Morris.

According to the Surgeon General's report there were treated from the war proper from May 1st, 1861 to June 30th, 1865 in the hospitals of the army 5,579,526 of diseases and cases of the whites, and 470,122 colored cases. There were deaths during that time in the hospital 161,891 whites and 23,465 coloreds, aggregating 185,356 deaths besides those killed in battle and others who came to their deaths elsewhere than in hospitals.

The Congress of the United States in public acts conferred honors on the following officers, individuals, soldiers, and seamen of the United States:[1331]

Brigadier General Nathaniel Lyon, Major General William S. Rosencrans, Major General Ulysses S. Grant, Major General Nathaniel P. Banks, Major General Ambrose Burnside, Major General Joseph Hooker, Major General George Meade, Major General Oliver O. Howard, Major General W. T. Sherman, Lieutenant Colonel Joseph Bailey, Brevet Major General Alfred H. Terry, Major General George H. Thomas and Major General Winfield S. Hancock.

---

[1331] Phisterer's Records, pg. 64.

*"It was Lincoln who appealed to the people against the judges when the judges went wrong, who advocated and secured what was practically the recall of the Dred Scott decision and who trusted the Constitution as a living force of righteousness."*

Theodore Roosevelt, President of the United States[1332]

# — 20 —

# THE *HABEAS CORPUS* CONTROVERSY

On the 27th of April, 1861 the president issued to General Scott the following general order: "You are engaged in suppressing an insurrection against the laws of the United States; if at any point or in the vicinity of any military line which is now or shall become between the city of Philadelphia and the city of Washington you find resistance which renders it necessary to suspend the writ of *habeas corpus* for the public safety, you personally or through the officers in command at the point at which resistance occurs, are authorized to suspend that writ." On July 2nd this order was extended to include the line to New York.

On the 10th of May, the commander of the forces of the United States on the Florida coast was empowered to exercise the right of suspension of the writ, "if he find it necessary to and to remove from the vicinity of the fortresses, all dangerous and suspected persons."

On May 25, General George Cadwalader[1333] was in command of Fort McHenry. John Merriman[1334] of Baltimore was charged with

---

1332 Lincoln in American Memory, pg. 165.

1333 General George Cadwalader was a lawyer who had been born in Pennsylvania. He had participated in the Mexican War. He commanded the First Division of General Patterson's Confederate Army in the Shenandoah Valley. www.absoluteastronomy.com/topics/George_cadawalader

1334 John Merriman was a southern sympathizer and secessionist from Maryland. www.csulb.edu/~crsmith/lincoln.html.

being a Lieutenant and holding a commission with a company that avowed its purpose of acting in armed hostility against the government. He was also charged with being in communication with the rebels of the South and was further charged with various other acts of treason. He was arrested and lodged in Fort McHenry as a military prisoner. The prisoner at once petitioned the Chief Justice of the United States, Judge Roger B. Taney,[1335] setting forth his arrest and praying for a writ of *habeas corpus* and the right to be heard. The writ was granted and on the 27th instant named as a day for a hearing.

General Cadwalader made no response, assuming his right under the authority of the President of the United States to suspend the writ of *habeas corpus* for the public safety and to hold anyone in arrest by military force who was dangerous to the safety or peace of the government; whereupon the chief justice issued his writ of attachment for the general directing the United States Marshal, Mr. Bonafant[1336] to produce General Cadwalader's body the next day—to answer for his contempt in refusing to produce the body of John Merriman. On that day the marshal replied that he went to the fort to serve the writ and "there was no answer to the writ."

Chief Justice Taney then gave his reasons for issuing the attachment which were because upon the face of the return the detention of the prisoner was unlawful upon two grounds. "First, the president under the Constitution and laws of the United States cannot suspend privileges of the writ of *habeas corpus* or authorize any military officer to do so. Second, a military officer has no right to arrest or detain a person not subject to the rules and articles of war for an offense against the United States except in and of the judicial authority and subject to its control, and if the party is arrested by the military it is the duty of the officer to deliver him over immediately to the civil authorities to be dealt with according to law." The chief justice reduced his opinion to writing and filed it in the office of the clerk of the circuit court. After this the chief justice further remarked "In relation to the present return I propose to say that the marshal has legally the right to summon out the *posse comitatus*[1337] to serve and bring into court the party named in the attachment; but it is apparent that he

---

[1335] Roger B. Taney—See pg. 96.

[1336] Washington Bonafant was the U. S. Marshal for the Baltimore District from 1861—1869. www.usmarshals.gov/district/md/general/history.htm

[1337] *Posse comitatus* are people assigned to help the police.

will be resisted in the discharge of that duty by a force notoriously superior to the *posse comitatus*, and such being the case, the court has no power under the law to order the necessary force to compel the appearance of the party. If however he were to be before the court, it would then impose the only punishment it is empowered to inflict—that by fine and imprisonment. Under these circumstances the court can barely say today. I shall reduce to writing the reasons under which I have acted and which have led me to the conclusion expressed in my opinion and shall report them with these proceedings to the President of the United States and call upon him to perform his constitutional duty to enforce the laws; in other words to enforce the process of this court. This is all this court has now the power to do."

Mr. Lincoln could not be made to see that it was his duty to enforce the laws in that way. His highest duty, he thought, was to suspend the technicalities of the law and if need be, to totally disregard all law on the statute book if necessary to preserve the life of the nation. This decision of the chief justice at this time was most embarrassing to the war powers then being exercised. The legal operations of the civil authorities had not been suspended by the declaration of martial law, and apprehended conflicts of authority would greatly embarrass the military operations of the government. At no point was a greater field for such obstruction than in Baltimore and Maryland. After due consideration, the administration determined upon the arrest of the chief justice. A warrant or order was issued for his arrest. Then arose the question of service. Who would make the arrest and where should be his imprisonment?

It was finally determined to place the order of arrest in the hands of the United States Marshal of the District of Columbia.[1338] This was done by the president with instruction by him to use the marshal's own discretion about making the arrest unless he should receive further orders from Mr. Lincoln. This writ was never executed, and the marshal never regretted the discretionary power delegated to him in the exercise of his official duty. The power of the president for making arbitrary arrests became at this time a question of greater importance.

---

[1338] Ward Hill Lamon, the author of this manuscript, was the U.S. Marshal of the District of Columbia. He was appointed for a four year term on July 26, 1861. Ward Hill Lamon: Lincoln's "Particular Friend," pg. 216.

Attorney General, Mr. Bates,[1339] wrote an elaborate opinion on the subject in support of the legal power. The opinion of many distinguished lawyers was sought by Mr. Lincoln. Among others, the Honorable Horace Binney,[1340] of Philadelphia, one of the oldest and most distinguished lawyers in the United States, who gave his opinion in this language, "In this matter of the suspension of the privilege of *habeas corpus*, the Constitution of the United States stands in the place of the English Act of Parliament. It ordains the suspension in the conditioned cases by the act of the competent department, as Parliament does from time to time. Neither is mandatory in suspending but only authoritative. Each leaves discretion to the executive power. The difference is that Parliament limits the time and provides for the effect by technical terms. The Constitution connects the suspension with the time of rebellion and provides for the effect as it did for the privilege by words that comprehend the right and deny for a season the enjoyment of it. It is fortunately confined to most dangerous times. In such times the people generally are willing and are often compelled to give up for a season, a portion of their freedom to preserve the right, and fortunately again it is that portion of the people for the most part who like to live on the margin of disobedience to the laws whose freedom is most in danger. The rest are rarely in want of *habeas corpus*."

Other eminent lawyers were consulted and all concurred in the conclusion that in cases of invasion from abroad or rebellion at home, the president may declare or exercise or authorize martial law at his discretion.

On September 24, 1862 a proclamation was issued ordering that during the existence of the insurrection, all rebels and insurgents within the United States—persons discouraging volunteers and enlistments, resisting military drafts, and in any way affording aid and comfort to the rebels should be subject to martial law and liable to trial and punishment by court-martial or military commission and the *habeas corpus* writ be suspended in respect to all person arrested or imprisoned by military authority or sentence of any court martial or military commission. The following year, 1863, Congress passed an act

---

1339 Edward Bates—See pg. 101.

1340 Horace Binney was a Philadelphia lawyer who came to Lincoln's defense. His pamphlet The Privilege of the Writ of Habeas Corpus under the Constitution attacking Justice Taney's position. www.csulb.edu/~crsmith/lincoln.html

giving to the president general authority to suspend the writ throughout the United States and in accordance therewith the president on the 15th of September of that year issued his proclamation for the general suspension of the writ of *habeas corpus* throughout the United States.

Mr. Lincoln's own views on this question may be found embodied in his reply to the New York Democrats dated June 12, 1863. What gave rise to this letter was a series of resolutions that were passed by the New York State Democratic convention, denying the right to make military arrests in states not in actual rebellion and denouncing the then recent assumption of a military commander (General Burnside[1341]) to seize and try citizens of Ohio (Clement C. Vallandigham) for no other reasons than words addressed to a public meeting in criticism of the course of the administration and in condemnation of the military order of that general. These resolutions were sent to the president for his consideration. They portended[1342] evil, coming from a state having the greatest population of any state in the Union. The Ohio Democrats held a state convention and sent resolutions for the consideration of the president. They deprecated[1343] any restraints upon free will, free thought, free speech, and free press, claiming that it is an inherent and constitutional right to discuss all measures of the government, denounced Mr. Vallandigham arrest and declared that they will not submit to the forcible violation of these constitutional rights in such cases.

The order of General Burnside under which Mr. Vallandigham was arrested and tried was what was known as General Order No. 38 which announced that "hereafter all persons found within our lines (within the Department of Ohio) who commit acts for the benefit of the enemies of our country, will be tried as spies and traitors and if convicted will suffer death." And this was added to the order, Viz. "the habit of declaring sympathy for the enemy will not be allowed in this department. Persons committing such offenses will be at once arrested with a view to being tried as above stated or sent beyond our lines, and into the lines of their friends. It must be distinctly understood that treason, expressed or implied, will not be tolerated in this department."

---

1341 General Ambrose Burnside—See pg. 171.

1342 Portended means threat of.

1343 Deprecated means averted.

Mr. Lincoln's letter in reply to the New York resolutions defining what he considers his power and duties as chief executive in time of war is as follows, to wit:

*Executive Mansion*
*Washington, June 12, 1863*
*Honorable Erastus Corning*[1344] *and others*[1345]

*Gentlemen: Your letter of May 19 including the resolutions of the public meeting held at Albany on the 16th of the same month was received several days ago.*

*The resolutions as I understand are resolvable into two propositions—first, the expression of purpose to sustain the cause of the Union, to secure peace through victory, and to support the Administration in every constitutional and lawful measure to suppress the rebellion; and secondly, a declaration of censure upon the Administration for supposed unconstitutional action, such as the making of military arrests. And, from the two propositions, a third is deduced, which is, that the gentlemen composing the meeting resolved on doing their part to maintain our common Government and country, despite the folly or wickedness, as they conceive, of any Administration. This position is eminently patriotic, and as such, I thank the meeting, and congratulate the nation for it. My own purpose is the same; so that the meeting and myself have a common object, and can have no difference, except in the choice of means or measures for effecting that object.*

*And here I ought to close this paper, and would close it if there were no apprehension that more injurious consequences than any merely personal to myself might follow the censures systematically cast upon me for doing what, in my view of duty, I could not forebear. The resolutions promise to support me in every constitutional and lawful measure to suppress the rebellion; and I have not knowingly employed, nor shall knowingly employ, any other. But the meeting, by their resolutions, assert and argue that certain military arrests, and proceedings following them, for which I am ultimately responsible, are unconstitutional. I think they are not. The resolutions quote from the Constitution the definition of treason, and also the limiting safeguards and guarantees therein provided for the citizen on*

---

1344 Erastus Corning was President of the New York Central Railroad. He was a Democratic businessman who was also involved in manufacturing and banking. He served as mayor, State Senator and U.S. Congressman. www.mrlincolnandnewyork.org

1345 Eli Perry, Peter Gansevoort, Peter Monteith, Samuel W. Gibbs, John Niblack, H.W. McClellan, Lemuel W. Rogers, William Seymour, Jeremiah Osborn, Wm. S. Padock, J.B. Sanders, Edward Mulcahy, D.V.N. Radcliffe, William A. Rice, Edward Newcomb, R. W. Peckham Jr., M. A. Nolan, John R. Nessel, and C. W. Weeks. Political History of the United States during the Great Rebellion, pg. 162

*trials of treason, and on his being held to answer for capital and otherwise infamous crimes, and, in criminal prosecutions, his right to a speedy and public trial by an impartial jury. They proceed to resolve "that these safeguards of the rights of the citizen against the pretension of arbitrary power were intended more especially for his protection in times of civil commotion." And, apparently to demonstrate the proposition, the resolutions proceed: "They were secured substantially to the English people after years of protracted civil war, and were adopted into our Constitution at the close of the revolution." Would not the demonstration have been better, if it could have been truly said that these safeguards had been adopted and applied during the civil wars and during our revolution, instead of after the one and at the close of the other? I, too, am devotedly for them after civil war, and before civil war, and at all times, "except when, in cases of rebellion or invasion, the public safety may require" their suspension. The resolutions proceed to us that these safeguards "have stood the test of seventy-six years of trial, under our republican system, under circumstances which show that while they constitute the foundations of all free government, they are the elements of enduring stability of the republic." No one denies that they have so stood the test up to the beginning of the present rebellion, if we accept a certain occurrence at New Orleans; nor does anyone question that they will stand the same test much longer after the rebellion closes. But these provisions of the Constitution have no application to the case we have in hand, because arrests complained of were not made for treason—that is, not for the treason defined in the Constitution, and upon the conviction of which the punishment is death—nor yet were they made to hold persons to answer for any capitol or otherwise infamous crimes; nor were the proceedings following, in any constitutional or legal sense, "criminal prosecutions." The arrests were made on totally different grounds, and the proceedings following accorded with the grounds of the arrests. Let us consider the real case with which we are dealing, and apply to it the parts of the Constitution plainly made for each case.*

*Prior to my installation here it had been calculated that any State had a lawful right to secede from the national Union, and that it would be expedient to exercise the right whenever the devotees to the doctrine should fail to elect a President to their own liking. I was elected contrary to their liking; and, accordingly, so far as it was legally possible, they had taken seven States out of the Union, had seized many of the United States forts, and had fired on the United States flag, all before I was inaugurated, and, of course, before I had done any official act whatsoever. The rebellion thus began soon ran into the present civil war; and in certain respects, it began on very unequal terms between the parties. The insurgents had been preparing for it more than thirty years, while the government had taken no steps to resist them. The former had carefully considered all the means which could be turned to their account. It undoubtedly was a well-pondered reliance with them that in their own unrestricted efforts to destroy the Union, Constitution and law, all together, the Government would, in great degree, be restrained by the same Constitution and law from arresting their programs. Their sympathizers pervaded all departments of the Government and nearly all communities of people. From this material, under cover of "liberty of speech," "liberty of the press," and "habeas corpus," they helped to keep on foot amongst us a most efficient corps of spies, informants, suppliers, aiders and abettors of their cause in a thousand ways. They knew that in times such as they were inaugurating, by the Constitution itself, the "habeas corpus" might be suspended; but they also knew they had friends who would make a question as to who was to suspended it; meanwhile their spies and others might remain at large to help on their cause. Or if, as has happened, the Executive would suspend the writ, without ruinous waste of time, instantaneous of arresting of innocent persons might occur, as are always likely to occur in such cases; and then a clamor would be raise in regard to this, which might be, at least, for some service to the insurgent cause. It needed no very keen perception to discover this part of the enemies program, so soon as by open hostilities their machinery was fairly put in motion. Yet, thoroughly imbued*[1346] *with a reverence for the guaranteed rights of individuals, I was slow to adopt the strong measures as being within the exceptions of the Constitution, and as indispensable to the public safety. Nothing is better known to history than that courts of justice are utterly incompetent to such cases. Civil courts are organized chiefly for the trials of individuals, or, at most, a few individuals acting in concert; and this in quiet times, and on charges of crimes well defined in the law. Even in times of peace bands of horse-thieves and robbers frequently grow too numerous and powerful for ordinary courts of justice. But what comparison, in numbers, have such bands ever borne to insurgent sympathizers even in many of the loyal States? Again, a jury too frequently has at least one member more ready to hang the panel than to hang the traitor. And yet again, he who dissuades one man from volunteering, or induces one soldier to desert, weakens the Union cause as much as he who kills a Union soldier in battle. Yet this dissuasion or inducement may be so conducted as to be no defined crime of which any civil court would take cognizance.*

*Our is a case of rebellion—so called by the resolutions before me—in fact, a clear, flagrant, and gigantic case of rebellion; and the provisions of the Constitution that "the privilege of the writ of habeas corpus shall not be suspended, unless when in cases of rebellion or invasion, the public safety may require it," is the provision which specifically applies to our present case. This provision plainly attests the understanding of those who made the Constitution, that ordinary courts of justice*

---

[1346] Imbued means saturated.

*are inadequate to "cases of rebellion"—attests their purpose that, in such cases, men may be held in custody who the courts, acting on ordinary rules, would discharge. Habeas corpus does not discharge men who are proved to be guilty of defined crimes; and its suspension is allowed by the Constitution on purpose that men may be arrested and held who cannot be proved to be guilty of defined crimes, "when, in cases of rebellion or invasion, the public safety may require it."*

*This is precisely our present case—a case of rebellion, wherein the public safety does require the suspension. Indeed, arrest by process of courts and arrests in cases of rebellion, do not proceed altogether upon the same basis. The former is directed at the small percentage of ordinary and continuous perpetration of crime, while the latter is directed at sudden and extensive uprisings, against the Government, which, at most, will succeed or fail in no great length of time. In the latter case, arrests are made, not so much for what has been done, as for what probably would be done. The latter is more for the preventative and less for the vindictive than the former. In such cases the purposes of men are much more easily understood than in cases of ordinary crime. The man who stands by and says nothing when the peril of his Government is discussed, cannot be misunderstood. If not hindered, he is sure to help the enemy; much more, if he talks ambiguously—talks for his country with "buts" and "ifs" and "ands." Oh how little the constitutional provisions I have quoted will be rendered, if arrests shall never be made till defined crimes shall have been committed, may be illustrated by a few notable examples. General John C. Breckinridge,*[1347] *General Robert E. Lee,*[1348] *General Joseph E. Johnston,*[1349] *General John B. Magruder,*[1350] *General William Preston,*[1351] *General Simon B. Buckner,*[1352] *and Commodore Franklin Buchanan*[1353] *now occupying the highest places in the rebel war service, were all within the power of the Government since the rebellion began, and were nearly as well known to be traitors then as now. Unquestionably had we seized and held them, the insurgent cause would be much weaker. But no one of them had then committed any crime defined in the law. Every one of them, if arrested, would have been discharged on habeas corpus were the writ allowed to operate. In view of these and other similar cases, I think the*

---

1347 John C. Breckinridge—See pg. 48.
1348 Robert E. Lee—See pg. 119.
1349 Joseph E. Johnston—See pg. 129.
1350 John B. Magruder—See pg. 143.
1351 William Preston—See pg. 85.
1352 Simon B. Buckner—See pg. 172.
1353 Franklin Buchanan was a Maryland native and one of the U.S. Navy's most experienced officers. He was commanding officer of the *CSS Virginia* and later founding Superintendent of the U.S. Naval Academy. The Confederate Navy, pg. 8.

*time not unlikely to come when I shall be blamed for having made too few arrests rather than too many.*

*By the third resolution, the meeting indicated their opinion that military arrests may be constitutional in localities where rebellion actually exists, but that such arrests are unconstitutional where rebellion or insurrection does not actually exist. They insist that such arrests shall not be made "outside of the lines of necessary military occupation and the scenes of insurrection." Inasmuch, however, as the Constitution makes no such distinction, I am unable to believe that there is any such constitutional distinction. I concede that the class of arrests complained of can be constitutional only when, in cases of rebellion of invasion, the public safety may require them; and I insist that in such cases they are constitutional wherever the public safety does requires them; as well as in places to which they may prevent the rebellion extending as in those where it may be already prevailing; as well as where they may restrain mischievous interference with the raising and supplying of armies to suppress the rebellion, as where the rebellion may actually be; as well where they may restrain the enticing men out of the army; as where they would prevent mutiny in the army; equally constitutional in all places where they will conduce to the public safety, as against the dangers of rebellion or invasion. Take the peculiar case mentioned by the meeting. It is asserted, in substance, that Mr. Vallandigham*[1354] *was, by military commander, seized and tried "for no other reason than words addressed to a public meeting, in criticism of the Administration, and in condemnation of the military orders of the general." Now, if there be no mistake about this; if this section is the truth and the whole truth; if there was no other reason for the arrest, then I concede that the arrest was wrong. But the arrest, as I understand, was made for a very different reason. Mr. Vallandigham avows his hospitality to the war on the part of the Union; and the arrest was made because he was laboring with some affect, to prevent the raising of troops; to encourage desertion from the army; and to leave the rebellion without adequate military force to suppress it. He was not arrested because he was damaging the political prospects of the Administration, of the personal interests of the commanding general, but because he was damaging the army, upon the existence and vigor of which the life of the nation depends. He was warring upon the military, and this gave the military constitutional jurisdiction to lay hands upon him. If Mr. Vallandigham was not damaging the military power of the country, then his arrest was made on mistake of fact, which I would be glad to correct on reasonably satisfactory evidence.*

*I understand the meeting, whose resolutions I am considering, to be in favor of suppressing the rebellion by military force—by armies. Long experience has shown*

---

1354 Clement C. Vallandigham —See pg. 245.

*the armies cannot be maintained unless desertion shall be punished by the severe penalty of death. The case requires, and the law and the Constitution sanction, this punishment. Must I shoot a simple-minded soldier boy who deserts, while I must not touch the hair of a wily agitator who induces him to desert? This is none the less injurious when affected by getting a father, or brother, or friend, into a public meeting and there working upon his feelings till he is persuaded to write the soldier boy that he is fighting in a bad cause, for a wicked Administration of a contemptible Government, too weak to arrest and punish him if he shall desert. I think that, in such a case, to silence the agitator and save the boy is not only constitutional, but withal a great mercy.*

*If I be wrong on this question of constitutional powers, my error lies in believing that certain proceedings are constitutional when, in cases of rebellion or invasion, the public safety requires them, which would not be constitutional when, in the absence of rebellion or invasion, the public safely does not require them: in other words, that the Constitution is not, in its application, in all respects the same, in cases of rebellion and invasion involving the public safety, as it is in times of profound peace and public security. The Constitution itself makes the distinction; and I can no more be persuaded that the Government can constitutionally take no strong measures in time of rebellion, because it can be shown that the same could not be lawful taken in time of peace, than I could be persuaded that a particular drug is not good medicine for the sick man because it can be shown to not be good food for the well one. Nor am I able to appreciate the danger apprehended by the meeting, that the American people will, by means of military arrests during the rebellion, lose the right of public discussion, the liberty of speech and press, the law of evidence, trial by jury, and habeas corpus, throughout the indefinite peaceful future, which I trust lies before them, any more than I am able to believe that a man could contract so strong an appetite for emotion during temporary illness as to the persist in feeding upon them during the remainder of his beautiful life.*

*In giving the resolutions that earnest consideration which you request, I cannot overlook the fact that the meeting speak as "Democrats." Not can I, with full respect for their known intelligence, and the fairly presumed deliberation with which they prepared their resolutions, be permitted to suppose that this occurred by accident, or in any way other than that they preferred to designate themselves as "Democrats" rather than "American citizens." In this time of national peril I would have preferred to meet you on a level one step higher than any party platform, because I am sure that, from such more elevated position, we could do better battle for the country we all love than we possibly can from those lower ones where, from force of habit, the prejudices of the past, and selfish hopes of the future, we are sure to expend much of our ingenuity and strength finding fault with, and aiming blows at each other. But, since you have denied me this, I will yet be thankful of the country's sake, that not all Democrats have done so. He on whose discretionary judgment Mr. Vallandigham was arrested and tried is a Democrat, having no old party affiliation with me; and the judge who rejected the constitutional view expressed in these resolutions, by refusing to discharge Mr. Vallandigham of habeas corpus, is a Democrat of better days than these, having received his judicial mantle at the hands of President Jackson.*[1355] *And still more, of all those Democrats who are nobly exposing their lives and shedding their blood on the battle field, I have learned that many approve the course taken with Mr. Vallandigham, while I have not heard of a single one condemning it. I cannot assert that there are none such. And the name of President Jackson recalls an instance of pertinent history. After the battle of New Orleans and while the fact that the treaty of peace had been concluded was well known in the city, but before official knowledge of it had arrived, General Jackson still maintained martial law of military law. Now, that it could be said the war was over, the clamor against martial law, which had existed from the first, grew more furious. Among other things, a Mr. Louillier*[1356] *published a denunciatory newspaper article. General Jackson arrested him. A lawyer by the name of Morel procured U.S. Judge Hall*[1357] *to order a writ of habeas corpus to relieve Mr. Louillier. General Jackson arrested both the lawyer and the judge. A Mr. Hollander ventured to say of some part of the matter that "it was a dirty trick." General Jackson arrested him. When the officer undertook to serve the writ of habeas corpus, General Jackson took it from him, and sent him away with a copy. Holding the judge in custody a few days, the general sent him beyond the limits of his engagement, and set him at liberty, with an order to remain till the ratification of the peace should be regularly announced, or until the British should have left the northern coast. A day or two elapsed, the ratification of the treaty of peace was regularly announced, and the judge and others were fairly liberated. A few days more and the judge called General Jackson into court and fined him $1000 for having arrested him and the others named. The General paid the fine, and there the matter rested for nearly thirty years, when Congress refunded principal*

---

1355 Mr. Lincoln is referring to the fact that Chief Justice Roger B. Taney had been appointed by President Andrew Jackson to that seat on the bench on March 15, 1836. Appleton's Cyclopaedia of American Biography, pg. 28.

1356 Mr. Louillier was a member of the state legislature who was arrested by General Jackson for exciting sedition amongst Jackson's troops. www.famousamerican.net/dominickaugustinehall

1357 Judge Diminick Augustine Hall was a federal district judge of the territory of New Orleans. Chestofbooks.com/reference/American-cyclopaedia-4/Dominick-augustine-hall.html

*and interest. The late Senator Douglas,*[1358] *then in the House of Representatives, took a leading part in the debate, in which the constitutional question was much discussed. I am not prepared to say whom the journals would show to have voted for the measure.*

*It may be remarked: First, that we had the same Constitution then as now; secondly, that we then had a case of invasion, and now we have a case of rebellion; and thirdly, that the permanent right of the people to public discussion, the liberty of speech and of the press, the trial by jury, the law of evidence, and the habeas corpus, suffered no detriment whatever by the conduct of General Jackson or its subsequent approval by the American Congress.*

*And yet, let me say, that in my own discretion, I do not know whether I would have ordered the arrest of Mr. Vallandigham. While I cannot shift the responsibility from myself, I hold that, as a general rule, the commander in the field is a better judge of the necessity in any particular case. Of course, I must practice a general directory and revisory*[1359] *power in the matter.*

*One of the resolutions expresses the opinion of the meeting that arbitrary arrests will have the effect to divide and distract those who should be united in suppressing the rebellion, and I am specifically called on to discharge Mr. Vallandigham. I regard this as, at least a fair appeal to me on the expediency of exercising a constitutional power which I think exists. In response to such an appeal I have to say, it gave me pain when I learned the Mr. Vallandigham had been arrested—that is, I was pained that there should have seemed to be a necessity for arresting him—and that it will afford me great pleasure to discharge him so soon as I can, by any means, as I believe the public safety will not suffer by it.*

*I further say, that as the war progressed, it appears to me, opinion and action, which were in great confusion at first, take shape and fall into more regular channels, so that the necessity for strong dealing with them gradually decreases. I have every reason to desire that it should cease altogether, and far from the least in my regard for the opinions and wishes of those who like the meeting in Albany declare their purpose to sustain the Government in every constitutional and lawful measure to suppress the rebellion. Still, I must continue to do so much as may seem to be required by the pubic safety.*

*A. Lincoln*[1360]

Neither the decision of the Chief Justice of the United States, the remonstrance and deprecation of the New York convention, the

---

1358 Senator Stephen A. Douglas—See pg. 34.

1359 Revisory means the ability to correct or improve.

1360 History of the United States during the Great Rebellion, pgs. 162—167.

threats of the Ohio Democracy, nor the formidable army of the South had the effect of deterring Mr. Lincoln from his settled and determined duty. An enemy to the country within or without the Union lines, he regarded as a traitor and preferred to have all such either killed, or in a bunch to themselves, to having them scattered among loyal people who were striving to suppress the rebellion and by coercive means to restore peace and quiet to the country. Many things were necessarily done or authorized that were not specifically provided for by the Constitution and law: the higher law of necessity in the face of danger to life and country justified them in the absence of provisions. Duty stimulated by indomitable[1361] courage, provided an unwritten law to meet the extraordinary emergency of dishonor, life or death in the struggle for the right. Once engaged in the war little time was given for amendment to the Constitution or the enactment of laws to meet the case in hand. Had there been provision for organic or statutory law defining the belligerent treatment of citizens of one section by the other in time of peace it may be doubted whether it would have been observed in a citizens' internal war and more than a treaty stipulation of peace and amity[1362] between nations would be observed when one of the nations invades the other with a hostile army, threatening the lives of the other high contracting party. In the midst of a fight there is little time to think of introductions, compliments, courtesies, modes, apologies, or inquiries as to who commenced the fuss.

Who had the right to complain of a violation of the Constitution and law? There was a square issue between the sections, and that was, shall the Union be preserved or sundered[1363] and divided into two confederacies? There could not possibly be a neutral ground upon which to stand. He that was not for the Union was against it. If in times of war those who were for it were satisfied to violate the laws that were made for the government in times of peace to the end of putting down the insurrection against law and order, who had a right to complain? The Confederates in the very outset had set at defiance all the laws and had foresworn all allegiance to the Constitution and the government.

---

1361 Indomitable means unconquerable.
1362 Amity means good will.
1363 Sundered means broken.

With all its violations that glorious old instrument survived the war and with slight repairs in the shape of amendments it is again called into active service and not unlike another "Constitution" in name of war memory, dating back to 1812, while subduing a foreign enemy and the *guerre á outrance*,[1364] like the confederates went under, it went again on duty unimpaired by neglect or abuse, but after repairs strengthened in its power for service.

There was a large class of non-combatants in the North as well as in the South who constantly clamored and inveighed[1365] against this necessary violation and supposed violation of the Constitution during the progress of the war who pretended to regard its sacrifice with a greater abhorrence than loyal men did the sacrifice of all the men killed in the engagements for its support. In reality these men generally had already forfeited their allegiance and abjured[1366] the binding force and effect of that instrument upon their loyalty and citizenship. Loyalty in the loyal breasts of the men engaged in the war like a tornado swept away every obstruction to its progress in restoring peace and security to the country.

---

1364 *Guerre á outrance* means war to the death.
1365 Inveighed means railed.
1366 Abjured means rejected.

*"My politics are short and sweet, like an old woman's dance.*
*I am in favor of a national bank."*
Abraham Lincoln, 1832[1367]

# — 21 —

# THE FINANCIAL SITUATION

The public debt of the United States in October, 1863, was $1,228,635,613.48, which was drawing an average rate of interest of three point ninety-five percent. At that time however the amount of the national debt to each person in the British government was $133.55. That of France was $61.38 while that of the United States was $44.94 to each citizen. About this time according to Confederate statements their debt amounted to $163.00 to each person. (A man with a wife and six children would owe $1304.00 to the Confederate government.) October the first, 1863, the debt of the Confederate states was $784,363,139.00. To give some idea to the cost of the war, the military attack alone on the city of Charleston on the 7th of April, 1863 cost the government $150,000,000.00. At this time the U. S. Government had treasury notes and fractional currency in circulation to the amount of $394,920,956.00, and there were in addition thereto $142,750,000.00 certificates of indebtedness in circulation.

It may not be uninteresting to the reader to know the amount of money the war has cost the United States government since its foundation; in less than a century it expanded.

1st—the war of revolution from 1775 to 1782 –$135,193,703.
2nd—Indian War in the Ohio Territory 1790
3rd—the war with the Barbary states—1803-1804
4th—Tecumsen War—1807

[1367] www.lewrockwell.com/dilorenzo/dilorenzo30.htm

5th—war with Great Britain 1812 to 1815—$107,159,000.
6th—Algerian War 1815
7th—The first Seminole War 1817
8th—the Blackhawk War of 1832
9th—the second Seminole War of 1845
10th—the Mexican War 1846-1848—$66,000,000
11th—the Mormon War 1838, 1844, and 1857-1858.
12th—the war of the rebellion 1861-1865—$3,000,000,000.

It is a striking instance, worthy of note, showing the progressiveness, magnitude and great inherent power of this nation in referring to the fact that one single attack of the fortified city of Charleston, South Carolina during this war cost half as much as all the wars the nation had had up to the time of the rebellion including the war of the revolution. The war of the rebellion surpassed in magnitude any war in history, and would doubtless have continued to the present time if the South had not become exhausted in resources and decimated in population. It was a struggle for greater stakes than ever before contended for by force of arms. In the short space of four years, it cost more lives, destroyed more property and necessitated the expenditure of more money than any other war the history records since the foundation of the world.

## National Banking

Mr. Hamilton[1368] on the 9th of January 1790, during the first session of the first Congress being then Secretary of the Treasury of the new republic, made his report on the settlement of the public debt, which consisted of three recommendations;

First - that the foreign debt of the confederacy be assumed and paid in full.

Second - that the domestic debt of the confederacy which at that time had become a synonym of worthlessness, should also be paid at its par value.

Third - that the debts incurred by the states during the revolution and remaining unpaid should be assumed and paid in full by the federal government.

---

1368 Alexander Hamilton—See pg. 101.

His first recommendation was adopted promptly and unanimously. The second was opposed by Mr. Madison[1369] and many of the anti-federalists on the ground that the domestic debt was held by speculators who bought it at a heavy discount and would gain usurious[1370] interest on their investment. This argument was met by Mr. Hamilton and his supporters urging that if only for that reason they should be paid in full which would teach the holders of the United States securities not to sell them at a discount.

With Mr. Hamilton's policy it was urged, if adopted, the national credit would be strengthened for all time to come. This recommendation as well as the third was adopted, but afterwards, reconsidered and defeated. After the adoption of the third recommendation, and its reconsideration and rejection, Mr. Hamilton secured its final adoption by a bargain which excited the deep indignation of the anti-federalists and one of the effects was to make Mr. Hamilton very much disliked and so unpopular with the anti-federalists which soured his acknowledged talents that his party deemed it prudent never to nominate him for any elective office afterwards—wherein the Secretary of the Treasury incurred the displeasure of the opposing party to the administration when a national capital was to be selected.

The federalists agreed that the capital should be established on the Potomac River (where it now stands) after remaining ten years at Philadelphia, and through a bargain and the influence of Mr. Hamilton, two of the anti-federalist members from the Potomac region agreed in turn to vote for the third resolution, which was then adopted. The immediate effect was to appreciate the credit of the United States and enrich the holders of the continental debt. This state of things was not permitted to long exist.

During the second session, which met during December 1790, Mr. Hamilton recommended the establishment of a national bank to act as financial agent of the government. This excited further party contests and involved the new question of federal powers—he was supported in this measure by the federalists, who claimed it as an incidental power to the undoubted authority to pass all laws necessary for the collection of revenues and taxes. There was a constitutional right to charter a bank for the purpose of facilitating those objects. Its

---

1369 James Madison was the 4th U.S. President and one of the Founding Fathers. He was President from 1809—1817. www.answers.com/topic/james-madison

1370 Usurious means exorbitant.

constitutionality was not denied by the opposing party, under certain circumstances, but they urged it was unnecessary, though it might be convenient, and thence it was beyond the power of Congress.

The difference of opinion of the subject engendered continued with partisan bitterness for half a century afterwards, and the same may be said that in a modified spirit between political parties until the present time. The bill for the charter of the bank passed both houses of Congress. Then the fight was renewed in opportunities and remonstrances against the president signing it, so it would become law.

The president demanded the written opinions of his Cabinet—able papers were written by the members of the Cabinet on this subject and it is doubtful whether the argument portrayed then have ever been improved upon by subsequent statesmen on that subject. Mr. Hamilton's views upon the question were adopted by Mr. Washington[1371] over Mr. Jefferson and Mr. Randolph[1372] and he signed the bill. The bank thus created continued until 1811, when on a change of parties, the anti-federalists coming into power, refused to re-charter it. Four years afterwards, however, in 1816 another national bank was chartered by Congress which caused intense strife and violent attacks by the partisans which lasted until 1836, when the bank ceased to exist.

Repeated attempts after this time were made by the party known as "loose constructionists" to re-charter that institution without success until the war of the rebellion made it necessary to issue the green-back currency which took the place of a national bank with power to make forced loans.

For the present acquirable system of national finances the country is more indebted to the late Salmon P. Chase[1373] than to any other man.

### Financial Conditions

At the outbreak of the Civil War the financial condition of the government was of great concern and consideration to Mr. Lincoln

---

[1371] George Washington—See pg. 7.

[1372] Edmund Jennings Randolph is considered one of the country's founding fathers. He served as Governor of Virginia, Secretary of State to George Washington and as the first Attorney General of the Untied States. www.nndb.com/people/099/000049949

[1373] Salmon P. Chase—See pg. 98.

and the country. The necessity to increase receipts of the government gave rise to the first legislation of Congress in 1862 and 1863, which organized the enhanced tariff duty and the vast revenue derived from the authorized system of internal revenue taxes in ten years from this inauguration (say 1863 to 1873) produced the sum of $3,739,136,870; averaging $374,000,000 per annum, besides or excluding all receipts from loans. The current expenses rendered necessary to sustain the immense army in the field and pay the interest on the rapidly growing public debt and necessitated the extension of the tax gatherers over pretty much every character of production or consumption. The tariff duties on all imports were raised, in many instances 50, 70 and 100 percent, above former rates and placed upon new commodities formerly free from taxation. A direct taxation of twenty million of dollars per annum was appropriated among the states. The income tax was the first to have ever been known in the history of the American government, but one was now levied for the first time. It imposed payment of three percent on all annual incomes over six hundred dollars, five percent on all below five thousand dollars and ten percent on the excess over five thousand dollars

On February 25, 1863 and June 3, 1864, Congress passed acts establishing the national bank system of the United States—the act of 1864 provided that the aggregate circulation of the banks so established should not exceed three hundred millions of dollars; not limiting the number of banks. That any place with a population of six thousand people or less might have a bank with a capital of not less than fifty thousand dollars, in those places with a population of between six thousand and fifty thousand must have a capital of not less than one hundred thousand dollars and those places with a population of over fifty thousand must have capital of not less than two hundred thousand dollars.

Each bank was required to deposit with the United States Treasury bonds of the national issue to the extent of one-third at least of its capital (and not less than fifty thousand dollars in any case) as security for creditors. Each bank was to report its situation quarterly to the comptroller of the currency.

As of the end of the year 1870, there were in the United States 1,627 national banks having an aggregate capital of $436,000,000 with a combined circulation of $299,720,000—being but one hundred and seventy-one thousand dollars under the limit prescribed by the bank establishing act of Congress.

The system of national banking together with the authorized issue of national bonds proved a great success and relieved the country of any embarrassment for want of funds for the war purpose, and, at the same time, was a source of immense revenue to the bankers. A person desiring to go into the banking business during the year 1863-4, with a hundred thousand dollars in gold could sell his hundred thousand dollars in the market for two hundred and fifty thousand of green-back currency, take his green-backs to the United States Treasury, exchange them for two hundred and fifty thousand dollars in bonds, deposit the bonds in the treasury for which he would draw six percent per annum interest in gold, payable semi-annually. He was then authorized to start his bank and issue ninety percent of his capital in bonds of bank currency for banking operations. Many millions were made by this system of banking and at the same time the nation was able to secure all the sinews of war necessary for its purpose. The year after Lincoln's death the public debt of the United States was greater than any time from the foundation of the government until present time. It was at that time $2,773,236,173.69. Since that time the amount has been greatly reduced. The amount of revenue alone from the income tax of 1863 was $2,741,857—1864, $20,292,733—1865, $32,050,017—1866, $71,984,160—aggregated as $127,058,767.

In addition to the above, there was collected interest on United States securities and property of citizens residing abroad during these years of $442,885. Great Britain's receipts for the years above stated respectively $54,415,000—$45,510,600—$39,930,000—$31,610,000—aggregating $171,465,600 in a time of profound peace amounting to $45,000,000 more than the United States in the time of her war.

At the close of the war, the Confederate state's government had outstanding confederate state's currency alone of $64,465,963. From the time of the first issue of this kind of currency, March 9, 1861, (first emission) $1,000,000 dollars there was a progressive decline and fall in its value. In December 1861 it took $120 to purchase $100 in specie—in 1862, $300—in 1863, $1,900—in 1864, $5,000—in March, 1865, $6000 for one dollar in specie.[1374]

---

[1374] Specie is a gold or silver coin.

The Confederate state's notes were based on the faith and credit of their government. They were made a legal tender for all debts, public and private, and it was made by their laws a felony for anybody to take it at par—the only security for its redemption being a pledge of the whole taxable resources of their people. Every one in the Confederacy was constrained to support by every motive of interest and patriotism that could influence man. The currency was nominal[1375] and was redeemable six months after peace should be restored between the Confederate government and the United States.

England was at one time fated to become temporarily an irredeemable paper money country, and her finance minister, under whose reign she became so was thus satirized in a current epigram of the day: "Of Augustus and Rome, the poets still warble. How he found it of brick and left it of marble. So of Pitt and England, we may say without vapor, that he found it of gold, and left it of paper."

The following lines on the Confederate paper currency were written by Major S. A. Jones, of the Texas brigade, shortly after the surrender of General Lee's army at Appomattox County Courthouse. This had been printed on the backs of many Confederate bills:

In Memoriam. Respectfully dedicated to the holders of Confederate Treasury notes.

Representing nothing on God's earth now,
and naught in the waters below it,
of a pledge of a nation that is dead and gone,
keep it dear friend and show it.

Too poor to possess the precious ores,
and too much of a stranger to borrow,
we issued today our promise to pay,
and hoped to redeem on the morrow.

The days rolled on and the weeks became years,
But our coffers were empty still.
Coin was so rare that the treasury quaked,
If a dollar should roll in the till.

---

1375 Nominal means not real.

We knew it had hardly a value in gold,
Yet, as gold our soldiers received it.
It gazed in ones eyes with a promise to pay,
And each patriot soldier believed it.

Keep it as it tells our history all o'er
For its birth to its dreams to the last.
Modest, and born of the angel hope
Like the hope of success—it passed.

Judging by this standard of redemption and faith it has met—peace has not been restored—and it may be well apprehended that if the Confederate arms had succeeded the people would have never submitted to the taxation requisite to the payment of so vast an amount of local currency, which never could have been made available except as a domestic circulation medium—like the continental money issued during the revolutionary war. It went into a state of orphanage because its redeemer did no longer live. There was in the case of the revolution of 1776 (unlike the case of the Confederacy) a change of allegiance of the people but no change in obligation to redeem their promises to pay—the sacred obligations incurred affecting their independence in a new form of government. One of the most shameful acts ever perpetrated by any government, this new republic of the United States was guilty by virtually repudiating her outstanding continental money and promises to pay.

The amount outstanding was $359,546,825. Congress by Act of August 4, 1790, determined that the bills of credit issued by authority of the United States should be funded in the loan providing for the full amount of the domestic debt, "at the rate of one hundred dollars in the said bills for one dollar in specie." The very initiation of the reform by the new government had its culmination in practical repudiation of its bills of credit and sacred obligations to pay its just debts. By the Act of 1790 Congress virtually resolved that to act in good faith with her citizens and discharge her promises would be unjust, impolitic and destructive of public and private confidence and of the virtue which is the basis of republican government.

Continental money was the currency the patriot soldiers the revolutionary war had been paid for six long years of service and suffering. The soldier who retained his credit notes in the hope that grateful government would sometime redeem its own credit and relieve him necessitous[1376] circumstances was eventually forced either gratuitously to give up the whole or receive the scaled amount due him under the Act of 1790. Say a soldiers pay was nine dollars (it was not so much as that) per month. He served six years. His aggregate pay was $648. This amount in paper he presented to the treasury and received therefore $648, which would give to him the full and liberal sum of fifty-four cents for each and every month of his services or one cent and eight mills per day in full compensation. There can be no doubt that this grateful liberality on the part of the new republic was appreciated by the scar worn veteran republicans.

As an instance of the appreciation of the ingratitude of the nation, this story was told by the Honorable Thomas H. Benton,[1377] of Maryland: "General George Rogers Clark[1378] who had rendered invaluable and singularly eminent services to his country during the war, being unpaid, and was ruthlessly neglected and unrecognized until in his old age. When in almost a starving condition, having lived for many years in squalid poverty, now being cared for by the charity of an aged sister, Congress at last passed a resolution of thanks to him for his services and ordered to be presented to him a handsomely mounted and engraved sword. A committee of Congress waited upon him in his far western neglected poverty stricken home, read to him the resolution, and presented the sword. Without one word in response but in order to show the extent of his appreciation of his long neglect by an ungrateful people, he took the sword in his old trembling hands, placed it across his knee, and in an effort and power unusual to one of his years, he broke the sword in two pieces. Then he rose from his seat and with tottering steps, he stooped and picked up the fragments and threw them out of the door of his cabin; then he resumed his chair and maintained a dignified silence until his astonished visitors departed from his humble home. He had no further

[1376] Necessitous means needy.

[1377] Honorable Thomas H. Benton was a five-time U.S. Senator and the father-in-law of General John Frémont. bioguide.congress.gov/scripts/biodisplay.pl?index=b000398

[1378] General George Rogers Clark (1752-1818) was the highest ranking military officer in the western frontier during the American Revolution. His younger brother, William Clark, was part of the Lewis and Clark Expedition. www.answers.com/topic/george-rogers-clark

use of his country's sword, nor the calling presence of his prosperous country's representatives to mock his old age and infirmities."

Paper money may become a necessity indispensable to any nation in an emergency and its integrity depends alone on the virtue of its people. Such an emergency for the second or third time arose in the United States government at the second revolution by the American people. There is an immense volume of it now in existence, but it is founded on a solid basis and the integrity of its redemption will never be doubted. Whatever may be said in the bad faith in some cases, our government has been guilty of in individual claims. No government had a more safe and solid system of secured credit than the United States has today and her paper is and is likely to continue at par with specie. In her prosperous condition, her immensity of power and the elevated position she occupies and is destined to occupy among the nations of the earth, the United States beyond question will never be unmindful of her obligations due to credit obtained for the promotion of her existence in the time of her trial. Henceforth it is to be hoped she will be honorably careful for the purity of her paper money and all national obligation.

It little affects the prosperity of any nation whose paper money is equal in value to specie within it own dominion, whether its circulating medium is paper credit or gold or silver, or whether its paper money is made a legal tender for all the internal public and private debts or gold and silver coin be the only standard of domestic values for the acquittance for commercial obligations. Today there is more concern and agitation in the United States about the standard of the precious metals and the coinage of one of them at the depreciated number of grains to the dollar than there is about the legal tender provision of paper money.

When the war began, the present necessity for prompt action excused the president as he supposed, for securing bond or security for the faithful performance of the duties, and by the orders issued by either of the parties named as authorized to act in case of inability to consult with others. Mr. Lincoln also directed the Secretary of the Treasury[1379] to advance without requiring security, two million of dollars of the public money to the Honorable John A. Dix,[1380] George

---

[1379] The Secretary of State was Salmon P. Chase.

[1380] John A. Dix—See pg. 63.

Opdyke,[1381] and Richard M. Blatchford[1382] of New York, to be used by them to requisition as should be directly necessary upon the consequent military and naval measures necessary for the defense and support of the government, requiring them only to act without compensation and to report their transactions when duly called upon.

If there had not been so essential of an account as the great number of persons who had been disloyal to the government in the different departments, it would have been dangerous to have transacted this business through the regular channels, through the routine of office. For this presidential reason alone, Mr. Lincoln deemed it proper to confide the important trust to citizens favorably known for their ability, loyalty, integrity and patriotism. These orders had to be transmitted by private messenger who pursued devious ways and circuitous routes to the seacoast cities inland across the state of Maryland, Pennsylvania and Ohio, taking in the northern lakes in order to reach their destination.

These orders and directions were without the authority of law but who will at this day doubt that had it not been for these and similar measures taken at that crisis, the government would have been overthrown during the first quarter of the first year of Mr. Lincoln's administration. These trusts were fulfilled with promptness and fidelity, but on the 30th day of April, 1862, Congress passed a resolution of censure on the late Secretary of War Mr. Cameron[1383] for investing Alexander Cummings[1384] with the control of large sums of public money without authority.

In response to this resolution Mr. Lincoln came promptly forward and in a message dated May 29, 1862, after stating what he had done and authorized to be done and giving his reasons for so doing, he concluded his message in these characteristically magnanimous remarks: "Congress should see that I should be wanting equally in candor and in justice if I should leave the censure expressed in this resolution to rest exclusively or chiefly upon Mr. Cameron. The same sentiment is unanimously entertained by the heads of departments

---

1381 George Opdyke—See pg. 257.

1382 Richard M. Blatchford was an attorney and financier who lived in New York. www.ronulrich.com/rfuged/nti87818.htm.

1383 Simon Cameron—See pg. 97.

1384 Alexander Cummings was third territorial governor of Colorado and a civil war general. He used his influence to be appointed to the War Department as a special purchasing agent. search.intlius.com/Alexander-Cummings-(territorial-governor)

who participated in the proceedings which the House of Representatives has censured. It is due for Mr. Cameron to say that although he fully approved the proceedings, they were not moved or suggested by himself, and that not only the president but other heads of the departments were at least equally responsible for whatever error, wrong or failure was committed in the premises."

*"The South had gained the monopoly of an article which had come to be a necessity of the world. Europe must have cotton and she could get it only from the South.... Nay the North itself could not live without cotton. Cotton was king."*[1385]

# — 22 —

# IMPORTANCE OF COTTON

The consumption of cotton in Europe is very great and about fifty-five percent of the grand total is consumed in England. The crop in the United States then amounted to 3,797,000 bales worth $247,000,000. The following year, when the war was inevitable, the crop was worth but the sum of $189,000,000 and the demand was in excess of the supply. This state of things continued until long after the termination of the war. The crop of 1880 was 5,746,414 bales.

The great and increasing demand for it towards the close of the last century caused the Americans to turn their attention to its production, until at the breaking out of the civil war, it had become the stable product of the southern United States and cotton was regarded as "king" of the nation's products. Such as had been the success of producing it, that the exportation of it which was 138,328 bales in 1792 (there being no exportation before 1790) amounted just before the war of the rebellion to four-fifths of the enormous quantity in all Europe, and in 1870, but thirty percent of it consumed on that continent was furnished by the United States. The relative manufacture of cotton may be estimated by the number of spindles employed which are established at 40,000,000 throughout the world, of which more that 21,000,000 are employed in Great Britain, 5,000,000 in France, and 6,000,000 in the United States.

---

[1385] Harpers Pictorial History of the Great Rebellion, pg. 124.

A brief history of this great staple as a commercial commodity may not be deemed improper in this connection. From the most reliable information we could gather it was brought to Spain by the Mahommedan[1386] conqueror of that country. Pliny,[1387] early in the Christian era, mentions its growth in upper Egypt on the side of Arabia "where robes for the Egyptian priests were cotton." From Spain it spread to other parts of south Europe but to this day it has never proved an article of great importance in agricultural commerce of those countries. India supplied the greatest amounts of cotton fabrics used in Europe until the rise of the English manufacturers in the latter part of the last century. Cotton was introduced into England about the close of the 16th century. A great amount of Flemmings, on account of religious persecution about this time, fled to England and established manufacturers at Bolton and Manchester. Until the brilliant improvements in its manufacture which long afterwards followed, it was merely a domestic production and yielded but a domestic trade.

The first improvement or invention was a spinning jenny, invented by James Hargreaves[1388] in 1767; then came the spinning frame, by Sir Richard Arkwright,[1389] in 1769. This was followed by the mule jenny, invented by Samuel Compton,[1390] in 1779; and it was succeeded by the power loom, invented by Cartwright[1391] in 1787. At first the raw cotton for England's manufactures was obtained from the Levant[1392] in the south of Europe, with lesser quantities from India and Bourbon. Eventually the United States supplied the principal demand of Great Britain. The whole of the product of cotton in the United States was in the South and when the war broke out it was the backbone—the

---

1386 Mahommedan refers to the Islamic prophet Mohammad. www.answers.com/topic/mohammedan-2

1387 Pliny was an ancient Roman statesman. www.eyewitnesstohistory.com/Pompeii.htm

1388 James Hargreaves was an English inventor credited with the spinning Jenny—a machine where a number of spindles were placed side by side so that several threads could be spun at once. www.answers.com/topic/james-hargreaves

1389 Sir Richard Arkwright was the English inventor of the spinning frame, a machine making possible the production of inexpensive yarn into calico and greatly expanding the cotton industry. www.answers.com/topic/richard-arkwright

1390 Samuel Compton was the English inventor of the spinning mule that spun yarn into muslin. inventors.about.com/library/inventors/blspinningmule.htm

1391 Edmund Cartwright was credited with inventing mechanical weaving and wool combing machines. inventors.about.com/od/cstartinventors/a/power-loom.htm

1392 The Levant were biblical lands in western Asia lying between Egypt and Mesopotamia. www.answers.com/topic/levant-1

banking capital upon which the Confederacy relied for support and financial credit to defray the expenses of the war. The cotton produced had to run the chances of the blockade and would have been inadequate for its purposes without the indirect cooperation of the British government, in effecting a system of blockade running that would accommodate the necessities of the Confederacy and at the same time furnish England with the means of keeping her immense manufacturers supplied with cotton.

The policy of the administration was to break the backbone of the Confederacy by destroying the traffic in cotton with foreign governments. The cotton market was the Confederacy's whole dependence for national credit and for being furnished with the munitions of war, with funds to pay their troops and the incidental expenses connected with the war.

After a time the executive was permitted to carry out his policy by authorizing under certain restrictions, the cotton which was impracticable for the Confederacy and Great Britain to run through the blockade to foreign ports, to be brought through the lines and disposed of as other commercial products of the United States.

This policy adopted by Mr. Lincoln gave great dissatisfaction at first to a portion of the representatives of the Republican Party. Much opposition was manifested against it. This became a source of immense revenue to the government (likewise to many individuals) and yielded little financial support to the Confederacy, being the means of weakening the credit of the national southern prospects.

It may be well doubted if this policy had not been adopted and carried out to a moderate degree of success, the Confederacy would have succeeded in establishing and maintaining its independence as a free and independent nation, not withstanding the disparity in point of numbers engaged in the strife. No people ever fought for supremacy with greater courage and desperation and greater conviction of right—irrepressible on both sides of the conflict in the history of the known world.

Contraband trade—trading in such goods or products, imported or exported as would afford aid and comfort to the enemy—was expressly prohibited. Cotton, therefore, occupied an anomalous[1393] and peculiar status, so far as belligerent rights of traffic were concerned,

---

1393 Anomalous means abnormal.

when recognized by either of the belligerent powers engaged. Restrictions were by law placed on trading for cotton in the South, establishing that nothing contraband should be given in exchange for it, which greatly embarrassed the trade, and afforded facilities and inducements to the blockade runners and encouraging trade with foreign governments.

Later Mr. Lincoln became so thoroughly imbued[1394] with the policy of stripping the South of this main resource and credit afforded by the cotton crop, that he was willing to permit individuals to have brought it into the Union lines and allow the payment for it to be in arms and munitions of war or any other prohibited commodity believing that as soon as the South was deprived of this resource, their power would be so weaken as to make capitulation[1395] a speedy necessity, resulting in the termination of further bloodshed.

After General Grant was appointed commander of all the armies, Mr. Lincoln sought to interfere as little as possible with the military affairs of police, as will be shown by the following letter written by him to General Grant:

*Executive Mansion, Washington, April 30, 1864*
*Lieutenant General Grant:*

*Not expecting to see you before the spring campaign opens, I wish to express in this way my entire satisfaction with what you have done up to this time, so far as I understand it. The particulars of your plan I neither know, nor seek to know. You are vigilant and self-reliant and restraints or constraints upon you, while I am very anxious that any great disaster or capture of our men in any great numbers shall be avoided, I know that these points are less likely to escape your attention than they would be mine.*

*If there be anything wanting which would be in my power, do not fail to let me know it. And now with a brave army and a just cause, may God sustain you.*

*Yours very truly*
*(Signed) A. Lincoln*

General Grant had hitherto concurred in Mr. Lincoln's cotton policy, so much so that General Grant had given a permit to bring out cotton from within the Confederate lines to his own father. Large permits had been given by Mr. Lincoln to Mr. Maddox of Maryland and

---

[1394] Imbued means impressed.
[1395] Capitulation means surrender.

was also given to General Singelton,[1396] of Illinois, to go through the lines to Richmond to arrange for the purchase of all the cotton and tobacco remaining in the Confederacy they could possibly obtain. The Honorable E. B. Washburne[1397] of Illinois had always opposed this cotton policy. He was the intimate friend of General Grant and with a single exception had been General Grant's most earnest supporter and defender throughout the war. For some reason, which has never been satisfactorily explained, Mr. Washburne determined to thwart the cotton/tobacco scheme and to that end visited Mr. Lincoln. They differed widely as to the propriety of the measure and the interview terminated in an unfriendly discussion the result of which Mr. Washburne left the White House in no amiable honor, saying with feeling "I will show you that I will see about this." He then took the train to the headquarters of the army and had an interview with General Grant which resulted in the general's promptly issuing an order rendering Mr. Lincoln's passes and permits inoperative and of no avail. Mr. Washburne based his opposition on the ground that it was a palpable[1398] violation of the Non-Intercourse Act[1399] of Congress approved July 17, 1861 and the president's proclamation pursuant thereof August 18, 1861.

The trade of cotton, tobacco, resin, etc. products of the South was carried on generally under permits from Hanson A. Risley[1400] the sole general agent for their purchase in the insurrectionary states. A copy of the permits in blank we were here given with the usual endorsement appended thereto by the president:

---

[1396] General James Washington Singleton was born in Winchester, Virginia. He moved to Mt, Sterling, Illinois where he was an attorney and a colleague of Mr. Lincoln. He was also an associate of the author, Ward Hill Lamon. Winchester-Frederick County Historical Society Journal, "Local Area Confidants of Abraham Lincoln" pgs. 9 - 11 & 28.

[1397] Honorable Elihu B. Washburne—See pg. 91.

[1398] Palpable means obvious.

[1399] Congressional Act declared that "all goods, and chattels, wares and merchandise" coming from a state proclaimed by President Lincoln in insurrection and going into other parts of the United States should be forfeited. www.supreme.justice.com/us/80/358/case.html

[1400] Hanson A. Risley was from New York. He managed the contracts and special permits in the Treasury Department. The plan was designed to bring down the price of gold prices and at the same time strengthen the Yankee greenbacks. www.shout.net/~bigred/mc080209.html

*"I, Hanson A. Risley, agent for the purchase of products for the insurrectionist states, on behalf of the government of the United States at ____ do hereby certify that I have agreed to purchase from ____, ____ bales of cotton, which product is represented, are or will be near the national military line, in the state of _____, on or before the ____ day of ______ and which it is stipulated will be delivered to _________ at ________ unless he is prohibited from so doing by the authority of the United States; I therefore request safe conduct for the said __________, his agents and his means of transportation and said products from such point or near the national military line, to ______ where the product so transported are to be sold and delivered to ______ agent and company under the stipulation referred to above and pursuant to regulations prescribed by the Secretary of the Treasury.*

*Signed) Hanson A. Risley, Supt., Spl. At. TD*[1401] *which paper was required to be endorsed by the president as follows:*

*"An authorized agent of the Treasury Department having with the approval of the Secretary of the Treasury contracted for the cotton above mentioned and the party having agreed to sell and deliver the same to such agent. It is ordered that the cotton moving in compliance with and for fulfillment of said contract and being transported to said agent or under his direction shall be free from seizure or detention by any officers of the government and commanders of military departments, districts, posts and detachments, naval stations, gunboats, flotillas, and fleets will observe this order and give the said ____________ his agents and his transports free and unmolested passage for the purpose of seeing the said cotton or any part thereof, through the line, except blockade lines, (it not be intended in any event to violate the blockade) and safe conduct within our lines while the same is moving in strict compliance with the regulations of the Secretary of the Treasury and for the fulfillment of the said contract with the agent of the government.*

*Signed,*
*Abraham Lincoln*

The product then by the treasury regulation was to be delivered to the local treasury agent. It was then to be sold by him in the market, one-fourth of the proceeds of the sale to be retained by the agent for the United States and the other three-fourths to be delivered to the contractor.[1402]

---

1401 Abbreviations stand for Special Agent, Treasury Department.

1402 The author of this manuscript, Ward Hill Lamon, fails to mention here that he also was involved in cotton permits. A letter to Mr. Lamon from David O. Laws dated January 18, 1865 refers to "the taking of 50,000 to 100,000 bales of cotton with the understanding that we take three-fourths of the net proceeds in 7.30s or other government bonds."

*A summary of the British Parliament's feelings can be summed up as follows: "the strong antipathy to the North, the strong sympathy to the South, and the passionate wish to have cotton."*

Minister Lord Granville, British Parliament[1403]

# — 23 —

# FOREIGN DIPLOMACY

Immediately after the passage of the act of July 13 closing the ports, a course strongly urged by Mr. Lincoln, he directed the Secretary of State to "inform our minister at London that since his interview with Lord John Russell, the Congress of the United States has by law asserted the right of this government to close the ports of this country which have been seized by the insurgents." He further authorized Mr. Seward to inform Mr. Adams[1404] that he understood and appreciated fully the purpose of Lord Russell in connecting the measure, when it was in prospect, with what had taken place in regard to a law of New Grenada, in Lord Russell's gratuitous remarks to our minister on that occasion were unmistakable in their intent and import. They were significant and required no special illustration, interpretation, or translation.

Mr. Lincoln also desired her majesty's government to know that he was in full accord with Congress in the principal of the law which authorized the closing of the ports seized by the insurgents, and he further distinctly desired it to be understood in Great Britain as well as elsewhere that he intended to put it into execution and to maintain it with all the means at his command, at hazard of whatever consequenc-

---

1403 Abraham Lincoln: A Biography, pg. 189. Lord Granville was Sir William George Granville Vernaldes Vernon Harcourt was a British lawyer and liberal politician. He often condemned the widespread support of the Confederacy by the British. www.1911encyclopedia.org/Sir_William_George_Granville_Harcourt

1404 Charles Francis Adams—See. pg. 27.

es and whenever the safety of this nation required it. From this time until the close of the rebellion, the English government evinced[1405] a spirit of hostility in all her diplomacy towards the United States. To a faithful observer, no doubts would be entertained that England on the slightest cause would have declared war against the United States in her crippled condition had not other conditions made such course undesirable—the known friendly relations with Russia with the United States, and her sympathy manifested in behalf of the Union in the struggle going on may have been one of the unfavorable conditions that influenced her majesty's government to neither recognize the Confederate states government nor declare war against the United States on her own account. No man in either government realized and understood the state of things more fully than Mr. Lincoln. He was constantly apprehensive of danger from this source. He believed his course was the true one, however, and if the worst should come, he was ready to accept the issue. Mr. Seward was more timid. He sought conciliatory measures. Mr. Seward was a cautious diplomat. He tempered the wind to the shorn lamb. He sought in every possible way to appease the British arrogance, and the result was that our government did not order the ports to be closed, but they were blockaded.

Mr. Lincoln soon saw and realized what he supposed from the first was the purpose of the English government—the establishment, throughout the war, of the English ports of Nassau, Bermuda, and Halifax as entre-points for elicit traffic from the rebels and as shelters for rebel cruiser to harass and destroy our commerce. This was made the means for opening the English ports throughout the world to the *Alabama*,[1406] and such like rovers of her class, which were made to sweep our merchant ships from the ocean for the aggrandizement[1407] of England.

The United States submitted to many like indignities in deference to the royal arrogance of England during the struggle for the restoration of the Union. One of England's greatest statesmen, Sir

---

[1405] Evinced means exhibited.

[1406] *Alabama* was a 220 foot cruiser with 148 men and 8 guns. The British built was credited with destroying sixty Union ships during the war. Warships of the Civil War Navies, pg. 209.

[1407] Aggrandizement means embellishment.

Vernon Harcourt,[1408] in his amazement in our submission and pusillanimity,[1409] warned his government against proceeding too far in its demands: "For," said he, "what we have most to fear is not Americans will yield too little, but that we shall accept too much."

The *Alabama* was a rebel cruiser that as built by the Laird's[1410] of Birkenhead, England, for the Confederate states' government under the superintendency of Captain James D. Bullock,[1411] who was the agent of the Confederacy. The apprehension of the American agents that the vessel was intended as a free-booter was during the process of her construction repeatedly brought to the attention of the English authorities. Remonstrances[1412] were urged by the American minister against the vessel's being allowed to be launched from an English port for the purpose of despoiling and plundering American commerce. No attention was paid to this protest and England in palpable[1413] violation of international law, and in bad faith permitted the vessel to sail by a "ruse" under pretense of making a trial trip with a large party of ladies and gentlemen on her on the 28th of July, 1862. She was permitted to go out of English waters. It was then conveniently arranged that a tugboat should meet the ship in the channel and take off the guests, while the free-booter, now called the *Hull 290*,[1414] that being the number of her register in the yard where she was built and was so called up to the time of her leaving the yard, proceeded on her voyage to the island of Terceira,[1415] among the Azores, where a transport had preceded her with war materials. Captain Raphael Semmes,[1416] with his officers, carried by the "bahama" met her.

---

1408 Sir William George Granville Venaldes Vernon Harcourt was a British lawyer and liberal politician. He often condemned the widespread support of the Confederacy by the British. www.answers.com/topic/william-vernon-harcourt.

1409 Pusillanimity means cowardliness.

1410 Laird's Ship Builders—British firm that built the *Alabama*. Warships of the Civil War Navies, pg. 252.

1411 Captain James D. Bullock was a Confederate who organized the receipt of 18 ships from the British to trade cotton for arms and munitions. Lincoln and the Civil War, pg. 275

1412 Remonstrances are protests.

1413 Palpable means obvious.

1414 *Hull 290* was the official name of the *Alabama*. Warships of Civil War Navies, pg. 209.

1415 Terceira is an island located in the Azores in the Atlantic Ocean.

1416 Captain Raphael Semmes—See pg. 301.

These vessels arrived August 20, 1862, at Terceira. The transfer was completed on the following Saturday night and on Sunday morning. Outside of the marine league the two vessels were lashed together and the transfer was made of the armament and sorties. The cruiser was then and afterwards known as the *Alabama* under the confederate state flag, and she was put in commission. Men from the crews of the several ships then in port signed articles and formed the nucleus of the *Alabama*'s crew—the full compliment being made up of the crews of prize vessels. They then commenced the cruise of 22 months—the like of which is not recorded in history.

The ravages up to this time of the *Sumter*[1417] on American commerce had been great. This was haled by friendly welcome and this vessel was supplied in British ports. Her ravages upon American commerce were now supplemented by the *Alabama* and *Florida*,[1418] English built and manned chiefly by English men.

These cruisers, to some extent, became masters of the seas in piracy, directed against American commerce, fostered and protected by British connivance.[1419] This soon aroused the indignation of Mr. Lincoln and the whole country. The indignation was greatly increased and aggravated by the conduct of the British government in excluding all United States cruisers from English ports in China. Not withstanding, the seas of that empire were then infested by pirates and the whole commercial world was interested in their suppression.

Little hospitality was extended to our national ships in English ports anywhere—while it was notorious that semi-pirates and buccaneers with no recognized nationality—substantially English vessels sailing under the Confederate flag—were plundering and practically destroying our commerce to the injury to the United States and the benefit of Great Britain. This covert state of hostility by a pretended friendly nation causing such wrongs and outrages if committed in a time of profound peace would have produced and justified a war with England which might have resulted in more calamity and havoc to English commerce than has ever been dreamed

---

1417 *Sumter* captured and destroyed 18 Union ships. Warships of the Civil War Navies, pg. 214.

1418 *Florida* was a 191 foot ship with a crew of 52 and seven guns. She captured thirty-three Union prizes. She was sunk in Newport News on November 28, 1864. Warships of the Civil War Navies, pg. 211.

1419 Connivance means passive consent.

of in English philosophy and diplomacy. The condition of the federal government was then such that it was forced to forebear and open rupture or to seek that redress due for British impudence and oppression, humiliating as was the trial, the United States government had to tamely submit to the indignity, but doubtless will not soon forget the insult.

To the majority of the Union people of the United States it would require proof as strong as holy writ to convince them of the propriety of the course pursued by the British government in the face of the fact that the English capital was largely engaged in the illicit traffic with the Confederates and in running and evading the blockade—menacing at every step the federal action by unfriendly conduct of her ministry—never putting forth an arm to prevent, but with characteristic craft connived a tall scheme that militated[1420] against the success of the Union cause.

The Union American people have no reason for admiration, nor are they under grateful obligation to the administration of Palmerston[1421] and Russell,[1422] during their terrible struggle.

Fifteen millions of dollars was afterwards awarded against England[1423] and was paid to the United States by her for the deprivations[1424] committed by the *Alabama* and other cruisers outfitted within her realm.

Now, when the dark days are passed and peace and prosperity are again restored, it is a source of pride and gratification that in addition to this award our navy without the assistance of privateers (England's special admiration) captured more than thirty millions of dollars worth of property engaged in illicit traffic and running the blockade, a greater portion of which was English capital.

Many distinguished American statesmen advocated the privateer retaliatory process—Mr. Lincoln ever cautious and firm, maintained a conservative course and would commit himself to no scheme or policy that would unnecessarily endanger the national welfare. He realized

---

1420 Militated means to effect.

1421 Henry John Temple Palmerston, known as Lord Palmerston was the Prime Minister of the British government. Lincoln and the Civil War, pg. 92, and The Two American Presidents, pg. 294.

1422 Lord John Russell—See pg. 128.

1423 The award was decided by the courts on September 14, 1872. www.brainyhistory.com/topics/c/civil.html

1424 Deprivations are losses.

that there was a limit, however, to American forbearance, but was slow to act on this important matter notwithstanding the significant sense of the American people expressed by the act of Congress on the 3rd of March, 1863.[1425] He was heard to say about this time, that he was in doubt whether Great Britain was inspired most by a spirit of unscrupulous greed, her love for our enemies, or her enmity[1426] to us.

Russia with her fleet already in American waters was a friend of the United States government and her demonstration without doubt deterred Great Britain from taking a decided stand in favor of the South, by encouraging her belligerent rights and involving us in a war with England on slightest justification or provocation. At this time the United States had many sympathizers among the people of England, but the natural grasping disposition of that powerful government would never have hesitated to have pounced down upon this government crippled as she was where so great a stake might have been won but for the silent and protecting care of the friendly power of Russia well prepared for and indifferent to a naval fight with the most powerful nation on earth.

The real disposition of England towards the United States during her embarrassment is exemplified in her course on the occasion of the first pretense of trouble and annoyance in the matter of the mail on the *Peterhoff*,[1427] a vessel which had been captured as a prize and the mail turned over to the prize commissioner's office. The prize court had directed that the mail should be opened in order to see what letters were enclosed relating to the cargo on board the ship, and requested that the Secretary of the Navy could open the packages and open such letters as appeared to relate to the cargo on board or to the assignee mentioned in the manifest and to take charge of the residue of the mail with the view of forwarding it to its destination. With this request or direction the English counsul in New York, Mr. Archibald,[1428] refused to acquiesce and protested against the direction

---

1425 The Enrollment Act required enrollment of every male citizen and those immigrants who had filed for citizenship who were between the ages of 20 and 45 for service in the Union Army. www.encyclopedia/com/doc/1G2-3407400085.html

1426 Enmity means hatred.

1427 *Peterhoff* was a British a warship that captured the Union ship *Vanderbilt* off the coast of St. Thomas on February 25, 1862. Warships of the Civil War Navies, pg. 80.

1428 Sir Edward Mortimer Archibald served for 26 years as British consul to New York. www.biographi.ca/009004-119.01-e/php?&id_nbr=5343

of the court. He immediately informed Lord Lyons,[1429] her majesty's minister at Washington, who immediately wrote to Secretary of State Seward, remonstrating against the action of the court and asking the secretary to telegraph orders to stop it. This the secretary declined to do, alleging that it was not the providence of the State Department and it would be an unwarrantable interference for him to do so. Mr. Seward said that the court would not likely be governed or influenced by anything he might do on the subject of naval concern. He, however, advised the Secretary of the Navy[1430] to send word to the court to give up the mail. The Secretary of the Navy refused to do this and urged that it would be a palpable[1431] violation of international law, the judge being supposed to know his duty it might be regarded as impertinence[1432] of him to interfere in the matter. The Secretary of the Navy insisted that if the court gave up the mail without explanation, it would in all probability destroy the best and perhaps the only evidence that the vessel was a proper prize. The best evidence thereof was to be found in the mail bags, and the surrender of the mail bags would work great wrong to the government as well as to the captors of the vessel.

Previous to this time the Secretary of State had some correspondence from Lord Lyons on the subject of the mail on captured vessels. It would seem that the state department was somewhat embarrassed by the case in point in view of the correspondence, for he had virtually pledged the government that the mail should be given up without search, which was a concession if officially made of abandoning of national rights that would be most injurious to the navy and country while engaged in war. Lord Lyons presumed upon the correspondence whether official or unofficial and that it had been read and received as authority in Parliament and our government would be held to the promises made therein. The correspondence on the part of Mr. Seward as Lord Lyons knew was not an executive order, nor had it the force and effect of an act of Congress or treaty stipulation and was in no sense an administrative measure. The law on the subject of search is well settled, not only by the decisions of courts involving international rights in regard to it, but the founders of this government foresaw the necessity of a statute providing for just such a case, and

---

1429 Lord Lyons—See pg. 121.
1430 Giddeon Welles—See pg. 101.
1431 Palpable means obvious.
1432 Impertinence means inappropriate.

enacted the law of 1789 in these words: "All papers, charter parties, bills of ladings, passports and other writings whatsoever found on board any ships which shall be taken shall be carefully preserved and the originals sent to the courts of justice for maritime affairs." This law was reenacted and confirmed by Congress in 1800, and by a number of subsequent enactments. The imbroglio[1433] became a question of serious interest.

Mr. Lincoln was greatly concerned, not only about Mr. Seward's correspondence but how Mr. Seward and the country could be relieved of the consequences of it. Mr. Lincoln most deeply sympathized with Mr. Seward, but was at a loss to see his way out of the difficulty. He did not want to see the efficiency of the navy impaired nor yield a right that would result injuriously to our nation's interests. He inquired if Lord Lyons for the British government had abandoned the right of search in case of war. The response was that he had not, but Mr. Seward said he had no doubt that he would agree to do so. When the whole thing came to be explained Mr. Seward's only justification consisted of a disposition to pacify the unfriendly feeling of Great Britain which he knew to be hostile at this time. And it was his constant labor and he considered it his bounden[1434] duty to placate that government in their demands as far as possible. He made the extraordinary concession in the interest of peace. The chairman of foreign relations in the Senate, Mr. Sumner,[1435] was consulted by Mr. Lincoln. He had great confidence in Mr. Sumner's sagacity[1436] and familiarity with the questions of international law. Mr. Sumner was clearly of the opinion that most important right had been compromised by the concession; but the argument of Mr. Seward that the British government was sensitive and that if we opened and examined the mails they would surely avail themselves of this as a pretense and justification to declare war. Mr. Seward prevailed because Mr. Lincoln

---

[1433] Imbroglio means difficult situation.

[1434] Bounden means binding.

[1435] Charles Sumner was from Massachusetts and educated at Harvard College. He was an eloquent speaker, a lawyer and a member of the Whig Party. He was a Radical Republican U.S. Senator. Following a passionate speech in the Senate in May, 1856, he was severely beaten over the body by the cane of leading abolitionist proponent Preston Brooks. Sumner suffered greatly from the beating, but eventually returned to the Senate. Two Roads to Sumter, pg. 119 and Appleton's Cyclopaedia of American Biography, Vol. V., pgs. 744—750

[1436] Sagacity means keen judgment.

was very apprehensive of war with that power and yielded under the pressure of expediency, humiliating as it was, to avert the consequences of the threatening attitude that England had assumed.

Lord Lyons prevailed in his unreasonable and unjust demands and the *Peterhoff* mails were surrendered. Even this did not satisfy the British Minister, but he must demand and receive further explanation and apology for the violation of the sacredness of neutrality committed at Key West on the *Peterhoff*. The policy adopted of the immunity of search stimulated and encouraged an immense commerce to spring up at the neutral port of Matamoras, Mexico. The trade was principally illicit with the rebels of the South at Brownsville, Texas with a guarantee of immunity of the mails. Very shortly after this time a line of British mail packets to Matamoras was established. The *Peterhoff* was one of the line, and when captured she was an experimental advanced steamer of the proposed line. She had been an old rebel blockade runner. This line was secure from danger now in taking on mail and taking it to a neutral port, consequently it was enabled and did carry letters and contraband freight licensed by the subterfuge[1437] of diplomacy to the insurgent regions of the southern Confederacy.

This however is not the only instance during the civil war that the government of the United States yielded to the unreasonable demands of Great Britain solely in the spirit of conciliation and as a necessity to avert the dangerous, threatening belligerent tendencies characterizing the conduct of that government throughout the long period of America trouble. The whole scheme of search diplomacy was deliberately planned on the part of the English representative, as Mr. Lincoln was afterwards led to believe and acknowledge, to evade the blockade and open to the rebels free communication abroad through the English mails by way of the Rio Grande River. Mr. Lincoln now saw that the situation was such that he was powerless to prevent this communication effected by strategy and fraud on the part of England for the benefit of the Confederacy and to the great detriment of the United States government. The only way left open to prevent it was to effect a treaty with the Mexican Republic by which he could blockade the Rio Grande River, which at the time might have easily been effected.

[1437] Subterfuge means deception.

Here he was met with another necessity for conciliation in placating Louis Napoleon[1438] of France, who was sustaining and supporting the *sio-disant*[1439] empire of Maximillian,[1440] and he deemed it prudent to forego the chances of this mode of avoidance of his pending troubles in this particular time to avoid a war with France, another unfriendly power. After the mails of the *Peterhoff* had been given up the vessel itself or its appraised value was restored to her owners, the want of that evidence to condemn her which had been lost by restoring the mails containing the only proof available for her libel. In a case in the English courts after the war was over, involving a question about the Matamoras line of steamers, it was made evidence that the *Peterhoff* was a proper subject of prize and that the mails contained the proof that would have assured her condemnation in the American courts. This ungenerous strategic diplomacy on the part of the British government forced upon and for prudential reasons acquiesced in by the United States in her embarrassed and crippled condition cost the United States perhaps one hundred thousand soldiers and millions of dollars besides prolonging the war for a period long beyond the time it would have lasted otherwise. In this England ignominiously[1441] made traffic and gain to the amount of many thousand of millions of dollars. It mocked at our weakness and like hungry wolves fed on our calamity and feasted on our misfortune.

It is but justice however to acknowledge, and it is done with pride and gratitude, that the Royal Victoria, Queen of England,[1442] and her equally noble consort Prince Albert[1443] together with the Duke of Southerland the Right Honorable John Bright,[1444] Mr. Mill,[1445] with a few others, with a large class of the common or middle class of Great Britain sympathized with the North. This sympathy was the exception and not the rule in that kingdom. The persons just named, the Queen included, were however powerless for good in the matter of

---

1438 Louis Napoleon Bonaparte—See pg. 2.

1439 *Sio-disant* means pretend.

1440 Maximillian was Emperor of Mexico. The U.S. Government refused to recognize his government. www.infoplease.com/cele/people/A0832311.html

1441 Ignominiously means dishonorably.

1442 Queen Victoria—See pg. 169.

1443 Prince Albert was the husband of Queen Victoria. hstory1800v.about.com/od/leaders/a/prince-albert-html.htm

1444 Right Honorable John Bright was British radical and Liberal statesman. www.absoluteastronomy.com/topics.John_Bight

1445 John Stuart Mill was a liberal British politician. *New York Times*, May 7, 1865.

government control and direction, her majesty occupying about the same humiliating position to her government that Mr. Lincoln at one time acknowledged in his that was "he had very little influence in his administration." We are forced to contend ourselves with the reflection that it is natural for all aristocrats to oppose all republics and all governments by the people, and they usually manifest their hatred to democracy by preying on its misfortune and contributing to its downfall as a type of the aristocratic and be it said autocratic appreciation of our war and our rights in English circles just after the fall of the southern Confederacy. We here refer to the indignantly elegant vent of pent up malignantly[1446] felt for the North published in the *London Evening Herald* a leading journal of English aristocracy.

In October 1862 the Spanish Minister Senor Don Gabriel Garcia y Tassara[1447] set up the claim that the Dominion of Spain extended six miles instead of three from the coast of Cuba. It was at first regarded with but little apprehension by the administration but owing to the persistency of the minister's claim it became a serious question not so much as to the international rule in such case but how to dispose of the question without provoking a war with Spain or to surrender rights long since settled by international law and universal usage. There was no principle or rule better settled by common consent and the practice of maritime nations than that a marine league of three miles off the open sea was the extent of sovereign dominion. The demand bore on its face a suspicion of collusion and a simultaneous action of the minister of Great Britain on the subject germane to the question at this time and gave strength to such a conclusion. If this claim had been conceded it would have afforded wonderful protection to the Confederates of the South and given great facilities and immunity to blockade runners, in which the English people were greatly interested and in which many of them were actively engaged. The claim of the Spanish Minister was based upon the principle that the maritime jurisdiction of every sovereignty extends the length of a cannon shot from the shore and claimed that she had fixed the limit for herself at six miles without making general or specific arrangements for the purpose with other states, and this done in the face of settled

---

1446 Malignantly means evil.

1447 Senor Don Gabriel Garcia y Tassara was her Catholic Majesty of Spain. www.latinamericanstudies.org/19-century/US-Spain-Cuba-1864.pdf

provision of law that the jurisdiction of a state extends a distance of a marine league or cannon range beyond its shore.

True a marine league is a fixed and definite distance—a cannon range cannot be fixed except by a conventional agreement for the determination of jurisdictional domain. Mr. Lincoln took this view of the question, but said little, and let Mr. Seward, the Secretary of State, the Secretary of the Navy and the Spanish Minister settle it. The result was very much to the chagrin of the Secretary of the Navy,[1448] a submission of the question to the arbitration of the king of Belgium,[1449]with a proposition for a convention of nations to settle the question which fortunately delayed the settlement of the issue between the United States and Spain. Mr. Lincoln in a general conversation said he thought the Spanish government had chosen a very inopportune time for the settlement of this question, considering the friendly relations hitherto existing between the governments. He admitted that the improvements in modern ordinance affecting of range of cannon ball might be discussed to advantage, and in future settled by treaty stipulation or a convention of nations, but he was grieved that Spain should seek this opportunity to embarrass us in our misfortunes by giving such an inopportune, unparalleled, novel interpretation to the laws of nations. It seemed, he said, that Spain and England both were just ready to jump on us and both had been seeking an excuse to do so.

It is a strange coincidence that Mr. Stuart,[1450] her Britannic majesty's charge d'affairs, on the 10th of October at the same time this correspondence was going on with Spain in regard to gun shot range and dominion, should write a letter to our Secretary of State expressing apprehension that the steamer *Bermuda*[1451] (a vessel in the maritime prize court) might be purchased by the secretary and taken for the use of the Naval Department prior to her condemnation, and suggestion to remonstrance against it. Mr. Seward promptly responded to this, without examination into the case, unguardedly said unofficially and admitted that Mr. Stuart's apprehension was

---

1448 Giddeon Welles—See pg. 101.

1449 King Leopold I of Belgium served 34 years as king, from 1831 to 1865. www.absoluteastronomy.com/topics/leopold_I_of_Belgium

1450 William Stuart served as charge d'affairs in Washington, D. C. www.ocean.otr.usm.edu/~w416373/ps%2033/british%20mediation.pdf

1451 *Bermuda* was a 226 foot blockade runner captured off the Bahamas by the Union ship *Mercedita*. Warships of the Civil War Navies, pg. 222.

unfounded, as such a measure would afford ground for serious complaint on the part of Great Britain. Yet in fact and in truth the policy of the Navy Department was to do the very thing complained of by Mr. Stuart.

Secretary Welles had to have a navy and had adopted a system by which to improvise one. He had before this time appointed a board consisting of a naval construction engineer and an ordinance officer empowering the board to make a thorough examination of every prize vessel deemed suitable for navy service, and on favorable report he deposited the amount of the appraised value with the register of the court and had her immediately taken to the navy yard, fitted and armed for duty. The Secretary of the Navy was availing himself of every suitable steamer to be found in the country that could be made efficient for the defense of the blockade. Our blockade was very extensive, so extensive that Sir John Russell[1452] of her Britannic majesty's Cabinet at the beginning of our war troubles pronounced it an impossibility to maintain and defend yet afterwards he admitted it was effective. At the time the blockade was proclaimed, it was impossible to build and vessels could not be purchased from our merchant service sufficient to enforce it. Therefore it became necessary for the secretary to make a standing order for obtaining from the courts such prizes as were in possession of the prize commissioners and liable to condemnation. Of course this proceeding on the part of the Naval Department became most annoying to the open as well as the secret enemies with their allies to this government on account of their being largely engaged in illicit traffic and running the blockade. These vessels were eagerly sought for the contraband trade, and hence the machinery of the state craft of England was invoked for the nefarious[1453] purpose of furnishing facilities and for sapping the vitals of this government when it was bleeding at every pore.

Mr. Lincoln was distressed by this new embarrassment caused by Mr. Stuart's unwarrantable demand and said it was time the Gordian Knot[1454] was out and regardless of consequences coincided with the Secretary of the Navy whom he regarded as having special charge of the police of the seas in purchasing the *Bermuda* and putting her in

---

1452 Sir John Russell—See pg. 128.

1453 Nefarious means wicked.

1454 Gordian Knot—See pg. 319.

immediate service. Mr. Lincoln endorsed the policy adopted by the Naval Department utilizing all vessels taken as prize in the hands of the prize commissioners. What made the demand of the English representatives the more unreasonable and wanton, was the fact that there was at that time a British law authorizing the sale of a ship before a decision of the appellate court had been announced. In a conversation with Mr. Welles, the Naval Secretary, concerning the outcome of the correspondence, Mr. Lincoln said: "If the jury must hang in this case, be it so; we have some international rights left after all the concessions that we have made, in the interest of peace and conciliation, and some of them that remain to us must be respected. If we do not exert ourselves and demand a recognition of our rights we would better lay down our arms and surrender to our enemies with a general acknowledgement of our subservience[1455] to foreign pressure."

Sometime after during the year of 1864 Secretary Welles speaking of another complication which Spain attempted to draw the government of the United States into, in regards to reclaiming her possessions in San Domingo, said in his book that Spain was sick of her European alliance and was beginning to manifest a more friendly spirit towards our country she possessed that the government had never been fully identified with Palmerston and Louis Napoleon in their intrigue for European intervention. At the beginning of the American troubles Spain had committed herself to some extent and had been induced to recover her possessions in San Domingo. She had failed, had severed herself from the alliance, sought to preserve our friendship and give no offense to our countrymen whose sympathies in the present affairs were enlisted on behalf of the Negroes. The pressure was great, he says, on both sides, and the question a great and delicate one, what position we should take and what course to pursue. On the one side Spain whose favor we wished to consolidate, and on the other the appeal of the Negroes against Spanish oppression. Mr. Seward, in detailing the embarrassment of attending the negotiations for Mr. Lincoln, Mr. Welles says that Mr. Lincoln's countenance indicated that his mind was relieved before Mr. Seward had concluded. He remarked that the Secretary of State reminded him of an interview between the two Negroes in Tennessee; one was a preacher who with the crude and strange notions of the ignorance of his race was

---

[1455] Subservience means a willingness to serve another's purposes.

endeavoring to admonish and enlighten his brother African of the importance of religion and the danger of the future "Dare are," said Josh, the preacher, "two roads befoe you, Joe; be careful which of dem you take. One of dem roads leads straight to hell—de oder goes right to damnation." Joe opened his eyes with affright and under the inspired eloquence and awful danger before him exclaimed, "Take which road you please. I shall go through the woods"

"I am not willing" said the president, "to assume any new troubles or responsibilities at this time and shall therefore avoid going one place with Spain or with the Negro to the other, but shall take to the woods: we will maintain an honest and strict neutrality."

*"I can't spare this man; he fights."*

Abraham Lincoln of criticism of General Grant

# — 24 —

# GENERAL GRANT OVERCOMES HIS TROUBLES

Like Mr. Lincoln, the great Napoleon of the American army, General Grant had his trials and annoyances during the war of the rebellion. His very position elicited discussion and criticism. The humble position from which he so rapidly arose to the command of the army, naturally engendered jealousies throughout military circles. Our war was no exception in this and other counts rise—that the men engaged in it were inspired with great patriotism, never will be doubted, but heroism has undoubtedly played an important part. Ambition for fame laudably inspired true patriotism, and in some instances the inspiration exceeded its proper limits, in rivalry by unworthy attempt to supplant deserved fame by calumny[1456] and detraction, yet it is perhaps true that General Grant was freer from jealously from his co-commanders than any other general officer of the army.

Before the fall of Vicksburg,[1457] General Grant was distrusted and disliked by General Halleck,[1458] the general-in-chief of the armies. During the Tennessee campaign this feeling on the part of General Halleck had assumed proportions dangerous to General Grant's security and command, so much so that General Halleck, in response to an inquiry from Washington to know where General Grant was, telegraphed that he was "drunk somewhere in the rear of the army." It

---

[1456] Calumny means slander.

[1457] July 4, 1863. www.historynet.com/the-fall-of-vicksburg.htm

[1458] General Henry Wager Halleck—See pg. 158.

was pretty generally asserted that General Grant at the battle of Shiloh had been surprised while drunk. But General Halleck himself put this charge to rest on the 2nd day of May, 1862, in his dispatch wherein he said "The newspaper accounts that our divisions were surprised were utterly false; every division had notice of the enemies approach hours before the battle commenced."

Shortly after this battle, however, General Halleck assumed the command in person of the western army, deposing General Grant, and making him nominally second in command; General Grant was not consulted in any of the operations, being considered as a disgrace. This was a bitter trial, a terrible ordeal for General Grant to pass through. He naturally thought he had been unjustly dealt with by his superior officer and seriously thought of leaving the army by resigning his position. From this step, however, he was dissuaded by General Sherman and other friends. In a short time after this General Halleck was called to Washington and General Grant resumed command with the odium and suspicion still resting upon him.

A large class of the American people looked upon excessive indulgence in intoxicating beverages with great displeasure, and these charges whether true or false, seriously affected General Grant's reputation and were magnified to the extent of lessening his effectiveness in the service for the time being. Without doubt, "the evil that men do lives after them; the good is oft interred with their bones." Not so with the hero patriot of the second American revolution. "For trifles light as air are to the jealous confirmation strong as proofs of holy writ." But in the candid judgment of mankind General Grant eventually again rose to his former dignified and untrammeled[1459] position.

General Halleck and the country generally, when Vicksburg was invested[1460] by General Grant, felt great doubt as to the outcome. When the victory was at last won and Vicksburg had fallen, then it was that the country at large and the general-in-chief in particular, who appreciated the wisdom in Mr. Lincoln persistently standing by General Grant in good report and evil report in the face of all opposition to him. General Halleck sunk all and sent the following congratulatory dispatch to General Grant: "Your report dated July the 6th of your campaign in Mississippi ending in the capitulation of

---

1459 Untrammeled means not restrained.

1460 Invested means surrounded.

Vicksburg was received last evening. Your narrative of the operations is brief, soldierly and in every respect credible and satisfactory. In boldness of plan, rapidity of execution, and brilliancy of routs, these operations will compare favorably with those of Napoleon[1461] at Ulm. You and your army have deserved well the gratitude of your country and it will be the boast of your children that their fathers were the heroic army that opened the Mississippi." This dispatch breathed nothing of envy, nothing of hatred, no want of trustfulness, but genuine gratulation[1462] to the heroes of great deeds.

---

1461 Napoleon Bonaparte—See pg. 2.
1462 Gratulation means showing congratulations.

*"Such was Lincoln's adroit planning and exquisite tact in crisis that the complaining Senators...found after they shot their bolt that the President was still in command, with the Cabinet unchanged."*

James G. Randall, from his book *Midstream*[1463]

# — 25 —

# RADICAL MEN OF THE NORTH GO ON THE ATTACK

One of the most pregnant causes for differences and dissentions between Mr. Lincoln and the radical men of his party grew out of the generous terms granted to the rebels by his amnesty proclamation,[1464] and its restrictive prohibition against all but qualified voters such as were entitled to that franchise under the laws prior to the rebellion, to vote in the re-establishment of the suspended state governments. This prohibition gave great concern to a large class of Republicans. They were confidently relying upon permanent party ascendancy in the South, by the votes of the colored population, trained for the work by adventurers that the war had created who were by the proclamation expressly excluded from voting.

In this Mr. Lincoln was patriotically influenced by the motive and purpose of maintaining republican government in preference to

---

1463 Lincoln in American Memory, pg. 309.

1464 Mr. Lincoln's amnesty proclamation delivered to Congress on the second Tuesday in December 81863 provided that all Confederates excepting holders of public office, army generals and navy officers above the rank of Lieutenant, former U.S. Congressmen, judges, and anyone found guilty of mistreating prisoners of war, be given a full executive pardon upon taking the oath of loyalty to the federal government, support the Emancipation Proclamation and obedience to all lawful acts in reference to slavery. And as soon as one-tenth of the 1860 voters took the oath the state could be reinstated and allowed representation in Congress. The Civil War a Narrative, pg. 880 - 881.

securing permanent ascendancy of his party, which he regarded as of subordinate importance to the great principles involved. Mr. Lincoln had long been regarded by certain members of his party as too conservative for the times and surroundings. This proclamation was made the excuse for open hostility to him and his administration. He was attacked in all possible ways when opportunity arose affording excuse for such attack by members of Congress while in session and, while not in session, by the radical politicians in season and out of season, by orators, charlatans and the leading newspaper publishers.

A fair sample of the attacks of the latter class of patriots may be found in the letter written by the Hon. Murat Halsted,[1465] editor of the *Cincinnati Commercial* to the Hon. Samuel P. Chase, who was Secretary of the Treasury of Mr. Lincoln's Cabinet. This letter is given space in these pages not so much as to the monstrosity of the base sentiments it contained as to give the readers a specimen and type of the literature published, and secretly circulated, by many of the leading Republican journals of the country about that time. There were other Republican editors in the large cities, in New York, Chicago and elsewhere, who entertained like sentiments and were not by any means backward in giving publicity to their antagonism to the policy of the administration, as to the head, in such language as might be calculated as to inspire the assassination of the executive. Many of the friends of Mr. Lincoln after his death, could not refrain from the harrowing thought that if John Wilkes Booth[1466] had wrapped his bullet in the shred of one of these newspapers, he might have lodged a vindication of the crime in the brain of his victim. The executive succession of all times is a great stake to be played by both the conscientious and unscrupulous politician. In time of war, no less than the time of peace, are the basest intrigues and passions as well as the noblest ambitions that can animate[1467] the humans' breast, brought into action, for the achievement of individual supremacy and power to govern. It has been so in all ages of the world. Men from the remotest period to the

---

[1465] Honorable Murat Halsted was a journalist and editor of the *Cincinnati Commercial* and established a Sunday newspaper in Cincinnati. He was a supporter of the Republican Party. Appleton's Cyclopaedia of American Biography, Vol. III., pg. 54.
[1466] John Wilkes Booth was a member of the prominent Booth family of Maryland involved in the theater. He assassinated Abraham Lincoln at the Ford's Theater on Good Friday, April 14, 1865. *Baltimore Sun*, October 5, 1992.
[1467] Animate means to rouse.

present time have been governed by the interests, likes and dislikes, prepossessions, prejudice, loves and hates.

Nearly eight hundred years before the Christian era Amulius[1468] secured the Roman throne by murdering all his brothers, uncles and nephews. Later Herod[1469] slaughtered the innocents under two years of age intending to destroy our Savior. For the gratification of his wanton desires Nero[1470] set fire to Rome and then persecuted the Christians because of the destruction of the city. Still later Madame de Pompadour[1471] filled the bastille with victims of her petty spite, and more recently still, Lolla Montez[1472] set her dogs on the students at Munich for doubting the political wisdom of the mistress of the king of Bavaria. And now the reason of the assassination of Abraham Lincoln appears not in the records of history.

The following is the letter referred to above.

*Office Cincinnati Daily and Weekly Commercial*
*Cincinnati, February 19, 1863*
*Gov. Chase*[1473]
*My dear sir:*

*I wrote you a somewhat fantastic letter the other day but that I suppose now is not strange.*

*I write this morning to send you a breviated*[1474] *letter I have from our Army in front of Vicksburg. It is from a close observer who endeavors to tell the truth.*

*There has never has been a more thoroughly disgusted, disheartened, demoralized army than this is, and all because it is under such men as Grant and Sherman.*[1475] *Disease is disseminating its ranks, and while hundreds of poor fellows are dying of smallpox and every other conceivable malady, the medical*

---

1468 Amulius was a character in Roman mythology. www.pantheon.org/articles/a/amulius.html

1469 King Herod was the King of the Roman Empire from 73 to 4 B.C. who murdered members of his own family. www.answers.com/topic/herod-the-great

1470 Nero was Roman Emperor from A.D. 27—68. www.answers.com/topic/nero

1471 Madame de Pompadour was a lady who used her beauty to influence the French court. She lived from 1721 to 1764. www.answers.com/topic/madame-de-pompadour

1472 Lolla Montez was an adventurer, entertainer and dancer who caused several political commotions and was expelled from Bavaria. Appleton's Cyclopaedia of American Biography, Vol. IV., pg. 368.

1473 Governor Salmon Portland Chase—See pg. 98.

1474 Breviated means abbreviated.

1475 William T. Sherman—See pg. 160.

*department is inflicted with delirium tremens.*[1476] *In Memphis, smallpox patients are made to walk through the streets from camps to hospitals while drunken doctors ride from bar-rooms to whore houses in government ambulances. How is it that Grant, who was behind at Fort Henry, drunk at Donelson, surprised and whipped at Shiloh and driven back from Oxford, Mississippi, is still in command?*

*Gov. Chase, these things are true. Our noble Army of the Mississippi is being wasted by the foolish, drunken, stupid Grant. He cannot organize or control or fight an army. I have no personal feeling about it, but I know he is an ass.*

*There is not amongst the whole list of retired major generals a man who is not Grant's superior. McClellan, Frémont, McDowell,*[1477] *Burnside,*[1478] *Franklin,*[1479] *even Pope*[1480] *or Sumner*[1481] *would be an improvement upon the present commander of the Army of the Mississippi. We will wake up some of these days and find we will have no Army of the Mississippi.*

*Then there is awful discouragement at the way the foolish old Hunter,*[1482] *who is thought to be a great man, because he is not insane on his prejudice of the Negro question, is doing.*

*In God's name what is he waiting for? More reinforcements? Pity he cannot die and get out of the way as Mitchell*[1483] *did.*

*But to stop this growling and come to something more practical.*

*The army west and east is being weakened hourly by desertion. It is the great evil. The thing needed to stop it is for the president to give each commander of departments the power to shoot deserters. They must be shot by the dozens. The president's weak, puling,*[1484] *piddling humanitarianism is death and hell to the army. Can't you take him by the throat and knock his head against the wall until he is brought to his senses on the war business? I do not speak wantonly when I say that it was doing God's service to kill him if it were not feared that Hamlin*[1485] *were not a bigger fool than he is.*

*And yet the pitiful Congress twaddles*[1486] *weakly in the private caucus about political matters, as if a little more Negro would do everything.*

---

1476 *Delirium tremens* are violent tremors caused by drinking too much alcohol.
1477 General Irvin McDowell—See pg. 137.
1478 General Ambrose Everett Burnside—See pg. 171.
1479 Major General William B. Franklin—See pg. 211.
1480 Brigadier General John Pope—See pg. 180.
1481 General Edwin Sumner—See pg. 166.
1482 General David Hunter—See pg. 138.
1483 Ormsby McKnight Mitchell—See pg. 185.
1484 Puling means whining.
1485 Hannibal Hamlin—See pg. 95.
1486 Twaddles mean acting silly.

*The proclamation is a positive nuisance to every truly loyal man in the west. It is a weapon in the hands of the butter-nuts. If it is made a party test, Vallandigham*[1487] *would be elected governor of Ohio. Do not think I am talking at random. Alas, I know what I am talking about.*

*What is wanted:*

*A general for our Army of the Mississippi.*

*Deserters shot by orders of the commanders of the departments.*

*Less dependence on the nigger and more on the white man*

*The consolidation of the fragment of the regiments.*

*Arrest and try Henry May*[1488] *and Wendell Phillips*[1489] *for treason.*

*Suppress the New York Tribune and the New York World.*

*M. Halstead*

Just such infamous sediments as are expressed in this letter, coming from so high of a source, backed up by the leaders in Republican journalism—journals that shamelessly and treasonably poisoned the public mind and manufactured a false public sentiment against the executive of the nation. The general officers in the field engaged in the fierce struggle with the enemy could not be otherwise than dangerous and embolden[1490] evil disposed persons to commit outrage and violence with the confidence and impunity for their acts. The conspiracy which Booth and the others first formed for kidnapping Abraham Lincoln was doubtless the offspring of such treasonable utterances and the devilish purpose, fed and fanned by the echoes of just such northern patriots until it culminated in a most foul and unnatural murder.

Further on we will have occasion to allude to this subject again.

At the expense of drawing the author into a position which may give him a partisan, unsavory reputation, in the interests of truth, he must state that the general emancipation of slavery and questions growing out of the local District of Columbia proclamation of freedom to the slave under the District Emancipation Act[1491] were

---

1487 Clement L. Vallandigham—See pg. 245.

1488 Henry May was born in Washington, D.C. where he was an attorney. He served in the U.S. Congress. Appleton's Cyclopaedia of American Biography, Vol. IV., pg. 272.

1489 Wendell Phillips—See pg. 8.

1490 Embolden means brave.

1491 District of Columbia Emancipation Act was passed on April 15, 1862. Mr. Lincoln had supported this legislation when he was a U.S. Congressman in 1849. The act caused almost as many problems as slavery itself. The Negroes were not allowed to

sources from which the most fruitful pretenses for the justification for abuse of the executive ever emanated. The subject was fruitful of evil in the pretense of good.

The Fugitive Slave Act[1492] was yet in force. The District of Columbia Emancipation Law had gone into effect. Maryland and Virginia slaves were constantly seeking a refuge of safety from slavery. The District of Columbia was a depot for them but was not an asylum under the law in existence. The effect of the passage of the law without the concomitant[1493] protection and relief made it most embarrassing and complicated for all the local judicial, ministerial and executive officers. Slavery was abolished in the territory. The law was plain enough on that subject.

The object now of the radical members of Congress[1494] was to make slavery as offensive and as hideous as possible. In order the more effectively to bring about this state of things, runaway slaves coming in to the District were sought to be canonized and given a place in history by a bugle blast in the United States Senate. The lower house of Congress depicted the horrors of the arrest of a man and brother under the law who were by the Declaration of Independence declared free without reference to what the Constitution said afterwards on the subject, if the necessity of the act of Congress freeing slaves in the territory to which unemancipated slaves were unauthorized to come. The issue which prevailed during the presidential campaign of 1864 between the president supported by the moderate Republicans and the radical Congress was kept alive long after the death of Mr. Lincoln and for years after the close of the war up to the time of the final reconstruction of the rebellious states, as late as the year 1866. The fierce struggle for supremacy between the two factions was very bitter. Many person who had been most temperate in speech throughout the stormy clash of arms now became most fierce and intemperate in supporting their respective theories of the proper treatment towards their rebellious brethren and the erring sister states until the Union was almost in as great a danger from

---

attend schools in the District of Columbia, could not ride streetcars, and couldn't be heard in courts of law. Lincoln's Emancipation Proclamation, pgs. 82 & 88.

1492 Fugitive Slave Act—See pg. 17.

1493 Concomitant means accompanying.

1494 The core of the legislative opposition came from Senator Benjamin Wade of Ohio, Senator Zachariah Chandler of Michigan, and Congressman George Julian of Indiana. The Odd Couple Who Hanged Mary Surratt, pg. 65.

aspiring and contending Republicans as it had been from the enemy just conquered and subdued.

Before and after the compensated abolition of slavery, the execution of the Fugitive Slave Law in the District of Columbia became a question much discussed by Congress and was a frightful scandal to radical members. The District had become the asylum of runaway slaves from the border states, particularly from the rebel state of Virginia and the quasi-loyal state of Maryland. The Fugitive Slave Law remained in force and no attempt was made by Congress to repeal it or provide for the protection of the executive officers whose duty it was to enforce it. Mr. Lincoln was appealed to for instructions. The subject gave him great concern, but he could see no way out of the difficulty but to have the law executed.[1495]

As far as the state of Virginia was concerned, according to the theory of the administration, seceded states were yet part and parcel of the Union. The state was still one of the United States and all Congressional laws of the statute book in force in regard to her as well as states not in rebellion; which made the question one of great embarrassment.

During the month of August in the year 1861, the Confiscation Act[1496] had gone into effect. The military governor of the District assumed that by virtue of this law which gave liberty to all slaves that had been employed by the rebels for insurrectionary purposes, that necessarily all slaves that came into the District from whatever section had been thus employed and were consequently free. It became his duty to give them military protection as free persons.

This state of things caused a fearful responsibility to rest upon the shoulders of the civil executive authorities and if persisted, it would inevitably have ruined financially the persons whose duty it was to execute the slave laws in force in the District. The president gave private instructions to the civil officers to execute the laws until Congress modified or repealed them. In doing this Mr. Lincoln said,

---

[1495] The man who had to enforce the fugitive slave law was the Federal Marshal of the District of Columbia, the author, Ward Hill Lamon. Ward Hill Lamon, Lincoln's "Particular Friend," pgs. 214 and 258.

[1496] The Confiscation Act gave liberty to all slaves who had been employed by the rebels for insurrectionary purposes. The War Department interpreted this to mean that slaves of disloyal southern owners were now "contraband of war." Ward Hill Lamon: Lincoln's "Particular Friend," pg. 258 and www.hsitory.wmd.edu/freedman/conact1.htm

"You will receive much adverse criticism and a good deal of down right abuse from members of Congress. This," he said, "is certain to come, but it will not be so much intended for you as for me. As our friend Senator Hale, the other day said the Senate, 'We must not strike too high, nor too low, but we must strike between wind and water—the marshal is the man to hit.'[1497] And I say 'We will have to stand it, whatever they send."'[1498]

Martial law had not been declared. There was not even a temporary suspension of civil authority even in exceptional cases in the District of Columbia. It was therefore only a question of time. And the time soon came for a conflict between civil and military authority. It was conceded by all that the temporary rule of military authority was virtually necessary to the preservation of the federal capital when in danger, but at this time there was no pretense of danger from the rebels in arms. The civil courts in the District were in full power for the adjudication of all cases arising within their jurisdiction and nothing but a pressing military necessity could give countenance or pretense for the abrogation[1499] of civil law.

The conflict grew out of an order of the military governor to take a female fugitive slave from the custody of the marshal. She belonged in Maryland. The deputies to whom the order was shown declined to obey the demand for the delivery of the fugitive into the hands of the military, giving as the reason for their refusal that she was being held under due process of law, and that they were without authority to give her up without order of the court. Military officers with strong guard then arrested the deputy marshals, seized the jail, released the slave and left a military guard in charge of the captured jail. The marshal afterwards (he being temporarily absent at the time of the seizure)[1500]

---

1497 Radical opposition leader Senator Hale decided the best way to get at Mr. Lincoln was not a frontal assault, but an assault on his friend, Ward Hill Lamon. Recollections of Abraham Lincoln, pg. 255.

1498 Mr. Lincoln told Congressman Kellogg of Illinois: "Kellogg, you fellows at the other end of the Avenue seem determined to deprived me of every friend I have who is near me and whom I trust. Now, let me tell you sir, he (Lamon) is the most unselfish man I ever saw; is discreet, powerful and a most desperate man in an emergency I ever saw or expect to see. He is my friend and as long as I have the great responsibility on me, I intend to insist on his being with me, and I will stick by him at all hazards." Recollections of Abraham Lincoln, pg. xxxv.

1499 Abrogation means abolishment.

1500 The author does not tell us why the federal marshal (Ward Hill Lamon) was not present in this instance.

arrested the military guard, recaptured the jail, liberated the prisoners placed therein by the military and held the military guards as prisoners in the jail. Things now had assumed rather fearful proportions and danger of bloodshed was imminent. The marshal backed by police and other civilian authorities together with the citizens of Washington opposed the military governor with forces under his command intended for the defense of the city. The matter was eventually laid before the president.

Mr. Lincoln called to his aid the Attorney General[1501]who gave a prompt but decisive opinion that the civil authority outranked in authority the military in the present state of things in the District of Columbia and gave the further opinion that the military governor's conduct was misguided and unauthorized, however philanthropic may have been his purpose or intentions.

No one will doubt that General Wadsworth[1502] was not only a philanthropist but a true and undoubted patriot. He made many sacrifices in the cause of his country, and afterwards yielded up his life in the struggle, gallantly fighting at the battle of Wilderness on the 6th day of May 1864.

Reconciling the differences on the subject of supremacy of authority by no means reconciled or put to rest the perturbed aggressive spirit in Congress in opposition to the president's policy. The friends of the aggressive policy must live, and Mr. Lincoln and his administration be sunk into oblivion, or Mr. Lincoln and his adherents must live and his opponents must go to their political graves. That was the issue. The emphasized zeal of the opposition prompted the enthusiastic adherents of this opposing policy in Congress to make the district jail an objective point in the furtherance of their ends and objects. They made personal visits to that institution and examined all the inmates whose color was not of orthodox albino-anglo American tint. They would hear the story of the prisoners' wrongs and injuries, and then would straightaway proceed to the halls of Congress and make known their wonderful discoveries. Detectives were employed by them to make daily reports of the cruelty and wrongs to the poor down-trodden colored inmates of the jail, which reports were soon

---

1501 Edward Bates was Attorney General. See pg. 101.

1502 Brigadier General James S. Wadsworth was the appointed military governor of the District of Columbia. He was a strong abolitionist. Ward Hill Lamon, Lincoln's "Particular Friend," pg. 288.

dressed up in pathetic and classic language of the occasion. Professional and amateur demigod politicians made sensational speeches, sometimes written for them by department clerks and professional speechwriters, and Rome was made to howl in the halls of the American Congress. Mr. Lincoln and his beastly Negro captors were denounced in unmeasured terms.

The jail was by now, the necessities of its surroundings, made the receptacle for prisoners of all kinds, civil, military and state. Orders from the War Department were issued to the custodian of the jail[1503] to allow no person whatsoever to communicate with the military or state prisoners without an order from the War Department. The Chairman of the District committee for the District of Columbia in the Senate and certain others of that committee claimed the right by virtue of their position in the face of the orders of the Secretary of War to go in and examine all prisoners in the jail, and in furtherance of this pretended right, made daily visits and violated Secretary of War Stanton's orders.

The situation became unbearable and the marshal sent in his resignation.

*January 31, 1862*
*Washington, D.C.*
*Abraham Lincoln, President*
*Sir:*

*I hereby resign my office as Marshal for the District of Columbia. Your invariable friendship and kindness for a long course of years which you have extended to me impel me to vie the reasons for this course. There appears to be a studious effort upon the part of the more radical portion of that party which placed you in power to pursue me with reckless persecution, and I am now under condemnation by the United States Senate for doing what I am sure meets your approval, but by the course pursued by that honorable body I fear you will be driven to the necessity either sustaining the action of that body, or breaking with them and sustaining me, which you cannot afford to do under the circumstances.*

*I appreciate your embarrassing position in the matter, and feel as unselfish in the premises as you have ever felt and acted towards me in the course of fourteen years of uninterrupted friendship; now when our country is in danger, I deem it proper, having your successful administration of the Government more at heart than my own*

[1503] The author, Ward Hill Lamon as U.S. Federal Marshal of the District of Columbia was custodian of the jail. Recollections of Abraham Lincoln, pg. xxxiii.

*pecuniary interests, to relieve you of this embarrassment by resigning that office which you were kind enough to confide to my charge, and in doing so allow me to assure you that you have my best wishes for your health and happiness, for your successful administration of this government, the speedy restoration to peace, and a long and useful life in the enjoyment of your present high and responsible office.*

*I have the honor to be your friend and obedient servant,*

*Ward H. Lamon*[1504]

This, however, was not accepted.

The official opinion of the Attorney General was again evoked by the president, and he gave his views as to the duties of the custodian heterogeneous mass of prisoners in the jail which resulted in the request of the president to the Attorney General to prepare such an order as was proper for the marshal to sign, giving notice of what would be required for admission into the jail of others than prisoners, and having unrestrained intercourse with its inmates. The paper prepared in the Attorney General's office was signed and sent forth and before the close of the day on which it was signed, resolutions were passed in Congress declaring the marshal in contempt of that body for having presumed to that issue they deemed a contemptuous restriction of their rights. A committee was appointed to wait on the president and to demand the instant dismissal of that insolent officer. The president showed the committee the resignation of that officer already in his hands and informed them that he would neither accept the resignation nor dismiss him from office, and giving his reasons for this action.

After this the opposition became more and more acrimonious and offensive towards Mr. Lincoln and his administration. The leaders of the opposition now resorted to every means in their power except violence to oppose him for his recalibrations,[1505] want of respect and disobedience to the behests of the ranking co-ordinate branch of the government, Congress having made the offensive laws and the president's duty was to execute them.

Soon the marshal's office was made the subject of legislation in Congress to shear it of its power and reduce its emoluments.[1506] The

---

1504 Recollections of Abraham Lincoln, pgs. xxxiv & xxxv.

1505 Recalibrations means redeterminations.

1506 Emoluments are fees. The Marshal received a base salary of $6000 plus additional fees for feeding and transporting prisoners. The radicals in Congress reduced and

custody of the jail and its prisoners was soon given a warden and shortly after that an act was passed relieving that office from the duties of attending the Supreme Court of the United States by providing a special marshal for that court, leaving the office still one great responsibility but without remuneration commensurate with its duties. Before the appointment of the warden to the jail and the duty revolved around him to perform all the acts—before that time obligatory upon the marshal—the district court had sentenced two men to be hanged for murder on a day subsequent to the passage of the warden act. The marshal refused to become the hangman.[1507] Congress again passed a resolution denouncing his conduct and instituted an investigation into the facts. The order of the court was that the marshal should hang the condemned men, but Congress had unconsciously relieved him of that painful duty. The warden had no order for their execution and could not perform the service with any more propriety than the marshal. The result was by the effects of the blundering legislation super induced by hasty factious zeal, to injure an object of their dislike, Congress nullified the solemn acts of the United States District Courts and restored to life and liberty and immunity from punishment two miscreants whose lives had been forfeited and who should have been hung. This fiasco of legislative jail delivery was a source of great annoyance and some amusement to Mr. Lincoln. In speaking of certain members and the part they had taken in this and other petty acts of annoyance he said, "I have great sympathy for these men, because of their temper and their weakness, but I am thankful that the good Lord has given to the vicious ox short horns for if their physical courage was equal to their vicious dispositions some of us in this neck of the woods would get hurt certain for their blood upon the moon."

The kick was continued to the last and Mr. Lincoln adhered to his policy to the end. The following is a letter defining more explicitly his policy in answer to the adverse criticism made upon it by Mr. Horace Greeley under date of August 22, 1862.

---

eventually took away all those emoluments from Mr. Lamon. Ward Hill Lamon: Lincoln's "Particular Friend," pg. 347.

[1507] The two men sentenced to hang were Jeremiah Hendricks and Emmanuel Pollard. Instead their sentences were commuted to life in prison because there was no one legally in position to execute them. Attorney General Bates ruled, "that the marshal no longer has any duty or lawful power to execute any sentence of death upon any man imprisoned in the jails of the District of Columbia." Ward Hill Lamon: Lincoln's "Particular Friend," pgs. 337 & 347.

On August 20, 1862, Greeley released an open letter to Mr. Lincoln, "A Prayer of Twenty Millions," in which he urged immediate emancipation of southern slaves. Greeley wrote:

*"We complain that the Union cause has suffered, and is now suffering immensely, from mistaken deference to Rebel Slavery. Had you, Sir, in your Inaugural Address, unmistakably given notice that, in case the Rebellion already commenced were persisted in, and your efforts to preserve the Union and enforce the laws should be resisted by armed force, you would recognize no loyal person as rightfully held in Slavery by a traitor, we believe the Rebellion would therein have received a staggering if not fatal blow. At that moment, according to the returns of the most recent elections, the Unionists were a large majority of the voters of the Slave States. But they were composed in good part of the aged, the feeble, the wealthy, the timid, the young, the reckless, the aspiring, the adventurous, had already been largely lured by the gamblers and negro-traders, the politicians by trade and the conspirators by instinct, into the toils of Treason. Had you then proclaimed that Rebellion would strike the shackles from the slaves of every traitor, the wealthy and the cautious would have been supplied with a powerful inducement to remain loyal. As it was, every coward in the South soon became a traitor from fear; for Loyalty was perilous, while Treason seemed comparatively safe. Hence the boasted unanimity of the South a unanimity based on Rebel terrorism and the fact that immunity and safety were found on that side, danger and probable death on ours. The Rebels from the first have been eager to confiscate, imprison, scourge and kill: we have fought wolves with the devices of sheep. The result is just what might have been expected. Tens of thousands are fighting in the Rebel ranks to-day whose, original bias and natural leanings would have led them into ours."*[1508]

Mr. Lincoln wrote his reply to Mr. Greeley for the *National Intelligencer* in Washington:

*I would save the Union. I would save it the shortest way under the Constitution. The sooner the national authority can be restored; the nearer the Union will be 'the Union as it was.' If there be those who would not save the Union, unless they could at the same time save slavery, I do not agree with them. If there be those who would not save the Union unless they could at the same time destroy slavery, I do not agree with them. My paramount object in this struggle is to save the Union, and is not either to save or to destroy slavery. If I could save the Union without*

---

1508 www.abrahamlincolnsclassroom.org/Library/newsletter.asp?ID=128&CRLI=176

*freeing any slave I would do it, and if I could save it by freeing all the slaves I would do it; and if I could save it by freeing some and leaving others alone I would also do that. What I do about slavery, and the colored race, I do because I believe it helps to save the Union; and what I forbear, I forbear because I do not believe it would help to save the Union. I shall do less whenever I shall believe what I am doing hurts the cause, and I shall do more whenever I shall believe doing more will help the cause. I shall try to correct errors when shown to be errors; and I shall adopt new views so fast as they shall appear to be true views. I have here stated my purpose according to my view of official duty; and I intend no mortification and my oft-expressed personal wish that all men every where could be free.*

*Yours,*

*A. Lincoln*[1509]

Mr. Greeley contended that the policies Mr. Lincoln "seemed to be pursuing in respect to slaves" were "duly influenced by fossil politicians hailing from the Border States" and that Mr. Lincoln "failed to see all attempts to put down the rebellion and at the same time uphold its inciting cause (slavery) are preposterous and futile."[1510]

Here is a letter from Mr. Lincoln to Mr. A. G. Hodges of Frankfort, Kentucky on the issue.

*Executive Mansion*
*Washington, April 4, 1864*
*A. G. Hodges,*[1511] *Esq., Frankfort, Ky.*
*Mr. Dear Sir:*

*You asked me to put in writing the substance of what I verbally said the other day, in your presence, to Governor Bramlette*[1512] *and Senator Dixon.*[1513] *It was about as follows: "I am naturally anti-slavery. If slavery is not wrong, nothing is wrong. I cannot remember when I did not so think and feel, and yet I have never understood that the Presidency conferred upon me an unrestricted right to act*

---

1509 www.civilwarhome.com/lincolngreeley.htm

1510 Team of Rivals, pgs. 470 & 471.

1511 Albert G. Hodges was editor of the *Kentucky Commonwealth* newspaper. condor.depaul.edu/ntps/Abraham_Lincoln_an_Abolitionist_Lincoln_letter_Hodges.htm

1512 Governor Thomas E. Bramlette was Governor of Kentucky from Sept. 1, 1863—September 3, 1867. www.branlete.com/document/govbram.htm

1513 Archibald Dixon was a Whig who was elected Lt. Governor of Kentucky in 1844 and was U.S. Senator from 1852—1855. www.powerset.com/explore/go/Archibald-Dixon

*officially upon this judgment and feeling. It was in the oath I took that I would do the best of my ability preserve, protect and defend the Constitution of the United States. I could not take the office without taking the oath. Nor was it my view that I might take my oath to get power, and break the oath in using the power. I understood too that in ordinary and civil administration of this oath even forbids me to practically indulge my primary abstract judgment on the moral question of slavery. I had publicly declared this many times and in many ways. And I aver that, to this day, I have done no official act in mere deference to my abstract judgment and feelings on slavery.*

*I did understand, however, that my oath to preserve the Constitution to the best of my ability, imposed upon me the duty of preserving by every indispensable means, that Government—that nation, of which that Constitution was the organic law. Was it possible to lose the nation and yet preserve the Constitution? By general law, life and limb must be protected; yet often a limb must be amputated to save a life; but a life is never wisely given to save a limb. I felt that measures, otherwise unconstitutional, might become lawful, by becoming indispensable to the preservation of the Constitution, through the preservation of the nation. Right or wrong, I assumed this ground, and now avow it. I could not feel that, to the best of my ability, I had even tried to preserve the Constitution, if, to save slavery or any minor matter, I should permit the wreck of Government, country and Constitution altogether. When early in the war General Frémont attempted military emancipation I forbade it, because I did not then think it an indispensable necessity. When, still later, General Cameron, then Secretary of War, suggested the arming of the blacks, I objected, because I did not yet think if an indispensable necessity. When, still later, General Hunter attempted military emancipation, I again forbade it, because I did not think the indispensable necessity had come.*

*When in March and May, and July, 1862, I made earnest and successive appeals to the Border States to favor compensated emancipation, I believed the indispensable necessity for military emancipation and arming of blacks would come, unless averted by that measure. They declined the proposition and I was, in my best judgment, driven to the alternative of either surrendering the Union, and with it the Constitution, or of laying strong hand upon the colored element. I chose the latter. In choosing it, I hoped for greater gain than loss, but of this I was not entirely confident. More than a year of trial now shows no loss by it in our foreign relations, none in our home popular sentiment, none in our white military force, no loss in any way now, or anywhere. On the contrary, it shows a gain of quite a hundred and thirty thousand soldiers, seamen and laborers. These are palatable facts; about which, as facts, there can be no caviling.*[1514] *We have the men; and we could not have had them without the measure.*

*And now let any Union man who complains of this measure, test himself by writing down in one line, that he is for subduing the rebellion by force of armies; and in the next, that he is for taking three hundred and fifty thousand from the Union side, and placing them where they would be best for the measure he condemns. If he cannot face his case so stated, it is only because he cannot face the truth.*

*I add a word which was not in the verbal conversation. In telling this tale, I attempt no compliment to my own sagacity.*[1515] *I claim not to have controlled events, but confess plainly that events have controlled me. Now at the end of three years of struggle, the nation's condition is not what either party, or any man desired, or expected. God alone can claim it. Whither it is tending seems plain. If God now wills the removal of a great wrong, and wills also that we of the North, as well as you in the South, shall pay fairly for our complicity in that wrong, impartial history will find therein new causes to attest and revere the justice and goodness of God.*

*Yours Truly,*
*A. Lincoln*

As late as January 1864 on this subject Mr. Lincoln wrote the following letter for the publishers of the *North American Review*, in which he uses unmistakable language defining the "President's policy."

*Executive Mansion*
*Washington, January 16, 1864*
*Messers. Chosey and Nichols:*[1516]

*The number for this month and year of the North American Review was duly received, and for which please accept my thanks. Of course, I am not the most impartial judge, yet with due allowance for this, I venture to hope that the article entitled "The Presidential Policy" will be of value to the country. I fear I am not quite worthy of all which is therein kindly said of me personally.*

*The sentence of twelve lines, commencing at the top of page 252, I would wish to be not exactly as it is. In what is there expressed the writer has not correctly*

---

1514 Caviling means quibbling.
1515 Sagacity means judgment.
1516 Messers. Chosey and Nichols were the publishers of the North American Review. www.americancivilwar.com/civilwar/spproduct/C001/B001ESQL75.htm

*understood me. I have never had a theory that secession could absolve states or people of their obligations. Precisely the contrary is asserted in the Inaugural address; and it was because of my belief in the continuation of these obligations that I was puzzled, for a trial, as to denying the legal rights of those citizens who remain individually innocent of treason or rebellion.*

*But I mean no more now than to merely call your attention to this point.*

*Yours Respectfully,*

*A. Lincoln*[1517]

The sentence referred to in the *North American Review* is as follows: "Even so long ago as when Mr. Lincoln not yet convinced of the danger and magnitude of crisis, was endeavoring to persuade of Union majorities in the South, and to carry on a war that was half peace in the hope of a peace that would have been war, while he was still enforcing the Fugitive Slave Law under some theory that secession, however it might solve some states from their obligation, could not escheat[1518] them from their claims under the Constitution and that slave holders in rebellion had alone among mortals the privilege of having their cake and eating it at the same time—the enemies of free government were striving to persuade the people that the war was an abolition crusade; to rebel without reason was proclaimed as one of the rights of man; while it was carefully kept out of sight that to suppress rebellion was the first duty of government."

To this the editors of the *North American Review* appended a note as follows:

*"Nothing could have been further from the intention of the editors than to misrepresent the opinions of the president. They merely meant that in their judgment the policy of the administration was at first such as practically to concede to any rebel who might choose to profess loyalty rights under the Constitution whose corresponding obligations he repudiated."*

It is of interest to hear from William T. Sherman on the subject of the war at this point,

---

[1517] History of the Rebellion, pg. 336.

[1518] Escheat means relieve.

*Headquarters, Military Division of the Mississippi*
*Near Atlanta, Georgia (in the field)*
*August 10, 1864*
*Daniel M. Martin,*[1519] *Sand Mountain*
*Dear Friend*

*When in Larkinsville last winter I enquired after you and could get no positive answer. I wih you would have sent me your letter of January 22—which I have just received—for I could have made you feel at ease at once. Indeed I do remember our old times about Bellefonte and the ride we took to the corn mills and the little farm where I admired the handsome colt and tried to buy it. Time has worn on and you are an old man, in want and suffering and I am no longer young, but leading a hostile army on the very road I came when I left Bellefonte and at this moment pouring into Atlanta the dreaded missiles of war seeking the lives of its people. And yet I am the same William Tecumseh Sherman that you knew in 1844, with as warm a heart as ever, and anxious that peace and plenty shall prevail in this land, and to prove it I defy Jefferson Davis,*[1520] *General Lee*[1521] *and General Hood*[1522] *to make the sacrifice for peace that I will personally and officially.*

*I will today lay down my power and my honor—already won—will strip myself naked and my wife and child stark naked in the world as we came, and begin life anew, if the people of the South will but cease the war, elect their members to Congress and let them settle, by argument or reason, the questions growing out of slavery, instead of trying to divide the country into two angry halves, to quarrel and fight to the end of time. Our country cannot be divided by an east and west line, and must be one, and if we must fight, let us fight now and not bequeath it to our children.*

*I was never a politician but resigned from the army and lived in California till 1857 when I came back with my wife and three children who wanted to be near home—Mr. Ewing's not Mr. Corwin's—but had the old army so grounded in my composition that civil pursuits were too tame and I accepted an offer as president of Louisiana Military Academy. Therefore at the time of Lincoln's election I was in Alexandria on Red River.*

*I saw and you must have seen, the southern politicians wanted to bring about secession—separation. They could have elected Mr. Douglas*[1523] *but they so managed the Lincoln's election was made certain and after they had accomplished*

---

1519 Daniel Martin was a friend of William Tecumseh Sherman
1520 Jefferson Davis—See pg. 18.
1521 Robert E. Lee—See pg. 119.
1522 John Bell Hood—See pg. 309.
1523 Stephen A. Douglas—See pg. 34.

*this, was it honest or fair for them to allege it was a cause of war? Did not Mr. Breckinridge,*[1524] *as vice-president in his seat, declare Mr. Lincoln the lawfully elected president? Was it ever pretended the president was our government? Don't you know that Congress makes laws, the Supreme Court judges them and the president exercises them? Don't you know that Mr. Lincoln of himself could not take away your rights?*

*Now I was in Louisiana and while the planters and mechanics and industrious people were happy and prosperous the politicians and busybodies were scheming and plotting and got legislation to pass an ordinance of secession which was submitted to the people, who voted against it; yet the politicians voted the state out, proceeded to take possession of the United States Mint, the forts, the arsenal, and tore down our flag and insulted it. This too before Mr. Lincoln had gone to Washington. I saw these things and begged Bragg*[1525] *and Beauregard*[1526] *and Governor Moore*[1527] *and a host of personal friends, to beware in that was high treason. But they answered: The North was made up of mean manufacturers, of traders, of farmers, who would not fight. The people of the North never dreamed of interfering with the slaves or the property of the South. They simply voted as they had a right to do, and they could not understand why the people of the South should begin to take possession of the United States forts and arsenals till our government had done something wrong—something oppressive. The South began the war. You know it. I and millions of others living in the South know it. But the people of the North were as innocent as your grand children. Even after forts had been taken, public arms stolen from our arsenals and distributed among the angry militia, the brave and honest freemen of the North could not realize the fact and did not until Beauregard began to fire upon the garrison of United States troops in a fort built by the common treasury of the whole country. Then, as a mighty upheaval, the people rose and began to think of war, and not until then.*

*I resigned my post in Louisiana in March 1861 because of the public act on the part of the state in seizing the United States arsenal at Baton Rogue and went to St. Louis where I readily got lucrative employment hoping some change would yet avert war. But it came, and I with all of my military education had to choose. I repeat, that then as now I had as much love of the honest people of the South as any man living. Had they remained true to the country I would have resisted, even with arms, any attack upon their rights—even their slave rights. But when they tore down our old flag and spit upon it, and called us cowards and dared us to the*

---

1524 John C. Breckinridge—See pg. 48.

1525 Braxton Bragg—See pg. 189.

1526 Pierre Beauregard—See pg. 112.

1527 Governor Thomas Overton Moore—See pg. 78 footnote.

*contest, then I took up arms to maintain the integrity of our country and to punish the men who challenged us to conflict. Is this not a true picture? Suppose the North had patiently submitted, what would have been the verdict of history and the world? Nothing else but that the North was craven and coward. Will you say the North is craven and coward now?*

*Cruel and inhumane as this war has been, and may still continue to be, it was forced upon us. We had no choice. And we have no choice yet. We must go on even to the end of time; even if it result in the taking of a million lives and desolating the whole land leaving a desert behind. We must maintain the integrity of the country. And the day will come when the grandchild you love so well will bless us who fought that the United States of America should not sink into infamy and worse than Mexican anarchy, by the act of Southern politicians who care no more of you or such as you as they care for Hottentots.*[1528]

*I have never underrated the magnitude of this war for I know the size of the South and the difficulty in operating in it. But I also know that the Northern races have, ever since the world began, had more patience and perseverance than the Southern races. And so will it be now; we will persevere to the end. All mankind shall recognize within us a brave and stubborn race, not to be deterred by the magnitude of the danger. Only three years have passed and that is but a minute in the nation's life, and see where we are. Where are the haughty planters of Louisiana who compared our hard working white of the North to their Negroes?*

*The defeats we have sustained have hardly made a pause in our course and the vaunted braves of Tennessee, Mississippi, Louisiana, Missouri etc. instead of running rough-shod over the freemen of the North are engaged in stealing horses and robbing your old people for a living, while our armies now tread in every Southern state, and your biggest armies in Virginia and Georgia lie behind forts, and dare not come out and fight us cowards of the North, who have come 500 miles into their country to accept the challenge.*

*But my dear old friend, I have bored you too much. My handwriting is not plain, but you have time to study it out, and as you can understand I have a great deal of writing to do and it must be done in a hurry. Talk it over with your neighbors and ask yourself if, in your trials and tribulations, if you have suffered more from the Union soldiery that you would have built your barn where lightening was sure to burn or tear it down? Their course has provoked the punishment of an indignant God and government. I care not a straw for niggers. The moment the master rebels the Negro is free, of course, for he is a slave only by law, and the law*

---

1528 Hottentots are African tribesmen.

*broken, he is free. I command in all Tennessee, Kentucky, Mississippi, Alabama and Georgia. The paper I endorse will be of service to you.*

*Love to Mrs. Martin.*

*Signed,*

*William Tecumseh Sherman, Major General*

It is germane to consider at this point the Edgerton Resolutions[1529]

*January 25, 1864*

*Whereas the House on the 17th day of December last adopted, with but one dissenting vote, the following resolutions, to wit "Resolved that we hold it to be the duty of Congress to pass all necessary bills to supply man and money, and the duty of the people to render every aid in their power to the constituted authority of the government in the crushing out of the rebellion, and in bringing the leaders thereof to condign[1530] punishment." Therefore in explanation of the foregoing resolution and in further expression of the opinion and purpose of this House, "Resolved that the aid hitherto liberally supplied in men and money by the people of the United States to enable the Federal Executive to prosecute the existing Civil War, has been supplied by all citizens truly faithful to the Federal Union and Constitution, for the purpose and no other expressed in the resolution adopted by Congress on July, 1861 declaration of the object of the war, and commonly known as the 'Crittenden resolution' and public faith, true Christian humanity, and wise statesmanship alike demand strict adherence by the 'constitutional authorities of the Government' to the purpose or object of the war, as thus declared by Congress and accepted by the people."*

*That the demand of the President, by his proclamation of December 8, 1863 that the people of the States wherein rebellion exists shall swear to abide by and support his proclamation of emancipation (in other words change or submit to the change at is dictation of their state constitution, local laws, and domestic institutions not incorporated with the Constitution of the United States) before each State of the people will by him be considered to have ceased to be in rebellion and entitled to their Constitutional rights of State government, in harmony, with the Government of the United States, is, in the judgment of the House, an oppressive and unconditional demand, the tendency and the effect of which, if persisted in and enforced by war, will be to substantially change the object and character of the war on the part of the Federal Government from one to preserve, support and defend the Constitution of the United States as the supreme law of the land, to a revolutionary war against the constitutional rights and sovereignty of Federal States and virtually*

---

1529 History of the Rebellion, pg. 573.

1530 Condign means deserved.

*subversive of the constitutional government of the United States; and as such a war we now record our disapproval.*

*That in view of the immense power of war demanded by the President and supplied to him by patriotic people and hitherto wielded by him according to his own will, with little deference or regard to the opinions and conditions of the very large number, if not the majority of the faithful Union citizens of the United States who have doubted or disapproved his policy in conduct of the war and his extra and imaginary assumptions of executive power, and in view of the dangers to the constitutional liberty and the manifold evils that ever attend civil war, we desire peace, and the replacement under its healthful and benign influence, with the least possible waste of blood and treasure of the people, of all the relations and functions of constitutional government, State and Federal, now disturbed and endearing; and we therefore deprecate*[1531] *all vindictive and revolutionary measures and policy, military or civil, in tending to divide the Union men of the country to aggravate the evils and to intensify the animosities of the war and prolong its duration; and we advise, and do cordially invite and pledge our cooperation in negotiations, proposals, and efforts for peace upon the lands of a restoration of the Federal Union under the Constitution as it is, leaving to the free constitutional action of the people the question of amendments to the Federal Constitution and leaving also to the people of each State, as their unquestioned right, the right and the free exercise, to form, regulate, and control their State constitution, laws and domestic institutions in their own way, subject only to the Constitution of the United States.*

---

1531 Deprecate means to express disapproval of.

*"Hill, your apprehension of harm to me from some hidden enemy is downright foolishness. For a long time you have been trying to keep somebody–the Lord knows who–from killing me."*

As told to the author, Ward Hill Lamon,
by Abraham Lincoln in early 1865[1532]

# — 26 —

# CONSPIRACY AGAINST THE PRESIDENTS

The first conspiracy syndicate that was organized in Washington City had not for its object assassination; but the abduction of the president from the White House. The conspirators planned to take him South and hold him hostage to affect more easily favorable terms and concessions by the North to the end that peace between the sections might be established in a way that would prevent a war. These it would seem were the motives that inspired the conspirators of that organization.

The organization was now complete, and secrecy was maintained among the distinguished gentlemen composing it. It was composed principally with men from the South, but some resident Washingtonians and a few New Yorkers were initiated into their secrets.

Sometime in the month of December, 1860 while the leaders of the South were most dissatisfied with President Buchanan and he was struggling between two fires, the radical secession and the conservative national element represented in his Cabinet, a move was put on foot to abduct the president shortly after the return of Mr. Cushing[1533] from

---

1532 Recollections of Abraham Lincoln, pgs. 117 & 118.

1533 Caleb Cushing was of Massachusetts was chairman of the National Democratic Convention in Baltimore in 1860. www.answers.com/topic/caleb-cushing

the South where he had been sent by the administration to negotiate for peace with the southern people in convention. A few choice spirits organized a meeting in Washington in which it was proposed that President Buchanan should be kidnapped and taken off to a secure place in the South which was indicated. At this time it was thought this would necessitate the recall of Mr. Breckinridge to the executive chair, and under his ruling the whole South would feel a security against being (as Mr. Wigfall[1534] and others who called the meeting said) "trapped into war." At this meeting this policy was determined. Mr. Wigfall was the leader of the conspiracy and the conspirators had determined that President Buchanan had to go. It was not their purpose to kill him, but they wanted to get him out of the way. Now to get him safely out of Washington they could not contrive without the cooperation of Mr. Floyd.[1535]

Mr. Wigfall is said to have gone on Christmas night to the house of Mr. Floyd, taking with him one other gentleman. The proposed abduction was explained to Mr. Floyd which the proprietor of the plan earnestly advocated. Mr. Floyd heard the emissaries through. Then in a most empathetic manner he refused to give aid or countenance to such a diabolical conspiracy. Disappointed at Mr. Floyd's non-concurrence and expressed disapproval, Mr. Wigfall lost his temper, became very angry and is said to have deported himself with his usual inclination to bluster.

Mr. Cushing had been sent by Mr. Buchanan to the South Carolina secession convention to treat and make terms, &c. but his mission proved an ignoble[1536] failure and led to a most acrimonious[1537] discussion in this secret Washington organization, which eventually became a permanent institution. In this conclave was said to have first risen the question and proposition of detaching the city of New York not only from the Union but from the state of New York as well, the object being to make it kind of a free and independent city like Hamburg. Here were discussed all the matters bearing on secession and dismemberment of the Union. A watchful vigilance was kept up of every movement of the president and the administration ever ready

1534 Lewis T. Wigfall—See pg. 102.

1535 John B. Floyd was President Buchanan's Secretary of War. See pg. 42.

1536 Ignoble means dishonorable.

1537 Acrimonious means harsh.

to seize upon the first opportunity to abduct the executive. No opportunity arose to steal Mr. Buchanan while in office.

The organization was continued, however, in order to abduct Mr. Lincoln afterwards and there came as the favorable opportunity of doing this about the time Mr. Lincoln made the Soldiers' Home[1538] his summer residence. But their plans were thwarted by the vigilance of friends[1539] watchful of Mr. Lincoln's personal safety who had from the first of his presidential career been apprehensive of such danger or even a greater one. Those fears had been strengthened and confirmed by an ascertained knowledge of the intentions and operations of this secret conclave. Added to the other precautions a strong guard of cavalry[1540] was detailed to escort the president to and from the presidential mansion and his summer residence.

Up to the time of the assassination it was believed that it was not the intention of the organization to have Mr. Lincoln murdered, but that they did intend to spirit him away through the Confederate lines. He was, however, never free from danger of being murdered through other agencies. After the capitulation of General Lee, the better class, the thinking people of the South, began to learn and realize the nobility of his character, the tenderness of heart and the disposition of Mr. Lincoln. They seemed to know and realize then that their greatest interest—life, liberty and property—depended greatly upon him and they had begun to believe that he would be their greatest friend. When the assassination occurred they deprecated[1541] the murder and sincerely mourned his death, which was like an irreparable loss to them and the nation.[1542]

---

[1538] The Soldier's Home was built in 1842 by Washington banker George W. Riggs and was used to take care of elderly or injured soldiers. It contained five large buildings and several cottages. It is located about three miles north of the White House near Silver Springs, Maryland. It was used by Mr. Lincoln as an escape from the White House. It is still used as a Soldier's Home today. The Lincoln Cottage is a national historic landmark open to the public. Lincoln's Sanctuary, pgs. xi & xii and www.lincolncottage.org..

[1539] Mr. Stanton and the author, Ward Hill Lamon were two of Mr. Lincoln's main "friends" who watched out for his safety. Ward Hill Lamon: Lincoln's "Particular Friend," pgs. 367 & 368.

[1540] The 11th New York Cavalry of about 80 horsemen was assigned to this duty. Lincoln's Sanctuary, pg. 59.

[1541] Deprecated means disapproval of.

[1542] General Joseph Johnston said of the South when he heard of Mr. Lincoln's death, "Mr. Lincoln was the best friend they had" and the assassination was "the greatest possible calamity to the South." Abraham Lincoln, The War Years, pg. 869.

There never was an hour from the time Mr. Lincoln entered Washington on the 23rd of February, 1861 to the 15th of April, 1865 that he was not in danger of his life from violence. Beyond question had it not been for the constant and persistent watchfulness of his friends by day and night, he would have been murdered long before he was. He never could be persuaded to believe that he was in the least danger whatever, nor did the Cabinet and friends general among him realize that there was any danger. The apathy and assumed security only had the affect of inspiring those whose business it was to guard him to redouble their energy in their watchfulness over him.

Very shortly after the installation of Mr. Lincoln in the presidential chair, a citizen of Washington, a gentleman of prominent position, got into some complication and was charged with serious offenses. He was arrested upon these charges by an official holding a post of high trust and responsibility.[1543] The case threatened to result greatly to the detriment of the accused. The official who arrested him became satisfied the prisoner was possessed of more knowledge of some crookedness that one man ought to enjoy alone and was desirous of sharing that knowledge and upon a square proposition that he could be granted immunity from the charge, and the matter hushed up.

The officer went to Mr. Lincoln and told him that he was satisfied that it would be greatly to the interests of the public service if he could be given discretionary powers to save harmless a man who resided in the District of Columbia against who charges of a serious nature were made, and who had been already arrested under said charge. The party accused was a man of high character and well connected, in a position to know the secrets of the enemy in conspiracy and could place valuable information in his hands under a promise of protection. The matter was of such character and importance that he thought immunity should be guaranteed in good faith to the party imparting the information and for other prudential reasons he thought it wise that he alone be entrusted with the promised information.

Mr. Lincoln, after serious deliberation, said to the officer, "In your judgment I have great confidence. I am sure you would not ask for anything that was not for the best interests of the country. Go ahead, do what you think best about it, and I will stand by you."

---

[1543] This official was the author, Ward Hill Lamon, U.S. Marshal of the District of Columbia. Lincoln: The War Years, pg. 869.

The implicated man yielded to the proposition. The confession was made however, on the express condition that the officer would pledge his word of honor that neither the name of the unfortunate or the name of the conspirators he would implicate should be made public unless in the judgment of the official it became absolutely necessary.

No absolute necessity ever having arisen, the names were never divulged; yet, the information received through this source was invaluable. The officer concluded that no good to the country and much harm to the individual would result if he were to violate the confidence of the promise made to an unfortunate man whose services had been of such inestimable[1544] value.

The officer here mentioned just three days previous to Mr. Lincoln's assassination was sent to Richmond on a special mission connected government affairs in relating to the reorganization of the state.

The following is a facsimile of the pass he bore and is probably the last autographic one that Mr. Lincoln gave to anyone:

*Allow the bearer ____________ and friend, with ordinary baggage to pass from Washington to Richmond and return. April 11, 1865*[1545]

On the eve of his departure from Washington, this officer had urged upon Mr. Usher, Secretary of the Interior, to persuade Mr. Lincoln to exercise extreme caution and to go out as little as possible while he was absent, and to particularly avoid the theater. Mr. Usher[1546] went to see Mr. Lincoln who pooh-poohed the counsel with the remark, "What does anyone want to massacre me for?"

---

[1544] Inestimable means excellent.

[1545] Recollections of Abraham Lincoln, pg, 280.

[1546] Mr. J. P. Usher was Mr. Lincoln's Secretary of the Interior.

Allow the bearer, W. H,
Lamon & friend, with ordin
ary baggage to pass from
Washington to Richmond
and return —

April 11. 1865 . A. Lincoln

Copy of actual pass as mentioned on the previous page

*"The country must be saved under principles of the Declaration of Independence which promised 'liberty for all.' If it can't be saved upon that principle, it will be truly awful. I was about to say I would rather then be assassinated on this spot than surrender it."*

Abraham Lincoln, Philadelphia speech,
February 22, 1861[1547]

# — 27 —

# ABRAHAM LINCOLN'S ASSASSINATION

From Walt Whitman's[1548] vivid description of the scene at Ford's Theater.

The day, April 14, 1865, seems to have been a pleasant one throughout the whole land—the moral atmosphere pleasant—too, the long storm, so dark, so fratricidal[1549] full of blood and doubt and gloom and over, ended at last by the sun rise of an absolute national victory, and utter breaking down of secessionism, we almost doubted our senses. Lee had capitulated beneath the apple tree at Appomattox; the other armies, the flags of the revolt quickly followed. And could it really be then a bout of all the affairs of this world of woe and passion, of failure and disorder and dismay was there really to come the confirmed unerring sign of peace like a shaft of pure light, of rightful rule of God?

But I must not dwell on accessories, the deed hastens. The popular afternoon paper *The Little Evening Star* had scattered all over its third page divided among the advertisements in a sensational manner, in a

---

[1547] The Lincoln Train to Washington, pg. 277.

[1548] Walt Whitman is a famous poet. He spent much of his time in Washington visiting the sick and wounded soldiers in the area hospital. Lincoln's Sanctuary, pg. 1 and whitmanarchive.org

[1549] Fratricidal means killing ones own brother.

hundred different places: "The president and his lady will be at the theater this evening." Lincoln was fond of the theater. I have myself seen him there several times. I remember thinking how funny it was, that he, in some respects the leading actor in the greatest and stormiest drama known to real history stage through centuries, to sit there and be so completely interested in those human jack-straws moving about with their silly gestures, foreign spirit and flatulent[1550] text. So the day as I say was propitious.[1551] Early herbage, early flowers were out. I remember where I was stopping at the time, the season being advanced. There were many lilacs in full bloom by one of those caprices[1552] that enter and give tinge to events without being at all a part of them. I find myself always reminded of that day by the sight and odor of these blossoms. It never fails.

On this occasion the theater was crowded. Many ladies in rich and gay costumes. Officers in their uniforms, many well-known citizens, young folks, the usual cluster of gas lights, the usual magnetism of so many people, cheerful with perfume, music of violins and flutes—and over all, a saturating, that vast, vague, wonder, victory, the nation's victory, the triumph of the Union filling the air, the thought, the scent, with exhilaration more than all perfumes.

The president came betimes[1553] and with his wife, witnessed the play from the large stage boxes of the second tier, two thrown into one, and profusely draped with the national flag. The acts and scenes of the piece, one of those singularly witless compositions which have at least the merit of giving the entire relief to an audience engaged in mental action or business excitements and cares during the day, as it makes not the slightest calls on either the moral, emotional, aesthetic or spiritual nature—a piece (*Our American Cousin*) in which among other characters is a so-called Yankee—certainly such one as was never seen, or at least like it never seen in North America, is introduced in England with a varied *foll-der-oll*[1554] of talk, plot, scenery and such phantasmagoria[1555] as goes to wake up a popular modern drama—had progressed through perhaps a couple of its acts when in

---

1550 Flatulent means inflated.

1551 Propitious means a good omen.

1552 Caprices are feelings.

1553 Betimes means early.

1554 *Foll-der-oll* means a bit of nonsense.

1555 Phantasmagoria means fever.

the midst of the comedy or tragedy, or non-such, or whatever it is called, or to offset it or to finish it out as if nature and the great muse's mockery of these four mimics come interpolated[1556] that scene not really or exactly to be described at all (for on the many hundreds who were there) it seems to this hour to have left little but a passing blur—a dream—a blot—and yet partially to be described as I now proceed to give it.

There is a scene in the play representing the modern parlor in which two unprecedented English ladies are presented by the unprecedented and impossible Yankee that he is not a man of fortune, and therefore undesirable for marriage hatching purposes; after which the comments being finished, the dramatic trio make exit leaving the stage clear for the moment. There was a pause, a hush, as it were. At this period came the murder of Abraham Lincoln, great as that was with all its manifold train circling around it and stretching into the future for many centuries in the politics, history, art, &c. of the new world, in point of fact, the main thing, the actual murder transpired with the quiet and simplicity of any commonest occurrence—the bursting of a bud or pod in the growth of vegetation—for instance.

Through the general hum following the stage pause, with the change of position &c., came the muffled sound of a pistol shot, which not one hundredth of the audience heard at the time—yet a moment's hush—somehow surely a vague started thrill—and then through the ornamented drapery starred and striped space way of the president's box, a sudden figure. A man raises himself with hands and feet, stands a moment on the railing, leaps below to the stage (a distance of perhaps fourteen or fifteen feet), falls out of position—catching himself, his boot heel in the copious drapery (the American flag), falls on one knee, quickly recovers himself, rises as if nothing had happened (he really sprains his ankle, but unfelt then) and the figure, Booth, the murderer, dressed in plain black broad cloth, bare headed, with a full head of glossy raven hair, and his eyes, like some animals flashing with light and resolution, yet with a certain strange calmness, holds, aloft in one hand a large knife—fully towards the audience, his face a statuesque beauty, lit by those basilisk[1557] eyes, flashing with desperation, perhaps insanity—launches out in a firm and steady voice

---

[1556] Interpolated means altered.
[1557] Basilisk means lizard-like.

the words "*sic semper tyrannis*"[1558]—and then walks with neither slow nor very rapid pace diagonally across the back of the stage and disappears. Had all this not terrible scene—making the mimic one preposterous—had it not been all rehearsed in blank by Booth beforehand?

A moment's hush, incredulous—a scream—the cry of murder—Mrs. Lincoln leaning out of the box with ashy cheeks and lips, with involuntary cry pointing to the retreating figure, "He has killed the president." And still a moment's strange incredulous[1559] suspense—and then the deluge!!! Then that mixture of horror, noiseless uncertainty (the sound, somewhere back, of a horse's hoofs clattering with speed), the people burst through chairs and railings and break them up—that noise adds to the queerness of the scene—there is extricable[1560] confusion and terror—women faint—quite feeble persons fall and are trampled on—many cries of agony are heard—the broad stage suddenly fills to suffocation with a dense and motley crowd like some horrible carnival—the audience rush generally upon it—at least the strong men do—the actors and actresses are there in their play costumes and painted faces in moral fright showing through the rouge—some trembling, some in tears, the screams and calls—confused talk—redoubled, trebled—two or three manage to pass up water from the stage to the president's box—others try to clamber up.

In the midst of all this the soldiers of the president's guard with others, suddenly drawn to the scene, burst in—some two hundred altogether—they storm the house, through all the tiers, especially the upper ones, inflamed with fury, literally charging the audience with fixed bayonets, muskets and pistols, shouting "Clear out, clear out, you sons of b's." Such the wild scene or a suggestion of it, rather inside the playhouse that night. Outside too, in the atmosphere of shock, crowds of people filled with frenzy ready to seize an outlet for it came near committing murder several times on innocent individuals. One such cause was especially exciting. The infuriated crowd, through some chance, got started against one man, either through words he uttered or perhaps without any cause at all and were proceeding at once to hang him on a neighboring lamp post when he was rescued by a few heroic policemen, who placed him in their midst and fought their way

---

1558 *Sic semper tyrannis* is Latin for "thus ever to tyrants." Lincoln and Liberty, pg. 316.
1559 Incredulous means not believable.
1560 Extricable means tangled.

slowly and amidst great peril towards the station house. It was a fitting episode of the entire affair. The crowd rushing and eddying to and fro—the night, the yells, the pale faces, many frightened people, trying in vain, to extricate themselves—the attacked man not yet freed from the jaws of death—looking like a corpse—the silent, resolute, half a dozen policemen with no weapons but their clubs, yet stern and steady through all the eddying swarms—made indeed a fitting side scene to the tragedy of the murder. They gained the station house with the protected man whom they placed in security for the night, and discharged him in the morning. In the midst of that night, pandemonium of senseless hate, infuriated soldiers, the audience and the crowd and the stage and all its actors and actresses—its paint pots, spangles and gas lights—the life blood from those veins—the best and the sweetest of the land dripped slowly down and death's ooze already begins its little bubbles on the lips.

Such hurriedly sketched were the accompaniments to the death of President Lincoln. So suddenly, and in murder and horror, unsurpassed he was taken from us. But his death was painless.

When the dreaded tragedy occurred the general sentiment was that had this officer been at his post in the exercise of his wonton vigilance, the catastrophe would have been averted. Recovering from the stunning affect of the assassination and Payne's[1561] murderous assault, Mr. Seward's first exclamation was "Where was ______?[1562] This would not have occurred if he had been here."

Mr. Lincoln at all times manifested a total indifference to danger to his person while the marshal and some others never were free from apprehension of the greatest peril that he was daily subjected to,[1563] yet with all the sleepless nights and the precautions taken he was assassinated by J. Wilkes Booth on the night of April 14, 1865 in Ford's Theater on 10th Street in Washington City at the hour of ten o'clock and thirty minutes p.m. And at twenty-two minutes past seven

---

1561 Lewis Payne was one of the Lincoln conspirators. His assignment was to kill Mr. Steward, which he failed to do. The Lincoln Murder Conspiracies, pg. 56.

1562 What Mr. Seward actually said was "Where was Lamon?" Ward Hill Lamon: Lincoln's "Particular Friend," pg. 381. (The reader may wonder where Mr. Lincoln's personal body guard and the author of this manuscript, Ward Hill Lamon, was on this night. See editor's notes pg. ii)

1563 The author, Ward Hill Lamon, and Allan Pinkerton (See pg. 92) both had investigated numerous plots to harm Mr. Lincoln. Allan Pinkerton, The First Private Eye, pg. 177

o'clock a.m. on the following morning he died of the wound inflicted by a pistol ball in the back part of his head directed by the hand of his foul murderer at the house of a Mr. Peterson situated across the street from the theater to which he was conveyed.

Mr. Lincoln's body was then taken to the White House where it lay in state. On Monday the 17th a meeting of the members of Congress was held in the Capitol to take into consideration what was necessary and proper to be done about his funeral &c. The Honorable La Fayette Foster[1564] of Connecticut presided at this meeting and on the 18th (Tuesday) at ten o'clock, the doors of the White House were thrown open and at least 25,000 persons availed themselves of the opportunity of looking upon the familiar face of him whose eyes were now closed in death. No more solemn spectacle was ever witnessed. On the 19th the funeral ceremonies were solemnized in the east room of the presidential mansion. The funeral address was delivered by Rev. Dr. Gurley.[1565] The remains were then taken to the Capitol where they were again exposed to the public view, and viewed by thousands of mourning people, until the 21st instant when the funeral train took up the march and on the way to the final resting place of honored dead in the western city of Springfield, Illinois home of his early affections, trials, and ambitions. On the same day the train bearing his body and its sad and mournful escort reached Baltimore at ten o'clock a.m. It left for Harrisburg the next morning.[1566] Here the body was again exposed in the state capitol during that evening and from seven o'clock p.m. until nine o'clock a.m. the next day when the train left for Philadelphia.

The remains were then taken to Independence Hall where they remained from ten a.m. until twelve p.m. and the next day (Sunday) from six a.m. until ten a.m. On Monday the body was again viewed by a vast multitude of people. At this last hour April 24th the procession

---

1564 Honorable LaFayette S. Foster served as U.S. Senator from 1855—1867. He was President *Pro Tempore* of the Senate and first in line for the presidency had the conspirators also killed Vice - President Andrew Johnson. www.infoplease.com/biography/us/congress/foster-lafayette-sabine.html

1565 Rev. Dr. Phineas D. Gurley was the pastor of the Lincoln family's church. He also gave the Benediction at the funeral ceremony in Springfield, Illinois. The War Years, Vol. III, pg. 886 and When Lincoln Died, pg. 133.

1566 Harrisburg, Pennsylvania is the capital of the Commonwealth of Pennsylvania. Mr. Lincoln spoke to the legislature in Harrisburg on his train trip to his inauguration. The Life of Abraham Lincoln, pg. 234 and The President Travels by Train, pg. 22.

resumed its march arriving at Kensington Station where appropriate ceremonies were had. And at four p.m. the train left for New York where the normal ceremonies were paid and the remains viewed by an immense concourse of sorrowful people. At four p.m. on Tuesday April 25th the train left for Albany and reached there at midnight. At one o'clock a.m. Wednesday the 26th the casket lid was again removed and from that time until two p.m. the body was viewed by an immense throng of people. At four p.m. the train was again on its way and reached Buffalo at seven a.m. on Thursday the 27th. From nine p.m. that evening until eight p.m. on the 28th the sacred remains were exposed and viewed by the people there. At ten p.m. the train left for Cleveland reaching there at seven a.m. on Saturday where similar services were performed, after which Chicago was reached on the 1st of May at nine a.m. The remains were then exposed in the rotunda of the court house where an immense crowd of his former fellow citizens took a last lingering look at what was left of their friend and chosen leader. On the 3rd the procession reached Springfield, the former home of the living and sepulcher of the late president, where the body was taken to the state house over the entrance which was written—"He left us shorn up by our prayers, he returned embalmed in our tears." These lines were suggested by the sentiments he uttered to his old friends and fellow citizens of Springfield on the day he left for Washington, February 11, 1861.

Thousands upon thousands of people of all classes, all ages, and all sexes embraced this opportunity of viewing the features the last time of their friend, their country's pride and humanity's greatest nobleman. At ten o'clock a.m. Thursday May 4, 1865, Abraham Lincoln's body was born to Oak Ridge Cemetery where it now rests in peace from the troubles of life—his fame pictured on the canvas of time, lined in his martyr's blood, by the sublime artist of eternity, will never need defense by a finite agency.

*"General, there's no such thing as reconstruction.*
*These states have not gone out of the Union.*
*Therefore reconstruction is unnecessary."*
Andrew Johnson to John A. Logan, May 31, 1865[1567]

# — 28 —

# PRESIDENT ANDREW JOHNSON

Mr. Lincoln's successor to the presidency, the Honorable Andrew Johnson, was not long in exciting Congressional antagonism, greater even than the political difference between his late predecessor and that honorable body. That Mr. Johnson was patriotic and honest in his purposes there can be no reasonable doubt, though he was unfortunate in his modes, methods and means. He should be credited with an honest purpose of administering the government as nearly in the line marked out and determined by his predecessor as possible. He did not take into consideration the changed condition of things.

The assassination of Mr. Lincoln had a wonderful affect on the public mind—men who before that time were in favor of liberal reconstruction of the rebellious states, now changed from a feeling of forgiveness and the advocacy of conservative policy to that of bitter hatred, and favored the most rigid punishment of the southern people by all constitutional means. The altered condition of public sentiment which the assassination of Mr. Lincoln created was disregarded by Mr. Johnson and he was assured by place seekers—sycophants[1568] and southern sympathizers, flatterers and advisors that his cause and position was a strong one and his strength was irresistible. He had an established character for firmness, but that qualification, admirable in

[1567] Andrew Johnson and Reconstruction, pg. 91.
[1568] Sycophants are accusers.

itself, when based on the principles of justice and expediency, fitting proper conditions, now proved his downfall.

He was eventually arraigned for impeachment by Congress for a series of charges, tried and was acquitted.[1569] Great injury doubtless would have resulted to our free institutions had his trial proved otherwise. No unprejudiced reader, after examining the record of that trial—the arguments particularly of the managers appointed on behalf of Congress to manage the trial, will not admit that Mr. Johnson was charged with one series of charges and upon which he never was tried; but the trial seemed to be for the charge of "pure cussedness." Mr. Johnson had been unfortunate in the selection of his advisors outside of his Cabinet. It was but natural that the Republicans had cause to complain of his course in the administration of the complicated public affairs then existing. Before the presidential election he had been in accord with the most radical creed of that party and had sought and received their suffrages. Upon his succession to office, his mind seemed to have undergone a change, which led to the charge of baseness and with having made an alliance with the enemies of the Union. Extravagant rumors were in circulation about him, which Republicans gave credulous[1570] ear. The committee or certain members of it charged with investigation of the president's official conduct, were seriously impressed by such rumors.

One of the most appalling of the rumors was that General Grant had been approached by President Johnson to use the army for the purpose of sustaining himself in revolutionary measures which he had in contemplation. These rumors did General Grant a great injustice. But recently, since the death of General Grant,[1571] some sensational parties have endeavored to make it appear that General Grant was aware of a revolutionary purpose on the part of Mr. Johnson while president, and that he, General Grant, had been approached by him on that subject to give him the support of the army in carrying them out. This rumor sought to be established as fact amounted to this: whether if it should be determined to constitute a Congress of Democratic members from the North and admit rebel members from the South,

---

[1569] He escaped impeachment by one vote. The Odd Couple Who Hanged Mary Surratt, pg. 84.

[1570] Credulous means inclined to believe.

[1571] General Grant died on July 23, 1885 at Saratoga, New York. Appleton's Cyclopaedia of American Biography, Vol. II., pg. 709.

President Johnson could rely on General Grant with the army to sustain such a movement by force, if necessary. There was apprehension at this time, that Mr. Johnson was capable, if the army could be made to sustain of overthrowing the legitimacy of the Congress of the United States by some such means that resorted to by Cromwell[1572] closing the session of the long parliament of England.

With General Grant's known and established patriotism, and high sense of personal dignity and official honor, it could not be doubted for one moment by any fair minded man divested of prejudice, that he would not have listened to such a monstrous proposition, and that he would have promptly exposed, and denounced anyone guilty of making it as a traitor to his country. Had President Johnson been tried for treason on such a charge, backed and supported by such testimony, instead of paltry misdemeanors upon which he had been tried, little doubt can be entertained that he would have been convicted and rendered infamous for all coming time.

Reviving the charge at this late day, as it has been done after the death of General Grant, or indeed at any time, that he was in possession of the facts, that a proposition had been made directly to him of such a treasonable nature by the chief executive of the nation, and he had tactically remained silent in regard to it, cannot be construed in any other light as doing great injustice the memory of that wonderful man. It implies a want of circumspection[1573] and probity[1574] and demeanor for which the General of the United States Army had ever been so eminently[1575] characterized.

That President Johnson at the time was advised and urged to pursue such a course as indicated in these charges, there can be no doubt. This fact is within the knowledge of the writer. It is also within the knowledge of the writer that Mr. Johnson indignantly rebuked his advisors thereto, and that he replied to them excitedly, that such a course were to be pursued by him under the military menace, it would not only be revolutionary in its character, but would justly subject him to the charge of downright treason—a direct attempt of the executive

---

1572 Oliver Cromwell was the first Lord Protector of the Commonwealth of England, Ireland and Scotland, serving from 1653—1658.
www.newworldencyclopedia.org/entry/oliver_cromwell

1573 Circumspection means being discreet.

1574 Probity means honesty.

1575 Eminently means highly.

to overthrow the established usages and forms of the government proceedings.

Mr. Johnson did not hesitate then, and in that presence to declare it as his firm and deliberate conviction that the pretended seceded states never having the constitutional power to segregate themselves from the Union by their own voluntary act, were still integral parts of the United States and still retained their suspended right of representation in Congress under the apportioned act of Congress of 1860, whenever they might renew their demand for representation in the federal expenditures of that government. In justice to Mr. Johnson and in the interest of truth and history, it is proper to state that he repudiated[1576] the proposition to use the army to enforce the rights of the class of people which rights he was ready to acknowledge. He recognized at the same time the right of the coordinate legislative branch of the government as an independent body, being the judges of their own membership and of the persons who should be permitted to compose that body.

And it is further true that a strong effort was made to influence President Johnson to invoke the auxiliary power of the army to enforce southern right of representation in Congress at the time and in connection with the appointment of Major General Hancock[1577] to assume the military command of the provisional government of the state of Louisiana. This Mr. Johnson rejected with all such counsels, and by doing so he incurred the personal enmity[1578] of several of his self-constituted counselors, newly made friends, and coadjutors,[1579] many of whom were in Ohio and Kentucky at that time ready and eager for cooperation in such revolutionary movements and in fact, in any movement whatever, however desperate and lawless, that would secure ascendancy over radical rule in the government of the public affairs of the nation.

There were many idle persons at this time in the country, many whom four years had unfitted for the ordinary vocations in life, full of adventure who would not have required great persuasion to engage in any enterprise having as its object a change in the existing state of things under any leader in whom they might have confidence, if for no

---

1576 Repudiated means disowned.

1577 Major General Winfield Scott Hancock—See pg. 188.

1578 Enmity is hatred.

1579 Coadjutors are assistants.

other object, the mere love of adventurous employment would be a sufficient incentive to action. Happily, however, this class embraced but a meager minority of the people. The great majority were governed in all things under those prudential restraints, that all loyal people instinctively impose on themselves in times of great public excitement and danger.

This disposition to scourge the people of the South who had eventually laid down their arms and asked to be allowed to come back to their alliance with the Constitution and again have a voice in the affairs of the restored government on a fair basis of representation was not partaken of by the men who had done the fighting—the soldiers of war—but alone by the soldiers of fortune. As a type of literature and an index to the feeling prevalent among those who had taken some part in the war other than for speculative purposes, the following extract from a letter written in September 1866 by a civilian is given:

"A good citizen can no more adhere to the dominating faction in Congress at this critical moment in our country's affairs than he could have given 'aid and comfort' to the public enemy in the late war. The claim that any partisan majority in the National Legislature represents the people at large in a closer and more direct manner than the President is false and in fact theory. Representatives are elected by single districts and Senators by State Legislatures.[1580] The latter often plot, bargain and buy the way to their seats, while the former are floated in upon petty local questions or little trades in county politics.

On the contrary the President is chosen by the whole people, voting on the same day, and is essentially and solely their representative, their tribune, armed with their veto and charged especially to 'preserve, protect, and defend' their Constitution. They, the people, ordained and established it as 'the supreme law of the land.'

Mr. Johnson is not the first President who has had to look to the holiest part of the oath and shield that sacred instrument against the assaults of a fierce faction, which claimed to represent the country. An old neighbor of his, sprung from the loins of the people, like himself, fought this same battle over many years ago. The victorious issue on that occasion amply demonstrated the wisdom of our fathers in

---

[1580] At this time U.S. Senators were not elected by the vote of the people in their district but by the vote of the state legislature.
www.encarta.msn.com/encyclopedia_761586759_3/senate.html

making the President, by organic law, the peculiar representative of the whole people, to check the follies and restrain that license of Congress to which deliberate assemblies are always subject.

If by any fault of his own or by the hapless failure of the people to come to his aid, Andrew Johnson should go down in the terrible conflict forced upon him that would be a vital result to the country. He will be impeached. The phrase goes that he will be *punished before trial*; but that is not the word. The triumphant faction will merely wreak a terrible and cowardly revenge upon him. He will be declared suspended, deposed, perhaps murdered. A revolutionist will assume his office. Henceforth the election of the President is taken out of the hands of the people and lodged with Congress. That body can make and unmake Presidents in a day or an hour. Will it be said that Congress will not set such a precedent; because the Radicals cannot always expect to possess this power? If they succeed now, they intend, by force and fraud, to hold that power at least until this generation has passed away. The present is merely a desperate struggle to that end. Confessedly acting outside the Constitution, claiming the right to disfranchise the people or exclude the representatives of any State which may not agree with them and holding in the hollow of their hands the ten 'rotten boroughs of the South,' to return Radical Congressmen, white or black, as they may dictate, they will possess the power to accomplish any purpose, however revolutionary, however atrocious.

Even now, with the form of government still unchanged, without a usurper in the Presidential chair, are not the representatives of Kentucky and the defrauded Senators of New Jersey and Maryland, to say nothing of the ten Southern States, driven from the seats to which they were elected? And further, will the five monarchs then be withdrawn from one-third of our common country, and our free system of government extended to the unfortunate people? On the contrary, we may expect that they will make them despots in name, show and parade as well as fact. They may put crowns on their heads, and scepters in their hands, and set them to doing deeds of tyranny; beside which the past will appear as innocent pastime. We will then present to the world a spectacle even more singular than we do now. We shall have a patent State, a pretended *free republican constitutional* government located at Washington, with five outlying despotisms, blighting its territory, plundering and decimating its people. Can such monsters be born of free, popular government?

But you may say the Radicals will withdraw the viceroys as soon as the Negroes are put in possession of those States and the whites are sufficiently ground beneath the black heels. Not to mention here that this would be very unpleasant to the 'great Union majorities' which Mr. Greeley and others always claimed in those States. I do not believe that such a purpose exists. Military, despotic, unlimited power is never abandoned except under compulsion. Despotism is delicious to the despot, and when people are freed from his power they achieve it by their own good swords. In the meantime, it would be cruel pleasantry to compare the condition of those States with that of Ireland, Hungary, Canada, or any other people on the globe. They produce but half what their industries ought to make now, but when the Negro and the soldier contend over the entirely ruined and prostrate country, they will produce nothing. The great staples will disappear from our commerce. We have said the North must carry the debt of the war without aid from the quarter where we had a right to expect it. The President's hands are tied by a tenure of office bill, passed to shield a horde of corrupt officials fastened upon the Government, and all banded together in one great combination to elect a Radical President. Revenue to the amount of hundreds of millions (witness whiskey frauds alone) remain uncollected, through the unparalleled corruption of financial agents. Not only must one-third of our territory be made desolate; not only must the laboring North be taxed to support a standing army and Negro governments in ten States, but must be fleeced and mortgaged in a way of these stupendous frauds to insure its own subjugation in the Radical party.

But we all hope that the hour of our deliverance is at hand. Every State that speaks from California to Maine, speaks in defense of the Constitution and the President who upholds it. If the coming elections result as the late ones have we will see the fallen framework of our constitutional Government reared again, and the pillars of republican liberty fixed to stand unmoved forever."[1581]

---

1581 The letter was unsigned.

*"The depiction of Booth in some places as 'our Brutus'–the last protagonist of Southern Chivalry–contributed to the northern belief that the assassination was a plot of the Confederate government."*

John S. Wise of Virginia[1582]

# — 29 —

# The Assassination of Abraham Lincoln— A Confederate Plot

Immediately after the assassination of President Lincoln, there was intense excitement in Washington, as well as throughout the country, and a pretty general belief among the loyal element of the people that persons of so-called high authority in the Confederate States' government were directly responsible for his murder. This feeling seemed to intensify from day to day until the second of May following, when President Johnson issued his proclamation as follows:
Proclamation, by the President of the United States

*Whereas it appears from evidence in the Bureau of Military Justice that the atrocious murder of the late president and the attempted murder of the Honorable William H. Seward, Secretary of State, was incited, concerted and procured by and between Jefferson Davis, late of Richmond, Virginia and Jacob Thompson,*[1583] *Clement C. Clay,*[1584] *Beverley Tucker,*[1585] *George M. Sanders,*[1586] *W. C.*

---

[1582] Lincoln in American Memory, pg. 45.

[1583] Jacob Thompson—See page 60.

[1584] Clement C. Clay—See pg. 137.

[1585] Beverley Tucker was the purchasing agent for the Confederate government. He was trying to negotiate trade arrangements with Canadian officials, trading Canada's

*Cleary*[1587] *and other rebels and traitors against the government of the United States harbored in Canada.*

*Now, therefore, to the end that justice may be done, I, Andrew Johnson, President of the United States, do offer for the arrest of said persons or either of them within the limits of the United States so they can be brought to trial, the following rewards: $100,000 for the arrest of Jefferson Davis; $25,000 for the arrest of Clement C. Clay; $25,000 for the arrest of Jacob Thompson of Mississippi; $25,000 for the arrest of George M. Sanders; $25,000 for the arrest of Beverly Tucker; $10,000 for the arrest William W. Cleary, clerk of C. C. Clay.*

*The Provost Marshal General of the United States is directed to cause a description of said persons with notice of the above reward be published.*

*(signed) Andrew Johnson*

*In the testimony, W.H. Hunter,*[1588] *secretary of the United States*

Some of the persons accused had held high positions under the Confederate government and all of whom had, through life, the single blemish of treason attached to them, for rebelling against the established government. Each had enjoyed the confidence of their fellow citizens and were on unblemished reputation as private gentlemen. The morbid excitement of the public mind now gave color enough to the accusations against them to satisfy a large class of people of their guilt, which subjected them to all ignominy[1589] scarcely less virulent that would have attached upon full proof of guilt and conviction.

Subsequently it transpired that the accusations were based on a false state of facts. Naturally enough under the excitement produced by Mr. Lincoln's assassination, the heads of the federal government

---

bacon for the Confederacy's cotton. The Two American Presidents, pg. 339 and The Lincoln Conspiracies, pg. 15.

[1586] George M. Sanders was from Kentucky. He developed the theory that any political leader who acted like a tyrant, like he thought Mr. Lincoln was doing, ought to be murdered. He was the leader of the conspirators sent to Montreal. He was trying to encourage the Canadians to raid American towns along the border. The Two American Presidents. Pg. 339 and The Lincoln Conspiracies, pg. 15.

[1587] William C. Cleary declared himself an agent of the Confederacy according to testimony in front of Judge John Bingham. www.law.umkc.edu/faculty/projects/ftrials/lincolnconspiraccy/binghamclose.html

[1588] W. H. Hunter was acting Secretary of State. Harpers Pictorial History of the Great Rebellion, pg. 788.

[1589] Ignominy means disgrace.

were easily misled and betrayed into the action they had taken under the testimony of irresponsible enthusiasts which afterwards proved to be unreliable and untrue.

The accused, Clay, Thompson,[1590] Sanders, Tucker and Cleary were all in Canada at the time the proclamation was issued. The proclamation was based principally on statements of three detectives, Viz.[1591] Sanford Conover,[1592] Richard Montgomery[1593] and James B. Merritt[1594] who professed to have had many conversations with the accused before and after the assassination in the dominion of Canada, in which Mr. Thompson acknowledged that he was aware of the purpose to kill President Lincoln, also the purpose of poisoning the Croton Water Works,[1595] introducing yellow fever into the northern cities and armies and of also firing[1596] of the New York hotels.

Conversations were also held where Mr. Thompson admitted that he had received dispatches brought to him by John Surratt[1597] (one of the actual conspirators, who was a party to Lincoln's murder) and to other conversations with Mr. Thompson about the assassination both before and subsequent to the act. These detectives gave similar testimony to the Bureau of Military Justice at Washington against the

---

[1590] According to John Wilkes Booth's papers, Thompson, Tucker, Sanders, Dr. Blackwell of Kentucky, Mr. Lee, and Dr. M.A. Pallen met in October 1864 in Lawrence Hall in Montreal. Thompson, Tucker, Sanders, Dr. Blackwell, Mr. Lee and Dr. Pallen met with John Wilkes Booth in October 1864 in St. Lawrence Hall in Montreal according to Booth's papers. The Odd Couple Who Hanged Mary Surratt, pg. 45

[1591] Viz. stands for videlicet which means namely.

[1592] Sanford Conover, one of the detectives, was also an anonymous correspondent for the *New York Tribune* newspaper. The Lincoln Murder Conspiracies, pg. 71

[1593] Richard Montgomery, one of the detectives, was also a U.S. spy. The Lincoln Murder Conspiracies, pg. 71.

[1594] James B. Merritt was a doctor from Ayr, Southern Canada West (now Ontario). The Lincoln Murder Conspiracies, pg. 71

[1595] Croton Water Works were a series of dams and aqueducts developed along the Croton River to provide drinking water for the city of New York. www.water-industry.org/water-facts/croton_1.htm.

[1596] Firings means setting on fire. Actually on November 25, 1864 conspirators set fire to three hotels in New York and the Barnum Museum. Thirty two fires were planned in all. The fire at the La Farge Hotel interrupted a performance by John Wilkes Booth and his brothers Junius Brutus Booth Jr. and Edwin Booth at the Winter Garden Theater. The Lincoln Murder Conspiracies, pg. 19.

[1597] John Surratt was one of the Lincoln conspirators who fled to Europe. His mother Mary Surratt was hanged with three other conspirators. He was later captured and returned to the U.S. for trial and was found innocent. The Assassination of Abraham Lincoln, History or Myth, pg. 222.

others named who were then in Canada. James B. Merritt said that he was present at a meeting at Montreal, about the middle of February when Colonel Steele,[1598] Captain Scott and George Young[1599] were present when a position to kill President Lincoln was discussed, and a letter was read from Jefferson Davis, approbating[1600] whatever might be done on this behalf.

At the military court in Washington subsequently, the whole of the statements of these detectives proved to be false and not in a single instance where they fixed a time and place was there not a satisfactory alibi proven.[1601] Mr. Merritt's testimony about the meeting in Montreal about the middle of February where the proposition to kill Mr. Lincoln and the letter from Jefferson Davis approving whatever might be done were discussed, turned out to be an infamous fabrication. Abundant proof was adduced[1602] to show that Messers. Steele, Scott and Young were not in Montreal at anytime during the month of February, and on the contrary, they were all at Windsor several hundred miles distant during the whole of that month. It eventually turned out after a patient and thorough trial before a military commission that these men, Messers. Conover (whose real name was Dunham), Montgomery and Merritt were all men of desperate character. It was satisfactorily and clearly proved that they were a trio of perjured villains who severely and collectively deserved to be hung as high as hay men and for the same reason. The lives of these Mordecais[1603] were saved, and these hay men fled the country before the infliction of an indignant country's righteous retribution was visited upon them.

---

1598 Colonel Steele had been heard to say that the tyrant (Lincoln) should never serve another term.
www.law.umkc.edu/faculty/projects/ftrials/lincolnconspiraccy/binghamclose.html

1599 George Young had been overheard saying that Lincoln should never have been nominated for his 2nd term.
www.law.umkc.edu/faculty/projects/ftrials/lincolnconspiraccy/binghamclose.html

1600 Approbating means officially sanctioning.

1601 It was also determined that the principal object of their mission which was well funded was to buy up newspapers in the West to affect the defeat of Abraham Lincoln in the 1864 election. The Lincoln Conspiracies, pg. 15

1602 Adduced means brought forward.

1603 Mordecai was the son of Jair of the tribe of Benjamin. He is one of the main characters in the book of Esther in the Hebrew Bible.
www.christiananswers.net/dictionary/mordecai.html

*"But both men were necessary to compete our history. Neither could have done the other's work."*

Rutherford B. Hayes, on Lincoln and Washington, 1865.[1604]

# — 30 —

# PARALLELS— WASHINGTON AND LINCOLN

### THE ADMINISTRATIONS OF WASHINGTON AND LINCOLN

England after the treaty of peace in 1783 did not accredit a minister resident to the United States until October 1791. She persistently until then refused to carry out her obligations by the treaty of peace which bound her to surrender her military posts on United States soil and to pay for slaves carried away by her armies. This refusal upon her part to evacuate the western coast was grounded on the pretended unjustifiable neglect of the United States to enforce the article of that treaty which provided for the payment of debts due British subjects. England was during this time guilty of many other unwarrantable acts in bad faith to her treaty stipulations for which offenses she offered no justification except her arbitrary sovereign will. She seemed to be stimulated by an assumption that the United States was her secret enemy and was soon expected to be the ally of France with which the government of Great Britain was at war. The United States had every reason to believe that the agents of Great Britain were interfering to prevent treaties of peace with the savages of the northwest, and were exciting them to renewed outrages on the frontier settlements.

About this time there was an unexpected treaty made between Portugal and Algers, the result of which was Algeriene pirates made

1604 Lincoln in American Memory, pg. 29.

warfare upon the Atlantic against the unprotected American commerce, and it was understood that this was brought about by English intervention. The bad motives and purposes were attributed to that government aiding and abetting the piracy.

There was at this time a growing grievance produced by the impressments[1605] of the American seaman, under the delusive color of resemblance to the English subjects; Great Britain went so far as to order on the 8th of June, 1793, that all vessels should be stopped which were bound for France with corn, and compel them to change their course and put into an English port. On the 6th of November following this outrage on American commerce was supplemented by a further order that all such vessels should be seized and sent to Great Britain for trial by English courts. On the other hand, the sympathies of the American people were aroused for their sister republic, France, even though she may have been the aggressor in declaring war against Great Britain and Holland. There had been a treaty in 1778[1606] which was still in force which bound France and the United States to offensive as well as defensive alliance. England now saw that the United States was in a position to drift easily into a war as an ally of France. France, in view of the past, had a natural right to expect more than a friendly relation from the United States. To disappoint these expectations was an unpopular course to adopt by the administration. The people were ready to help France: the consequences of involving the new republic in another war were well weighed by President George Washington. He consulted with his Cabinet, the result of which was the unanimous sentiment not withstanding the inevitable unpopularity of the act and the seemingly bad faith it involved. The former treaty should be nullified by the change in government of France and by the declaration of neutrality of the republic and her belligerent enemies. It was at once determined upon and issued.

This course by the government aroused the most intensely angry opposition. For this the president was assailed personally. The reader may find a parallel in the case of President Lincoln's proclamation of amnesty and reconstruction during the war of rebellion. President Washington was accused by the extreme republicans as Mr. Lincoln

---

1605 Impressments are seizings.

1606 Treaty of Alliance with France was a defensive alliance between the U. S. and France to aid each other in the event of an attack from the British. www.infoplease/t/his/treaty-of-alliance

was, of being an enemy to his country, to France and to republican institutions, of usurping the functions of Congress in the decision and announcement of peace and war and as setting at naught a treaty whose observance the faith of the country was pledged.

When Citizen Genét [1607] (as he was called) who had been accredited by the French Republic to be minister to the United States reached Charleston, South Carolina, in April (1793) by demonstration of enthusiasm manifested by the people and the cordiality of his reception he was mislead and so blinded to the improprieties of his position that he entered on and persisted in a course which could only have been justified or pardonable if he had acted on the soil of the French republic.

Mr. Genét assumed the right and acted on it by commissioning cruisers from the American ports which captured British vessels in American waters—created courts for the trial and condemnation of prize vessels and began to raise money and enlist men for the service of France. In due course this was complained of by the British agent as a violation of the neutrality and Mr. Jefferson promptly informed Mr. Genét that he must cease to persist in his courses. Two of his American recruits were arrested and sent to jail.

Citizen Genét's manners and style of diplomacy about this time became very offensive to the president. The following is told to have occurred during the interview between them: Mr. Genét was urging upon the president with all his assurances the duty of the United States to make common cause with France against England and took occasion to say: "Mr. President, it is a melancholy and distressing proof of the slavery of mankind that the tree of liberty could never be made to flourish without having its roots watered with human blood." Then, enlarging on the subject, made reference to the president and the former condition of the United States in such language as greatly irritated the president.

President Washington turned upon the Frenchman and with more than his usual animation and said: "Born free and a citizen of a free country, my fervent thanksgiving ascends to the immortal throne of grace in humble acknowledgement for having been made instrumental in vindicating and perpetuating to my countrymen the inestimable

---

[1607] Citizen Edmond-Charles Genét was French Ambassador to the United States during the French Revolution. www.answers.com/topic/citizen-genet

rights and liberties vouchsafed to every man at his birth by the eternal God that rules the universe."

Mr. Genét had gone up to his headquarters at Philadelphia where he persisted in breaking the law and disturbing the peace in various ways. He remonstrated in the most undiplomatic and offensive language against the imprisonment of the two recruits. In all this he was upheld and encouraged by the more violent republicans in imitation of the Jacobins[1608] of France. To such Republicans, no less, in the case of President Lincoln was the character and past services of President Washington, a bar to the meanest denunciation of his conduct.

The insolence of Mr. Genét and his adherents during the summer of 793, continued to become more and more insolent, offensive and intolerant. About this time a libel vessel in the harbor in Boston was rescued from the United States marshal by the French counsel aided by a body of marines from a French war vessel in the harbor. An American privateer under French colors left Philadelphia in defiance of an order from the federal government. These and many other outrages were committed against American rights and the dignity of the government which had been tolerated, but the time came when Chief Justice Jay[1609] and United States Senator King[1610] of New York declared over their own signatures that Mr. Genét had declared his intention to appeal from the government to the people. The American government then asked his recall, which was made the following winter.

Many things in the diplomatic policy of France during the late war of rebellion recall to mind these relations and actions. France's connection with the tripartite[1611] treaty—England's right of search on the high seas—the violation of both Great Britain and France of the neutrality pretensions of those governments by surreptitiously giving aid and comfort to the enemies of the United States in the Confederate state lines—by constant menaces, running the blockade,

---

1608 The Jacobins of France were the largest and most powerful group in France during the French Revolution. www.britannica.com/ebchecked/topic/299007

1609 Chief Justice John Jay was President of the Continental Congress 1778 - 1779 and first Chief Justice of the Supreme Court, serving from 1789—1795. www.oyez.org/justices/john_jay

1610 Senator Rufus King was the first U.S. Senator from New York. He served from 1789—1796 and from 1813—1825. www.answers.com/topic/rufus-king

1611 Tripartite means three party.

and furnishing contraband stores, protecting rebel cruisers, allowing rebel privateers to be built in their harbors, and keeping up communication with the enemy in direct violation of the international law and amenity between recognized friendly nationalities all combine to contrast and parallel the government relations in times of war, and afford a basis of a correct estimate of friendly disposition in times of peace.

We ask to be pardoned by the readers by again going back to the early history of our county. There are many parallel cases of interest in administration of the government and its people and the diplomacy between it and other governments then and later. The hostility of Great Britain against the United States after the revolutionary war (as well as that of France) was kept up until in December 1793. Mr. Jefferson, in an official report advised friendly arrangements for their cessation, if possible, and in default, active retaliation upon the offending nation. Mr. Madison[1612] on January 4th, 1794, introduced resolutions imposing prohibitory duties upon English goods. For two months these resolutions were debated but failed adoption.

President Washington, seeing the difficulty the country was likely to be involved in by the policy advocated by either of the opposing parties, on the 16th of April took an unlooked for step towards conciliation by nominating Chief Justice Jay to be envoy extraordinary to England to affect a peace by a new treaty. This nomination was confirmed, the federalists having a small majority in the Senate. Every means was used by the republicans to halt or defeat the mission in every possible way. They offered resolutions prohibiting trade entirely with England, which effort was fortunately defeated. Party feelings ran so high at this time that resolutions for censure of Mr. Hamilton for his management of the treasury were introduced and acrimoniously[1613] defeated. The alarm produced and made it prudent for the conservative members of Congress to resort to the expedient of distracting the public mind by offering and adopting an amendment to the constitution known as the 11th amendment,[1614] which has enabled

---

1612 James Madison—See pg. 356.

1613 Acrimoniously means angrily.

1614 11th Amendment—Adopted in 1798 saying "the judicial power of the United States shall not be construed to any suit in law or equity, commenced or prosecuted against one of the United States by citizens of another state or by citizens or subjects of any foreign state." The U. S. Constitution, pg 47.

so many states to repudiate[1615] their honest obligations with impunity.[1616] Justice Jay soon affected his treaty[1617] and presented it for ratification. It was not such a one as the president wished but he felt that a treaty of some kind was necessary and saw then that no better one could be obtained, and he therefore signed it.

It was not uncommon at this time to indulge in criticism of President Washington's policy, but his approval of the treaty brought out the most reckless aspirations upon his public as well as his private character, such as were never equaled in the history of the republic against the chief magistrate, except in the case of Mr. Lincoln, at the time he issued his proclamation of amnesty and reconstruction during the late war. The aspirations of his character caused General Washington to say: "I would rather be in my grave than in the presidency." At one time smarting under the galling attacks of the extreme Republicans, Mr. Lincoln declared "he would rather be dead than be president."

President Washington was charged by the extreme republicans of that day with usurpation,[1618] treason to his country and hostility to her interests—President Lincoln was charged with the same ignoble[1619] purposes by the extreme Republicans of his day. Washington was accused of having shown incapacity during the old revolution as President Lincoln was during the late attempt at revolution. President Washington was charged with embezzling the public funds while president—a like charge, thanks be to the greatest ruler of the universe, no man in the 19th century has found base enough to make such a dastardly charge against Abraham Lincoln. George Washington was threatened with impeachment and an assassination—President Lincoln was not only threatened and menaced, but was actually murdered. Mr. Washington, in derision,[1620] had been called the step father of his country and Mr. Lincoln "The Judas Iscariot of his party." Soon, however, each of these distinguished patriots and statesmen's unyielding common sense justified their executive actions,

---

1615 Repudiate means reject.

1616 Impunity means without punishment.

1617 The Treaty of Jay of 1794 was between the United States and Britain and helped avert war. www.earlyamerican.com/earlyamerican/milestones/jaytreaty

1618 Usurpation means illegal seizure of power.

1619 Ignoble means not honorable.

1620 Derision means mockery.

and the fruits of their labors proved their wisdom, and put to shame their abusive opponents and enemies.

History presents many contradictions and many curious contributions of inconsistencies of defecations and detractions of these two great men. To many of their present admirers, time may have lent us enchantments to the view (or more properly speaking preview). Public sentiment has changed many scoffers and calumniators[1621] to idolatrous worshippers. Many persons whips either of these two great men with livid regard and treated each as typical heathens but since their deaths metaphorically know no God but them—no fame could longer be made by envenomed[1622] strikes at these shining lights crendation[1623] was sought in pagan-like impious worship. The real friends and admirers of Abraham Lincoln claim for him only that he was a man—human—mortal—a finite being. General Washington was nothing more. Each of them had, like other men, amiable weaknesses and may have had some small vices strictly speaking. Their greatness as men is all their greatness. Their greatness as a God would not compare favorably with the greatness of the Almighty ever-knowing God. There is no God but God. There is one God and none other and He rules the universe. Once venerated dieties ruled but one of the tribes of his people and we are held accountable to the people and to Him. God gives no accounting of his doings.

---

1621 Calumniators are false accusers.

1622 Envenomed means embittered.

1623 Crendation means the state of having battlements.

*"He exercised no government of any kind over his household. His children did much as they pleased. Many of their antics he approved, and he restrained them in nothing."*

William Herndon[1624]

# — 31 —

# ABRAHAM LINCOLN— THE FAMILY MAN

Mr. Lincoln had always been an early riser. After he went to the White House to live, he necessarily was irregular in the times he rose in the morning, owing to the exciting events occurring which often kept him up late at night and sometimes almost until morning. He breakfasted at 9 o'clock a.m., lunched at 2 and dined at 6. In his family circle he never failed in his endeavors to make all as happy as possible. He loved his family, was devoted to his children, particularly to Thomas, who he always called "Tad". His whole heart seemed to be centered in this child after the death of his second son William[1625] during the year 1862. "Willie" as he was called up to the time of his death was the apple of his father's eye. He was an exceedingly bright and promising boy, and gave evidence of wonderful genius and talent. Willie had learned to make diagrams and maps of battles and sketches with great facility, proficiency and accuracy, in which his father took the greatest pride and never failed to encourage and assist him. He died in the 9th year of his age, which was a terrible blow to Mr. Lincoln yet he had an abiding faith in an overruling providence - believed "What is to be will be" is a true maxim, and the decrees of God could

1624 William Herndon (See pg. ii) Lincoln in American Memory, pg. 132.

1625 William Lincoln died February 20, 1862 of typhoid fever. The Sword of Lincoln, pg. 61.

not be altered—endeavored to control himself in all things—that God was just—but all powerful.

At times when he was in the home circle resting from his labors, his wife would read him newspaper criticisms of his course and administration. He would often check her and say: "Save me from that. I have enough to bear without that—if I am right I will live; if I am wrong I will die." And would quickly turn the subject to one more agreeable. With the pressing affairs of the state upon him, when he would withdraw from his office duties to mingle in the enjoyment of the domestic circle he would frequently lie down on his back in the middle of the floor and have a romp with Tad which always seemed to bring relief from his disturbing cares.

As this child seemed to be regarded by Mr. Lincoln after the death of his son William as the connecting link between himself and posterity in the later years of his life—the one animate object in whom all his hopes for the future were centered, space is given to another occurrence illustrative of Mr. Lincoln's domestic relations representing another phase of his character, showing his characteristic for firmness and indomitable will even where his affections were most deeply concerned.

In one of the vacant and unoccupied rooms in the presidential mansion, this boy Tad as he was called, had with the aid of the servants in leisure hours fitted up a mini-theater with a stage, orchestra, stalls, parquets, and all the paraphernalia of an improvised theater. About this time some photographer after the review of Burnside's Division of the Army of the Potomac came to the White House to make some stereoscopic studies of the president's office for a Mr. Carpenter,[1626] an artist of reputation (the same person who painted Mr. Lincoln's portrait) and who had been a great deal about the house. These artists needed a dark closet in which to develop their pictures; there was such a closet attached to Tad's theater; which could be used without disturbing the theater outfit. With the sanction of Mr. Lincoln, Mr. Carpenter led the artist to the closet without the knowledge or permission of Tad. Several pictures had been taken before Tad discovered the invasion upon his prerogative. When Tad took in the situation, there was a tumult and uproar. Tad took great offense at their occupancy of his theater without consent, and declared

---

[1626] Artist Francis B. Carpenter spent about six months in the White House studying Mr. Lincoln prior to painting his portrait. The Story-Life of Lincoln, pg. 318.

it an indignity which he would not tolerate. He locked the door and refused them admission, and carried off the key. There was no way of getting into the room left them. All their chemicals and instruments were in this room; they hunted up the young theater manager, remonstrated, coaxed and wheedled[1627] him, but it was of no use. He flew into an indignant passion and blamed Mr. Carpenter for the outrage. He declared "that they should neither use his room or go into it for their property. No one said he has any business in my room that I don't invite to it, and I never invited you."

At this time Mr. Lincoln was sitting for his photograph in another room. Tad came in. His father said to him very mildly, "Tad, go and unlock the door." The offended youth went off into his mother's room very angry, muttering and positively refused to obey the command of his father. Mr. Carpenter followed him into the passage and tried to pacify him without effect and returned to Mr. Lincoln and inquired, "Has not the boy opened the door?" "No," said he. "He has gone off in a great pet." Mr. Lincoln's lips became firmly compressed, and then suddenly rising from his chair strode across the room and into the passage with the air of a person bent on punishing for disobedience of orders. He soon found Tad and got the key, then went to the door of the theater, unlocked it and said "There go ahead now, it is all right." He and Mr. Carpenter went back to his office leaving the artist in Tad's room. "Tad" said he, half apologetically "is a peculiar child. He was violently excited when I went to him. I said, 'Tad, do you know you are making your father a great deal of trouble?' He burst into tears instantly and gave me up the keys."

All Mr. Lincoln's feelings seemed to be concentrated in sympathetic affection for the temporary unhappiness of his dearly loved little pet. His firmness, however, manifested itself at home as well as abroad.

The incident related of a few pages back of Mrs. Lincoln's reading to Mr. Lincoln the adverse criticisms in the newspapers when he uttered the memorable words "if I am right, I will live; if I am wrong I will die" was after the death of Willie in February, 1862. His utterance may be attributable to the fact of a visit paid to him at that time by Reverend Doctor Vinton[1628] of the Trinity Church, New York. Doctor

---

1627 Wheedled means coaxed.

1628 Rev. Dr. Francis Vinton was rector of the Trinity Episcopal Church of New York City. www.ttf.org/index/update/february-2009

Vinton was an acquaintance of Mrs. Lincoln and her sister Mrs. Edwards[1629] of Illinois who was, at that time, staying with the family at the White House. At this time Mr. Lincoln had given way to great grief and a deep melancholy—despondency had taken possession of him. The doctor chided him for showing such a rebellious disposition to the decrees of providence. Dr. Vinton told Mr. Lincoln without reserve that the indulgence of such feelings though natural was sinful and that it was not worthy of one who believed in religion; that he had duties to the living greater than any other man as the chosen father and leader of the people and that he was unfitting himself for these great responsibilities by sinfully giving way to his grief. The doctor then went on to say "to mourn the departed as lost belonged to hedonism, not to Christianity. Your son," he said, "is alive in paradise." Then he quoted the passage from scriptures, "God is not the God of the dead, but the living, for all live in him."

When Mr. Lincoln heard these words, "Your son is alive" he was startled and exclaimed "Alive, alive. You surely mock me!" Mr. Lincoln became very much affected. The doctor continued "Seek not your son among the dead for he is not there. He lives today in paradise." He continued "Did not the angel patriarch mourn his son for dead, 'Joseph is not, and Simeon is not, and ye will take Benjamin also.' Joseph and Simeon both lived though he believed it not—the fact that Joseph being taken away from him was eventually the fact of saving the whole family." He then told Mr. Lincoln that God had called his son to his upper kingdom and that his own, like Joseph, had gone with God's good providence to be the salvation of his father's household and that it was a part of the Lord's plans for the ultimate happiness of him and his.

This consolation so earnestly ministered by the respected divine had great affect on Mr. Lincoln and aided in soon bringing him back to his original self and in refitting him for the duties so urgently pressing upon him.

During the first year of the war owing to the great press of business it was at times difficult to get to the president. Four or five distinguished gentlemen from Kentucky who had come to visit the

---

[1629] Mrs. Ninian W. Edwards (Elizabeth Todd) was Mary Todd Lincoln's sister who lived in Springfield, Illinois. Abraham Lincoln and Mary Todd were married in their home in Springfield on November 4, 1842. Mrs. Lincoln died in her house on July 16, 1882. The Story-Life of Lincoln, pgs. 167 & 671 and Seaport Autographs, pg. 20.

president as commissioners or agents from that state had been endeavoring to see Mr. Lincoln for a number of days without success. Mr. Lincoln having learned the object of their intended visit to him through some source or other, wanted to avoid the interview if possible and had given them no chance for presenting themselves. One day after waiting in the lobby for several hours they had about given up the effort in despair and in no amiable terms expressed the disappointment. They turned to the head of the stairs and saying something about "seeing old Abe." Tad caught at these words and asked them if they wanted to see "old Abe," laughing at the time. They replied, "Yes."

"Wait a minute," said Tad and he rushed to his father's office and said "Papa. May I introduce some friends to you?"

His father, always indulgent and ready to make him happy said, "Yes, my son. I will see your friends."

Tad went to them again and asked a very dignified gentleman of the party what his name was. He was told his name. Then Tad said, "Come gentlemen," and they did so. Leading them up to Mr. Lincoln, Tad with much dignity said, "Papa let me introduce you to Judge _______ of Kentucky" and quickly added "Now judge you introduce the other gentlemen." The introductions were gone through with and they turned out to be the gentleman Mr. Lincoln had been avoiding for a week. Mr. Lincoln reached for the boy and took him on his lap, kissed him, and told him that it was all right. Tad had introduced his friends like the little gentleman that he was. Tad was about 8 years old at the time.

Mr. Lincoln was pleased with Tad's diplomacy and often laughed and told others of the incident. One day while caressing the boy he asked Tad why he called those gentlemen his friends?

"Well," he said. "I have seen them so often and they looked so good and sorry and said they were from Kentucky. I thought they must be our friends."

"That is right my son," said Mr. Lincoln. "I would have the whole human race your friends and mine, if it were possible."

Thomas (Tad)[1630] died on the fifteenth day of July 1871, universally regretted and his death may well be considered a great misfortune to the country. In life he had given singular promise of being a worthy

---

[1630] Tad Lincoln was born on April 4, 1853. www.lincolnstudies.com/archives/348

son of his illustrious father. Mr. Lincoln had another son, besides the two mentioned (William and Thomas) whom he called Robert Todd Lincoln[1631] who is still living.

1631 Robert Todd Lincoln—See pg. iii.

*"Lincoln blended in his character the most yielding flexibility with the most unflinching firmness, childlike simplicity and statesmanlike wisdom and masterly strength, but over and around all was thrown the matter of unquestionable integrity."*

Cordelia Hovey of Wisconsin, agent of the U.S. Sanitary Commission[1632]

# — 32 —

# ABRAHAM LINCOLN'S CHARACTER

Mr. Lincoln had great fidelity to his friendships. Once a friend, always a friend. The deserving lowborn commanded his respect and consideration with the high born and distinguished alike. An instance of this may be found in what he said on one occasion to an Austrian count. During the rebellion the Austrian minister to his government introduced to Mr. Lincoln a count, a subject to the Austrian government, who was desirous of obtaining a position in the American army. Being introduced by the accredited minister of Austria there was no further recommendation necessary to secure the appointment, but fearing that his importance might not be fully appreciated by the Republican president, the count was particular in impressing the fact upon him that he bore that title and that family was ancient and highly respectable. Mr. Lincoln listened with attention until this unnecessary commendation was mentioned, and then with a merry twinkle in his eye he tapped the aristocratic sprig of hereditary nobility on the shoulder in the most fatherly way as if the gentleman had made a confession to some unfortunate episode in family lineage for which he was in no wise responsible, saying, "Never mind. You shall be treated with just as much consideration for all that. I will see to it that your bearing a title shan't hurt you."

---

1632 Lincoln in American Memory, pg. 107.

In conversation with him one night about the time General Burnside[1633] was relieved, the author was urging upon Mr. Lincoln the necessity for looking well to the fact that there was a scheme afoot to depose him, and to appoint a military dictator in his stead. He laughed and said, "I think for a man of accredited courage you are the most panicked person I ever knew. You can see more dangers to me than all the other friends I have; you are all the time exercised about somebody taking my life; murdering me; now you have discovered a new danger. Now you think the people of this great government are likely to turn me out of office. I do not fear this from the people anymore than I fear assassination from an individual. Now to show you my appreciation of what my French friends would call a *coup d'etat*,[1634] let me read you a letter I have written to General Hooker,[1635] whom I have just appointed to the command of the Army of the Potomac." He then opened the drawer of his table and took up a letter and read it in substance if not in *totidem verbis* [1636] as follows:

*Executive Mansion*
*Washington, D.C.*
*January 26, 1863*
*Major General Hooker*
*General:*

*I have placed you at the head of the Army of the Potomac. Of course I have done this upon what appears to be sufficient reasons: yet I think it is best for you to know that there are some things in regard to which I am not quite satisfied with you. I believe you to be a brave and skilful soldier—which of course I like—I also believe you do not mix politics with your profession—in which you are right. You have confidence in yourself which is a valuable if not indispensable quality. You are ambitious which within reasonable bounds does good rather than harm.*

*But I think that during General Burnside's command of the army you have taken consul with your ambition and thwarted him as much as you could, in which you did a great wrong to the country and to a most meritorious and honorable brother officer. I have heard in such a way as to believe it of your saying that both the country and the army needed a dictator. Of course it was not for this but in spite of it that I have given you the command. Only those generals who gain success can*

---

1633 General Ambrose Burnside—See pg. 171.

1634 *Coup d'etat* is seizure of the government by an opposing group.

1635 General Joseph Hooker—See pg. 195.

1636 *Totidem verbis* means in so many words.

*set up dictators. What I ask of you is military success and I will risk the dictatorship. The government will support you to the utmost of its ability, which is neither more nor less than it has done and will do for all of its commanders. I much fear that the spirit in which you aided to infuse into the army of criticizing their commander and withholding confidence from him will now turn upon you and I shall assist you as far as I can to put it down. Neither you nor Napoleon, if he were alive again, could get any good out of an army while such a spirit prevails in it, and now beware of rashness; beware of rashness but with energy and sleepless vigilance, go forward and give us victories.*

*Yours very truly,*
*A. Lincoln*

This letter has been published heretofore but by what authority we are unable to state; yet we vouch for its authenticity. General Hooker referred to this letter afterward with great feeling and said of it, "it is just such a letter as a father might have written to his son; it was a great rebuke to me at the time." If the letter was published during the life time of General Hooker, the author is not aware of that fact.

Referring to the conversation alluded to above, Mr. Lincoln told the following story: "A couple of emigrants from the Emerald Isle many years ago were making their way westward and seeking for labor; a large pond of water was in their way and they were greeted by a chorus of bull frogs, a kind of music new to them. B-A-U-M, B-A-U-M. This terrified the emigrants and they both grasp to their shillelaghs[1637] and crept in the direction the music came from with a hope of catching a view of the enemy, but they were unable to see him. After watching for some time they could not ascertain from whence the music came. At last a happy thought occurred to one of them. He pulled the sleeve of the other and said, 'Be Jeses, Jamie, it is my opinion it is nothing but a noise.'"

In early days of Illinois (1842) Mr. Lincoln was challenged by Mr. Shields[1638] to fight a duel.[1639] The challenge was accepted, and Mr.

---

1637 Shillelaghs are Irish walking sticks. www.fashionablecanes.com/Irish_shillelagh/html

1638 General James Shields—See pg. 174.

1639 Mr. Lincoln had written an article in the *Sangamo Journal* attacking the Democratic administration of Illinois and criticizing the state auditor (Mr. Shields). After demanding a retraction which he did not get, Mr. Shields challenged Mr. Lincoln to a dual. Note—Shields was nine inches shorter than Mr. Lincoln. Lincoln: The Presidential Archives, pg. 41.

Lincoln chose Dr. Merriman,[1640] an old friend of his who was a splendid swordsman, for his second. Mr. Shields was a small man with short arms, while Mr. Lincoln was a tall, muscular man with long armed patronage, possession Herculean strength. Mr. Lincoln chose broad swords as the weapons[1641] for the deadly strife, not knowing anything more about the expert use of that weapon that a Hottentot[1642] does about Christianity. Relying entirely upon his own physical strength with advantage of length of arm, his hope was of becoming dexterous of its use under the tutelage of his second. He knew that Mr. Shields was dead shot with a pistol. The duel was by interposition of mutual friends preventing from taking place and the differences between the belligerents were accommodated and satisfactorily settled.

Some little time after this on meeting Usher F. Linder,[1643] one of the shrewdest lawyers and one of the most eloquent orators the west ever produced, at Danville court, seeing Lincoln in his walk making passes with a stick he held in his hand such as is made in the broad sword exercise, asked why he had selected that weapon in which to fight Mr. Shields. With a twinkle in his eye he replied to tell the truth: "Mr. Linder, I did not want to kill Mr. Shields and I felt sure of being able to disarm him. I had about a month to practice the broad sword exercise under an experienced teacher, and I did not want the darn fellow to kill me either, which I have reason to fear he would have done, if pistols had been selected."

In his early life Mr. Lincoln had been very ambitious to go to Congress and that ambition was gratified in the fall of 1846, by his election to that body. After this hope had been realized he was still unsatisfied. There was an unrest—a longing for something else—something more, and that "something more" was eventually realized to his promotion afterwards to the highest official distinction that can be obtained under a Republican government.

---

1640 Dr. Edward H. Merriman was a Springfield, Illinois physician. www.wikisource.org/wiki/The_Life_of Abraham_Lincoln_(Holland)/Chapter_VII

1641 Mr. Lincoln's letter to Mr. Shields setting down the requirements called for the use of "cavalry broad swords of the largest size precisely equal in all respects—and such as now used by the cavalry company at Jacksonville." Lincoln: The Presidential Archives, pg. 41.

1642 Hottentot is an African tribesman. See pg. 297.

1643 Usher F. Linder was an Illinois lawyer who employed Abraham Lincoln in the famous *In re Bryant* case. www.lawpracticeofabrahamlincoln.org

Just after his election to Congress in October, 1846, he wrote to his most intimate personal friend Mr. Joshua F. Speed[1644] of Illinois as follows: "Being elected to Congress, though I am grateful to our friends for having done it, has not pleased me as much as I expected."

When he wrote this letter, he must have been in one of his quaintest moods, and for its peculiarity its concluding paragraph of the letter is given: "We have another boy born the 10th of March.[1645] He is very much a child as Bob[1646] was at his age, rather of a longer order. Bob is short and low, and expect always will be. He talks very plainly, almost as plainly as anybody. He is quite smart enough. I sometimes fear he is one of the rare ripe sort that are smarter at five than ever after. A great deal of that sort of mischief is the offspring of the animal spirit. Since I began this letter, a messenger came to tell me Bob was lost, but by the time I reached the house his mother had found him and whipped him and by now very likely he has run away again."

He then went on to give another illustration by telling another anecdote which was 'a traveler on the frontier on horseback lost his reckoning. A terrible thunder storm was a brewing, and to add to his further trouble his horse gave out and left him stranded in the storm. The peals of thunder were frightful and the lightening afforded him the only clue to his way. A bolt seemed to crash the very earth beneath him which brought him to his knees. He was not a praying man, but as he had been brought involuntary to a humble and suppliant position, he bethought himself to offer up a petition for his deliverance. His prayer was after this fashion. "Oh Lord, hear my prayer this time for though you knowest that it is not often that I call upon thee. And Lord, if it is all the same to you, give me a little more light and a little less noise! I hope,' said he, 'that we will have a little more light and a little less noise."'

"I hope," said Mr. Lincoln, "that we may have a much stronger disposition manifested hereafter, on the part of our civilian warriors,

---

[1644] Joshua Speed was an old friend from Springfield. He operated the A. Y. Ellis store where Mr. Lincoln stayed for four years after first arriving in Springfield in April, 1837. Lincoln and the Civil War, pg. 292, Lincoln's Herndon, pg. 14 - 15 and the Two American Presidents, pg. 38.

[1645] Birth of Edward Baker Lincoln was March 10, 1846. www.freebase.com/view/cn/edward_baker_lincoln

[1646] Bob refers to Robert Todd Lincoln.

to unite in suppressing the rebellion and a little less noise as to how and by whom the chief executive office shall be administered."

During the year 1861, a gentleman by the name of Rexford (New York) who had been present at the Chicago convention which nominated Mr. Lincoln for president, and who was a great friend of Mr. Seward, and an earnest advocate in that convention for Mr. Seward's nomination visited Washington and called with a mutual friend of his and Mr. Lincoln's to pay his respects to the president. This gentleman (Rexford) was a very clerical looking gentleman in all respects except in the manner of his supporting an immense gold watch fob chain with its usual accompaniment of a large topaz seal. He was a large, fleshy man, rubicund[1647] in appearance with an exceedingly homely countenance and dignified in demeanor; he dressed in a neatly fitting forked-tailed coat with brass buttons, a ruffled shirt of faultless beauty, orange colored gloves and carried a large gold headed cane. His whole appearance was one of dignified uncomeliness[1648] betoking[1649] no sign of the sparkling wit, good humor, and thorough knowledge of the world that really characterized the man.

After the introduction ceremonies were over, the conversations turned upon different subjects and Mr. Lincoln gradually showed evidence of a change of opinion about the character of his visitor. His visitor had noticed that Mr. Lincoln had appeared somewhat restrained and somewhat embarrassed by the commencement of the interview. At length he determined to break the ice for more free and unrestrained intercourse, and did so by saying, "Mr. President, I have no business with you whatever. I merely called to pay my respects, and to say to you, I think you are doing everything for the good of the country that is in the power of man to do, and as one of your constituents, I now say, do as you damn please, and I will support you."

After this Mr. Lincoln jumped to his feet and impetuously grasp him by his hand and said: "Why Mr. Rexford, I took you to be a reverend gentleman who had come to preach to me and tell me how to take Richmond." They had both risen from their chairs. Mr. Lincoln seemed to enjoy the relief from his misconceived anticipation from an unprofitable interview. He then said: "Sit down my friend, sit

---

[1647] Rubicund means ruddy.

[1648] Uncomeliness means not pleasant.

[1649] Betoking means showing.

down. I am delighted to see you. You must stay and lunch with us." They lunched together with the family, and the good cheer, fun and the anecdotes that followed could only have been produced and enjoyed by two such unique and congenial characters.

One day Mr. Lincoln sat in his office in deep meditation, after arousing himself from his reverie, he said to a gentleman in his office whose presence he had not before then noticed: "Do you know I think General ______ is a philosopher. He is really a great man. This war has not produced another such man. He has grappled with that greatest of ancient and wise admonition 'know thyself' and certainly he is as intimately acquainted with himself, knows for what he is fitted as well as for what he is unfitted as any man living, for much to my relief and greatly to the interest of the service to which he is resigned his position in the army. I am in hopes some other dress parade commander will study over this advisory self-examination of 'know thyself' and follow his example. If they will only do so, I would be greatly relieved. They will have done their duty and the country will be benefited."

In the state of West Virginia at the time when the most lively operations were being enacted by the opposing armies, one of the Union generals allowed himself and his command to be drawn or were forced into a dangerous position, from which it was feared at Washington he would be unable to extricate himself without the loss of his whole command. In speaking of this fiasco, Mr. Lincoln said: "General ______ reminds me of a man out west who was engaged in what they call heading up a hogshead, and he worked diligently for some time driving down the hoops. But when he would get his work nearly done, the head of the vessel would fall in. He was for a time greatly annoyed at this but suddenly a bright idea struck him. He put his little son, quite a lad at the time inside of the hogshead, to make him hold up its head. This was done. It never occurred to him until the job was done, how he was to get the boy out again. He was securely fastened up inside the hogshead. Now," said Mr. Lincoln, "this is a fair sample of the way some people always do business. They can succeed better in getting themselves and others bottled up than in getting themselves uncorked again."

Mr. Lincoln once said in a speech: "Twenty-two years ago Judge Douglas[1650] and I, first became acquainted. We were both young then—he younger than I. Even then we were both ambitious, I perhaps quite as much as he. With me the race for ambition has been a failure—a flat failure: with him it has been one of splendid success. His name fills the nation and is not unknown even in foreign lands. I affect no contempt for the high eminence he has reached—so reached as the oppressed of my species might have shared with me in my elevation—had I succeeded as he has—I would rather stand on that eminence than wear the richest crown that ever pressed a monarch's brow." At the time that these sentiments were uttered, he little expected to wear a crown far more brilliant than was ever worn by his successful rival and more dazzling than ever worn by any man of his generation.

As a striking instance of Mr. Lincoln's wonderful power of turning everything to his own advantage in the way of response or repartee during the exciting campaign between him and Judge Douglas, in 1858, whilst he was making a speech in Charleston, in Coles County, Illinois, a rude fellow of rather unsavory reputation interrupted him by asking if it was true if he entered the state of Illinois barefooted, and driving a yoke of oxen. Mr. Lincoln paused for a moment and looked steadily at the political blackguard,[1651] and knew that he could prove the truth of the charge implied in the question by a dozen or more of his acquaintances in the crowd, any one of who was more respectable than his notorious questioner; he realized the ignoble[1652] purpose of the question to be a reminder of his early life involving his poverty which the question viewed as a degradation of his manhood. To this cruel impertinence[1653] he did not at once respond but it seemed to inspire him with great animation. He went on to show by his argument what free institutions had done for himself and all of the poor like himself. And with great power he portrayed the evils of slavery to the white man generally, wherever it existed. He said it was only natural that he hated slavery in all of its forms.

"Yes," he said, "we will speak for freedom and against slavery as long as the constitution of our country guarantees free speech until

---

[1650] Judge Stephen A. Douglas—See pg. 34.
[1651] Blackguard means scoundrel.
[1652] Ignoble is someone who is mean.
[1653] Impertinence means uncivil remark.

everywhere on this wide land the sun shall shine and the sun shall fall and the wind shall blow upon no man who goes forth to unrequited toil."

A trite fact of his slavery characteristics might be found in the incidents which occurred in his professional practice shortly after Governor Bissell[1654] was elected Governor of Illinois. An old Negro woman came into the office of Lincoln and Herndon[1655] in Springfield, Illinois and narrated her troubles which amounted to this: She and her offspring had been born in Kentucky and were liberated slaves. Their owner, a gentleman by the name of Hinkle had brought the whole family along with his family into Illinois and had given all his bondsmen and bondswomen freedom. The son of this woman had recently gone down the Mississippi in the capacity of a servant or deckhand on a team boat. After arriving in New Orleans, and going ashore, he was at once arrested by the police under the law then in force against Negroes from other states and was at once confined in a prison. Afterwards he was brought out and tried. The result he was fined in accordance with the laws then in force in the state of Louisiana. The boat to which he belonged at this time having left on her return trip, he was sold or was in imminent danger of being subjected to that dire alternative to satisfy his fine and the expenses attending thereupon.

Lincoln, after hearing her story, was very much moved. He said to Herndon, "Go you over to the state house. See Governor Bissell, state this case to him, and see if something cannot be done to liberate this freeman from his difficulty."

At once Mr. Herndon made his inquiry—returned—and reported that the governor was pained to say that he could see no legal or constitutional way of justifying any action he might take in furthering his desire in the situation. Mr. Lincoln became very much excited and jumped to his feet and said: "By the eternal, I'll have that Negro back here again or I will have twenty years of agitation in Illinois. I will see that the governor of a free state does have the legal and constitutional right to demand the liberation of a manumitted slave, to the

---

[1654]William Henry Bissell was Governor of Illinois from 1857 until his death in 1860. Governor Bissel had appointed the author, Ward Hill Lamon as state agent for all swamp and overflow lands in Vermilion County, Illinois. Ward Hill Lamon, Lincoln's "Particular Friend," pgs. 102 & 103.

[1655] William Herndon—See pg. ii.

restoration of his liberty, and the right to return to the home of his adoption. That Negro is a free man and he is entitled to the liberty of freedom, if not equality, which is as dear to him as sacred a right to him as any one of us. He has got to be brought back to his home."

The irate advocate of the oppressed race was saved from the alternative of his resolve, at least in the direct form proposed by him. A New Orleans correspondence was affected which caused the release of the Negro upon payment of the amount of the fine and expenses required which was furnished by Lincoln and Herndon, and the Negro was returned to his mother.

While he was practicing law in Illinois, he was employed in a case against a railroad company in the county of Vermilion in that state. The case was concluded in his favor, except as to the pronouncement of the judgment. Before this was done he rose and stated that his opponent had not proven all that was justly due to them in off-set and proceeded to state briefly that justice required that an allowance should be made against his client for a certain amount, which the court at once acquiesced in, and immediately proceeded to announce his judgment in accordance therewith. He was ever ready to sink his selfish love of victory as well as for his partiality for his client's favor and interest for exact justice.

Mr. Lincoln was always proud of his adopted state and Springfield—and its people never ceased to be special objects of his affection and admiration, yet, after he had left town and bidden his old friends and neighbors farewell to enter upon his new duties of government of national affairs, his memories would often wander back to the scenes of his early struggles; the place where he was married in the days of his early manhood, the place where his children were born and the country from unpromising youth he developed into majestic manhood; the retrospect was always the source of unfeigned pleasure and satisfaction to him and with all this he used to delight in telling the following story, not by way of casting any reproach upon his former home, and its people, but purely in a spirit of innocent and mirthful humor and amusement.

Many years ago, the honored Thompson Campbell[1656] was Secretary of State of the state of Illinois. He was a talented and

[1656] Thompson Campbell was an Irish immigrant who moved to Galena, Illinois. He was Illinois Secretary of State (1843—1846) and a member of the U.S. Congress. bioguide.congress.goc/scripts.biodisplay.pl?index=C000102

distinguished man, full of dry humor, had eminent social qualities and was a great friend of Mr. Lincoln. One day Mr. Lincoln said in a time when the legislature was not in session, "a very meek, cadaverous looking, clerical looking individual with a white neck cloth and other accompaniments of dress in keeping" came into Mr. Campbell's office, introduced himself, and stated that he had learned that he (Mr. Campbell) had the letting of the legislative hall; that he wished to secure it if possible for the purpose of delivering a course of lectures to the people of Springfield. Mr. Campbell said, "May I ask what is to be the subject of your lectures?"

"Certainly," was the reply, and with a brave, demure and solemn countenance he informed him that "the course he proposed to deliver was on the second coming of our Lord."

"It is of no use," said Campbell. "If you will take my advice you will not waste your time in this city, for it is my private opinion if the Lord has ever been in Springfield once, he will never come the second time."

In another instance a man wished to use the legislative hall to solicit people wanting to be insured. Mr. Campbell insisted that "Our people insure with no company except the Hartford and the Aetna. Many agents of your company have issued policies here before, but there have been but a few insurances. The people are joined to their idols. And you had better let them alone."

"But," said Mr. Lincoln, "Mr. Campbell let them have the legislative chamber to let him try his hand on them."

In the long years of intimate personal relations with Mr. Lincoln we can recall but two instances where he did not appear to advantage in his intercourse with his fellow men. The first case was that of his being employed with Mr. Edwin M. Stanton[1657] in the McCormick[1658] reaper infringement case in the United States circuit court in Cincinnati, in 1858, which has already been referred to in these pages. The other case was at Mr. Grinnell's[1659] breakfast in New York City on the 20th of February, 1861, whilst on his way from Springfield to Washington, at which many of the wealthiest men of that city were present. The

---

[1657] Edwin M. Stanton—See pg. 45.

[1658] Cyrus McCormick—See pg. 166 footnote.

[1659] Josiah Bushnell Grinnell was an abolitionist minister, a conductor on the Underground Railroad and an associate of John Brown. He was the benefactor of Grinnell College in Iowa. www.answers.com/topic/Josiah-bushnell-grinnell

breakfast itself was gorgeous in all its appointments. Nothing was lacking that the greatest epicure[1660] could possibly desire. And the silver plate as well as the cuisine bore testimony to luxurious wealth. But as social or political entertainment, the breakfast was a flat failure. Nobody seemed at his ease, and Mr. Lincoln least of all.

There seemed to be a realizing sense of an ill-assorted company of aristocrats to meet with a primitive child of nature, with the rich men of the nation coming in contact with a poor man of the people causing painful restraint to a sociable entertainment. Mr. Thurlow Weed[1661] who was present was particularly vexed at the failure of harmonious enjoyment and free and unrestrained intercourse. It was very apparent that Mr. Lincoln had made a bad impression upon the assembled millionaires, and someone had the bad taste to unnecessarily remark to him that he would not meet so many millionaires at any other table in New York. This had the affect of provoking the already embarrassed state of things by calling forth this reply from Mr. Lincoln: "Oh, indeed, is that so? Well that is all right. I am a millionaire myself. I got a minority of a million in the vote last November." Considering the occasion and the company, this might have been a light and frivolous thing for the president to say, and certainly it was so accepted by all company, except for a few personal friends of Mr. Lincoln present. Unfortunate as it was it showed that he appreciated the real difficulties of his position and was thinking more of the people than of the millionaires. These wealthy gentlemen were too much depressed by the mercantile situation of the country to excuse what they deemed an inadequate sense of presidential gravity and dignity, but as these gentlemen became better acquainted with his nobleness of character and the surpassing fitness for his position in the great struggle for the life of the nation, as time went on, the contempt gendered at the breakfast table changed to admiration and without exception, these men proffered their good will and support together with their millions in aid of suppressing the rebellion.

During the year 1861 it was difficult to preserve peace and good order in the city of Washington. Riots and disturbances were occurring daily and some of them were of a serious and sometimes dangerous nature. The authorities were in constant apprehension owing to the disloyal sentiment prevailing that a riot might occur of such magnitude

---

1660 An epicure is someone who takes pleasure in eating and drinking.

1661 Thurlow Weed—see page 21.

as to endanger the safety of the capital, which necessitated the utmost vigilance upon their part to preserve order.

On one occasion when the fears of the loyal element of the city were excited to fever heat when a free fight near the Old National Theater occurred about eleven o'clock one night. An officer in passing the place observed what was going on. Seeing the great number of persons engaged, he felt it to be his duty to command peace. The imperative tone of his command for the moment stopped the fighting—but the leader, a great bull, roughly pushed back the officer and told him to leave there or he would whip him. The officer again advanced and said, "I arrest you" and in attempting to place his hand on the man's shoulder, the bully struck out a fearful blow at the officer's face which was parried[1662] and instantly followed by a blow from the fist of the officer striking the fellow under the chin and knocking him senseless. Blood soon issued from the bully's mouth, nose and ears. A surgeon soon arrived and at first said it was a case beyond the skill of surgery and that the man's neck was broken. Soon the officer had other doctors in attendance. By the time of their arrival, it was ascertained that the man's neck was not broken, but that he had a concussion to the brain to that extent that it might prove fatal. The crowd soon dispersed. The injured man was conveyed on a litter to comfortable quarters where all medical skills of the officer could procure was employed in the hope of saving the life of the man whose death he apprehended from the blow of his hand in the discharge of his official duty. Conscious that he was, he was in no wise to blame, yet he felt a sincere regret to feel that he had been unfortunate enough to kill a fellow being.

Being on terms of intimacy with the president about two o'clock that night he went to the presidential mansion, woke up Mr. Lincoln and requested him to come to his office after which he told him his story. Mr. Lincoln listened with great interest until the narrative was completed and then asked a few questions and afterwards remarked, "I am sorry that you have had to kill the man, but these are times of war and a great many men deserve killing. This one according to your story is one of them that should be killed; so give yourself no uneasiness about the matter. I will stand by you."

---

[1662] Parried means evaded.

"That is not why I came to you. I know I did my duty and had no fear of your disapproval of what I did," replied the officer and then added. "Why I came to you is I feel great grief over the affair and I wanted to talk to you about it."

Mr. Lincoln said with a smile, placing his hand on the officer's shoulder, "You go home now and get some sleep, but let me give you this piece of advice. Hereafter when you have occasion to strike a man with your fist; strike him with a club or something that won't kill him."

The officer then went home but not to sleep. The occurrence had a great affect on him and was a real source of discomfort to his mind during the fourteen months the unfortunate invalid lived. The incident left sincere regret impressed upon him ever after. But in the after years the conciliatory and kindly views prompted by Mr. Lincoln's kind heart and his fidelity to friendship on this occasion to relieve him often occurred to him and to this day is cherished in his memory with feelings of consecration.[1663]

General James B. Fry,[1664] the Provost Marshal during Mr. Lincoln's administration, was designated by the Secretary of War as a special escort to accompany Mr. Lincoln to Gettysburg upon the anniversary of the battle at that place. The general upon arriving at the White House found the president late in his preparation for the trip. The general remarked to him that it was late and there was little time to lose in getting to the train on time. "Well," said Mr. Lincoln, "I feel about like how the convict did in Illinois when he was going to the gallows, passing along the road in custody of the sheriff and seeing people eager for the execution. They kept crowding and jostling each other past him. He at last called out, 'Boys, you need not be in such a hurry to get ahead, for there won't be any fun till I get there.'"

On another occasion he said to General Fry, "You are in charge of the appointment office of the War Department?"

He replied, "Yes."

"Now here I have a basketful of letters making application for office. I have examined some of them and have brief memoranda on some, but there are too many for me to examine all of them. Take them and examine them yourself, and such as are proper for further

---

[1663] The incident is well known by the author, Ward Hill Lamon, as he was the officer who struck the man, killing him in the above mentioned incident. *The Daily Commercial*, Bloomington, Illinois, November 20, 1879.

[1664] James B. Fry—See pg. 239.

action or consideration hand over to the Secretary of War and file the others." On one of the letters Mr. Lincoln had written

*"This day Mrs. ________ called upon me. She is the wife of Major ________ of the regular army. She wants her husband made a Brigadier General. She is a saucy little woman and I think she will torment me until I have to do it."*

*Signed,*

*A. Lincoln.*

It was but a short time after this that the little woman's husband was appointed.

*"Sleep hath its own world, a boundary between the things misnamed–death and existence. Sleep hath its own world, and a wide real of wild reality. And dreams in their development have breath, and tears and tortures, and the touch of joy; they leave a weight upon our waking thoughts,they take a weight from our waking toils, they do divide our being."*

A favorite poem of Abraham Lincoln
from Byron's "Dreams."[1665]

# — 33 — ABRAHAM LINCOLN'S VISIONS AND DREAMS

On the day of Mr. Lincoln's re-nomination for the presidency at Baltimore he was much engaged at the War Department receiving and answering dispatches from and to General Grant then in front of Richmond. He remained at the war office until lunch time, then went home, and after his lunch he did not go into his office, but returned to the War Department. On his arrival there the first dispatch received was the announcement of the nomination of Andrew Johnson for vice-president. "This is strange," said he. "I thought it was usual to nominate the president before nominating the vice."

The operator looked astonished and said, "Mr. President, have you not heard of your nomination? It was sent to the White House two hours ago."

He replied, "No. I did not see it, but it is all right. I shall see it probably on my return." He afterwards in speaking about this incident said, "A singular thing happened to me the day I was nominated in

1665 Recollections of Abraham Lincoln, pg. 122.

Chicago four years ago. On returning home in the afternoon from downtown where I had been enjoying a game of ball with the boys, on going upstairs to Mrs. Lincoln's room and feeling tired I laid down upon a lounge in the room directly opposite a dressing case upon which was a looking glass. In that glass I distinctly saw two images reflecting of myself which were in all respects alike except that one of them was somewhat paler than the other. I thought this strange and got up and walked around, then laid down again and a like result presented itself to my view which made me feel somewhat uncomfortable for the time being. Something occurred to distract my mind and I thought no more of it just then. On the following day, while on the street I was again reminded of the occurrence and the disagreeable sensation it had produced on me. I was still bothered over the phenomenon never having seen anything like it before. To give the matter a further test on going home that day I placed myself in the same position as nearly as I could and again the same affect was produced. I then began to think that it was the natural result of some principle of refraction or optics that I knew nothing about and entirely dismissed the subject from my mind. But recently" he said, "the subject recurred to me and I endeavored again to produce the same affect at the White House by arranging the mirror and the couch in as nearly the same position as before as possible, but I could not produce the same effect."

From conversations with him there can be little doubt that he as well as Mrs. Lincoln regarded this circumstance first spoken of as an omen of his re-election.

On one occasion when Mrs. Lincoln was present, Mr. Lincoln said, "It is strange how much there is in the Bible about dreams. There are I think some sixteen different chapters in the Old Testament and four in the New Testament in which dreams are mentioned and there are many other passages which refer to visions. If we believe the Bible we must accept the fact that in those days God and his angels came to men in their sleep in dreams. Now days dreams are regarded as very foolish things and are seldom told except among old women and young men and maidens in love."

Mrs. Lincoln asked if he believed in dreams. He answered that he could not say he did, but said he, "I had one the other night that has haunted me ever since, and after it happened the first time I opened the Bible and strange as it may appear, it was at the passage relating to

Jacob's dream. I turned to other passages and read them as in keeping with my own thought turning in that direction." The subject caused him to look serious and reflect, which attracted the attention of Mrs. Lincoln.

She remarked, "You frighten me with your solemn looks."

He then remarked, "I fear I have done wrong to mention the subject at all, but somehow or other the thing has gotten possession of me." Mrs. Lincoln disclaimed any belief in them. "All right, then," he said. "You will not be troubled by mine."

Being then urged to tell his dream he commenced and warmed to the subject. When Mrs. Lincoln grew more and more interested and with all her contempt for dreams she was visibly moved and much excited. His revelation was as follows: "About ten days ago I retired at night quite late. I had been up waiting for important dispatches from the front and could not have been long in bed before I fell into a slumber for I was very weary. I soon began to dream. There was great stillness about me and I heard weeping. I thought that I got up and wandered downstairs. The same stillness was there. As I went from room to room. I heard mourning and weeping again. At length I came to the end room which I entered and there before me was a magnificent dais on which was a corpse. Here there were sentries stationed and a crowd of people standing around. I said to one of the soldiers, 'Who is dead in the White House?' He answered, 'The president. He was killed by an assassin.' I then heard great wailing and distress all over the house which woke me from my dream, but I did not sleep anymore that night."

Little Tad who was intensely interested at the relation asked, "Father. Does it mean anything?"

"No, no, my son," he answered with a smile. "It is only a dream."

Mrs. Lincoln remarked, "It was a horrible one. I am glad I do not believe in dreams, or I should be in terror from this time forth. I really wish you had not told it."

"Well," said Mr. Lincoln, "let us say no more about it and try and forget all about it."

The relation of this dream was only a short time before his death. He did not often refer to it, but on one occasion while speaking of the safe guards around the presidential mansion to protect him from danger menacing his life, he said it was nonsense and the marshal's apprehension[1666] of any harm to his person was down right foolishness. In noticing the precautionary measures for his safety for a long time he said "They are trying to keep somebody, Lord knows who, from killing me." He then added. "Although I do not believe in any danger yet seeing means adopted for my protection has impressed me so that I actually dreamed the other night that the president was assassinated at the White House, but it seems fortunately that I was not the fellow that was killed."

He then related the dream, after which he jokingly remarked that in this case the fellow that was to kill me tried his hand on another first as I thought. He was like an old farmer in Illinois whose family at one time was very sick by eating greens occasioned by some poisonous "yarb" that had got into the mess. Some of the family were in danger of dying from it. There was a half-witted boy named Jake in this family, and always afterwards when they had greens the head of the family would say, "Now before running another risk with these things we will first try them on Jake. If he stands it we are all right." He then said, "Just so with me. As long as this imaginary assassin continues to exercise his amusement on others I can stand it, and I really think I am more in danger of dying from eating spinach or greens than I am from being killed by an assassin." He then again became serious and said, "I think the Lord in his own good time and way will work out this thing all right. We must trust in his wisdom and protection."

The most remarkable circumstance of its nature that ever occurred in the life of Mr. Lincoln was related by him to General Grant and others on the morning of the day of his assassination. There was a Cabinet meeting held that morning at which General Grant was present. During an interval of the discussion of the subject in hand, Mr. Lincoln turned to General Grant and asked him if he had heard from General Sherman who was then confronting General Johnston. The reply was in the negative, but the general added that he was in hourly expectation of receiving dispatches from him announcing the surrender of General Johnston. Mr. Lincoln then with great impressiveness said, "We will hear very soon now and the news will be important."

General Grant asked him why he thought so. "Because," said he, "I had a dream last night and ever since the war began I have had the

[1666] The author, Ward Hill Lamon, is the marshal he is referring to. Ward Hill Lamon, Lincoln's "Particular Friend," pg. 216.

same dream before every important military event that has occurred." He said it was so before Bull Run, Antietam, Gettysburg, and in fact all the important events. Turning to Mr. Welles, Secretary of the Navy, he said, "My dream is in your line, for in it I saw a ship sailing rapidly, and I am satisfied it portends some important national event, not so much from the fact of my having this dream, insignificant in itself as it may be, but it greatly impresses me because of its frequent occurrence and is always followed by important events."

After this Mr. Lincoln became unusually cheerful and continued so throughout the day. In the afternoon he ordered a carriage for a drive. Mrs. Lincoln asked him if he would like to have anyone accompany them. He answered, "No Mary. I prefer that we ride by ourselves today." Mrs. Lincoln said afterwards that she had never seen him look more supremely happy than he was on this occasion. In reply to a remark of hers indicating this fact, he responded "And well, I may feel so, Mary, for I consider this the day the war has come to a close. Now," said he, "we must both be more cheerful in the future for between this terrible war and the loss of our darling Willie, we have suffered much misery; but we must try to be happier in the future."

*"For a man so relentless with himself in the performance of his own duty, Lincoln's charity toward others was little short of phenomenal."*

General John Eaton[1667]

# — 34 —

# ABRAHAM LINCOLN'S ACTIONS

A striking exemplification of Mr. Lincoln's views may be found in what he said to two ladies from Tennessee during the war. Their husbands were prisoners of war at Johnson's Island[1668] and the ladies made application to the president for their release. At each interview one of these ladies would urge as a reason why her husband should be liberated was that he was a religious man. Eventually Mr. Lincoln gave the order for their discharge from prison with these remarks. "You say your husband is a religious man. Tell him when you meet him that I say I am not much of a judge of religion but in my opinion the religion which sets men to rebel and fight against the government because they think that the government does not sufficiently help some men to eat their bread in the sweat of other man's faces is not the sort of religion upon which can get people to heaven."

Mr. Lincoln at all times gave great respect to religious people and sacred subjects. He always showed a deference to ministers of the gospel and was disposed at all times to listen with that respectful attention and reverence due to their sacred calling. During the progress of the war he was in its early stages visited daily almost by reverend gentlemen sometimes singly and at other times as committees. They came from all sections of the country, sometimes for the speedy proclamation of emancipation of the slaves, sometimes

---

1667 Lincoln in American Memory, pg. 105.

1668 Johnson's Island is in Sandusky Bay, Ohio. It was a prison camp for Confederate officers. www.johnsonisland.org

to urge strict observance of the Sabbath day by the army, and at other times in the interest of other Christian objects such as urging something to be done or to be prevented from being done, and not infrequently to urge the appointment of some favorite to office. These visitations were for a long time tolerated patiently, but eventually became too frequent to be compatible to the public service. They had become somewhat vexatious,[1669] not only because of their frequency but because of the exacting tone of these advisors and their arbitrary assumption of diplomatic rights of members plenipotentiary[1670] in the secular affairs of the administration, protesting the blundering acts of commissions and omission to that misguided body.

Some time early in the war a clergy man said in Mr. Lincoln's presence that he "hoped the Lord was on our side."

"I am not at all concerned about that," replied Mr. Lincoln, "for I know the Lord is always on the side of the right. But it is my constant anxiety and prayer that I and this nation would be on the Lord's side."

On one occasion after patiently listening to a lengthy fault-finding personal sermon from a western delegation, the text of which was blunders of the administration, Mr. Lincoln with more than his usual animation said to them: "Gentlemen, suppose all the property you were worth was in gold and you had placed it in the hands of Blondin to carry it across the Niagara River on a rope. Would you snake the cable or keep shouting to him 'Blondin stand up a little straighter, Blondin stoop a little more, go a little faster, lean a little more to the north, lean a little more to the south?' No, you would hold your breath as well as your tongue and keep your hands off until he was safe over. The government is carrying an immense weight; untold treasures are in our hands. The persons managing the ship of state in the storm are doing the best they can. Don't badger the pilot. Keep silent and we will get you safe across." He then said, "Good day gentlemen. I have duties pressing upon me that must be attended to at once."

They had scarcely gone out of the room when another party was admitted who plied him with all sorts of questions until he was quite irritated and disturbed. One question asked him was how many men the rebels had in the field. Mr. Lincoln politely but enthusiastically answered "1,200,000 according to his best authority." His listener looked aghast and in astonishment exclaimed, "Good heavens."

---

1669 Vexatious means annoying.

1670 Plenipotentiary means someone who is invested to transmit official business.

"Yes, sir. 1,200,000 no doubt about it. You see all of our generals when they get whipped say the enemy outnumbered them from three or five to one, and I must believe them. We have 400,000 men in the field. Three times four makes twelve. Don't you see it? It is plain to be seen as a nose on a man's face. At the rate things are now going with the great amount of speculation and the small crop of fighting, it will take a long time to overcome 1,200,000 rebels in arms."

During his presidency Mr. Lincoln was always delighted to see his western friends and always gave them as cordial a welcome as circumstance would justify. At all times when the proprieties justified, he met them on old familiar footing and at once fell into his former habits and accustomed ways of entertaining with anecdotes and unrestrained, free and easy conversation. He never alluded to himself as president or as occupying the presidency, always spoke of his office as "this place," and would often say to an old friend "call me Mr. Lincoln. Mr. President is entirely too formal for us."

Shortly after the first inauguration an old and respected friend accompanied by his wife visited Washington, and as a matter of course paid their respects to the president and his family, having been on intimate social terms with them for many years. It was proposed that at a certain time Mr. and Mrs. Lincoln would call at the hotel where they were stopping and take them out for a ride in the new presidential carriage, a gorgeous and grandly caparisoned[1671] and accoutred[1672] establishments the like of which the party had seldom seen before that time. As close as the intimacy was, the two men had never seen each other with gloves on in their lives, except for protection from the cold winter. Both gentlemen realizing the proprietary of their use in the changed condition of things discussed mentally[1673] the use of gloves on this occasion. The subject of gloves had from the time of the commencement of Mr. Lincoln's official career given him great trouble and he hated the sight of them, except as they might be needed for warmth instead of ornament. Their use was also discussed by the respective wives of each of their husbands. They decided the gloves were the proper things. Mr. Lincoln reluctantly yielded to this decree and placed his in his pocket to be used or not used according to circumstances.

---

[1671] Caparisoned means adorned.

[1672] Accoutred means furnished.

[1673] Mentally means intellectually.

On arriving at the hotel, much to Mr. Lincoln's surprise he found his friend had doubtlessly yielded to his wife's persuasion and was gloved in the most approved style. The friend taking in the situation hardly had been seated in the carriage when he began taking off the clinging kids,[1674] at the same time Mr. Lincoln began to draw his on. Seeing what was happening, they both burst into a hardy laugh and Mr. Lincoln explained, "Oh, why should the spirits of mortals be proud?"

They with one accord each said "this glove nuisance is none of my doings." Mr. Lincoln then added, "I suppose it is polite to wear these things but it is positively uncomfortable for us to do so. Let us put them in our pockets. That is the best place for them and we shall be able to act more like folks in our bare hands." After this the ride was as enjoyable as any one they had ever taken in the early days in a lumber wagon over the prairies of Illinois.

At one time Captain Mix,[1675] commander of the president's body guard,[1676] was accompanying him from the Soldier's Home[1677] to the White House, with Mr. Lincoln riding in his carriage at the time. On the way they overtook a straggler some distance from the rear of his regiment marching into Washington. The soldier was heavily loaded with camp equipage and whiskey. Mr. Lincoln accosted him with the question, "My lad, what is that?"

"It's a regiment," the soldier sulkily replied, plodding on steadily and keeping his gaze upon the ground.

"Yes," said Mr. Lincoln, "I see that but I want to know what regiment it is."

"____ Pennsylvania," the man replied, looking neither to the right nor the left.

After passing on Mr. Lincoln turned to Captain Mix and said with a merry laugh, "It is evident that chap smells no blood of royalty in his establishment."

---

1674 Kids refers to kid gloves.

1675 Captain James B. Mix was in charge of Company A of the cavalry escort for Mr. Lincoln's trips to and from the Soldier's home. Lincoln Sanctuary, pgs. 84 & 114.

1676 From the 11th New York Cavalry assigned by the author, Ward Hill Lamon and Mr. Stanton to accompany the president while off the grounds of the White House. Ward Hill Lamon, Lincoln's "Particular Friend," pgs. 367 & 368 and Lincoln's Sanctuary, pg. 59.

1677 Mr. Lincoln went to the Soldier's Home almost every night in the summer as a respite from the White House. Lincoln Sanctuary, pgs. 2 & 3.

Mr. Lincoln used to tell the following story on Andrew Johnson, which he said Col. Moody[1678] "the fighting Methodist parson" as he was called in Tennessee vouches for the truth of: "Moody happened to be in Nashville the day it was reported that General Buell[1679] had decided to evacuate the city. Johnston at the time was provisional governor. It was said that the rebels had been strongly reinforced and were within two days march of the capital of that state.[1680] There was great excitement at that time in the city. Moody said he visited Johnston. He found him in his offices closeted with two other gentlemen who were walking the floor with him, one on each side. Shortly after he entered the office these gentlemen retired. Johnston was laboring under great excitement and coming up to Moody he said, 'Moody, in forty-eight hours we will all be in the hands of the rebels.' He then commenced waling the floor again, chaffing like a caged tiger. Suddenly he turned to Moody and said, 'Moody can you pray?'"

"Yes, that's my business."

"Well Moody I wish you would pray." And down both of them went upon their knees. The prayer was an earnest and fervent one. And soon Johnston began to respond in true Methodist style. During his devotional enthusiasm Johnston crawled onto his hands and knees over to where Moody was praying and threw his arms around Moody's neck, manifesting the deepest reverential emotion. Any one who would have witnessed the scene would never have thought of either actor as a gentle savage, but only as a devout sincere Christian. The prayer was at length concluded with a hardy "Amen." From both of them as they arose, Johnson drew a long breath as if relieved, and said with great emphasis, "Now Moody I feel better." Shortly afterwards he asked if Moody would stand by him. "Most certainly I will," was the answer. "Well," he said, I know I can depend on you." Then he commenced to walk the floor again, but suddenly turned around—the whole current of his thoughts seemed to have changed from a trustful and entire reliance on God for help and said, "Now, Moody, I don't want you to think I have suddenly become a religious man because I asked you to pray. I am sorry to say it, but I am not and never was a

---

1678 Colonel Granville Moody was born in New England but joined his brother in Ohio. He was the head of the 74th Ohio Infantry Regiment. www.ohiocivilwar.com/cw74.html

1679 Don Carlos Buell—See pg. 158.

1680 The capital of Tennessee is Nashville.

religious man, but no one knows this better than you do; yet, Moody, there is one thing true about it. I do believe in Almighty God but I wish I may be d—d if Nashville shall be surrendered to the rebels."

Mr. Lincoln at no time in his life could tolerate anything like persecution. His whole nature appeared to rebel against any appearance of such a thing and he never failed to act in the promptest manner when any such case was brought to his attention. One of the most celebrated cases every tried by any court martial during the war was that of Franklin W. Smith[1681] and his brother, charged with defrauding the government. These men bore a high character of integrity. At this time however, court martials were seldom invoked for any other purpose than to convict the accused, regardless of the facts of the case. The Smiths shared the usual fate of persons whose charges were submitted to such an arbitrament.[1682] They had been kept in prison, their papers seized, their business destroyed and their reputations ruined, followed by a conviction. After the judgment of court their case was submitted to the president for his approval.

The case was such a remarkable one, and was regarded as so monstrous in its unjust and unwarrantable conclusion that Mr. Lincoln after a full and careful investigation of it annulled the whole proceeding. What is very remarkable that the record of the president's decision could never be found afterwards in the Navy Department. No exact copy can be obtained of it. Someone in the office, however, familiar with the tenor and effect of it, furnished, as nearly its wording as possible. It is as follows, which was presented to the Boston Board of Trade and embraced the sentiment if not the exact words of the remarkable document.

*"Whereas Franklin W. Smith had transactions with the Navy Department to the amount of a million and a quarter of dollars, and whereas he had a chance to steal at least a quarter million of dollars and was only charged with stealing $2,200 and the question now is about his stealing one hundred. I don't believe he stole anything at all. Therefore, the record and the findings are disapproved, declared null and void, and the defendants are fully discharged."*

---

1681 Franklin W. Smith and his brother, Benjamin B. Smith were businessmen from Boston who had been arrested, were kept in prison, and had their business and reputation damaged. In the trial they were found guilty. www.rickwalton.com/lincoln/line086.htm

1682 Arbitrament means the power of deciding for oneself.

Mr. Lincoln upon taking up residence in the White House had so long watched the Confederate flag (which was in plain view from the window of his office) in Alexandria, and the fact of Colonel Ellsworth[1683] being killed by a citizen of that place combined to arouse in him sentiments and feelings of no kindly nature toward the inhabitants of that city without exception where they had not manifested openly their loyalty to the old flag. After the war had become fairly inaugurated and several battles had been fought, a lady from Alexandria visited Mr. Lincoln importuned[1684] him to give an order for the release of a certain church in that place which had been seized and used as a hospital. He asked and was told the name of the church and that there were but three or four wounded persons occupying it. The inhabitants wanted to worship in it. Mr. Lincoln asked her if she had applied to the post surgeon in Alexandria to give it up. She answered that she had and that she could do nothing with him. "Well," said he, "Madame. That is the end of it then. We put him there to attend to just such business, and it is reasonable to suppose that he knows better what should be done under the circumstances that I do."

More for the purpose of testing the sentiments of this visitor than for any other purpose, he said, "You said you live in Alexandria. How much would you be willing to subscribe to towards building a hospital there?"

She replied, "You may be aware Mr. Lincoln that our property has been very much embarrassed by the war and I could not afford to give much for that purpose."

"Yes," said Mr. Lincoln, "and the war is not over yet, and I expect we will have another fight soon, and that church may be very useful as a hospital in which to nurse our poor wounded soldiers. It is my candid opinion that God wants that church for our wounded fellows more than he does for the secess people to worship in. So Madame, if you will excuse me. I can do nothing for you."

Afterwards in speaking of this incident Mr. Lincoln said that the lass as a representative of her class in Alexandria reminded him of a story of a young man who had an aged father and mother owning considerable property. The young man being an only son and believing that old people had lived out their usefulness assassinated them both.

---

1683 Ephrain Ellsworth—See pg. 123.

1684 Importuned means urged.

He was accused, tried and convicted of the murder. When the judge came to pass sentence on him and called him upon him to give any reason he might have why the sentence of death should not be passed upon him, he with great promptness replied that he hoped the court would be lenient upon him because he was a poor orphan.

After commencement of hostilities in 1861 the state of Kentucky had to be handled by the administration with great care, to prevent her from passing secession resolutions and casting her lot with the other southern states. Her people as a whole wanted no part of the war—wanted to remain neutral—noncombatant—desiring to be left alone and undisturbed. War was raging in Tennessee and something had to be done and done soon. The Kentucky people remonstrated[1685] and insisted that no troops should be sent through the state for the purpose of putting down the war in Tennessee or any other southern state. The repeated remonstrances[1686] of this kind set Mr. Lincoln to thinking seriously what was best to be done, as there was a pressing necessity for immediate action. In the midst of his perplexities he said, "I am a good deal like the farmer who was returning to his home one night. He found his two little sons fast asleep with a hideous serpent leisurely crawling over their bodies. He dared not strike the serpent for fear of killing or wounding his children. So in agony in mind and apprehension he waited until the reptile moved off. Now," said he, "I do not want to act in a hurry about this matter for I don't want to hurt any of the children in Kentucky if I can help it. But that serpent has got to be taken out of Tennessee, neutrality or no neutrality."

Mr. Lincoln was stern and resolute whenever duty called him to act, and yet his great good heart would sometimes manifest itself on the side of mercy at the expense of discipline in the army. At one time there were twenty-four deserters sentenced by court martial to be shot and the warrants for their execution were sent to the president for his approval. He refused to sign the warrants. The commanding general of the troops to which these unfortunate men belonged left his command and went to Washington and urged their punishment. He said, "Mr. President, unless these men are made examples of, the army itself is in danger. Mercy to the few is cruelty to the many."

---

[1685] Remonstrated means demonstrated.

[1686] Remonstrances are protests.

Mr. Lincoln replied, "General, there are already too many weeping widows in the United States. For God sake do not ask me to add to that number, for I tell you plainly I will not do it."

The following incident will illustrate another phase of his character. A slave trader who had been convicted for being engaged in the prohibited slave trade then confined in Newburyport, Massachusetts jail petitioned for a pardon. He had been sentenced to imprisonment for five years and to pay a fine of $1000. The petition was accompanied by a letter to the Honorable John B. Alley,[1687] a member of Congress from Lynn, Massachusetts. Mr. Alley presented the papers to the president, with a letter from the prisoner acknowledging his guilt and the justice of his sentence. He had served out the term of the imprisonment but was still held on account of the fine not being paid. Mr. Lincoln was much moved by the pathetic appeal. He then, after pausing for some time, said to Mr. Alley, "My friend. This appeal is very touching to my feelings and no one knows my weakness better than you. It is to be possible that I am too easily moved by appeals for mercy. I must say that if this man had been guilty of the foulest murder that the arm of man could perpetrate I might forgive him on such an appeal; but the man who could go to Africa and rob her of her children and then sell them into international bondage with no other motive than that which is furnished by dollars and cents, is so much worse than the most depraved murderer that he can never receive pardon at my hand. No, sir, he may rot in jail before he shall have liberty by any act of mine."

At one time when things were at a standstill and the armies were taking things easy and no aggressive movements could be induced by the anxious Washington authorities, Mr. Lincoln went to General McClellan's[1688] headquarters to have a talk with him, but for some reason he was unable to get an audience with the general. Being to his disappointment naturally there was a feeling of inexcusable indifference to his presence apparent upon the part of the commander of the Union forces which created in the mind of the president an impression that in the general's opinion he was an unimportant factor in what was going on. He returned to the White House very much disturbed at what had occurred and immediately sent for the two other

---

[1687] John Bassatt Alley was a shoe manufacturer and U. S. Congressman from 1852 to 1867. dbpedia.org/resource/John_B_Alley

[1688] General George McClellan—See pg. 123.

general officers to have a consultation. On their approach he told them he must have someone to talk to about the situation as he could not see General McClellan. He had sent for them to get their opinion to the possibility or probability of soon commencing active operations with the Army of the Potomac. He said he desired an expression of their opinion about the matter for it was his opinion if something was not done and soon, that the bottom would fall out of the whole thing. He intended "if General McClellan did not want to use the army, I propose to borrow it from him, provided he could see how it could be made to do something, for if McClellan can't fish, he ought to cut bait at a time like this."

About the first time Mr. Lincoln contemplated leaving Washington he was to attend some gathering of the people of Baltimore, Philadelphia or New York (in which city is not now recollected). A committee waited on him and urged his attendance on the occasion saying that they were sure Mr. Garrett[1689] the president of the only road going out of Washington east would take great pleasure in furnishing a special train of cars for him. "Well," he said, "I have no doubt of that. I know Mr. Garrett well and like him very much, but if I were to believe (which I don't) everything some people say of him, about his secess principles he might say to you as what was said by a superintendent of a railroad to a son of one of my predecessors in office, some few years after the death of President Harrison.[1690] The son of the incumbent of this office, contemplating an excursion for this father, somewhere or other, went to order a special train of cars. At the time politics were very bitter between the Whigs and the Democrats and the railroad superintendent happened to be an uncompromising Whig. The son made know his demand which was bluntly refused by the railroad official saying that his road was not running special trains for the accommodation of a president, just then. 'What?' said the young man. 'Did you not furnish a special train for the funeral of General Harrison?' 'Yes,' said the superintendent very calmly, 'and if you will only bring your father here in that shape you shall have the best train on the road.'"

---

[1689]John W. Garrett—See pg. 218.

[1690] President William Henry Harrison was the 9th President of the United States. He was the first President to die in office. He died on April 4, 1841 of pneumonia/scurvy after serving in office for only 31 days. www.answers.com/topic/william-henry-harrision

"But gentlemen," said Mr. Lincoln, "I have no doubt of Mr. Garrett's loyalty for the government or of his respect for me personally and I will take pleasure in going."

*"Lincoln actually believed that popular government was practical. He actually listened to people. He knew them so well that he understood what they said when he listened. He was indeed the world's best guide in government by the people."*

Ida Tarbell, in Gideon Welles' diary as published in *Atlantic Monthly*[1691]

# — 35 —

# ABRAHAM LINCOLN—THE LEADER

In the personal magnetism, moral courage, eloquent speech, political shrewdness, common sense and ability, Mr. Lincoln stood preeminent. It may be well doubted whether any man ever lived on the American continent who was his peer in that combination of qualities required to make a man a great leader, competent to hold his party together, and to overcome such difficulties and restore peace to a distracted and shattered country such as was his fortune or misfortune to govern. With him there was method in his every move. He never trifled; he was charged with much over-seriousness—melancholy was misconstrued as discouragement, and was also charged by the more serious with a disposition to indulge too much anecdote telling to elucidate[1692] his ideas on all questions whether grave or gay; but it is notable that he never told an anecdote that did not "point a moral." Many of them were more forcible than polite; that is true. They often served to subject him to adverse criticism among the elite, especially when this class of persons was made the object of his illustrations and with the imputation[1693] of a want of veneration amounting to moral

[1691] Lincoln in American Memory, pg. 161.

[1692] Elucidate means to explain.

[1693] Imputation means attribution.

obliquity.[1694] He was often charged. He stooped to no vindication in life, but left this to be recorded in history as neglect or loving reference whichever someone would choose to indicate. In his role of elucidation[1695] he was epigrammatic.[1696] He indulged in no studied phrases; he was no fumbler of words. His most abounded language expressive of all passions, and trite with exemplifications,[1697] novel in literary or political history. They with all their crudities[1698] and censured blemishes stand the test of criticism with any that can be culled or found in the saying or speeches of any other politician or statesman.

General Fry was thrown into very close and intimate relations with Mr. Lincoln during the war. In the year 1885 in the *New York Tribune* he gave the following pen picture of the president: "I never saw him when he appeared to be anything but a great man and a very ugly one; his expression in repose was sad and dull, but his ever recurring humor at short intervals flashed forth with the brilliance of an electric light. I have observed but two well defined expressions in his countenance—one that of a pure, thoughtful honest man absorbed in a sense of duty and responsibility—the other that of a humorist so full of fun that he could not keep all of it in. His power of analysis was wonderful. He strengthened every case he stated and no anecdote or joke every lost form or effect from his telling. He invariably carried the listener with him to the climax and when that was reached in relating a humorous story, he laughed all over. His large mouth assumed unexpected and comical shape. The skin on his nose gathered into wrinkles. His eyes though partially closed emitted infectious rays of fun. It was not only the aptness of his stories, but his way of telling them and his own unmitigated[1699] enjoyment that gave them zest and even among the gravest men and upon the most serious occasions. Nevertheless, Mr. Lincoln, though a good listener, was not a good conversationalist. When he talked he told a story or argued a case but it should be remembered that during the entire four years of his presidency—from the spring of 1861 until his death in 1865, civil war prevailed. It bore

[1694] Obliquity means divergence.
[1695] Elucidation means explainer.
[1696] Epigrammatic means witty.
[1697] Exemplifications means showing be example.
[1698] Crudities means crudeness.
[1699] Unmitigated means absolute.

heaviest upon him and his mind, was daily, hourly even upon the duties of his high office; so as he might have expressed it, he was either lifting with all his might at the butt end of the log or sitting upon it for rest and recreation.

Mr. Lincoln was as nearly master of himself as it is possible for a man clothed with great authority and engaged in the affairs of public life to become. He had no bad habits and if he was not wholly free from the passions of human nature, it is quite certain that passion but rarely, if ever, governed his actions. If he deviated from the straight course of justice it was usually from indulgence for the minor faults or weaknesses of his fellow men observed. He had but one craving he could not overcome—that was for a second term of the presidency. He was fully conscious of the grip this had upon him and said in a way of apology for it, "No one knows what that gnawing is till he has had it."

It will be acknowledged Mr. Lincoln lacked dignity in outward appearance. When he was silent and not in action, he was not interesting to the observer. He would attract attention then only from his angularity and ungainly form, length of stature and serious aspect. In speech he never failed to interest to such an extent as to obscure all personal defect and gain for himself the respect of all within the sound of his voice. To hear him once was to know him always. His voice and his subject buried in oblivion all thought of his personal appearance except as a man who was the wonder of the age, a colloquial[1700] entertainer. He fully realized that he was formed by nature all right but not molded by art in his physical architecture owing to his habits, education associations and former surroundings to be ornamental, or to be able to preside with graceful dignity in doing the honors of the White House expected of the chief magistrate. In speaking of his want of polish, the light accomplishment and adaptation as presiding dignitary at the presidential mansion he said: "I guess I will leave all the fancy work to others and will browse around in the utility departments best I can." He, however, soon showed that he was master of a style of elevated and forcible, non-descript crudity[1701] of dignity unknown and never before then recognized by orthodox diplomats. In diplomacy and statesmanship an American statesman will compare favorably with that of the most favored nations on the

[1700] Colloquial means informal.
[1701] Crudity means unrefined.

earth. No American of any period of our history could state a cause or write a paper on public import with more impressive seriousness circumspection and grave dignity than Abraham Lincoln.

His speeches with Judge Douglas on the slavery question in 1858, his speech at Cooper Institute in New York, his first and second inaugural address, his messages to Congress, his emancipation proclamation and other proclamations, his Gettysburg speech and his writings compare most favorably to the speeches and state papers of revolution when Washington, Adams,[1702] Jefferson, Dickerson,[1703] Jay,[1704] Hamilton and other immortal statesman figured. The papers written by Mr. Lincoln, for force of diction, adaptation intensity of grasp and effectiveness fitting the condition occasioning their promulgation[1705] are unequalled in modern times in this or any other country. He was by no means vain of the accomplishment of these achievements. He realized his work and regarded it as a matter of course. His appreciation of anything accomplished by himself was modest, regarding it as a duty discharged, rather than an accomplishment of which to be proud. The hard lines that have been drawn of him and the fearfully hard life he led from his infancy through youth to raw manhood had not embittered[1706] him but it was ever before his view and cast a gloom of sadness over his existence.

Yet he was genial,[1707] ever genial, tender and social. He never bewailed[1708] the hardships he suffered nor exalted in the triumphs he accomplished. He felt in going to Washington that he would not be at home in all circles, but he had an abiding faith in the practical accomplishments of his destiny, not only as a faithful servant, but as a leader of the people in times that tried men's souls. He is likely to be in all coming time the acknowledged monumental figure of the group of intellectual giants which the republic has produced, and as time progresses it will doubtless be said of him as Bolingbrook said of

---

1702 John Adams was the 2nd U.S. President serving from 1797-1801. www.whitehouse.gov/aboout/president/johnadams

1703 John Dickinson was a delegate the United States Constitutional Convention from Pennsylvania. www.answers.com/topic/john-dickinson

1704 Justice John Jay—See pg. 439.

1705 Promulgation means declaration.

1706 Embittered means caused ill feelings.

1707 Genial means kindly.

1708 Bewailed means lamented.

Marlsborough. "He is so great a man that it is forgotten that he ever had weakness."

Mr. Lincoln's great ambition was to leave the country and the world better than he found it. And it is a source of gratification to his friends to contemplate the great work of his life in efficient assistance in blotting out chattel slavery from the face of the American republic as the fruition of that ambition. The sound of the last hostile gun had scarcely died away when crime in its most unpardonable wickedness ushered his soul into eternity ere[1709] the great plaudits of a respectively reunited people relieved from the blemish of a bondmen population that had met his respective and grateful ear. There was now no living man who could fill the place of the fallen dead in the hearts of the admiring people. When reconstruction would have been relatively easy of accomplishment with him at the head of the affairs of state, the untimeliness of his death, the manner of his "taking off" made it a task of no easy accomplishment for his successor.

About two thousand years previous to this period, history gives us an account of one man in Rome, who was the prototype of Mr. Lincoln in many respects. After the people had assumed the prerogative claimed exclusively by the Senate to suspend the Constitution in a time of great danger to the Commonwealth, and placed Carus Marius at the head of affairs as the only safety for the republic. Marius had previously been consul, but custom having the effect of law prevailed, that a consul was not eligible for a second election. The crisis then upon them, the people disregarded the custom and re-elected him as their only salvation after the battle of "Orange" between the Romans and the Cimbri where the former are said to have lost 80,000 of their soldiers and 40,000 camp followers. The Senate was now in a great state of perturbation.[1710] They could have appointed him dictator and the emergency would have justified it, but for reasons of their own they refused to do so.

The Constitution was suspended and the ineligibility clause or custom was abrogated[1711] by the will of the people, without the concurrence of the Senate. The significant acknowledgement that the empire, which had won by the sword, must be held by the sword. The

---

[1709] Ere means before his time.
[1710] Perturbation means disturbance.
[1711] Abrogated means nullified.

sword itself must be held by the hand that could make it most effective. The country had to be saved, constitution or no constitution.

There were many points of comparison between the military campaigns; between the Romans and the Cimbri and the campaigns between the Union and Confederate forces. Had the Cimbri turned after whipping the Romans at the battle of Orange and re-crossed the Alps into Italy, the taking of Rome would have been made easy and natural, which had they done so might have terminated the mighty power of that great republic as was done about 500 years afterwards by Alaric when in its decline. If on the other hand the Confederates after the first battle of Bull Run had crossed the Potomac River and taken the city of Washington, the capital of the United States, what would have been the result we leave to conjecture. The Germans and Tuetons did not embrace the favorable moment for seizing Rome and delay enabled Marius to place himself in position to repel any attack that could have been made on the city. So with the Confederates after the battle of Bull Run when the way was clear, for some unaccountable reason they did not opportunely embrace the advance by seizing the capital, its treasure, before the American Marius could place himself in a defensive position.

There is a striking similarity between these two men—Carus Marius and Abraham Lincoln. Both were self-made men. The father of each moved in the humble walks of life—small farmers. And both their sons being bred to the plough and inured[1712] to manual labor; both belonging naturally to the common people, and all their sympathies and natural instincts were essentially with that class and opposed to aristocracy in any form or condition. It was by the medium of their sentiments of democracy that so eminently marked their success in the leadership in their respective governments in times of great peril. It may be conjectured that at the time alluded to the Roman Senate was composed pretty much of corrupt partisans who had little to expect from the rule of an honest man like Marius. Clothed with aristocratic power after the destinies of Rome were relieved of their impending peril and embarrassment, corruption, and rascality,[1713] Marius eventually conquered the Germans and other opposing forces as Mr. Lincoln did the opposing Confederates. Historians differ about some characteristics of the great Roman; some

---

[1712] Inured means accustomed to.

[1713] Rascality means the actions of a rascal.

attribute to him cruelty and tyrannical disposition. If the charge of cruelty and tyranny is true, this is a striking instance of dissimilarity between him and his American prototype. And strange it is that Marius lived in a time of consulary[1714] government in Rome. But to be murdered was the usual end exceptionally distinguished Romans and yet he lived without danger and died a natural death, while Mr. Lincoln in his country so noted for its freedom from violence and for the order and peacefulness of its citizens after the grand achievements of suppressing internal strife and restoring amity among its people, was stricken to death by the hand of an assassin.

Feeling engendered between the sections during the progress of the war was fast subsiding after the capitulation at Appomattox, but Mr. Lincoln's unnatural murder revived and re-engendered with redoubled the fury the subdued hate of the North against the South, and made reasonable terms on which the government could be reconstructed most difficult, if not impossible. Owing it the condition of affairs and Mr. Lincoln's popularity previous to his death, he would have been the only man in the nation who could have reinstated satisfactorily all the wheels of the old machinery of state into harmonious working order. All the prejudice of the great mass of the American people that had existed for so many years—the candid thinkers will now admit that it was to such men as William Lloyd Garrison,[1715] Wendell Phillips[1716] and Joshua R. Giddings[1717] that made Mr. Lincoln the possible Moses[1718] to conduct the oppressed children in bondage through the wilderness as freemen, after centuries of suffering and oppression and unrequited toil, ignorant, penniless and naked from the homes of their earthly masters surrounded by wealth and luxury, created by their labor and sweat of their brows. These men, called abolitionists, the designation which had become a term of derision and opprobrium[1719] for a quarter of a century despised, shunned and dreaded, now hailed as the anointed philanthropists, the country is indebted, not only for the freedom of the Negro, but for the impunity of free speech, the toleration of opinion, for the limit of authority, for the relation of the

---

[1714] Consulary means republic.
[1715] William Lloyd Garrison—See pg. 8.
[1716] Wendell Phillips—See pg. 8.
[1717] Joshua R. Giddings—See pg. 20.
[1718] Moses was a Biblical figure who led his people to freedom.
[1719] Opprobrium means shameful conduct.

citizen to the law, for the government of as well as for defining states rights and nationality; but this indebtedness cost hundreds of thousands of lives, and also countless millions of dollars.

They made public opinion by their appeals, conscience and the moral senses of mankind, awakened the necessity to exterminate human slavery through the agency and power of Christianity and when that opinion was fairly established, the Republican Party used it effectively under the pressure of a military necessity. After the issue was decided, and the struggle was over, the hostile strife had ceased, and belligerents had capitulated, the country was again instantly disturbed and horrified by the inhuman murder of the liberator of mankind, the patriotic statesman and the greatest man that ever adorned the annals of American history. With his death the most brilliant light of the age went out, and his spirit went prematurely forth to mingle with the heavenly hosts that had preceded him to that haven where the weary are at rest.

*"Yon marble minstrel's voiceless stone,*
*In deathless song shall tell*
*When many a vanished year hath flown*
*The story how he fell.*
*Nor wreck nor change nor winters blight*
*Nor time's remorseless doom*
*Can dim one ray of holy light*
*That guilds his glorious tomb."*

*"The most striking fact of our time, of a psychological kind, is the growth of Lincoln's fame since the earth closed over his remains."*

Horace White, publisher and editor of the *Chicago Tribune* newspaper[1720]

# — 36 —

# SUMMARY

Of all great characters who have played the most tragical[1721] drama on the real stage of life throughout Christendom, the epoch that marked the American civil war produced in Abraham Lincoln the most remarkable character that ever appeared. The living now realize it from observation; posterity will see it in the record of the historian and creations of the poets. There have not been many such periods as the one marked by the rise, progress and termination of America's civil war. It records the most eventful pages in history. It tested the power of self-government of the people and made the government stronger, by means of the test. It will require the rare literary powers to convey to those who follow, to paint the picture for posterity equal to the reality. The crisis which settled at so great cost the question as to whether a government of the people, for the people and by the people could stand, produced its heroes and villains, its triumphs and its sorrows, its loves, its hatreds, its passionate admirers and deadliest enemies. Time, the assuager[1722] of all griefs, has in a measure subdued and mollified the passions and estrangements created but still enemies are denounced, friends are extolled; conflicting emotions still exist; hopes and fears are alike and indulged and divided public opinion as to what constitutes patriotism in civil government.

---

1720 Lincoln in American Memory, pg. 141.

1721 Tragical means fateful.

1722 Assuagers are pacifiers.

An irreconcilable conflict of rights or supposed rights between the sections will remain an open question, at least during the present generation in this government. It is not our purpose to sit in judgment on the rights or the wrongs of revolution. Under oppression, real or imaginary, to oppose or not to admit this right under certain conditions would be to slander our birthright and heritage of American independence. But what causes justify revolution and were they sufficient to justify rebellion in the late civil war? It is not the purpose of these pages to discuss, admit or deny. Previous to dissensions growing out of political rights claimed and denied, in regard to an institution constitutionally recognized in one section, prohibited by statutory enactments in the other, all citizens of the whole country were a unit upon all subjects of human interests. Religion, morals, politics, poetry, and all the speculative problems of life—one people, one country and all struggling after one and the same object. Few distractions were seriously recognized.

The South claimed distinction over the North for birth, culture and honor, and the North claimed distinction for wealth, progress and education. Each section in truth and in fact, had enough of all the worthy qualities boasted of by both necessary to make them not only the happiest but the most prosperous and honorable people in the world. Nothing but a vital question like slavery involving wealth, service, and moral and religious questions could ever have involved the people in a war with themselves. The political questions being now settled there will be no change in the structure of society. The main question being settled, the minor ones of birth, culture and education if not settled harmoniously will be tolerated with amicable forebearance. It can well be said that no people ever showed greater devotion nor ever set forth braver armies of greater generals than met in this bloody conflict. True it is that the lesson taught by the result is one of disastrous augury[1723] to speculative mankind, and forces the conclusion that valor and strategy, however great, are vain when opposed to inherent right and the immutable[1724] principles of justice, particularly when supported by the superiority of numbers when the loss of one man in battle was irreparable on the one side of the conflict, when the loss of thousands on the other was regarded with indifference. Without doubt, relative numbers of the belligerents had

---

[1723] Augury means omen.
[1724] Immutable means unchanged.

much to do with the decision of the struggle. Justice and candor force us to acknowledge that no braver or more united people ever drew swords in defense of civil rights and national independence than were forced to yield obedience to laws of their own established government, mourn a lost cause and bury the hope of establishing a new and separate republic.

Doubtless in the near future the results of this bloody struggle, after the passions of the opposing parties have entirely subsided, there will be universally regarded as presages[1725] of good to the cause of liberty and the future of mankind. Happily there are to be the casual observers but two visible causes now left unsettled in the body politic of a threatening nature, from which any serious apprehensions may be felt for the safety and perpetuity of the nation. One is corruption in party organization and management and the other is the conflict between capitol and labor. This latter is assuming the proportions of an undissolvable conflict. Corporations assume to control the direction in which labor and capital shall be employed. If ever American society and the United States government are overthrown, it will be from one or both of these causes, for they are kindred grievances, with closely allied interests forming an immense corrupting power of evil.

[1725] Presages are predictions.

# Postscript

# ABRAHAM LINCOLN ACCORDING TO WARD HILL LAMON

No one knew Mr. Lincoln better. None loved him more than I. My friendship did not begin with his official career. I was near him in private life; I was near him in the darkest hours of the great struggle; I was near him when the first rational hope of peace dawned upon the land. In truth, I might say without offense to the people of his State and mine, that I retained his confidence unshaken as he retained my affection unbroken, until his own life was offered up the last great sacrifice to domestic accord, on the very threshold of peace, and in the actual blaze and glory of the nation's triumph.[1726]

It was my good fortune to have known Mr. Lincoln very long and well—so long and so intimately, that, as the shadow brightens and the years recede, I am more and more impressed by the rugged grandeur and nobility of his character, his strength of intellect, and his singular purity of heart. Surely I am the last man on earth to say or do aught in derogation[1727] of his matchless worth, or to criticize the fair frame of who he was, during eighteen of the most eventful years of my life,[1728] as constant, considerable and never failing friends.[1729]

In conclusion, I may say that my friendship with Mr. Lincoln was of no recent hot-house growth. Unlike that of many who have made me the subject of hostile criticism, it antedates the beginning of his presidential term and the dawn of his political triumphs. I had the good fortune to be in intimate association with his private life when it

---

[1726] Recollections of Abraham Lincoln, pg. 22.

[1727] Derogation means detraction.

[1728] Mr. Lamon met Mr. Lincoln in 1847. Recollections of Abraham Lincoln, pg. 14.

[1729] The Real Lincoln, pg. 225 & 226.

was humble and obscure, and I was near him too in the darkest hours of his executive responsibilities, until, indeed, the first rays of God-given peace broke upon the land… Is it, therefore, likely that words of mine, written or spoken, should do purposed injustice to his memory?[1730]

An army of his command was powerless to defend his person from the assassin's bullet, but myriads of earthly foes to humanity will ever be powerless to efface[1731] one single lineament from the tracing of his national and infinite portrait. A man never dies until his work is done. He still lives—his death was the birth of his enduring and eternal renown.[1732]

The Author
January 6, 1828—May 7, 1893

1730 Recollections of Abraham Lincoln, pg. 22.
1731 Efface means to destroy.
1732 Ward Hill Lamon: Lincoln's "Particular Friend," pg. 391 and Recollections of Abraham Lincoln, pg. xxxviii.

# Bibliography


Appleton's Cyclopaedia of American Biography, D. Appleton & Co., 1889.

Barnes, Frank—Fort Sumter National Monument South Carolina, National Park Service Historical Handbook Series No. 12, Washington, D.C., 1961.

Barton, William E.—The Life of Abraham Lincoln, The Bobbs-Merrill Company, Indianapolis, Indiana, 1925.

Borreson, Ralph—When Lincoln Died, Appleton-Century, New York, 1965.

Burlington, Michael—The Inner World of Abraham Lincoln, University of Illinois Press, 1997.

Bushong, Milliard K., Ph. D.—The History of Jefferson County, Carr Publishing, 1972.

Canby, Courtlandt—Lincoln and the Civil War, George Braziller, Inc. New York, 1960.

Cashen, Joan—The First Lady of the Confederacy, The Belknap Press of Harvard University Press, Cambridge, Massachusetts, 2006.

Catton, William and Bruce—Two Roads to Sumter, Orion Publishing Group, London, 1963.

Catton, Bruce—A Stillness at Appomattox, Doubleday and Company, Garden City, New York, 1953.

Catton, Bruce—Grant Takes Command, Little, Brown and Co., Boston, 1968.

Chadwick, Bruce—The Two American Presidents, Birch Lane Press, Secaucus, NJ, 1999.

Charnwood, Lord—Abraham Lincoln: A Biography, Madison Books, Lanham., MD., 1996.

Cohen, Stan—The Thundering Voice of Jehovah, Pictorial Histories Publishing Company, Missoula, Montana, 1999.

Commanger, Henry Steele—The Blue and The Gray, Bobbs-Merritt Co., Indianapolis, Indiana, 1882.

Corseon, Oscar Taylor—Abraham Lincoln: His Words and Deeds, F. A. Owen Publishing Co., Dansville, New York, 1927.

Cosky, John M.—The Confederate Navy, The Museum of the Confederacy, Richmond, Virginia, 2005.

Davis, Burke—The Civil War: Strange and Fascinating Facts, Holt, Rinehart and Winston, New York, 1960.

Davis, Jefferson—The Rise and Fall of the Confederate Government, D. Appleton and Company, New York, 1881.

Davis, Kenneth C.—Don't Know Much About the Civil War?, William Morrow and Co, Inc., New York, 1996.

Donald, David Herbert—Lincoln's Herndon, Da Capo Press, New York, 1848.

Fischer, David Hackett—Liberty and Freedom, Oxford University Press, Oxford, 2005.

Flood, Charles Bracelen—Lee: The Last Years, Houghton, Mifflin and Co., Boston, 1981.

Foote, Shelby—The Civil War a Narrative, Random House, New York, 1963.

Foote, Shelby—Civil War a Narrative, Parts I—IX, Random House, New York, 1974.

Guelzo, Allen C.—Lincoln's Emancipation Proclamation, The End of Slavery in America, Simon and Schuster, New York, 2004.

Guernsey, Alfred H. and Alden, Henry M.—Harpers Pictorial History of the Great Rebellion of the United States, The Fairfax Press, New York, originally published in 1866 (Reprinted edition called "Harpers Pictorial History of the Civil War").

Hamand, Lavern A.—"Ward Hill Lamon: Lincoln's Particular Friend"—doctoral thesis for the University of Illinois, 1949.

Hanchett, William—The Lincoln Murder Conspiracies, University of Illinois Press, Urbana and Chicago, 1983.

Holzer, Harold—"Incognito Into Baltimore", *Civil War Times*, Dec. 2008, pgs. 36-41.

Horner, Harlan Hoyt—Lincoln and Greeley, Greenwood Press, 1971.

Hutton, James V., Jr. —"General James Washington Singleton and Colonel Ward Hill Lamon—Local Area Confidantes to Abraham Lincoln" Winchester/Frederick County Historical Society Journal, Vol. XVI, 2004, pages 1-63.

Hutton, James V., Jr.—Miss Dolly, The Remarkable Daughter of Ward Hill Lamon, Friend and Bodyguard of Abraham Lincoln, James Hutton Jr., Winchester, Virginia, 2003.

Johannsen, Robert W.—The Union in Crisis, 1850-1877, The Free Press, New York, 1965.

Lamon, Ward Hill—Recollections of Abraham Lincoln, University of Nebraska Press, Lincoln and London, 1994.

Lamon, Ward Hill—The Life of Abraham Lincoln, From His Birth tc His Inauguration as President, University of Nebraska Press, Lincoln and London, 1999 (Originally published by James R. Osgood and Co., Boston, 1872).

Lewis, Lloyd—The Assassination of Abraham Lincoln, History or Myth, MJF Books, New York, 1929.

McKitrick, Eric L.—Andrew Johnson and Reconstruction, The University of Chicago Press, Chicago, IL, 1960.

McPherson, Edward—History of the Rebellion, Philip and Solomons, 1865.

MacKay, James—Allan Pinkerton, The First Private Eye, John Wiley and Sons, New York, 1996.

Miller, Francis Trevelyn—The Armies and The Leaders, Caste Books, New York, 1957.

Perrett, Geofrey—Lincoln's War, Random House, New York 2004.

Peterson, Merrill D.—Lincoln in American Memory, Oxford University Press, Oxford, 1964.

Pinster, Matthew—Lincoln's Sanctuary, Abraham Lincoln and the Soldier's Hime, Oxford University Press, Oxford, 2003.

Pollard, Edward A.—Southern History of the War, Fairfax Press, originally published in 1866.

Potter, David—Lincoln and His Party in the Secession Crisis, Yale University Press, 1942.

Randal, J. D.—Lincoln The President, Dodd, Mead and Company, New York, 1953.

Sandberg, Carl—The War Years, Dell Publishing Company, Laurel edition, 1974.

Schildt, John—Four Days in October, published by the author, Chewsville, Maryland, 1982.

Shaw, Albert—Abraham Lincoln, His Path to the Presidency, and the Year After his Election, The Relevant Reviews Corporation, New York, 1930.

Silverstone, Paul H.—Warships of the Civil War Navies, Naval Institute Press, Annapolis, Maryland, 1989.

Thomas, Emory M.—The Confederate Nation, History Club Books, New York, 1979.

Wallace, Lewis—Lew Wallace: Autobiography, Harpers and Brothers, 1906.

Waugh, John C.—Reelecting Lincoln: The battle for the 1864 Presidency, Crown Publishing, Inc., New York, 1997.

Wert, Jeffery—The Sword of Lincoln, The Army of the Potomac, Simon and Schuster, new York, 2005.

Wertz, Jay and Bearrs, Edwin—Smithsonian's Great Battles and Battlefields of the Civil War, William Morrow and Co., Inc., New York, 1997.

White, Ronald C., Jr. —The Eloquent President, Random House, New York, NY, 2005.

Williams, T. Harry—Lincoln and the Generals, Alfred A, Knopf Inc., 1952.

Wills, Chuck—Lincoln: The Presidential Archives, Dorling Kindersley Ltd., London, 2007.

Withers, Bob –The President Travels by train, TLC Publishing Company, Marceline, Missouri, 1996.

Yearns, W. Buck editor—The Confederate Governors, The University of Georgia Press, Athens, 1985.

Military Operations in Jefferson County, Virginia 1861—1865, edited by James C. Holland, 2004.

*Harpers New Monthly Magazine*, June 1868.

"The Railsplitter and the Railroads", *Trains Magazine*, February 2009, pgs. 28- 39, Peter A. Hansen.

Seaport Autographs, Bicentennial Catalog, Part I, Number 111, Winter 2008-2009.

Antietam Battlefield, National Park Service brochure

*New York Times*, May 13, 1863.

Berkeley County Historical Society Journal, 1979.

Official Program of the Dedication of the National Cemetery in Gettysburg, November 19, 1863.

The U. S. Constitution, 11th printing, Oak Hill Publishing, Naperville, Illinois, 2007.

Monocacy Battlefield, National Park brochure

Teachingamericanhistory.org, 1860 State of the Union Address, James Buchanan.

*Harpers New Weekly Magazine*, June 1868.
*New York Herald*, February 28, 1861.
*Charleston Mercury*, June 18, 1858.
*Harpers Weekly*, December 14, 1863.
*Illinois - Springfield Times*, June 2, 2005.
*Berkeley County Journal*, 1979, pg. 16 and Miss Dolly, pg. 1.
*Richmond Daily Dispatch*, March 9, 1863.
*The Daily Commercial,* Bloomington, Illinois, November 20, 1879.
Cyrus F. Jenkins Civil War Diary, Nov. 1, 1861.
*Harpers Weekly*, July 5, 1862.

# Index

The Life of Abraham Lincoln—Index (fn means footnote)

## *Other Books by Bob O'Connor*

*"The Perfect Steel Trap Harpers Ferry 1859"*—Named finalist in the Best Book Awards

*"The Virginian Who Might Have Saved Lincoln"*—also available on Audio Books—Named finalist in the Indie Book Awards—Named Finalist in the Best Book Awards

*"Catesby: Eyewitness to the Civil War"*

*"The U.S. Colored Troops at Andersonville Prison"*—Non-fiction

*"The Centennial History of Ranson, West Virginia"*—1910-2010"—Non-fiction

All are available at the author's website—
www.boboconnorbooks.com